AMERICAN MEDIA HISTORY

SECOND EDITION

Anthony R. Fellow
California State University, Fullerton

WADSWORTH
CENGAGE Learning™

Australia • Brazil • Japan • Korea • Mexico • Singapore • Spain • United Kingdom • United States

American Media History, Second Edition
Anthony R. Fellow

Publisher: Michael Rosenberg

Assistant Editors: Rebekah Matthews and Megan Garvey

Marketing Manager: Erin Mitchell

Content Project Manager: Jessica Rasile

Associate Technology Project Manager: Jessica Badiner

Marketing Communications Manager: Christine Dobberpuhl

Production Technology Analyst: Jamison MacLachlan

Art Director: Linda Helcher

Print Buyer: Susan Carroll

Text Permissions Manager: Mardell Glinski-Schultz

Image Manager: Leitha Etheridge-Sims

Production Service/Compositor: Pre-Press PMG

Cover Designer: Stuart Kunkler

Cover Image: © Jakub Semeniuk/istockphoto

Cover note: The *New England Courant* was one of the first American newspapers, first published circa 1721.

For product information and technology assistance, contact us at
Cengage Learning Academic Resource Center, 1-800-423-0563
For permission to use material from this text or product, submit all requests online at **www.cengage.com/permissions**.
Further permissions questions can be e-mailed to
permissionrequest@cengage.com.

Library of Congress Control Number: 2008940353

ISBN-13: 978-0-495-56775-2

ISBN-10: 0-495-56775-2

Wadsworth
20 Channel Center Street
Boston, MA 02210
USA

Cengage Learning products are represented in Canada by Nelson Education, Ltd.

For your course and learning solutions, visit
www.cengage.com

Purchase any of our products at your local college store or at our preferred online store **www.ichapters.com**

Printed in Canada
1 2 3 4 5 6 7 13 12 11 10 09

This book is dedicated to my grandparents, Lucy and Joseph Anziano, who arrived at Ellis Island from Italy during the great immigration wave. They came with nothing but a dream. They built a business and reared a family during an era of depression and poverty. Grandmother Lucy became my hero. She taught us to be the best, achieve the most, and never give up.

Rose and Anthony Fellow, first-generation Italians who settled in Connecticut, set an example of service to one another and mankind. Grandfather Fellow was a beloved community leader. Grandmother Rose, who reared eight children following the early death of her husband, showed the stuff of which heroes are made. She taught us the meaning of love.

And to my Father, Raymond J. Fellow, a member of America's greatest generation and one of America's great dads.

They truly were grand people, the type of people that made America great.

ABOUT THE AUTHOR

ANTHONY R. FELLOW, Ph.D., chair of the Department of Communications at California State University, Fullerton, was a daily newspaper reporter and editor for ten years before obtaining his doctorate at the Annenberg School of Communication, University of Southern California, where he also has served as an adjunct professor. He is co-author of the *Copy Editors Handbook for Newspapers* and *News Writing in a Multimedia World*.

CONTENTS

PART 2 | 1833–1860 A NEW POLITICS, A NEW PRESS   83

CHAPTER 4   A PRESS FOR THE MASSES   85

PART 3 | 1860–1900 THE AGE OF NEW JOURNALISM   111

CHAPTER 5   A DIVIDED NATION, A DIVIDED MEDIA   113

CHAPTER 6   THE YELLOW PRESS AND THE *TIMES*   145

PREFACE

American Media History is the story of a nation. It is the story of events in the long battle to disseminate information, entertainment, and opinion in a democratic society. It is the story of the men and women whose inventions, ideas, and struggles helped shape the nation and its media system and fought to keep both free.

The story includes an impressive array of characters, including James Franklin, one of the first rebel printers in the New World; Samuel Adams whose powerful pen fomented dissent in the colonies; James Gordon Bennett who advanced communications for the masses; and Ida Tarbell and the muckrakers who exposed the wrongs of the nation.

Some of the players in the nation's story set standards for aspiring media professionals to emulate. Edward R. Murrow, Eric Sevareid, Margaret Bourke-White, Ernie Pyle, Walter Cronkite, Ruben Salazar, and Christiane Amonpour still inspire many to pursue careers in journalism and photography.

Other characters in America's media playbill provided information that many didn't want to read or hear about. Their revelations tarnished the image of the world's greatest democracy, but those stories also showed that democracy works. They included Carl Bernstein and Robert Woodward's Watergate coverage, Morley Safer's "The Burning of the Village of Cam Ne," and Matt Drudge's account of the sexual tryst of a president.

Still other stories, such as the congressional investigations into communists in the motion-picture business and government, the struggles in the civil rights movement, and the lies of Iran Contra, darkened America's door. Only a free press could provide accounts of those stories to further inform the people whose lives are affected.

This edition of *American Media History* includes a new Chapter 11, which looks at the history of advertising and its social, economic and political impact.

Chapter 13 presents stories of more modern heroes—technological wizards that have ushered in the fourth technological revolution and, perhaps, the most revolutionary after the invention of writing and the invention of the alphabet and the invention of the printing press.

They include Charles Babbage, John Vincent Atanasoff, Clifford Berry, and, of course, Bill Gates and Steve Job. The chapter includes one of the most complete histories of the computer and the story of the Internet as well as the invention of social networking in cyberspace, including MySpace, Facebook, Second Life, and YouTube, that could be found in a media history book. Finally, new material on the ethnic and alternative press in the information age has been added as well as the impact of mega mergers and their impact on the future of media and democracy.

The idea for *American Media History* came about from my own teaching need. I have assigned almost every available textbook for this course. Although there was much valuable content in each of the available books, none told the stories in a way that would get my students excited about how these stories affect the profession they are pursuing. The goal was to write a book that brought the stories to life for the student by focusing on individuals and their contributions and to place these stories within a broader social and cultural context.

When I first began teaching media history, I began to collect the best chapters written on media history and compiled them into a book of readings. Most chapters came from John Tebbel's *The Media in America*. His book the closest to writing media history as a colorful and interesting story. I contacted Tebbel, a professor emeritus from Columbia University and distinguished author of some forty books, to see if he would be willing to begin a new project. He agreed. Thus, the bulk of some of the early chapters, many of which have been rewritten, appeared in his popular *Media in America*.

Each chapter attempts to cover the development of a medium. Of course, some media overlap from chapter to chapter. I tried to fit it into a timeline in order to show the development of media over time.

American Media History ends with the history of computers, the Internet, the World Wide Web, and what they have wrought and what is on the horizon. The goal was to write a readable story of a fascinating nation and the story of the development of its complex and fascinating media system. I hope I have succeeded.

ACKNOWLEDGMENTS

There were many reviewers who, along the way, provided excellent feedback to help me in shaping this manuscript. My thanks go to the following: Christopher B. Daly, Boston University; Bill Kovarik, Radford University; Louis Liebovich, University of Illinois; Peter E. Mayeux, University of Nebraska–Lincoln; Jane S. McConnell, Minnesota State University, Mankato; Robert M. Ogles, Purdue University; Ruth Bayard Smith, Montclair State University; Charles R. St. Cyr, California State University, Northridge. I am especially grateful to the reviewers whose feedback helped shape this second edition: Mike Applin, Louisiana State University; Jeanni Atkins, University of Mississippi; Donna Bertazzoni, Hood College; Brian Cogan, Molloy College; Sandy Ellis, University of Wisconsin, River Falls;

Doug Ferguson, College of Charleston; Don Godfrey, Arizona State University; Neil Goldstein, Montgomery County Community College; Donna Halper, Emerson College; Larry Lain, University of Dayton; William Lingle, Linfield College; Shawn Murphy, SUNY Plattsburgh; Daniel Panici, University of Southern Maine; Pamela Parry, Belmont University; James Phipps, Cedarville University; Eric Schaefer, Emerson College; Dolores Sierra, Black Hawk College; Sam Terilli, University of Miami; and Alex Wainer, Palm Beach Atlantic University.

Additionally, I appreciate the assistance of the team at Cengage Wadsworth: Rebekah Matthews, editorial assistant; Jessica Rasile, content project manager; and Michael Rosenberg, publisher.

Thanks are due to many friends, colleagues, and family who helped bring this book to publication. John Tebbel, the esteemed media historian who died in 2004, allowed me to use some material from one of his previously published books. Professor Robert E. Blackmon was the first to spark an interest in the subject when I was enrolled in his undergraduate media history course. His love of books, journalism, and media history continues to inspire me. He also hired me for my first university teaching position and allowed me to teach media history.

My love of the subject got another boost when I became a faculty member at California State University, Fullerton. I am indebted to my former colleagues Ted C. Smythe, professor emeritus, and Terry Hynes, now senior vice chancellor for academic and student affairs at the University of Nebraska, Omaha, who welcomed me and allowed me to teach History & Philosophy of American Mass Communications. Our many luncheons were spent talking about media history as well as sharing teaching techniques. One couldn't ask for better colleagues.

My present colleagues are just as wonderful. Gail Love wrote the chapter "Advertising as a Social, Economic, and Political Force." Others wrote the American Media Profiles. Thomas N. Clanin wrote about Nellie Bly and Robert Abbott; Beth Evans wrote about Helen Thomas and Barbara Walters; Carolyn Johnson wrote about Jane Swisshelm and Margaret Bourke-White; Andi Stein wrote about P. T. Barnum; and Darren Williams, my student assistant, wrote about Steve Jobs. Two California State University, Long Beach, journalism professors also contributed to this edition. Chris Burnett wrote the section on the gay and lesbian press, and Judith Frutig made substantial contributions to the chapter "The Press and the Founding of a Nation." Fred Glienna and Suzanne Schenkel, my former university classmates, also enrolled in Professor Blackmon's media history course, wrote the profiles of I. F. Stone and Bill Gates, respectively.

I also appreciate the encouraging words of two of America's greatest historians when I mentioned this project to them. Thank you to Doris Kearns Goodwin, author of numerous books, including *Team of Rivals: The Political Genius of Abraham Lincoln; No Ordinary Time: Franklin and Eleanor Roosevelt: The Home Front in World War II;* and David McCullough, author of *John Adams* and *1776.*

Special thanks go to my wife, Clara Potes-Fellow, a noted media specialist, who wrote parts of the last chapter. Her encouragement and suggestions are much appreciated.

Finally, a big thank you to the thousands of students I have taught in media history. Many of their suggestions improved the book. I especially want to thank my recent graduate students whose interest in the topic produced some fascinating research about the newest technologies. Some of that research found its way into this edition. They include Ginger Ammon, Michael Delgado, Erin DeWolf, Richard Favela, Leslie Fehr, Julie Guevara, David Kuhn, Bianca Oros, Debra Smith, and Jessica Yoshikawara and my student assistant Darren Williams. They and future students are the reason this book was published. I hope they find it an interesting story about the greatest media system in the greatest nation on the earth.

Anthony R. Fellow, Ph.D.
California State University, Fullerton

INTRODUCTION

Before the American Experience

German printer Johannes Gutenberg topped many lists as "the person of the millennium." It was a fitting tribute to the fifteenth-century inventor of movable type. His invention revolutionized the spreading of information that changed political and social structures. Until Gutenberg's invention in 1450, European cultures were primarily oral or scribal cultures. Town criers, ministers from the pulpit, and bartenders disseminated information or news. Town criers, for example, broadcast royal edicts, police regulations, and important community events, such as births, marriages of princes, war news, and treaties of peace or alliance.

These correspondents were important in ancient Rome, where news traveled by foot. For example, William Shakespeare's accounts of ancient Rome in the days of Coriolanus (a Roman military and political leader) and Julius Caesar are filled with tales of messengers delivering written intelligence.[1] The Roman elite who resided in the provinces sent their personal correspondents to Rome to obtain information, especially commercial and political news. Correspondents culled information from the *acta diurna*, a hand-lettered prototype of today's newspaper that was posted on walls of the Roman Forum between 59 BC and AD 222. Oral communications also played a major role in the American colonies after 1750, though some colonists were reading colonial newspapers in the early 1700s. Colonial churches were hubs of information in early British America. While ministers delivered their sermons from the pulpit, colonists seeking goods and services gathered in the back of the church to conduct their business.

THE IMPACT OF THE PRINTING PRESS

Though China appeared to have movable type in the eleventh century, printing remained undeveloped for centuries; in the West, it followed quickly on the heels of Gutenberg's press four centuries later. Before Gutenberg, the ability to read and write was confined to the great merchants and to the first two estates—the nobility and clergy.[2]

Gutenberg's invention shattered the medieval world and gave rise to modernism. It ripped apart the social and structural fabric of life in Western Europe and reconnected it in new ways that gave shape to modern patterns. His invention provided the soil from which sprang modern history, science, popular literature, the emergence of the nation-state—so much of everything by which we define modernity.[3] It was the engine behind societal, cultural, familial, and industrial changes that culminated in the Renaissance, the Reformation, and the scientific revolution.

The printing press brought about a number of changes. It allowed the production of cheap literature and the reproduction of documents without error. It also enabled information to be preserved, affected social relationships, and inspired new forms of writing.

AMERICAN MEDIA PROFILE | JOHANNES GUTENBERG 1400–1467

Key Color/Index Stock/Photolibrary

It has been said that Johannes Gutenberg's story is one of a genius that almost went awry. Many parts of his inventions had been around for years. As early as the eighth century, China, Japan, and Korea carved blocks of whole pages made of wood or stone to print books. By the eleventh century, letters were carved in wet clay and then baked. This did not prove workable, but the principle was used by the Koreans to make movable metal type.

Gutenberg introduced an invention and a technique. He fashioned a hand mold that created multiple letters in metal types. He then created a technique, the gathering of type together in a frame to make up a page of metal type. His machine allowed small blocks of letters to be moved so written material could be printed and mass-produced.

His invention has been called the "third revolution," after the invention of writing and the invention of the alphabet. The world knows much about his invention, but he was not famous during his lifetime. Thus, the world knows little about the man who ignited one of the greatest revolutions in the history of mankind.

Gutenberg was born in Mainz, Germany, sometime around 1400 to Friele Gansfleisch and Else Wyrich, or so the world's printers have traditionally said for centuries. The Gutenberg name was taken from the home of his father and his paternal ancestors: "zu Laden zu Gutenberg." Family names were rare at this time. If an upper-crust nonaristocrat was known by anything other than a Christian name, it was almost always by the name of his house or estate.

He likely spent little time in Mainz. When his family migrated to Strasbourg, he joined the goldsmiths' guild. Gutenberg wanted to make money—lots of money. In the city of Aachen, he and three other partners had an opportunity to do just that. In 1165, Charlemagne, founder of the empire, was

Scribes witnessed the first impact of the printing press. Then they disappeared. An Italian businessman, Vespaniano da Bisticci, employed forty-five scribes to produce 200 books for Cosimo de Medici's library in the 1460s and pretended to despise the new invention. By 1478 he was out of business. The scribes copied printed typefaces to hold back the flood, to no avail. The scribes were gone, and so were the illuminators, as their work of decorating capitals and margins went by the wayside.[4]

Printed materials were now cheap enough to reach the masses. This had tremendous ramifications. Knowledge was no longer the exclusive property of the privileged classes. For example, gifted students no longer needed to sit at the feet of a gifted master in order to learn a language or academic skill.[5]

The ability to reproduce scientific, technical, and religious documents and manuscripts in their exact form meant that errors which persisted through generations could be corrected. Printing allowed wide dissemination of accurate knowledge from the sources of Western thought, both classical and Christian. It also allowed people to form an accurate picture of their past. In medieval scribal culture accuracy of manuscripts could not be checked without visiting every library. Thus, scholars, who traveled from one book collection to another, now were able to remain at home.

AMERICAN MEDIA PROFILE | **CONTINUED**

declared a saint by the church. By Gutenberg's time, pilgrimages of tens of thousands of people visited the city hoping for a miracle or some life-changing experience. They bought little metal badges decorated with the image of a saint or two as evidence of their visit.

The holy relics were said to have powerful charms, and that a mirror, if held in a certain way, could absorb the healing power of the relic. Everyone wanted one of these. Gutenberg had a plan to mass-produce 32,000 mirrors, but he needed some kind of press to do it. Thus, some type of press was on Gutenberg's mind long before the printing press. However, a plague hit the area, bringing a halt to the pilgrimages and Gutenberg's business.

At the time, his partners heard rumors that Gutenberg had another type of press in mind. Around 1444 almost every European city had in place the elements for Gutenberg's invention. Procopius Waldvogel in Avignon had two alphabets and various metal forms, and he was offering to teach "the art of artificial writing" to a schoolteacher. However, he vanished without a trace. A second threat to Gutenberg's invention arose in Holland, where a maker of block books named Laurens, whose surname was Coster, lived. For years rumors circulated in Haarlem that Coster made the invention which Gutenberg stole. A nineteenth-century statue of Coster looks out on the Market Square there. However, most in the town like the story but give the nod to Gutenberg as the inventor of the printing press.

Loans and a partnership with the wealthy Johann Fust helped Gutenberg finance his idea, which he kept secret for years. For their first project they printed the Bible, completed in the years 1453–1455. However, the partnership soured, and Fust sued his partner to recover the money, plus interest, he lent to the inventor. Gutenberg's machinery and type then became the property of Fust.

Little is known of Gutenberg after this. He likely spent his declining years in the court of Archbishop Adolf of Nassau. His appointment to the court, on January 18, 1465, saved him from homelessness. He was given an allowance for clothing and other necessities. It is likely he died at Mainz toward the end of 1467 or the beginning of 1468. He was buried in a Franciscan church, which no longer stands.

Type also enabled the preservation of information. This meant that knowledge could be shared. It increased discussions, which ushered in the Enlightenment, an eighteenth-century intellectual movement that took place primarily in London and Paris. Those involved in the movement believed that human reason could be used to combat ignorance, superstition, and tyranny. Their goal was to build a better world by challenging religious doctrine, especially embodied in the Catholic Church, and the domination of society by a hereditary aristocracy. Enlightenment thinkers questioned the notion that only the church and monarchy were privy to the truth. They insisted on something they called "reason," which consisted of common sense, observation, and their own unacknowledged prejudices in favor of skepticism and freedom.

The printing revolution also inspired new forms of writing. Before the printing press, popular literature was a rarity. In a castle tower near Bordeaux, Michael Eyguem de Montaigne, the great French Renaissance thinker, would write in 1572 what he called "essays," telling readers about himself. Somewhere an unknown writer would produce the first true novel (*The Life of Lazarillo de Tormes*, 1554) of the new medium.[6]

Movable type also made it possible to directly address anyone, anywhere, in his or her own language. Furthermore, it allowed all forms of written communication to be categorized. Indexes facilitated the retrieval of information and rid the world of the arcane cataloguing system developed by the monks. Jon Man writes that the indexer contributed to the growth of democracy. For example, the statutes on which English law was based were unknown to the general public until the sixteenth century when John Rastell and his son William published every statute since 1327. Monarchs and parliaments could no longer escape the fact that their rulings could be displayed to any literate person, and that they or their descendants would be answerable.[7]

The printing revolution affected social relationships. The advent of printing led to the creation of a new kind of shop structure; to a regrouping that entailed closer contacts among diversely skilled workers and encouraged new forms of cross-cultural interchange. With this regrouping, printer-merchants achieved a sense of prestige in cities. Their shops became meeting places and educational centers, forces for commercial and academic change. The master printer emerged as a social force, coordinating financial sources, authors, proofreaders, suppliers, and salesmen. Printers enlarged their markets, printing handbills, circulars, and catalogs advertising their products. These master printers also functioned, in a sense, as deans of mini-universities, attracting multilingual scholars, who were gathering and dispersing information.[8]

The impact on social relations also could be seen in the evolution of the work of priests. These men of the church, once isolated from the rest of academia, began to work with university professors and other members of society. University professors, in turn, came into closer contact with metalworkers and mechanics.

The printing press also had a tremendous impact on the church's relationship with the outside world. The church at first welcomed the printing press. It looked upon this new invention as a gift from God to raise cash for the crusades against the Turks. However, the printing press eventually posed a threat to the nobility and the clergy. It contributed to the end of church-dominated control of book publishing and its lock on ideas. It allowed dissemination of new and radical ideas that brought about changes and revolts.

Certainly the printing press accelerated Protestant protagonist Martin Luther's revolt against the authority of the Roman Catholic Church. He is said to have written most of the books printed in Germany between 1518 and 1525. Luther also used the printing press to reproduce and circulate his "Ninety-Five Theses," which denounced the church's sale of indulgences, bits of paper that freed one of sin. Since 1476 one could buy an indulgence for a dead person to save them from further suffering in purgatory, a state of limbo and cleansing before proceeding to heaven. In 1515 Pope Leo X needed money to finish the Vatican's basilica over the tomb of the supposed bones of St. Peter. He raised the cash by authorizing the selling of indulgences.

Such practices horrified some leaders, such as Luther, who believed that buying indulgences was something lazy Christians did to avoid good work. He considered indulgences a mockery upon his God. On All Saints' Day in 1517, he nailed his "theses" to the door of Wittenberg's castle church. He initiated a break that could not be stopped. It culminated in the Peace of Augsburg in 1555, contributing to a division of Europe into Protestant and Catholic areas. Each faction then attempted to control the printing press.

THE PRINTING PRESS IN EARLY ENGLAND

Hearing of Gutenberg's invention, William Caxton traveled from his home in England to Germany, where he was determined to learn as much as he could about printing. While in Germany, he printed what many believe to be the first book in English. It was his own translation of *Le Recueil des Histoires de Troyes*. He called it the *Recuyell of the Historyes of Troye* (or *History of Troy*), and shipped it to England. When he returned to London in 1476, he opened a print shop.

During the next fifteen years, Caxton's shop published about 100 books, including such famous works as Chaucer's *Canterbury Tales* and Sir Thomas Malory's *The Noble Histories of King Arthur and of Certain of His Knights*. Caxton never founded a newspaper, and it took more than a century for any Englishman to do so.

Though the illiteracy rate was still very high, the masses now had a means of communicating with one another. They were able to learn about each other as well as identify problems they had in common. Thus, Gutenberg's invention of movable type, combined with the establishment of the Caxton Press, threatened European authoritarian regimes.

Control of information didn't arise with the invention of the printing press. In about AD 496, Pope Gelasius I issued one of the first catalogues of censored books. Those caught reading such works faced excommunication from the church. Later popes, such as Pope Innocent IV in 1252, gave inquisitors permission to use torture against heretics (those who spoke or wrote against the church). From the eleventh to fifteenth centuries, several thousand "heretics" were burned at the stake or strangled to death.

By the early fifteenth century, the church was so powerful that it ordered the bones of the religious leader John Wycliffe (1330?–1384) to be dug up, burned, and thrown into England's Thames River. One of Wycliffe's offenses was that he translated the Bible from Latin to English without church approval. Leaders feared the masses might form dangerous opinions about religion and challenge the clergy itself.[9]

As early as 1275, the English Parliament outlawed "any slanderous News ... or false News or Tales where by discord or occasion of discord or slander may grow between the King and his people or the great men of the Realm ..." Parliament reenacted the statute in 1379 to prevent "subversion and destruction" by means of false speech.[10]

The invention of printing magnified the danger of such opinions. The printed word could cause agitation and rebellion, making it a very dangerous occupation. Henry VIII (1491–1547; reigned 1509–1547) understood that. He remained loyal as a young man to the teachings of the Catholic Church and the pope. But he challenged the church's supremacy in 1529, when Pope Clement VII refused to grant him a divorce from his first wife, Catherine of Aragon, to whom he had been married for twenty years, so he could marry Anne Boleyn. The Reformation Parliament (1529–1536) then declared the king the supreme head of the new Church of England. Thus separated from the Catholic Church, the king married his beloved Boleyn.

Henry VIII then seized the Catholic monasteries in the name of the Crown and persecuted Catholics and non-Catholics who did not accept him as head of the Church of England. He silenced the press during the last two decades of his reign, allowing only official orders or printed materials that praised the monarch of the now independent church.

To maintain power, the Crown established an elaborate system of prior restraints (the censorship of materials before publication). Henry VIII took over a system for the censorship of heretical manuscripts, long established by the Catholic Church and approved by Parliament, and applied it to writings on any subject.[11]

The Crown, over time, established three agencies responsible for overseeing what was printed. They included: the Stationers' Company, the Court of High Commission, and the Court of Star Chamber. The Stationers' Company was a group of select printers who had extraordinary powers of search and seizure. If a print shop published without authority, the company had the authority to mar its type and chop up the illegal presses. The Court of High Commission, which the Crown set aside as the highest ecclesiastical tribunal, controlled the Stationers' Company and did the actual licensing. The Court of Star Chamber imposed fines and imprisonment. It shared its jurisdiction over the trial of offenders with the Court of the High Commission.

When Henry VIII's daughter Mary (1516–1558; reigned 1553–1558) was proclaimed queen, after the death of her stepbrother Edward VI, she repealed her father's orders establishing a separate church and proclaimed England as once again accepting the doctrines of Catholicism. Queen Mary was tagged "Bloody Mary" after a rampage ended in the execution of more than 300 people she or the church labeled as heretics.

Her firm hand silenced freedom of speech and the press by controlling the Stationers' Company, which had existed in England since 1357 as a guild for writers. Under Queen Mary, the Stationers' Company became a "watchdog" of sorts, issuing licenses and authorizing searches and seizures of unauthorized works. This guild of printers selected by the Crown had the power to smash open the doors of those publishing without authority and destroy illegal printing presses.

Upon Queen Mary's death, Elizabeth (1533–1603; reigned 1558–1603) ascended to the throne. During her forty-five-year reign, she re-established the power of the Crown and its authority over the Church of England. She instituted mandatory attendance at Sunday church services, thus establishing an effective system of communication while also lessening the influence of the non-authorized religions. Queen Elizabeth's rage against Catholics was fanned when Philip II of Spain launched the Spanish Armada of 120 ships against England. Philip II, who had been King of England when he was married to Queen Mary, was hoping to avenge the death of his wife and destroy Protestantism in the only European country in which it was the dominant religious belief.[12] Queen Elizabeth ordered the execution of more than 200 Catholics during her reign of terror.

Under Queen Elizabeth, the Star Chamber reestablished the Stationers' Company, which had the responsibility to regulate printing. Heavy fines could be expected if a work was heresy. She defined heresy as anything that denied the existence of God, accepted any tenets of the Catholic religion, or attacked the queen or her ministers. She ordered one writer, William Carter, who had written an incendiary pro-Catholic pamphlet, tortured and hanged.

During the reign of James I (1566–1625; reigned 1603–1625), the first English colonies were established in North America and the first English-language weekly news sheets, called *corrantos* (meaning *current* and *put together* in Latin), were printed in Amsterdam. George Veseler and Broer Jonson were the author-printers of these *corrantos* from December 2, 1620, to September 18, 1621. About twenty-five or thirty of these news sheets were imported into England by Nathaniel Butter in 1621. Butter and his associate Thomas Archer eventually printed their own *corrantos*. They included some original materials, but most of their content was pirated from the Amsterdam sheets.[13] King James I, however, issued a proclamation opposing the *corrantos*. He believed they threatened England's security. It was more likely he was upset because they wrote about his indecisive foreign policy maneuverings during the Thirty Years War (a number of declared and undeclared wars, which took place in central Europe from 1618 to 1648).

King James I imprisoned Archer when he refused to stop publishing the *corrantos*. However, he eventually gave permission for Butter and Nicholas Bourne to print a weekly newspaper, *The Continuation of Our Weekly News,* if all articles were submitted for approval. About twenty-three issues of the newspaper were published from 1621 to 1642, reaching an average circulation of 250 to 500 copies.[14]

The Star Chamber's power increased further when Charles I (1600–1649; reigned 1625–1649) became king. He appointed William Laud to be privy counsel. Laud, in turn, used the Star Chamber to once again control the Stationers' Company and expand its domain as an arm to regulate printing in England. Before 1637 only printers had to be licensed. Now all books had to be licensed and registered by the Stationers' Company.

The outcome proved brutal for those who did not comply. For example, in 1633, printer John Twyn was accused of having printed a pamphlet that advocated the overthrow of an absolute monarch if the policies proved to be oppressive to the people. He supposedly knew of a plot to kill the royal family but refused to reveal the names of the perpetrators. He was sentenced to be hanged, cut down while still alive, and then emasculated, disemboweled, quartered, and beheaded—the standard punishment for treason.[15]

Four years later, Willliam Prynne, a lawyer and theologian, was brought before the Star Chamber. He was charged with a series of offenses, including heresy and sedition, after writing a pamphlet opposing a liberalization of social customs. He was opposed to long hair and all forms of alcohol. He attacked the arts, writing that actresses were little better than whores. He also attacked the English stage, where Shakespeare's plays were being performed, as the source of England's immorality and evil.

Prynne and two others were sentenced to the pillory, to have their noses slit and their ears cut off, and to pay a fine of 5,000 shillings; then they were sent to prison. There Prynne had the letters S.L., for seditious libeler, burned onto his cheeks.

Parliament abolished the Star Chamber in 1641, but on June 14, 1643, it passed an act in which it exerted greater control over the licensing of books. The Stationers' Company strictly enforced the new act. English poet John Milton, author of *Paradise Lost*, was cited as one of its worst violators.

JOHN MILTON AND BRITISH ROOTS OF FREE EXPRESSION

Milton had written a number of pamphlets, all unlicensed, attacking the Church of England and the ruling by Charles I that no pamphlets could be printed without a church license. A number of Milton's pamphlets derailed the church's concept of marriage and divorce. At the time, Milton was displeased with his sixteen-year-old bride. However, adultery was the only recognized reason for divorce. He wrote that incompatibility might be a greater crime against God and humanity.

Milton considered the church's absurd and self-destructive threats of licensing to silence opposing voices an even greater crime against humanity. His appeal to the complaints lodged against him was published under the title of *Areopagitica*[16] on November 24, 1644, and delivered to Parliament. It is considered "the finest argument ever written against the stupidities and futilities of censorship."[17]

Milton argued that whenever truth and falsehood come to grips with each other—in what today we describe as "the marketplace of ideas"—it will always be truth that emerges triumphant. His plea came to be known as "the self-righting principle," the idea that truth needs no companion in the arena of that marketplace, that truth wins even without the authority of someone in power.[18] "For who knows not that Truth is strong next to the Almighty; she needs no policies, nor stratagems, nor licensing to make her victorious," Milton wrote.[19]

Furthermore, understanding, as well as decency and goodness, can only come about by taking into consideration all sides of issues, according to Milton.

> Since knowledge and survey of vice is so necessary to the constituting of human virtue, and the scanning of error to the confirmation of truth, how can we more safely, and with less danger, scout into the regions of sin and falsity than by reading all manner of tractates and hearing all manner of reason? And this is the benefit which may be had of books promiscuously read.[20]

This became one of the enduring elements in the belief system of modern journalists.[21]

THOMAS HOBBES AND JOHN LOCKE

Seven years after Milton's *Areopagitica*, Thomas Hobbes set forth the doctrine of social contract, which stands today as the philosophical underpinning of the American experiment.[22] In his *Leviathan*, published in 1651, Hobbes looked at man as savage and unprincipled. Authority and control were necessary if man was to survive in a social setting. In other words, Hobbes argued the solution of man's human depravity was the political state—or, to use his terminology, the commonwealth.[23]

Under Hobbes' notion of a social contract, the commonwealth or sovereign state would guarantee peace and order. The obligation of the citizens was to swear obedience to the sovereign state, which would be ruled by an absolute, all-powerful force. In Hobbes' view, that force was a monarch. Perhaps Hobbes' call for a monarch was influenced by the times in which he lived. He feared civil warfare, which Britain was experiencing, more than anything. A century later, John Locke, one of England's greatest philosophers, wrote that the worst evil was "to be subject to the inconstant, uncertain, arbitrary will of another man."[24] He wrote that at a time when England's civil wars had ended and a period of relative calm and stability existed.

Locke, considered "the father of American democracy," refuted the notion of divine right; rulers were not the product of divine right, and they did not rule by divine right. In *Two Treatises on Government*, Locke wrote that a ruler lost the right to rule if he or she ignored community needs.

His notion that some things are self-evident ("among these life, liberty, and the pursuit of happiness") found their way into the American Declaration of Independence. In addition, his name is forever associated with two notions that are associated with the American belief system and the professional ideology of American journalists. The first is his contract theory, which holds that government thrives under the consent of the governed. The second is the doctrine of the right of revolution, which holds that a people have the absolute right, indeed the duty, to rise up against tyrannical leaders and throw the rascals out, by force and violence if that is necessary. These two fundamental beliefs underpin America's basic fundamental civil liberties—the freedom to say what one wants and the freedom to print and publish opinions and beliefs.[25]

The most perfect government for Locke would be one run by lawmakers, not a monarch. However, he was not recommending a democracy. He, like Hobbes, used the term *commonwealth* to define his community of men, which was constituted only for procuring, preserving, and advancing their own civil interests, which he called life, liberty, health, and the possession of outward things, such as money, land, houses, furniture, and the like.

However, Locke had no toleration for those who disrupted the commonwealth. "No opinions contrary to human society or to those moral rules which are necessary to the preservation of civil society, are to be tolerated by the magistrate," he wrote in *A Letter Concerning Toleration*.[26] He also proposed punishment of any who will not "teach the duty of tolerating all men in matters of mere religion."[27] He, like Milton and Hobbes, did not tolerate seditious utterances. Locke wrote that if any person exercising his religion might behave "seditiously, and contrary to public peace," he was punishable "in the same manner, and not otherwise than as if in a fair or market."[28]

"CATO'S LETTERS"

Two English essayists clashed with Parliament, as well as with Milton, Hobbes, and Locke, on the concept of seditious libel in early English libertarian thought. John Trenchard (1662–1723) and Thomas Gordon (1685–1750) wrote under the pseudonym "Cato," a name they selected to honor Cato the Younger, who had committed suicide rather than live under the rule of Julius Caesar. Between 1720 and 1723, they wrote about 197 "Cato" letters in the *Independent Whig*, then in the *London Journal* and *British Journal*.

Their essays made them the most popular and most controversial authors in England. They wrote about religious and personal freedoms, the rights of citizens, and the responsibilities of government to protect its citizens. They distinguished from libel against the government, which they said was always unlawful, and libel against those who govern. Rulers, they said, should laugh at the libels but not prosecute because of them. The public, they wrote, had a duty to expose public wickedness, and these exposures could never be a libel. "Cato's" letters on the subject formed the essence of Andrew Hamilton's defense in the celebrated New York trial of John Peter Zenger.

Their fifteenth article, published on February 4, 1720, dealt with freedom of the press. They wrote:

> Without freedom of thought, there can be no such thing as wisdom and no such thing as public liberty, without freedom of speech: Which is the right of every man, as far as by it he does not hurt and control the right of another; and this is the only check which it ought to suffer, the only bounds that it ought to know.[29]

The obligation as well as the right of the press was to engage in political criticism, condemn public measures injurious to the people, and expose corruption in high office. This led, ultimately, to a theory of the press as the "fourth estate," a watchdog of government on behalf of the people.[30]

"Cato's Letters" extolling press freedom in a republican society became important in the development of American political ideas. Their letters were quoted "in every colonial newspaper from Boston to Savannah."[31] Benjamin Franklin reprinted their essay "Freedom of the Speech" in the *New-England Courant* after his brother, James Franklin, was imprisoned by the Massachusetts legislature.[32] The *Boston Gazette* reprinted the essay on free speech at least seven times.[33] Cato's Letters were on John Adams's must-read list for Americans.[34] And Thomas Jefferson had a personal copy in his home library.[35] In the history of political liberty as well as of freedom of speech and press, no eighteenth-century work exerted more influence than "Cato's Letters."[36]

CONCLUSION

Gutenberg's invention, which was perfected over time by others, including the English printer William Caxton, eventually posed a threat to those in power. What the world saw and continues to see is that when governments feel secure, they are more likely to extend freedom of speech, religion, and the press to their citizenry.

Governments found many ways to silence opposition. Several attempts were made to arrest John Trenchard and Thomas Gordon for writing "Cato's Letters." When such attempts failed, government officials bought off the editor of the *London Journal*, forcing the writers to publish their works in the weaker *British Journal*.[37] This ended their influence.

Still other rulers ignored their pleas. For example, the Crown didn't pay much attention to John Milton's assault on censorship, which is why he escaped prosecution. It was not until 1728, after the most dramatic confrontation on censorship in the American colonies, the trial of John Peter Zenger, discussed in Chapter 1, that a new edition of the *Areopagitica* was published. It set off a serious clamor for an end to censorship and for freedom of expression.

Many of the early colonists in the New World were familiar with the works of Milton, Hobbes, Locke, and "Cato." Jefferson read Locke's *Two Treatises on Government* three times. As the colonies matured, the treatises of these English philosophers, poets, and essayists circulated among the people and were quoted widely, especially by the nation's founders. Their philosophies, especially those of Locke, provided the blueprints for revolutionary thought in the American colonies. They became the underpinnings of the American experience and of the nation's greatest documents—the Declaration of Independence and the U.S. Constitution.

1690–1833 THE PRESS IN EARLY AMERICA

The Massachusetts Bay Colony would be not only the cradle of the New World's journalism but also a hotbed of revolutionary ideas that would foment in a new nation called America. However, it would take time—84 years to found a newspaper and 156 years to found a new nation.

It was a long time, indeed, when one considers that two of the Pilgrims—William Brewster and Edward Winslow—who landed at Plymouth in December 1620 were printers. Not until 1704 did the first continuous newspaper appear—in a colony of religious exiles who settled around Boston ten years after the arrival of the Pilgrims.

The Massachusetts Bay Colony was unlike the Plymouth settlement. It had the fastest population growth, the highest educational level, and the greatest degree of self-government. Boston, the colonies' largest town, had a population between 7,000 and 12,000. It also had the largest concentration of literate elites, who had both the skill to read papers and the money to buy them.

In 1638, six years after the founding of the settlement, the Massachusetts Bay Colony established Harvard College and grammar schools to prepare boys for Harvard. It also had the first press, located in Cambridge, in the English colonies. Its purpose was to print religious texts for schools and colleges.

Boston's high literacy rate, propensity toward self-government, and cultural leadership provided the basis for the development of the first newspaper, the *Boston-News Letter*. Newspapers also appeared in other colonies, including Maryland, Virginia, and South Carolina. The growth of newspapers accompanied a rapid expansion in population from 251,000 in 1700 to 1,171,000 in 1750.

Boston also had the most vociferous patriots; they used the press to kindle the flames of revolution. Samuel Adams, a palsied, fifty-three-year-old dubbed by a Tory as "that Machiavellian of Chaos," had been inciting a riot for a decade. He "eats little, drinks little, sleeps little, thinks much," muttered Joseph Galloway (a less than ardent defender of American rights who eventually became loyal to England).

This master of propaganda created an interlocked network of town committees, called the Sons of Liberty, throughout the colonies to obtain information about patriotic behavior or of British perfidy. Such information would find its way into his *Journal of Occurrences,* a widely circulated diary disseminating a parade of loathsome incidents sprinkled with editorial comment designed to agitate sentiment against the British.

In Philadelphia, where he traveled as a delegate to the Continental Congress, Adams sought to "instruct the unenlightened, convince the doubting, and fortify the timid." While Congress—hoping for reconciliation—dawdled throughout the fall and winter of 1775, Adams argued for independence. His audiences were the rowdies found in taverns and dockside gangs. "Would you believe it," a British officer wrote, "that this immense continent from New England to Georgia is moved and directed by one man?" To Jefferson, Adams was the "Man of the Revolution."

It was Adams who pushed for "the just liberty of the press." The Constitution was approved only when a Bill of Rights was promised. When states refused to ratify the first two amendments, number three became the First Amendment, known the world over as a cornerstone of liberty, protecting individual freedoms—of religion, speech, press, assembly, and petition—needed for democracies to thrive.

Following the adoption of the U.S. Constitution in the spring of 1789, the new nation witnessed one of the most politically and journalistically vigorous periods in its history. From 1783 to 1833, intensified party divisions shaped the American political system, and the press played a critical role in determining the direction of that system.

THE COLONIAL YEARS

Less than a century after Johannes Gutenberg's invention of movable type, printing was brought to the Americas, a part of the world unknown fifty years earlier. When Father Juan de Zumárraga, first bishop of Mexico, arrived in Mexico in 1528, he perceived that if the church could establish a printing press in the new colony, his task of making converts of the Indians would be made immeasurably easier, and the press, the enemy of illiteracy, would be firmly controlled.

Father Zumárraga was responsible for the negotiations that brought Juan Pablos, an Italian from Brescia, to the New World as its first printer. Pablos had been working for Seville's leading printer, Juan Cromberger. He printed his first book in Mexico City in 1539, although there is some scholarly debate about whether it was the first in the New World; one may have been printed three years earlier.

In any case, Pablos' primitive equipment had turned out thirty-seven books before he died in the 1560s. He created the kind of cottage industry in printing and publishing that prevailed in North America for the next 250 years. The technology he used changed so slowly that no substantial breakthrough occurred until the early nineteenth century. The cottage-industry character of publishing did not begin to change in the American colonies until after the Revolution transformed them into states. Both printing and learning were firmly controlled by the Roman Catholic Church during the early years of North American colonial development.

Meanwhile, the powerful elite of Europe that controlled the printing press also thought that the relatively low degree of literacy among workers and peasants prevented "disobedience and heresy," as they put it. However, they were astonished when the peasants talked about "the rights of man" in the list of the grievances that they drew up on the eve of the French Revolution in 1789. Long before that time, the rapid growth of newspapers guaranteed that such grievances would be circulated and trickle down to those who were still unable to read.

The bourgeoisie, the middle class, played a key role in this development. Not revolutionary people by nature, they nevertheless provided most of the writers and readers who created public opinion. Pamphlets, newspapers, reading clubs, and private societies were the instruments by which they spread the new ideas about religious, intellectual, political, and economic freedom.

It was the bourgeoisie, too, who determined the establishment of the media in America. These were men of comfortable means who settled on the banks of the James River in Virginia. In the Massachusetts Bay Colony, the first settlers included an unusually high percentage of university-trained men. William Brewster, however, was the only man among the earlier Plymouth settlers who had gone to college, although he had never graduated. In the first decade after Governor John Winthrop led the pioneers ashore, nearly a hundred of the 25,000 settlers who followed were Oxford and Cambridge graduates, and fifty had advanced degrees. They were the intellectual elite, who determined what would be done with printing.

These early settlers were not imbued with the idea of democracy. Governor John Winthrop called democracy "the meanest and worst of all forms of government." Sir William Berkeley, governor of Virginia in 1671, wrote home to his sovereign, Charles II, describing his difficulties with the colony. Nevertheless, he told the king that a glimmer of hope existed. Berkeley said: "I thank God, there are no free schools nor printing, and I hope we shall not have these [for a] hundred years; for learning has brought disobedience, and heresy, and sects into the world, and printing has divulged them, and libels against the best government. God keep us from both."

For these refugees from Old World tyranny and oppression democracy meant that the new freedom they were establishing applied only to them. Opposition from those who dissented would not be tolerated. In the case of religious freedom, this kind of authoritarianism did not last long. Dissent was in the bones of these men, and Roger Williams' insistence on full freedom of conscience, not mere toleration, was only the first step in a process of revolt that led to widespread religious freedom in the colonies. Williams, banished from the Massachusetts Bay Colony for expressing religious opinion different from the official Puritan doctrine, established Rhode Island in 1636.

This freedom was not extended to the media. The colonial political leaders drew on the experiences of religion and concluded that authority and loyalty were best guaranteed by control of the printing press. And they controlled it rigidly for a long period of time. The press had a dual advantage for those in authority; it confirmed and propagandized at the same time.

It is hardly surprising, then, that the first item to emerge from a press in America was the Freeman's Oath in 1639 by Stephen Day. Every resident more than twenty years old who had been a householder for at least six months had to subscribe before he could become a citizen of the colony. The uncompromising voice of ecclesiastical and civil authority is heard in its language: "I do solemnly bind myself in the sight of God, which I shall be called upon to give my voice touching any such matter of this State, in which freemen are to deal, I will give my vote, and suffrage as I shall judge in mine own conscience may best conduce and tend to the public weal of that body, without respect of persons, or favor of any man."

Similarly, the early colonial authorities learned not to put all their trust in the Freeman's Oath. First, they ensured the loyalty of printers by forbidding anyone to own a press or to publish anything on it without a license. Then, they regulated the flow of ecclesiastical and government job printing, on which the printer's income was nearly completely dependent, so that only the loyal got work.

PRINTING IN BRITISH AMERICA

As a consequence, the establishment of printing in America, and the resulting rise of the media, was slow and sometimes painful. The beginnings are still a matter of controversy, but the facts, briefly, appear to be these:

In the early summer of 1638, the Reverend Jose Glover sailed out of London, bound for Boston, on the ship *John*, together with a company of fellow Puritans in flight from Archbishop William Laud's attempt to purge the Anglican faith of all Nonconformist elements. Glover had a printing press, which he had bought for twenty pounds. He also had paper worth another forty pounds, and a font of type. In their company was a locksmith, Stephen Day (sometimes Daye), who was not a printer but an ambitious man who wanted to establish an iron foundry in the New World.

Day was long regarded as the man who operated the first press, but it appears possible that a printer, name unknown, was on board and died on the way over, but not before teaching his craft to Day's eighteen-year-old son Matthew, and his brother, Stephen Jr. The Reverend Glover also died en route, and soon after the ship docked in Boston in mid-September 1638, his widow married John Duster, who would become the first president of Harvard. He set up the press as an adjunct of the new college in Cambridge and placed the Days in charge.

This was the celebrated Cambridge Press, which established book publishing, the first medium in America. Its production under the Days and their successors, primarily the numerous Green family, was notable for many things, but chiefly for the first book to be printed in America, after the press had turned out the Oath and an almanac. It was the *Whole Book of Psalmes*, better known as the *Bay Psalm Book*, which appeared in 1640; it remains the prime bibliographical treasure in America today.

Glover originally intended the press to be a fountainhead for Puritan tracts, but the long struggle in England ended with the deposing of Archbishop Laud and the outbreak of civil war. Puritans were now relieved temporarily from persecution and censorship, and no longer needed a new power center in the Massachusetts Bay Colony. As a result, Harvard became a provincial college instead of a Puritan propaganda factory, and the press was turned to local uses, supplying the needs of the college and the community. It was under the college's general supervision when the General Court (as the legislature was called) set up a licensing board to run it.

Before the Cambridge Press came to an end in 1692, it turned out more than 200 books, pamphlets, and broadsides. Its importance lies not so much in what it printed, although the *Bay Psalm Book* had its particular significance, but in the fact that it existed at all, and so early. The Cambridge Press was functioning before printing was practiced in many of the major cities of England and Scotland. Canada did not have a press until 1751. If one measures by the number of imprints, rather than by quality, Boston was the second publishing center of the British Empire by 1700.

Nevertheless, book publishing was slow to rise as an industry. What was produced accurately reflected the character of society. More than a third of the output was theology, a fifth of it was literature, and a little less than a half is categorized as social science, such as collections of laws, proceedings of the assembly, or government proclamations, along with a smattering of essays and treatises. Sermons comprised most of the theology, together with pamphlets and a few books on theological doctrine.

Most of these early books were paperbound, for the practical reason that paperbacks were cheaper, as they are today. Some of them anticipated modern paperbacks in their use of the "skyline," the phrase or sentence on a cover that summarizes the content, and is in effect a sales message. "The happiness and pleasure of unity in the Christian societies considered," reads the skyline above the title on a Boston sermon.

For a century or more, the sermon-publishing business was dominated by that "great Mather copy-factory," as the critic and historian John T. Winterich once called the prolific Mather family, the most notable of whom were Richard, Moses, Increase, and Cotton. The Mathers produced no fewer than 621 published works; Increase and Cotton between them accounted for 546 of these. Cotton, writing in seven languages, alone produced 444. Many were translated into Indian tongues.

Little creative literature appeared on the early publishing lists during the first fifty years of the colonies, and there was a similar and simultaneous lack in post-Elizabethan England. In America, the reason was a simple one. The authorities who controlled the press used it as a civil and ecclesiastical tool. They were not interested in employing it to promote literature. Those few colonists who were concerned with literature sent their work to London to be published.

Colonial America, however, was not devoid of literary culture. It flourished in the private libraries of those affluent citizens who were able to import a wide variety of books through local booksellers. An intellectual such as Cotton Mather had a library of more than 3,000 volumes, one of the largest in the world.

The Mathers published their own work because they were motivated by the powerful urge to proselytize. Other intellectuals did not want to see their own efforts in print, and in fact they looked down on printing and publishing as a grubby business, on a par with the theater and even lower in social status. To preserve dignity, these people had their literary manuscripts copied and circulated among their friends, if they were not sent to London for publication. Oddly enough, then, anti-intellectualism where the media were concerned did not originate in the lower classes in America, but among upper-level intellectuals.

This reluctance to support a local industry was not the greatest handicap to the rise of book publishing, however. Government control was the real deterrent. The Massachusetts General Court was so afraid of "the general diffusion of printing" that it gave the Cambridge Press a half century of monopoly before it began to license other printers. There was an attempt to establish a press in Pennsylvania near the end of the seventeenth century, but the authorities quickly ended it. No printing of any kind was permitted in Virginia until 1730.

Only the rise of an intellectual community among the better-educated university men of the Massachusetts Bay Colony made the continued growth of book publishing possible. In time, poetry, history, and biography began to appear on lists that once included only theology, schoolbooks, official publications, Harvard theses, almanacs, and proselytizing religious books in the Algonquin language.

As the output of the Cambridge Press began to broaden in the hands of the Day family's successors, notably Samuel Green and Marmaduke Johnson, the authorities became increasingly anxious about what it was printing. The General Court attempted to restrict what little liberty the press enjoyed. In the legislature's law of 1665, establishing a new board of licensers (who were really censors) there was a clause prohibiting a printing press in any Massachusetts town except Cambridge. Johnson himself was censured in 1668 for publishing an innocuous fictionalized book of travel, not for what was in it but because he had published it without permission. In the same year, the General Court forbade the press to print a translation of Thomas á Kempis's *Imitation of Christ* unless it dropped its papal doctrines.

By the end of the seventeenth century, book publishing in America had begun to forecast the future of printing in the New World. Book publishing, as would be newspapers, was in the hands of printers, who were sometimes publishers themselves. At various times they practiced their trade on behalf of others, usually booksellers, who also might be publishers as well. Copyright was unknown in America, and censorship was rigid. But the evidence of things to come was in the variety of work emerging from these presses. Most of the categories of modern publishing were in existence, and the growing population guaranteed that an even wider variety of publications would soon be demanded. But the technology of bookmaking was advancing scarcely at all, and the products of the presses were not distinguished for their craftsmanship or beauty.

At the end of the seventeenth century, book publishing was still a century away from being a modern industry; only the groundwork existed. What was primarily needed was freedom from restrictions of every kind so that books could become the free forum in an open society that they were obviously destined to be.

It would be wrong, however, to view the colonial printer as the protagonist in a constant struggle between freedom and tyranny. It is easy to look at it that way now, with the advantage of contemporary hindsight. But it would be wrong to fall prey to the popular mythology that freedom was an early preoccupation of the American colonists. Unfortunately for the romanticists of history, that was not the case.

The conflicts already cited merely illustrate the nature of the controls. Most early printers did not look at them as a form of tyranny. They were loyal citizens who would not have thought of printing without a license or of offending the authorities in any other way. For the most part, they were faithful and loyal subjects of the king. Defiance and rebellion came later.

The Crown itself, in fact, rarely intervened directly with printers in what they printed. Local governments, especially the royal governors, who represented the Crown and conducted its affairs in constant fear of losing their positions of power, exerted the controls.

In the seventeenth century control from London rested on the Parliamentary Press Restriction Act, forbidding the publishing of anything to which the printer's name and the place of publication had not been imprinted. Among those in England who loudly opposed this act and disobeyed it whenever they dared were the Quakers. Yet it was these same Quakers who in 1693 charged the first Philadelphia printer, Andrew Bradford, with violating that act in printing pamphlets concerning a religious controversy. When they could not prove the charge, the Quaker leaders put Bradford in jail anyway. It took the governor to release both him and his impounded equipment, after which he moved to New York.

Some printers felt so confined by the heavy hand of Massachusetts authority that they went elsewhere in the hope of finding a better climate. Others were content to stay and share in the well-being of this most prosperous of colonies and even to take advantage of financial assistance offered by the royal governor to begin a newspaper. Only a relative few chafed against the ruthless and complete suppression of press freedom that prevailed well into the eighteenth century.

BENJAMIN HARRIS, PRINTER

The most celebrated among those who offended the authorities was Benjamin Harris, a former London bookseller and publisher, who on September 25, 1690, offered for the first time a periodical that looked like a newspaper.[1] It also was a publication that ordinary colonists could afford and understand. His *Publick Occurrences Both Foreign and Domestick* extended the function of the coffeehouse. The paper was filled with gossip and information he picked up from people who frequented it. Harris was witty and printed the truth as he saw it.

It had no more than appeared, however, before it was suppressed, after only one issue. The primary reason was the familiar one: Harris had neglected to get a license from the authorities. Perhaps he also believed, mistakenly, that the comparative new freedom of the press which had accompanied Protestant King William's accession to the English throne extended to the colonies.

Beyond his basic mistake was the irritation of the authorities over two items in the paper. Significantly, they had to do with the government's foreign and domestic policies. One concerned the mistreatment of prisoners taken captive by the Mohawk Indians during the bloody border warfare between the colonies and Canada. No one doubted this story unless it was Harris himself, who noted, "This possible, we have not so exactly related the Circumstances of this business, but this Account, is as near exactness, as any that could be had in the midst of many various reports about it." Nevertheless, the recital of atrocities would certainly displease the Indians who heard about it, and whom the authorities were, for the moment, trying to enlist on their side against the French. Harris referred to them as "miserable salvages" (an old word for savages).

The other item was more embarrassing, both politically and in terms of conventional morals. "France," Harris reported, meaning its king, "is in much trouble (and fear) not only with us but also with his Son, who has revolted against him lately, and has great reason if reports be true, that the Father used to lie with the Son's Wife."[2]

In themselves, these items would not have been seriously damaging—except that everyone was aware that nothing could be published in the colony without a license. Since the public had no way of knowing that Harris did not have one, it would have been assumed that these stories were printed with the government's knowledge and consent. People reading *Publick Occurrences* in England, France, or elsewhere, consequently, would have reason to believe that the authorities had blessed the publication's insult of valuable Indian allies and the French monarch in a single issue. No wonder it was suppressed and all but a few copies were destroyed.

Harris made no further attempt at newspaper publishing, but even so, his career in the colony was remarkable. He had come to Boston as a stranger, and he left it eight years later, to return to England, as the colony's leading printer, bookseller, and coffeehouse proprietor, as well as the compiler and publisher of the most successful book of the eighteenth century in America. That was the *New-England Primer*, issued in the same year as his newspaper fiasco, and one of the truly remarkable volumes in publishing history. Sometimes called "The Little Bible of New England," this teaching tool for the secular alphabet and religious morality continued to sell for nearly two centuries, and it profoundly influenced generations of Americans. It laid the foundations for children's literature in America. Millions learned to read from it, and at the same time were indoctrinated by such familiar rhymes as "In Adam's fall/we sinned all." From later editions they learned to say, "Now I lay me down to sleep...."

The *Primer* was Harris' lasting contribution to the media in America, far more significant than his abortive attempt to establish a newspaper, which won him a permanent place in the history of American journalism. But the lesson of the paper's demise was not lost on his contemporaries. Obviously, the publication of news had to have official sanction. Although there was an equally obvious necessity to disseminate information as the colony grew and word of mouth no longer sufficed, no one appeared eager to publish an approved gazette. Nearly seventy years of colonizing preceded Harris's paper, and it took fourteen more before someone dared try again.

JOHN CAMPBELL, FAVORED PRINTER

It was logical that the Boston post office should begin where Harris had left off in publishing a newspaper. John Campbell, the sober Scot who functioned as postmaster at the turn of the century, was a man who served at a pivotal point in the city. The post office was the news center, as it would be in American small towns from that day to this, a place where news and gossip were traded freely. Campbell also possessed an instant means of distribution in the postboys who carried the mail.

The civil authorities considered a postmaster a safe choice as publisher, since he owed his job to them and, consequently, was unlikely to print anything that might offend. In Campbell's case little danger existed. He was a conservative bureaucrat who was pleased to print in large type under the title of his *Boston News-Letter*, when it appeared on April 24, 1704, "Published by Authority." In the "ears," those boxes on each side of the title, were the insignia of his distribution methods. The one on the left depicted a sailing ship, signifying that most of the news, or at least the news not already known to the *News-Letter*'s readers, came from abroad. It was already four months old by the time it got to Boston. In the other ear was the figure of a galloping postboy, soon a familiar symbol on the front pages of colonial newspapers.

Campbell had no trouble with the authorities, as might be expected, but his paper was soon in other difficulties. The local news, since it had been duly approved, was dull and most of it had been conveyed by word of mouth before it appeared.[3] As for the news from abroad, letters from home kept the colonists apprised of what was happening to friends and relatives left behind. Many had lost interest in the larger affairs of England and the Continent. At home, in the world outside Boston, no large events were occurring in the continuing struggle with the Canadians and their Indian allies. George Washington had not yet led his Virginia militia into the bush skirmish that would touch off the American phase of the Seven Years' War, or the French and Indian War, as later generations of Americans were taught to call it.

As a publisher, Campbell conducted his newspaper business with one hand, and with the other he ran the affairs of the post office and his private interests. As these interests prospered, the *News-Letter* continued to be unprofitable; it had few readers and fewer advertisers. Nevertheless, when Campbell lost the postmastership in 1718, he refused to turn over his newspaper along with the job to his successor, William Brooker. He ran the paper in an even more desultory way until 1722, when he sold it to his printer, Bartholomew Green, whose father had been the proprietor of the Cambridge Press.

Brooker was so angry with Campbell for not relinquishing the *News-Letter* that he started his own paper, the *Boston Gazette*, which proved to be fully as dull as its rival. He gave the printing contract to a young Bostonian, James Franklin, but it was a brief arrangement, because Brooker lost the postmastership in less than a year. He was succeeded by Philip Musgrave, who inherited the paper and transferred the printing contract to a friend. Now it was Franklin's turn to be angry. He immediately founded his own newspaper, the *New-England Courant*, on August 7, 1721, and suddenly there were three newspapers in Boston. The newspaper business in America had begun.

JAMES FRANKLIN, REBEL PRINTER

The *New-England Courant* was the first American newspaper worthy of the name—and for good reason. It was in the hands of James Franklin, an excellent printer. In James' sixteen-year-old apprentice, his brother Ben, the press had acquired its first real writer. Some of his friends had tried to talk James out of starting the paper, Ben recalled later, deeming it "not likely to succeed." James persisted, however, and his brother, "after having worked in composing the types and printing off the sheets," was "employed to carry the papers through the streets to the customers."[4]

As it happened, the newspaper saved James's struggling business, which had been trying to compete with several other printers in a community of no more than 12,000 people. Not enough job printing existed to go around. Since Ben had come to him as an apprentice at the age of twelve in 1718, the brothers had been compelled to turn out all kinds of odd jobs, including Ben's ballads; the issuance of pamphlets; and even printed linens, calicos, and silks.

The *Courant* arrived on the scene at a critical moment in the colony's history. For the first time, serious dissent against the ruling authority existed. It was not yet political. Dissenters were finding the iron rule of the Mathers, allied with the civil administrators, stifling to religious freedom. Congregationalism had been the most powerful force in the colony from the beginning, but now enough Episcopalians, Deists, Baptists, and others existed to form a core of resistance. Two of these dissenters helped Franklin launch his paper. They were John Checkley, a bookseller and apothecary who had already been in trouble with the authorities, and William Douglass, a Scottish doctor, who had the only medical degree (earned in Edinburgh, Leyden, and Paris) in America when he arrived in Boston.

Checkley and Douglass had seen how valuable the press could be as a propaganda medium. Dull as the *News-Letter* and *Gazette* had been, they were obviously effective as an arm of government. Presumably the dissenters also observed that the printer could be as useful in a variety of ways. Operating within a pattern that would persist for decades, Checkley was a publisher whose output included books, pamphlets, broadsides, job printing, and now newspapers. In a short time, magazines would join this list.

All these activities attracted a broad variety of people to print shops; they ranged from intellectuals eager to circulate their ideas, to businessmen needing advertising. Other citizens came, too, because the front of the shop displayed not only books and newspapers but also candy, violin strings, and many of the sundries that would soon be the stock of a general store, and later of that great American institution, the drugstore. The press usually occupied its own space at the rear of the shop. This was the pattern of the colonial print shop, and it was repeated in town after town as the presses moved westward during the eighteenth and nineteenth centuries.

Obviously, the products of such a shop could be no better than the talents and character of the man who operated the press; consequently some were typographically admirable, printed on excellent paper, while others were merely competent. The newspapers that came off these presses, written primarily by the printers themselves or by the postmasters, before Franklin arrived, were badly done, quite innocent of syntax and grammar.

As the media began to develop, the printer became more and more the operating craftsman, while the content of what he printed was more and more the province of editors and writers. Editors of newspapers, as the eighteenth century advanced, were likely to be young intellectuals with a talent for writing, who gathered around themselves men of their own stripe. As young men, they were quite naturally in revolt against the establishment. First they defied the local civic and religious authorities, and later the Crown itself. When there was no editor as the focal point, the young dissenters simply used the printer as the tool in their dissent.

In the case of the *Courant*, it was Checkley, Douglass, and their friends using the paper against the Mathers, but ironically, the issue on which they chose to oppose their powerful enemy in the first number of the paper was one of the few on which the Mathers happened to be indisputably right. The *Courant* appeared for the first time in 1721 on an August day in the middle of a steaming summer during which smallpox had been rampant.[5] Authorities had been fighting it with an inoculation Cotton Mather had heard about from one of his slaves, who had undergone the procedure in Africa. Following this lead, Mather had discovered in a London newspaper that the inoculation was being practiced in Constantinople. He then obtained some of the serum, the fluid from a smallpox pustule. He persuaded a Boston doctor, Zabdiel Boylston, to inoculate two of his slaves and his six-year-old son. Boylston's inoculations were so successful that he had to set up a clinic and became the hero of the hour.[6]

Instead of attacking the substance of the inoculation, Douglass, in the *Courant*, opposed the "doubtful and dangerous practice" of inoculation itself, calling it "the practice of Greek old women." He quickly acquired the support of doctors, select-men, and other citizens, who used the *Courant* as a club to beat Boylston and Mather, whose lives were threatened during the controversy. This was the first time a newspaper attacked the ruling establishment in British America.[7]

James Franklin tried to stay a little above the struggle and assert a printer's impartiality.[8] The Mathers struck back through the pen of Increase's grandson, Thomas Walter, with the broadside, *The Little-Compton Scourge*, or *The Anti-Courant*. The language of the *Courant* and *Anti-Courant* set the tone for the next 100 years or more of American journalism. Walter asserted that the *Courant* appealed only to "men of passion and resentment." Checkley, in the *Courant's* third issue, called Walter an "obscene and fuddling Merry-Andrew," a drunkard and a debauchee.

It is hardly surprising that Cotton Mather found the *Courant* intolerable. He dubbed its writers the "Hell-Fire Club," and characterized them in terms that would make the language of latter-day authoritarians seem unimaginative. He declared passionately that "the practice of supporting and publishing every week a libel on purpose to lessen and blacken and burlesque the virtuous and principal ministers of religion in a country, and render the services of their ministry despicable, even detestable, to the people, is a wickedness that was never known before in any country, Christian, Turkish, or Pagan, on the face of the earth."[9]

As the smallpox issue died down, so did the passions on both sides. The *Courant's* scant space—it was only a single sheet, printed on both sides—was devoted to shipping reports, snippets of information from neighboring towns, and letters from Europe. Its real substance was in letters to the editor from the Boston wits, poking fun at the city's morals and manners while being circumspect in what they said about the authorities.

These letters were signed with pseudonyms in the fashion of the day, conceits like "Timothy Turnstone," "Tom Penshallow," "Ichabod Henroost," and "Abigail Afterwit." One that appeared on April 2, 1722, was the first prose that can be authentically attributed to Benjamin Franklin. He signed himself "Silence Dogood," and wrote in the guise of a prudish widow of a country minister writing to the publisher. Speaking convincingly as a woman, Franklin wrote about manners and morals, scoffed at women's clothes and their pride of dress, lashed out at the hypocrisy in religion, and lampooned Harvard College students, which he considered his best work.

James Franklin promised to provide the paper's readers once every fortnight "with a short Epistle, which I presume will add somewhat to their entertainment." Ben suspected correctly that his brother "would object to printing anything of mine in his paper if he knew it to be mine"; consequently he slid his contributions under the shop door anonymously.[10] Franklin biographer Walter Isaacson notes that the Silence Dogood letters are so historically notable because they were among the first examples of a quintessential American genre of humor: the wry, homespun mix of folksy tales and pointed observations.[11]

Authorities made no attempt to suppress the Silence Dogood columns attesting to how far press freedom had come since Harris' day. They had reason enough, but the colony was larger now. The paper enjoyed some popular support, and the magistrates felt they had to be wary. Nevertheless, they waited only until they had a good enough reason to suppress it. They believed they had when the paper published a fictitious letter from Newport that satirized what young Boston intellectuals considered the establishment's bureaucratic slowness in dealing with public problems. The letter reported pirates off the coast, and added that the government was fitting a ship to go out after them, "to be commanded by Captain Peter Papillon, and tis thought he will sail some time this month, wind and weather permitting."[12]

This, at least, was contemptuous, the Council thought, and it had James Franklin arrested and thrown into jail. He apologized within a week, and he got out in a month when the *Courant*'s erstwhile enemy, Dr. Boylston, certified that his health had been impaired in prison. While James was incarcerated, Ben had operated the shop.

James was eventually liberated, but he was unrepentant. He began to attack the magistrates and the religious authorities again. In January 1723 he went too far once more. "There are many persons who seem to be more than ordinary religious," he wrote, "but yet are on several accounts worse, by far, than those who pretend to no religion at all." The Council had no doubt who the "many persons" were, and it reverted to the harsh kind of control that had always been exercised with dissenters. James was forbidden to publish not only the *Courant*, but "any other pamphlet or paper of the like nature, except it first be supervised by the Secretary of this Province."[13]

The *Courant*'s influential friends rallied around. At their suggestion, James made his brother publisher, giving him a release from his indenture for the purpose, so that if the authorities charged that the apprentice was merely acting for the printer, Ben would have a duly executed paper to show them. Privately, however, James insisted that his brother sign new indentures, although there is no record that he did.

In Ben's hands, the paper took on a different tone. The *Courant*'s masthead on February 11, 1723, read: "Printed and sold by Benjamin Franklin." He assured his readers that "the present undertaking ... is designed purely for the diversion and merriment of the reader" and to "entertain the town with the most comical and diverting incidents of human life." He had the overwhelming talent to fulfill that promise, and at the same time to keep on prodding the authorities so deftly that they scarcely knew they were being prodded. At seventeen he was, as Franklin biographer Carl Van Doren put it, "the best mind in Boston and ... the best apprentice in the world."[14] His excellence, at once made plain in his editing and

| **BENJAMIN FRANKLIN 1706–1790**

"Benjamin Franklin is the founding father who winks at us," Walter Isaacson writes in the most recent biography of "the first great American."

Colleagues found it hard to imagine touching the austere George Washington on the shoulder, and Thomas Jefferson and John Adams were just as intimidating, Isaacson writes. However, Americans address Franklin using his nickname and know him by his letters, almanacs, essays, and autobiography. And "this founding yuppie," as David Brooks in the *Weekly Standard* called him, likely would feel more at home in modern-day America than any of his colonial brethren.

He climbed the social ladder, moving from runaway apprentice to the most sought-after American in Europe. Along the way "he moved through this world in a humorous mastery of it," Franklin biographer Carl Van Doren writes.

Some have called him the first real newspaper editor in American history. Colonists were first introduced to Franklin by his "Silence Dogood" articles published in James Franklin's *New-England Courant.* Tired of the beatings he received as an indentured apprentice to his brother, he fled Boston for Philadelphia, where he eventually established his own newspaper. His *Pennsylvania Gazette* was the best edited, the most interesting, and the most profitable newspaper in the colonies. He also could be sinister, or downright deceptive. For example, in Philadelphia he successfully maneuvered to have one of his enemies ousted as clerk of the assembly and postmaster so he could be appointed.

Though he was happy to be known throughout his life as "B. Franklin, printer," he has been called America's best philosopher, best inventor, best writer, best business strategist, and best diplomat. He believed that one could best serve God by serving his fellow man. And his service to mankind was remarkable, Isaacson writes. By flying a kite he showed that lightning was electricity. He invented the

in the Silence Dogood letters, earned him extravagant praise, and it proved too much for a jealous older brother.

After a few weeks James Franklin returned to the *Courant* and treated Franklin as an apprentice. Once again Ben was subjected to occasional beatings. The situation became intolerable, and, as Ben wrote later, "I took upon me to assert my freedom."[15] Fearing his brother would prevent him from leaving, he left secretly on the evening of September 25, 1723, aboard a sloop bound for New York and Philadelphia, where he soon would make further contributions to media history.

BENJAMIN FRANKLIN, CAUTIOUS PRINTER

When he arrived in New York on his runaway voyage, Franklin met the colony's only printer, William Bradford, who had earlier supported James Franklin's fight against the Boston authorities. He suggested that Ben continue to Philadelphia and contact his son Andrew, who ran the family print shop and published the weekly newspaper, the *American Weekly Mercury*, there. The young Bradford had no work for the runaway and introduced him to Samuel Keimer, another printer.

AMERICAN MEDIA PROFILE   **CONTINUED**

---

lightning rod, clean-burning stoves, and bifocal glasses. He launched a variety of community organizations, including a hospital, a fire brigade, a militia, a lending library, and a home-delivery system. He also devised a system of paper currency, personally drawing the leaf designs for the notes so no one could counterfeit them.

It took some time before he abandoned his enthusiasm for the British Empire and his hopes that the New World would remain part of it. For ten years, he worked to bridge the breach between the two continents. However, in July 1775 he publicly supported rebellion from England. He could no longer tolerate Britain's attempt to subordinate the colonies by mercantile rules and taxes. He believed in the wisdom of the common citizen, the necessity of a democracy, and an end to tyranny.

He devised the Albany Plan of 1754, which called for an inter-Colonial Congress, a loose confederation of states. However, the new confederation would remain part of the empire. One year later, he revised his Albany Plan. His new plan called for a division of powers between a powerful central government and those of the states. It would become the American federal system.

Franklin was chosen by a congressional committee acting in great secrecy to embark on his most dangerous and complex mission—to form an alliance with France. His diplomatic maneuverings in 1778 sealed the course of the Revolution and altered the world's balance of power. Franklin was able to obtain treaties of friendship and alliance from the French, who enjoyed an amiable relationship with England. He played the British and French emissaries off each other. Word leaked to the French that England might sign a pact that would include America's support for Britain's attempt to capture France's island in the West Indies. The French signed the pact with one stipulation: America could not make peace with England without France's approval. The treaties were approved. Historian Edmund Morgan called it "the greatest diplomatic victory the United States has ever achieved."

At age eighty-two, a month after personally presenting a copy of the new Constitution to the Pennsylvania Assembly, he accepted reelection as the state's president. He had been employed fifty years in public offices. Two years later, on April 17, 1790, he died when an abscess in his lung burst. Some 20,000 mourners watched his funeral procession. It was the largest gathering ever in Philadelphia.

After promising to hire Ben as soon as he had work, Keimer told him his plans for luring away Andrew Bradford's business.

He was soon working for Keimer while living with the younger Bradford. Keimer finally saw the arrangement as a conflict and suggested he live somewhere else. He was able to rent a room from John Read, who eventually would become his father-in-law.[16]

During his first winter in Philadelphia, Franklin enjoyed a freedom he had never felt before. His brother could not bully him, and he was respected as a skilled workman instead of an apprentice people took for granted.[17]

However, it would not take long for Franklin to tire of Keimer, who hijacked his idea to start a second newspaper in Philadelphia. Franklin and one of Keimer's apprentices, Hugh Meredith, made secret plans to open a competing print shop once Meredith's servitude was completed. On December 24, 1728, Keimer usurped their idea and introduced the *Universal Instructor in All Arts and Sciences;* and the *Pennsylvania Gazette.* Furious at the outright theft of his newspaper idea, Franklin published several articles in the *Mercury* under the name "Busy-Body," attacking the *Instructor.* These attacks, coupled with the dullness of the paper, drove Keimer out of business within a year, as his circulation dropped to ninety. He left for Barbados while Franklin and Meredith took over the paper.[18] Meredith eventually allowed Franklin to buy him out. Franklin was twenty-four years old.

In his brief stint as editor of the *Courant*, Franklin proved more cautious than his rebel brother. As editor of the *Pennsylvania Gazette*, he resisted making his newspaper fiercely partisan. He expressed his beliefs in the *Gazette*'s most famous editorial, "Apology for Printers," a strong defense for a free press. In it he said: "Printers are educated in the belief that when men differ in opinion, both sides ought equally to have the advantage of being heard by the public; and that when Truth and Error have fair play, the reformer is always an overmatch for the latter."[19]

It was not in Franklin's nature to be dogmatic or extreme about any principle. Instead, he thought, a sensible balance was needed. He believed that the rights of printers were balanced by their duty to be responsible.[20]

His treatise may help account for the *Pennsylvania Gazette*'s success in its war with the young Bradford's *American Weekly Mercury*. Bradford, the colony's postmaster, at first ordered his carriers not to distribute the *Gazette* to its subscribers. Franklin, however, was always one step ahead of his rival. Franklin also was deceptive. He bribed the carriers to deliver it secretly.[21]

He then set out to take Bradford's job as the official printer for the Pennsylvania Assembly. "He [Bradford] had printed an Address of the House to the Governor in a coarse blundering manner; We reprinted it elegantly and correctly, and sent one to every Member. They were sensible of the Difference, it strengthen'd the Hands of Our Friends in the House, and they voted us their Printers for the Year ensuing."[22] Franklin eventually became clerk of the Assembly and postmaster of Philadelphia, which helped him to get news for his newspaper and to keep rival publishers from sending their publications through the mails.[23]

If that wasn't enough to disturb Bradford, the young Franklin would publish the most interesting and the most profitable newspaper in British America. Simply, Franklin had an innate ability to know what people wanted to read.

Though he had high-minded principles, he also knew that sex sells. The week after he printed his "Apology for Printers," Franklin wrote about a husband who caught his wife in bed with a man named Stonecutter. The distraught husband attempted to cut off the interloper's head with a knife. He also included a story about a sex-starved woman who wanted to divorce her husband because he could not satisfy her.[24] He also published the first recorded abortion debate in the New World. He knew the topic would sell newspapers.

Franklin also attracted readers with gossip and crime stories. One of the stories dealt with a couple charged with murdering the man's daughter from a previous marriage. Though the couple neglected the girl, who was forced "to lie and rot in her nastiness," a physician said she would have died from something else. The judge ordered the couple burned on the hand. The light sentence outraged Franklin.[25] His use of sensationalism would be repeated in the 1830s with the penny press and 1890s in the age of new journalism.

In addition, Franklin's *Pennsylvania Gazette* included serious foreign and domestic news. He also carried letters to the editor. Many he wrote and answered himself. Whether in news stories or editorial comments, Franklin drew upon his experiences at the *New-England Courant* and kept discreet what he said about civil authorities.[26]

He also knew the value of advertising, and he is considered one of the continent's first advertising copywriters. He grouped advertisements together on one page and then separated them from each other using lines or white space.[27]

Finally, Franklin continued to champion freedom of the press as he did in his "An Apology for Printers." That freedom would undergo numerous tests in British America.

TESTS OF PRESS FREEDOM

According to First Amendment scholar Leonard Levy, the persistent image of colonial America as a society in which freedom of expression was cherished is a hallucination of sentiment that ignores history.[28] They just didn't understand that freedom of thought and expression meant equal freedom for others, especially those with hated ideas. This was evident in two of British America's most celebrated cases involving William Bradford and John Peter Zenger.

WILLIAM BRADFORD AND PRESS FREEDOM

William Bradford, whose family became one of the first printing dynasties in America, was involved in 1692 in the first criminal trial in the New World involving freedom of the press. He had supported a separatist Quaker faction led by George Keith, whose heretical views caused his dismissal as headmaster of the Friends' school in Philadelphia. Forbidden to defend himself at Quaker meetings, Keith and a supporter, Thomas Budd, wrote a number of tracts. They hired Bradford to print them.

Bradford, along with Keith and Budd, was jailed for four months before going to trial. For the first time in the New World, Bradford made the contention, which would be repeated forty years later in the Zenger case, that the jury should determine the *law* and *fact* of a case in sedition trials. Under English law, as well as that of most of the colonies, when seditious libel (criticism of government) was charged, the judge would determine the *law*. Simply, if a judge determined the publication or utterance was "Malitious [*sic*] and Seditious" then a crime had been committed. The jury's duty was to determine the *fact* of publication, the authorship of the material, which could be determined by the printer's imprint or the seizure of the publication in his shop. If this was established, the printer would be found guilty of a crime and punished.[29]

When the magistrate overseeing the Bradford trial instructed the jury that they were "only to try, whether Bradford printed it or not." Bradford responded, "This is wrong, for the jury are judges in law as well as the matter of fact." It was the jury's duty, he said, "to find also, whether this be a seditious paper or not, and whether it does tend to the weakening of the hands of the magistrates."[30]

However, the charges against Bradford were dropped when, as the story goes, a juror asked to view a frame of hand-set type and accidentally bumped it with his cane. "The types fell from the frame ... formed a confused heap, and prevented further investigations,"[31] since a pile of scattered printer's type was poor evidence on which to convict him. Bradford went back to jail to await a second trial. However, one year later he was suddenly released.

He then fled Pennsylvania and moved his press to Manhattan Island in 1693. Now well into his sixties, he had seen three papers started in Boston and witnessed his son Andrew's success in printing Pennsylvania's first newspaper, *The American Weekly Mercury*. By November 8, 1725, the elder Bradford was ready to start New York's first newspaper, the *New York Gazette*. It was a poorly printed two-page affair so official in character that its rival, the *Journal*, launched eight years later, was quite justified in describing it as filled with "dry, senseless Stuff," and insincere tributes.[32]

However, Bradford witnessed a sedition trial in which his earlier plea would be tested again. This time it was in New York City, where the inhabitants suffered under a rule far more oppressive than anything the intellectual Mathers might have conceived. Governor William Cosby was perhaps the worst of the colonial administrators the Crown had sent to America. Lazy, lecherous, and dissolute, he ruled by whim through his flatterers and favored cronies. He had antagonized the middle-class merchants with excessive taxes. The respectable lower classes were offended by Cosby's display of ostentation. It was not so much the immorality, but the fact that they were financing it.

Like so many arrogant rulers past and present, Cosby went a step too far by deposing one of the colony's best-loved elder statesmen, Chief Justice Lewis Morris. He then appointed to succeed him young James DeLancey, the son of Oliver DeLancey, a rich merchant who was one of Cosby's friends. This appointment of a young man only recently returned from his training at Temple Bar, London, to replace a veteran jurist of high reputation affronted almost everyone.

Nothing could be expected from Bradford as a defender of Morris; his profitable business would be far too valuable for him to risk. Instead of supporting Zenger, who faced charges similar to those Bradford had to grapple with in Pennsylvania, he did the unthinkable. He wrote in his *Gazette* that men should be responsible for what they write: "Tis the abuse not the use of the press that is criminal and ought to be punished."[33]

JOHN PETER ZENGER AND PRESS FREEDOM

Zenger, a poor printer who was an immigrant refugee from Germany, served a term as Bradford's apprentice until he could set up a print shop for himself. He printed Morris' side of the story in a pamphlet, following the chief justice's ouster, and the jurist's friends saw their opportunity. They helped him establish the *Journal* on November 5, 1733. However, some historians suggest that Zenger's benefactors started the newspaper because they wanted more business and political influence in the colony.

Zenger has been so idealized in the annals of journalism that his real contribution to the historic case that bears his name has been obscured. He was an untalented writer and an indifferent printer. He had fled from authoritarian rule in Europe, and he had the courage to place his struggling business and possibly his life as well at the service of Morris and his friends.[34] It was not an inconsiderable risk, to be a stalking horse for determined men who meant to make an assault on a royal governor. James Franklin had used his friends as much as they had used him to poke dangerous fun at the rulers of Massachusetts. And although Franklin faced jail and suppression for his actions, at least he had the knowledge that the clergy and magistrates of Boston were not monsters. No one could predict what a savage tyrant like Cosby might do.

At first Cosby did no more than conduct a counter campaign against the *Journal* through Bradford's *Gazette*, but it was an uneven contest. The *Gazette's* heavy-handed vituperation, in the accepted style of the day, was no match for the satiric pens of Morris' friends, particularly the real editor of the *Journal*. He was an accomplished young lawyer named James Alexander, who drew on *Cato's Letters*, Swift's *Tale of a Tub*, and Addison's essays to score his points.[35] Through the columns of the *Journal*, like a bright thread, ran the appeal to freedom from tyranny, and the plea for representative government.

Cosby did not miss these implications and in time his patience, scant at best, ran out. He tried through DeLancey to get a grand jury indictment for libel against Zenger, but the jurors, ordinary citizens who hated Cosby, refused to hand it up. Frustrated, the governor instructed his handpicked council to do the job, and it obediently issued a warrant on its own behalf on November 17, 1734, that sent Zenger to jail "for printing and publishing several seditious libels."[36] He was charged with criminal libel, much more serious than the civil variety since it involved imprisonment as well as a fine.

Zenger wrote about his arrest in the *Journal* and said he would continue to "entertain" the reader "thro' the Hole of the Door of the Prison" with the help of his wife and "servants."[37] Once they had the printer in jail, Cosby and DeLancey persecuted him mercilessly. Reasonable bail was refused. His lawyers made a desperate effort to attack DeLancey's commission so that he would be prevented from sitting on the case. DeLancey disqualified them and appointed one of his friends to represent Zenger. This lawyer was not without conscience, however; he asked for a month's delay to prepare his case, a standard procedure DeLancey could not very well deny.

During that month, while the Morris faction plotted their course, the pending case became the talk of the colonies. Whatever the legal issues might be, even the most illiterate citizen could understand the morality of the situation: an unpopular, tyrannical governor opposed to a respectable judge with no ties to the ruling class, and a poor printer made the victim of their quarrel.

Zenger's disbarred ex-lawyers, James Alexander and William Smith, interested Ben Franklin in the case. It probably was Franklin's persuasion that stirred his friend, Andrew Hamilton, the great liberal Philadelphia lawyer, then in his eighties, to the point of accepting one more battle for liberty. Hamilton likely had issues of his own. While speaker of the Pennsylvania Assembly, he took part in prosecuting William Bradford's son Andrew when he criticized the Pennsylvania Assembly and attacked Hamilton personally. He apparently relished the opportunity to defend Zenger, who competed with William Bradford, the father of his old enemy, Andrew Bradford.[38]

Hamilton arrived in New York in the blazing summer heat of August 4, 1735, and sat quietly in the back of the room while the jury was being impaneled. He heard John Chambers, the attorney appointed by DeLancey, enter a plea of "not guilty" to the charges. Then, with the sense of drama that marked his courtroom appearances, he rose and came to the bar, a striking figure with his white hair falling to his shoulders, his ancient body erect, and his eyes keen. DeLancey and his fellow justice, Frederick Philipse, who were hearing the case, had to greet him with respect, and could hardly deny his request to appear for the defense.

Turning his body so that he was addressing the jury as much as the justices, Hamilton began in his resonant actor's voice: "I cannot think it proper to deny the publication of a complaint which I think is the right of every free-born subject to make. Therefore I'll save Mr. Attorney General the trouble of examining his witnesses to that point; and I do confess (for my client) that he both printed and published the two papers set forth in the information. I do hope in so doing he has committed no crime."

Those in the courtroom who were familiar with the law turned to each other in astonishment. Under the statutes, the jury had only to decide whether the defendant had actually made the publications. Hamilton had opened his case by admitting it.

Puzzled but grateful, the attorney general replied, "Then, if your honors please, since Mr. Hamilton has confessed the fact, I think our witnesses may be discharged; we have no further occasion for them." With publication admitted, he continued, nothing further was left for the jury to do but to bring in a verdict of guilty.

"Not so, neither, Mr. Attorney," Hamilton answered cooly. "There are two sides to that bargain. I hope it is not our bare printing or publishing a paper that will make it a libel. You will have something more to do before you make my client a libeler. For the words themselves must be libelous—that is, false, malicious, and seditious—or else we are not guilty." On this point of law, Attorney General Richard Bradley and Hamilton stood before the bench and argued. The old lawyer cited the Magna Carta (a charter of English liberty granted under considerable duress by King John on June 15, 1215) and the abolition of the Star Chamber. Bradley simply said that the law was the law. He was right, but Hamilton's superb courtroom manner had even the partisan justices momentarily hypnotized. It was only when he asserted that "the falsehood makes the scandal, and both the libel," and added he would "prove these very papers that are called libel to be true," that DeLancey interposed. Young and unqualified though he might be, he had been to Temple Bar and he knew something about English law.

"You cannot be admitted, Mr. Hamilton," he admonished, "to give the truth of a libel in evidence. The court is of the opinion you ought not to be permitted to prove the facts in the papers." He was correct, and he cited a long list of precedents to prove it. Hamilton listened patiently. He knew the citations by heart.

"Those are Star Chamber cases," he said, when DeLancey had finished, "and I was in hopes that practice had been dead with that court."

Confused and angered by this unexpected reply, DeLancey responded to it as a young man in his special circumstances might. "The court have delivered their opinion," he said coldly, "and we expect you will use us with good manners. You are not permitted to argue against this court."

It was the answer Hamilton had been waiting for. He knew he had no case in law, but he had provoked DeLancey into acting in the arbitrary way every man on the jury would recognize as Cosby's. Taking his cue, Hamilton then proceeded to give a magnificent, historic performance.

Bowing to the chief justice with a courtly "I thank you," he turned his back on both judges and addressed the jury in a ringing voice. "Then it is to you, gentlemen," he began, "that we must now appeal for witnesses to the truth of the facts we have offered, and are denied the liberty to prove.... I beg leave to lay it down as a standing rule in such cases that the suppressing of evidence ought always to be taken for the strongest evidence, and I hope it will have that weight with you."

DeLancey interrupted. Doggedly, he pointed out that the jury had no right under the law to do any more than decide whether Zenger had published the papers. It was the prerogative of the judges to decide whether they were libelous. Hamilton continued:

> A proper confidence in a court is commendable, but as the verdict (whatever it is) will be yours, you ought to refer no part of your duty to the discretion of other persons. If you should be of opinion that there is no falsehood in Mr. Zenger's papers, you will, nay (pardon me for the expression), you *ought* to say so; because you do not know whether others (I mean the court) may be of that opinion. It is your right to do so, and there is much depending upon your resolution, as well as upon your integrity.

The justices and every lawyer in the courtroom could see what Hamilton was doing. He was telling the jury to be free men, to follow their consciences and assert the liberties guaranteed them by English law. His voice ringing in the tense courtroom, he confirmed those liberties for them in the words so often cited by press historians:

> Old and weak as I am, I should think it my duty, if required to go to the utmost part of the land where my service could be of any use in assisting to quench the flame of persecutions upon informations, set on foot by the government to deprive a people of the right of remonstrating (and complaining too) of the arbitrary attempts of men in power. Men who injure and oppress the people under their administration provoke them to cry out and complain, and then make that very complaint the foundation for new oppressions and prosecutions....
>
> The question before the court and you, gentlemen of the jury, is not of small nor private concern. It is not the cause of the poor printer, nor of New York alone, which you are now trying. No! It may in its consequences affect every free man that lives under a British government on the main of America. It is the best cause. It is the cause of liberty, and I make no doubt but your upright conduct this day will not only entitle you to the love and esteem of your fellow citizens, but every man who prefers freedom to a life of slavery will bless and honor you as men who have baffled the attempt of tyranny, and by an impartial and incorrupt verdict have laid a noble foundation for securing to ourselves, our posterity and our neighbors that to which nature and the laws of our country have given us a right—the liberty—both of exposing and opposing arbitrary power (in these parts of the world at least) by speaking and writing—truth.[39]

THE ZENGER VERDICT

Justice DeLancey must have realized that he was defeated, after this moving appeal to the passions and prejudices of the jury, but he clung to what he knew. He gave what amounted to a directed verdict, insisting again that the jury could not go beyond deciding the fact of publication, which had already been admitted. That left the question of libel to the justices. But the jury was transformed. In the afterglow of Hamilton's words, they saw themselves as free men upholding the ancient rights of Magna Carta. The jury brought in a unanimous verdict of not guilty. Supporters carried Hamilton to the Black Horse Tavern to celebrate.[40]

The chief justice did not then do what he had the power to do. He could have set aside the verdict as being in direct contradiction to the law, as it was. He could even have cited Hamilton for contempt. That he did neither of these things indicated that the British government in the New World, in spite of the excesses of men like Cosby, was inclined at this point to move cautiously in its relations with the colonists. It was plain to DeLancey that the verdict was not simply the result of Hamilton's histrionics; these had only been the key that unlocked the expression of a deep and intense popular feeling. He could see it in the faces of the inspired jury, and in the electric atmosphere of the courtroom, which erupted in riotous cheering after the verdict.

Hamilton's victory was no more than a moral one, however. The principle he argued—the jury's right to determine both *law* and *fact*—was not recognized either in England or America until more than a half century later. The verdict of the Zenger jury, as DeLancey maintained, was contrary to the law. In those days, the recognized principle was, "The greater the truth, the greater the libel." Nor did the verdict have any immediate effect on the law. Truth as a defense was not recognized generally in America until 1804, when another Hamilton, the more famous Alexander, argued and lost a libel case which nevertheless stirred the lawmakers to belated reform.

Zenger might well have been rearrested after his trial, but Cosby too was cautious, primarily because Morris had gone to England to argue his case against the governor personally with the Crown. While Cosby was awaiting the result, he fell ill and died the following March. Zenger published a verbatim account of the trial, which made him momentarily famous in the colonies and got him appointments as public printer in both New Jersey and New York. However, he was not competent enough to take advantage of the opportunities that came to him, and he died poor in 1746. Ironically, he was the one who achieved lasting recognition, while Hamilton, the real hero of the case, is known today only to scholars and students of American history.

ANNA ZENGER AND COLONIAL WOMEN OF THE PRESS

Zenger spent nine months in prison awaiting trial. During that time, his wife, Anna Zenger, ran the *Journal*. She would pick up materials from her husband's jail cell and then have them set in type and printed.[41]

Journalism was one of the first occupations open to respectable women. Most women got positions when they had to take over publishing their husband's newspapers when they were jailed for thwarting the royal governors, as in Zenger's case, or, more likely, following the early deaths of their printer husbands.

Though colonial women shared hardships with their husbands, they were legally the property of men, though some inherited property. Most women could not read or write, and the few who were educated were given training in manners, morals, and social and household practices.[42] About thirty colonial women are known to have been printers, publishers, or typesetters. Of these, six served as official printers for colonial governments and one for a city government, while sixteen published newspapers, pamphlets, and tracts.[43]

Dinah Nuthead, a widow, successfully petitioned the colonial legislature in 1696 at Annapolis, Maryland, for a license to print legal forms; she was the first actual woman printer in the New World.[44] However, James Franklin's wife, Ann, was the first woman in the New World to be involved in printing a newspaper. When Franklin's *New-England Courant* ceased publication in 1726, he moved his family to Rhode Island, where he founded the colony's first newspaper, the *Rhode Island Gazette*. Ann, a skilled typesetter, helped her husband, who suffered from a variety of illnesses, finally taking over his printing house when he died in 1735.[45] Twenty-five years later she and her son, James Jr., began the *Newport Mercury*. When her son died in 1762, she took over the paper, and eventually obtained a partner. The two continued the *Mercury* until Ann's death the following year.[46]

One of the earliest woman publishers was Elizabeth Timothy, who took over the helm following the death of her husband, Lewis, in 1738. Elizabeth's readers learned in that first issue that she was not only the printer but also the publisher.[47] What she lacked in writing, grammar, and type-composing skills, she compensated for with strict and innovative financial strategies and advertising regulations. Elizabeth ruled that if an advertiser did not pay the quarterly advertising rate on time, his ads would be terminated. She often bartered subscriptions to the *Gazette* for goods and then advertised the goods for sale in the paper.[48] Her paper was lively and printed foreign as well as colonial news, literary works, and columns with varying viewpoints.

Like Timothy, Sarah Updike Goddard relieved her ill husband of his duties in 1755, becoming postmistress of New London, Rhode Island. She also was the matriarch of colonial America's most unusual printing family. Sarah and her daughter, Mary Katherine Goddard, undertook the financial risk and practical editing and printing of four papers associated with Sarah's son, William Goddard, whom she apprenticed to printer James Parker, of New Haven. He was nominally and legally owner of the four papers, but he had a habit of leaving his mother and sister in charge of the publications while he did other things.[49]

Five years after the death of her husband in 1757, Sarah moved to Providence, Rhode Island, to finance the establishment of twenty-two-year-old William's first newspaper, the *Providence Gazette, and Country Journal*. However, it was not a profitable venture, and he suspended it three years later, leaving the print shop under the direction of his mother while he ventured to New York. Mother and daughter maintained the printing office under the title Sarah Goddard and Company (Mary Goddard and a printer), while William hopped from one job to another. They printed broadsides, pamphlets, stationery, books, and an almanac, which was very popular with local housewives and farmers. The first book they published was written by a woman. They also attempted a special issue of the paper, entitled *A Providence Gazette Extraordinary*, which appeared August 24, 1765.

Meanwhile, the mercurial William, now in Philadelphia, began *The Pennsylvania Chronicle, and Universal Advertiser*, making history of sorts. The first issue on January 26, 1767, was on the largest scale yet attempted in America,[50] a large folio with four columns instead of the usual three. However, William's poor management and his relationships with his silent partners sent him back to his mother. At first, she declined his invitation to come to Philadelphia, but she eventually sold her shop and newspaper to her partner, John Carter. She and Mary Katherine managed and operated William's newly established newspaper, which was on its way to being one of the best-edited pre-Revolution newspapers. Unfortunately, Sarah died a year after the move and the burden fell to Mary Katherine.[51]

While Mary Katherine published the *Chronicle*, William took off again. This time he went to Baltimore to start a third paper, the *Maryland Journal and Baltimore Advertiser*, Maryland's third and Baltimore's first newspaper. But William couldn't sit still and he was off again. He called on his sister to take over the *Journal*, which she ran for eight years. In 1775 she was appointed Baltimore's postmistress. She held the position for fourteen years before being removed because of sex discrimination: a new postmaster demanded she be replaced by a man.[52] The postal district was to be enlarged. According to George Washington's newly appointed postmaster general, Samuel Osgood, the travel necessary to oversee the operation would be too strenuous and inappropriate for a woman.[53] In addition to her publisher and postmistress duties, Mary Katherine started a paper mill in 1776.[54]

Her *Journal* became a popular instrument of revolt. It was among the loudest voices of the rebellious colonies seeking independence from England. She attacked the cruelty of British soldiers and opened her columns to patriot propagandists, such as Thomas Paine. She also printed the first official copy of the Declaration of Independence authorized by Congress on January 18, 1777, with the names of all the signers.[55]

CONCLUSION

New World settlers talked a good game about democracy, freedom of religion, and freedom of the press. However, to them *democracy* meant that the new freedom they were establishing was meant only for those who believed in the philosophy of their particular colony. Dissent would not be tolerated.

As for *freedom of religion*, two American colonies, the only ones in the British Empire, were established with provisions for complete religious freedom. They were Maryland, established in 1632 by George Calvert, and Rhode Island, established in 1636 by the Reverend Roger Williams. Williams was banished from the Massachusetts Bay Colony for expressing religious opinions different from the official Puritan doctrine. Many Puritans had fled England because of religious persecution. However, once in British America, they began persecuting members of other religions, particularly those who did not practice Christianity or Puritanism. In 1646 the Massachusetts Act Against Heresy made it a crime against the state to deny belief in the immortality of the soul, the resurrection of Jesus, or the need for repentance. Virginia in the 1600s prescribed the death penalty for those who were convicted of blasphemy, as defined by the state.

Freedom of the press was suppressed by the heavy hands of authorities, despite the efforts of dissenters. Books, the first medium in the colonies, and then newspapers needed the approval of the government before being published. Benjamin Harris was among the first to be subjected to prior restraint laws—or censorship before publication—in the New World. His attempt to print something that looked like a newspaper was halted after the first issue. James Franklin also knew the difficulties of writing about local controversies and was imprisoned.

William Bradford may have been the first American martyr to the cause of a free press as well as to the jury's power to decide the law in libel cases. However, no evidence exists that he was a consistent champion of a free press.[56] Once Bradford became the official printer of New York, he chastised John Peter Zenger for having published "pieces tending to set the province in a flame, and to raise sedition and tumults."[57] Though numerous tests of press freedom occurred in the colonies, none was as significant as the Zenger trial. That trial established no legal precedents, but it did have a powerful effect on other juries, which were now emboldened to uphold critics of government, no matter what the law might be. This was particularly important in the turbulent decades before the Revolution, when partisan newspapers exhibited little, if any, regard for the truth in their propagandistic zeal. The Zenger trial also encouraged citizens to believe that colonial laws, as laid down and interpreted by the governors and their councils, were not immutable and could be changed by popular demand. In all this, the newspaper had emerged as the vehicle of popular revolt.

The Press and the Revolution

John Peter Zenger's triumphant vindication in challenging authorities just may have been the most significant and dramatic of all events connected with the history of early New York journalism. It also was an early sign of things to come. First, it had a tremendous influence upon popular feelings about the importance of a free press and how it could be used as an instrument of revolt. Second, it got some to thinking about the concept of liberty.

However, it would take more than thirty years from the end of colonial America's most famous trial, in 1735, to Parliament's enactment of the Stamp Act, in 1765, that those seeking liberty would witness the power of the press in manipulating public opinion on a grand scale. "Since the inception of the controversy," Arthur M. Schlesinger tells us, "the patriots exhibited extraordinary skill in manipulating public opinion, playing upon the emotions of the ignorant as well as the minds of the educated."[1]

That is a fair summary of the Americans as propagandists, and it would apply as well to the loyalist or Tory press, which was just as skillful but outnumbered. Revisionist historians who see the Revolution as an economic conflict fail to understand people's deep, fundamental emotions, which the newspapers of the time so clearly reveal. It was not greed for control of maritime commerce or political arguments over the power to tax that impelled writers to refer to their king as the ruling "savage of Great-Britain," and to charge that he thirsted "for the blood of America."

It is true, however, that the use of the press as a propaganda instrument has distorted our view of the character of the Revolution. To read the colonial newspapers, one would be justified in believing, as generations of schoolchildren have been taught, that the revolt against the Crown was the result of intolerable abuses suffered by downtrodden colonists. Once they had enough, they rose up and defeated the best the British army could offer, and so won their independence.

A RELUCTANT REVOLUTION

In reality, the Revolution was an extremely reluctant revolution from the beginning. A decade before the war broke out, very little sentiment for any open rebellion existed, and there was no general demand for independence.

First of all, the colonies, as Benjamin Franklin attested, felt closer to England than they did to one another.[2] Franklin, like many in colonial America, thought himself as much an Englishman as an American.[3] He did not believe that independence would come about in his lifetime and saw no reason why it ever should, so long as England treated the colonies as equals. Franklin saw America as the future center of the British Empire. He thought his task was to guide growth, to make life useful and beneficial to the people of the future greatest empire in the world.[4]

However, his views changed even before the first shots were fired. Two events caused that change: the end of the Seven Years' War and the Stamp Act.

THE SEVEN YEARS' WAR

Americans were as joyous as their British compatriots when the Treaty of Paris ended the Seven Years' War (known as the French and Indian War in the New World) in 1763. The war, which erupted in 1756, was the result of years of rivalry between Britain and France about French land claims in Canada and the territory near the Mississippi River all the way to Louisiana. France's expansion into the Ohio River valley repeatedly brought it into conflict with claims of the British colonies, especially those of Virginia. However, the British were hampered by France's success in gaining the support of the Indians and fostering rivalries among the American colonies. The British victory strengthened the American colonies by removing the French in the north and south. This guaranteed the security of the entire eastern seaboard from upper Canada to Florida, and opened the Mississippi River Valley for development.

Franklin had hoped to avoid further English intrusion into the New World. In 1754 he proposed his Albany Plan of Union, which called upon the colonies to unite under a president-general appointed by the king. "The colonies, so united, would have been sufficiently strong to have defended themselves; there would have been no need of troops from England; of course, the subsequent pretence for taxing America and the bloody contest it occasioned, would have been avoided," Franklin wrote.[5] Pennsylvania's governor sent the plan to the assembly on a day Franklin was absent. It was rejected. Franklin's ideas about colonial union and self-government proved premature for colonists frightened about British unified control. However, his ideas would eventually generate a "continental groundswell of opinion."[6]

The Seven Years' War left Great Britain nearly bankrupt. The conflict had saddled her with an enormous debt and created fresh territorial responsibilities in two hemispheres. Britain wanted the colonies to share in the cost of defending them; at first glance, this was not an unreasonable request. However, she also wanted to reign in the colonies and to make them more attached to the empire.

The colonists were not particularly grateful for what the British had done to save them from the French and their Indian allies. They were under the impression that they had saved themselves—with some help from the British, of course. The colonies looked forward more to the opportunities the end of the conflict would bring than to the responsibilities of being part of the empire. To recoup her losses and reign in her colonies, Britain inaugurated a series of taxes, set forth in the Sugar Act of 1764 and the Stamp Act of 1765.

THE STAMP ACT OF 1765

Under the 1764 Sugar Act, the molasses duty was halved to threepence a gallon, making its payment cost-competitive with bribery. That was the good news for the Americans. The bad news was that George Grenville, who spoke for the ministry in Parliament, actually expected them to pay the tax. To make sure they did, he required colonial merchants to document each and every shipment leaving or entering an American port. Another regulation transferred the cases of accused smugglers to special admiralty courts, whose judges were much less sympathetic to violations of the law than colonial juries had been.[7]

However, a single piece of British legislation in 1765 was enough to turn the newspapers into political organs of the most virulent kind. Word of the Stamp Act reached the colonies the last week of May 1765. By November 1, the Crown stated, almost everything written or printed on paper, including pamphlets, newspapers, advertisements, diplomas, bills, legal documents, ship's papers, and playing cards, except for books and personal letters, would be required to carry revenue stamps, which could cost as much as ten pounds.

Often cited as a particularly unjust example of "taxation without representation," the Stamp Act, from the British point of view, was completely defensible; from an historical perspective it is not difficult to understand British reasoning. First, ample precedent existed in England for taxing printed matter. For over half a century, a stamp tax had been in force there, and the system was not generally regarded as intolerable.[8] Second, Britain had been nearly bankrupted by the long war with France. Her navy had opened up the sea again to American commerce. Tax money was absolutely essential to put England on its feet, and the Crown turned to its colonies for taxes in no greater proportion than were levied against its subjects at home.

Consequently, when the Stamp Act was passed, the colonists were outraged, even though the levies fell on everyone. The notion that it was the tax on tea that started the trouble is another part of American mythology. In reality, the blow fell heaviest on newsprint and legal documents, so the two most offended segments of the population were those capable of doing the most harm to the mother country—publishers and lawyers. The *Boston Gazette* reported that Virginia was in a state of "utmost consternation."[9]

The publishers were divided on the question of resistance. A minority simply declared that they could no longer carry on their businesses profitably and suspended publication of their papers. Such actions aroused citizens who relied on these journals to advertise their wares and get their news. For example, the publisher of the

New York Gazette and Post-Boy received an anonymous letter threatening "imminent Danger" to his "house, Person, and Effects" if he suspended his "useful paper by groundless fear of the detestable Stamp-Act." Its printer, John Holt, then told his readers that he was going to continue publishing on unstamped paper. He said it was the "unanimous sentiment" that the Stamp Act was not legal, as well as impractical to execute, since no printer could apply for the stamped paper "without certain Destruction to his Person and Property from the General Resentment of his Countrymen."[10]

The majority, like the *New York Gazette* and *Post-Boy*, fought the law by evading it. If a newspaper was published without its masthead or title, it was technically not a newspaper, and therefore not taxable. A much bolder evasion was to publish without the required tax stamp on each issue, and to explain editorially that the publisher had tried to buy stamps but found none available. That was quite literally true in those places where angry mobs had succeeded in stopping the sale.

Publishers agreed with near-unanimity that the tax was a direct assault on their freedom, and it is quite possible the king's ministers intended this to be an additional benefit. The *Pennsylvania Journal and Weekly Advertiser* proclaimed that the press was dead, and appeared in the shape of a tombstone with its column rules turned over to make heavy black divisions. A skull and crossbones also appeared on its front page,[11] as they did in the *Boston Gazette* and the *Maryland Gazette*.

As soon as he arrived in London, Franklin did all he could to convince Grenville to repeal the act, which he called "the mother of mischief."[12] Grenville, however, resisted any change. He held strong to the notion that Parliament was sovereign, and that the right of taxation was an essential part of its power. Furthermore, members of Parliament voiced that Americans talked of liberty, but what they wanted was stingily to pay as little as possible. British officials believed that if Parliament yielded now there was no telling how far the Americans would go. Repealing the act, they said, would humiliate Parliament and be treacherous for Britain.[13]

Parliament, seeing the futility of trying to impose and enforce the act, repealed it on March 8, 1766. The repeal was so popular that people in America and England did not pay attention to its accompanying act, the Declaratory Act of 1766, which reaffirmed Parliament's right to pass any law it wished, binding the British colonies "in all cases whatsoever"—even taxes.[14] However, jubilant Americans praised Franklin, an agent for Pennsylvania in London, as the hero who won the repeal. It was the first time he ever spoke so long before so large an audience, and he never did again.[15]

The repeal quieted America for a while. However, Franklin was still uneasy. His vision for an imperial union had been shattered. In January, he had come to doubt that his dream of America as the center of the British Empire would ever materialize. "The breach between the two countries is grown wider, and in danger of becoming irreparable," Franklin wrote.[16]

VOICES ON THE ROAD TO REVOLUTION

A polarization began to take place. It was not a simple division between the have-not mobs of Boston and New York against the privilege and position represented by the Crown and its rich friends in the colonies. Such a division existed and grew, whipped on by radicals like Samuel Adams. But the tax was also an affront to these same rich friends, whose viewpoints were identical with those of conservative capitalists who insisted on the sanctity of property rights and free enterprise. The arbitrary action of government, whether it was the king's, as in this case, or a provincial assembly's, was as offensive to them as it was to the conservative community in the 1930s when Franklin Roosevelt proposed his social legislation.

How to deal with the taxes and the mother country was another matter. What emerged were three political ideas—Tory, Whig, and Patriot—that began to dominate newspapers before the Revolution. Causes attract zealots, and the writers and editors attracted to these conflicting ideas of the social order were nothing if not zealots. Each represented about a third of the colonists.

The Tories, best exemplified by James Rivington and Hugh Gaine, remained loyal to their country and refused to bear arms against the British in the War of Independence. The Whigs, represented by John Dickinson, "the Penman of the Revolution," were a rising capitalist faction who mildly opposed the Tory point of view. Simply, they were fence-sitters who supported the Patriots after the first shots were fired. Finally, the Patriots' philosophy was best represented by Isaiah Thomas, Samuel Adams, "the Master of the Puppets" and the leading radical, and Thomas Paine. Interestingly, except for Thomas, many of the most important Patriots weren't editors but contributors to some of the most important newspapers of the period.

With varying degrees of skill, even brilliance, they told what they were convinced was the truth, and at the same time they denounced those who did not agree with them as liars and worse.

In the decade or so before the Revolution broke into armed conflict, the young editors who spoke for the democratic view easily dominated the war of ideas. Their influence cannot be underestimated, although many historians have virtually ignored them. They lashed out fiercely at the establishment, or Tory, papers, and at the embryonic ideas of Whigs who believed until the last moment that conciliation and compromise would save their properties. They argued their own cause with fervor and dedication, if not with much devotion to the truth.

It was not difficult to kindle the patriotism of those in the great port cities, where the British tax collectors, civil servants, and soldiers were constantly under everyone's nose. But the settlers who had moved into the interior were so occupied with their own hard lives that they would have had little knowledge of what was going on in the centers of revolt if the newspapers of Boston, New York, and Philadelphia had not reached them.

A conscious effort existed on the part of these city editors to woo the farmers and convince them of their cause. It was a propagandistic campaign in which truth was the first victim. One paper, for example, depicted the British as so hungry for tax money that they meant to tax kissing. What unity existed in the colonies for the war, when it began, was the result of such newspaper stories. Reaching the farthest settlements of the Ohio River Valley weeks or months late, they were read by people who feared the Indians far more than they did the British. Nevertheless, slowly and painfully, the will to resist British rule was crystallized among large numbers of colonists.

The language of these papers was intemperate and defiant, to say the least, and there was no way of knowing when the authorities might be goaded beyond their reluctant tolerance. Moreover, it was a time when the mindless mob did not hesitate to stop writers who were afraid to sign their names. The proprietors of the papers, whether they wrote for them or not, and most did, could not hide their identities. By the time war came, a few leaders had emerged, representing the Tory, Whig, and Patriot voices.

JAMES RIVINGTON, THE TORY VOICE

Governing by virtue of property, heredity, position, and tradition was basic to the Tory philosophy. Though tagged traitors, because of their opposition to taking up arms against Britain, in reality they were the loyalists while others plotted treasonous acts against the mother country.

The colonies' most famous and exciting Tory newspaper publisher was James Rivington, familiarly known as "Jemmy." His father had been the Church of England's official publisher, as the family had been for generations. Rivington came to America in 1762 to recoup his fortunes, lost mostly at the Newmarket races. He began as a Philadelphia bookseller, prospered, and opened branches in Boston and New York, thus becoming the first chain store book operator in America.

Seeking other outlets for his vivacious personality, Rivington in 1773 began to publish in New York *Rivington's New York Gazetteer, or the Connecticut, New Jersey, Hudson's River and Quebec Weekly Advertiser*. It circulated in all these and other places, as far as the West Indies and England itself, but most of its 3,600 copies were distributed in New York City. Typically, Rivington asserted it circulated "thro' every colony of North-America, most of the English, French, Spanish, Dutch, and Danish West India islands, the principal cities and towns of Great Britain, France, Ireland, and the Mediterranean."[17]

He announced in two Massachusetts newspapers that he would strive to please readers of all "Views and Inclinations: and eschew personal Satire, and acrimonious Censures on any Society or Class of Men."[18] "Few men, perhaps," he wrote, "were better qualified ... to publish a newspaper," and as for the *Gazette*, "no newspaper in the colonies was better printed, or was more copiously furnished with foreign intelligence."[19]

Its editorial policy was proclaimed in equally flowery prose: "Never to admit any Performance, calculated to injure Virtue, Religion, or other public Happiness, to wound a Neighbor's Reputation, or to raise a blush in the face of Virgin Innocence."[20] Rivington added that he would print both sides of public questions, and in the beginning, at least, that was the one part of his policy he was scrupulous about. "The printer of a newspaper," he declared, "ought to be neutral in all cases where his own press is employed." He vowed to publish all views and all pamphlets submitted to him, "Whether of the Whig or Tory flavour."[21] This merited him respect, despite the fact that the Patriot rebels were not interested in fair and objective reporting.

As the war neared, Rivington found it as hard to be objective in New York. Finally, Rivington told his readers:

> The Printer is bold to affirm that his press has been open to publication from ALL PARTIES...He has considered his press in the light of a public office, to which every man has a right to have recourse. But the moment he ventured to publish sentiments which were opposed to the dangerous views and designs of certain demagogues, he found himself held up as an enemy of his country.[22]

Then, in November 1775, a Sons of Liberty mob, in pursuit of freedom, swept down on Rivington's shop and destroyed it. He was understandably bitter, because he had been attempting to cover both sides of public issues, as he had promised, in spite of his own Tory sympathies. He had even carried Patriot versions of events from other papers when he knew them to be untrue. But the Patriots disdained impartiality; for them there was only one truth, and that was their own. Completely disillusioned, and hardened in his own attitudes, Rivington went back to England.

He returned two years later, after the British had occupied New York in November 1775, and started another newspaper, the *New York Royal Gazette*. It was an entirely different paper, a strong Tory paper, as he turned the full force of his clever, nasty pen against the Patriots and all their works, with telling effect. From General Washington on down, the rebels suffered from his savage wit and were outraged by the paper's unprincipled charges against them. Rivington apparently had no remorse about spreading any kind of rumor that seemed likely to upset the Continentals.

He created scandals that even such formidable figures of virtue as Washington were busy denying years later. No doubt it was his experience with Rivington that caused Washington to have a distaste for newspapers. It became a passionate hatred when he was president. General Ethan Allen, whom Rivington pursued with ridicule through the war years, swore he would "lick Rivington the very first opportunity" he had when the conflict ended.[23] He tried earnestly to carry out his promise, but Rivington disarmed him with two bottles of ten-year-old Madeira and soft words. Governor William Livingston was just as vocal when he declared: "If Rivington is taken, I must have one of his ears; Governor Clinton [of New York] is entitled to the other; and General Washington, if he pleases, may take his head."[24]

The Patriots of New York, restored to power, were not so forgiving, although Rivington expediently apologized for his wartime conduct. Some of those who did not forgive him were journeyman printers, who remembered his opposition to their strike of November 1778, the first labor walkout in America. Other master printers had yielded almost at once; Rivington held out for five days. Another of the unforgiving was a Patriot whom Rivington had ridiculed during the war. Encountering the editor in the street, this man set upon Rivington and beat him.

Nothing could save him, not even the disclosure that he had been a double agent, in one of Washington's spy networks in New York. Rivington supposedly had stolen the British navy's signal codebook, which, in the hands of Admiral de Grasse, the French naval commander at Yorktown, undoubtedly played a major role in the Franco-American victory. Although documentary proof of this activity did not come to light until 1959, it is almost as difficult to believe today as it was for Rivington's contemporaries to accept in 1782. Probably the answer—at least the only reasonable one—is that his truly outrageous attacks on Washington and the other Continental commanders, particularly the abuse and ridicule he heaped on the general himself, must have occurred before he accepted the double agent's role. But the motivation for that move is still not known.[25]

Rivington's newspaper career overshadowed his considerable accomplishments as bookseller and publisher. He imported books from London, pirated and published some on his own account, and, before the war, brought out American editions of *Robinson Crusoe* and other children's books. By 1776, he had published no fewer than thirty-eight books, pamphlets, broadsides, and almanacs.

After the war, aged fifty-eight and with no other means of making a living, he turned once more to bookselling, and with considerable courage opened up trade with his old enemy Isaiah Thomas and the rising young Philadelphia publisher Mathew Carey. He even opened up a second shop, and did a little publishing. After he fell into debtors' prison as a result of bad debts of others with whom he had done business, he never recovered. Not long after his release, he died on the Fourth of July, 1802, just before his seventy-eighth birthday.

Aside from the street in lower Manhattan named for him much later, Rivington left behind a reputation that has grown with the years. The series of political pamphlets he published were a considerable influence in the course of the Revolution. His power as a publisher can be measured by the fact that so much of what he printed was destroyed by the irate Patriots. He was printer, publisher, stationer, king's printer, propagandist, and businessman. But more than any of these, he was a bookseller, with a sure instinct for knowing which books and magazines would be most popular with the public. He made a real contribution to American life in his time by providing the public with the best works, particularly those by British authors.

HUGH GAINE, TURNCOAT EDITOR

Another noted Tory editor of a somewhat different stripe was Hugh Gaine, an opportunistic Irishman who had come to New York from Belfast in 1753 and founded the *New-York Mercury*. As the war approached, he tried to maintain a

---

AMERICAN MEDIA PROFILE | **THOMAS PAINE 1737–1809**

Hulton Archive/Getty Images

Thomas Paine was truly "the godfather of the American nation," for he did more than any other individual to bring about the Declaration of Independence, Paine biographer W. E. Woodward writes. The title is not meant to diminish the work of Revolutionary leaders Thomas Jefferson, John Hancock, and Samuel Adams. It is meant, however, to underscore his efforts as a writer in bringing all diverse revolutionary activities together and giving them a common aim—the establishment of American independence.

Paine, a dismal failure in most of his early pursuits, left England in 1774 for Philadelphia, armed with a letter of introduction from Benjamin Franklin, who met and took a liking to the young man when he was in London. Printer Robert Aitken immediately offered him a position on his *Pennsylvania Magazine*. He eventually became its editor.

While in the New World, Paine began associating with leading advocates of political change. Such revolutionary impulses moved him to anonymously publish, in January 1776, a pamphlet titled *Common Sense*. In it he condemned monarchy, saying it was folly of a strong, self-reliant people to take orders from a nation across the seas. He also pointed out that many of the British rules, conceived by stupid officeholders, were utterly senseless, lacking all sound ideas of America and her people.

The pamphlet, simple in style as an ordinary conversation between friends, sold an astonishing 150,000 copies, adding fuel to the revolutionary movement. "The cause of America," he said, "is in a great

nonpartisan stance, like Rivington, but he too failed. His fantasy of obtaining revenue from both sides ended when the Sons of Liberty, those strident enemies of objective journalism, hinted at his total destruction if he did not advocate their cause.

As the British moved into New York after defeating Washington at Brooklyn and White Plains, Gaine prudently moved to New Jersey, where he continued to publish the *Mercury* in Newark, as an exceedingly mild Patriot paper. He was not happy there. Supply was difficult, and he missed the good friends and good drink he had left behind in New York. Surveying the military situation from the standpoint of ignorance, he thought that the war would soon be over and the British would win it, so he concluded it would be best to switch to the winning side. He returned to New York and was welcomed by the British, who had been publishing their version of the *Mercury* in the same shop.

As a convert, Gaine proved to be more Tory than the Tories. Those who had known him as at least a mild Patriot must have been astonished to read in the *Mercury*: "The shattered Remains of the Rebel Army, 'tis said, are got over into the Jersies. Humanity cannot but pity a Set of poor misguided Men who are thus led on to Destruction, by despicable and desperate leaders, against every idea of Reason and Duty, and without the least prospect of Success."[26]

His later versions of war news were so wildly partisan that it was difficult even for the British to believe some of them. In any case, he was not the kind of man to endear himself to the British leaders. A hardworking, serious, frugal man, Gaine was not particularly congenial to a British commander like General Sir William Howe,

---

AMERICAN MEDIA PROFILE   **CONTINUED**

measure the cause of all mankind." He became famous overnight, adding converts to his cause and crippling the Tory cause.

Once the Revolutionary War began, Paine published a series of *Crisis* papers, telling soldiers that "these are the times that try men's souls." The papers, thirteen in all, were designed to buoy the courage of the soldiers and inspire dejected patriots to keep fighting for independence. In the second *Crisis* paper, Paine created the expression the *United States of America*, becoming the first to name the new country. In later papers, he would suggest a union of the states instead of a long string of small independent republics.

Paine had more on his plate than agitating a break from Britain. He proposed a number of innovative ideas. For example, he is credited with starting the movement for women's emancipation and being the first major writer with a large audience who called for the abolition of slavery. He advocated a tax to care for the elderly, pushed the single-tax theories later identified with Henry George, and proposed a turn to internationalism, at a time when it was thought pure lunacy. In his *Rights of Man*, he called for what today would be a League of Nations and a World Court.

He also proposed a toast to "world revolution," but he was not an early Communist. Like Jefferson, he believed in individualism. He regarded the state as a "necessary evil"; the less of it the better.

To his enemies, and they were many, Paine was a "demon of discord." He fell out of favor with some Americans when he printed a *Letter to George Washington*. In it he denounced Washington for not lifting a finger while Paine was imprisoned in France. He also wasted no time in condemning John Adams. However, it was Adams who said in the early 1780s, when the colonies had won their freedom, "history is to ascribe the Revolution to Thomas Paine."

who felt himself much more akin to a man who loved drink and women like Jemmy Rivington. Consequently, when Rivington returned, he got most of the Tory business, and Gaine was left with precious little from his switch of allegiance.

Like Rivington's, Gaine's newspaper career ended in failure, but his book publishing was more successful. Most of his publishing occurred before the Revolution. He produced editions of the classics, poetry, and music, and an ambitious two-volume *Journal* of the votes and proceedings in the General Assembly.

Philadelphia also had an equivalent of Gaine, in the person of Benjamin Towne, publisher of the *Pennsylvania Evening Post*, one of three Tory papers. The *Post* had begun as a Patriot organ, and was first in the city to print the Declaration of Independence. When the British occupiers came, Towne switched his politics and began competing successfully with his old Tory rivals when they returned to the city. After the British evacuation, these editors fled once more—all except Towne, who succeeded in selling himself to the returning Americans, who permitted him to keep publishing.

As Gaine had discovered, however, it was easier to placate authority, particularly military commanders, than it was to erase the memories of common citizens. Advertisers did not return to the *Post* in any great number, and neither did subscribers. Patriot writers did not believe he reformed and refused to write for him.

More and more the censorship of newspapers had passed from governmental authority to public opinion, and some editors found it harsher than the old order. It was possible to conciliate, bargain with, or otherwise deal with governments, but there was no way to argue with an angry mob of Patriots who insisted that a paper print only the propaganda of its cause.

Although the most colorful editors of the Revolution were in Boston and New York, Philadelphia could boast three excellent newspapers during that period, and one of them had considerable distinction. It was William Bradford III's *Pennsylvania Journal*, which from the beginning made no attempt to be nonpartisan. Bradford, third in a line of famous printers, was an unabashed Patriot. He fought the Stamp Act, was among the first to come out flatly for independence, and published the first of Thomas Paine's *Crisis* papers. On the side, he operated a coffeehouse, conducted a marine-insurance business, and published books. A man of conviction, this veteran of the French and Indian Wars enlisted in the Continental army at age fifty-seven, and ended the war as a colonel. But the British occupation of Philadelphia ruined his business, and field duty so impaired his health that he could never get started again.

JOHN DICKINSON, THE WHIG VOICE

A number of factions opposed the Tory philosophy, including the Whigs, which represented a rising capitalist faction that believed more in property rights than human rights. They had a very narrow idea of liberty. Even their cry of "no taxation without representation" was focused upon the economic aspects of the New World's struggle with the mother country. Most noted was the wealthy and sophisticated Pennsylvania lawyer John Dickinson, who was tagged the "Penman of the Revolution."

He was given that name because he was neither a publisher nor printer. He wrote a series of letters anonymously. Almost all partisan essays were signed with the names of classical heroes or invented characters, such as "Farmer in Pennsylvania." Anonymous or pseudonymous writing were traditional practices in the press by this time. Unidentified writing helped preserve the impression that newspaper essays and pamphlets were spontaneous expressions of American public opinion, and it camouflaged the sheer extent of the efforts of many prolific writers.[27] The use of pen names also helped to protect the identity and safety of anonymous writers.

Dickinson's "Letters from a Farmer in Pennsylvania to the Inhabitants of the British Colonies" were published in the *Pennsylvania Chronicle* in twelve successive installments from December 2, 1767, to February 15, 1768. In these letters he denounced the Townshend Acts.

After Parliament repealed the Stamp Act, calm reigned—but only for a while. Britain still needed revenue to pay her war debt, and Chancellor of the Exchequer Charles Townshend was determined that the colonies should pay a fair share. He knew that levying a direct tax would reignite the Stamp Act protests, so he proposed in May 1767 a new series of tariffs. Approved by Parliament in late June, the Townshend Acts placed new import duties on glass, lead, paints, paper, and tea—products that were in high demand. The act also revived the writs of assistance (a general search warrant issued by the courts to assist the British government in enforcing trade and navigation laws) and made the Crown directly responsible for the payment of colonial governors' salaries (so they couldn't be held hostage by colonial assemblies). It also reduced North American troop deployments while simultaneously shifting the financial burden of supplying the soldiers entirely onto the colonists.[28]

Dickinson attacked the new taxes, rejecting the distinction between internal and external taxes. The Townshend Act was an external tax, as opposed to the internal tax of the Stamp Act. He distinguished between taxation as incidental to the regulation of imperial trade and taxation primarily for purposes of revenue. Only Parliament could impose the first; only the provincial legislatures the second.

He likened the Townshend exactions to a "bird sent out over the waters, to discover, whether the waves, that lately agitated this part of the world, are yet subsided," and laid down as maxims *that we cannot be HAPPY, without being FREE*—that we cannot be free, *without being secure in our property*—that *we* cannot be secure in our property, *if, without our consent, others may, as by right, take it away.*"[29]

His argument was so masterful that all but three newspapers of the time published the letters. They also came out in pamphlet form several weeks after the *Chronicle* run. The endless speculation provoked by the mystery of the "Farmer's" identity further whetted popular interest.[30]

Though Dickinson realized that public opinion, especially in his colony of Pennsylvania, was mixed, he feared that New England and Virginia radicals were forcing rebellion on the rest of America. Dickinson, and most Whigs of the time, believed that separating from England was not the answer. They believed that difficulties with England could be worked out. However, his letters were important to the revolutionary movement. First, they moved merchants and businessmen to question British policy. Second, the "Letters" also came from a distant colony, not New England, thus elevating the local partisan bickering to the plane of a continental struggle for basic liberties.[31]

The British Whigs, oddly enough, were the greatest thorn in the side of their American counterparts. They, for instance, supported commercial restrictions on colonial businesses that could have very well destroyed their American rivals.

In response to the Townshend Act, the Massachusetts House of Representatives adopted on February 11, 1768, a letter that was circulated among the assemblies of all the colonies. It stated grievances similar to those adopted by the Stamp Act Congress in 1765. The colonies again boycotted English goods, which contributed to tensions that resulted in the British occupation of Boston on October 1, 1768. On April 12, 1770, Parliament repealed the importation duties of the Townshend Act on all materials except tea.

Samuel Adams could conceive of no greater compliment to the Philadelphian than to say after meeting him, "He is a true Bostonian."[32]

ISAIAH THOMAS, THE PATRIOT VOICE

While the Tories were interested in heredity rights and the Whigs in economic interests, the Patriots were interested in radical social change. The two most important Patriot voices were those of Isaiah Thomas and Samuel Adams. Thomas' *Massachusetts Spy*, which he started in Boston when he was only twenty-one, was the work of a man who was a master printer and one of the finest scholars of his time. He was so poor that he had to be apprenticed when he was only six years old to support his widowed mother. He rose to be the foremost book publisher of the post-Revolutionary era, a courageous newspaper editor, a noted historian, and the founder and first president of the American Antiquarian Society.

The *Spy* started out to be a voice of moderation, following the Whig line, and announced its good intentions in the same kind of language used by hundreds of papers in the next century, and abandoned with varying degrees of speed. A slogan under its masthead asserted that it was "A Weekly Political and Commercial Paper— Open to All Parties, but *influenced* by None." Perhaps no paper could have pursued such a policy for long in the tense years just before Lexington and Concord, but Thomas tried hard, until he lost his faith in the possibilities of conciliation. More and more, the *Spy* took on the coloration of the radical *Boston Gazette*, although it was much more reasoned, as well as better written and edited. Typographically, it was a work of art compared with its contemporaries.

Eventually, Thomas became a part of the underground conspiracy as the open break with Britain came nearer, and the *Spy* joined the *Gazette* on the list General Thomas Gage's officers were compiling of places to be captured and destroyed when the troops occupied Boston. Two nights before the occupation, Thomas loaded up his type and presses and hauled them across the Charles River to Watertown. He did not pause there, but went on to Worcester, Massachusetts.

In post-Revolutionary America, Thomas's Worcester shop was the wonder of the printing industry. It had 150 employees and seven presses, supplied by its own paper mill, and possessing its own bindery. Thomas had become America's leading publisher, publishing his newspaper, three magazines, and a distinguished list of more than 400 books, including Blackstone's *Commentaries*, Bunyan's *Pilgrim's Progress*, Defoe's *Robinson Crusoe*, more than 100 children's books, and (strictly under the counter) the first American edition of the erotic classic *Fanny Hill*, under its original title, *Memoirs of a Woman of Pleasure*. The apprentices Isaiah trained opened branches in eight other cities, utilizing his money and advice to do it. The *Spy* continued until 1804.

SAMUEL ADAMS, THE "MASTER OF THE PUPPETS"

Like Thomas, Bostonian Samuel Adams best represented the Patriot, radical, or democratic view. The master plan for change would be written by Adams, who eventually pulled the strings of the players that ignited a war and moved a nation unlike any other on the face of the earth. His enemies tagged him the "master of the puppets."

Like Dickinson, Adams wrote about Boston's suffering under the Townshend Acts and British military rule. This most radical of colonists used the chief radical newspaper in the colonies, the *Boston Gazette,* to set forth his political philosophy.

A member of Boston's radical Caucus Club—whose members were committed to independence—Adams' political philosophy was influenced by the writings of English philosopher John Locke, who believed that no government was absolute, that people have the right to overthrow governments that do not act for the public good. He also believed that governments should have distinct executive, legislative, and judicial branches.[33]

Two events in his life may have pulled him toward Locke. Adams, cousin of John, was the son of a very successful maltster, the merchant who steeped barley in water and prepared it for brewing. At the Old South Church, his father had been known as Deacon Adams, a godly man devoted to the Congregational faith. He also was a politician, at a time when the label was considered demeaning, and the crusade of his life was an economic scheme called the Land Bank.[34]

In 1740 Massachusetts slid into depression. The slide began in 1690 when the colony issued paper money, driving gold and silver coins from circulation, and creating inflated prices for goods. British merchants who were trading with Massachusetts were incensed as prices began to fluctuate. The king heard their cries and demanded that the governor veto any further issuance of paper money.

As tempers flared between the governor and the legislature over the measure, two joint-stock banking companies, or Land Banks, were formed to meet the crisis. The first, patronized by merchants, issued notes that could be redeemed in silver at the end of ten years. The second issued notes that could be exchanged for products or goods after twenty years. Adams' father invested in the latter. Along with Deacon Adams, approximately 800 were stockholders in the Land Banks. These Land Bankers not only controlled the legislature, but they had the power to remove the governor. However, in 1741, Parliament declared the Land Banks illegal. The Land Banks had to suspend their operations and redeem their script. Land Bank partners were held individually liable, driving each into ruin. Deacon Adams' fortune was wiped out.

His father's devastation would shape the political opinions of young Samuel Adams. Another controversy also would. Deacon Adams enrolled his son in the Harvard class of 1740, paying his tuition in molasses and flour.[35] There young Adams met evangelist George Whitefield, who led a religious revival known as the Great Awakening. Followers heeded Whitefield's call and gave up their fashionable clothes for Puritan gray garb. To his father's delight, Adams considered the clergy as a profession. But Adams changed course and studied law, to his mother's dismay. She, like most in British America, did not consider it a reputable profession and urged her son to nix such desires. He did and went back to Harvard for a master's degree. By the time he graduated in 1743, preachers at their pulpits pounded

AMERICAN MEDIA PROFILE | SAMUEL ADAMS 1722–1803

Samuel Adams was once described as one who "eats little, drinks little, sleeps little, thinks much, and is most indefatigable in the pursuit of his object." That object was independence from the British, which he pursued with a zeal that was scarcely interrupted and an energy that knew no fatigue.

The son of a Boston merchant and brewer, Adams proved to be an unsuccessful brewer and a poor businessman. However, like his cousin, John Adams, who was thirteen years younger, he was an excellent and very popular politician.

After obtaining a master's degree from Harvard, Adams began the study of law, which made his father very happy. But he eventually abandoned his law studies, obtained a sizable loan from his father, and lost every bit of it when he attempted to go into his own business. He was forced to join his father in the family brewery.

At his parents' death, he inherited a large estate, which included a home and the family brewery. Not one who could handle money, he spent most of it within ten years and took a job as a tax collector. If there was ever a man less suited for such work, it is hard to imagine him. Adams has been compared to Socrates and Abraham Lincoln because he was the least bitter of men and had a love for humble people. Thus, he would listen to the hard-luck stories of the underprivileged and, of course, collect no taxes.

the colony's rich and powerful for their lack of piety, while the Land Bankers took them to task for their greed. The young Adams agreed on both counts. He argued in his final Harvard paper that when the existence of the commonwealth was at stake it was lawful to resist even the highest civil authority.[36]

Adams believed that when a government, such as Parliament, ignored the basic rights of its colonies, the basic contracts that bound both entities no longer applied. According to Adams, the Stamp Act was such an example of the colonies' basic rights being ignored. In 1764, he drafted on behalf of the town of Boston the first public protest in the New World against the right of Parliament to tax the colonies. The final paragraph suggested a union of the colonies to fight the grievances.[37] It was printed in the *Boston Gazette*.

EDES AND GILL'S *BOSTON GAZETTE*

Samuel Adams found willing cohorts in *Boston Gazette* editors Benjamin Edes and John Gill, natives of Charlestown, Massachusetts, who had grown up there as friends. Edes was a politician, poorly educated but nevertheless possessed of a talent for writing inflammatory prose that reflected his radicalism.

When they came into control of the *Boston Gazette*, the city's second oldest paper, early in 1764, they boldly published it without license and quickly made its offices a gathering point for dissenters, who gravitated between the *Gazette*'s back rooms and the nearby Green Dragon tavern.

He found success in the political arena, where his great oratory skills were better put to use. He was elected in 1765 to the Massachusetts state legislature, where he became a vocal opponent of several laws, including the Tea Act, passed by the British Parliament to raise revenues in the American colonies. His wrath against the British was so great that his enormous Newfoundland, called "Queque," being continually badgered by the British troops in Boston, would attack a Redcoat whenever he saw one.

Besides enlisting "Queque" in his war with the Redcoats, Adams took his wrath out against the British in two ways. He used his able pen, writing essays in colonial newspapers, such as the *Boston Gazette*, and pamphlets. With the help of John Hancock, he organized the revolutionary Sons of Liberty and Committees of Correspondence that stirred up sentiment against the British. He acted as a master puppeteer, pulling the strings of his action groups as he plotted the Boston Tea Party and the Boston Massacre, the first instance of bloodshed between the British and the colonists.

A fed-up General Thomas Gage issued a warrant for his and Hancock's arrest. Gage had the power to send them to England for trial on a charge of treason. Paul Revere's famous 1775 ride to Lexington was to alert the two that the British were coming.

As a member of the Massachusetts legislature, he was the first to propose a "continental congress." He was eventually appointed to the Continental Congress, where he became a passionate advocate of independence from Britain. As one of its delegates, he signed the Declaration of Independence in 1776.

He retired from Congress in 1781 and became a leading member of the state convention to form a constitution. Eight years later he was appointed lieutenant governor, and upon the death of Hancock, he was chosen governor and was annually elected until 1797, when he retired from public life.

Boston was "the hotbed of sedition," and Edes' friends Sam Adams and James Otis, earnest and angry radicals, began writing for the paper under pseudonyms. Their political articles prepared the minds of the people for the idea of independence.[38]

The attacks under such names as "Populus" (Sam Adams) and "A True Patriot" (probably Edes) against the Crown and its governors provoked Governor Sir Francis Bernard to refer to the *Gazette* as "an infamous weekly paper which has swarmed with Libells of the most atrocious kind."[39] The *Gazette*, in turn, told the governor to "retreat or you are ruined."

Leading the revolt against the Stamp Act, the *Gazette* could claim at least a partial victory when the ministers retreated in May 1766 and repealed the part of it that applied to printers. There was jubilation and a growing sense of power in the shop at Court Street and Franklin Avenue, where the partners and their friends gathered to celebrate. These friends now included some others, soon to be illustrious, as John Adams, Josiah Quincy, and Joseph Warren. Their collective labors, as John Adams described them, consisted of "cooking up paragraphs, articles, & occurrences &, working the political machine!"

In this situation, the frustrated authorities got no help from the timid proprietors of the papers they controlled, and they were given no help from abroad, although they had generated a demand in Parliament to bring Edes and Gill to England for an examination of their part in the Stamp Act resistance. Nothing came of that move.

Only a few years earlier, the authorities would have found this intolerable. However, when the governor tried to bring an action against Edes and Gill, charging a "breach of privilege tending to overthrow all government," the Council refused to act, on the ground that they would "only be rescued by the mob." It was the mob that ruled now, not the Crown's representatives, and the *Gazette* was its mouthpiece. Edes himself was a member of a little revolutionary group called the Loyall Nine, an organized street gang in Boston, similar to the Sons of Liberty.

When Governor Bernard brought an action against Edes and Gill before the Council, the upper branch predictably supported him but the lower branch asserted that freedom of the press was "the great Bulwark of the Liberty of the People" and refused to act. A grand jury refused to indict.

Strengthened by these decisions, the publishers pursued Bernard relentlessly. Someone in the governor's office leaked to them the news that British soldiers were to be quartered in Boston to establish law and order, and the *Gazette* carried an account of it. Bernard pleaded with the Council to make Edes and Gill identify their sources, and disclose the names of their pseudonymous contributors, but the Council declined. Then an even more damaging leak occurred, in which the *Gazette* obtained, no one knows how, confidential letters the governor had sent to his British superiors in London. They described what was happening in the colony and referring in blunt, unflattering terms to the individuals, including several Council members, who were obstructing him. That resulted in a demand by the Council for his recall, and he sailed out of Boston Harbor for England on the first of August 1769, with the jubilant chiming of the church bells in his ears, celebrating his departure.

It was a victory for a free press, but hardly one for truth. The *Gazette* saluted Bernard's departure by describing him as "a Scourge to this Province, a Curse to North-America, and a Plague to the whole Empire." The governor was, in fact, an honest and conscientious public servant, a scholar with a talent for architecture; Harvard Hall, which he designed after a fire destroyed the college, is a present reminder of his abilities. He was a cultured man, an able administrator in the British colonial system who no doubt regarded the Sons of Liberty in much the same light as college presidents looked upon the students who were trashing libraries, looting offices, and paralyzing administrations in the late 1960s.

There was little opposition to them in Boston. The three other papers, two more or less kept alive by government printing contracts, were jointly, as John Adams described one of them, "harmless, dovelike, inoffensive." When the *Post-Boy* and the *News-Letter* issued a joint supplement, the *Massachusetts Gazette*, published on Mondays and Thursdays, it carried the old, familiar mark of government control, "Published by Authority." It was referred to derisively by the opposition as the "Court Gazette." In the last hours before the occupation, these two trumpeters dissolved their business, loaded their press and type on a wagon at night, and escaped to Watertown, where Edes continued publishing, moving back into Boston after the British left in March 1776. Gill remained in Boston and was arrested, but was later freed.

Consequently, the Massachusetts officials of the Crown were determined to start another paper, with a publisher who might be more successful in countering the *Gazette*. They chose John Mein, a pugnacious Scottish bookseller, whose loyalty was guaranteed. His Boston *Chronicle* appeared for the first time just before Christmas in 1767.

Within a month, the two papers were at each other's throats, and in the process set a pattern that persisted in the American press for the next century. The style was one of violent language, often followed by violent physical action, either by disgruntled readers or by the publishers themselves. In the first instance, the *Gazette* published a scathing article attacking something the *Chronicle* had printed. Mein demanded the writer's name (it was probably Otis, signing himself "Americus"), and Gill refused, whereupon Mein came at him with a club, for which he was taken to court and fined.

If Edes and Gill represented the rough-and-ready Patriot press, Mein demonstrated that the Loyalists could answer in the same tongue. To him, John Hancock was "Johnny Dupe, Esq." and Otis a "Muddlehead." Worse language was employed in his *Chronicle* to answer the daily libel in the *Gazette*. But he had no chance against the zealots who were crusading in the name of freedom; they intended the freedom to be for themselves, not for Mein.

They hanged him in effigy, boycotted his bookshop, disfigured his signs, and broke into his office at night with the intent to tar and feather him. After that, he went about armed, until he was attacked in the street one day by an organized mob, and during the scuffle, by ironic chance, he wounded a British soldier who happened to be passing by. Some Patriots hypocritically seized upon this as an opportunity to swear out a warrant against Mein. He had to flee by night to a British ship in the harbor, which took him to England.

THE SONS OF LIBERTY

Boston radicals now gravitated to Samuel Adams at the *Gazette* office. An agitator and propagandist, Adams also was faithful to his Puritan heritage, which meant emphasizing diligence, organization, and preparation.[40] Such talents were seen in his diligent maneuverings of the core revolutionary group, the Sons of Liberty, his organizing the Committees of Correspondence, and his preparing the *Journal of Occurrences*.

The Sons of Liberty came together to protest the Stamp Act in 1766, faded away after its repeal, then came to life two years later after the passage of the Townshend Acts. Though British authorities were leery of the agitators for independence, they also knew that many of the members remained loyal to the Crown. Many Sons of Liberty members said they were only defending their rights against royal officials.[41]

In addition to Edes, Adams' brigade included such notables as the *New York Journal's* John Holt; *South Carolina Gazette's* Peter Timothy; *Newport Mercury's* Solomon Southwick; *Massachusetts Spy's* Isaiah Thomas; *Pennsylvanian Chronicle's* William Goddard; *Pennsylvania Journal's* William Gradford III, though he refused to fully commit his paper to the Radical cause; and the engraver Paul Revere.

Providing the latest information to the revolutionary group were Committees of Correspondence. Adams proposed in 1772 that all the towns of Massachusetts appoint Committees of Correspondence to consult with one another about their common welfare. This was after Massachusetts Royal Governor Thomas

Hutchinson turned a deaf ear to the colonists' call to convene the legislature to deal with the Crown's order that judges be paid by the British Crown and not by the colony. Such action undermined the need for an independent judiciary.

Some eighty towns heeded Adams's call. Virginian Dabney Carr the next spring suggested that inter-Colonial Committees of Correspondence be established. Adams now had his own news service with his representatives covering every important meeting.

These reports, news stories if you will, chronicling dastardly deeds and events involving British troops, were published in the Adams-directed *Journal of Occurrences*. Such stories talked about British soldiers engaging in activities from spitting on the streets to attempted rape. Though most reports were probably false, it helped crystallize public opinion that the British troops were acting badly and that the Crown was ruthless in its punishment toward the Patriots. The *Journal* was then sent to various publishers who included the reports in their newspapers.

Simply, what Adams had plotted was a news network to gather reports of atrocities committed by the British that were printed in his *Journal*, thus spurring his revolutionary group to act. Reports of the Boston Massacre of 1770, the Tea Act of 1773, and the Intolerable Acts drove the Sons of Liberty to action. A number of Bostonians, including eleven-year-old Christopher Seider (sources disagree since his name could have been Christian Snider), gathered outside the home of Ebenezer Richardson, an informer for the local British customs inspectors, on a cold and windy February 22, 1770, morning. When the pelting of rocks broke most of his windows, Richardson picked up his unloaded musket. When the mob broke down his front door, he loaded it and fired into the crowd, wounding several and killing Seider. Adams and his Sons of Liberty organized the largest funeral procession ever seen on the American continent.

The Sons of Liberty were defiant three years later, when Parliament passed the Tea Act, giving a monopoly to the East India Company. It now could sell its tea directly through colonial agents, thus eliminating the American middlemen. Colonists felt that if the Crown could eliminate this profitable trade, it could eliminate others. Pushed by the Committees of Correspondence, newspapers, and the public, the Sons of Liberty on December 16, 1773, dressed as Indians boarded the *Dartmouth* and dumped its cargo overboard. It was the Sons of Liberty's Boston Tea Party.

The actions generated more stringent laws, which the colonists dubbed the Intolerable Acts, to punish Boston and her radicals. The measures included:

- the Coercive Acts, which included the Boston Port Bill, closing Boston Harbor to all commercial traffic until the colonists paid for the spoiled tea.
- the Administration of Justice Act, which authorized the transfer of legal cases involving royal officials charged with capital crimes to Great Britain.
- the Massachusetts Government Act, which made high elective officials subject to royal appointment, ending self-rule in the colony.
- the 1765 Quartering Act, which required civilians to open their homes to British soldiers when existing barracks were inadequate.
- the Quebec Act, which extended the Canadian border south into the Ohio River valley, giving Canada lands previously claimed by Massachusetts, Connecticut, and Virginia.

Topham/Image Works

A Currier and Ives lithograph dramatizes the Boston Tea Party, one of many events planned by Samuel Adams and his Sons of Liberty to protest England's taxation of the colonies.

Such acts confirmed Adams' view that independence was the only remedy for the trouble of the time and that war was inevitable. Through the inter-Colonial Committees of Correspondence, Massachusetts was invited to take the lead in calling for the First Continental Congress. Besides dealing with the Intolerable Acts, another issue that the First Continental Congress in Philadelphia debated was what to do with Hutchinson's replacement, General Thomas Gage. His authority was supported by the return of British soldiers to Boston. Delegates, however, were not about to have Boston radicals dictate the national agenda. Instead they agreed that if Gage attempted to rule by force, the residents of Massachusetts could respond in kind, and the other colonists would come to their aid.[42]

General Gage received orders to arrest Adams and his "willing and ready tool" John Hancock and send them over to London to be tried for high treason. Gage was intending to seize them at Lexington on April 19, 1775, but loyal Sons of Liberty member Paul Revere reached the Lexington residence of the Reverend Jonas Clarke, where Adams and Hancock were lodging. As the story goes, Sergeant William Munroe, who was guarding the house, told Revere to keep the noise down because people were sleeping. "Noise!" Revere allegedly barked. "You'll have noise enough before long. The regulars are coming out!"[43]

The two escaped to Woburn and then to Philadelphia in time for the second session of the Continental Congress. On the morning of April 19, 1775, the "shot heard 'round the world'" was fired at the battles of Lexington and Concord, igniting a war, foreseen and diligently planned and organized by the "master of the puppets."

DECLARATION OF INDEPENDENCE

On July 2, 1776, more than a year after the skirmish at Lexington and Concord, the Continental Congress took the most treasonable step by declaring the colonies independent of Great Britain in approving the motion offered by Richard Henry Lee of Virginia and seconded by John Adams of Massachusetts. About to go to press that day, Benjamin Towne added this line in his triweekly *Pennsylvania Evening Post*: "This day the CONTINENTAL CONGRESS declared the UNITED COLONIES FREE and INDEPENDENT STATES."[44]

However, most did not hear about the separation until weeks later. The *Pennsylvania Journal* and the *Pennsylvania Gazette* told its readers July 3, while *New-York Gazette and Weekly Mercury* readers learned about it on July 8. *Boston Gazette* readers learned a week later. It wasn't until July 10 that the *Massachusetts Spy* announced that it was reporting a rumor that the Congress had repudiated "that Monster of imperious domination and cruelty—Great Britain! Which we hope is true."[45]

The purpose of the Declaration of Independence, penned by Thomas Jefferson and edited by Franklin and Adams, was to explain why the colonists' decision to separate from Great Britain was reasonable and just. In it Jefferson stressed that governments derive their legitimacy from "the consent of the governed" and that a government without such consent had no authority to rule. He said people can change their form of government if that government becomes oppressive. It was the ablest piece of writing born of the long controversy, a resounding exposition of "unalienable rights" that ever since has reverberated through the country and world.[46]

After the official Declaration was adopted, on the evening of Thursday, July 4, the Congress on Friday and Saturday sent copies to the legislative assemblies, conventions, and similar bodies, as well as to the military commanders. Congress approached John Dunlap, printer of the *Pennsylvania Packet or The General Advertiser*, to print broadsides of the document. An exuberant Samuel Adams exalted: "Was there ever, a Revolution brot about, especially so important as this without great internal Tumults & violent Convulsions!" The people, he said, looked on the Declaration of Independence "as though it were a Decree promulgated from Heaven."[47]

When the skirmish at Lexington and Concord occurred, it precipitated a war that only a small minority of colonists really wanted. That was why the conduct of the war itself proved to be so difficult. There was little agreement on objectives, many of those who fought were halfhearted about it, and great numbers fled the militia at the first opportunity, leaving in the middle of a battle if that was when their terms of enlistment expired. The British had little more appetite for the conflict, and a good case could be made for the argument that this was a major reason for their ultimate defeat.

If the Revolution had an authentic hero, it was George Washington. His unruly militia, dependent on the ragged ranks of the Continental army, was beset on every side by treachery and treason. He was in constant struggle with a Continental Congress so divided and weak that it could not provide him with the men and money he needed. He also lacked any real support from a population that was far more self-seeking than patriotic. Yet against all this, Washington stood firm, a monument to patience and persistence. His army lost every major battle of the war except the two decisive ones, at Saratoga and Yorktown, and there is little doubt that the contest would have been lost entirely without the help of the French.

NEWSPAPERS AS A REVOLUTIONARY FORCE

Newspapers played a key role in the events of the Revolution (including those preceding and following actual warfare). Magazines were not yet strong enough to take a major part, and the impact made by book publishing was confined largely to pamphlets, if in fact one counts them as books.

Approximately thirty-seven newspapers were in operation at the start of the Revolution, on April 19, 1775. During the six years of warfare, another thirty-five newspapers were started. Of these about fifteen were Tory organs. Most of the others advocated the Patriot view.

A number of factors made these newspapers a potent medium for the Revolution. One factor was the youth of their proprietors. In New England, several young men were heads of lively newspapers, some in partnership with their fathers and others who had inherited their presses. In the South, William Parks was not yet thirty when he established the *Maryland Gazette* at Annapolis in 1727, and nine years later founded the *Virginia Gazette* in Williamsburg, Virginia. Having learned his art from the finest printers in England, and enjoying the benefit of an excellent education, Parks gave the educated English gentry who had settled in the Tidewater South a typographically superior, well-written newspaper much appreciated by Washington, Jefferson, and other future leaders of the republic who lived there.

Another factor was the Crown's move to stop licensing newspapers. This led to a proliferation of them. By 1750, there were fourteen weeklies in the six colonies with the highest population. They had become an essential part of colonial life, not only as carriers of news but as the transmission belt between producer and consumer. Nevertheless, they were becoming closely allied with the spectacular rise of business in pre-Revolutionary America; by midcentury, circulations were substantial enough, when aided by advertising revenue, to make a few publishers reasonably rich. That kind of success made it possible to produce papers with more news in them, and to publish them more often, sometimes as frequently as three times a week.

Although the newspapers of the Revolution were valuable to each side in providing a unifying force and a platform for political conviction, they obviously divided the country even further by their unbridled partisanship. It may well be that the familiar saying "You can't believe everything you read in the newspapers" had its roots in the press of the Revolution, when people believed only what was in the papers that represented their own political convictions.

Such disaffection, along with the wartime difficulties of getting newsprint and paper, reduced the number of journals from thirty-seven in 1775 to twenty after the guns were silenced at Yorktown. That would not include eighteen started and discontinued during the war. But other new starters were more fortunate, so that the net loss was only two at the time hostilities ended.

Physically, newspapers did not improve during the Revolution (as one would expect), but their quality was raised because of the influx into journalism of young and talented people. Compare, for example, the typical notice of a local death in the *New London Gazette*—"Last Monday there died here Mr. Edward Ashby, a very inoffensive man in the hundred and ninth year of his Age"—with Rivington's coverage of the same kind of event: "On Monday afternoon, the Spirit of that facetious, good-tempered, inoffensive Convivialist Mr. John Levine, ascended to the Skies."

One of the most astute observers of the role of the press in the Revolution was Ambrose Serle, in charge of the Royalist press in New York, who wrote home to Lord Dartmouth in 1776 about the American papers: "One is astonished to see with what avidity they are sought after, and how implicitly they are believed, by the great Bulk of the People.... Government may find it expedient, in the Sum of things, to employ this popular Engine."

Government did. As every politician could not help observing, the press had already surpassed the pamphlet and the sermon as a propaganda instrument, and people were beginning to depend on it for their information, right or wrong. It was a situation ripe for exploitation, and that was exactly what happened when the Revolution was over and the new nation began.

THE REVOLUTIONARY WAR'S IMPACT ON THE PRESS

Taxes levied by the Crown unleashed a newspaper offensive that had profound impacts on American journalism. Those impacts included increases in readership, new ways of distributing newspapers, greater frequency of publication, and the development of the newspaper editorial, which sparked debates on the issue of press freedom.

Readership   The prolonged war generated a thirst for news and views, with some 40,000 homes reading a newspaper. Rivington had a pre-Revolutionary War circulation of approximately 3,600, while Thomas' circulation was 3,500. The Patriot newspaper, *Connecticut Courant,* of Hartford became a circulation leader after the occupation of New York by the British in 1776. Its circulation leaped to 8,000. A number of London papers during those years might well have been jealous of those figures.[48]

The colonists' appetite for news allowed publications to increase their editions from just once a week to two or three times a week, with some newspapers thriving in communities that never possessed any. Benjamin Towne's *Pennsylvania Evening Post*, which experimented with both triweekly and semiweekly issues, evolved after the war into America's pioneer daily. Starting on May 30, 1783, it lasted only one month. However, the next year another Philadelphia newspaper, the *Pennsylvania Packet,* published by John Dunlap and his partner, David C. Claypoole, converted their triweekly to a daily on September 21, 1784. It continued to publish for nearly half a century; its most famous subscriber was George Washington, of Mount Vernon, Virginia. Dailies began springing up in such cities as New York, Baltimore, and Charleston by 1790.[49]

Distribution   Bad roads, the interference of military campaigns, and poor financing culminated in a partial breakdown of the colonial postal system, hastening the need for a new newspaper distribution technique. Private post riders, who had been in vogue before the beginning of hostilities, as well as trained pigeons carried competing newspapers from town to town, collecting subscription fees. They also carried tear sheets so other colonial printers and publications could share stories and comments. In larger towns, printers hired delivery boys (they might also be older men).[50]

Editorials   For the first time, a distinction was made between news and comment in some newspapers. Printers even struck out boldly, signing partisan statements and sometimes inserting pungent italicized or bracketed comments in news reports.[51] For example, the publisher of the *New York Journal* used italics to denote comments in reports by Adams' *Journal of Occurrences*.[52]

This partisan style of newswriting, in which commentary or comments followed the lead or other paragraphs of news stories, led to the forerunner of today's newspaper editorial. The following death and marriage notices that appeared in newspapers at the time illustrate the trend:

> Last Monday there died here Mr. Edward Ashby, a very inoffensive man, in the hundred and ninth year of his Age.
>
> Last Sunday evening was married here Mr. Daniel Shaw, of Marlborough, to Miss Grace Coit, of this Town, a young Lady embellish'd with every Qualification requisite to render a married life agreeable.
>
> On Monday afternoon, the sprit of that facetious, good tempered inoffensive Convivialist Mr. John Levine, ascended to the Skies.[53]

FREEDOM OF THE PRESS

Newspapers' growing use of editorial comments inescapably involved them in freedom of the press issues. At least as they understood it, Revolutionary leaders placed great importance on freedom of the press. John Adams, for example, said that he knew of no "means of information … more sacred … than … [a free] press."[54] On the eve of the Revolutionary War, the First Continental Congress underscored the point in 1774 in its "Address to the Inhabitants of Quebec." The document, aimed at explaining to a largely alien audience the political rights that Americans felt they must defend against ministerial encroachment, set freedom of the press among the five foundation stones of English liberty.[55] It read:

> The last right we shall mention regards the freedom of the press. The importance of this consists, besides the advancement of truth, science, morality and arts in general, in its diffusion of liberal sentiments on the administration of government, its ready communication of thoughts between subjects, and its consequential promotion of union among them, whereby oppressive officials are shamed or intimidated into more honorable and just modes of conducting affairs.[56]

The most significant phrase in the Quebec declaration of 1774 stressed the diffusion of "liberal sentiments." However, loyalist sentiments were simply suppressed.[57] Patriots heralded freedom of the press as a virtue, especially the unlimited liberty to praise the American cause. Criticism of that cause brought the zealots of patriotism with tar and feathers.[58] Simply, liberty of speech belonged solely to those who spoke the speech of liberty.[59]

John Adams went so far as to propose that one's adherence to the independence movement be the legal test of loyalty. Such a test, he said, would stop unfriendly papers and "produce no more seditious or traitorous speculations." Like Adams, Francis Hopkinson, a member of the Continental Congress and a signer of the Declaration of Independence, saw the press as one of the most important privileges in a free government. However, he also warned against its abuses. He said:

> When this privilege is manifestly abused, and the press becomes an engine for sowing the most dangerous dissensions, for spreading false alarms, and undermining the very foundations of government, ought not that government upon the plain principles of self-preservation to silence by its own authority, such a daring violator of its peace, and tear from its bosom the serpent that would sting it to death?[60]

Hopkinson spoke for many at a time when Tories were afforded no relief. His words also generated the following question: Did the revolution bring about a truly free press, one that would tolerate various points of view? All but two state constitutions included the words of Virginia's Bill of Rights: "the freedom of the press is one of the great bulwarks of liberty, and can never be restrained but by despotic governments." Maryland's constitution stated, "the liberty of the press ought to be inviolably preserved."[61]

Maryland also provided two test cases on the question of whether a newspaper could disseminate unpopular sentiments at this time. Vagabond printer William Goddard published on February 25, 1777, in the *Maryland Journal* an article by the future U.S. Supreme Court Justice Samuel Chase, who wrote under the pen name of "Tom Tell-Truth." When he satirically suggested acceptance of the British peace proposals, the Whig Club of Baltimore demanded that Goddard reveal the source and the writer repudiate the "clumsy irony." Goddard refused and was ordered to leave the vicinity.

On July 6, 1779, Goddard was in the hot seat again. This time he published an anonymous article against General Washington by the lately court-martialed General Charles Lee. A mob descended upon a frightened Goddard, who identified the writer and was forced into temporarily disowning Lee's views. Both times the state legislature, citing Maryland's Bill of Rights, supported Goddard's right to editorial independence.[62] Freedom of the press had come a long way.

However, when the Constitutional Convention assembled in 1787, a free-press clause was not on the delegates' minds. Charles Pinckney, of South Carolina, proposed a free-press clause for the Constitution, but it was rejected by a slight majority. Members of state ratifying conventions, on the other hand, were alarmed at its omission. So was Samuel Adams, who wanted to safeguard "the just liberty of the press." Seeing the writing on the wall when Congress met for the first time under the new Constitution, it added a national Bill of Rights. The First Amendment stated that Congress shall make no law "abridging the freedom of speech, or of the press."[63] The Revolutionary War era ended with a priceless gift to American journalism and the democratic process—a free press.

CONCLUSION

Tory, Whig, and Patriot political ideas dominated newspapers before the Revolution. Causes attract zealots, and the writers and editors attracted to these conflicting ideas of the social order were nothing if not zealots. With varying degrees of skill, even brilliance, they told what they were convinced was the truth, and at the same time denounced those who did not agree with them as liars and worse.

In the decade or so before the Revolution broke out in armed conflict, the young editors who spoke for the democratic view easily dominated the war of ideas. Their influence cannot be underestimated, although many historians have virtually ignored them. They lashed out fiercely at the establishment, or Tory, papers, and at the Whigs who believed until the last moment that conciliation and compromise would save their properties. They argued their own cause with fervor and dedication, if not with much devotion to the truth.

The first work of Revolutionary newspapers was not the planning of a new society but rather the exposure of injustices in the old. Newspaper editors knew what they were doing in this collective endeavor, and they exalted in their mission. The language of these papers was intemperate and defiant, to say the least, and there was no way of knowing when the authorities might be goaded beyond their reluctant tolerance. Moreover, it was a time when the mindless mob did not hesitate to invoke violent repression in the name of liberty.

Much of the newspaper war was collective and anonymous, but the proprietors of the papers, whether they wrote for them or not, and most did, could not hide their identity. By the time war came, a few leaders, the most noted being the young Benjamin Edes and John Gill, had emerged. They, along with Sam Adams and John Dickinson, fueled the flames of revolution.

Although newspapers of the Revolution were valuable to each side in providing a unifying force and a platform for political conviction, they obviously divided the country even further by their unbridled partisanship. Readers basically believed only what represented their own political convictions.

Now others wondered if government would find the popular engine an expedient tool. Government did. Politicians could not help but notice that the press had already exceeded the pamphlet and the sermon as a major communications instrument, and people were beginning to depend on it for their information, right or wrong. It was a situation ripe for exploitation, and that was exactly what happened when the Revolutionary War was over and the new nation took shape.[64]

THE PRESS AND THE FOUNDING OF A NATION

After the Revolution, powerful men exploited the power of the press to shape public opinion and the direction of the nation and its politics. This was a time of great change. Since the end of the Revolution, America had existed as a confederation, but the 1780s marked a new era in politics and journalism. The new Constitution, adopted in 1789, transformed the loose grouping of the United States into a unified nation. As new printers and publishers appeared on the scene, the revolutionary press gave way to a nation-building press that began to report on the great debates shaping the form and character of the new government.

During the Revolution, the Tory party had disappeared as a political force. Now, among a deeply divided people still not certain whether they had traded British rule for control by an American aristocracy—and even more uncertain about how to govern themselves—two new sides had formed: the Federalists, or Hamiltonians, who wanted a strong, centralized federal government, and the Anti-Federalists, or Jeffersonians, who held to the sentiment of Thomas Paine, "that government is best which governs least."

A two-party system was emerging, and a bitter power struggle was under way. From the beginning, battle lines were drawn over the very nature of the new government, and leaders of both parties recognized the need to appeal to public opinion. In the process, the Federalists and Anti-Federalists each created their own newspapers to enlighten and encourage the public debate from their viewpoint. This new, partisan press featured powerful newspaper editors siding with the parties that supported and, in some cases, financed them.

For the Federalists, John Fenno published the first issue of the *Gazette of the United States* in April 1789. Two years later, Philip Freneau launched the Anti-Federalist's *National Gazette.* Fenno and Freneau's newspapers were like shots fired over the bows of opposing battleships. The party press era would go down as one of the most vivid and vitriolic periods in American history.

With the nation's political system taking shape, one of the most important roles of this press was to serve as a watchdog over the opposition party. It was a rough-and-tumble process of discovery and disclosure. At times the partisanship turned sufficiently violent that the national government—with limited success—tried to legislate against the practice. Some historians have called this period the "dark ages of journalism" because of the scurrility of the press. Adding to the tension was the war between Great Britain and France. At one point, the Federalists, holding control of the national government, succeeded in passing the oppressive (but short-lived) Alien and Sedition Acts for the purpose of silencing the voices of their Anti-Federalist opponents.

Both political parties had come to realize a singular fact that had been the essence of American public life since the first colonists had stepped ashore in the early 1660s: public opinion was the foundation of public policy. "Give to any set of men the command of the press, and you give them the command of the country," the Federalist judge Alexander Addison wrote in the *Columbian Centinel* in 1799, "for you give them the command of public opinion, which commands everything."[1]

The Signing of the Constitution of the United States in 1787, 1940 (oil on canvas) by Howard Chandler Christy (1873–1952) © Hall of Representatives, Washington D.C., USA/The Bridgeman Art Library

George Washington presides over the second Constitutional Convention in 1787 in a painting by Howard Chandler Christie.

To John Adams, from the Commonwealth of Massachusetts, as to others, dissolution itself was the greatest single threat to the American experiment. "The fate of this government," he had written earlier from New York to his former law clerk, William Tudor, "depends absolutely upon raising it above the state governments."[2] He knew that Americans were accustomed to putting their interests of community or region ahead of those of the union except during war, and not always then. Immediately following the Revolution, General Nathanael Green had written to General George Washington from South Carolina that "many people secretly wish that every state be completely independent and that as soon as our public debts are liquidated that Congress should be no more."[3]

Soon after the Constitution was ratified, as legislators arrived in New York for the first session of the new Congress, two major issues were at stake: (1) the level of power granted to the national government as opposed to power reserved for the states; and (2) the absence of a Bill of Rights.

The outcome for both would be anything but certain.

THE BILL OF RIGHTS AND PRESS FREEDOM

In the first session of Congress, the Bill of Rights was drawn up and submitted to the states to ratify. Of overriding concern to the press was the First Amendment:

> Congress shall make no law respecting an establishment of religion, or prohibiting the free exercise thereof; or abridging the freedom of speech, or of the press; or the right of the people peaceably to assemble, and to petition the Government for a redress of grievances.

Supporters of the Constitution—the Federalists—had argued for a strong national government. Opponents—the Anti-Federalists—contended that the Constitution, as written, would create a centralized and potentially despotic government and, at the same time, give no guarantees for freedom of religion, speech, press, or assembly or any right to petition the government. The concept of a free press was rooted in the thinking of many legislators. It was, for example, included in the Virginia Declaration of Rights, coauthored by James Madison; in the Massachusetts Constitution, written by John Adams; and debated and discussed in the general correspondence of many of the authors and defenders of the Declaration of Independence. "No government ought to be without censors and where the press is free, no one ever will," Thomas Jefferson told George Washington in 1792.[4] But in the debate over the necessity for a Bill of Rights, there were powerful voices on both sides; neither Benjamin Franklin nor James Madison, for example, thought such language was necessary. The record of the congressional discussions is sketchy; it is impossible to be certain what Congress had in mind.

It was the Federalists' contention that a Bill of Rights was unnecessary because powers not specifically given to the federal government would be preserved and upheld by the states. At least two delegates, George Mason, of Virginia, and Eldridge Gerry, of Massachusetts, skeptical of democracy without restraint, walked out of the convention. In the following weeks they were joined in their opposition by Thomas Paine and Samuel Adams, who demanded a Bill of Rights as a condition of approving the Constitution.

These views supporting a Bill of Rights attracted other powerful supporters who were serving abroad in London and Paris when the Constitution was debated and written. Reading the Constitution for the first time, John Adams—who was then serving as ambassador to Britain—voiced his overall satisfaction with the document but expressed immediate concerns about the absence of a Bill of Rights.

"What think you of a Declaration of Rights? Should not such a thing have preceded the model?" John Adams wrote to Thomas Jefferson in France.[5] Although Jefferson said almost nothing publicly, he had much to say in private correspondence with James Madison. "I do not like...the omission of a bill of rights providing clearly and without the aid of sophisms for freedom of religion, freedom of the press, protection against standing armies, restriction against monopolies, the eternal and unremitting force of the habeas corpus laws, and trials by jury in all matters of fact triable by the laws of the land and not by the law of nations."[6]

Madison argued that public opinion expressed during the Revolution had been more powerful in determining civil rights than legislation had, but he also acknowledged the logic of Jefferson's observations. "The political truths declared in that solemn manner acquire by degrees the character of fundamental maxims of free Government," he wrote, "and as they become incorporated with the national sentiment, counteract the impulses of interest and passion."[7]

The document itself had been drafted behind closed convention doors. No reporters were allowed inside to hear or record the proceedings. Even so, when the proposed Constitution was released to the public, virtually every newspaper in the country printed a copy and opened its columns to discussions of it. In the early weeks, editorial support for adopting the Constitution was so strong that Anti-Federalist supporters complained their views weren't getting a fair hearing. Editors responded that they were printing what they received, and if they were publishing fewer articles opposing the Constitution, it was because fewer articles were submitted to them.

Of the avalanche of articles that were published in favor of adoption, the most widely talked about and republished was a series called the *Federalist Papers*. Co-authored by Alexander Hamilton, James Madison, and John Jay, each man signed his contributions by the pen name of "Publius." Their articles appeared first as editorials in the semiweekly *New York Independent Journal* between October 1787 and April 1788. In time, the series was reprinted in newspapers throughout the country. Eventually, they were published in a pamphlet and, in an extended form, as a book. There were eighty-five articles in all. To this day, the series is recognized as one of the most insightful works ever written on America's constitutional form of government.

By the time New Hampshire became the ninth state to ratify the Constitution, it was June 1788 and the debate had established national recognition for the two-party system. Supporters of the Constitution were being called Federalists. They were men engaged, for the most part, in commerce, manufacturing, and banking, property owners, mostly, who were more interested in preserving and extending their economic advantages than in risking social experiments. The opponents of the Constitution were being called Anti-Federalists and, as a group, they largely comprised the agrarian class. They were small farmers and city wage earners, supported by intellectuals and political philosophers, who wanted to continue the social reforms that had brought on the American Revolution in the first place.

Even after the Constitution was amended to include the Bill of Rights, Federalists, led by Alexander Hamilton, and Anti-Federalists, led by Thomas Jefferson and his protégé, James Madison, continued to do battle over issues critical to the new republic. Of particular interest were the federal government's assumption of state debts and the question of whom the United States should support in overseas conflicts between France and Great Britain. The record of the congressional discussions when the Bill of Rights was drafted is sketchy; it is impossible to know what Congress had in mind when they drafted it. Considered word for word, the First Amendment is almost everything a free press advocate might hope for, but most scholars doubt that the majority of the framers intended the First Amendment to be an absolute prohibition on any government actions that might curtail the freedom of the press.

Whatever the first Congress may have intended, it was only a few years later that the Federalists and the Anti-Federalists had each established their own party-controlled newspapers. Then, too, it was only a few years later that Congress passed laws that seemed to be a flagrant violation of the First Amendment when, in 1798, Congress approved the Alien and Sedition Acts, a group of laws designed to silence political dissent in preparation for a war with France.

THE FEDERALISTS AND FEDERALIST EDITORS

The *Federalist Papers* established Alexander Hamilton as leader of the party. It was Hamilton who wrote the largest number of Federalist essays—possibly fifty of them. James Madison is believed to have written thirty of them. John Jay, a noted New York lawyer and a member of both Continental Congresses, probably wrote the other five.

Hamilton was one of the most respected and yet reviled men in the government, a revolutionary who considered the framework of the British government he revolted against to be "the best in the world."[8] Brilliant to the point of genius, he was an immigrant of illegitimate birth who arrived in New York from the West Indies at the age of fifteen. In less than a decade, he had distinguished himself as a scholar at King's College (later Columbia University), and had become a student leader of the unrest that led to the Revolution. While serving as an officer under General George Washington, Hamilton began campaigning for a convention to enlarge the powers of the federal government. He favored government support of commerce and believed that the way to make government work was to encourage an educated, well-to-do ruling class, whose special interests would be closely tied to the interests of the nation. "We should be rescued from democracy," Hamilton insisted, and he looked forward to a restoration of an aristocracy.[9] To survive, Hamilton thought the nation would have to be what it had not been under the Articles of Confederation—firmly united, with the separatist tendencies of the states kept in check, able to defend itself against attack from outside forces, and dependable in economic matters.

When it came to the economy, Hamilton believed it was his duty to establish the nation's economic credit regardless of the cost to citizens. He had no compassion for Shays' Rebellion, as it came to be known after one of its leaders, Daniel Shays, a former captain in the Continental army. The rebellion protested heavy and rising taxes and court actions brought against indebted farmers who, in many cases, were losing their land.

Hamilton was a veteran himself, but his inclinations would have been to put down Shays' Rebellion by force rather than by reason. Yet his great success was not as a military man but as the author of the *Federalist Papers*. As one of Hamilton's biographers observed:

> He was a natural journalist and pamphleteer—one of the fathers of the American editorial. His perspicacity, penetration, powers of condensation, and clarity of expression were those of a premier editorial writer. These same qualities made him a pamphleteer without peer.[10]

Hamilton's coauthors of the *Federalist Papers* were his fellow Federalist leaders. Hamilton was commonly linked with Madison, although they were unlikely compatriots. Madison was a Virginia statesman, a tiny and sickly looking man who dressed always in black and emerged as a formidable figure in the House of Representatives on the strength of his penetrating intelligence. He was often called the "Father of the Constitution" and the "Father of the Bill of Rights." Although he supported Hamilton's views, Madison considered Jefferson to be his mentor. On the basis of his relationship with Jefferson, he wrote and secured the adoption of the Bill of Rights in return for sufficient votes to ratify the constitutional package. The third *Federalist Papers* author, John Jay, was prevented by illness from writing more than five of the essays. Jay was a New Yorker, a noted lawyer, and member of both Continental Congresses, who served as minister to Spain and would become the first chief justice of the Supreme Court under President Washington.

Few people in the country understood the press as well as Hamilton did. He had traveled the colonies and read the newspapers from Boston to Virginia, observing along the way that a government or a politician could have no better friend than a newspaper dedicated to party or personal interest. He saw, too, that the best way to be certain of a newspaper's dedication was to handpick its editor and control him. Consequently, in 1789, he established what became, in effect, the official organ of the Federalist administration, the *Gazette of the United States*.

On April 15, 1789, fifteen days before Washington took the oath of office as the first president of the United States, John Fenno published its first issue. The appearance of the *Gazette*, as it was called, marked the beginning of the party press era.

THE FEDERALIST EDITORS: FENNO, COBBETT, AND RUSSELL

The *Gazette* was founded and subsidized with money supplied by Hamilton and other prominent Federalists who were always ready to supply more if it were to be needed. Hamilton himself was the paper's chief contributor. His editor, John Fenno, was a thirty-eight-year-old Boston schoolteacher, who had kept General Artemas Ward's orderly book during the Revolution.

Before the *Gazette* appeared, New York, even as the nation's capital, had no strong Federalist newspaper. Hamilton intended the *Gazette* to be the official Federalist organ in the battle to determine the nature of the American government.

To Fenno, its purpose was "to hold up the people's own government, in a favorable point of light," he wrote, "and to impress just ideas of its administration by exhibiting FACTS, comprise the outline of this paper."[11]

The *Gazette* quickly became the leading paper of the national Federalist Party, circulating to party leaders and printers in all thirteen states. To meet its operating expenses, Hamilton, who was now serving as secretary of the treasury, gave Fenno the printing of government contracts, including all of the printing from the Treasury Department and much of the Senate's. Fenno's newspaper carried some foreign news, but focused on reports from the debates in the House of Representatives on taxes, tariffs, and smuggling. When Thomas Jefferson was forced to resign from Washington's cabinet in 1793 over charges of scandal, Fenno's paper castigated him and, at the same time, defended Hamilton against Anti-Federalist charges that bankers, speculators, and wealthy merchants had gained far more than their due under his aegis in the Treasury. When the capital was transferred to Philadelphia, Fenno and the *Gazette* moved too because of the stipulation in his proposal to Hamilton that the paper be "published at the seat of government."[12]

With the *Gazette* gone, New York City was once again left without a strong Federalist organ. To fill the vacuum, two more publishers moved in. On the more scathing side was William Cobbett with *Porcupine's Gazette*, and on the temperate side was Benjamin Russell with the *Columbian*. Cobbett was considered by many to be the best writer of the period. He was an immigrant, an English printer and bookseller, who lived in America for only six years, from 1794 to 1800, but in that short time he eclipsed John Fenno, still the official subsidized party editor, as the Federalists' leading journalistic advocate. When Cobbett launched *Porcupine's Gazette* in 1797, it was a lively daily newspaper, taking its name from Cobbett's own pen name, "Peter Porcupine." Cobbett vowed to his readers that he would never be impartial. "Professions of impartiality I shall make none," he said.[13] Cobbett quickly demonstrated that he was a master of invective and willing to attack his peers. He especially appeared to enjoy antagonizing his Anti-Federalist rival, Benjamin Bache, editor of the Philadelphia *Aurora*. At one point, Cobbett called Bache "that public pest and bane of decency." At another time, he called the *Aurora* "Mother Bache's filthy dishcloth."[14]

As for Russell, his moderation existed only in the highly charged atmosphere of the party press era. In 1798, when a Federalist Congress passed the Alien and Sedition Acts, Russell wrote, "It is Patriotism to write in favor of our Government; it is Sedition to write against it."[15] Russell was pro-British and anti-French, an advocate of an American aristocracy and, in time, an enemy of Thomas Jefferson.

THE ANTI-FEDERALISTS AND ANTI-FEDERALIST EDITORS

The colossus of the Anti-Federalists was Jefferson, who served as secretary of state in Washington's cabinet and vice president in President Washington's cabinet before assuming the presidency himself. Jefferson was the direct opposite of his colleague Hamilton, and not just in ideology. Jefferson was convinced that no other people in the world were as well off as the independent, rural landowners of the

United States. Having lived in London and Paris, and having seen firsthand the wretched condition of European cities, he was convinced that the benefits of American farmers and city wage earners must be protected and maintained.

To Jefferson a decentralized, states'-rights government was strong enough; he would have been content with no more government than was necessary to preserve internal order. Although Hamilton insisted upon responsible government—one to protect property and aid commerce—Jefferson was more interested in a responsive government, more concerned with the current needs of the people than with security. He believed that the primary means of communication was the newspaper, and since the political system was based ultimately on the will of the people, he thought that appealing to public opinion became crucial. "The basis of our government being the opinion of the people, the very first object should be to keep that right," Jefferson famously wrote to Edward Carrington, "and were it left to me to decide whether we should have a government without newspapers or newspapers without a government, I should not hesitate a moment to prefer the latter. But I should mean that every man should receive those papers and be capable of reading them."[16]

ANTI-FEDERALIST EDITORS: FRENEAU AND BACHE

Fighting the Federalists' newspapers were a number of prominent Anti-Federalist papers. Many of the harshest attacks on Hamilton's economic policies—along with some of the more biting criticisms of President Washington—came from the *National Gazette*, a newspaper just getting started in Philadelphia in 1791 as an antidote to the partisan Federalist views of the *Gazette of the United States*. When it became known that the editor of the *National Gazette*, Freneau, had been encouraged by Madison and Jefferson to establish the paper, and that he was employed by Jefferson as a translator in the State Department, it appeared that Jefferson himself had an invisible hand in the attacks. Freneau's most vicious swipes were aimed at Hamilton, whom Freneau delighted in vilifying. Adding to the insults, his anti-Hamilton diatribes were almost always accompanied by lavish praise for Jefferson.

Publicly, President Washington claimed to disregard newspaper abuse; privately, he asked Jefferson to intercede with Freneau and remove him from the State Department. Instead, Jefferson insisted that Freneau and his paper were saving the country from a return to the monarchy and persuaded Washington that it would be a grave misstep to impede on the freedom of the press.

Perhaps more aggravating for the president was the unrelenting feud between Jefferson and Hamilton, the two highest officers in his cabinet. Animosity between them had reached the point where they could hardly stand to be in the same room. Each was certain the other was a dangerous man intent on dominating the government; both complained privately about the other to the president.

As for Freneau, money didn't bring him to the capital, Madison did. Madison was Freneau's classmate at Princeton, and he brought him to Jefferson's attention. Freneau saw himself as a journalistic crusader. Under his editorship, the early editions of the *National Gazette* were mild enough, until one day he let loose a barrage at Hamilton over the injustices of debt funding. The pen name he used was "Brutus," and Hamilton immediately realized that he had a journalistic foe who could match him. Day after day, Freneau let loose with verbal volleys. They were colorful and articulate and even less gifted Anti-Federalist editors began picking up these exchanges.

Freneau was proving to be such an irritant that Hamilton made the mistake of responding. He wrote an unsigned article for Fenno's *United States Gazette* that said a government employee shouldn't criticize its policies. Freneau fired back that the stipend he received from Jefferson's State Department did not muzzle him. With Hamilton's identity as a writer revealed, he accused Jefferson of being the real author of the *National Gazette* attacks. The quarrel between the cabinet officers had to be refereed by President Washington, who found the breach beyond repair.

Hamilton, for his part, disliked and distrusted the French nation, while, for the good of the American economy, he favored better relations with Britain. Jefferson disliked and distrusted the British nation, while seeing in the French Revolution the embodiment of the ideals of the American Revolution. There was only one issue on which the two cabinet members could agree: for the sake of the country, they both said, Washington must serve a second term. For he alone could hold the union together.

In the *National Gazette*, Freneau warned that "plain American republicans" stood to "be overwhelmed by those monarchical writers…who were spreading their poisoned doctrines through this blessed continent." To commemorate the Fourth of July Independence Day, the *National Gazette* declared, "another revolution must and will be brought about in favor of the people."[17]

The upshot of the exchange was this: Seeing themselves as representing the true spirit of republican ideals, Jefferson, Madison, Freneau, and others allied with them began calling themselves Republicans,[18] implying that that the Federalists were no friends of democracy, but rather monarchists. Although there was some doubt whether it was Jefferson or Madison who led the Republicans, there was no doubt who led the Federalists. Hamilton was more than a match for anyone.

In the same way, Freneau's *National Gazette*, for all his good writing, was no match for Fenno's *Gazette of the United States*. In the end, it was a matter of cash. The *National Gazette* was strapped for operating money. There were no deep-pocket sponsors to rescue him as Fenno had under Hamilton's sponsorship. Jefferson offered help for a while, but when he left the cabinet in 1793, Freneau lost his financial support, and the newspaper closed.

One of the journalists who stepped into the breach left by Freneau was Benjamin Franklin Bache, the grandson of Benjamin Franklin. Bache founded the *Philadelphia General Advertiser*, better known as the *Aurora*, in 1791. He was a mercurial young man, brilliant but also impetuous. Friends called him Benny, but Philadelphians referred to him as "Lighting Rod Junior," only partially in remembrance of his distinguished relative.

Bache started the paper in 1790, at age twenty-one, and at first it seemed that he meant to improve the quality of journalism rather than debase it further. The *Aurora* was the first paper to attempt to provide a full account of the proceedings in Congress, at a painstaking length that the other papers did not emulate. But Bache was an angry young man, a strong Anti-Federalist, and he soon began to devote his news columns to a virulent campaign against President Washington and the Federalists that far surpassed anything the *National Gazette* had attempted.

Bache accused Washington of overdrawing his salary, professed to regard most of his acts as unconstitutional, and reprinted forged and long-since discredited letters of Washington that the British had used in Rivington's paper in 1776.

Bache had been brought up in England and France by his grandfather and was sympathetic to the French cause. When John Jay came back from London in 1795 with the treaty he had negotiated with Great Britain in support of the anti-French party headed by Hamilton and others, Bache reacted.

Like Freneau before him, Bache resorted to personal attack in his campaign to wreck the Federalist Party. He even tried to besmirch the character of Washington, who was already known as the "Father of His County." Bache wrote in the December 23, 1796, issue of the *Aurora*:

> If ever a nation was debauched by a man, the American nation has been debauched by Washington. If ever a nation has suffered from the improper influence of a man, the American nation has suffered from the influence of Washington. If ever a nation was deceived by a man, the American nation has been deceived by Washington. Let his conduct then be an example to future ages. Let it serve to be a warning that no man may be an idol.[19]

The retaliation was swift, and it came from his rival editors. Federalists trashed the *Aurora* offices and beat Bache. Fenno caned Bache in the street. In the

---

AMERICAN MEDIA PROFILE | **PHILIP FRENEAU 1752–1832**

Courtesy of StanKlos.com

Thomas Jefferson knew he had just the right man in Philip Freneau to edit the *National Gazette* as a counter to Alexander Hamilton's Federalist mouthpiece, the *Gazette of the United States*.

Freneau had a rebellious spirit and energy that was matched only by his talent as a writer. He was a formidable adversary on the battlefield of print, according to James Madison, his roommate while attending Princeton. Other rebels such as Aaron Burr, William Bradford, and Harry Lee gravitated to their room to debate the affairs of state.

Of these rebels, Freneau proved the most vocal advocate for the cause of liberty. He supported Jefferson's Republican principles. Jefferson later praised Freneau for having "saved our Constitution which was galloping fast into monarchy." On the other hand, George Washington referred to him as "that rascal Freneau," whose powerful pen condemned the president's foreign policy.

At Princeton, Freneau, of Huguenot extraction, began writing newspaper articles and poems on liberty. Freneau and Hugh Henry Brackenridge, another Princeton classmate who supported Jefferson's politics, collaborated on *Father Bombo's Pilgrimage to Mecca in Arabia,* a snapshot of eighteenth-century American manners. It is considered one of the first works of prose fiction written in America. They also composed the patriotic poem "The Rising Glory of America," which embodied their revolutionary spirit. It was read at their Princeton commencement.

Freneau studied theology for two years, then struggled to determine what direction his life should take. He certainly was interested in promoting the revolutionary cause and performing public service. However,

Porcupine's Gazette, Cobbett slammed him with words. He called Bache an "atrocious wretch."

THE ROLE OF THE PRESS IN POLITICAL COVERAGE

The press was the most important medium for the distribution of news and views. Its function continued to grow along many of the traditional lines of publishing that were established in the Colonial and Revolutionary periods. But now there was a new element: the emergence of newspapers acting as a spokesman for the two political parties.

Most newspapers were still weeklies, but with so much news to read, circulation numbers were up and more people were subscribing to and buying them, in order to follow the most recent news, ads, and opinions. However, the financial lifeblood of these papers was not from subscriptions but from political parties. When the politicians' influence dried up, so did the newspaper. For example, Freneau's paper folded after Jefferson left Washington's cabinet.

The position of editor was becoming more important and prestigious. The most important operators were printers, who also served as writers, typesetters, pressmen, and as circulation and advertising managers.

AMERICAN MEDIA PROFILE   **CONTINUED**

the romantic poet within him won out, and he sailed for the West Indies for two years. After hearing about the Declaration of Independence, he hurried home to New Jersey from Bermuda to take part in the Revolutionary War. He joined the military and served as a ship captain. During the war, he was captured by the British and spent weeks in jail. Freneau barely escaped death, and the experience left him a physical wreck, which only instilled in him a greater hatred of the British.

He turned to his pen and wrote the poem "The Prison Ship" about the cruelties inflicted on him by the British. His other revolutionary works, such as "American Liberty," "A Political Litany," and "A Midnight Consultation," earned him fame and the titles of "Poet of the Revolution" and "Father of American Literature."

Madison then introduced Freneau to Jefferson, promoting him as the only writer who would be a match for Federalists Hamilton and John Fenno, editor of the *Gazette of the United States*. Jefferson offered Freneau a small subsidy as State Department translator if he took the job. Freneau was not lured by the money but by the opportunity to use his powerful pen against his adversaries—the Federalists.

He is considered the first powerful crusading editor in America. His verbal and written bullets assailed against the Federalists during journalism's darkest days. Of President Washington, he said, "The first magistrate of a country... seldom knows the real state of the nation, particularly if he be buoyed up by official importance to think it beneath his dignity to mix occasionally with the people."

When Jefferson left Washington's cabinet, Freneau lost his financial support. Furthermore, he lost his staff when a yellow fever epidemic plagued the city. He closed the *National Gazette* office and returned to the sea, where he wrote some of his most important work, including "The Wilde Honeysuckle" and "The Indian Burying Ground."

Party divisions and antagonisms were deepening between Federalists and Anti-Federalists. Just as the Revolutionary press advanced the agenda of Whigs, Tories, and Patriots, now the party press was advancing the agenda of Federalists and Anti-Federalists.

Both Federalist and Anti-Federalist press outlets became essential to spreading their agendas and ideas. Newspapers were a natural source of political cohesion and sense of nationalism. However, the role of the reporter in writing for these publications would certainly be disdainful to today's journalists. The role of the reporter was to improve what the politician said.

As political arguments were being developed, a closer association was growing between politicians and editors. Politicians took a strong hand in the reporting process. For example, the great orator Daniel Webster withheld addresses from the printer until what he said escaped the memory of his audience. He then could freely change what he had said.[20] Martin Van Buren, whose contemporaries called him "the Little Magician," collected all the reporters' notes in the Senate, lost them, and kept his own version of the speeches a secret. Simply, political leaders had what they would never again enjoy: separate worlds for what they said and what they published.[21]

In the partisan period, the overriding purpose was to serve a partisan cause. Election campaigns included no speechmaking at all, which meant newspapers needed to expand their news hole to develop additional space for the text of speeches, announcements, and news events.

WASHINGTON AND THE PRESS

During the party press era, Washington was a target of Anti-Federalist editors. He was not unprepared for the attacks, but he was quick to say that knowing they were coming did not make them easier to take. As a Virginia planter, he had regarded the press as an advertising convenience, offering land for sale and noting the escape of two runaway slaves for whose return he promised a reward of twenty dollars each. As a military field commander, though, he depended on newspapers as a source of information. In the process, he developed an ambivalent attitude toward the press. It is an attitude repeated in the lives of most other presidents.

It was a simple ambivalence. Like those who followed him, Washington approved the newspapers when they were useful to his work or helped to publicize his views; he was against them when they persisted in printing things that were not useful, or when they attacked him. He was known to complain in private about the way the press treated him, but publicly the president maintained his support of a free press to provide citizens with the information they needed to survive in a republic.

Several characteristics of a twentieth-century free press emerged during Washington's two terms in the nation's highest office. They included the freedom to criticize an incumbent president without suffering retribution; the ability to obtain information about government activities through a variety of sources both openly and through leaks; and the ability to manage the press, as Washington himself did in leaking a copy of his farewell address to a friendly Philadelphia printer.

Long before the issue of a free press came to a crisis state in the Lincoln administration, Washington was writing to the president of the Congress: "It is much to be wished that our Printers were more discreet in many of their Publications. We see almost in every Paper, Proclamations or accounts transmitted by the Enemy, of an injurious nature. If some hint or caution could be given them on the Subject, it might be of material Service."[22]

Before he became president, Washington complained that he was the recipient of too many "Gazettes," some sent without his subscription order. He had little time to read them, he wrote to a friend, and when he did, found them "more troublesome, than Profitable." He thought they were inaccurate and meddlesome, but on principle he felt compelled to defend them against any attempt to restrict their circulation.

Even when they were complimentary—and the Federalist press treated him like a deity—he did not trust them. As he became president, he observed gloomily that the day would soon come when "the extravagant (and I may say undue) praises which they are heaping upon me at this moment" would be turned to "equally extravagant (that I will fondly hope unmerited) censures." In fact, that prophecy came true almost at once, as the Anti-Federalist press revived the old charge that he had misappropriated Virginia property belonging to his old friend and patron, Lord Fairfax. But there was no open quarrel between the president and the newspapers until he was drawn unwillingly into the public battle between his two cabinet members, Hamilton and Jefferson.

When he left the presidency, Washington canceled most of his newspaper subscriptions, although he renewed many of them in the quiet of Mount Vernon. Yet, at the same time, he continued to believe that the public should be fully informed. He wrote to Secretary of State Timothy Pickering: "The crisis, in my opinion, calls loudly for plain-dealing, that the Citizens at large may be well informed, and decide, with respect to public measures, upon a thorough knowledge of facts. *Concealment* is a species of mis-information; and misrepresentation and false alarms found the ground work of opposition."[23]

Despite all that he suffered, Washington continued to believe in the broad principles of the Bill of Rights, including the First Amendment, and since he was also a firm believer in the ultimate judgment of history, he refused to use the press as a personal political weapon, and did not always approve those who used it on his behalf.

He spent the last evening of his life reading newspapers. Tobias Lear, his faithful secretary, tells in his diary how he and the president sat up until after nine o'clock going through the gazettes that had just arrived from the post office. "When he met with anything which he thought diverting or interesting," Lear tells us, "he would read it aloud as well as his hoarseness would permit. He desired me to read to him the debates of the Virginia Assembly, on the election of a Senator and Governor; which I did—and, on hearing Mr. Madison's observations respecting Mr. Monroe, he appeared much affected; and spoke with some degree of asperity on the subject, which I endeavored to moderate, as I always did on such occasions."

A few hours later Washington was dead, and so great was the nation's grief that even the Anti-Federalist press was momentarily silenced.

ADAMS AND THE PRESS

The character of the press did not change in the least, however, with Adams' election to the presidency, nor could it, because it still had no prime reason for existence except to be the tool of the two political parties. Its news function, even a substantial part of its advertising, was subverted to that purpose.

Adams was a far different kind of man and a far different president. He was tougher-minded and more combative. A skilled writer on his own account, he contributed articles and essays to various newspapers for more than forty years of his life, although he had no formal connection with any of them. As president, he suffered most from what was happening in this third term of Federalist administration, which saw a growing consolidation of political and economic power in the hands of a relatively few people who were benefiting financially and politically from the government. Meanwhile, the Anti-Federalists, still out of power, and many of their supporters, out of pocket as well, raged and snarled at what they conceived to be the triumph of the haves over the have-nots.

Like Washington, Adams believed that the press ought to present America in the best possible light, and he followed his predecessor's policy of public silence in the face of newspaper attacks. Similarly, he was against carrying on political controversies in the press.

Long after his retirement, Adams continued to write for the press, in the interest of better public understanding, as he thought, but he did not forgive the newspapers. He wrote to a friend in 1815:

> One party reads the newspapers and pamphlets of its own church, and interdicts all writings of the opposite complexion. The other party condemns all such as heresy, and will not read or suffer to be read, as far as its influence extends, any thing but its own libels... . With us, the press is under a virtual imprimatur, to such a degree, that I do not believe I could get these letters to you printed in a newspaper in Boston.... Have not narrow bigotry, the most envious malignity, the most base, vulgar, sordid, fishwoman scurrility, and the most palpable lies, a plenary indulgence, and an unbounded licentiousness. If there is ever to be an amelioration of the conditions of mankind, philosophers, theologians, legislators, politicians and moralists will find that the regulation of the press is the most difficult, dangerous, and important problem they have to resolve. Mankind cannot now be governed without it, nor at present with it. Instead of a consolation, it is an aggravation to know that this kind of ignorance ... runs through every State in the Union....[24]

JEFFERSON AND THE PRESS

Nothing appeared to shake Jefferson's belief in a free press. He defended the right of his detractors to print when others would have silenced them, and he rarely chose to defend himself. Basically, he believed it was more important to be informed than to be governed, an idea that steadily lost ground in the late twentieth century.

He is often quoted as saying: "The basis of our government being the opinion of the people, the very first object should be to keep that right; and were it left to me to decide whether we should have the government without newspapers, or newspapers without a government, I should not hesitate a moment to prefer the latter." The quotation usually ends there, but his real wisdom lies in the sentence that follows: "But I should mean that every man should receive those papers, and be capable of reading them." Jefferson understood that the effectiveness of the press in a democracy is in proportion to the number of people who are able to read its publications and who take the time to do it. Those who choose to remain ignorant rather than informed deserve more government and less freedom of information.

Jefferson was a complicated man. He advocated a free press but believed in the restriction of newspapers on the state level. He vigorously supported the Bill of Rights but argued that a few carefully selected libel prosecutions should restore the credibility and quality of the press.

ALIEN AND SEDITION ACTS OF 1798

In 1798 the Federalists passed the Alien and Sedition Acts, a group of laws that were designed to silence political dissent in preparation for war with France. At this time, John Adams was president. There was growing fear of French émigrés in America, who, according to the French consul in Philadelphia, numbered 245,000 or more. Many were aristocrats who had fled the Terror, but the majority were refugees from slave uprisings in the Caribbean island of San Domingo. In Philadelphia a number of French-language newspapers had been established. There were French restaurants, French booksellers, French schools, and French boardinghouses. The French-speaking people, it seemed, were everywhere. The war clamor was at a pitch, and who could measure the threat they posed in the event of war with France?

The Alien Acts included a Naturalization Act, which extended the required period of residence to qualify for citizenship from five to fourteen years, and the Alien Act, which granted the president the legal right to expel any foreigner he considered "dangerous." In the view of the vice president, the Alien Act was something worthy of the ninth century.

Of greater consequence was the Sedition Act, which made any "false, scandalous, and malicious" writing against the government, Congress, or the president, or any attempt "to excite against them … the hatred of the good people of the United States, or to stir up sedition," crimes punishable by fine and imprisonment. Though it was clearly a violation of the First Amendment to the Constitution guaranteeing freedom of speech, its Federalist proponents in Congress, and President Adams himself, insisted it was a war measure. They also thought it an improvement on the existing common law, in that proof of the truth of the libel could be used as a legitimate defense in sedition cases.

Still, the real and obvious intent was to stifle the Anti-Federalist press, and of those arrested and convicted under the law, nearly all were Anti-Federalist editors. A Newark man was fined $100 for wishing out loud that a cannon wadding would lodge in President Adams' backside; a county official in New York was manacled and driven 200 miles to jail for making an anti-administration remark. In all, there were fourteen indictments under the Sedition Act. Eleven trials resulted and eight of the convictions involved newspapers—all Anti-Federalist.

When Jefferson ran against Adams for president in 1800, he made the Alien and Sedition Acts a major campaign issue, and public discontent over these laws was an important factor in his victory. Soon after his inauguration, Jefferson ordered pardons of those who had been convicted under the Sedition Act, however, his record as a champion of a free press was not without blemish. During his presidency, Jefferson was the target of harsh personal attacks by opposition Federalist newspapers. Although he publicly defended the right of his opponents to express their views, he was eventually so annoyed that he encouraged his supporters to prosecute some of his critics in state courts.

The Sedition Act expired in 1801, and it was more than 100 years before Congress again attempted to make criticism of the government a federal crime. However, prosecutions did not end with the expiration of the Sedition Act. In 1803, after Harry Croswell, editor of the Federalist *Wasp*, brought down the ire of the White House when he reprinted a charge from another newspaper that Thomas Jefferson had paid an Anti-Federalist editor, James Callender, to criticize John Adams. He also would print the story about Jefferson's fathering a child with his slave Sally Hemings. Jefferson agreed with some of his supporters that the government should make an example of Croswell by prosecuting him for seditious libel.

The trial court found Croswell guilty, and he appealed to a higher state court. His defense attorney, Alexander Hamilton, argued that truth plus "good motives for justifiable means" should be a defense. This has since been called the Hamilton Defense. Despite Hamilton's efforts, Croswell lost when the appellate panel deadlocked. Despite the trial's outcome, the New York legislature then passed a libel act that made truth a complete defense and gave the jury the power to decide both law and fact. These were the same principles argued in the first seditious libel trials in the New World.

However, Hamilton didn't live long enough to enjoy the recognition: A newspaper account of something he said during the trial led to the infamous duel in which he was killed by Aaron Burr, then the vice president of the United States.

THE PARTY PRESS IN RETROSPECT

In his *Brief Retrospect of the Eighteenth Century*, Samuel Miller diagnosed with some insight the reasons for the dismal character of the press and why the initial post-Revolutionary pattern had persisted. He wrote:

> In the United States the frequency of Elections leads to a corresponding frequency of struggle between political parties; these struggles naturally engender mischievous passions, and every species of coarse invective; and, unhappily, too many of the conductors of our public prints have neither the discernment, the firmness, nor the virtue to reject from their pages the foul ebullitions of prejudice and malice. Had they more diligence, or greater talents, they might render their Gazettes interesting, by filling them with materials of a more intrusive and dignified kind; but, wanting these qualifications, they must give such materials, accompanied with such a seasoning as circumstances furnish. Of what kind these are no one is ignorant.[25]

Large elements of truth exist in Miller's assessment, yet it does not produce the more balanced view that historical hindsight provides today. The "Gazettes," one must remember, were not in the hands of publishers and editors as we think of them now. Rather the "Gazettes" were controlled by the contending political parties and their leaders—from the highest to the secondary levels. These leaders, who mostly concealed their support, both financial and literary, comprised, generally speaking, the intellectuals of the day.

Aside from Hamilton and the presidents, there were lesser figures who nevertheless qualified as men of intellect and culture—people like Noah Webster, whose *American Minerva* represented only an episode in his varied life, was a Federalist organ whose invective was limited by Webster's own moderate personality. His defense of Jay's Treaty, for example, was a model of public discussion in a newspaper. Moreover, his editorials running in the same place in every edition were the prototype of the editorial page in America, while his semiweekly edition, the *Herald*, intended "for country readers," was the first bulldog, or updated, edition.

William Cobbett was another man of intellect during the party press era. He was the English political refugee who signed himself "Peter Porcupine," and whose *Porcupine's Gazette* lived up to Cobbett's opening pronouncement: "Professions of impartiality I shall make none." His slashing pen—he described Benjamin Franklin as a "crafty and lecherous old hypocrite … whose very statue seems to gloat on the wenches as they walk the State House yard"—got him into endless trouble, and he finally had to flee to England, but he no more fit Miller's scathing description of newspaper proprietors than many of the others.

If the press was scurrilous, it was also a reflection of the times. The presence of great men like Washington, Hamilton, Adams, and Jefferson obscures the fact that the American party political system was already producing lying, manipulating, cheating, violent, and the other dismal attributes which have always gone hand in hand with its virtues. These were at a disgraceful peak in the first three presidential administrations because the system was new and unrefined, still far from enjoying the benefits of public relations and advertising techniques.

When Miller asserted that more talented editors would fill their pages with "Materials of a more instructive and dignified kind," he was expressing in the language of his time what we still hear as pleas to "print the good news not the bad," to publish "what's right with America, not what's wrong." In fact, everything that was wrong with America can be found in the pages of the late eighteenth-century and early nineteenth-century press. They reflect a nation that was still half civilized, violent, poorly educated, and profoundly uncertain of how its newly devised political system ought to work, and deeply divided still on exactly what form the system should take. All of this was in the newspapers, which have always faithfully reflected their times. The people were already cynical about their political leaders. It was not lost on them that when these leaders deplored the excesses of the press, they seldom disavowed the papers that were excessive in their praise.

CONCLUSION

The party press era has been called the "dark days of journalism." The aim of the vindictive stories and opinions found in these newspapers was to sway public opinion in an effort to shape the new government. Alexander Hamilton and his

Federalists, who advocated a strong central government, were pitted against Thomas Jefferson and his Anti-Federalists, who argued for states' rights.

Hamilton and Jefferson knew that public opinion was the foundation of public policy. They also knew the growing power of the press and its usefulness as an instrument in educating the people as to what shape that public policy and new government should take. Hamilton used and financially supported the *Gazette of the United States* while the *National Gazette* supported Jefferson's philosophy. Their verbal arrows were among the most poisonous in the nation's history.

The practices of the party press were far from the professionalism of today's media. The role of the reporter was merely to enhance the words and stature of the politician. As political arguments were being developed, a closer association was growing between politicians and editors. Politicians took a strong hand in the reporting process. It was easy then. A cloud of secrecy prevailed over officials and their deliberations and decisions.

However, as the nation entered the nineteenth century, the party press era was winding down. Fenno and Bache had both died in a yellow fever epidemic that swept Philadelphia in the summer of 1798. Freneau was driven out by the same fever and retired to his New Jersey farm. Cobbett left the country in the wake of a libel suit that forced him into bankruptcy. Bache's widow married her husband's assistant, William Duane, whose wife had also died of the fever. The *Aurora* continued to support Jefferson and the Republicans, but its tone under Duane was much more reasonable. Duane had the courage of Freneau but without the shrillness. His writing was as colorful as Cobbett's but was without Cobbett's recklessness. Like his newspaper colleagues, Duane suffered for the cause: he was beaten by hoodlums and arrested under the Sedition Act.

By 1808, public response to the excesses of the party press was already in evidence. "It is high time," the *Washington Monitor* observed, "that some effort should be made to purify the presses of the United States, from their froth, their spume, and their coarse vulgarisms. Newspapers of all descriptions teem with bombastic invective, with ridiculous jargon and empty declamation. The popular taste becomes vitiated, and is prepared to receive the pestilential banquet of every noxious creature that wields a pen or controls a pen."

By the end of President Jefferson's second term in 1809, profound changes were stirring in the nation. In another twenty-five years, the news media would be almost unrecognizable as the press force that documented and recorded America's first full century of freedom and independence.

1833–1860: A NEW POLITICS, A NEW PRESS

This was one of the most dynamic and colorful, yet tragic, periods in American history. Social, economic, political, and cultural conditions of the age fostered a new journalism. Readers, for once, were able to read newspapers instead of "viewspapers."

America's first press for the masses was born in a period when the nation's population increased from 12 million to 30 million, including 2.5 million English, Irish, Welsh, and German immigrants who poured into the country. The population increase produced more potential subscribers for existing papers and, likewise, increased the number of newspapers. In 1830 some 1,300 newspapers were published; by 1860, the year Abraham Lincoln was elected president, the number of newspapers had increased to 4,051. That of the number of dailies increased from 25 to 387.

It was the era of the Machine Age, with the steam engine answering the demand for more power and faster-turning machines. In 1840 the value of manufactured products reached $483 million. Twenty years later the figure was almost four times greater—about $1.9 billion. Industrialization brought about mass production, which lowered the costs of goods and created the need for advertising.

The era also saw improvements in transportation. "The true history of the United States," wrote an English observer, "is the history of transportation." Pioneer ingenuity built wagon homes to cross a continent, flatboats to float rivers, sharp ships to knife waves, and it developed steam engines to run boats and railroads. In the 1790s a rash of road building was carried out, mostly by states or private companies, which expected to profit from tolls. From 1816 to 1840

Americans built 3,226 miles of canals. In an effort to speed messages between east and west on the new transportation, the Pony Express began its spectacular eighteen-month life in April 1860. It was fast, with riders making the 2,000-mile trip from Missouri to California in eight days. However, it was not fast enough to compete with the telegraph, completed in October 1861.

In politics, it was the era of the common man. Unlike his predecessor, Andrew Jackson entered office without any definite program to set before Congress. He did bring with him a deep belief in his kinship with the people. Martin Van Buren later said: President Jackson felt that the people were his "blood relations—the only blood relations he had...[he believed that] to labor for the good of the masses was a special mission assigned to him by his Creator."

Simply, Jackson's political philosophy was one of faith in the common man; belief in political equality; belief in equal economic opportunity; and hatred of monopoly, special privilege, and the intricacies of capitalistic finance. This wave of democracy wiped away property restrictions on voting and other barriers to political suffrage for the masses.

It was this democratization of business and politics in the 1830s that best explains the revolution in journalism in the same period, according to Michael Schudson. Some historians claim that the nation's growing literacy spurred the development of the cheap press. Others attribute it to advances in technology and changes in printing, transportation, and communications. Still others, such as Frederic Hudson, who wrote the first comprehensive history of American journalism, claimed that newspapers of the 1830s were so dull that a change was needed and that it occurred naturally.

For Schudson, the cheap press was a product of the Jacksonian spirit of individualism in business enterprise and independence in politics. The penny papers contributed to the extensive development of the free market by making advertising more available to more people and by transforming the newspaper from something to be borrowed to a product one brought home and read. A new press reflected the new politics.

The new politics, though, would foster one of the bloodiest wars in this nation's history. Civil War journalism also would see the press coming of age as the modern news story, among other inventions, was developed.

A PRESS FOR THE MASSES

On September 3, 1833, when the *New York Sun* first appeared on the streets, a line was crossed in media history, a line that sharply divided the past from the present. The *Sun*'s runaway success laid the foundation for three other great New York metropolitan dailies—James Gordon Bennett's *Herald*, Horace Greeley's *Tribune*, and Henry Raymond's *Times*.

These newspapers marked a far more radical change in media structure and influence than anything that had happened before. Between 1833 and the end of the century, the newspaper was established as a capitalist institution, placed firmly in private hands, and freed of both government control and political parties. It was no less politically committed, but now the commitment came from private entrepreneurs who owed their power—and it was the kind of power the press had never enjoyed before—to unprecedented circulations and the force of their own personalities and those of the men and women who wrote for them.

The most prominent of the new publishers, who also were editors, were eccentric in varying degrees. They were restless, egocentric, and combative, possessed of a certain cynicism, and devoted to the making of newspapers, although Greeley and Raymond were politically ambitious as well. By today's standards, truth and responsibility were not always their hallmarks, but in comparison with what had gone before, these ethical ideas were now beginning to blossom where nothing had grown before. The editors might be as partisan as their predecessors in some respects, but what they did was done in their own right, not as party minions. That was true even of Greeley and Raymond, who were practicing politicians.

Although the newspapers they produced were sometimes guilty of excesses reminiscent of the past, the competition of these strong-minded men for readers produced a constantly refined conception of news. This made the papers entirely different from anything that had gone before. News—distorted on occasion, perhaps, but news—was the criterion by which they lived. With the development of the cylinder press, they were now speaking to mass audiences.

In overcrowded, rowdy, pushy New York City, where politicians manipulated the Irish and German immigrant masses shamelessly, the new generation of personal publishers was soon an important force. The newspapers they produced were read far beyond the borders of the city or state. Greeley's *Tribune*, in fact, was read and heeded nearly everywhere in the country, and for the first time that much-abused phrase "the power of the press" began to take on a new and different meaning.

A VERY DIFFERENT NEWSPAPER

The idea of a cheap newspaper was not new. By 1826, a number of editors were experimenting with gossip, sporting news, and a cheap press. For example, a New York weekly, *Hawk and Buzzard*, survived for six years by titillating its reading audience with gossip. William T. Porter's *Spirit of the Times*, introduced in 1831, had a successful twenty-five-year run covering racing, the out-of-doors, and other frivolous topics.

Meanwhile, Seba Smith's *Portland* (Maine) *Daily Courier*, which began in 1829, sparked a number of cheap Boston papers, including the *Morning Post*, *Transcript*, and *Mercantile Journal*. All of these papers sold for four dollars a year.[1]

Perhaps the penny paper's greatest inspiration came from Charles Knight's very successful 1832 *Penny Magazine*. It was published for the Society for the Diffusion of Useful Knowledge, with the aim of educating and improving England's poor. Within a year, it attained a circulation of more than 20,000. It even boasted of a large American audience.[2]

Many American printers were well aware of the *Penny Magazine*'s success. One of them was Benjamin H. Day.

BENJAMIN DAY AND THE *NEW YORK SUN*

Day was a New Englander who had learned his craft on the excellent newspaper in Springfield, Massachusetts, the *Republican*, operated by Samuel Bowles. He had come down to New York as a compositor, but in the depression of 1833, which was casting a premonitory shadow toward the crash three years later, he started the *Sun* as a desperate gamble. He reasoned that a penny paper would prove popular in hard times, and that a substantial untapped market existed in the immigrant masses who could not afford six cents. He was right, and the paper was an instantaneous success.

His innovations were many, which included advances in news, advertising, and circulation. Day stretched the definition of news by introducing a new meaning of

Library of Congress Prints and Photographs Division [LC-USZ62-68002]

The penny press pushed technology. Here, pressmen work on a linotype machine in a penny press composing room. The machine allowed editors to mass-produce their papers and distribute timely extras.

sensationalism, which came to be defined as reliance on human-interest stories. Everything and everyone, especially the underdogs of society—the butcher, the baker, the shoemaker, the mistress, and the prostitute—was news. What he did was to place emphasis on the common person as he or she was reflected in the political, educational, and social life of the day. His formula was to blend stories of murder, catastrophe, and love with elements of pathos to produce the human side of the news. Simply, the *Sun* mirrored the life of the urban masses.

The police and court reporting talents of George W. Wisner added to the *Sun*'s success. The job of the nation's first police reporter, paid four dollars per week, was to mimic human-interest stories first utilized by the *London Morning Herald* in its report of the Bow Street court. Exploitation of the tragicomedy of drunkenness, theft, assaults, and streetwalking pushed the *Morning Herald*'s circulation to new heights.[3]

Every day the *Sun* would print some bawdy news or feature story. Nine times out of ten, the stories dealt with crime, which exploited the weaknesses and errors that comprised human life. Take, for example, an 1841 sex murder. The victim, Mary Cecilia Rogers, was a beautiful cigar girl, the magnet at John Anderson's tobacco shop. Though the murderer was never apprehended, the mystery played into a sensational crime story. However, Day used the story to condemn employment of girls as attractions in retail stores. It became the basis for Edgar Allan Poe's *The Mystery of Marie Roget.*

Another story was based on the sensational Robinson-Jewett murder case. Ellen Jewett was a New Yorker who was murdered in 1836. The handsome and wealthy Richard P. Robinson was indicted for the murder. For two months, Day and some of his fellow editors kept the story alive, exploring every aspect of the steamy story. Thus, circulation skyrocketed.

One story was taken in good humor by readers and competing newspapers. The *Sun* devoted four columns to reporter Richard Adams Locke's story about the moon's extraordinary vegetation and animal life, which, he reported, a scientist had seen through his high-powered telescope. He wrote about winged men and women living on the lunar body. Other editors were fooled by the "moon hoax" until the *Journal of Commerce* exposed it.

It has been suggested that the hoax was a clever attempt by the *Sun* to outwit the six-penny papers of New York City. The *Sun* and other penny papers were disturbed by the fact that the six-penny papers were reprinting their stories.[4]

In addition, Day revolutionized advertising practices by instituting a cash-in-advance policy. In the days of the six-cent newspapers, advertisements were sold on an annual basis for thirty dollars or forty dollars. He introduced "Help Wanted" columns for factory workers. Like its news columns, the *Sun*'s advertising appealed to the masses. That appeal may have been helped by Day's insistence that ads use display type, capital-letter headlines, and tiny cuts, or illustrations.

Finally, Day introduced an aggressive business spirit to sell his newspaper. Until this time, newspapers were delivered only to subscribers who paid six dollars to ten dollars a year in advance. Day reached across the Atlantic and put into practice the London Plan, with the shrill cries of newsboys hawking their newspapers on the streets. Day charged the newsboys sixty-seven cents a hundred if they paid cash and seventy-five cents if they took their papers out on credit. In so doing, he created a new entrepreneurial group. This plan also helped the *Sun* reach new circulation heights. In six months, it had a circulation of 8,000.

JAMES GORDON BENNETT AND THE *NEW YORK HERALD*

Broke and out of a job, James Gordon Bennett tried unsuccessfully to join Day's *Sun.* Day turned him down. The *Sun*'s editor, out of necessity, did all the work himself. Years later, Day would call Bennett "the veriest reptile that ever defiled the paths of decency; whose only chance of dying an upright man will be that of hanging perpendicularly upon a rope."[5]

When Bennett knocked on Day's door, he already had a great deal of journalism experience. His Catholic parents insisted he be educated at the seminary, hoping their son would become a priest. He quit before taking holy orders and in 1819 emigrated from Scotland to Halifax, where he got a job teaching school. He had been desperately poor there and in Boston, where he obtained a job clerking and proofreading. He then obtained a badly paying publishing job at the *Charleston* (South Carolina) *Courier,* where he translated news of South American republics from Spanish-language newspapers. He got his first newspaper job on the *New York Courier,* a

Albert Harlingue/Roger-Viollet/Image Works

James Gordon Bennett founded the *New York Herald* in 1835 and made it "a bundle of detonating firecrackers."

Sunday paper, where the series he wrote exposing sharp practices in the city's business world made him perhaps the first real investigative reporter in America.

After the associate editor of the *New York Enquirer* was killed in a duel, Bennett got the job if not the title and was soon the paper's correspondent in Washington, where he produced some penetrating articles about politicians, which would now be called profiles. James Watson Webb, the editor of the *Courier*, bought the *Enquirer* and merged the papers, making Bennett the editor.

It was a brief and uneasy alliance. Webb was a flamboyant, swashbuckling opportunist who still wanted to be called "major," even though he had been compelled to leave the army after he had fought several duels. He was a violent, arrogant man with no visible principles. When he suddenly switched loyalty from Andrew Jackson to the Whig camp, it was too much for young Bennett, whose long years of poverty had made him an ardent populist and Jackson supporter; he resigned.

Unable to find work, the forty-year-old Bennett, disillusioned and deep in debt with only $500 to his name, decided to rent quarters in a Wall Street basement and set up a desk made of wide planks laid across two flour barrels. The paper, the *New York Morning Herald*, that his press cranked out was unimpressive to look at, a four-page double sheet, ten and a half inches wide and fourteen inches long.

The only thing in it that foreshadowed the future was the prospectus on the second page of its premier issue on May 6, 1835. Quintessentially Bennett, it read:

> Our only guide shall be good sound practical common sense, applicable to the businesses and bosoms of men engaged in everyday life. We shall support no party, be the organ of no faction or coterie, and care nothing for any election or any candidate from President down to constable. We shall endeavor to record facts, on every public and proper subject, stripped of verbiage and coloring, with comments suitable, just, independent, fearless and good-tempered.... [6]

His professed independence was nothing new. His brand of independence was. The *Herald* became a politician-hating organ by puncturing their pretensions, embarrassing their schemes, insulting them, and making them look foolish and criminal.[7] They were called "schemers," "tricksters," "loafers," "frauds," "parasites," "spoilsmen," "thieves," and "vagabonds." The press was no longer a servant to politicians. "The age of politicians," he wrote, "is past and gone. We are at the beginning of a new period, in which all contests shall be decided by the independent press, working independently of parties and cliques and guided only by national instincts."[8] Simply, Bennett saw his press as the fourth branch of government.

Finally, no editor before Bennett promised "to record facts, stripped of verbiage and coloring." Previously facts could hardly be separated from fancy and propaganda in the news. Bennett, of course, proved to be far from objective, but he was the first to declare an intention to try to present the news as fairly and accurately as possible.

Within six months he was outselling the *Sun* and the *Transcript*. However, a fire on Ann Street razed the plant that printed the *New York Morning Herald*. The paper was suspended for nineteen days. It returned as the *Herald* with a promise to be "larger, livelier, better, prettier, saucier, and more independent than ever." He told readers that the type and presses may have been destroyed, but the *Herald*'s "soul was saved—its spirit is exuberant as ever."[9]

JAMES GORDON BENNETT AS INNOVATOR

Bennett was the man who almost single-handedly changed the course of journalism history, and he would have been the first to admit it, if charged. The eccentric father of an even more eccentric son, he brought to the making of newspapers an entirely fresh concept. He redefined the concept of news, organized the news business, and, most importantly, introduced newspaper competition. Such achievements, plus the fact that his newspaper was on strong financial ground, attracting large number of advertisers, made his newspaper financially independent of politicians.[10]

Imitating Day's concept of news, Bennett gave his readers primarily local news, at first, of an unvarnished kind—the kind that mass-circulation tabloids were purveying so successfully in the 1920s. In a rare, expanding city, Bennett reported the news of sin and corruption in a blunt, accurate style, far different from the wordy, mock-elegant manner that had become standard. He realized that "there was more journalistic money to be made in recording gossip that interested bar-rooms, workshops, race courses, and tenement houses, than in consulting the tastes of drawing rooms and libraries."[11]

His goal in covering the news was to make people face things realistically and to foster an informed citizenry. He wrote: "I speak on every occasion the words of truth and soberness. I have seen human depravity to the core—I proclaim each morning on 15,000 sheets of thought and intellect the deep guilt that is encrusting our society."[12]

He saw the daily newspaper as the greatest organ of social life. "Books have had their day—the theatres have had their day—the temple of religion has had its day," he wrote. "A newspaper can be made to take the lead of all these in the great movements of human thought and human civilization. A newspaper can send more souls to Heaven, and save more from Hell, than all the churches or chapels in New York—besides making money at the same time. Let it be tried."[13]

And he believed God was on his side. "I know and feel I shall succeed," he said. "Nothing can prevent ... success but God Almighty, and he happens to be entirely on my side. Get out of my way, ye driveling editors and driveling politicians."[14]

It was difficult to separate Bennett's overwhelming personality from the hard, brilliant work he did in the newsroom, but it was there that he made his lasting contribution. He made the *Herald* "a bundle of detonating firecrackers" on New York streets.[15] What he did was to organize the business of news gathering and editing in the pattern that prevails today. He set up a city staff of reporters who went out on more or less regular beats as well as handled spot news.

He also introduced sections that covered sports, entertainment, and business news. Bennett himself covered Wall Street and business news with a thoroughness never seen before, and frequently with savage criticism of the money changers. A former economics teacher, Bennett wrote what he called the "money page." He also introduced sections devoted to the coverage of women and pioneered society news. In 1855 he hired reformer Jane Cunningham Croly, known as "Jennie June," one of America's most quoted and most prolific women writers, and the first woman to syndicate her features. She interviewed such notables as Louisa May Alcott, Phoebe Cary, Robert G. Ingersoll, and Oscar Wilde.[16]

In addition to providing readers with more national news, Bennett went to Europe in 1838 and organized a staff of six—the first foreign correspondents—to cover the Continent. At home he extended the *Herald*'s national coverage with correspondents in strategic cities, and made a particular effort to get the news from the South, utilizing Samuel Morse's new telegraph as soon as it was invented. In Washington, he organized the first bureau to cover the capital, and had its members admitted to sessions of Congress.

His editorials, too, were totally unlike the pontifications that were the stock in trade of other editors. He slashed away in his half-mocking, populist manner at churchmen, politicians, businessmen, and other establishment figures. He spared no one and respected no one, which was exactly what delighted his readers. In New York, as elsewhere, the war between the haves and the have-nots had begun, and Bennett, whose early poverty and frustration had left him with an almost Marxist hatred of the business world, was the friend of the have-nots.

The effects of these innovations made others want to emulate him, and for the first time, getting and printing the news became the chief object of newspapers. Bennett spared nothing to get the news first, establishing another journalistic criterion. His exploitation of modern technology was paired with the use of such traditional methods as horse expresses and even carrier pigeons.[17]

During 1838–1839 Bennett established a pony express from Washington to New York and a pigeon express between Washington and Baltimore. He developed the latter with Arunah S. Abell, of the *Baltimore Sun*, and D. H. Craig, of the *Boston Daily Mail*. The pigeons would eventually be trained to carry pellets of news northward to Philadelphia and New York. The terminal point for the winged messengers would be a bird coop on the top of the *Herald* building. That coop was maintained for many years after the telegraph had been perfected.[18] As for new technology, Bennett was the first to understand the commercial value of the telegraph and used it more than anyone in the nation.[19]

The opposition despaired of beating the *Herald*. Some editors resolved to try out the old adage, "If you can't beat 'em, join 'em." David Hale, of the *Journal of Commerce*, for example, entered the office of the despised *Herald*. He wasted little time in proposing to join the *Herald* in getting the news. The two editors eventually worked out an arrangement. Their venture would become instrumental in forming the Associated Press.[20]

His fast packets cruised off Sandy Hook, intercepting ships bringing dispatches from Europe and getting them into his paper hours before the steamers could dock. When the locomotive was introduced to America in 1849, Bennett used it to get his *Herald* to readers in Newark, Patterson, Albany, Troy, Poughkeepsie, and Philadelphia. Once he met a ship bearing important European news at Halifax and carried the dispatch cases himself by hired locomotive through Boston, Worcester, and New London, then by ferry to Long Island, where another locomotive whisked him to New York.

Like Day, he demanded cash in advance from advertisers. In 1847, he went a step further than his rivals. He asked that ads be changed daily, set in small type, and devoid of any illustrations. His goal was to give the small retailer the same advantage as a large manufacturer. He also included personal advertisements:

> Leone: I have received your note of yesterday and this morning. The answer is in the Post Office.
>
> If Louisa wishes to hear from a friend she may send a note, appointing a time and place to OPAL.[21]

He generated about three pages of advertisements, with about forty advertisements per column. No full-page advertisements were allowed. His paper was a financial success, allowing the *Herald* to appear in double sheets of eight pages and then in triple sheets of twelve pages to accommodate the volume of advertising. In 1856, Bennett's paper made $186,258 in advertising revenue. Ten years later, the *Herald* made $196,366 in a three-month period.[22]

JAMES GORDON BENNETT AND THE GREAT MORAL WAR

Balanced against this extraordinary enterprise, which was making Bennett richer by the day, was the exhibitionism that distressed his friends and made him more enemies than any other man in town. His enemies detested his exploitation of crime news and his delight in stories of illicit sexual relations.[23] They also deplored his ability to make himself a subject of news, as well as his ability to give his paper notoriety by attacking competing editors.[24] Simply, rival editors found it hard to understand his success. For one thing, he published a paper filled with sauciness. For another, he deserted the penny press by raising the price of his newspaper to two cents. "Such success could not but excite envy," Bennett writes in his memoirs.

> Accordingly, antagonists began to gather all the terrible energies which selfishness could animate for a renewal of ancient hostilities—and men were so weak as to suppose that, by the force of their own desires, they could carry out their nefarious and tyrannical designs, particularly as they seemed to be sustained by those unprincipled cliques of politicians with whom neither character nor truth—neither honor nor honest—avails anything as a barrier to acts promoted by the most degrading and ignoble passions.[25]

They were envious, he said, because five years after the *Herald* began, no fewer than six Wall Street journals were discontinued, and in the course of its envied career, no fewer than twenty daily newspapers were projected, published, and permitted to perish for lack of public favor.[26]

In an effort to cloud his success and stop his attacks on men and morals, a united opposition swung into action in May of 1840. New Yorkers were treated to what was later called "the Moral War," which would last an entire year. Park Benjamin, of the *Evening Signal*, opened the first salvo and was quickly joined by Mordecai Noah, of the *Evening Star*, and Webb, of the *Courier and Enquirer*, as well as other editors who had long-standing accounts to settle.[27]

Venting all their pent-up anger, the editors ransacked the dictionary for every mean and offensive word or phrase to be found. Benjamin called him a "daring infidel," "habitual liar," "Prince of Darkness," "profligate adventurer," "venal wretch," "contemptible libeler," and "pestilential scoundrel."[28] Noah referred to him as "a turkey buzzard," "rascal," "rogue," "cheat," "common bandit," "a humbug," and "a polluter of the press."[29]

His former employer, Major Webb, had become his chief enemy, and the two engaged in an unseemly scuffle when they met on Wall Street one day. Reporting this incident, Bennett concluded: "I may be attacked, I may be assailed, I may be killed, I may be murdered, but I never will succumb. I never will abandon the cause of truth, morals, and virtue."[30]

Nearly everything in the *Herald* was likely to offend someone. "All we Catholics are devilish holy," Bennett would remark in one of his ambivalent statements about the church in whose faith he had been reared. The death of a beloved brother under the rigors of one of the harsher priestly orders had left him with bitterness toward the church that he scarcely bothered to suppress.[31]

When the militant Catholic archbishop John Hughes pushed the New York legislature to pass a measure to allow state funds to be used to support parochial schools, Bennett commented that "his mind must be blinded to all facts—to all truths—save the dogmas and driveling of the Catholic Church in the last stage of decrepitude."[32] Hughes called Bennett an apostate and even went so far as to excommunicate him from the Catholic Church. "Considering his talents, his want of principle, and the power of doing mischief which circumstances have placed within his reach," Hughes wrote, "I regard him as decidedly the most dangerous man, to the peace and safety of a community, that I have ever known, or ever read of."[33]

Always he fought the conventional morality of his day, ordering his reporters to write "leg" instead of "limb," except when he himself satirically referred to the "branches" of dancers. Similarly, the *Herald* used "shirts" for "linen" and "pantaloons" for what was usually termed "inexpressibles." Once he lashed out: "Petticoats—petticoats—petticoats—petticoats—there, you fastidious fools. Vent your mawkishness on that!"[34]

The climax of the Moral War came on June 1, 1840, when Bennett announced his approaching marriage on the front page of the *Herald* in headlines and a story that seemed incredible even to his friends. He had met a pretty Irish girl, Henrietta Agnes Crean, at a party, and pursued her with his characteristic arrogance, which may well have frightened her into consent. Henrietta found herself celebrated with this glaring headline:

TO THE READERS OF THE HERALD—DECLARATION OF LOVE—CAUGHT AT LAST—GOING TO BE MARRIED—NEW MOVEMENT IN CIVILIZATION.

The story that followed began:

> I am going to be married in a few days. The weather is so beautiful; times are getting so good; the prospects of political and moral reform so auspicious, that I cannot resist the divine instinct of honest nature any longer; so I am going to be married to one of the most splendid women in intellect, in heart, in soul, in property, in person, in manner, that I have yet seen in the course of my interesting pilgrimage through human life.... I cannot stop in my career. I must fulfill that awful destiny which the Almighty Father has written against my name, in the broad letters of life, against the wall of heaven. I must give the world a pattern of happy wedded life, with all the charities that spring from a nuptial love.[35]

While his readers were still recovering from this proclamation, Bennett and his Henrietta were married and took an entirely conventional honeymoon trip to Niagara Falls, an excursion that the bridegroom improved by sending back daily dispatches on the state of the American countryside. On their return to New York, Bennett intended to install his bride in the Astor House until the home he was building for her was completed. However, he discovered that his enemies had gone so far as to persuade the courtly proprietor of the Astor House, Charles Stetson (whose more enduring fame rested on the hat named for him), to refuse him the hospitality of the hotel.

Bennett's reaction was typical. "These blockheads are determined to make me the greatest man of the age," he wrote. "Newspaper abuse made Mr. Van Buren chief magistrate of this republic—and newspaper abuse will make me the chief editor of this country. Well—*so be it, I can't help it.*"[36]

In spite of the *Herald*'s and Bennett's success, it was not an influential newspaper, although many believed it to be. It was, in fact, the first large daily to demonstrate that even though a paper dominates its circulation field and apparently has a loyal readership, it does not follow necessarily that these readers will accept its politics. The *Herald*'s readers liked its news coverage, and were entertained by Bennett's eccentricity, but they often voted contrary to what Bennett advised them. The power of the press, it appeared, was not necessarily political. Bennett did not succeed in changing the morality of his day, either on Wall Street or in the living room, any more than he succeeded in influencing local or national politics in a significant way. The power to inform that the *Herald* created with its national and international news coverage was far more lasting.

Another New York eccentric and Bennett's chief rival as time went on demonstrated that it was possible for a newspaper to influence not only its own locality but also the nation as a whole. The unlikely vehicle for this demonstration was Horace Greeley, who founded his *New York Tribune* in 1841.

HORACE GREELEY AND THE *NEW YORK TRIBUNE*

To most Americans today the name Greeley is remembered, if at all, for a passing remark taken out of context: "Go West, young man." He was an eccentric, like Bennett, but this was a different kind of deviation. Where Bennett was intensely egocentric, Greeley was a liberal reformer whose dreams were for humanity.

Hulton Archives/Getty Images

Horace Greeley, founder of the *New York Tribune*, became one of the most respected penny press editors in the nation. His *Tribune*, next to the *Bible*, was one of the most respected publications in the nation.

He was so widely known everywhere in the country that he became a popular legend in his own time, much as William Randolph Hearst was in his time.

His restless, crusading spirit dominated the American journalistic scene from 1830 to 1870. Although other editors and literary figures viewed him with some contempt (William Cullen Bryant, the elegant editor of the *Post*, would not even speak to him), his was the only journalistic voice heard from New York to California. A good many people in the country refused to believe anything in the papers was so unless "Uncle Horace," as he was affectionately known, confirmed it in the *Tribune*.

A master showman, an amiable medicine man, he has been referred to as "the most conspicuous figure in Broadway's midday throng," "his stature like a bent hoop, appearing to occupy both sides of the street" that "one might take him for an elder rustic, come to the city to sell a load of turnips and cabbage." Greeley stood an inch or two under six feet and carried perhaps 145 pounds on his long legs; "his head was twenty-three and one-half inches in circumference, and doctors who have studied it say the brain within was very large, and in all the right places."[37]

AMERICAN MEDIA PROFILE | WILLIAM CULLEN BRYANT 1794–1878

Hulton Archive/Getty Images

Truth gets well if she is run over by a locomotive, while error dies of lockjaw if she scratches her finger.

William Cullen Bryant

No man ever entered upon a career with less illusion and with less ambition to become a full-time journalist than did William Cullen Bryant when he took up his labors in the newspaper field. Yet his journalistic achievements have been duplicated by few, writes biographer Curtiss S. Johnson in *Politics and a Belly-ful: The Journalistic Career of William Cullen Bryant*.

Today he is generally known only as a poet; perhaps as the author of "Thanatopsis" or "To a Waterfowl." However, for thirty-two years he edited a daily newspaper—the *New York Evening Post*. Founded by Alexander Hamilton in 1801, the *Post* is the only surviving New York newspaper that dates back to the beginning of the nineteenth century.

Hamilton and his friends tapped William Coleman, an attorney who was probably one of the best educated journalists of his day. Coleman also was a great admirer of Bryant's works, and was the first to reprint "Thanatopsis" when Bryant visited New York in 1825. When Coleman was injured in an accident in 1826, he hired Bryant, who was editor in chief, in fact although not in name. At the time, Bryant looked upon journalism as beneath him. However, he had no other job offers. A year later, he still questioned if he had found his niche, since his creative energies had not been completely satisfied with newspaper work.

Coleman, who had been paralyzed from the waist down since the accident, died on July 14, 1829. Bryant finally received the title of editor in chief and a share in the newspaper's ownership. At the helm, Bryant delighted in literary hoaxes. He once gave a fictitious source for a Latin quotation in order to confound his readers and revel in the ensuing confusion. However, his sense of journalistic integrity overtook his humorous ways.

Vernon Parenting writes of his "round moon-face, eyes blinking through spectacles, and a fringe of whiskers that invited the pencil of the cartoonist."[38] And Don Seitz writes that his voice was high and shrill. "There was no charm of flowing periods or sonorous appeal. He screeched until hearers put fingers in their ears, but his speech bored through to the protected eardrum; there was no stopping its pervasive penetration."[39]

In his usually rumpled but clean suit and wearing a frock coat and white hat, he could be seen talking endlessly to people, in New York and elsewhere. Those who thought Bennett might have more than a touch of paranoia were certain that Greeley was out of his mind, but they could not be outraged, or hurt, or angry about him, as they were about the *Herald*'s publisher. Instead, they told stories of Greeley's eccentricities, adding steadily to his legend.

They recalled, for example, how Greeley, an ardent vegetarian, once absent-mindedly ate a large steak under the impression it was Graham bread. They repeated with delight the incident of the visitor who poured out a tirade in Greeley's office, and when the editor seemed to be paying no attention, exclaimed, "I've

---

AMERICAN MEDIA PROFILE | **CONTINUED**

Bryant is credited with pioneering the meaningful editorial page. As an editorial writer, he had no peer, except for Horace Greeley, whom he loathed. It was natural for a free-trade Democrat such as Bryant to dislike Greeley, an ardent protectionist and Whig. But his dislike of one of America's most influential editors was not based on political disagreements. He just could not stand Greeley's jumping from one utopian scheme to another, and was disdainful of his adoption of such causes as temperance, anti-tobacco, women's rights, and spiritualism, according to Johnson. He also could not forgive Greeley's violent outburst to a *Post* editorial in 1849. He wrote in the *New York Tribune*, "You lie, villain! Wilfully, wickedly, basely lie." Bryant did all he could to thwart Greeley's run for the presidency. He wrote "Why Mr. Greeley Should Not Be Supported for the Presidency" following Greeley's nomination by the Liberal Republicans and the Democrats in the 1872 election. He then went on a crusade, writing almost daily editorials to hurt Greeley's chances of victory.

Though an effective editorial writer, Bryant was not a purveyor of news like James Gordon Bennett. Bryant believed the chief function of a newspaper was to point the way rather than tell the story. He was more a reformer than newsman, and he felt more comfortable pointing out a wrong in society.

Many considered his liberal thinking far ahead of his day. He supported free trade, the right for the laboring man to bargain collectively, and the end of slavery. He pleaded for equality among races and outlined the need for and aims of civil rights legislation which would be passed in the latter half of the twentieth century.

Despite his contributions to journalism, Bryant is honored more as the first and greatest American poet, except possibly for Walt Whitman and Edgar Allen Poe, during his lifetime. One of his poems suggested the month in which he wanted to die:

in flowery June
When brooks send up a cheerful tune,
And groves a joyous sound

Bryant died June 12, 1878.

treated you like a gentleman, which obviously you're not." To which Uncle Horace responded mildly, "Who in hell ever said I was?" He was a strong-minded man who kept a goat in the backyard behind his house on East Nineteenth Street. When his fellow Union League Club members censured him for befriending Jefferson Davis after the Civil War, he called them "narrow-minded blockheads" and dared them to throw him out of the club.

In the *Tribune*, Greeley created a newspaper as legendary as he was, a training ground for other editors. It was a forum for every liberal idea directed to the betterment of humanity, without regard for its real merits, since Greeley's agile mind leaped from idea to idea. He was likely to go whooping off after another before his readers had fully absorbed one.

Like Bennett, Greeley had come out of poverty, in his case a New Hampshire farm, from which his father went to debtor's prison. He got his education from the Bible and from working as a printer's apprentice. Arriving in New York in 1831, he looked the prototype of the Alger hero, with everything he owned in the world slung over his shoulder in a bandanna, and his total wealth, ten dollars, in his pocket.

THE *NEW YORK TRIBUNE*

After a discouraging start on the first penny paper in New York, the *Morning Post*, which died within three weeks, Greeley was invited by Bennett to join him in establishing the *New York Herald*. Greeley declined and started his own Whig weekly, the *New-Yorker*, on the proverbial shoestring. Its editorial page spoke with so much vigor and obvious talent that Thurlow Weed, the political boss of New York state, was attracted and hired young Greeley to edit some campaign papers for him. Out of his savings from this successful venture, Greeley launched the *Tribune* on April 10, 1841, when he was only thirty. He supplemented the thousand dollars he had saved with another thousand dollars he had borrowed; half the total went for printing equipment.

Bennett had a six-year head start, but Greeley's editorial genius, expressed in a different way, enabled him to achieve the same immediate success. The *Tribune* reached a circulation of 11,000 in just seven weeks, although it never matched the *Herald* or its other competitors in number of readers. Often it was behind with the news, and sometimes it was unpopular politically. But no paper could equal its national influence. That was because the whole staff, from Greeley on down, believed that the "New Morning Journal of Politics, Literature and General Intelligence," as Greeley called the *Tribune* in its first issue, really meant it when the publisher promised it would "advance the interests of the people, and promote their Moral, Political and Social Well-being."

Furthermore, he wrote that "the immoral and degrading Police reports, advertisements, and other matter which have been allowed to disgrace the columns of our leading Penny Papers, will be carefully excluded from this, and no exertion spared to render it worthy of the virtuous and refined, and a welcome visitant at the family fireside."[40]

His contributions to media's development are many. He put together a talented editorial staff to further his goal to publish a newspaper that relied on rationalism, not sensationalism, and he published editorial pages that were the heart of his paper, the reason for its remarkable influence. The *Tribune*'s editorial pages were the most influential in the nation, despite Greeley's many personal "isms," such as vegetarianism, spiritualism, socialism, Fourierism, and associationism, which many found odd.

His news staff was the ablest in America, operating under the direction of Charles A. Dana, who would, after the war, create his own distinctive newspaper from the remnants of Day's *Sun*. Greeley was publisher; Dana was editor; and Uncle Horace's old friend from Brook Farm days, Margaret Fuller, was literary editor for some time. Bayard Taylor wrote travel sketches and the editorials Greeley didn't write. Since the *Tribune* directed a large part of its appeal to farmers, it also had an agricultural editor, Solon Robinson. For a time, Karl Marx was its London correspondent, but he quit when Greeley wanted to cut his ten-dollar weekly salary to five dollars.

By 1854, the *Tribune* had ten associate editors and fourteen reporters, with an outside staff of thirty-eight regular correspondents. Its weekly edition, condensing what had been printed in the daily, went to the remotest corners of the United States and was passed from family to family. As Taylor remarked, "The *Tribune* comes next to the Bible all through the West." According to historian James Ford Rhodes, it was "a power never before or since known in this country."[41]

EDITORIAL INFLUENCE OF THE "GREAT MORAL ORGAN"

When Greeley summed up his philosophy in 1850 under the title "Hints Toward Reforms," it was easy to see why the *Tribune* was known far and wide as the "Great Moral Organ." He believed that "the avocations of Life, and the usages and structure of Society, the relations of Power to Humanity, of Wealth to Poverty, of master to servant, must all be fused in the crucible of Human Brotherhood, and whatever abides not the test rejected."

Greeley lived in an America that was in transition from an agricultural to an industrial society. This was a highly painful process full of dislocations, maladjustments, indignities, oppressions, and injustices, along with the normal complement of evil and stupidity. To a man like Greeley, with a highly developed but largely unfocused moral sense, many of these things were intolerable, to be fought with whatever weapon lay at hand. That was why he preached thrift although he never practiced it himself: it was good for humanity. He could ally himself with the conservative Whigs because they were fighting slavery, but he also horrified them because he thought of himself as a philosophical socialist.

Greeley fought hard for his beliefs, with a splendid disregard for consistency. He helped establish the Republican Party and was at home within its inner circle. When it failed to live up to his standards, he did not hesitate to run against it for the presidency in 1872, with the help of Democrats.

He was for labor unions and free homesteading but he was also for vegetarianism and spiritualism. For example, Greeley readily accepted the vegetarian doctrines of flour faddist Sylvester Graham, a Connecticut man who invented the flour that bears his name, and that is still popular. Graham, a Presbyterian clergy-man, eventually gave up the pulpit to preach his doctrines of health. According to Greeley, Graham preached against the use of tea, coffee, tobacco, opium, beer, brandy, and gin, and rejected all spices and condiments save a little salt. Instead, he taught, that "the ripe, sound berry of wheat or rye, being ground to the requisite fineness, should in no manner be sifted, but should be made into loaves and eaten precisely as the mill stones deliver it."[42] However, Graham's death in 1854 at fifty-seven doesn't say much for his health regimen. Furthermore, Greeley's own death at a young age is a poor testimony to those who don't imbibe alcohol or eat meat.

One of his most ardent crusades was to lift the laboring class "out of ignorance, inefficiency, dependence and want."[43] This led him to turn his attention, and space on his editorial page, to a brand of socialism espoused by Albert Brisbane, who was telling New Yorkers about Brook Farm, a 1840s American social experiment in the socialist mold of Charles Fourier, a French Communist who died in 1837.[44] It was an attempt to establish the kingdom of God on earth; that kingdom in which "The Will of God shall be done as it is in Heaven."[45]

Simply, it was a scheme of curing the ills of capitalism by a form of collective living called "associationism." For five years or so Greeley preached that imported French brand of socialism, known as Fourierism, which advocated cooperative ownership of land and homes. His bright young assistant, Henry J. Raymond, sneered at Fourierism as a "stupendous humbug." He wrote a friend, "Some delectable asses here (among whom I am sorry to say is Greeley) have started a plan for reorganizing society."[46] However, when Greeley finally lost interest in this idea, he never mentioned it again.

Not all of his crusades were ineffective, by any means. As a printer himself and an advocate of unionism, which was related to his belief in associationism, he organized the New York Printers' Union and became its first president. He believed in trade agreements jointly negotiated by employers and employees, declaring that they should be regarded as morally binding. And he said that those who refused to abide by them should be "shunned alike by journeymen and customers."[47] It would not be too farfetched to credit Greeley as one of the nation's pioneers in collective bargaining.[48]

He had other successes. As a teetotaler, he used the influence of his paper to get state prohibition laws passed. As a humanitarian, he was against capital punishment and succeeded in persuading several states to repeal laws permitting death by hanging. After a two-hour interview with Brigham Young, which made newspaper history because it was the first interview conducted in question-and-answer form, he found himself opposed to Young's views on polygamy. He considered this practice an infringement on the natural rights of women. Through his paper he brought so much pressure to bear on Congress from his aroused readers that polygamy was outlawed three years later.

Occasionally he supported the right things for what some considered the wrong reasons. As a Whig, for example, he came out strongly in favor of protective tariffs, not because he wanted to protect the nation's industrialists but because he thought the high standards of labor would be protected by them. His fellow Whigs, during their uneasy alliance, were confused when they read editorials arguing for protectionism and socialism in the same issue of the *Tribune*. The Whigs had something to thank him for, however. Greeley almost single-handedly sold the idea of high tariffs to the nation's farmers, with whom his paper had its greatest influence. He sold it so well that it is still an article of faith in most parts of the rural community. In conjunction with the various restrictive tariffs that Congress passed later in the century, the measure probably caused more economic damage to the country than any other political idea.

Many of Greeley's crusades stemmed from his passion to make the country strong internally. His "Go West, young man, and grow up with the country," was part of the *Tribune*'s westward expansion campaign. Greeley constantly urged the federal government to aid the young men who took his advice by passing a federal homestead law, and helping to build railroads and telegraph lines—all propositions that horrified his Whig friends and their Republican successors.[49]

If he were alive today, Greeley would probably be just as unclassifiable as he was in his own time. He was for what the Republicans would now call "creeping socialism," but he was also an isolationist in today's terms, and would be in sympathy with the Republican right wing. He believed that laissez-faire was suicidal, leading to the "anarchy of individualism," yet he preached the rights of the individual. He put his ultimate trust in the fundamental goodness of humanity, a romantic view that accurately forecast his total failure in politics.

THE PENNY PRESS AND THE MEXICAN WAR

The new power of the press demonstrated by Greeley's editorial successes was not enough to change the course of national events when a determined president was directing them. The Mexican War of 1846 was a case in point.

For Bennett, America's war with Mexico provided an exciting opportunity for the *Herald* to show off its expertise in covering the news. He wrote, "We are on the verge of vast and unknown changes in the destiny of the nation."[50] For Greeley, it was a moral outrage.[51] It was, he wrote, a war "in which Heaven must take part against us."[52]

The war with Mexico is an example of one of democracy's more sordid failures, and although it has been explored and analyzed by many historians, it has somehow failed to linger in the American consciousness. It began on the morning of May 11, 1846, when President James Polk sent a special message to Congress declaring that America had been invaded by Mexico, that American blood had been shed, and that "war exists, and, notwithstanding all our efforts to avoid it, exists by the act of Mexico herself." Polk wanted Congress to declare a war that was already under way.

Whether the Mexicans had actually invaded was a question. They had crossed the Rio Grande, but whether that was the boundary with Texas, annexed only five months before, had been a matter of dispute. There was more to the boundary dispute, however. Polk was under pressure from businessmen who suffered losses in Mexico as the result of its revolution. Although $8.5 million had been claimed, a commission had determined in 1840 that only about a quarter of this amount was valid; the rest of the claims were either fraudulent or padded. The Mexican government had defaulted on payment of the valid claims after three installments. American corporations and states were at the time in default to the British for more than $200 million, but nothing was said about that.

These and other grievances had led Polk to set General Zachary Taylor in motion toward the Rio Grande, with a resulting skirmish between a cavalry force and a reconnoitering party. That was the war the president asked Congress to declare after it was begun. An uproar arose on the Hill, particularly when members read the draft of a House bill, accompanying the message, which authorized the president to accept volunteers and militia. Its hawkish preamble stated blandly, "Whereas, by the act of … Mexico, a state of war exists between that government and the United States," and the president was authorized to exert his powers as commander in chief. In brief, Polk was calling it a defensive war when the opposite was obviously true.

The war divided the country. In Washington, the Whigs, both the North and the South, opposed it, and the Democrats supported it, although divisions in the parties existed because of the slavery question. Some thought the administration wanted to take Mexico and extend slavery there and through Central America, and Southern Whigs who opposed the war were hardly aghast at this idea.

Those who embraced the idea of Manifest Destiny (the supposed inevitability of the continued territorial expansion of U.S. boundaries westward to the Pacific, and even beyond), such as Bennett, were just like those who tried to sanctify the war in Vietnam and did so by depicting the United States as the defender of liberty in the world. In Polk's day, those who believed in Manifest Destiny were more frank about it: They were unabashed in proclaiming their desire to absorb all of Mexico, and they had no strong objections to extending slavery. The antislavery people termed them "doughfaces."

As the bloody conflict continued, the Whigs denounced it as unconstitutional, but they continued voting supplies for it because they did not want to be accused of depriving troops in the field. By praising the troops and exalting the generals, especially if they were Whigs, they were able to marshal so much popular sentiment against the unpopular war that they got control of the House, and consequently of the budget. It proved a humiliating setback for the Polk administration.

But Polk defended the war, insisting that the Mexicans had invaded the country, attacking the Whigs who claimed the opposite, and charging them with giving "aid and comfort to the enemy." The Whigs called this presidential attack "an artful perversion of the truth … to make the people believe a lie."

Whether the president lied or told the truth, the conflict marked the beginning of modern war correspondence, and Bennett was not about to sit still and accept official statements by the government. He was determined to be the first to publish news from the trouble spot. He had a "sense of urgency and an open fisted entrepreneurs' desire to beat the opposition with the freshest battlefield reports, casualty lists, or campaign dispatches from the armies of Scott and Taylor." If he needed two dozen express riders and four dozen fast horses to bring the news to a Southern telegraph point, so be it. He would pay the price.[53]

Bennett was aided by a 2,000-mile communications network that included a courier system between New York and New Orleans, pony express, and railroads.

His couriers outsped the couriers of the U.S. mail, a forbidden practice in the eyes of the postmaster general, who ordered it ended.

Included in his communications network were 130 miles of telegraph lines; this was the first war in which news was transmitted via the telegraph. The *Herald*'s reports of battles and casualty lists outstripped the rest of the American press by days and provided Washington with its first word on distant encounters.[54] In an effort to cut expenses and shorten time in publishing fresh news, a number of newspapers began to cooperate in using the telegraph lines. The system was so efficient that President Polk first heard about America's victory at Vera Cruz from a telegram sent by the publisher of the *Baltimore Sun*.[55] This attempt at sharing the telegraph lines would culminate in an agreement between the *Journal of Commerce*, the *Herald*, the *Sun*, the *Express*, the *Courier and Enquirer*, and the *Tribune* on January 11, 1849, forming the New York Harbor News Association. Many consider this the formal origin of the Associated Press.[56]

Despite Bennett's efforts, his correspondents, as well as others from American newspapers, had a hard time getting into Mexican cities. Thus, many newspapers reprinted reports provided by correspondents of *La Patria* of New Orleans. It became the first Spanish-language daily in the United States.[57]

The *Herald*'s enterprise in reporting culminated in the biggest scoop of the war when its Washington correspondent John Nugent procured a copy of the Treaty of Guadalupe Hildalgo, which ended the war, giving California, New Mexico, and the Rio Grande boundary to the United States. But the Senate wanted to keep the peace treaty a secret because Mexico had not yet signed it. However, Bennett's *Herald* printed the complete text of the treaty and days later printed Polk's confidential correspondence to the Senate.[58]

The Polk administration, as well as the Senate, were annoyed at Nugent, who admitted he had a copy of the text but refused to reveal his source. He was confined by the Senate sergeant at arms for almost a month, which infuriated Bennett, who saw it as a breach of freedom of the press. Nugent was eventually released without having to reveal his sources.[59]

Meanwhile, Greeley was outspoken and sarcastic in his opposition to the war. "So far as our government can effect it, the laws of Heaven are suspended and those of Hell established in their stead." He quoted Shakespeare:

> Thrice is he armed who hath his quarrel just,
>
> And he but naked, though locked up in steel,
>
> Whose conscience with injustice is corrupted.[60]

Bennett branded Greeley "a traitor," and Webb attempted to incite a mob for subverting the national interest. Greeley told his critics that he had a higher definition of patriotism than blind allegiance to wrongheadedness. He said: "Our Country, right or wrong... it is madness, it is idiocy, to wish to struggle for her success in the wrong; for such success can only be more calamitous than failure, since it increases our Nation's guilt."[61]

Greeley was adamant that America's vast new territories gained from the war never be subjected to the curse of slavery. No compromise on the issue of slavery existed for the crusading editor. He wrote that Congress had no more right to legalize slavery than it would have to legalize "Polygamy, Dueling, counterfeiting, Cannibalism or any other iniquity condemned by and gradually receding before the moral and religious sentiment of the civilized and Christian world."[62]

In the end, the opposition press led by Greeley won a victory of sorts. It had not been able to stop the war, although it had amply exposed its perfidy. However, it helped to get the treaty ending it adopted in a form Polk would have preferred not to accept, by capitalizing on the country's great desire for peace, and by constantly reminding voters that the war was draining the nation of resources needed to meet its urgent domestic needs.

It was on the whole, a rather hollow victory. If the editor of the most influential paper in the country, Greeley of the *Tribune*, could do no more about the war than to get the treaty modified, then the press could be said to have lost power, compared with the pressures the partisan papers had been able to bring on government in earlier days. Still, it had shown itself able to rally opinion and, perhaps even more important, had provided an outlet for dissent that the other media could hardly satisfy so well, in these circumstances.

Whether they were justified or not, politicians all the way from mayors to the president himself were fearful of press power, particularly of its most influential voices, such as those of Bennett and Greeley.

To all politicians in those contentious times before the Civil War, when passion was increasingly the watchword of the hour, the arrival of the *New York Times* and its young publisher, Henry Jarvis Raymond, must have come as a considerable relief. Some sectors of the public may have welcomed him, too—those who were tired of Bennett's sensationalism and cynical views, or those equally weary of Greeley's liberal high-mindedness.

HENRY JARVIS RAYMOND AND THE *NEW YORK TIMES*

Henry Raymond was neither eccentric nor populist in his opinions. The son of a well-to-do upper New York state farmer, he had a degree from the University of Vermont, where he had studied so hard that his health was impaired. At Vermont, he had begun contributing to Greeley's *New-Yorker*, so it was quite natural that after his graduation he came to ask the editor for a job with his new *Tribune*. He was no raw recruit from the country. Money had given him the opportunity to travel in Europe and to know some of the influential men of his time, and he was worldly by comparison with most of his contemporaries in the business. Greeley astutely made him his chief assistant, at eight dollars a week.

No other figure like Raymond exists in media history, just as no other paper exists like the *Times*. A born nonpartisan in a journalistic sense, Raymond at the same time was paradoxically in love with politics. In the back of his mind stirred that worm of ambition which has made and ruined so many careers, the urge to rise and rise in public office until—the White House itself! From the beginning, Raymond was afflicted with that disease, which, as Bernard Baruch often observed, would impel a man to get up from his deathbed and start walking toward Washington.

As Greeley's assistant, Raymond applied sound principles of newspaper management, which seemed to come naturally to him, and saved the *Tribune* from disaster during its first few struggling months. He had the help of a friend in the business office, a Vermonter named George Jones, and in their spare time these two men planned their own newspaper.

The venture had to be postponed for lack of capital. Jones went to work for a bank in Albany, and after two years with Greeley, Raymond quit and moved to the *Courier and Enquirer*, where he soon got himself so deeply involved in Whig politics that newspapering was almost a sideline. He was elected to the state assembly in 1849, and after his reelection to a second term, became speaker in 1851. After a brief tour of duty as editor of *Harper's New Monthly Magazine*, he and Jones, with whom he had been corresponding, contrived to accumulate the astonishing capital sum of $100,000, and with it they established the *New York-Daily Times* in 1851. Only ten years before, Greeley had started the *Tribune* with $2,000 and sixteen years previously Bennett had started with $500.

Raymond proposed to cover all the news of the day with special attention to "legal, criminal, commercial and financial transactions in the City of New York, to political and personal movements in all parts of the United States, and to the early publication of reliable intelligence from both continents." In addition, the new paper promised to include "literary reviews and intelligence, prepared by competent persons, and giving a clear, impartial, and satisfactory review of the current literature of the day; criticisms of music, drama, painting, and of whatever in any department of art may merit or engage attention."[63]

In the usual declaration of principles that appears in the inaugural edition, Raymond set the tone for his paper in words which have been its guidelines for more than a century: "We do not mean to write as if we were in a passion—unless that shall really be the case; and we shall make it a point to get into a passion as rarely as possible."[64]

He intended the *Times* to be enlightened and decent: "the best and the cheapest daily family newspaper in the United States." According to Dana, who would take over the *New York Sun* in 1868, Raymond "aimed at a middle line between the mental eccentricity of the *Tribune* and the moral eccentricity of the *Herald*."[65] His conservative voice countered most of the popular press of the day.

Coming as they did at a time when the country was beginning to be torn apart, these words were greeted with utter disbelief by old hands in politics and newspaper-making. But Raymond meant them, and he carried out his policy successfully. He made the *Times* the kind of newspaper it tries to be—balanced, accurate, written and edited on the highest level—despite its recent ethical dilemmas. It also would be complete, carrying texts of speeches and treaties, and establishing itself as "a newspaper of record." Its rational fairness, free of abuse and passion, was immediately in striking contrast to nearly every other newspaper in the country.

WHY A PRESS FOR THE MASSES?

What Benjamin Day had started and James Gordon Bennett had refined was a press for the masses. The question is: What precipitated such a press at such a time?

AMERICAN MEDIA PROFILE | ANDREW JACKSON 1767–1845

Early biographers painted Andrew Jackson as a "man of the people" who championed poor workers and small farmers against the rich and privileged politicians. By 1980, however, a different portrait emerged. The former general now was seen as a ruthless political entrepreneur, an opportunist who engaged in dubious maneuvers. Ten years later, social historians looked at the Age of Andrew Jackson as a phase of an Age of Revolution that began in 1776 and ended with the Civil War.

Jackson's election in 1828 coincided with a new era in American journalism. The tremendous growth of the press from 1810 to 1828 made it a force in the nation's life. It marked the last gasp of a press that served political parties or candidates. It also served as a turning point in the relationship between the president and the press.

America has had no president before or since like Jackson. Unlike John Quincy Adams, the European-educated son of a president, Jackson lacked class and culture. He was tall, arrogant, craggy, rough—and a deeply opinionated self-made man. In his mind, the people did not elevate him to the presidency to administer congressional laws. They put him there to lead as he did his armies at Horseshoe Bend and New Orleans.

Although his predecessors assailed the press in polite terms, Jackson did not. John Tebbel and Sara Mills Watts relate in their book *The Presidents and the Press* the story of a note that had fallen accidentally to the floor of the House of Representatives. It came into the hands of Francis Blair, editor of the administration's paper *The Globe*. It expressed the opinion that the story of how Jackson had shed his blood in the Revolution was only an electioneering tale. Blair described the note to Jackson, who flew into a rage and bellowed, "The damned, infernal scoundrel! Put your finger here, Mr. Blair." The editor gently placed a digit on the long dent in the president's head, a reminder of the British officer's sword that had been applied there when Jackson refused to clean the Redcoat's boots fifty years before.

To understand his relationship with the press, one must understand the Jacksonian movement. Arthur Schlesinger Jr. in *The Age of Jackson* writes that the Jacksonians believed that there was a deep-rooted

Frederick Hudson, the first to write a comprehensive history of American journalism, attributes the rise of the penny press as a natural development of the modern newspaper. He writes that newspapers were so dull during the 1830s that a revolution was needed, and it occurred naturally.[66] In a 1931 essay, Walter Lippmann suggested that any nation's press will naturally pass through four stages of development. First, the press is a monopoly controlled by government. Second, it is controlled by political parties, not government. Third, it breaks from government and parties by becoming commercially profitable. Lastly, the press passes through a professional stage, in which reporters are so conscientious about pursuing objective facts that they are free from the changing tastes and prejudices of the public.[67]

For Augustus Maverick that pursuit of objective facts is what brought about the birth of the *New York Times*. He writes that natural forces were at work as readers hungered for something better than the unsatisfactory newspapers of the day.[68]

---

conflict in society between the farmers and laborers on the one hand and the business community on the other. The latter held the upper hand in this conflict through its networks of banks and corporations, and its control of education and the press. Thus, those who produced all the wealth were left poor.

Historians Allen Nevins and Henry Steele Commager summarize Jackson's creed as "faith in the common man; belief in political equality; belief in equal economic opportunity; hatred of monopoly and special privilege." He drew to his side a class of people who had previously been denied the opportunity to participate in the power to which they felt entitled. One such class was journalists. By courting newspaper editors, Jackson became the first president to support the powers of the press by offering its editors the privilege of governmental influence. He proceeded to fill many offices with newspaper editors. He also appointed two newspapermen to his Kitchen Cabinet, a small group of intimate "good-old- boy" companions who discussed public and party affairs, as well as helped draft Jackson's messages to Congress. They were Blair and Amos Kendall, the president's press secretary—the first in the nation's history. Another newspaperman in the Jackson camp was Mordecai Noah, of the *New York Enquirer*. Not only was it a well-edited paper, it produced the first Washington correspondent, James Gordon Bennett, who would eventually become the first modern publisher-editor.

America's seventh president looked at the press as a tool to help him reform business, government, and politics. In politics, Jackson brought the two-party system back. During his campaigns for president in 1824, 1828, and 1832, Jackson supporters organized the Democratic Party, while his opponents formed first the National Republican Party and then the Whigs. Party loyalty became a staple of American politics for the first time.

Jackson believed that in a democracy political parties best solved conflicts. Pushing a more democratic agenda, the Jacksonians were instrumental in changing the way presidential candidates were chosen. Prior to 1828, parties met secretly in the Capitol and selected their party's candidate. Jacksonians believed it was more democratic to select the party's candidate at nominating conventions.

The democratization in business and politics, according to Michael Schudson, in *Discovering the News*, suggests a framework for understanding the revolution in journalism during this period. The Jacksonian spirit and politics allowed the rise of a commercial middle class that radically affected every stratum of society. The founding of the penny papers is evidence of the new kind of entrepreneur and the new type of enterprise the 1830s encouraged.

Other historians credit a rise in literacy for the birth of the penny press. The nation saw a 233 percent increase in population between 1833 and 1860. During the same period, public education developed and illiteracy dropped to 9 percent, calculated on the basis of whites over twenty years of age.[69]

Still others attribute the development of the penny press to technological development. Certainly, a number of technological innovations occurred during the 1830s. The hand-powered press gave way to steam power and the flatbed press to a cylinder press, making it possible to print more sheets per hour. In addition, technological developments improved the manufacturing of paper.

Improvements in transportation, with the development of canals and, especially, railroads, allowed paper mills to transport their newsprint to distant places instead of just selling it to local markets.

Sociologist Michael Schudson, however, says it was not an increase in literacy or advances in technology or transportation that caused the penny press to develop. For example, if literacy was a primary cause of the penny press, then why didn't advanced literate societies such as Sweden and Scotland produce a penny press? He also writes that although technology was a major factor during the nineteenth century in expanding the newspaper press, its impact came too late to explain its development. Day's *Sun*, for instance, was printed on a flatbed hand-run press making two 200 impressions an hour. Within a few months, he purchased a cylinder press, which made one 1,000 impressions an hour.[70] If anything, the penny press pushed technological innovations.

Instead, the penny press developed in the context of Jacksonian democracy, or the Age of Egalitarianism, according to Schudson. It was characterized by the rise of the common people. For example, a new urban middle class of merchants, tradesmen, and craftsmen arose and were able to wield influence in politics and business. The penny press responded to the needs of a "democratic market society" created by the growth of mass democracy. This was fostered by the policies of President Jackson, a marketplace ideology, and an urban society. The qualities of the penny press included independence from political parties; low prices; high circulation; and an emphasis on news, timeliness, and sensation. The penny press contributed directly to the extension of the market by opening up advertising and by making the newspaper something cheap enough to be consumed at home.[71]

At the time, Isaac Pray observed that matches, which replaced the tin box and flint and steel, became popular about the same time as the penny press and had this same effect: "The cheap matches and the cheap newspapers were sold in every street. Families before this, had borrowed coals of fire and newspapers of their richer neighbors. With the reduced prices, each family had a pride in keeping its own match-box, and in taking its favorite daily journal."[72]

CONCLUSION

Two truths have governed the economics of the newspaper business: one is that well-to-do readers are more attractive to advertisers; the second is that poorer readers build higher circulation. At various periods in journalism history, publishers have honored one of these truths at the expense of the other.[73] Following the American Revolution, more than half of the newspapers in New York; Boston, Baltimore, Philadelphia, Charleston, Washington, D.C., and New Orleans featured the words "advertiser," "commercial," or "mercantile" in their titles. Their publishers catered to the more elite members of society, those who could pay a high price for advertised goods and services. They also could afford to pay six cents for a copy of a newspaper or the eight to ten dollars for a subscription. This guaranteed low circulations, since the average non-farmworker earned seventy-five cents a day.

The second truth was realized when Benjamin Day published the first successful penny newspaper on September 3, 1833. This new paper provided information not much different from that served up by Benjamin Harris. And, most important, readers could get the "pauper papers" for one cent. Day's model of a cheap press was quickly adopted, and readers, who previously could not purchase the more elite mercantile and political newspapers, found these newspapers affordable.

The penny press revolutionized the way news was *financed, produced, distributed*, and *consumed*. The common man was now reading "newspapers" not "viewspapers." Newspapers included political news, local—not just foreign—news including news from the local police, from the courts, from the streets, and from private households. News, for the first time, reflected not just commerce or politics but social news. The need for news expanded newspaper organizations, making them large-scale businesses with production, editorial, and advertising departments.

News became less political, though no less colorful, because most of these publishers were no longer wedded to any political party.[74] They could not afford to offend anyone with different political beliefs, because they needed mass audiences to attract advertisers—now the foundation of their economic success.

Andrew Jackson's belief in the common man and economic equality ushered in a democratic market society, which contributed more than anything else to the birth of the penny press. The Jacksonian era brought about an explosion in public prints. The printed word rose suddenly to prominence and became as powerful as the new president himself and played just as important a role in the democratizing of America as Jackson.[75]

Once established, the penny press pushed technology as far as it could go. Bennett, for example, introduced newspaper competition and demanded faster methods to get the news and faster presses to print the news. The telegraph was introduced in the 1840s. Methods to produce cheap and abundant paper from wood pulp instead of rags came about in 1844, making it possible for newspapers to be produced quickly and in mass quantities. This allowed publishers to reach the mass audiences they needed to attract advertisers and make money.

Newspapers now began to draw people into some kind of commonality of interest and learning. They gave people things that they could understand. As much as any other force in the Jacksonian era, the papers that began to flourish in the big eastern cities forged a new and vibrant sense of community, a sense of our own peculiar nationhood.[76]

On the eve of the Civil War, these prosperous newspapers were organized to get the news. They were independent of government and party, but many of them were as violently partisan as ever, and that too would have an effect on the approaching Civil War. In the dark years ahead, it was not only the Union that was to be tested, but the media themselves, and most particularly newspapers. For these new newspapers, it would be the greatest test of the First Amendment and all it implied.

1860–1900 THE AGE OF NEW JOURNALISM

At some point between the Civil War and the turn of the century, every aspect of American life, including its media, was transformed by a powerful revolution. Urbanization and industrialization were at the center of this dynamism.

In 1860 there were no cities with a population of a million, and only two, New York and Philadelphia, had a population of more than half a million. On January 1, 1892, immigrants—about 5,000 a day—began landing at Ellis Island, in New York harbor. The immigrant wave pushed the nation's population to 76 million by 1900. Within a decade, New York City's population jumped to 1.5 million. Philadelphia became the nation's second largest city, with 1 million people.

For about $30, an immigrant could travel from Europe to the New World. One of those immigrants was Andrew Carnegie, who arrived from Scotland in 1849 at the age of thirteen. He soon made a living earning $4.80 a month as a bobbin boy in a Pittsburgh textile mill. By 1901 his steel empire assured him of a guaranteed retirement income of a million dollars a month for life.

In the early 1860s, a second industry, the oil business, began to flourish. In the middle of the Civil War, John D. Rockefeller formed a partnership that would produce 3,000 barrels of oil a day, one-tenth of the industry's output. Within a decade, his Standard Oil Company controlled nine-tenths of the nation's oil-refining capacity.

Modern America rose directly from the foundations laid by such moguls, yet the methods they used to gain and hold power are generally unattractive to the modern eye. A good many Americans lived in squalor. Most obvious among the oppressed were immigrants, Southern freedmen and blacks in the North, women workers, and mine and factory workers. Many families were able to survive in America only because their children could earn money in sweatshops. Child labor and similar iniquities vanished from the American scene only after organized labor became strong enough to push through reforms.

The underlying economic trends of the industrial age were reflected in the nation's politics. With the exception of two Cleveland administrations (1885–1889, 1893–1897), Republicans won all the presidential elections between the Civil War and the end of the century. The Republican Party's membership included captains of industry, farmers of the Middle West, new immigrants, federal jobholders and pensioners, freed blacks, and thousands of small businessmen.

The Democratic Party became the minority party, composed of farmers and mechanics. It turned to industrial eastern cities for leadership among lawyers, merchants, financiers, and officeholders.

Political corruption was notorious in Washington and in large cities and small towns in the post–Civil War era. Corruption flourished with the administration of Ulysses S. Grant, who had defeated Horace Greeley in the 1872 presidential race. City machines became instruments for bilking taxpayers, furthering criminal behavior, and lining the pockets of the boss and his followers. No boss was more notorious than William M. Tweed, who controlled New York City. By 1860, his power extended to the state legislature and the governor. New York's Tweed Ring collected millions of dollars from builders and contractors who built the municipal courthouse at inflated costs and then kicked back part of the money to Boss Tweed and his Tammany Hall henchmen.

Muckrakers of the era exposed these injustices in the nation's first national medium, magazines. For instance, in St. Louis, Lincoln Steffens reported that "franchises worth millions were generated without one cent of cash to the city, and with provision for only the smallest future payment; several companies which refused to pay blackmail had to leave; citizens were robbed more and more boldly; pay-rolls were padded with the names of non-existent persons."

Newspapers reflected the urban trends of American life and the problems of urban America—corruption, inefficiency of government, and crime. Increases in populations were able to support newspapers. By the end of the century, about 1,630 newspapers were published in the afternoon and 595 in the morning.

Joseph Pulitzer, one of the many immigrants who helped to build the new America of the post–Civil War period, and his rival, William Randolph Hearst, capitalized on problems of the period as circulation builders, culminating in the creation of a "new journalism."

A Divided Nation, a Divided Media

On the eve of the Civil War, the penny press editors of New York were already caught up in the struggle. In his new building, at the corner of Fulton and Nassau streets, James Gordon Bennett discovered that as he got richer, he had more in common with the business community than he had supposed. Since the impending conflict was highly unpopular with businessmen, Bennett found himself supporting Senator Stephen A. Douglas, of Illinois, the Democratic Party's 1860 presidential candidate. Some local politicians remembered that Bennett had once worked in Charleston, South Carolina. Thus abolitionists (members of the movement that agitated for emancipation of slaves) began charging him with being pro-Southern.

Bennett, of course, had his own unique solution for the nation's family quarrel. Let the seceding states go, he said in the *Herald*, and then reorganize the Republic under the South's new constitution, leaving out the New England states. It is doubtful whether Bennett really believed in this harebrained idea. However, the paper's readers took him seriously, and a mob of several thousand gathered outside the *Herald*'s new building with the intention of burning it down.

Narrowly saved from this disaster, Bennett thought better of his politics after Fort Sumter was fired on. Overnight he switched parties, turned over his yacht to the Union, and offered his son as a sacrificial lamb, ordering him to enlist in the navy. After completing these rituals, he supported Abraham Lincoln in a lukewarm way.

By 1861, as darkness fell on the land, editors such as Bennett were taking sides in what Robert Penn Warren called "the greatest single event in American history"—the Civil War (1861–1865).[1] Four years later, when the darkness lifted, the nation and its journalism were not the same, nor would they ever be. The Union was saved and the slaves were freed. However, the United States of America emerged with a confirmed sense of destiny and a new sense of military and economic competence, which made it the world power it is today.

ROOTS OF THE CONFLICT

Political and cultural differences between the North and South led to the Civil War. States' rights, economic parity, slavery, and the election of Abraham Lincoln as president accounted for the sectional conflicts leading to war. Some of these differences existed since the nation was first established. One needs only to turn to the vigorous debates at the Constitutional Convention in Philadelphia, the fighting over the Kentucky and Virginia Resolutions of 1798, which were passed in opposition to the Alien and Sedition Acts of 1798. The resolutions declared that the Constitution merely established a compact among the states and that the federal government had no right to exercise powers not specifically delegated to it under the terms of the compact.

States' rights, as advocated by Thomas Jefferson and James Madison, authors of the Kentucky and Virginia Resolutions, and *economic parity* boiled over with the presidency of Andrew Jackson. One of the first problems he had to deal with was South Carolina, a state that evolved politically from ardent nationalism to nullification. South Carolina's states' rights advocates asserted that states have the right to declare null and void any federal law that they deem unconstitutional. The doctrine was based on the theory that the Union is a voluntary compact of states and that the federal government has no right to exercise powers not specifically assigned to it by the U.S. Constitution.

Many South Carolinians, who became prosperous as cultivators of cotton, supported the national republic. However, by 1819, the state's economic fortunes skidded into a decline as world prices for cotton tumbled and newer states were producing the product more cheaply.

Vice President John C. Calhoun, of South Carolina, to President Jackson's dismay, talked of nullification. He argued that prior to the adoption of the Constitution the states had been independent and sovereign. Furthermore, he said, the states created the federal government and endowed it with strictly limited powers. Thus, a state had the right to call a state convention and nullify any act of Congress that exceeded the authority granted by the Constitution.

President Jackson, however, outmaneuvered the Carolina radicals when Congress passed the Compromise Tariff of 1833. The tariff provided that rates on protected imports to the United States would be lowered in gradual stages to 20 percent in mid-1842. Leaders cried that the rate was nearly double what South Carolinians wanted, but the state accepted the compromise figures. However, it also learned a lesson—if South Carolina was going to be successful against Northern "tyranny" in the future, it would have to solicit the cooperation of the other slave states.

Political battles between North and South over states' rights and economic parity were just two differences dividing the nation. Culturally the South was dominated by *pro-slavery sentiment* whereas the North developed a more liberal philosophy of reform and democracy. Over the years, the executive, legislative, and judicial branches of government as well as political parties attempted to forge a compromise on the slavery issue. However, the two societies, one slave and one free, expanded their animosity at a quickening rate within a single nation-state.

Finally, *the nomination of Lincoln for president* drove a painful wedge between the North and the South. On June 16, 1858, when he was campaigning for the Senate seat held by Douglas, Lincoln said, "A house divided against itself cannot stand." He didn't invent the phrase. However, the idea behind it was original and revolutionary:

> I believe this government cannot endure, permanently half slave and half free.
>
> I do not expect the Union will be dissolved—I do not expect the house to *fall*—but I *do* expect it will cease to be divided.
>
> It will become all one thing, or all the other.
>
> Either the *opponents* of slavery will arrest the further spread of it, and place it where the public mind shall rest in the belief that it is in course of ultimate extinction; or its *advocates* will push it forward, till it shall become alike lawful in *all* the States, *old* as well as *new*—*North* as well as *South*.[2]

Southern extremists had promised that a Lincoln victory would hasten secession. They feared Northern political and economic domination after the Republicans were able to win the presidency without any electoral votes from the South. Two days after Lincoln's election, South Carolina, the bastion of Southern sectionalism, became the first Southern state to announce its intention to secede.

The South's cry for economic parity, the clash of cultures over the issue of slavery, and Lincoln's election served as catalysts that culminated in the War Between the States. More than 3 million Americans fought in it and some 558,052, 2 percent of the nation's population, died in it. And it cost $5.183 billion.

BEFORE THE STORM

The debate over slavery and states' rights in the press had grown to a furious tempo even before the first shots were fired, on April 12, 1861. The war of words over slavery started in the early 1800s, and the debate over slavery in the press was virulent and exhausting.

As early as 1821, the *New York Commercial Advertiser* declared that slavery was "shedding sectional animosity" upon the nation.[3] From 1821 to 1839, Benjamin Lundy, one of the earliest and most influential abolitionist editors, published the *Genius of Universal Emancipation*, a newspaper that took up the cause of his Union Humane Society. This organization advocated civil rights for free blacks and freedom for enslaved blacks.[4]

He quickly attracted a following, including a young William Lloyd Garrison, who with twelve of his supporters, organized the New England Anti-Slavery Society in 1832 and the American Anti-Slavery Society one year later. These were the first organizations dedicated to promoting immediate emancipation.

At about the same time, Elijah Lovejoy and Lewis Tappan with James Birney organized the American and Foreign Anti-Slavery Society. They used their printing presses to whip the antislavery cry to a feverish pitch. However, none was more influential than Garrison.

WILLIAM LLOYD GARRISON AND THE *LIBERATOR*

Garrison's *Liberator* had no more than 4,000 subscribers at any one time, but it was the most eloquent of the abolitionist organs. It was the voice of the New England Anti-Slavery Society, and the longest-surviving antislavery organ, publishing for some thirty-five years. Other abolitionist organizations had magazines or newspapers, but none had Garrison's fiery pen to command. Few periodicals have ever been so ardently loved or hated as the *Liberator*.

After an apprenticeship on his hometown newspaper, the *Newburyport* (Massachusetts) *Herald* and then Lundy's *Genius of Universal Emancipation*, Garrison founded the *Liberator*, his own weekly paper. From its first issue on January 1, 1831, until the end of the Civil War, in 1865, when the last issue was published, he eloquently, steadfastly, and passionately advocated the immediate emancipation of all slaves and rights for all blacks. His writings were not only directed at blacks. He also wanted to educate slaveholders about the evils of the system they supported.

Garrison was a pacifist. He opposed slave uprisings and other violent resistance, believing that only through persuasion could slavery end. And he was firm in his belief that slavery must be abolished. In the first issue of the *Liberator*, he wrote:

> On this subject I do not wish to think, or speak, or write with moderation.... Tell a man whose house is on fire to give a moderate alarm; tell him to moderately rescue his wife from the hands of a ravisher ... but urge me not to use moderation in a cause like the present.... I will not retreat a single inch—AND I WILL BE HEARD.[5]

Despite his rhetorical flourishes, Garrison did not expect to see an end to slavery in his lifetime. However, he said it was his right to express his view of enslavement, even to the point of accusing slaveholders of godlessness.

Garrison rose to fame following the August 1831 revolt led by the slave Nat Turner, a religious fanatic who was convinced that it was his mission in life to free his fellow slaves. Approximately sixty white people were killed by Turner's group during the rebellion. And the blacks involved in Turner's rebellion in Southampton County took to the countryside. A heavy reinforcement of troops and militia stopped the uprising, which saw hundreds of black people massacred without a trial.

Garrison also antagonized his critics by advocating the rights of women, like many abolitionist editors. He wrote, "As our object is universal emancipation—to redeem woman as well as man from a servile to an equal condition—we shall go for the RIGHTS OF WOMEN to their utmost extent."[6]

As the debate grew more strident on the eve of the war, mass meetings were held in New York and Boston to protest what many regarded as unwarranted revolutionary provocation by the *Liberator*. A tumultuous meeting in Boston resulted in mob violence against Garrison and the destruction of his press. In Charleston another mob rifled mailbags and burned Northern antislavery papers.

Some of the magazine press believed that newspapers, reflecting the interests of businessmen who were generally in favor of the status quo, were inciting the mobs. After the sacking of the *Liberator*, the great Methodist organ, *Zion's Herald* came to Garrison's defense with an angry cry: "And this is the land of LIBERTY! Our soul is sick at such hypocrisy! ... Who are the authors of this riot? The daily press of this city."[7]

LOVEJOY, BIRNEY, AND TAPPAN

Followers of Garrison, called "Garrisonians," established a number of antislavery newspapers supporting his type of radicalism. Elijah Lovejoy was the most loyal Garrisonian. Others, such as James Birney and Lewis Tappan, broke from Garrison's aggressive demands for abolition and established a more moderate antislavery stand.

Lovejoy, a Presbyterian minister, was violently anti-Catholic and antislavery. Simply, he considered slavery a product of the pope, and he advocated those views on the editorial pages of the *St. Louis Observer*, the abolitionist paper he established in 1833. St. Louis was not antislavery until the great wave of immigration of German refugees in 1848.

St. Louis did not support Lovejoy. He became even more unpopular after he criticized a judge, a Catholic judge at that, for giving people accused of burning a mulatto sailor alive a light sentence. Usually such a crime committed by one or two people would be punishable by death. Infuriated St. Louis residents presented Lovejoy with a resolution saying that First Amendment freedom of expression rights did not extend to editors such as him.

Fearing for his family after a mob smashed his office, Lovejoy fled across the Mississippi River to Alton, Illinois. However, he was just as unpopular in Alton; there he set up the *Alton Observer*, which denounced injustices against the black man. He also organized a state antislavery society, to the dismay of Alton residents who mostly favored slavery. They were determined that his press would never function. He refused to give up his fight and leave Alton. Lovejoy predicted in 1837 that "God has not slumbered nor has his Justice been an indifferent spectator of the scene.... In due time they [the souls of dead slaves] will descend in awful curses upon this land, unless averted by the speedy repentance of us all."[8]

He died while trying to defend his press after an attack by a mob. John Quincy Adams said that the murder sent "a shock as of an earthquake throughout this continent."[9]

Breaking from the radicalism of Garrison and Lovejoy, abolitionist editors Birney and Tappan created newspapers that were more moderate in their approach to slavery. Birney, a wealthy Alabama lawyer who turned his back on the aristocratic life of a planter, moved to Kentucky. There he organized the Kentucky Society for the Gradual Relief of the State from Slavery.

To the dismay of other abolitionist editors, Birney advocated the colonization of slaves, telling them to return to Africa. Earlier, in 1819, Congress passed an Anti-Slave Trade Act, which was intended to suppress the slave trade by returning captured slaves to Africa. Congress at the time appropriated $100,000 to help a shipload of eighty-eight colonists return to the West African coast, where, two years later, the nation of Liberia was founded.

Using an inheritance, Birney took his slaves to Ohio. There he emancipated them and joined the antislavery cause. In Cincinnati Birney published the *Philanthropist*, but anti-abolitionists didn't want it to succeed. Violent mobs raided the building in 1836 and destroyed the press. They were on their way to burn down Birney's home when his son intervened and deflected the mob. Birney, fortunately, was away. However, he realized it was time to leave Cincinnati. He left his paper to Gamaliel Bailey, a physician who joined Birney in the editorial control of the *Philanthropist*, the year before. Bailey's office was attacked three times by pro-slavery mobs, and finally the entire establishment was destroyed. In 1847 Bailey fled to Washington, D.C., where he edited Tappan's antislavery publication, the *National Era*, until his death.

Tappan broke with Garrison's aggressive demands and formed the American and Foreign Anti-Slavery Society. His *National Era* would continue to "help coordinate anti-slavery sentiments and action among government officials." It achieved the largest circulation of any abolitionist newspaper; it grew to 25,000 in 1853. He published installments of Harriet Beecher Stowe's popular *Uncle Tom's Cabin* in 1852 and 1853 and Nathaniel Hawthorne's short story "The Great Stone Face," and this contributed to the newspaper's success.

THE BLACK PRESS

Others of the black press joined these vocal abolitionists. Black writers and editors of antislavery beliefs had been issuing their work sporadically in the North since

---

AMERICAN MEDIA PROFILE | HARRIET BEECHER STOWE 1811–1896

Hulton Archive/Getty Images

"So you're the little woman who wrote the book that started this great war," President Abraham Lincoln greeted Harriet Beecher Stowe when she visited the White House on a November day in 1862. By the time of their meeting, *Uncle Tom's Cabin*, the book Lincoln said started the Civil War, was an international best seller.

Tolstoy called the novel, which eventually sold 3 million copies worldwide and was translated into thirty-seven languages, a great work of literature "flowing from the love of God and man." Alfred Kazin called it "the most powerful and most enduring work of art ever written about American slavery."

Congressional passage of the Fugitive Slave Act of 1850 and a personal tragedy drove Stowe to write her novel. The act granted Southerners the right to pursue fugitive slaves into Free States and made it illegal to assist an escaped slave. Such inhumanity moved Stowe to tears. She further understood the horror of being separated from family following the death of her infant son from cholera.

In the story, slave Eliza Harris escapes from her Kentucky plantation home with her child, who is to be sold. She successfully eludes hired slave catchers as she heads north with the help of the Underground Railroad, whose work deeply touched Stowe. However, another slave, Uncle Tom, is not so lucky. He is sent "down the river" for sale at least three times, and ultimately endures a martyr's death when he is

Phillis Wheatley's poetry was published in 1770. The first black periodical, *Freedom's Journal*, was published in 1827 by Samuel Cornish and John B. Russwurm. Black historians believe that it was easier to launch a magazine or newspaper at that time than it was in 1861, when repression more than offset the slow rise of literacy in the black population.

Russwurm, the leading spirit of *Freedom's Journal*, started to counter the attacks of New York papers devoted to hate-mongering blacks. The first black college graduate in America, he earned a degree from Bowdoin in 1828.

Few black people could afford to buy the *Journal*. (White abolitionists also supported it.) Its name was changed to the *Rights of All*; then it was quietly suspended in 1830. Russwurm went on to teach school in Liberia, where he published the *Liberia Herald* and eventually became governor.

No black publication, however, had greater impact on the public than a pamphlet written by a *Journal* contributor David Walker, titled "Appeal in Four Articles Together with a Preamble to the Coloured Citizens of the World." Walker advocated that slaves free themselves through violence. Walker was a freedman from North Carolina who opened a secondhand clothing store in Boston in 1827 and held meetings designed to lay plans for a slave insurrection. He had only a little education, but he was an able writer, and his fiery pamphlet was like a slap in the face to the South. In Louisiana and elsewhere, men, whether white or black, who possessed it were thrown into jail. The mayor of Savannah wrote to the mayor of Boston and demanded that Walker be punished. Although the Bostonian expressed his own disapproval, he made no move against Walker. In Virginia, the

---

AMERICAN MEDIA PROFILE   **CONTINUED**

beaten by his last owner. A man of strength and moral nerve, Tom says in the midst of the deadly beating, "Mas'r, if you was sick, or in trouble, or dying, and I could save ye, I'd give ye my heart's blood, and, if taking every drop of blood in this poor old body would save your precious soul, I'd give 'em freely, as the Lord gave his for me."

What Stowe did was to shatter the myth that some magnanimous masters treated their slaves with any semblance of kindness. She showed that even kindly slave owners would sell their slaves for cash.

Her book pushed the antislavery movement. Frederick Douglass praised the book for its "keen and quiet wit, power of argumentation, exalted sense of justice, and enlightened and comprehensive philosophy."

Stowe's book also made her one of America's best-paid and most famous writers and a celebrity in America and Europe, where she spoke out against slavery. She refuted those who were leery of the authenticity of her work and who dismissed her work as abolitionist propaganda in a second book, *A Key to Uncle Tom's Cabin*. Here she documented many of the stories, including those she heard from fugitive slaves with whom she came into contact. From them she learned about life in the South and how cruel slavery was.

A second novel, *Dred: A Tale of the Great Dismal Swamp*, told the story of a dramatic slave rebellion. She also wrote *The Pearl of Orr's Island* (1862), *Old-Town Folks* (1869), and *Pogamic People* (1878), all partly based on the childhood of her husband, Calvin Stowe, a professor at Lane Theological Seminary in Ohio, where her father served as president. In addition, she wrote political columns for the *Independent* and the *Atlantic Monthly*.

However, her favor with American magazines soured as they changed their focus and found that her passionate stands against social justice were deemed overly sentimental.

legislature, stirred to a towering passion by the pamphlet, nearly passed a bill that would not only have prohibited such "seditious" literature but would have ended the education of free black people.

A number of other black authors in the North wrote books, articles, pamphlets, and poetry. Probably the most compelling were stories of escaped slaves, including such well-known figures as Sojourner Truth, Frederick Douglass, and Josiah Henson, whose story was the inspiration for the literary character Uncle Tom. Mrs. Stowe had met him in Boston.

Altogether, some twenty-four magazines were published by black people before the Civil War began. Most appeared seldom or irregularly, and many were indistinguishable from pamphlets because they were published with few resources. Their names reflected pride and promise: *Mirror of Liberty*, the *Elevator*, the *Clarion*, the *Genius of Freedom*, the *Alienated American*, the *Ram's Horn*, and the *Colored American*. They were published primarily in New York City and elsewhere in that state, but others came from Pittsburgh, Cleveland, Cincinnati, and San Francisco. Their pages emphasized antislavery agitation.

Only one antebellum black periodical, the *Christian Recorder*, survived into the twentieth century. It was less a propaganda organ than a church newsmagazine and discussion forum. Its founder, the African Methodist Episcopal Church, had been organized in 1816 and within two years began a publishing department. Little market existed for the publication at first. Most potential readers lived in slave states, where they could not get an education, and were unable to read. By 1841, however, enough literate blacks lived in the North to support the *Christian Recorder*, intended to be a monthly magazine but issued quarterly for lack of funds. It brought news to church members for seven years, then became a weekly. It was renamed the *Christian Herald* in 1848, and later, in 1852, it was called the *Christian Recorder*.

Southern slaveholders and their Northern sympathizers regarded this magazine as an extremely dangerous publication. Its circulation was forbidden in the slave states. However, the U.S. Christian Commission, which was formed during the war to help the spiritual needs of Union soldiers, helped to get the magazine into the hands of Southern freedmen and black people in hospitals, as well as soldiers.

As a matter of rather strange principle, antislavery white people in the North did not want their publications to go to slaves. Even so, abolitionist literature did get into the hands of those who could read and write. When it did, they read accounts of revolutionary ideas of black leaders elsewhere in the world. It heartened them in their cause.

The most effective and important black publication was *The North Star*, edited by Frederick Douglass.

FREDERICK DOUGLASS AND *THE NORTH STAR*

Born in February 1818 on Holmes Hill Farm, near the town of Easton on Maryland's Eastern Shore, to a white father and a black slave mother, Frederick Baily, who would later change his name to Douglass, became the best-known black man in America.

He escaped from slavery in 1838 and settled in New Bedford, Massachusetts, where he became a popular speaker. There he was asked to subscribe to Garrison's

Liberator. "His paper took its place with me next to the Bible," Douglass wrote. "The *Liberator* was a paper after my own heart. It detested slavery—exposed hypocrisy and wickedness in high places—made no truce with the traffickers in the bodies and souls of men; it preached human brotherhood, denounced oppression, and with all the solemnity of God's word, demanded the complete emancipation of my race. I not only liked—I loved this paper and its editor."[10]

When Douglass was twenty-three years old, he saw his hero for the first time, in August 1841, at an abolitionist meeting in New Bedford. A few days later, Douglass spoke before the crowd attending the annual meeting of the Massachusetts branch of the American Anti-Slavery Society. His potential as a speaker was immediately recognized by Garrison, and he hired Douglass to be an agent for the society. As a traveling lecturer accompanying other abolitionist agents on tours of the Northern states, his job was to talk about his life and to sell subscriptions to the *Liberator* and another newspaper, the *Anti-Slavery Standard.* For most of the next ten years, Douglass was associated with the Garrisonian school of the antislavery movement. His early antislavery activities and beliefs had been strongly influenced by the strategies and principles of the Garrisonian abolitionists who had helped him get started in Massachusetts. Douglass formed his own views, and questioned Garrison's repudiation of the Constitution and rejection of political action as a means to end slavery.[11]

He became even better known with the 1845 publication of his autobiography, *Narrative of the Life of Frederick Douglass, an American Slave.* His story of the triumph of dignity, courage, and self-reliance over the evils of the brutal and degrading slave system, which he said sapped both master and slave of their freedom, became a best seller. His fame threatened his freedom since federal laws gave his owner, Thomas Auld, the right to seize his property as the fugitive slave Frederick Bailey.

Fearing a loss of freedom, Douglass traveled to Great Britain. He lectured on the evils of slavery from 1845 to 1847 in England and Ireland, an experience that changed his life in more ways than one. First, he had previously thought of emancipation simply as physical freedom. After being treated as a man and an equal abroad, he began to think of emancipation as social equality and economic freedom. Second, he was able to win his freedom after British sympathizers paid the slaveholder who legally still owned him.

Now a freedman, he returned to the United States and proclaimed the goal of immediate abolition of slavery. He established in 1847 *The North Star*, which would be the organ of the movement for the next seventeen years. It was a weekly, printed on a large sheet. It cost eighty dollars a week to produce and was sent to about 3,000 subscribers. In 1851, he merged *the North Star* with Gerrit Smith's *Liberty Party Paper* to form *Frederick Douglass' Paper*, which printed until 1860, to distinguish it from other papers that had "Star" in their titles. He also was aware of the selling value of his name.

Many argued with Douglass about establishing the paper. (So many other black periodicals had failed, they said, and he had no training for such an enterprise.) Although he welcomed the help of white people, Douglass replied "that the man who has *suffered the wrong* is the man to *demand redress*—that the man STRUCK is the man to CRY OUT—and that he who has *endured the cruel pangs of Slavery* is the man to *advocate Liberty*."[12]

The bigots of Rochester did not get this message. They burned his house, including twelve volumes of his paper. Bennett's *Herald* suggested that Douglass should be exiled to Canada and his presses thrown into a lake. But the black editor had white friends, "nonvoting abolitionists," as they were called. They included men like Horace Mann, Joshua Giddings, Charles Sumner, and William H. Seward, who held festivals and fairs to raise money for his paper. One special friend, Julia Griffiths Crofts, came to his rescue when Douglass mortgaged his house to pay expenses and the paper was heavily in debt. In a year of her efficient management, she enabled him to increase circulation from 2,000 to 4,000 copies, pay off debts, and retire the mortgage.

Meanwhile, Douglass served as an adviser to President Abraham Lincoln during the Civil War and fought for the adoption of constitutional amendments that guaranteed voting rights and other civil liberties for black people. On the night the Emancipation Proclamation was announced, Douglass wrote, "We were waiting and listening as for a bolt from the sky ... we were watching ... by the dim light of the stars for the dawn of a new day ... we were longing for the answer to the agonizing prayers of centuries."

Crowds cheered. The end of slavery was in sight.

THE PRESS ON THE EVE OF WAR

Editors in the North took up the cause of abolitionists and black editors long before the start of the Civil War. Greeley, for example, was so adamantly opposed to slavery that he bolted from the Whig Party. He broke from its bosses, New York governor William Seward and *Albany Evening Journal* editor Thurlow Weed, who shepherded Seward's political career. Seward was against slavery, but he took an increasingly moderate stand, perhaps in hopes of landing the Republican presidential nomination in 1860. For a time he tried to avert war by shoring up Union sentiment throughout the South. Eventually he would support Lincoln, who offered him the position of secretary of state. Like Greeley, Henry Raymond, publisher of the *New York Times*, left the Whig Party and helped found the new Republican Party, writing its first platform.

When Edmund Ruffin, an ardent supporter of states' rights and secession, was asked to fire the first shot against Fort Sumter on April 12, 1861, the press was prepared. (Ruffin also would fire the last shot of the war, when Robert E. Lee surrendered at Appomattox. Hearing the news, Ruffin committed suicide.) Never before in American history had the press been called upon to write about so moving a spectacle from day to day.[13] According to Edwin Lawrence Godkin, who became editor of *The Nation* in 1865, the world had not seen such large forces engaged and such desperate fighting since Napoleon's campaign in Russia. He described it as "vast, grandiose, sanguinary, checkered, full of brilliant episodes, of striking situations, of strange and varied incidents of all kinds."[14]

Approximately 2,500 newspapers were operating at the start of the U.S. Civil War. Of these, there were 283 dailies in the North and 80 in the South. New York had 17 dailies alone. The typical paper was four or eight pages and had few illustrations.

The war introduced the *special correspondent* and widespread use of the telegraph in both the North and the South. Special correspondents were sent anywhere at any time by their newspapers to gather the news in a timely and readable, but not necessarily accurate, fashion. They emerged at about the time of the development of the railroad and telegraph, both aids to news gathering. In addition, the Mexican War and the discovery of gold in California had already spurred newspaper enterprises and lusty competition, and set reporters traveling to the West.[15]

They transmitted their news of the Civil War via the telegraph. Some 50,000 miles of telegraph line, belonging to a half-dozen companies, crisscrossed the area between the eastern border of Kansas and the Atlantic in 1860.[16] However, the telegraph was a mixed blessing. It allowed the rapid transmission of news, but at great cost. For example, a 2,000-word newspaper column transmitted from Washington, D.C., to New York City cost about $100. That same story transmitted from New Orleans to New York might cost $450. That was a hefty sum; a reporter at this time likely earned less than $10 a week.[17] The *Herald*'s expenditures on war news from 1861 to 1865 ranged from $500,000 to $750,000 a year, but the effort brought James Gordon Bennett to the peak of his success: in 1864 one issue alone sold 132,000 copies.

THE CIVIL WAR PRESS IN THE NORTH

Some 350 correspondents accompanied the Northern armies to cover one bloody battle after another.[18] These newspapermen referred to themselves as the "Bohemian Brigade" because they were a colorful breed. They were rough, rowdy, courageous, competitive—occasionally even accurate—men who came to record the war surrounded by professional soldiers. They included some not-so-famous poets, preachers, schoolteachers, lawyers, and celebrities like Henry M. Stanley, a young Bavarian immigrant who was later assigned by the *New York Herald* to search for the missionary David Livingston in Africa.

Many correspondents were young, mostly in their late twenties, and were very well educated, holding degrees from Harvard, Yale, Columbia, Amherst, and Rensselaer, among others. Greeley expected his *New York Tribune* writers to stand out in the crowd. Some wore corduroy knickerbockers, buckskin jackets, high-topped boots of top grain leather, conspicuous gauntlets, and broad-brimmed hats.[19]

Correspondents were equipped with their standard tools—a revolver, field glasses, notebooks, a blanket, a sack for provisions, and a good horse. They worked long hours. A *New York Times* reporter, writing to his paper from Falmouth, Virginia, warned:

> If there are any men in Washington who lead dogs' lives, they are the correspondents of the daily papers. From morning to midnight they are on the watch for items, or "points," to use a common term among them, resting not from one week's end to the other, in their weary round of duties, and scarcely able to call one day in the seven their own, indeed, not at all if they are the victims of a Sunday edition.[20]

The modern concept of "balanced reporting" was unknown. Some correspondents slanted their copy to match the political slant of their newspapers, which fell into four categories. For Radical Republicans, led by such newspapers as the *New York Tribune* and *Philadelphia Inquirer*, the only reason to go to war was to obtain the abolition of slavery. Moderate Republicans, who supported abolition but saw the war more as a struggle to preserve the Union, were led by the *New York Times*, the *Cincinnati Commercial*, and the *Boston Journal*. Independents, such as the *New York Herald*, held a middle ground. Democrats in the North knew that they needed to reunite with the Democrats in the South if they were ever to be a strong national party. War then got in their way. They advocated settlement, not conquest; enlightened discourse, not battlefield victory.[21]

A correspondent sometimes found himself in the distinguished company of someone like the *New York Times* publisher Henry Raymond, who assigned himself to the field. His speed and accuracy were legendary, and his stories of Bull Run were acclaimed as masterpieces.

WOMEN CORRESPONDENTS OF THE NORTH

Among the Northern correspondents were three independent-minded women who were concerned about the abolition movement in addition to temperance and eliminating prostitution and gaining suffrage and higher education for women. The most noted was Jane Grey Swisshelm, who became the first Washington, D.C., woman correspondent when Greeley hired her for the *New York Tribune*. She won the equal right to sit in the Senate press gallery on April 17, 1850, with men—despite Vice President Millard Fillmore's warning that "the place would be very unpleasant for a lady."[22] In 1857 she separated from her husband and took her daughter to Minnesota, where she founded the abolitionist newspaper, the *St. Cloud Visiter*. It was similar to a sheet she had established earlier in Pittsburgh.

When James C. Shepley, a Democratic Minnesota lawyer, gave a public lecture attacking "strong-minded women," with Swisshelm the brunt of his attack, she retaliated. In her March 18, 1857, edition she said Shepley had failed to mention one kind of strong-minded woman, "frontier belles who sat up all night playing poker with men." He saw it as an undisguised attack on his wife. Her presses were smashed and the type thrown into the Mississippi River.[23]

Sara Clarke Lippincott, whose pseudonym was "Grace Greenwood," became the second Washington, D.C., woman correspondent. While junior editor of *Godey's Lady's Book*, Clarke contributed articles to the abolitionist paper the *National Era*. The *Godey's* editors thought her stories offended Southern readers and promptly fired her. The *National Era* immediately hired her as its Washington, D.C., correspondent. She also wrote for the *Saturday Evening Post* of Philadelphia.[24] She became a successful post–Civil War author of children's books and a popular lecturer on patriotic themes before joining the *New York Times*. She was a columnist from 1873 to 1878, and she wrote about corruption, about the cause of women government workers, and against Hayes' administration policies that permitted the return of white supremacy in the South.[25]

Laura Catherine Redden, who wrote under the pen name of "Howard Glyndon," was the third Washington woman correspondent. She was stricken at an early age by spinal meningitis, a disease that made her deaf and impaired her speech. However, she was able to report from the Senate press gallery during the U.S. Civil War. She wrote for the *St. Louis Republican*. Her fellow reporters knew she was a woman, but none of them was aware she also was deaf. She is thought to be the first deaf woman to succeed in the field of journalism and literature. Redden would eventually work for the *New York Sun* and *New York Times*. She also studied articulation with Alexander Graham Bell, who taught her to speak again.[26]

THE CIVIL WAR PRESS IN THE SOUTH

Few women wrote for the eighty newspapers published in the Confederacy at the start of the war. About 10 percent of these newspapers were dailies. The papers, typically four pages and varying from four to eight columns in width, were rarely profitable. As with the Northern press, many of the papers were highly partisan, surviving solely because of interest group subsidies.

Though the Southern press had few war correspondents, about 100 altogether, their performance in covering Civil War battles was just as good as that of Northern reporters in terms of reliability, readability, descriptive qualities, and the reporters' ability to convey the larger significance of the events they observed. The quality of their reporting was remarkable; their newspapers' constraints included labor shortages, rising subscription rates, paper shortages, and military censorship. When the Confederates called printers and editors to serve in the army, papers had to close. Those that survived had to raise their subscription prices. A year's subscription for a Southern newspaper was generally priced at $16 a year. By 1865 that cost soared to $100 and $125.[27] Eventually some slaves were trained to print newspapers as the labor force dwindled.

The Southern press also lacked ink and paper. Of the 555 paper factories in the United States reported by the census of 1860, only 24 were in the South. Meanwhile, blockades prevented paper shipments from the North, so many of the weeklies printed half sheets.

In some parts of the Confederacy the press depended exclusively on volunteer correspondents and the telegraph for coverage of military operations. Objective reporting and truth-telling by newspaper correspondents were not common practice, although the editors who employed them endorsed the principle of truthful reporting.[28] However, these correspondents were hampered in their efforts to tell the truth about military operations. News sometimes had to take a back seat to official military propaganda.

The Southern correspondents' task was so arduous because of the lack of guidance from a Confederate government ignorant of the art of public relations. And no one was less knowledgeable than Southern president Jefferson Davis. Unlike Lincoln, who constantly met with reporters, Davis seldom met or corresponded with them. He had little appreciation for the press as a medium of public opinion.[29]

MAGAZINES OF THE NORTH AND THE SOUTH

With the coming of war, magazines plunged into the conflict with the remainder of the press. Every issue of general magazines had material of some kind about

AMERICAN MEDIA PROFILE | JANE GREY CANNON SWISSHELM 1815–1884

Eugene S. Hill/Minnesota Historical Society

She was a feisty advocate of women's rights and a passionate participant in the antislavery cause. As a girl, she gained the nickname Wax Doll, because of her slight build and delicate features. But later, as a journalist, her contemporaries would say, "Beware of Sister Jane!"

Jane Grey Cannon Swisshelm was indeed a seminal woman journalist. She grew up in Pennsylvania Dutch country near Wilkinsburg. She learned about manual labor early on. Her father died when she was only eight years old, leaving her mother and her to fend for the family. Some of the money came from her knack for lace-making and other feminine needlework.

At fourteen, she was already teaching in the only school in her small village, a position she held until she married James Swisshelm in 1836 and moved to Louisville, Kentucky. Here she wrote her first vehement attack against slavery, which appeared in the *Louisville Journal* in 1842.

All during those early years she stumped whenever possible for the abolition of slavery and even became a member of the Underground Railroad. After just a couple of years in Kentucky with her husband, she returned to Pittsburgh to tend her ailing mother. Now she set her pen to work: she wrote caustic pieces against slavery and for the rights of married women for the *Spirit of Liberty*, the *Pittsburgh Gazette*, and the *Daily Commercial Journal*.

When her mother died in 1847, she used whatever legacy she was left to start the *Pittsburgh Saturday Visiter*. Her career as an editor began.

The weekly *Visiter* was an audacious little six-column sheet in which she advocated abolition, temperance, and woman suffrage, including property rights for women. She was sarcastic, spirited, convincing. And she certainly caught her male counterparts' attention.

In her autobiography, *Half a Century*, published in 1880, she writes, "It appeared that on some inauspicious morning, each one of three-fourths of the secular editors from Maine to Georgia had gone to the office suspecting nothing, when from some corner of his exchange list there sprang upon him such a horror as he had little thought to see.

the war. A few became violently partisan. Astonishingly, the *Knickerbocker* changed from a gently satiric review of New York life to a rabid Copperhead (pro-Southern) journal. Even periodicals devoted mostly to literature, such as the *Southern Literary Messenger*, followed the progress of the war closely.

Because they competed more directly with newspapers, weeklies made an effort to cover the war in depth. Magazines were among the foremost recorders of the struggle, playing a role different from that of newspapers or books. *Harper's Weekly*, for example, sent correspondents and artists, writing and sketching directly, to the battlefields to produce war reporting that ranked with the best in the newspapers. The woodcuts reproduced from the artists' sketches provided a valuable pictorial record of the war, supplementing the even more important photographic record being complied by Mathew Brady and others.

The magazines' coverage was a miracle in itself, since magazines were hit harder than newspapers by the emergencies of the war. Moreover, many of them were still trying to recover from the Panic of 1857, caused by the failure of the New York branch of the Ohio Life Insurance and Trust Company. It was

---

AMERICAN MEDIA PROFILE | CONTINUED

"A woman had started a political paper! A woman! ... Instantly he sprang to his feet and clutched his pantaloons, shouted to the assistant editor, ... called to the reporters and pressmen.... Here was a woman resolved to steal their pantaloons, their trousers.... The imminence of the peril called forth prompt action."

She was particularly proud of an article she published in 1850 exposing the private life of Daniel Webster. She liked to believe that this ruined his chances of becoming president. It's pretty obvious that she was a proponent of Abraham Lincoln, later becoming a personal friend of Mrs. Lincoln.

It should be noted here that two years after the start-up of the *Visiter*, she became the first woman to sit in the Senate press gallery, on April 17, 1850.

The marriage to Swisshelm did not go well for this outspoken writer. She divorced her husband and for no particular reason moved with her young daughter to St. Cloud, Minnesota, where she started the *St. Cloud Visiter* in 1857. However, her bold style was too much for those Midwesterners. The newspaper office was attacked by a pro-slavery mob, and the printing press was destroyed.

She quickly started the *St. Cloud Democrat*, a Republican paper which she ran until 1863. It was the middle of the Civil War. She learned of a dire need for nurses at the front and was one of the first to respond. Her autobiography relates graphic images of her experiences there.

Following the Civil War she took a clerical position in the Andrew Johnson administration and also started another newspaper, the *Reconstructionist*. In it, she attacked Johnson so severely that he ousted her from his employ!

Jane Swisshelm returned to Pennsylvania in 1866, to Swissvale, where she lived out her life and wrote her autobiography.

Surely, she tempered the landscape for female journalists. She was a prolific writer with strong convictions. Some of her columns are collected in a book, *Letters to Country Girls*. Her writings exhibit a vigorous style, both stinging and humorous. They called a spade a spade and gave women at that time the courage to poke around the edges of a male-dominated trade.

By Carolyn Johnson

---

one of the nation's major financial forces when it collapsed, following massive embezzlement. A series of other events, such as falling grain prices and widespread railroad failures, shook the public's confidence in the nation's financial structure. The panic had ended the careers of prominent periodicals like *Graham's*, the *Democratic Review*, and the *New-York Mirror*. The survivors had no more than recovered from the panic when the war came, bringing with it soaring costs, manpower problems, and severe disruption of distribution.

For Northern magazines, the last difficulty was the worst. Virtually overnight, magazine and book publishers lost their Southern market. That was particularly disastrous to magazines such as *Harper's* and *Godey's Lady's Book*.

For magazines in the South, the war meant absolute disaster. Most of their supplies—ink, paper, and machinery—came from the North, although their circulations were based more locally. In many cases they did not have the physical means or the manpower to continue business as the war dragged on. Others could not afford the ruinously high postage rates imposed by the Confederate government. In spite of these enormous difficulties, both magazine and book publishing survived. Some periodicals even managed to publish through the war, missing issues only rarely. Astonishingly, there were even a few new publications, although none survived for long.

Newspapers prospered where magazines could not, because papers were selling a commodity—news—that was in great demand. Some magazines also offered news of the war, and people were eager to read their accounts of events and personalities and to study the illustrative woodcuts they carried. But for immediate news, people turned to newspapers to learn the outcome of battles and to scan with anxious fear the daily casualty lists.

The more virulent of the magazines on both sides hesitated at nothing to keep hatred of the enemy alive during the war. In the North, *Continental Magazine* printed a poem about the widely believed myth that Southern ladies used the bones of dead Yankees to decorate their homes. In the South, the *Southern Monthly* declared, speaking of the Yankees, "They are a race too loathsome, too hateful, for us ever, under any circumstances, to be identified with them as one people."

The war years were the last in which magazines flourished as regional publications. Afterward, they became far more national in character, and those that were rooted nationally before the conflict began became the leaders of the modern era. Sectionalism and localism survived only in smaller periodicals.

LINCOLN AND THE PRESS

Abraham Lincoln upset the precedent of having an official newspaper, something that had existed since the beginning of political parties in the United States. However, the president did have what could be called an administration paper, something in the manner of Jackson. He had suggested to John W. Forney, proprietor of the Philadelphia *Press*, that he move to Washington, D.C., and establish the *Daily Morning Chronicle*, which became an administration mouthpiece. Forney was constantly at the White House, and was as close to Lincoln as any man in journalism or politics.

Collecting news in Washington became the free-for-all it has remained ever since. Lincoln received almost all reporters at the White House. Navy secretary Gideon Wells called it "an infirmity of the President." He noted in his diary that the president "permits the little newsmongers to come around him and be intimate.... He has great inquisitiveness. Likes to hear all the political gossip as much as Seward."[30]

Knowing Lincoln's curiosity, reporters would bring him news at odd hours when they had reason to believe it would interest him. John Russell Young and a fellow editor of the *Washington Chronicle*, for example, once had Lincoln awakened. With his eyes half closed, the president was told that the fall of Charleston was reported in a Southern paper. Lincoln asked, "What is the date of that paper?" Young replied that it was July 20. "July twentieth. Well, I have news from Charleston July twenty-second, and then the bombardment was going on vigorously." The two apologized. Young later wrote that the president was "so gentle over our regrets, so courteous, so much obliged for our coming—for did we not see it might have been news—... that we came from his presence as if dowered, and not as unseemly visitors who had robbed him of his peace."[31]

Time and again Lincoln sought out correspondents just returned from the front who could give him fresh information. He sent for Henry Villard, the *Tribune*'s tall young correspondent, on the morning after the Battle of Fredericksburg, telling him, "We are very anxious and have heard very little." Villard, who had seen it all, hurried back to the capital, and telegraphed a report to his paper so gloomy that Greeley would not print it until it could be confirmed. Villard repeated what he knew to Lincoln, who spent a half hour asking him detailed questions.

Perhaps his kindness toward the press could be attributed to Lincoln's awareness that his nomination had been achieved only with the help of the press. Specifically, *Chicago Tribune* editors Joseph Medill and Charles Ray had manipulated the convention and gotten their Illinois man nominated by giving away important posts in the new administration, without the candidate's knowledge, in return for swinging state delegations to the Lincoln nomination. Medill and Ray kept Lincoln carefully sequestered in his rooms in the Iroquois Hotel, seeing carefully selected visitors, until the nomination was achieved, when he was told how it had been accomplished. "You didn't leave much for me, boys, did you?" Lincoln observed wryly.[32] Later, he repudiated the promises, in whose making he had had no part, and this had not pleased Medill, who was strong for the Union but lukewarm about Lincoln. Medill, in fact, organized a stop-Lincoln movement in 1864. However, the president found the *Chicago Tribune* useful in fighting the *Chicago Times*, a vehemently Copperhead organ, and Bennett's assaults.

Something of the *Tribune*'s temper can be gleaned from its editorial advice to the *Herald* when Bennett was declaring General Grant "the People's Candidate" in 1864. Medill advised him that his paper would not be "allowed to paw and slobber over our Illinois General, and if it has any regard for its 'throat' or its 'fifth rib,' it will take warning and govern itself accordingly." For the *Herald* to advocate that was "a gross libel on him and an insult to his friends," the *Tribune* cried. "Unless it keeps its unclean and treacherous hands off of him, it may expect to get 'tomahawked.'" Bennett replied that the *Tribune* was "the sewer into which goes everything too dirty for its New York namesake to print."[33]

It was easy enough for Lincoln to identify his enemies in the press. They were editors such as Manton Marble, of the *New York World*; Wilber F. Storey, publisher of the *Chicago Times*; Samuel Medary, of the *Columbus Crisis*; Benjamin Wood, of the *New York Daily News*; Charles H. Olamphier, of the *Daily Illinois State Register*, in Springfield; and Marcus Mills "Brick" Pomeroy, of the *La Crosse* (Wisconsin) *Democrat*.

No president since Washington, and none afterward, endured so much from the press as Lincoln. He was accused of all kind of misconduct—drawing his salary in gold bars, drunkenness, granting pardons to get votes, needless slaughter of men for the sake of victories—even of treason.

In the Copperhead papers and some others, the president was referred to by such epithets as "a slang-whanging stump speaker," "half-witted usurper," "moleeyed," "the present turtle at the head of government," "the head ghoul at Washington," and others even less complimentary. There was not a major paper that Lincoln could depend on, except the *New York Times* and Samuel Bowles' *Springfield* (Massachusetts) *Republican*. The *Springfield* (Illinois) *Daily State Journal* was the only newspaper in the country that never wavered in its admiration for the president.

One of the prime centers of dissent was New York City, where the war was highly unpopular. New York had a leading Copperhead newspaper whose publisher was openly charged with disloyalty in Congress, a laboring mass whose sympathies were pro-Southern, a segment of businessmen who were against the war because it hurt their enterprises, and a Copperhead mayor. Nonetheless, the majority of its citizens, particularly the middle class, were abolitionist and pro–Lincoln.

New York's Irish and German laboring masses were against the war. They did not understand and were not interested in the ideology of the conflict and could foresee only fighting and perhaps dying for a remote cause, or else enduring the rigors of wartime living and the probable loss of jobs to liberated slaves drifting up from the South and flooding the labor market. Their customary bigotries were highly sharpened where black people were concerned.

Besides the Copperhead press, Lincoln had to contend with New York Mayor Fernando Wood, his outspoken foe. Wood declared that New York ought to establish itself as a free city and separate itself from the Union, becoming sovereign, like the South. In that way, he said, it could retain its trade and still keep its connections with the remainder of the country. Mayor Wood, whose administration was one of the most corrupt in the city's history, had a brother, Benjamin, who was a successful businessman. With the help of Mayor Wood, Benjamin Wood bought a thriving morning newspaper, the *Daily News* (not related to the present paper of the same name), and quickly made it one of the leading Copperhead dailies of the country, openly advocating the Confederate cause and urging the city to secede. At almost the same time, in 1861, he was elected to Congress.

The attacks of the *Daily News* on the administration finally acquired such harshness that the government could not ignore them. The New York postmaster was ordered to refuse to mail the paper. Benjamin Wood resorted to railway express, but the government put a stop to that by planting detectives on every express train leaving the city. When they spotted bundles of the *Daily News*, the papers were seized. Benjamin Wood could do little but suspend publication; an important part of the paper's revenue came from out-of-state circulation.

When publication was resumed nearly eighteen months later, it switched from morning to evening, but the paper was more virulent than before. The private war between Benjamin Wood and his brother against Lincoln and the Union came to a climax in 1863, when an editorial in the *News*, published just before the Battle of Gettysburg, helped to precipitate the draft riots. Vicious mobs of mostly Irish workingmen gathered in Central Park and marched on the city, fighting with police in the streets, burning a black-orphan asylum, lynching unfortunate black citizens who came in their path, and eventually succumbing only to federal troops hastily brought in from the battlefields of Pennsylvania. In five days of terror, more than 2,000 men and women were killed, and 8,000 more were injured; property damage was estimated at more than $5 million.

Wood's violent attacks kept him and the paper in constant trouble. At the time it was suspended, the *News* had been named in a grand jury presentment, with three other papers, charged with disloyal conduct. Then, in 1864, Congress itself moved against its disloyal member. In the House formal charges were brought against Wood for disloyal statements he had made on the floor. The charges were referred to the Judiciary Committee, and never were heard of again. As for the

News, until the last gun was fired, it continued to insist that the Union victories were frauds, and that the Southerners would never be defeated. "You may conquer, but you can never subdue them," Benjamin Wood wrote.

In addition to Copperhead press, labor, and mayor, the severe draft riots in New York and other cities in America provided more headaches for the administration. In 1863, the draft quotas aroused widespread protest in the cities. In Chicago, Medill headed a committee of three to go to Washington, D.C., and make a personal protest to Lincoln about the draft. The city had already sent 22,000 men and had endured heavy casualties among them.

Lincoln quietly heard the committee out, and then, as Medill recalled later, said:

> Gentlemen, after Boston, Chicago has been the chief instrument in bringing this war on the country. The Northwest has opposed the South as the Northeast has opposed the South. You called for war until we had it. You called for emancipation and I have given it to you. Whatever you have asked for you have had. Now you come here begging to be left off from the call for men which I have made to carry out the war which you have demanded. You ought to be ashamed of yourselves. I have a right to expect better things of you. Go home and raise your six thousand extra men. And you, Medill, are acting like a coward. You and your *Tribune* have had more influence than any paper in the Northwest in making the war. You can influence great masses, and yet you cry to be spared at a moment when your cause is suffering. Go home and send us those men.[34]

It may have been the only time in his life that Medill was abashed, and he had grace enough to admit it. "I couldn't say anything," he wrote later. "It was the first time I was ever whipped, and I didn't have an answer. We all got up and went out, and when the door closed, one of my colleagues said: 'Well, gentlemen, the old man is right. We ought to be ashamed of ourselves. Let us never say anything about this, but go home and raise the men.' And we did, six thousand men, making twenty-eight thousand in the war from a city of hundred and fifty-six thousand."[35]

Through all the abuse, Lincoln exhibited the greatest patience and leniency, which his enemies mistook for weakness. Frequently he used the papers as a sounding board. He particularly appreciated the New York Associated Press, which he respected for being unbiased. He often spoke openly to reporters covering the White House and thus, in a sense, introduced the modern presidential press conference, although it was not a formal procedure.

LINCOLN AND GREELEY

For a time President Lincoln valued Horace Greeley's cooperation so much that he gave him preferential treatment in the White House. Greeley, who had been a moving force in the abolitionist cause, was the best-known and most influential editor of the Civil War era. His support was considered important, both in Washington and in New York. The *Tribune*, the *Times*, and the *Herald* were the only three of the New York's seventeen daily newspapers to support the president and the war in any degree. Nine were defenders of slavery, and five others were definitely Southern sympathizers.

Greeley's enemies remarked skeptically that the editor might not have been so ardent an abolitionist if he had ever visited the South, since he was inclined to change his mind after firsthand examination. The South was the only section of America that Greeley had never visited, and his understanding of it was limited. But he knew that slavery was wrong, and he believed devoutly that secession would be fatal to the American idea. Southern travel would certainly not have converted him from those beliefs.

When it came down to the nub of the day's issues, however, those beliefs collided head on with Greeley's natural pacifism. He could not accept the idea of war. He was ready, at first, to let the Southern states go, as Bennett was, if that was the only way. In this his managing editor, Charles Dana, agreed with him. Dana, who had been as much of an idealist as Greeley, was becoming increasingly cynical about the world, but he still found himself in agreement with his employer on most large questions—except about labor unions, which he abhorred. The attack on Fort Sumter caused the severing of their relationship and changed their lives, as it did for so many thousands of others. Greeley was totally against the war in the beginning, and Dana was for it, so Greeley asked for his friend's resignation and got it.

Before he left, Dana had committed the *Tribune* to the war in Greeley's temporary absence and had given the Union forces a headline that became a ringing battle cry, "Forward to Richmond!" Lincoln and his cabinet were so pleased with this kind of support from an important paper that when Secretary of War Stanton heard about Dana's resignation, he offered the editor a job in the War Department. Dana was assigned to spy on General Ulysses S. Grant. He joined General Grant at headquarters and secretly provided Secretary of War Stanton with daily reports which would enable him to estimate what General Grant was doing and was capable of doing. As a reward, after Vicksburg, President Lincoln appointed Dana assistant secretary of war. As for Greeley, he continued to give the president uncertain support; Lincoln could not always be certain which side Greeley was on.

Greeley's rival was Henry Raymond, his former employee, who was referred to as "the little villain." The *Times* had double the *Tribune*'s city circulation, and Greeley was finding it his chief rival. Greeley and Raymond were also rivals in the political arena. Both were deep in the Whig politics of New York state, where Greeley found his ambitions blocked at every turn by his former assistant.

In the Whig struggle between the Northern Free-Soilers (those who opposed the further extension of slavery) and the slaveholding Southerners, Raymond won national attention at the Whig National Convention of 1852 for his eloquent advocacy of the Northern cause. Nevertheless, Greeley hoped that Thurlow Weed, the Whig boss in New York, would give him the nomination for governor. When Weed ignored him, Greeley humbled himself enough to ask for the lieutenant governor's job, but Weed gave the nomination to Raymond. "No other name could have been so bitterly humiliating to me," Greeley wrote. The ticket was elected.

When Greeley came to the convention of 1860, he was determined to support anyone who was against Weed and Seward. That is why Lincoln got the backing of the country's most influential newspaper, and it was of considerable help in electing him.

CENSORSHIP AND THE CIVIL WAR

Inevitably, during the Civil War, large questions were raised about the relationship between the press and the government. How much access to information should the press have during wartime? How does the government go about controlling the day's news? There were pro- and anti-war papers, all of them hotly partisan except for the *New York Times*. The perennial problem, which has never been solved, plagued both Washington and the editors: how to balance national security and the public's right to know.

The essential argument between the American media and the American military has always been about access. Access was all Florus Plympton, of the *Cincinnati Commercial*, wanted when he arrived in Kentucky in September 1861 to interview General William Tecumseh Sherman.

General Sherman, who abhorred the press, ordered the newsman to take the next train home. When the journalist protested that he had come to learn the truth, General Sherman exploded. "We do not want the truth about things; that is what we don't want. Truth, eh? No sir ... We do not want the enemy any better informed about what is going on here than he is."[36]

True, there were correspondents who gave General Sherman more than enough provocation to be angry and arbitrary in his treatment of them, particularly when they wrote stories disclosing military information in a dangerous way.

General Sherman was a commander who on occasion did not hesitate to attribute his own failures to information leaks in the papers. He never missed an opportunity to excoriate a correspondent or a newspaper—nor a chance to use a correspondent if he could be useful. At one point the press circulated a story that he was insane. A December 12 headline in the *Cincinnati Commercial*, for example, said, "GENERAL WILLIAM T. SHERMAN INSANE." And no doubt he was, in the nonclinical sense that applies to military men (and others) whose egocentricity pushes them beyond the limits of rationality.[37]

When one of Greeley's reporters filed a story that was a clear violation of censorship, General Sherman had him arrested as a spy, and would have had him shot if Lincoln had not intervened. This incident was serious enough to bring about a reform that was only logical. Correspondents were thereafter accredited, as they are today, and had to be acceptable to field commanders in order to gain accreditation. British correspondents were excluded; they had been a problem for the Union side because of Britain's sympathy with the Confederate cause.

In the end, these changes and a more relaxed attitude on the part of government and press led to enough cooperation that Sherman was able to make his march to the sea without disclosure of his plans in the newspapers at any stage.

In general, the correspondents enjoyed a freedom in their coverage that they do not have today. It matched the nearly complete freedom the press now enjoyed in its new prosperous, independent, and aggressive state. Every faction tried to use its own newspaper support to influence public opinion, in the classic manner, and sometimes they were successful enough to influence actual military decisions. Politicians and generals sometimes found themselves in an undignified scramble for press support, and those who ignored or resisted newspaper power, such as General George B. McClellan, often found themselves removed.

The press was in a familiar position in this struggle. Thanks to Bennett and the other New York giants, it was much more powerful, and its ability to gather and disseminate news had been enormously enhanced by the development of the telegraph and the railway. Balanced against these factors was the nearly total ignorance of the military commands, both North and South, on the subject of censorship; none of them had had the advantage of experience with it. There were, in addition, overwhelming tides of hate and bigotry washing over and nearly obliterating the national idealism that had prevailed since the Revolution.

During the Civil War, censorship—controlling news and editorial comment in a publication—was on a large scale and unstructured, since neither the government nor the press had any precedents to follow. The South was much better at censorship than the North at the beginning of the war. As the war progressed, the South lost leadership, structure, and resources, and thus its ability to manage the media. The North, on the other hand, increased its censorship of the media and was organized and effective by the end of the war. Censorship was carried out in a number of ways.

"MOB CENSORSHIP"

Horace Greeley's fervent opposition to slavery was enough to alienate the New York mobs who gathered in the draft riots of 1863; consequently the *Herald* and Greeley were on their list of prominent targets. These mindless men began with the destruction of the Enrollment Office, the draft headquarters at Third Avenue and Forty-Sixth Street, then rolled across the city, looting, burning, and killing.

Sidney Gay, the *Tribune*'s managing editor, a former Underground Railroad agent, watched the mob's progress with apprehension. He saw the crude banners—"NO DRAFT!" "KILL THE NIGGERS!"—and heard their shouts: "To the *Tribune!* We'll hang old Greeley to a sour apple tree." Gay warned Greeley and told him he ought to prepare to defend the building against the mob, but Greeley observed calmly, "It's just what I expected, and I have no doubt they will hang me. But I want no arms brought into the building."

Then the mob flowed into Printing House Square, and its raucous yells reached to the men inside: "Down with the *Tribune!* Down with the old white coat that thinks a nigger is as good as an Irishman!"[38]

Accounts vary as to what happened next. Some contemporary narratives say that Greeley left the building by a back door, hurried down an alley, and into a nearby tavern, Windust's Restaurant, where he often ate, and hid out under a table until the mob, giving up, went on to other mischief. A more heroic version, and one that seems more characteristic, says that he announced in his squeaky voice: "If I can't eat my dinner when I'm hungry, my life isn't worth anything to me." Then, clapping on his floppy hat, he took a friend's arm (possibly Gay's) and strode through the mob, unafraid, to his dinner. In any case, he and the *Tribune* escaped damage, except for a few stones thrown at the windows, but only because the most unmilitant of men, Raymond, came to his paper's rescue.

From his *Times* office, across the square, Raymond had watched the mob's threatening actions against the *Tribune* building, and remarked calmly that what the men required was "grape, and plenty of it." He organized a *Times* expeditionary force to go to the *Tribune*'s rescue. It was armed principally with two mitrialleuses—a new invention, a breech-loading machine gun with several barrels. Raymond gave one to a *Times* stockholder who happened to be there—it was Winston Churchill's grandfather, Leonard Walter Jerome—and took the other himself. Rifles were handed out to the reporters and printers.

With the aplomb of a general on the battlefield, Raymond sent sixteen *Times* men around the back way to relieve the besieged *Tribune* men. Meanwhile, 200 policemen, gathered from various parts of the city, poured into the square, pistols ready and nightsticks flying. When they were finished, more than fifty rioters were lying dead or injured.

When Greeley came back to work the next day, the square resembled a battlefield, littered with debris, overturned barricades, and smoke still rising from fires. In the *Tribune*'s office, he found Gay in charge of a veritable fortress, including a howitzer and several bombs. He ordered them taken away, but the rioters were once more gathering outside, and Greeley fearlessly walked out among them again, so the story goes, to hear Governor Horatio Seymour address the crowd and plead for order. Back in the office again, Greeley sat moodily in the newsroom with the reporters rather than be near the arsenal outside his office.

After soldiers from thirteen regiments had arrived in the city, order was restored. Vigilantes who called themselves Volunteer Specials helped patrol the streets, taking more credit than they deserved, some thought. One of them enraged the remnants of the mob anew by remarking that "the Irish cattle" had had "impressed on them a respect for order." Greeley apologized sardonically in the *Tribune*: "The Irish in the police department have won the respect of good citizens. They nobly shot down their fellow countrymen and women."[39]

CENSORSHIP BY ARMIES

In addition, combatant troops effectively censored newspapers or newsmen. When Union troops marched into Confederate cities, they sometimes took control of the newspapers. It happened to the *Picayune* when Union troops took New Orleans. It nearly happened to the *Appeal* when Union troops took Memphis. The *Appeal*, however, moved out of town rather than fall to the Yankees.

In the field, it was a different matter. When the editorial directors of the papers back home or their reporters were in conflict with military commanders, the commanders were likely to take punitive action against the correspondents.

VOLUNTARY CENSORSHIP

For the North, censorship in the field was firmly imposed after Bull Run. General McClellan, who understood the situation better than most commanders, called the correspondents together in 1861 and offered them a plan of voluntary censorship. Like most voluntary plans, this one did not work because there was no unanimity among the participants. Some papers were conscientious about it; some were not; some virtually ignored it.

To further confound the issue, the direction of censorship became an internal struggle between the State and War Departments. The voluntary system, rendered virtually useless by these handicaps, lasted three months. Then Congress took away the control from State and gave it to War, where Stanton, just coming into office, succeeded in improving matters.

In the South in May 1861, the Professional Congress of the Confederate States of America passed a bill giving President Jefferson Davis the power to censor the telegraph, though dispatches from reporters were seldom monitored. Postmasters were given the power to open and censor the mails.

Early in the war Southern reporters also were given voluntary censorship guidelines to follow. They were told by Secretary of War Leroy Walker to avoid publishing information that would hurt the Confederacy's efforts. Thus, information such as describing movements or armaments of Southern troops was considered off limits.

Those who couldn't follow the voluntary censorship guidelines were denied access to military battles. Punished Confederate newspapers had to scramble for news, most often relying on the Northern press to fill in gaps about activities of Southern troops.

FORMALIZED CENSORSHIP

In 1862 Stanton required correspondents to submit their copy to provost marshals who were instructed to delete only military information. The sole difficulty was in the administration of the order. Some generals and their provosts were concerned more with public relations than with the problem of censorship.

The press was infinitely more responsible in its coverage of the Civil War than it had been in previous history. For the first time, there was a great deal of factual, relatively unbiased news from the battlefields at a time of the most intense partisanship; that was a long step forward. In editorial columns, however, there was the same kind of irresponsibility that had always existed, and the treatment of Lincoln was inexcusable on any grounds. Until matters improved in the field and both correspondents and commanders got a better understanding of their responsibilities, some irresponsible reporting existed where purely military matters were concerned.

This irresponsibility, at home and in the field, brought the press into direct conflict with the government and produced the most serious threat to its freedom it had known since the Alien and Sedition Acts of 1798. Some historians justify the Lincoln administration's actions on the ground that it was a question of the Union's survival, but that takes us to the familiar ground of ends justifying means.

SUSPENSION

Lincoln was a liberal by nature, far more so than most of the others in his party, but in his overwhelming zeal to save the Union he permitted his government to employ high-handed infringements of fundamental freedoms. For example, writs of habeas corpus were suspended, and widespread censorship was instituted by the military and the post office.

Generals themselves sometimes became instruments of suppression. In the Northwest, General Ambrose E. Burnside arbitrarily seized and suppressed newspapers he thought were treasonous. Copperhead papers caused the biggest headaches for Lincoln and his generals. Burnside, for example, shut down the *Chicago Times* for two days for what he said were disloyal and incendiary sentiments.

Postmaster General Montgomery Blair used his power to deny the mails to newspapers he considered subversive, and he would not permit post offices to relay messages to enemy areas. In the constant search for traitors, telegrams between North and South were seized. Secretary Stanton and General Winfield Scott compelled the telegraph companies, illegally to be sure, to stop sending any information of a military nature, and naturally this affected the work of correspondents.

Secretary Stanton declared that "no news gatherer, nor any other person, for sordid or treasonable purposes can be suffered to intrude upon" national agents "to procure news by threats, or spy out official acts which the safety of the nation requires not to be disclosed." Under this doctrine, Secretary Stanton, and Seward as well, had some Copperhead editors thrown into Fort Lafayette, with no formal charges ever filed against them, and where civil-court remedies were unavailable to get them out.[40]

Meanwhile, suspensions in the South rarely occurred because pro-Union newspapers were effectively silenced by the Confederate military.

IMPACT OF THE CIVIL WAR ON THE PRESS

The Civil War had a tremendous impact on the nation's press. The press matured and became a big business. With the rise of the telegraph and special correspondents, a transformed journalism emerged from the Civil War. Circulation figures nearly doubled, and improved methods of printing, the introduction of Sunday editions, the growth of news agencies, and syndication followed this trend.

IMPROVED METHODS OF PRINTING

In 1861 Horace Greeley's *Tribune* introduced the process of *stereotyping*, making it possible for the first time to produce from the type form a solid plate the size of an entire page, curved to fit the printing cylinder. This process, which had been used for years in the book printing business, had many advantages. Pages could be duplicated an indefinite number of times at unheard-of speeds. In addition, several presses could be used at the same time to print the same edition of the newspaper. The *New York Times* and *Herald* soon adopted this process.[41]

In the composing room, William Bullock's 1863 invention, the *web perfecting press*, which printed both sides of a continuous roll of paper on the rotary press, guaranteed that the new market could be supplied in quantity. The press, first used by the *Philadelphia Inquirer*, was the prototype of the kind in common use today.

New typographical equipment led to new makeup techniques, including the *display headline*. Though introduced in 1856 by Raymond, such headlines were not common before the war. Even during the war, most newspapers displayed a story in a single column with six to twelve lines of a headline, depending on the importance of the story. By 1862 it was becoming general practice to move the war headlines from page two and three, where telegraphic news usually appeared, to the front page.

THE SUNDAY NEWSPAPER

Pressure for increased coverage of the war and demand for more advertising space necessitated the inauguration of *Sunday editions*. Until this time, it had been rare for dailies to publish Sunday editions, though there were a number of Sunday papers not associated with daily newspapers.

Many newspapers instituted the practice of issuing afternoon *"extras."* "They issue those evening editions to contradict the lies that they tell in the morning," it was said at the time.[42]

However, many newspapers feared that Sunday editions would offend their more religious readers. The *Chicago Tribune* reported that some newspaper, apparently unwilling to risk offending readers who were strict Sabbatarians, carried a Sunday dateline on the first page and a Monday dateline on the third as a sort of compromise.[43]

NEWS AGENCIES

Before the Civil War there were several loosely defined *news agencies* throughout the country. They included the Philadelphia Associated Press, the New York State Associated Press, the Southern Associated Press, and the Western Associated Press. Their aim was to provide news coverage on a regional basis.

News agencies became more popular during the Civil War as more and more Northern newspapers that could not afford correspondents found it expedient to obtain news from the New York Associated Press, an organization of seven morning newspapers founded in 1848. It collected news mostly for its own members but sold news to other papers as well. Its correspondents were called agents, not reporters. One could find an agent stationed at any important point in the country.

Costs of covering the war also brought about cooperative efforts. Strapped by rising costs, Southern editors formed a cooperative news agency. The Press Association of the Confederate States of America—"PA," in its familiar logotype—was one of the marvels of the war. All of the South's forty-three wartime dailies were members of it from 1863 to 1864.

Its news of the conflict was a model of objectivity, for the most part, and was sometimes more reliable than Northern reporting of the same event. J. S. Thrasher, its general manager, directed his correspondents to question reports, stick to the facts, send no rumors, and purge opinion from news dispatches.

SYNDICATION

Another marvel of the war was the birth of the *newspaper syndicate*. Ansel N. Kellogg, editor of the *Baraboo* (Wisconsin) *Republic*, was left without a staff when his printer, Joseph Weirich, joined the Union army. To continue publishing his paper, he ordered two pages of preprinted war news each week from the *Wisconsin State Journal*. By the end of 1861, fifteen other papers used this service.

Though Kellogg's efforts brought about the first continuous syndication, in 1841 Moses Yale Beach had first printed sheets containing a speech of President John Tyler and sold them to newspapers. Kellogg, publisher of the *New York Sun*, began publishing preprinted pages on a regular basis. Some feared that such activities would allow a handful of editors to control news for a large segment of the population. Eventually Kellogg sold his paper and traveled to Chicago, where he opened his own syndicate. He became a very rich man. His business served 1,400 newspapers and earned $200,000 a year.

THE CIVIL WAR AND THE PRACTICE OF JOURNALISM

The Civil War also had brought about sweeping and revolutionary changes in journalistic practices. In covering these incidents, the *Times* said that "New York newspapers gained their first realizing sense of two fundamental principles that have made them what they are to-day—first, the surpassing value of individual, competitive, triumphant enterprise in getting early and exclusive news, and second, the possibility of building up large circulations by striving unceasingly to meet a popular demand for prompt and adequate reports of the day-to-day doings of mankind the world over."[44]

The competitive nature of enterprise reporting brought about the saturation of on-the-spot reporting, visual journalism, and a new journalistic writing style.

SATURATION COVERAGE

Considered one of the milestones in the development of American journalism, however, was the news coverage of John Brown's Raid of 1859 and the subsequent trial and executions. Never before in American history had so many reporters and illustrators been sent by distant urban newspapers to cover a breaking story.[45]

Reporters learned that Brown attempted to establish some type of abolitionist republic in the Appalachian Mountains and make war on slavery with fugitive slaves and some whites. On the night of October 16, 1859, Brown seized the federal arsenal at Harper's Ferry. There he killed the town's mayor, and took some of the leading townspeople prisoner. By daybreak the neighboring militia was swarming about him, while the telegraph spread consternation through Virginia.

The next day Colonel Robert E. Lee found Brown with one son dead by his side and another son shot and dying. Eight days later the trial of Brown began in the courthouse of Charles Town, Virginia. On October 31 the jury brought in the verdict of murder, criminal conspiracy, and treason against the Commonwealth of Virginia. He was hanged on December 2, 1859.

Aside from the politics of the war, newspapers gave an outstanding example of what they could do. No war had ever been reported so freely and completely. Storey's *Chicago Times* boasted in November 1863: "There is not an important point in the country where we do not now maintain one or more special correspondents. We employ the magnetic telegraph at a cost of more than a thousand dollars annually, special messengers at a heavy outlay, and the express and mails only as they can be made useful."

But Bennett's genius made the *Herald* stand out above all others—audacious as always, amazingly complete, and nearly always accurate, with some forty correspondents covering the battles. War coverage cost Bennett more than a half million dollars, but the effort brought him to the peak of his success. The *Tribune* was its most serious competition, but Bennett had the satisfaction of knowing that Lincoln himself read the *Herald* above all others.

VISUAL JOURNALISM

An army of artists joined field reporters in covering John Brown's demise. And they would be a fixture for the rest of the war. Artists' woodcuts brought the war visually to the growing picture weeklies. Correspondents and artists, writing and sketching directly from the battlefields, produced war reporting that ranked with the best in the newspapers, and the woodcuts reproduced from the artists' sketches provided a valuable pictorial record of the war, supplementing the even more important photographic record being compiled by Brady and others.

The most noted were Frank Leslie's *Illustrated Newspaper* and *Harper's Weekly*. Leslie's boasted that one of its "trained corps of the first artists" had accompanied every important expedition "either by sea or land" and that it had published nearly 3,000 pictures of "battle, sieges, bombardments, stormings and other scenes, incidental to war," contributed by more than eighty artists. Meanwhile, woodcut illustrations helped Harper's achieve a circulation of 200,000 before the war.[46]

Mathew Brady and political cartoonist Thomas Nast would push visual journalism to new heights. Brady, who became intrigued by the daguerreotype, introduced by telegraph inventor Samuel F.B. Morse in 1839, became the first and most famous photographer to capture the war. He had the idea to put together a photographic history of the war. When he approached the government, officials

Matthew Brady/Getty Images

Civil War photographer Mathew Brady constructed a number of horsedrawn processing wagons, allowing him to capture Civil War battles.

wanted no part of it. So he invested $100,000 of his own money in salaries, equipment, and other expenses to fund about twelve photographers. He was counting on recouping his investments by selling the photographs to newspapers and magazines. However, technical limitations required that the photographs be converted to line drawings before printing, and this did not do justice to the photographs.

Eventually, Brady began taking pictures of Lincoln, who remarked on more than one occasion that "Brady and the Cooper Union speech made me president." The president gave him a press card, and by the end of the war he had twenty teams of photographers on the field. Each was equipped with one of his photographic carts. Using these black wagons that stored glass plates and doubled as darkrooms, Brady's troops captured the horror of war. In essence, he changed wartime reporting, and from then on it would be captured on film.

While Brady chronicled the war with his camera, Nast produced some of the most famous political cartoons in American media history. During the Civil War, he sent drawings to *Harper's Weekly*, where he became a regular staff member in 1862. Two years later, during the Democratic convention in Chicago, he was motivated to draw one of his most effective political cartoons. Nast, a radical Republican, was a fierce supporter of the Union and was angered when the Democrats declared the war a failure and called for peace on any terms. In a September 3, 1864, *Harper's Weekly* cartoon called "Compromise with the South," Nast depicted a downcast, unarmed, one-legged Union soldier with crutches shaking hands with a neatly groomed Southerner who is fully armed, smiling, and standing tall. Between them is a grave. The Southerner has one foot on the grave and has broken a knife lying there in two. One half of the knife reads "Northern" and the other "Power." Columbia, a female personification of the United States, is weeping beside the grave. The tombstone reads, "In memory of our Union-heroes who fell in a useless war." The image is said to have brought Nast "instant fame," and was reprinted widely by the Republicans in their effort to have Lincoln reelected.

Following the war, Nast's biting cartoons would capture the spirit of political corruption as exemplified by New York's Tammany Hall, which he depicted as a tiger, and its boss, William Magear Tweed, or "Boss" Tweed, as he was known. Nast's cartoons were so effective in depicting Tweed as a sleazy criminal that legend has it that the Boss dispatched his minions with the command, "Stop them damn pictures. I don't care what the papers write about me. My constituents can't read. But, damn it, they can see the pictures." Voters ousted Tweed and his compatriots in November 1871. An irony of history is that when Tweed escaped from jail and fled to Spain in 1876, he was arrested by a customs official who did not read English but recognized him from Nast's *Harper's Weekly* caricatures.

Nast also penned some of America's most famous symbols, including a roly-poly bearded Santa Claus visiting Union troops. However, William Cullen Bryant II, writing in the *New York Times* in 1883, suggested that it was Robert Walter Weir who drew Santa in 1837, three years before Nast's cartoon. He also popularized the donkey as the symbol for the Democratic Party and the elephant for the Republican Party. At his death, *Harper's Weekly* called him the "Father of American Caricature."

NEW REPORTING STYLE

The Civil War ushered in a new type of reporting, along with popularizing the use of illustrations. Readers were no longer content with editorials written by the dominant personalities or "lords of the penny press." Instead, readers now wanted news stories from correspondents in the field, and they wanted those news stories as soon as possible. Thus, reporters came into their own, and the American journalist emerged as an important player in the news business.

NEWSWRITING STYLE

In the North, particularly, the war considerably advanced newspaper technology. In using the telegraph as the chief transmitter of stories, correspondents learned to write more concisely, since transmission was expensive. Stories were more readable, and that became a hallmark of postwar mass journalism.

Timeliness became an important news element, changing dramatically the nature of news, and, perhaps, the concept of story. The telegraph also gave rise to the invention of the *summary lead*—that is, the first paragraph containing the who, what, when, where, and why of a story, still a standard form.

It also fostered the *inverted pyramid*, organizing the story by putting the most important facts first. Its origins are still being debated today. One story is that Civil War correspondents could not always be sure their entire dispatch would find its way through the precarious telegraph system, and so they tried to make sure that the essential facts would arrive if the rest of the story were cut off. Another story is that wire services used the inverted pyramid because they had to be impartial.

However, many dispute the importance of Civil War coverage in fashioning the inverted pyramid style of journalistic writing. Some have suggested that the first examples of such writing appeared in the 1870s and 1880s.[47]

It may be hasty to say that Secretary Stanton invented the inverted pyramid style of writing. However, he was among the first to write in a style that would replace narrative with a hierarchical ordering of facts.[48] For example, his terse and impartial dispatches came close to the inverted pyramid style of writing when most newswriting was still chronological and narrative.

CONCLUSION

The Civil War changed America and its press. When war erupted on April 12, 1861, some 2,500 newspapers, typically four or eight pages with few illustrations, were in operation. About 283 were dailies in the North and 80 in the South. The North had about 350 correspondents covering the war and the South had about 100.

The war had a tremendous impact on the nation's press. It matured and became *big business*. With the rise of the telegraph and special correspondents, the modern journalist emerged. Circulation figures nearly doubled, necessitating improved methods of printing, the introduction of Sunday editions, the growth of news agencies, and syndication.

The competitive nature of *enterprise reporting* brought about the saturation of *on-the-spot reporting*, a *new journalistic writing style*, and *visual journalism*.

Mathew Brady and his photographers who covered the battles would add another dimension to reporting. The public from now on would come to expect not only words but photographs or line drawings. It also would come to expect illustrations in the form of cartoons.

Finally, the Civil War did not really come to a close until that April night in 1865 when Lawrence Gobright, the Associated Press's man in Washington, flashed the fateful first bulletin: "The President was shot in a theater tonight, and perhaps mortally wounded." When the news reached the streets, there was a final outpouring of venom and hatred that had characterized the relationship between public and press from the beginning. Mobs swarmed into the offices of several Copperhead papers and destroyed presses and types, tarring and feathering or threatening to lynch the proprietors, if they could catch them. Plainly, the war had established the newspaper as a valuable and more responsible medium. It had not diminished its role in American life as the purveyor of a kind of freedom that the people it was intended to benefit were not sure they wanted.

THE YELLOW PRESS AND THE *TIMES*

CHAPTER **6**

The Civil War had changed America and American journalism. As historian Shelby Foote put it, the Civil War "made us an is." No longer did people say, "the United States are."[1] However, it would take decades to make the battered nation a truly united one. It had been such a bitter war, fought in 10,000 places—from New Mexico and Tennessee to Vermont and the Florida coast. Cities in the South were left in ruins, as were their fields of cotton and tobacco, the staples of their economic existence. Slaves were free, but true equality would continue to evade them.

The new role of the press as the primary source of news was ratified by newspaper coverage of President Abraham Lincoln's assassination. It was, according to Ted Smythe, a role that was hammered out in the post–Civil War era, and several characteristics vied for dominance: timeliness, accuracy, exclusiveness, sensationalism, entertainment, and impartiality.[2] News traveled through telegraph lines that now stretched from Maine to California, fostering evening newspapers and nationwide and sectional press associations. Also accelerating news transmission was the Atlantic cable, which was laid in 1866.[3]

Lincoln's death complicated the difficult task of Reconstruction in a nation which had grown to 75 million people by 1900. Some 16 million of them were immigrants, mostly from southern Europe. Change was rapid as the nation turned from its antebellum economic, political, and social organizations.

NEWSPAPERS AS PUBLIC DEFENDERS

Politically, corruption ran rampant throughout the nation in the post–Civil War era, and editors saw themselves as the only defense against such iniquities. The concept of the press as a "watchdog" over government and business, on behalf of the public, had been taking hold. James Bennett Sr. at first thought of himself as a public defender, but his idea changed as his wealth and his madness increased, and his son had no regard for the public interest at all.

Horace Greeley was a sincerely dedicated public defender, but he sadly permitted his personal thirst for the presidency to diffuse his dedication. Charles Dana could have been one of the most potent public defenders on record if he had not lost his early idealism. Henry J. Raymond was even more a creature of political ambition than Greeley, but the paper he created was the first to show, after he had gone, what a powerful role the newspaper could play on behalf of the public—the role Thomas Jefferson had envisioned.

After Raymond's death, the *Times* had been directed for a while by his friend and partner, George Jones, the business manager. He relied for editorial direction on three outstanding editors in succession: Louis J. Jennings, John Foord, and Charles R. Miller Jr. Jennings and Jones together directed the exposure of the Tweed Ring—one of the finest hours in the development of the *Times* and a significant episode in media history.

William Marcy Tweed, the sachem of Tammany Hall, was one of the most accomplished plunderers of a city that, like Boston and Chicago, had suffered from corrupt city governments almost since its founding. Tweed began his remarkable career as a member of the Common Council in 1852, and amassed a fortune through the prevalent mode of streetcar franchises, city land sales, and other such devices. In 1868, he and a gamy cast of municipal scoundrels were swept into New York's chief public offices by a Tammany landslide, and the most gigantic frauds in the city's history began.[4]

On July 8, 1871, the *Times* published an exposé of the Tweed regime. Tweed's answer to the charges provided some conception of the formidable task Jones faced. A month after they were made, Tweed held a giant rally in and outside Tammany Hall to demonstrate his support. Governor John T. Hoffman, who was in Tweed's pocket, sat beside the boss, and near him was Samuel J. Tilden, chairman of the Democratic State Committee. Jim Fisk was one of the principal speakers. More than a year earlier, on September 24, 1869, he and Jay Gould had precipitated Black Friday on the stock market when they attempted to corner the nation's gold supply. However, their shenanigan was stopped by the sale of $4 million in gold by the government.

Not long after the rally, Tweed solemnly called in eminent citizens to inspect the city's books, and in a few hours they certified the records as correct and well kept—a task that would have taken accountants three months to accomplish. One was John Jacob Astor, the city's chief landlord. Another was Moses Taylor, a banker and railroad investor who had been Cyrus T. Field's partner in laying the Atlantic cable; Field's brother, David, was later Tweed's chief lawyer. Present too was Edward Schell, another rich banker, one of whose four brothers, Augustus, later succeeded Tweed as a head of Tammany. Ironically, a fourth member was Marshall O. Roberts, one of the *Sun*'s owners, who had profiteered during the Civil War by chartering and selling steamships to the Union.

It was said that this ad hoc committee had been advised that they would get tax relief in return for their cooperation. Others asserted that they were threatened with sharp tax increases if they did *not* cooperate. Either way, Tweed controlled them. To underscore the point, he spoke to several of the *Times'* largest advertisers, who obliged by removing their advertising. At the same time, questions were raised about whether the paper really held title to the land it stood upon.

Rumors also persisted that the Tweed Ring paid hush money, in the form of lucrative advertising contracts, to a number of New York City newspapers. One historian wrote that some eighty-nine newspapers were on the Tweed payroll and that when the Tweed Ring came to an end, twenty-seven of these newspapers died.[5]

Meanwhile, a news article disclosed that Tweed had padded the city payroll with 1,300 people described as "rowdies, vagabonds, sneak thieves, gamblers, and shoulder-hitters." These hoodlums were engaged in such activities as painting park lamps on rainy days, making it necessary to redo them. The response to this revelation came from Jones's fellow editors, rather than from Tweed. The *Sun*, quite naturally, had already excoriated the *Times*, but so had the *World* and other papers. Now Dana himself sneered: "The decline of the *New York Times* in everything that entitled a newspaper to respect and confidence, has been rapid and complete. Its present editor [Jennings], who was dismissed from the *London Times* for improper conduct and untruthful writing, has sunk into a tedious monotony of slander and disregard of truth, and black-guard vituperation."[6]

There was no truth in this charge against Jennings. Dana did not like him because he was English, and because he was married to an actress, an occupation still only a step away from whoredom in the public mind.

Tweed was resourceful. He tried to buy control of the *Times* through a deal with Raymond's widow, who held thirty-four shares of the paper's stock, using Gould and Cyrus Field as front men. Jones saw through that plot easily and declared editorially that "no money" would persuade him to sell any of his own stock, which would be necessary for someone else to gain control.

As is so often the case, a single disgruntled individual, James O'Brien, who had been sheriff as well as head of the Young Democrats, broke Tweed. He was a Tammany insurgent with ambitions to get a larger share of the graft, and he hoped to replace Tweed. O'Brien had a friend and agent whom Tweed had just appointed county auditor, not knowing the connection between the men. Through this channel O'Brien obtained documentary proof of Tweed's corruption and laid it one night on Jennings's desk. It was material copied straight from the city ledgers.

There was a final move on Tweed's part to get Mrs. Raymond's stock. He took advantage of the fact that she had been separated from her husband, apparently over his affair with a Miss Eyting, and needed money. But that failed, too, and the *Times* laid before the public the proof that O'Brien had provided. Editorially, it reminded the other papers of their neglected duties as defenders of the public:

> We apprehend that no one will complain of a lack of facts and specifications in the articles to which we now call the reader's attention; and that not even the *Tribune* or any other of the eighteen dailies and weekly papers that have been gagged by Ring patronage will be able to find an excuse for ignoring the startling record presented here, on the ground that it is not sufficiently definite.[7]

Tweed was now alarmed enough to attempt a truly desperate maneuver. He sent his chief bagman, Controller Richard B. "Slippery Dick" Connolly, to offer Jones a bribe of $5 million if he would hold off and drop the case. Jones coldly refused. Connolly could not understand such honesty. "Why, with that sum you could go to Europe and live like a prince," he exclaimed.

"Yes, but I'd know I was a rascal," Jones said, and later observed wryly, "I don't think the devil will ever make a higher bid for me than that."[8]

Once the lid was off, the revelations followed rapidly, not only in the *Times* but in *Harper's Weekly*, where Thomas Nast's savage cartoons so aroused the public that Tweed tried to buy off the cartoonist with a $500,000 bribe.

When the entire fraud was disclosed by the press, it appeared that the Tweed gang had gotten away with a sum estimated at somewhere between $75 million and $200 million, only a fraction of which was returned. Confronted with the disintegration of the structure he had built, Tweed was revealed not only as a criminal but as a savage, contemptible man who could say, and mean it, "If I were twenty or thirty years younger, I would kill George Jones with my own bare hands."[9]

As it was, he had to face arrest and jail. He escaped but was captured in Spain by an official who recognized him from one of Nast's cartoons. Returned to the Ludlow Street jail, he died there. Connolly, however, got away with enough money to spend the rest of his life in luxury in Paris.

The Tweed Ring scandal provided the *Times* with an opportunity for a remarkable demonstration of courage, and defined a role for the media that everyone could understand. Partisans might argue, even in the face of the facts, that the papers were "out to get" Grant, but there was no way for anyone, even dedicated Democrats, to defend the Tweed Ring. The *Times* had obviously behaved admirably in the public interest against the most formidable odds.

This had been an honest effort on behalf of the public. Now another demonstration in New York and elsewhere showed how newspapers could pretend to play the role of public defender, while their real purpose was to gain circulation in a highly competitive situation. Jones was fighting for survival and for the public good. Joseph Pulitzer and William Randolph Hearst were fighting for circulation and consequently more money. Hearst, who didn't really need the money, also was engaged in a power struggle, one of the keys to his complex personality.

JOSEPH PULITZER

The publishers were complicated men. Pulitzer's life is still not well understood today, primarily because of the gloss laid over it by the *World*, the great newspaper he founded, and the prizes and the Columbia University School of Journalism he left behind him. Without question, he did make substantial contributions to the practice of newspapering, but his personal eccentricities, in the manner of the Bennetts, and his senseless struggle with young Hearst, diluted much of what he accomplished in his lifetime.

As a young man, he was a strong sight, "about six feet two and a half inches tall, ungainly in appearance, awkward in movement, lacking entirely in the art of human relations."[10] He was born in 1847, and his early life was bizarre, to say the least. He left his native Mako, Hungary, at seventeen because he could not abide the man his widowed mother, whom he idolized, had married. He had been given a good education by private tutors, but he was not suited for anything in particular.

His ambition was to be a soldier. This "tall, scraggy youth with long, thick black hair, large head, and oversized nose," as one of his biographers has described him, wandered about Europe looking for an army to join.[11] But even in a world torn by wars and revolutions, he could not find a recruiting sergeant who would take him. He was told he had weak eyes and an unpromising physique. He also may have given some indication of the approaching nervous disorder that would eventually make his life a living torture.

After being turned down by the Austrians, the French Foreign Legion, the British army, and even by the old sea captains in Hamburg, where he tried to ship as a common seaman, Pulitzer would have gone home from the North Sea port except that he fell in with an agent of the Union army in America. The agent was busy signing up promising young men who would get their passage, while he pocketed the $500 bounty given for these recruits, who would be substitutes for men who did not want to be drafted. Pulitzer signed up immediately.

Later he told several stories about his voyage to America. For a man whose watchword on his newspaper was accuracy, Pulitzer was extremely vague about the details of his early life. One story, the best, said that he found out about the bounty on the way over, jumped ship in Boston harbor, and collected the $500 himself. In any case, he enlisted for a year in the First New York (Lincoln) Cavalry, which had been organized by Colonel Carl Schurz.

Pulitzer found army life intolerable. He asked questions incessantly, and he despised anyone who withheld information. These were admirable qualities for journalism but hardly useful in the military. His skirmishes on the battlefield were far outnumbered by those he fought in the barracks and on the parade ground. Once he was nearly court-martialed when he struck a noncommissioned officer.

Out of the army in 1865, he was alone and broke in New York, sitting in City Hall Park with other unemployed people and staring out at the formidable façade of Park Row, where the offices of the *Times*, the *World*, the *Tribune*, the *Herald*, and the *Sun* were clustered. At the moment Pulitzer had no yearnings to work in them. He only wanted to get a job and learn English. When a man with a crude sense of humor told him the best place to learn the language was in St. Louis, he made his way there—to the city which had the largest concentration of German immigrants in the country.

At least he could use his native tongue in St. Louis, and he was soon working on the *Westliche Post*, the leading German-language daily. In his first year, he mastered English, obtained a certificate of naturalization, and became the city's leading reporter. His furious energy made him well known to everyone, particularly to the political leaders at the state house, where he spent a good deal of his time. Impressed with his vivid and knowledgeable reporting, these leaders decided he ought to run for the state house of representatives.

As a legislator, Pulitzer was the same explosive human being he had been as a reporter. Only a year after he was seated, he shot and wounded a well-known lobbyist, but his numerous friends saved him from serious trouble. He became one of St. Louis's three police commissioners, worked hard for the Liberal Republicans, and helped nominate Greeley in 1872. Pulitzer was one of several newspapermen who had backed Greeley and was deeply disappointed by Greeley's failure. He turned to the Democrats and became a lifelong member of the party.

THE *ST. LOUIS POST-DISPATCH*

Now Pulitzer began a series of intricate movements in the newspaper business. He acquired a part interest in the *Post*, sold it as a profit, bought the bankrupt *Staats-Zeitung* for next to nothing, and sold its AP franchise to the *Daily Globe* for a substantial profit. With this money he studied law, was admitted to the bar, married a distant cousin of Jefferson Davis, and in 1878 stood at a crossroads in his career.

He could have gone on to become a successful politician. Instead, he chose journalism, and bought the *St. Louis Dispatch*, a worthless paper that had been founded in 1864 at a sheriff's sale. He had enough resources, $2,700, to operate the paper for seventeen weeks, he estimated. Three days later, for $2,500, he purchased the *Post*, started by John A. Dillon in 1875, and merged it with the *Dispatch*. Dillon continued as a partner for one year, but John A. Cockerill was

Hulton Archive/Getty Images

Joseph Pulitzer, the Hungarian-born journalist and politician, changed journalism by inventing a news formula and rationalizing newspaper practices.

brought in to serve as his managing editor. The thirty-four-year-old Cockerill had met Pulitzer seven years earlier at the Cincinnati political convention. An experienced journalist, Cockerill was one of America's first foreign correspondents, having covered the Russo-Turkish War in 1877. He was painted as a born journalist, hard worker, and a hard taskmaster who was not well read but had lots of common sense.[12] When a clergyman objected to an irreligious cartoon, Cockerill shrieked, "My dear sir: Will you kindly go to hell?"[13]

In the first issue of the *St. Louis Post-Dispatch*, Pulitzer announced his new proactive editorial policy. He vowed that his newspaper "will serve no party but the people; will be no organ of 'Republicanism,' but the organ of truth; will follow no caucuses but its own convictions; will not support the 'Administration,' but criticize it; will oppose all frauds and shams wherever and whatever they are; will advocate principles and ideas rather than prejudices and partisanship."[14]

From its first day, the *Post-Dispatch* attacked corruption, inspired by Pulitzer's slogan, "Never drop a big thing until you have gone to the bottom of it." Thus he joined the ranks of the crusaders, to become the most vociferous of the public defenders. It has always been dangerous for the media to defend the public. In Pulitzer's case, he found trouble in 1882 when a prominent lawyer whose activities had been attacked came in person to call Cockerill to account, in the old manner, and was killed in the resulting quarrel. But in spite of this and other less sensational episodes, the *Post-Dispatch* won public acceptance and respect as a fearless newspaper of unblemished integrity.

THE *NEW YORK WORLD*

Pulitzer was soon a rich man, ready to conquer New York if the opportunity offered itself. On his way to Europe in May 1883, seeking escape from his growing nervous restlessness, he stopped off in New York, where Jay Gould's representatives sold him the *New York World* for $346,000. Gould thought he had concluded a shrewd deal, because the paper had been struggling for life ever since its founding as a penny religious daily. He knew Pulitzer could afford it. The *Post-Dispatch* was netting its publisher $85,000 a year by this time, and the *World* purchase was to be paid in installments.

Pulitzer believed he knew what to do with his acquisition. On the first day of publication under its new owner, the *World* printed something more than the usual grandiloquent statement of purpose. It was perhaps the first expression of journalistic idealism ever written. The statement declared the purpose of a newspaper to be as follows:

> An institution that should always fight for progress and reform, never tolerate injustice or corruption, always fight demagogues of all parties, never belong to any party, always oppose privileged classes and public plunderers, never lack sympathy with the poor, always remain devoted to the public welfare, never be satisfied with merely printing news, always be drastically independent, never be afraid to attack wrong, whether by predatory plutocracy or predatory poverty.[15]

He brought Cockerill on from the *St. Louis Post-Dispatch* to serve as managing editor. The old and new *World* would be as different as night and day. For example, it would no longer be the politically correct paper for "gentlemen." The new *World* utilized a neater and more modest typography with headlines in smaller and lighter-face type above stories of murder, mayhem, and mystery, which proved as sensational as those of the *Police Gazette*.[16]

To draw people into his many crusades, he first had to get them to read his paper. Thus, his front page featured two executions, one at Sing Sing, where the murderer refused to see a priest, shouting, "I am not a Catholic! I'm a Democrat!" and the other at Pittsburgh, where the condemned man yelled at his executioners, "Good-bye, all ye murderers! Yer hangin' an innocent man!" An account of a thunderstorm's toll on New Jersey ran under the headline "THE DEADLY LIGHTNING!" And with a subhead that said, "Six Lives and One Million Dollars Lost."[17]

Pulitzer was on his way to another success. One of his biggest boosters, William Nash, of the *Kansas City Star*, said, "There is scarcely a man west of the Allegheny mountains who does not wish Mr. Pulitzer success [and no one] doubts that he will carry the 'Western method' into the *World* office. His paper will no longer be the organ of the dudes and dudines of Fifth and Madison avenues.... It will devote itself to the news."[18]

The *World* was successful, and it became the most profitable newspaper ever published. By September 2, 1884, it reached a circulation of 100,000, and Pulitzer celebrated by firing off 100 guns in City Hall Park and giving every employee a tall silk hat. Two years later, circulation soared to 250,000. Pulitzer marked this milestone by presenting editors and advertisers with silver medals.[19] When he introduced the *Evening World* in 1887, the combined circulation of both editions was 374,000. Meanwhile, his Sunday edition reached 250,000 by the late eighties. Half of the Sunday edition, which consisted of thirty-six to forty pages, was advertising.[20]

PULITZER'S NEW JOURNALISM

Pulitzer's journalism "affected the character of the entire daily press of the country."[21] He upset the status quo and furnished a new formula for the metropolitan daily.[22] What Pulitzer did was to craft a new concept of news, utilize illustrations, develop the technique of the crusade, revitalize the editorial page, and rationalize the practice of selling advertising space.

NEWS

His chief contribution was the invention of the formula that Hearst later took up and made famous—*sex on the front page and a kind of spurious morality on the editorial page*. Hearst had no discernible public morality in any real sense; his private sense of morality, although not many people believed it, was impeccable only in the area of sexuality, where he was something of a puritan. Pulitzer professed the highest sense of morality in every respect, but where the welfare of his paper was concerned, he appeared ready to make any kind of concession that might prove necessary.

Pulitzer insisted that sensationalism as generally understood is to be avoided. "Cheap crimes are not to be seized upon to play up," he said. "A sensational story that is worth featuring is to be pushed to the limit. But no faking."[23]

He introduced a new definition of sensationalism. Now, it meant self-advertisement, defined as anything about newspaper layout and newspaper policy outside of basic news gathering. Self-advertisement techniques included illustrations, larger and darker headlines, and newspaper promotion of exclusive features. The *World*, for instance, regularly boasted its high circulation figures and that it printed more advertising than any other paper in the country on its front page.

Pulitzer knew what people wanted to read, and that is why the *World* had a mass audience. Cockerill, who often handled the news pages, defined news as "any hitherto unprinted occurrence which involves the violation of any one of the Ten Commandments and, if it involves a fracture of the Vth, VIth, VIIth, VIIIth, or IXth Commandments and by those people whose names people have heard and in whose doings they are specifically interested by knowledge of their official and social position, then it is great news."[24]

ILLUSTRATIONS

The *World*'s news columns also were peppered with illustrations, which were enhanced by color. Pulitzer abhorred pictures at first and once ordered they be removed from all pages. After witnessing a drop in circulation, Pulitzer reinstated them.[25] During the 1884 presidential campaign, the *World* introduced readers to political cartoons by Walt McDougall and Valerian Gribaye. The cartoon would become a daily fixture in newspapers by 1890.

STUNTS

Pulitzer not only had a nose for news, he created news—or stunts, as some critics called them. They were often entertaining, sometimes educational, and always attracted readers.[26] His most ambitious was sending Elizabeth Cochran, "Nellie Bly," who earlier had exposed the horrors of the asylum at Blackwell's Island, on a world voyage in an effort to beat the record of Phileas Fogg, the hero of Jules Verne's romance, *Around the World in Eighty Days*. To make the accounts more attractive to readers, Pulitzer invited them to guess how long it would take her to complete the trip. The winner would receive a free trip to Europe and $250 in spending money. Some 1 million readers participated.

CRUSADES

Though he didn't invent the crusade, Pulitzer stimulated circulation by constant exposés and stunts, using startling headlines. His most famous crusade was the collection of funds to build a pedestal for the Statute of Liberty after Congress refused to appropriate funds and a citizens' committee failed in its task. Pulitzer wrote that "the *World* is the people's paper, and it now appeals to the people to come forward and raise this money."[27] Some 120,000 men, women, and children sent contributions, some even pennies, to contribute the necessary $100,000.

Other crusades were directed against the New York Central Railroad, the Standard Oil Company, the Bell telephone monopoly, the Pacific Railroad lobbyists of 1887, a contractor who erected dangerous tenement houses, the Louisiana lottery, the white slave traffic, and New York aldermen who accepted bribes in connection

AMERICAN MEDIA PROFILE | NELLIE BLY 1864–1922

Library of Congress Prints and Photographs Division [LC-USZ62-59924]

Nellie Bly was hailed as the best reporter, male or female, in the United States when she died in 1922. She had covered a bloody labor strike, political change in the nation, and a world war during a career that spanned two centuries. A tireless advocate for the underclass, Bly was known both as a serious investigative journalist exposing social problems and as the creator of a new genre of sensationalistic news stories that became part of the era's newspaper circulation wars.

Bly is most famous for stories she wrote while traveling around the world in an attempt to beat Jules Verne's fictional character Phileas Fogg's record of eighty days. Her dispatches during what was basically a publicity stunt to sell newspapers captivated the nation and inspired a board game and a song.

Nellie Bly was born Elizabeth Jane Cochran in 1864 in Cochran Mills, Pennsylvania, a town founded by her wealthy father. Michael Cochran had ten children by his first wife. He remarried after she died and had five more children, including Elizabeth. He died when Elizabeth was six, and his will did not provide for his second family. The family was left penniless.

Elizabeth and her mother eventually moved to Pittsburgh, where her mother ran a boardinghouse while Elizabeth looked unsuccessfully for full-time work. Her career in writing was a result of her independent nature and empathy for the working class. A columnist for the *Pittsburgh Dispatch* criticized women who worked in factories or at other jobs outside the home. He called workingwomen "a monstrosity" and said they should be home raising children and cooking and cleaning for their husbands.

The column angered Elizabeth—who knew firsthand how difficult it was for young women to survive in Pittsburgh's poor, industrial neighborhoods—and she wrote a letter to the editor defending working women. The *Dispatch*'s editors were impressed with her writing and offered her a job. Writers in the nineteenth century used pen names, and the twenty-three-year-old took the name of a character in a Stephen Foster song: Nellie Bly.

Bly wrote a series of stories about the lives of factory girls in Pittsburgh. She wrote about the living conditions of the working poor and the state's unfair divorce laws. Her editors, however, preferred that she write about flower shows and fashions and other topics for the "women's page." She resisted and talked the paper into letting her go to Mexico and write about life there. Bly returned to Pittsburgh six months later and was once again assigned to cover women's news. She abruptly quit, leaving her boss a note, "I am off to New York. Look out for me. BLY."

Bly spent the next few months trying to get job interviews at newspapers that were not interested in hiring a female reporter. Perhaps trying to scare her away from a career in newspapers, John Cockerill, the managing editor of Joseph Pulitzer's *New York World*, dared her to find out how patients were really treated at the notorious Women's Lunatic Asylum, on Blackwell's Island in the East River. Officials for some time had denied rumors of inhumane treatment there, and delegations visiting the asylum never found anything wrong. The only way to find out what the facility was really like was to spend time there undercover. Bly checked into a rooming house and then pretended to be incoherent; police were called, and a judge remanded her to Blackwell's Island for treatment. Ten days later, Pulitzer's attorney secured her release.

Bly's series of stories described beating of patients and rancid food. She wrote in the first person of how the staff poured freezing water over her naked body. "The water was ice-cold," she wrote, "and I began to protest.... My teeth chattered and my limbs were goose-fleshed and blue with cold. Suddenly I got, one after the other, three buckets of water over my head—ice-cold water.... I think I experienced some of the sensations of a drowning person as they dragged me, gasping, shivering, and quaking, from the tub. For once I did look insane." She reported how she was forced to sit for hours in mind-numbing boredom and told of the doctors' indifference to the needs of their patients. She said that her ten days in the asylum nearly drove her mad and that she believed some of the women were committed because they didn't speak English; their confinement at Blackwell's had driven them insane.

Her stories were published around the country and resulted in increased funding for the asylum and improved conditions for its patients. The articles also helped a delighted Joseph Pulitzer sell more newspapers, and he gave her a full-time job and a bonus.

Bly's stories always sided with the poor and disenfranchised. She helped refine a new style of investigative reporting, often going undercover to get the story. Bly often wrote in the first person and was the central character in her articles. She shared her feelings and reactions, and her stories would often refer to her sparkling eyes or bright smile.

Her stories for the *World* included exposés on how police treated women prisoners, problems with inadequate health care for the poor, and political corruption. She also wrote numerous stories that today would be called "pseudo news," first-person accounts of personal exploits that, while they had no impact on readers' lives, were entertaining and helped sell newspapers. She also went around the world in sixty-seven hours, beating the time of Phileas Fogg, the main fictional character in Jule Verrne's 1873 novel *Around the World in Eighty Days*, by more than a week.

Her detractors called these stories "stunt journalism" whose only purpose was to attract readers. She described an ascent in a hot-air balloon and her descent into the ocean's depths in a diving bell. She posed as a chorus girl for a day and wrote about having to share a crowded dressing room.

Bly left journalism when she was thirty to marry Robert Seaman, the seventy-year-old president of American Steel Barrel Company and Iron Clad Manufacturing Company. She helped run his businesses and introduced labor reforms at the companies. She insisted that the 1,500 employees have health care and that they be taught to read, and she provided libraries and gymnasiums for them. Bly took over the operation of the companies after Seaman's death in 1910, but embezzlement by employees and costly lawsuits forced her into bankruptcy, and she lost the businesses within a few years.

In need of work, the journalist-turned-businesswoman returned to journalism, taking a job with the *Evening Journal* in New York. She was vacationing in Austria in August 1914 when World War I started, and she remained in Europe for four and a half years, covering the war as the only woman correspondent.

She used her fame and friendships to gain access to the war's Eastern Front. Her dispatches described misery endured by both soldiers and civilians. One of her dispatches described soldiers dying from the cold and cholera: "Human creatures they were, lying there in a manner our health authorities would prohibit for hogs or the meanest beasts. I staggered out into the muddy road. I would rather look on guns and hear the cutting of the air by a shot that brought kinder death." Bly was a columnist for the *Evening Journal* after the war and continued to write about the plight of the poor and homeless. She used her column as a conduit for social services and was especially active finding homes for orphans and abandoned children.

She was still writing for the *Evening Journal* in January 1922, when she contracted pneumonia and died. All the New York papers eulogized the fifty-eight-year-old woman. The *New York Journal* called her the "best reporter in America." The *New York Times* called her a "national character" and cited her "courage and liveliness."

By Thomas N. Clanin

with a streetcar franchise.[28] Pulitzer also offered poor New Yorkers free ice during the summer and dinners at Christmas.

EDITORIAL PAGE

Pulitzer also revitalized the editorial page, which interested him more than any other part of the newspaper. The *World* announced a ten-point editorial platform. It was for the taxing of luxuries, inheritances, large incomes, and monopolies. It advocated abolishing all special privileges possessed by corporations. It also demanded tariffs for revenue only, a civil service reform, severe punishment for corrupt officials, and punishment for employers who tried to coerce employees in elections.

It would have been difficult to find a better definition of the newspaper as public defender—against all other institutions including poverty, which had not yet been institutionalized. What Pulitzer really meant by "predatory poverty" is still a mystery. It may have been no more than rhetoric.

There is little doubt about what the rest of the platform meant. Like the early Bennett, Pulitzer meant to attack privilege and corrupt government, and there was a great deal to attack. But there was something puzzling in the way he went about it. On the front page of the *World* the mixture was as it had been, brewed by the elder Bennett and improved upon by Dana—a blend of sex, scandal, and corruption. On the editorial pages were well-written expressions of Pulitzer's intellectual idealism. In short, a front page for working people and an editorial page for intellectuals of Pulitzer's stripe. The result did not wholly please either class. The workers didn't know what Pulitzer was talking about on the editorial page, and the intellectuals deplored the *World*'s sensationalism.

ADVERTISING

Finally, he rationalized the practice of selling advertising space. He initiated the practice of selling such space on the basis of actual circulation and at fixed prices. Circulation became a public matter, an indicator of a newspaper's worth as an advertising medium.[29] Meanwhile, he stopped the practice of penalizing advertisers who used illustrations or broke column widths.[30]

By rationalizing newspaper business practices, he forged a new relationship between newspapers and advertisers. Until the 1880s, many publishers were hostile to advertisers, believing that they degraded the newspaper. However, the growth of department stores and the development of brand names and trademarks by national manufacturing concerns created a demand for advertising space, as did a Sunday edition of the newspaper.[31]

PULITZER'S *SUNDAY WORLD*

Pulitzer did not invent the Sunday edition. The *Boston Globe* published a Sunday edition briefly in 1833. James Gordon Bennett's *Herald* may have been the first to print a regular Sunday edition beginning in 1841. What Pulitzer did was to make the Sunday newspaper readable and interesting, despite those who thought it violated the Sabbath. Pulitzer did not regard his *Sunday World* as a desecration of the Sabbath, unless the paper was dull, which to Pulitzer was an unforgivable sin any day in the week.[32]

His *Sunday World* had fifty pages, compared to the twenty-four that ran on weekdays. The expanded *World* allowed Pulitzer to include special features about women, sports, and entertainment. His *Sunday World* also was the first to print halftone photographs on newsprint to illustrate these features and news stories.

Advertising accounted for half the pages, making the *Sunday World* a very profitable venture as circulation figures reached 266,000 in 1893 and climbed to 450,000 by the end of 1895.

Contributing to the *Sunday World*'s success was its editor, Morrill Goddard, a Dartmouth graduate and *World* city editor, who, like Pulitzer, had a talent for knowing what people wanted to read. He made the Sunday paper more sensational than the daily editions, with a "lavishly illustrated supplement style providing unsophisticated excitement in pseudo-science, sex and crime."[33]

Goddard filled the *Sunday World* with stories of romance and sex. Book reviews catering to the same sensations were turned into features, and suggestive headlines were attached. He also provided readers with dime novel features about the roaring West, with works from Buffalo Bill and Bret Harte, and travel stories that took readers on magic carpets to foreign lands. The freakish, the odd, the unique, and the unusual, as well as stories about science, were part of the Sunday fare. And he added a "Youth's Department" that included, among other things, puzzles and stories.[34]

Goddard also introduced readers to color supplements, including an eight-page comic section, in 1893. The highlight of this section was Richard F. Outcault's "Hogan's Alley," a social satire that depicted life in a New York tenement. The leader of the gang was a one-tooth ragamuffin, clothed by *World* printers in a bright yellow nightshirt.

However, Pulitzer watched in frustration as Hearst hired away Outcault and his "Yellow Kid" and the whole Sunday staff, including Goddard. Only Emma Jane Hogg, Goddard's secretary, remained. Pulitzer was able to get Goddard back by offering him a higher salary. That lasted a day. Hearst opened his purse, and Goddard left Pulitzer for good. George I. Luks took over the "Yellow Kid" for Pulitzer and Albert Brisbane, who had worked for Dana's *Sun*, was quickly moved into Goddard's place as Sunday editor.

The fight over the "Yellow Kid" was only one example of Pulitzer's innovation. Hearst liked what he saw and imitated it or outright took it from Pulitzer.

YELLOW JOURNALISM

The "Yellow Kid" came to symbolize the Pulitzer-Hearst brand of sensational journalism; "yellow journalism" as it was called. It was then applied indiscriminately to all publications associated with misconduct in news gathering. But where did the term that labeled this practice come from?

The origin of the term continues to spur debate among academics. Kobre writes that the style was stamped "yellow journalism" after a sensational magazine in England, *The Yellow Book*.[35] However, Campbell, author of the latest work on the subject, credits Ervin Wardman, the stern-looking editor of the defunct

New York Press. According to Campbell, it wasn't the Pulitzer-Hearst cartoon battle that inspired the term. It was Wardman's attempt to find a pithy and insulting substitute phrase for "new journalism." He early rejected "nude journalism," which suggested the absence of dignity and moral standards that defined the newspapers of Pulitzer and Hearst. He began to use the term *yellow journalism* relentlessly in his editorial comments about the *World* and *Journal.* The *New York Tribune* borrowed the term in mid-February 1897 and credited the *Press.*[36] However, legend has it that the term came about from the yellow nightshirt on the comic character introduced by Outcault.

"Yellow journalism," according to Mott, was founded upon "the familiar aspects of sensationalism—crime news, scandal and gossip, divorces and sex, and stress upon the reprint of disasters and sports." However, he said there was more to the term than being merely sensational; its "distinguishing characteristics" included:

- headlines, in black or red, that "screamed excitement, often about comparatively unimportant news,"
- pictures, many "without significance,"
- impostures and "frauds," such as "faked" interviews,
- a Sunday supplement, with color comics, and
- a "more or less ostentatious sympathy with the 'underdog,' with campaigns against abuses suffered by the common people."[37]

In short, Mott writes, the yellow papers contributed the following to modern journalism: "banner heads, free use of pictures, and the Sunday supplement."[38] Such journalism, which began with the *World* and *Journal* in 1896, spread like "a prairie fire," influencing nineteen out of twenty metropolitan newspapers.[39]

"Yellow journalism" was emulated throughout the nation for a number of reasons. First, it increased *circulation.* Two special groups of readers, immigrants and women, were attracted to the yellow press. The pictures, sensational stories, and easy editorials drew them. Department store advertising, directed chiefly to women in the home, also encouraged female readership.[40]

Second, yellow journalism was seen "as a *powerful democratizing force,* encouraging not only literacy in English but the embrace of American values."[41] "The foreign and the ignorant comprised the bulk of the American people," one defender of the yellow press said. "The principal problem that confronts us in our struggle to develop an American democracy is the education and uplifting of this vast mass ... the one institution that is successfully coping with this problem day after day, is the yellow press."[42]

Third, the public admired yellow journalism's *crusades* against the privileged and powerful interests, especially when they exposed corruption in municipal government, which probably encouraged muckraking journalism in the twentieth century.

Finally, readers appreciated its *enterprising reporting* by some of the ablest correspondents in the business. Josephus Daniels, editor of the conservative *Raleigh News and Observer,* wrote, "It is not because the people like stories of crime that they take the 'yellow journals.' It is because they want the news. They know that the *Journal* hires the ablest correspondents and spends the most money to get the fullest news."[43]

WILLIAM RANDOLPH HEARST

It is fascinating to speculate what might have happened if Hearst had never come to New York and "yellow journalism" had never become commonplace. Pulitzer might have dropped, or at least toned down, the sensationalism and wound up as a competitor of the *New York Times* instead of the *Journal*. There was no pretense about his editorial page; he meant what he said. But he also understood that stories of sex and crime sold newspapers, and it was necessary to meet Dana's *Sun* on those grounds if he expected to survive among the leaders. Dana's passing, so near Hearst's arrival, might have led to an alteration of a formula for which Pulitzer did not have much heart. His mind was on honest politics and the betterment of the human condition.

Hearst's mind was on making money. Among all the media entrepreneurs of the century, he was the only one who had been born rich, the son of Senator George Hearst, of California, who had made a fortune in Nevada silver. His life had been shaped by his beautiful, artistic, cultured mother—a sharp contrast to her rough-and-ready husband—who took Willie to Europe when he was only nine years old and gave him the grand tour. Young Hearst grew up with knowledge of art and culture gained from his mother, but he had inherited from his father a ruthless, driving ambition for power and achievement.

It was the kind of drive that made him drop out of Harvard at the end of his sophomore year. There he had lived luxuriously, learned nothing, and made contemptuous fun of the faculty, which included men of the stature of George Santayana and William James. While he was at Harvard, and on his frequent trips to New York, Hearst came to know and admire the *World*, particularly its front page. The editorial page left him indifferent; Hearst was no intellectual. He believed that Pulitzer had the right idea about making newspapers, and he conceived a passion to imitate him and, if possible, surpass him. Persuading his father to give him the *San Francisco Examiner*, which the senator had acquired in settlement of a political debt, he took over the paper when he was twenty-four years old and began his legendary career.

THE *SAN FRANCISCO EXAMINER*

Hearst made the *Examiner* more flamboyant and sensational than the *World*, without the New York paper's editorial idealism. Since he could afford to hire anyone he liked, he surrounded himself with a brilliant staff of editors and writers who doubled the paper's circulation in the first year. By 1893 it was up to 60,000, and he passed the rival *Chronicle*. The kind of paper Hearst created was best expressed by Arthur McEwen, its city editor, who said the *Examiner* was after the "gee whiz emotion." And any issue that did not cause its readers to rise out of their chairs and cry, "Great God!" was counted a failure.[44]

The ideas Hearst used were not particularly original. Essentially they were extensions and elaborations of what Bennett Sr. had done in the *Herald* and Pulitzer in the *World*. The emphasis was always on mass appeal, on the sensational and the so-called human-interest story. These were methods employed at the time by many American newspapers, but Hearst improved on them. The essence of the

Newspaper tycoon William Randolph Hearst was more an imitator of Joseph Pulitzer than an innovator. However, he did introduce new headline techniques and initiated reporting on the private lives of celebrities.

improvement was to get the best writers and reporters money could buy, and to add the new dimension of photography, done in the same sensational manner.

As a public defender, Hearst projected himself then and later as a man beyond the appeal of party politics. Actually, he supported nearly all the parties at one time or another—a St. George in search of dragons intent on devouring honest citizens and middle-class taxpayers. It was easy for Hearst to go beyond party politics, because he had no real political convictions of his own. Nonetheless, his crusades were among the most formidable in an era of crusading.

THE *NEW YORK MORNING JOURNAL*

This was the kind of man Hearst was when he came to New York in 1896, leaving the *Examiner* in competent hands, and revitalized a new morning paper he called the *Journal*, which once was owned by Pulitzer's brother. Hearst now meant to repeat his San Francisco success—as he had intended from the beginning. The West Coast was meant to be his schooling, the East Coast his graduation present.

Having only recently conquered Dana, Pulitzer understood that he must fight the front-page battle of sex and crime all over again, and he had little heart for the task. A general physical failure, perhaps induced by the long struggle with Dana, had compelled him to retire from day-to-day management of his paper in

1887. Worse, he was going blind, and his nervous affliction had half crippled him by this time. Its worst manifestation was an extreme sensitivity to noise. He had made his apartment soundproof, and found he could edit his paper from there in relative comfort, unless some thoughtless editor consulting him should drop something or crumple a piece of copy paper in his hand. That was enough to send Pulitzer into an acute attack of nervous frenzy.

As the disease developed, the restlessness it produced in him kept him traveling constantly. Like Bennett Jr., Pulitzer became a voluntary exile, moving about constantly for nearly twenty years, editing the *World* from wherever he happened to be. If he stopped at a hotel, he had to rent the rooms above and below and on both sides to ensure the quiet that was essential. Sometimes he crossed and recrossed the ocean without stopping. In spite of it all, he continued to edit the *World* closely and with incredible tenacity. Facing Hearst, he fought back, ill as he was, with courage but with the mistaken idea that he could beat the young man at his own game. He had established the *Evening World* in 1887, but the profits that Pulitzer had been able to build up through sound management could scarcely match the millions in family fortune that were Hearst's resources. Pulitzer dropped the price of the morning *World* to a penny, so that he would at least be fighting on even terms. The difference, however, was not only one of price. It lay in Hearst's genius for mass journalism, and Pulitzer's mistaken determination to hold that market no matter what it cost.

The Hearst formula was simple. He adopted Pulitzer's ideas wholesale, having admired them from the beginning, and then carried them a step further in extravagance and boldness. He could do this successfully because of his virtually unlimited resources and because he had a better sense of the mass mind than Pulitzer, although there was nothing in his background or his personality to account for it. It was sheer instinct.

On the front page of the daily edition, whose makeup was much like the *World*'s, the *Journal* carried on crusades that Pulitzer and his staff had completely overlooked. Hearst even hired Ella Reeve "Mother" Bloor, later a Communist Party heroine, to expose the evils of the packing industry, in the style of Upton Sinclair's *The Jungle*.

When it came to the editorial page, Hearst made no attempt to imitate Pulitzer's intellectual, high-minded appeal. He developed, instead, what he believed was a much more direct route to the masses. The editorials, most of which he wrote himself in the beginning, were done in his deliberate, distinctive style—short paragraphs, short sentences, and simple words. Their content represented what Hearst professed to believe at the moment, ideas that he thought would move his audience: the eight-hour day, the direct election of United States senators, woman suffrage, federal income taxes (they were considered a blow aimed at the rich in those days), the rights of labor, and municipal ownership of public services. It was, in essence, a socialist platform designed to mobilize opinion and to portray Hearst as the champion of the downtrodden masses, instead of as their exploiter.

One who was not fooled by what Hearst was doing was Edwin L. Godkin, who growled disdainfully on the editorial page of the *Post*: "A yellow journal is probably the nearest approach, in atmosphere, to hell existing in any Christian state, for in gambling houses, brothels, and even in brigands' caves there is a constant exhibition of fear of the police, which is in itself a sort of homage to morality or acknowledgement of its existence."[45]

It is difficult to understand today why a circulation war in New York between two strong-minded newspaper publishers should have an effect on national opinion. That effect has been exaggerated by newspaper historians and underestimated by academic historians, but there is no doubt that it existed. What Pulitzer and Hearst said and advocated was reprinted and discussed in other newspapers across the country, in pulpits, and from other public platforms. It was mistakenly believed by politicians that large blocs of voters could be swung by such strident appeals to the masses, and they respected the supposed power of this new mass medium.

Their respect no doubt diminished when Hearst ran for mayor of New York and was soundly defeated. It declined further after he was later elected to the House of Representatives, where his influence proved to be near zero, not solely because he so seldom appeared in Washington.

THE SPANISH-AMERICAN WAR OF 1898

The crucial test of the new mass-media power, particularly as it applied to Pulitzer and Hearst, came when their struggle coincided with the Spanish-American War. It is still widely believed that Hearst started the war. As proof the famous telegram, of dubious authenticity, from Hearst to the noted artist Frederic Remington is cited. Remington had asked to be relieved of his Cuban assignment because nothing much was happening. "Please remain," Hearst is said to have cabled. "You furnish the pictures and I'll furnish the war."[46] Later, Hearst was charged with having conspired to blow up the battleship *Maine* in Havana harbor so as to implement his promise, an act so utterly out of character that no one with the slightest knowledge of Hearst would believe it.[47]

In reality, Hearst's name is scarcely mentioned in present-day histories of the United States, and if it appears at all in specific studies of the Spanish-American War, it is usually no more than a footnote. The reason is that the war and the role of the media in it was a far more complicated matter than the flamboyant participation of Pulitzer and Hearst indicates. Even if neither had gone into publishing, the United States would have likely declared war on Spain in April of 1898. "That Hearst has received so large a measure of credit or blame for that 'glorious war' is a tribute to his genius as a self-promoter," according to Hearst biographer David Nasaw.[48]

The Spanish-American War of 1898 was the final chapter in Cuba's thirty-year struggle for independence. It also was a war waged on two fronts: sensational news accounts on the front pages of American newspapers and diplomatic maneuvering by the government in Washington, D.C.

The first chapter leading to war began in 1868, when Spanish authorities and Cuban revolutionaries began a bloody struggle regarding Cuban independence. Hearst, by the way, was five years old at the time. When it ended ten years later, an uneasy truce prevailed until the struggle resumed with even greater fervor in 1895. A year earlier the United States, which invested heavily in the Cuban economy by importing sugar, imposed the Wilson-Gorman tariff, which placed duties on Cuban sugar, leading to massive unemployment on the sugar plantations and to economic hardships. If that wasn't enough, disease killed more than one-fourth of the island's population.

The second chapter on the road to war occurred in early 1896, when Spain responded to the growing insurrection on the island. Some 150,000 troops were sent under the command of General Valeriano Weyler, a brutal soldier who predicted that blood would flow in Cuba. Weyler, dubbed "Butcher" Weyler by the American press, launched a reconcentration policy, forcing Cubans into concentration camps to prevent them from aiding the rebels with food and new recruits.

At the time, supporters of the Cuban revolution living in New York, called the Junta, supplied correspondents of Pulitzer's *World*, Hearst's *Journal*, and Dana's *Sun* with news of Cubans dying from starvation and disease behind barbed wire. The *Sunday Journal* reported that "[Weyler is] the prince of all cruel generals this century has seen … [Spain's] most ferocious and bloody soldier … the fiendish despot whose hand Cuba well knows…. Hundreds of Cuban women, maids and matrons, shudder."[49] A *Journal* editorial read:"Credible witnesses have testified that all prisoners captured by Weyler's forces are killed on the spot; that even helpless inmates of a hospital have not been spared, and that Weyler's intention seems to be to murder all the pacificos in the country."[50]

The *New York World*'s take on the story was provided by James Creelman, who wrote:

> No man's life, no man's property is safe. American citizens are imprisoned or slain without cause. American property is destroyed on all sides…. The horrors of the barbarous struggle for the extermination of the native population are witnessed in all parts of the country. Blood on the roadsides, blood on the doorsteps, blood, blood, blood! The old, the young, the weak, the crippled, all are butchered without mercy…. Not a word from Washington! Not a sign from the President.[51]

Cuban insurrectionists, who had freed territory from Spanish rule and proclaimed their own provisional government, rioted. That drove the United States to send the battleship *Maine* to Havana, where on February 15, 1898, it exploded, killing some 265 sailors, marines, and officers aboard. Hearst led an outcry, blaming the Spanish for the disaster, which probably was caused by mechanical problems.

The final chapter culminated on April 19, 1898, when Congress declared Cuba independent and gave President William McKinley the power to use military force to evict the Spanish. Spain would not budge and declared war on the United States fifteen days later. By the end of the war, some 5,400 Americans were dead. All but 379 of those deaths were caused by malaria and yellow fever.

PRESS COVERAGE OF THE WAR

Once the war started, both the *Journal* and the *World* spared no expense to cover it. The cost of the entire circulation struggle between Hearst and Pulitzer has been estimated at figures varying from $500,000 to $8 million. It is certainly higher than the lowest figure, because Hearst spent that much on his own account.

In early 1897, Hearst offered Richard Harding Davis, the prototype of the modern correspondent and something of a national hero in his own right, $3,000 a month plus expenses to be the *Journal*'s special correspondent in Cuba. Hearst also employed artist Frederic Remington, who illustrated Davis's articles.

Although its resources were considerably less, the *World* was not without distinguished coverage. To match Hearst's famous war correspondent, Pulitzer sent Stephen Crane, whose *Red Badge of Courage* had appeared in 1895, as a correspondent. Crane, who had been living from hand to mouth doing pieces for the *Tribune* and the *Herald*, responded by filing some of the war's best stories. They were not tales of battle, for the most part, but of soldiers and soldiering. He could cover the hard news just as capably, however, and proved it in his stories from Guantánamo Bay in June 1898, when the first American casualties were recorded: his detailed, informative story appeared on the *World*'s front page. He was later cited for his bravery under fire.

Later, he made the mistake of describing too accurately the behavior of New York's Seventy-first Regiment in the charge up San Juan Hill. This brought down the patriotic wrath of Hearst, who charged that Pulitzer was slandering the heroism of New York's own sons. Colonel Theodore Roosevelt did not forgive Pulitzer for printing the story, and later, when he was president, his active animosity toward him led to one of the more sordid presidential violations of the First Amendment. As for Crane, his cool disregard for his own safety in the field was, apparently, not only the result of personal courage but a feeling that his life was running out in any event. Soon after San Juan, he came home broken in health; he lived for only two more years.

Hearst's coverage of the war was accomplished in his usual magnificent style. He chartered a tramp steamer with a printing press and a small composing room. It was big enough to print an edition of the Journal, and Hearst set sail for Cuba himself with a crew of reporters and photographers.

The *Journal*'s men not only covered the war, they fought in it on occasion. Early in the conflict the beautiful Evangelina Cisneros, daughter of an insurgent leader, had been cast into an airless Havana prison for daring to protect her chastity against the brutal advances of a lust-crazed Spanish colonel. The incident was straight out of a bad movie, and Hearst twisted the plot and inflated this incredible episode to the proportions of an international incident. He took over the newsroom when he heard about Evangelina and barked out orders:

> Telegraph to our correspondent in Havana to wire every detail of this case. Get a petition to the Queen Regent of Spain for this girl's pardon. Enlist the women of America. Have them sign the petition. Wake up our correspondents all over the country. Have distinguished women sign first. Cable the petitions and the names to the Queen Regent. Notify our minister in Madrid. We can make a national issue of this case.... That girl must be saved if we have to take her out of prison by force or send a steamer to meet the vessel that carries her away—but that would be piracy, wouldn't it?[52]

When Spain refused to release Evangelina, Hearst ordered one of his reporters, named Karl Decker, to sail for Cuba and rescue the imprisoned girl. He was able to spring her from the dungeon and transport her to New York City. The *Journal* declared: "An American Newspaper Accomplishes at a Single Stroke What the Red

Tape of Diplomacy Failed to Bring About in Many Months." Once in the United States, Hearst dressed Evangelina like a princess and paraded her through the streets in a rally at Madison Square Garden. That was followed by dinner with President McKinley at the White House.[53]

His rescue of Evangelina was significant for many reasons, Nasaw notes. First, it embarrassed the Spanish. Second, it brought the United States closer to war in the Caribbean. Third, it bolstered Hearst's confidence that he was acting on behalf of the people of the United States—subverting, if need be, common sense and international law.[54]

But as Hearst wrote the twists and turns of Evangelina's plight, Spanish army officers, fearing that Spain might give in to the revolutionaries, incited riots in Havana on January 11, 1898. That is when President McKinley ordered the battleship U.S.S. *Maine* to sail from Key West to protect American interests in Cuba. In a little more than a month, the *Maine* exploded in Havana harbor. This new twist in Cuba's fight for independence fit right into Hearst's unfolding drama.

Returning to his apartment the night of the explosion, Hearst found his butler, George Thompson, waiting for him:

> "There's a telephone call from the office. They say it's important news."
>
> Hearst called the office. "Hello, what is the important news?"
>
> *"The battleship* Maine *has been blown up in Havana Harbor."*
>
> "Good heavens, what have you done with the story?"
>
> *"We have put it on the first page of course."*
>
> "Have you put anything else on the front page?"
>
> *"Only the other big news."*
>
> "There is not any other big news. Please spread the story all over the page. This means war."[55]

When Congress declared war, Hearst in four-inch-high type screamed: "NOW TO AVENGE THE MAINE!" Five days later, he celebrated the war declaration by setting off rockets from the *Journal*'s roof and offering $1,000 to the reader who had the best idea for conducting the war. A week later, the *Journal*'s front page asked: "How do you like the *Journal*'s war?"[56]

Though the cause of the explosion was unknown, the *Journal* laid blame inferentially or flatly on Spain. Its banner headline on February 17, 1898, read: "THE WARSHIP MAINE WAS SPLIT IN TWO BY AN ENEMY'S SECRET INFERNAL MACHINE." The page featured a seven-column drawing of the *Maine* anchored over mines, and a diagram showing wires leading from the mines to a Spanish fortress on shore. The caption read: "The Spaniards, it is believed, arranged to have the Maine anchored over one of the Harbor mines. Wires connected the mine with a powder magazine, and it is thought the explosion was caused by sending an electric current through the wire."

Though it was wishful thinking on Hearst's part to blame the Spaniards for the *Maine*'s demise, many readers took it for fact. To avenge the murder of American soldiers, the *Journal* offered a $50,000 reward to anyone who could solve the mystery of the *Maine*'s explosion.

In mid-June 1898, Hearst appointed himself a war correspondent, secured press credentials, and joined James Creelman, the paper's dignified chief correspondent, who was always "Mr. Creelman, even to other reporters," on a steamer bound for Cuba. At the battle of Guantánamo Bay, Hearst himself headed a foray in a steam launch. He landed on the beach and captured twenty-six frightened Spanish sailors stranded there, delivering them as prisoners of war. He made them sing "Three Cheers for George Washington."

As a climax of the *Journal*'s own war effort, Creelman personally led an infantry charge at the battle of El Caney, during which he was wounded. He wrote about what followed in his book, *On the Great Highway:*

> Someone knelt on the grass beside me and put his hand on my fevered head. Opening my eyes, I saw Mr. Hearst, the proprietor of the *New York Journal*, a straw hat with a bright ribbon on his head, a revolver at his belt, and a pencil and notebook in his hand. The man who had provoked the war had come to see the result with his own eyes, and finding one of the correspondents prostrate, was doing the work himself. Slowly he took down my story of the fight. Again and again the tinging of Mauser bullets interrupted. But he seemed unmoved. That battle had to be reported somehow.
>
> "I'm sorry you're hurt, but"—and his face was radiant with enthusiasm—"wasn't it a splendid fight? We must beat every paper in the world."[57]

Hearst may have felt sorry for his wounded correspondent, who was conscious and in great pain, but he left him lying on the beach waiting for the medics. He boarded his yacht and set off for Jamaica to file his exclusive, leaving Creelman to fend for himself.[58]

Governor Sadler, of Missouri, half seriously proposed at the time that Hearst send down 5,000 of his reporters to free Cuba. If he had thought of it in time, no doubt the publisher would have done it.

Meanwhile, Hearst and Pulitzer were claiming daily circulations of 1,250,000 each. Despite these circulation gains, both papers were losing money. They had purchased dispatch boats, hired correspondents, and published extras. The *Journal* sometimes printed as many as forty editions a day. Hearst alone spent $500,000 on ordinary expenses.[59] He also spent the $7,500,000 he got from his mother.[60]

The cost of the war was more than financial for Pulitzer, although that was serious in itself, since he had been compelled to reach deeply into his reserves. His precarious health was worse than ever, and he had seen his newspaper so lowered in public esteem during the battle with Hearst that it had been banned, along with the *Journal*, from a good many homes, clubs, and libraries. Taking on two such opponents as Dana and Hearst in succession had nearly wrecked both Pulitzer and the *World*. In the years remaining to him, he tried to mend the damage, and succeeded with his paper. However, his health was beyond repair.

MCKINLEY'S ASSASSINATION

After the Spanish-American War, Hearst was embroiled in another national story that would taint his image. During the 1900 presidential election, Hearst papers unceasingly attacked President McKinley. When Kentucky governor-elect William

Goebel was shot dead in an election dispute in February 1900, Ambrose Bierce, who was then writing for Hearst, had marked the occasion by suggesting in verse:

The bullet that pierced Goebel's breast
Can not be found in all the West;
Good reason, it is speeding here
To stretch McKinley on his bier.[61]

Then, days after McKinley's inauguration, Arthur Brisbane declared editorially in the *Journal*: "If bad institutions and bad men can be got rid of only by killing, then the killing must be done."[62] Bierce was not a clairvoyant, nor an accessory of assassins; his poetry only meant to convey that the kind of political violence that could kill Goebel might easily kill McKinley, as in fact it did. The *Journal*'s bloodthirsty editorial was no more than its usual overheated rhetoric; it is impossible to believe that Hearst or anyone else on the paper plotted to kill McKinley or encouraged anyone to do it.

The shooting of McKinley on September 6, 1901,was the act of one deranged man, twenty-eight-year-old Leon Czolgosz, an assassin acting alone. As in the case of Lee Harvey Oswald and President John Kennedy, true believers of conspiracy theory would have none of it. The least of the claims in the *Journal's* case was that Hearst's inflammatory editorials had inspired the assassin. Many thought that the publisher was part of a plot, and those who hated other publishers linked them with the plot too.

In short, the event made it possible for those who did not like the media to show their anger, as they had done from the beginnings of a free press. Once they had destroyed the type and burned down the print shops and done violence to the proprietors. Now they banned the *Journal* and sometimes the *World*, along with a few other offenders, from their clubs and libraries. Progress had been made.

The papers that had not attacked McKinley joined in the condemnation of the others, thus putting themselves squarely on the side of virtue. That was not enough to prevent a demand in some quarters for laws to limit press freedom where the president was involved. It took a magazine, the *Bookman*, to point out that the "respectable" papers had made violent attacks against the president too, and that no president had ever been killed because of newspaper influence, and that no connection existed between the assassination of McKinley and the attacks on him.

The assassination of McKinley marked the decline of "yellow journalism." In his first message to Congress, President Theodore Roosevelt said that McKinley's assassin had probably been inflamed by "reckless utterances of those who, on the stump and in the public press, appeal to dark and evil spirits."[63] The public agreed with the new president. They appeared to be tiring of Hearst's sensational papers. He was hanged in effigy in various parts of the United States. A decline in the *Journal's* circulation was further evidence of the public's disgust with Hearst's style of journalism.

Pulitzer's unhappiness about the war he had helped to foster also contributed to yellow journalism's demise. Pulitzer said he never wanted to go through another war, particularly one manipulated by the press.[64] His *World*, whose war with the *Journal* had gradually died down, showed a marked change by dropping the more objectionable features of the yellow style.[65]

| AMERICAN MEDIA PROFILE | ROBERT S. ABBOTT 1868–1940 |

Robert Sengstacke Abbott was one of the first African American millionaires in the nation, and his *Chicago Defender* weekly newspaper in its heyday was the country's largest and most influential African American newspaper. The *Defender* and other African American newspapers were the only news outlets that told the stories of heroic acts and successes in the African American community. White mainstream papers ignored minorities unless the stories were about crimes or threats to the white community. African Americans needed papers like the *Defender* to find role models who looked like them and shared their experiences.

In the decades before and after World War I, the *Defender* and other African American newspapers also reported on lynchings and other atrocities against minorities that were often ignored by the white press. Abbott's *Defender* was also a leading proponent of the great northern migration of African Americans after the Civil War.

Born in Georgia in 1868, Abbott left the South for the first time in 1893 to attend Colored American Day at the Columbian Exposition celebration in Chicago. The one-day event had been added to the exposition after African Americans protested that the celebration excluded their contributions to the nation. Abbott was then a young printing student at the Hampton Institute in Virginia. He saw and heard many African American leaders that day, including Frederick Douglass and Ida B. Wells. Historian Christopher Reed says that Abbott may have realized for the first time then that African Americans also could participate in the American dream.

Abbott finished his studies in Virginia and returned to Chicago to study law. He was the only African American in the class of 1899 at Kent College of Law. Abbott soon learned, however, that whites would not hire black attorneys and that there was not enough business in the African American community for him to prosper. He decided to go into the newspaper business.

The *Chicago Defender* was first published in 1905. The four-page paper had a press run of 300 copies.

By 1910, Abbott was using the same marketing tactics as William Randolph Hearst and Joseph Pulitzer to sell papers: sensational stories, large headlines, graphic images, and red ink. Abbott, however, didn't have to invent or exaggerate events for the *Defender*'s readers. He reported in graphic detail accounts of brutal lynchings, rapes, and tortures in the South. The paper's editorials boldly attacked segregation laws and atrocities against African Americans in the North and South.

"We are not Africans," Abbott wrote in 1920 about Marcus Garvey's proposal for a black nation in Africa at a time when the continent was controlled by European powers. "But rather [we are] Americans and have the right to live as equal citizens just like whites. We need the non-segregation and discrimination laws [that] have existed since the 1880s strictly enforced."

Perhaps the biggest factor marking yellow journalism's decline was the growth of the *New York Times*.

ADOLPH OCHS AND THE *NEW YORK TIMES*

Like Pulitzer and Hearst before him, *Times* publisher Adolph Ochs was convinced he would succeed in New York because he had succeeded elsewhere. Although he had the greatest respect for Ochs, Hearst wasn't about to follow his example.

AMERICAN MEDIA PROFILE	CONTINUED

Abbott also mocked the white press for its racism. Mainstream newspapers in the first decades of the twentieth century would put "Negro" in parentheses after the names of any African Americans mentioned in the paper. For example, "Jack Johnson (Negro) won the world heavyweight championship yesterday." Abbott, advocating equality between the races, referred to whites the same way: "Woodrow Wilson (white) declared war on Germany yesterday."

The *Defender* was selling more than 250,000 copies each week by the end of the 1920s and was distributed throughout the South. The paper played a major role in encouraging and helping the 1.25 million African Americans who left the South to find jobs in the North between World War I and the Great Depression. The *Defender* published train schedules and told Southern blacks what to expect in the North and how to act.

The northern migration was draining the South of cheap labor, and white authorities took steps to curb the exodus. Ignoring the First Amendment, cities in the South tried to ban or confiscate the paper. Abbott used black Pullman railroad sleeping-car workers and black entertainers to smuggle the papers into the South. The papers were passed around and read aloud in churches and other gathering places. It's estimated that each copy of the paper was read by up to five people.

The *Defender* offered more to its readers than crusading stories about civil rights abuses. The paper also ran articles about arts and fashion and profiles on blacks elsewhere in the world. Abbott's business thrived, and as his wealth grew he traveled extensively. He received many honorary degrees and other awards before he died in 1940.

Neither of his two marriages resulted in children, and Abbott had groomed his nephew, John H. Sengstacke, to take over the paper. Sengstacke continued *Defender*'s fight for equality and desegregation while improving its finances. The paper started publishing daily in 1956 as the *Chicago Daily Defender*, and in 1965 Sengstacke purchased other African American papers, to create Sengstacke Enterprises.

Sengstacke placed the newspaper company in a trust before his death in 1997 with instructions that it be sold. In 2002, Real Times Inc., which was run by Sengstacke's relative Thomas Picou, purchased the company for more than $10 million.

The *Defender* is not the powerful national voice today that it was seventy years ago. It has lost many of its readers to old age and to mainstream news media that are now more sensitive to the minority communities. Television networks and mainstream newspapers started paying attention to the African American community during the civil rights protests in the 1950s and 1960s, and they began hiring minority reporters to participate in covering the struggle for equal rights and other news in African American communities. Today, the mainstream papers tell the stories of heroic people and successes throughout their racially and ethnically diverse communities, and the African American newspapers have lost many of their readers.

By Thomas N. Clanin

When Edmond Coblentz, Hearst's editor of the *New York American*, suggested that the *American* should eliminate its women's page because the *New York Times* did not have one, Hearst responded:

> You mention the *Times* not having these things. I do not think that means a great deal. We have never run the kind of paper that the *Times* runs. The *Times* is an Ochs paper. Our papers are Hearst papers. There is a definite difference in everything, from political policies to news judgment, and character of the departments. In fact, it is desirable for us not to be like the *Times* but to be sufficiently different from the *Times*.[66]

The "definite difference" was obvious. Ochs saw himself as "a vendor of information," who defied the view that only the sensational newspaper could be a successful newspaper: "He in the end taught them [his competitors] that decency meant dollars."[67] Author Frank Presbrey confirmed that view by calling the *Times* "the world's most influential newspaper."[68]

Hearst, on the other hand, saw himself "as a minstrel and sage, ethical guide, social coach, financial adviser, confidant and strategist in affairs of the heart, culinary tutor, educator, house mother, prophet, purveyor of warm data on high life.... Every day of his life, he strives to exert his influence to the utmost."[69]

In August 1896 Ochs bought Henry Raymond's old newspaper, the *New York Times*, which was losing $2,500 a day and whose circulation had fallen to 9,000. At the time he was thirty-eight years old and a very successful publisher. The eldest of six children born to German immigrants in Knoxville, Tennessee, Ochs learned the printer's trade at fourteen as a "devil," or assistant, to the hand compositors on the *Knoxville Chronicle* and then became a business solicitor for the *Chattanooga Dispatch*. In 1878, at the age of twenty, he started the *Chattanooga Times* with actual cash in hand of $37.50, which he borrowed. Some $25 of that he had to pay out to keep his Associated Press wire going. However, the *Chattanooga Times* became one of the most lucrative newspapers in the South.

He came to New York to show that he could establish, as he said, "a decent, dignified and independent" paper against the competition of some of the most spectacularly sensational entrepreneurs who ever entered the ring. Unlike Pulitzer and Hearst, Ochs had a flair for what *New York Times* reporter Harrison Salisbury described as "understated public relations." For example, he ran a contest to select a slogan for his new paper. He eventually selected his own, which still appears on the *Times'* front page: "All the News That's Fit to Print." He took the slogan seriously by publishing a paper devoid of sensational or pornographic or "gaudily spiced reports of crime, sex or bloodshed." To this day, the *Times* does not publish comics, which increased circulation of his competitors. Ochs' headlines were discreet, and his business and financial columns did not offend bankers, merchants, and entrepreneurs of the day. His editorial pages were bland and wholesome. They lacked the shrillness or strong statements found in the newspapers of Pulitzer and Hearst.[70]

Ochs announced his newspaper policies in the *Times* on August 19, 1896:

> To undertake the management of *The New York Times*, with its great history for right-doing, and to attempt to keep bright the luster which Henry J. Raymond and George Jones have given it, is an extraordinary task.... It will be my earnest aim that *The New York Times* give the news, all the news, in concise and attractive form, in language that is parliamentary in good society, and give it as early, if not earlier than it can be learned through any other reliable medium; to give the news impartially, without fear or favor, regardless of any party, sect or interest involved; to make the columns of *The New York Times* a forum for the consideration of all questions of public importance, and to that end to invite intelligent discussion from all shades of opinion.

He also announced that he had no plan to change the character of the newspaper or its staff or its politics. He hoped the paper would continue to address select readers—"thoughtful, pure-minded people."

His attempt to increase that readership was a 180-degree turn from George Jones, who edited the paper from 1869 until his death in 1891. Jones boasted that no man had ever been asked to subscribe or advertise in the *Times*.[71] In 1898, Ochs became the first publisher to solicit circulation by telephone, offering a bicycle tour of France and England to the first 100 persons to bring in the most new subscribers. However, only the well-to-do had telephones, and this didn't bother Ochs. He was hoping to get school and college teachers to subscribe, stressing the theme "To be seen reading the *New York Times* is a stamp of respectability."[72]

He also promoted a "moral war" against the new journalism by using the advertising slogan, "It does not soil the breakfast cloth," to contrast it to the yellow journals.[73] Ochs hired Carr Van Anda, a former night editor of Dana's *New York Sun*, as managing editor. During his twenty-one years at the *Times*, Van Anda set high standards for news reporting, accuracy, completeness, and objectivity. He also was responsible for a number of *Times* innovations. On Ochs' orders, he brought the first rotogravure press to America from Germany in 1915. It was used for the *Times* Sunday supplement. He also founded the *New York Times* Index.

Ochs' formula for success worked. Within six years his *New York Times* was earning more than $200,000 a year, and within the decade he had it all in hand, safe and secure, the ownership his, no great obligations outstanding. Never again in his life would he face the threat of bankruptcy or financial debacle. His *Times* also would outlive Pulitzer's *World* and Hearst's *Journal* and continue to confirm Presbrey's view of it "as the world's most influential newspaper."

CONCLUSION

The nature of the press in America in 1895 gave newspapers a predominant role in the national debate that was then beginning. The wave of popular ten-cent magazines, like *McClure's* and *Munsey's*, had only just begun. New York had no fewer than fifteen dailies and more than twice as many weeklies, but even in a town as small as Emporia, Kansas, there were two dailies. The American newspaper was at the pinnacle of its glory and influence. The *New York World* was selling 374,000 newspapers in its morning and evening editions.

In these newspapers, two types of journalism emerged. One was *story-telling journalism*, which was practiced by Joseph Pulitzer's *New York World* and William Randolph Hearst's *New York Journal*. This, according to George Herbert Mead, idealized the "aesthetic function" of journalism. Simply, some parts of the news emphasize the "truth value of news," election results or stock market reports, for example. Other parts of the news emphasize the "enjoyability or consummatory value," an attempt to interpret readers' lives and to relate them to the nation, town, or class to which they belong. Mead said that the latter was the actual and proper function of a newspaper. Here the reporter is sent out to get a story, not the facts.[74]

In the *information model*, as practiced by Adolph Ochs' *New York Times*, the reporter's job is to bring back facts that can be verified. It is associated with fairness, objectivity, and scrupulous dispassion.

Competition for readers to meet the growing costs of producing newspapers pushed some to make them more popular. Publishers resorted to bigger headlines, color, pictures, and very often sensationalized coverage. What arose with the story-telling press, in particular, was a new "journalism with a soul," called *yellow journalism*. The yellow press demonstrated that the sex, sin, and violence sell newspapers.[75] Publishers realized that large circulations guaranteed them a more powerful voice. They became *champions of the powerless* in society and crusaders for working people by writing about unfair practices in government, industry, business, and social institutions. The public soon realized that powerful newspapers could have powerful effects on reforming these unethical and unfair practices.

The way journalists covered politics changed. The newspaper was emerging as an *impartial vehicle for news*. Richard L. Kaplan suggests that starting in 1865 journalism fundamentally altered how it reported on the words and deeds of politicians. Journalists proceeded to adopt the ideal of objectivity, a sober style of impartial, expert reporting. The press would be governed by a rigorous ethic of impartiality and public service, especially during America's Progressive Era,[76] which is discussed in the next chapter.

Finally, during this period the *newspaper as a cultural icon* was always at the forefront of the American consciousness. Newspaper people were portrayed in a pivotal role in popular culture, in the funny papers, in pulp fiction, in the movies. Newspapers gave pop culture the comic strip, whatever its future implications might be.[77]

By the 1920s some of the old warhorses would soon pass from the scene. The *New York Post*, the one-time paper of Alexander Hamilton and William Cullen Bryant, eventually became a lurid Rupert Murdoch tabloid. Joseph Pulitzer's *World* underwent a number of changes following his death in 1911. Herbert Bayard Swope, the *World*'s star reporter, eventually became managing editor. He took the fighting tradition of Pulitzer to a new level by going into real depth in some story or issue to arouse major public interest. His greatest contribution to American newspaper history, however, was his invention of the "op-ed" page. He added a page opposite the editorial page and filled it with columns, usually by writers from outside the paper. However, Pulitzer's sons sold the paper to Roy Howard in 1931. He immediately killed the morning *New York World* and merged the afternoon paper with his own *New York Telegram* to form the *New York World-Telegram*. Howard eventually purchased the *New York Sun* in 1950 and merged it with the *World* and *Telegram* to form the *New York World-Telegram & Sun*.

Meanwhile, when James Gordon Bennett died in 1872, his son, James Gordon Bennett Jr., an aging playboy and wine bibber, inherited the *New York Herald*. Bennett Jr., unlike his father, was frequently absent from the paper, thinking he could run the operation while partying in Paris. He did promote enterprise reporting. For example, he sent reporter Henry Stanley to Africa to look for the missing missionary David Livingstone. Stanley greeted the missionary with the now famous, "Dr. Livingston, I presume?"

At the age of seventy-three, Bennett Jr. married Baroness de Reuter, a widow of the Reuter news service family, and attempted to revitalize the failing newspaper. He founded the Paris edition of the *Herald* in 1887. It would eventually become the *International Herald Tribune*, the most important American newspaper published in Europe. Unfortunately, he had squandered his $40 million fortune before he died in 1918. The *Herald* eventually was purchased by magazine mogul Frank Munsey in 1920.

Finally, at Greeley's death in 1872, the *New York Tribune* passed into the hands of his associate editor, Whitelaw Reid. He, like his old boss, attempted to keep the paper on a more moral ground than other New York newspapers. When Reid died in 1912, he left the ailing newspaper, which then had a circulation of only 50,000, to his wealthy wife, Elisabeth Mills Reid.

Munsey then attempted to educate Mrs. Reid that New Yorkers would not support two Republican newspapers, and he offered to buy her out. When she refused, he suggested she buy his *Herald*. To his surprise, she did. Included in the $5-million price was the lucrative Paris edition of the paper.

MAGAZINES, MUCKRAKING, AND PUBLIC RELATIONS

Joseph Pulitzer's and William Randolph Hearst's new brand of journalism contributed to the rise of the muckrakers and their discovery of publicity. At the start of 1900, publicity was a bad thing, a really bad thing, as far as American businesses were concerned. Many liked the idea of operating in secrecy.

In America, the period from 1902 to 1912 has been called the Progressive Era, a period of reform in government and business. Playing a major role were "writers of exposure," whose investigations shocked readers. They demanded, through their leaders, reform in politics and industry. President Theodore Roosevelt labeled the writers "muckrakers." In direct response to the muckrakers, businesses began to feel that if publicity could be used against them, it also could be used for them. The public relations industry emerged.

ROBBER BARONS ON THE RISE

Muckraking came suddenly, unexpectedly, upon the American scene, according to historian Louis Filler. During the post–Civil War years, after all, the nation, politically and economically sound, had become very plainly the nation of the future. The Homestead Act of 1862 opened free lands in the West, now connected by new roads and the Union Pacific railroad. New inventions, such as the typewriter, industrial machinery, office devices, and the refrigerator car powered modernization.[1]

Emperors of business and finance, tagged "robber barons," gorged themselves on the nation's wealth. They and their principalities included: Jay Gould, William H. Vanderbilt, Collis P. Huntington, James J. Hill, and Edward H. Harriman, railroads; John D. Rockefeller, oil; Andrew Carnegie, steel; Jay Cooke and J. Pierpoint

Morgan, banking and finance; William A. Clark, mining; and Philip D. Armour, meatpacking. They won favor with state legislators, whom they bought and controlled. High protective tariff walls were erected. Such actions freed American manufacturers from foreign competition, allowing them to make exorbitant profits and forcing American consumers to pay more for goods.

The bankers and industrialists who made a handsome profit during the Civil War turned out to be "not pioneers but locusts."[2] Reaping such a cash bonanza, the new robber barons benefited from an immigration policy that provided cheap labor. Ignorant and unskilled Western Europeans, impoverished and suffering from political persecution, became the fodder for the great smoking mills.

The new immigrants were herded together in the great manufacturing cities. They lived in the most horrible conditions; whole families crowded together into dank cellars, or into firetrap tenements that had interior rooms, without windows, deprived of light and air. Drunkenness, vice, and crime flourished. This chaos led to the creation of a new power structure in American life—the political machine, dominated by an all-powerful political boss.[3] New York boss William Marcy Tweed, for example, set a record for public thievery that has never been surpassed. Politics became increasingly depraved. The stink of corruption was everywhere.[4]

ENTER THE MUCKRAKERS

Though impressed by American vitality and genius, a group of writers saw a nation drowning in political corruption that would have "sorely shocked the Founding Fathers."[5] According to historian Richard Hofstadter, the fundamental critical achievement of American Progressivism was the business of exposure, and journalists were the chief creative writers. It is hardly an exaggeration to say that the Progressive mind was characteristically a journalistic mind, and that its characteristic contribution was that of the socially responsible reporter-reformer. What these new writers did was to provide information that brought the "diffuse malaise of the public into focus."[6]

They focused primarily on three issues: corruption in government, the irresponsibility of trusts, and the exploitation of women and children. These "reporter-reformers," who included professionals and amateurs, stylists and tyros, were united by a shared concern for the physical and moral well-being of America. The nation then was dominated by laissez-faire, dedicated to the status quo, and in thrall to the dollar as a symbol of success. Journalists felt a sense of urgency to alert their fellow citizens to what had gone wrong and to the necessity of putting things right.

These reporter-reformers were unique, because for the first time they and a concentration of magazines hammered away at the ills of society. What makes this period important for study is that neither before nor since has there been in periodical literature anything that can compare to the relentless drive for exposure.

The typical article, factual though critical, was directed at the social conscience of the nation. It offered no cures. It offered no solutions. Its aim was to expose, not to solve.

Muckrakers cleaned house in America by naming names and pointing to sore spots in business and politics. They wrote about crooked politicians; corrupt policemen; exploitation of small boys and girls in mills, mines, factories, and sweat-shops; malefactions of capitalists; food adulteration; fraudulent claims for patents; prostitution across state lines; and unscrupulous business practices.

Certainly they weren't the first writers to expose the ills of America. Corrupt connections between business and government, the pervasiveness of graft, and the link between government and vice was nothing new. Since the 1870s, exposure to such ills had been a recurrent theme in American political life. As early as 1721, James Franklin's *New England Courant* introduced the New World to this litera-ture of exposure, offering for the first time a "crusade" type of journalism—edito-rial campaigns planned to produce some type of results. In the early 1870s, the *New York Times, Harper's Weekly*, and Thomas Nast went after the Tammany Hall political machine.

Thirty years later, however, muckrakers had a greater reach through national magazines and daily newspapers. The Progressive Era muckrakers were distin-guished from earlier writers of exposure by their reach—"their nationwide character and their capacity to draw nationwide attention, the presence of mass muckraking media with national circulations, and huge resources for the research that went into exposure."[7] The number of daily newspapers jumped from 574 in 1870, to 1,610 by 1899, to 2,600 by 1909.[8] In 1885 only four monthly magazines, which boasted a circulation of 100,000, existed. Within two decades their number had grown to twenty, with a total circulation of 5.5 million.[9] *McClure's* magazine, for example, had 120,000 readers two years after its founding in 1893. Its circulation soared to 370,000 and then to half a million by 1907.

What generated such large circulations? Rising circulations were fueled by a larger readership because of expansion of the high school system and urbanization. For example, in 1870 public schools had an enrollment of about 7 million pupils; by 1900 the attendance more than doubled, to an estimated 15.5 million. The illit-eracy rate in 1880 was 17 percent; in 1900 it dropped to 11 percent.

Urbanization also spurred the growth of newspapers and magazines. Uprooted farmers and villagers looked to these publications to make sense out of their new environments—which many found impersonal, corrupt, and cruel. The gossip, which filled many of these publications, provided a substitute for village gossip. To push circulation, editors offered human-interest stories, crusades, interviews, and stunts or promotional devices. A new type of human-interest story emerged. Where the old human-interest piece had played up the curious concern of the com-mon citizen with the affairs and antics of the rich, the new style exploited far more intensely the concern of comfortable people with the affairs of poor people. The slum sketch, the story of the poor and disinherited of the cities, became common-place. And it was just this interest of the secure world in the have-not world that provided the audience for muckracking.[10]

At the same time, mechanical costs dropped, a cheaper glazed paper was intro-duced, and photoengraving became quite inexpensive, permitting cheaper magazine prices for consumers.

Large circulations enabled editors to fund the muckraking efforts of their re-porters. McClure estimated that Ida Tarbell's controversial articles cost $4,000 each and those of Lincoln Steffens $2,000.[11]

MUCKRAKING MAGAZINES

The emergence of the ten-cent periodical as a powerful social force began with the founding of *McClure's* in June 1893; it forced its already established rivals, *Munsey's* and *Cosmopolitan*, to lower their prices to ten cents. *Peterson's* and *Godey's* also reduced their price to a dime. A flood of ten-cent periodicals followed, until Frank Munsey estimated in 1903 that they comprised about 85 percent of the total circulation of magazines in America. Besides his own (*Munsey's*, naturally), Munsey guessed correctly that the biggest moneymakers were *Argosy*, *Cosmopolitan*, and *McClure's*. Other magazines tried a five-cent price, and some even went down to one or two cents, but only the *Saturday Evening Post* did well at a nickel.

The basis of the ten-cent magazine's popular appeal was its liveliness and variety, its many and well-printed illustrations, its coverage of world events and progress at home and—most of all—its head-on confrontation with contemporary social problems. Business promoters who believed that they were newspapers in magazine form published them.

This was quite a contrast from the old, respectable magazines that were genteel and sedate enterprises selling at thirty-five cents a copy. Publishers of these magazines, such as *Atlantic*, *Harper's*, the *Century*, and *Scribner's*, were run by literary men who believed that magazines were a book in periodical form. Their circulations reached only 130,000.

Three leaders emerged in the ten-cent magazine field, and the personalities of the men who originated them could hardly have been more different. They included Frank Munsey, John Brisben Walker, and Samuel S. McClure.

MUNSEY'S

First to arrive was the *Argosy*, an offspring of Frank Munsey's fertile imagination. In the newspaper business, Munsey was known as the "Grand High Executioner of Journalism," because he bought and merged old and honorable papers ruthlessly, without regard for their traditions or ideals or even the needs of the community. Munsey was first and always the businessman with the morals of the counting house. His biography, *Forty Years—Forty Millions*, makes this clear. When it came to magazines, he was a resourceful innovator.

Beginning his career as a lonely boy in charge of the telegraph office in Augusta, Maine, he turned his superb talents to use as a salesman. He got to New York with borrowed money, and then persuaded magazine publisher E. G. Rideout to set him up in business; on December 2, 1883, he published the *Golden Argosy, Freighted with Treasures for Boys and Girls*. In 1888, the *Argosy* for children became *Argosy* for adults. Improving on this start, Munsey cleverly juggled his financing in a way that established a new adult magazine, *Munsey's Weekly*, in 1889, and this became simply *Munsey's*.

The adult *Argosy* was printed on rough paper called pulp. The paper gave its name to a whole category of cheap magazines that thrived through the twenties and early thirties. Their stories had little love interest; they were adventure and mystery tales, aimed at men and boys, by popular authors of outdoor stories. One of the serial writers was young Upton Sinclair.

Munsey's was not an immediate success. It did not catch on until the publisher brought it out as a ten-cent periodical in 1893. Its first issue at this price sold 20,000 copies; four years later, it was selling 700,000 a month.

The magazine did sell sex. Nudes were displayed legitimately in the department titled "Artists and Their Work," which led the magazine every month, and less cultured undraped female figures appeared in departments titled "The State" and "Types of Fair Women." Other magazines might be annoyed by *Munsey's* half-dressed women and undressed statuary; the proprietor abandoned them when his circulation was secure at more than half a million. The magazine also published fiction, both serials and short stories.

COSMOPOLITAN

Between the debuts of Munsey's two magazines, *Cosmopolitan* was launched. It began life in Rochester, New York, as a monthly published by a firm of printers and office-supply manufacturers. After various changes of ownership, it fell into the hands of John Brisben Walker, a remarkable man, then forty-one, who had made successive fortunes in iron manufacturing and real estate, and had been a successful newspaperman as well. As one critic put it, Walker "introduced the newspaper ideas of timeliness and dignified sensationalism into periodical literature."

Beginning in 1892 with the affiliation of William Dean Howells as coeditor, Walker put together a notable staff. The coeditorship lasted only four months, however. Walker could not work with anyone else. Like all the great magazine editors, he was the czar, the man who made all the decisions, and the magazine was to be whatever he made it. Because of his efforts, by the end of 1892 *Cosmopolitan* was among the best-illustrated magazines in the country, with more emphasis on public affairs than on fiction; it boasted a circulation of 300,000 by 1898. As one of the most important magazines dealing with domestic and foreign affairs, its coverage of the Spanish-American War ranked with the best magazine efforts, and its reports from abroad were often extraordinary.

Walker was well ahead of his time. In 1897 he was hard at work trying to revise what he termed the "frozen curricula" of universities, and as early as 1902, he proposed a world congress of nations. Walker, too, foresaw the eventual decline of the great American railways, and urged the government to nationalize them. Beginning in 1892, he began pushing the idea of "aerial navigation"; *Cosmopolitan* was far ahead of every other magazine in its acceptance and sponsorship of air transportation. Similarly, Walker did everything he could to promote the horseless carriage as soon as it appeared.

As editor, Walker was as ruthless and arbitrary as any of his nineteenth-century predecessors. When Tolstoy's *Resurrection* began to run in *Cosmopolitan* in 1899, he thought some of the sexual descriptions were offensive and deleted them. As the serial continued, he decided it would be impossible to make the book chaste enough for his pages and simply discontinued it. He much preferred writers like H. G. Wells and was the first to print *War of the Worlds* and *The First Man on the Moon*. He was also one of the first editors to recognize Jack London as a major writer.

Cosmopolitan did not get into the muckraking business until 1905, when Hearst acquired it for $400,000. To him, a magazine was only an extension of the

Sunday newspaper, except that more time could be spent on it to make it readable and "dressy." Under his direction *Cosmopolitan* became more sensational, like the Hearst papers, and passed easily, although rather late in the day, into muckraking.

McCLURE'S

McClure's was the last of the great ten-cent magazines, and it proved to be the most sensational in many ways. Samuel S. McClure was one of the great showmen of his time. Like so many other nineteenth-century publishing figures, McClure came from a background of poverty and clawed his way to the top. Irish-born, he came to this country, got an education at Knox College, and afterward went into the business of syndicating fiction and other feature material to newspapers. His partner was John Sanburn Phillips, a Midwesterner who had gone to school at Harvard and Leipzig.

When they decided to start a magazine in 1893, Phillips had $4,500, McClure only $2,800. But McClure had something more valuable, a natural flair for magazine making and the kind of personality that virtually ensured success.

An enthusiastic editor, McClure sent newspaper clippings from wherever he was, with sentences underscored for what he considered an idea for the magazine. "A week in the McClure office," wrote *McClure's* editor Ellery Sedgwick in her book *The Happy Profession*, "was the precise reversal of the six busy days described in the first chapter of Genesis. It seemed to end in a world without form and void. From Order came forth Chaos.... Yet with all his pokings and proddings the fires he kindled were brighter than any flames his staff could produce without him."[12]

McClure demanded two things from his writers: accuracy and a high standard of writing. The move toward reform, by the way, was not something McClure personally trumpeted. He just thought his readers wanted it. He may have stumbled into muckraking by accident.

Arthur and Lila Weinberg, in their definitive work, *The Muckrakers*, wrote that the unplanned but simultaneous publication of three articles in *McClure's* set muckraking on its "historic way" and more or less defined its future course. "It was while the January 1903 issue was being dummied that the editors discovered that Lincoln Steffens' article on Minneapolis, 'The Shame of Minneapolis,' Ida Tarbell's chapter on Standard Oil, and an article by Ray Stanndard Baker on 'The Right to Work' shared the same theme. The editors then inserted an editorial titled 'Concerning Three Articles in This Number of *McClure's*, and a Coincidence that May Set Us Thinking.'" Henceforth, the trumpeting of exposures became the theme for *McClure's*.[13]

McClure launched a wave of muckraking magazines. Some of the more important muckrakers for those magazines included *McClure's* own Tarbell and Steffens, and writers David Graham Phillips and Upton Sinclair.

IDA TARBELL

The writer who doubled *McClure's* circulation was Ida Tarbell, the queen of the muckrakers. One of the editors described her as "firm as the Statue of Liberty and holding up the lantern of integrity." Her subject in her first article for *McClure's* was "The Short Life of Napoleon Bonaparte," illustrated with pictures. She wrote the article "on the gallop," she later said, in just six weeks.

Following the success of that article, McClure put her to work immediately on a new project spawned in his active brain. Lincoln had been dead thirty years, but Sam's editorial instincts told him that people would never get tired of reading about him, particularly in a time when his honesty was in such contrast to the prevailing moral climate. At the moment, too, there were many people still living who could talk about him from personal knowledge. "Look, see, report," McClure instructed his new writer. The result was Tarbell's "Early Life of Lincoln," a series begun in the magazine in 1895; it meant the addition of 75,000 new readers. The series was full of previously unpublished material, and it was illustrated with many Lincoln portraits never printed before. However, her most famous assignment was on the horizon.

Reasoning that the public would like to hear more about the workings of big business, McClure decided to investigate the "Mother of Trusts," the Standard Oil Company. It was the creation of the remarkable titan of the new business class, John D. Rockefeller, "the Napoleon among businessmen." McClure assigned the topic to Tarbell. She pursued the record of a congressional investigation that was mysteriously suppressed. She then interviewed businessmen who had dealings with Rockefeller.

Louis Van Oeyen/WRHS/Getty Images

Ida Tarbell, one of the nation's early muckrakers, was the investigative journalist and chronicler of American industry who became famous for her classic "The History of the Standard Oil Company."

The first installment of her seventeen-part series, later published in book form as *The History of Standard Oil Company*, took five years of work before it was published in *McClure's* in November 1902. Her series was judged as probably the most sensational series of articles ever published by an American magazine. Tarbell discovered that unfair business practices squeezed out competitors. She found that the company monopolized trade by securing rebates and preferences from railroads by controlling pipelines, by local price cutting, by espionage, and by operating under the guise of small companies.

"When the business man who fights to secure special privileges, to crowd his competitor off the track by other than fair competitive methods, receives the same summary disdainful ostracism by their fellows that the doctor or lawyer who is 'unprofessional,' the athlete who abuses the rules receives, we shall have gone a long way toward making commerce a fit pursuit for our young men," Tarbell wrote.[14]

While Tarbell's articles exposed the company, the federal government sued Standard Oil. The case dragged through the courts for years, but on May 15, 1911, the U.S. Supreme Court issued a decree ordering the breakup of Standard Oil. The nation's highest courts decided, just as Tarbell had years earlier, that the company's object was "to drive others from the field and exclude them from their right to trade." It ruled that the great holding company must be broken up into separate corporations. At the time, Standard Oil controlled thirty-three companies, and Rockefeller held more than one-fourth of all the stock. When the shares were put on the market following the dissolution order, they were priced at $663 million. As a result, Standard Oil Company in New Jersey became Exxon; in New York, Mobil; in Ohio, Boron; in California, Chevron; and in Indiana, Amoco.

LINCOLN STEFFENS

The first installment of Tarbell's article appeared in *McClure's* just one month after Lincoln Steffens had broken muckraking ground with his "Tweed Days in St. Louis." Some experts consider Steffens the first muckraker. Others call him the muckraker of all muckrakers.

He was hired to be *McClure's* managing editor. However, McClure realized he hired an excellent writer but a poor editor. McClure eventually took Steffens aside and said he would have to go elsewhere to learn to be a magazine editor.

"How can I learn?" Steffens asked, hurt and angry.

"Not here," McClure said. "You can't learn or edit a magazine here in this office."

"Where then can I learn?" Steffens asked.

"Anywhere," McClure said. "Anywhere else. Get out of here, travel, go—somewhere. Go out in the advertising department. Ask them where they have transportation credit. Buy a railroad ticket, get on a train, and there, where it lands you, there you will learn to edit a magazine."[15]

Steffens found that the Lackawanna railroad owed the magazine money for advertising, and he ordered a ticket for Chicago. A friend told him to go on to St. Louis, where a prosecutor, Joseph Wingate Folk, was investigating bribery of the city's governing body. Folk found that the Suburban Railway Company had been granted a franchise, through the wholesale bribery of public officials, to run its line along St. Louis' streets.

Steffens had the story he was seeking, "Tweed Days in St. Louis," which implied that St. Louis was operating under a system similar to that of Boss Tweed in New York. The article was an indictment of the city's governing body, the House of Delegates.

Steffens wrote:

> There was a price for a grain elevator, a price for a short switch; side tracks were charged for by the linear foot ... a street improvement cost so much; wharf space was classified and precisely rated. As there was a scale for favorable legislation, so there was one for defeating bills. It made a difference in the price if there was opposition, and it made a difference whether the privilege asked was legitimate or not. But nothing was passed free of charge.[16]

A member of the House of Delegates admitted to the grand jury that his dividends from the bribery combined netted $25,000 in one year; a councilman stated that he was paid $50,000 for his vote on a single issue.[17]

"Was this the way things really were?" Steffens asked. "Were other cities equally corrupt?" He was convinced the answer was yes, and with McClure's support he set out to document it.

In Minneapolis he found graft in the hands of the mayor, Albert Alonzo Ames, and his appointed police chief, his brother Fred W. Ames. Steffens found that houses of prostitution, gambling dens, and illegal liquor joints paid off city officials. Clever crooks could be welcomed in the city if they played "fair" with the police.

Burglaries were common, many of them planned by the police. One case established on the court records was the robbery of the Pabst Brewing Company office. The officers persuaded an employee to learn the combination of the safe, and, with a burglar, to clean it out one night, while the police captain and the detectives stood guard outside.[18] The *Tribune* said that Ames and his gang created "a state of affairs in the municipal government of Minneapolis that discounts anything Tammany Hall ever dreamed of."[19] Ames fled the city.

In Philadelphia he found a political machine even more corrupt. Historian Fred J. Cook wrote in *The Muckrakers* that a hotelman told Steffens how when he went to vote, he was told that he had "voted already." When he protested and threatened to kick up a terrible fuss, he was finally permitted to vote, "but they called in a couple of gangsters to offset my ballot by voting the other way—in the names of George Washington and Benjamin Franklin."[20]

In St. Louis he found payoffs to state legislators to pass or defeat bills pending before them. From the assembly, bribery spread into other departments. He wrote: "Men empowered to issue peddlers' licenses and permits to citizens who wished to erect an awning or use a portion of the sidewalk for storage purposes charged an amount in excess of the prices stipulated by law, and pocketed the difference. The city's money was loaned at interest, and the interest was converted into private bank accounts."[21] One official was so "incited by Steffens' articles" that he pursued municipal graft prosecutions in 1903, which "raised him to the governorship of the state the following year."[22]

In 1904, Steffens collected the articles he had written for *McClure's* and published them in a book called *The Shame of the Cities*. He found that the greed of all classes for special privileges and for special dispensations was the underlying factor in the wholesale corruption of American city government. He did not blame the politicians, businessmen, or any one class: "... no one class is at fault," he wrote, "nor any one breed, nor any particular interest or group of interests. The misgovernment of the American people is misgovernment by the American people."[23]

His work elicited widespread shock. Disturbed by the implications of Steffens's work, former president Grover Cleveland told him, "I can't believe it." He told Steffens, "I'm not doubting your report.... It is the picture as a whole that I cannot accept. No, no, I don't doubt that either. It is true. I have seen it myself in office. I simply cannot make my imagination look at it as it is. It is too terrible. You will have to repeat and repeat that story, in other states, to get it through our heads."[24]

Steffens did just that, with a lot of help from his fellow muckrakers, including David Graham Phillips, whose investigation of U.S. congressmen would have even greater ramifications.

DAVID GRAHAM PHILLIPS

Cosmopolitan, late in joining the muckrakers, produced one of the most important investigations. David Graham Phillips wrote "The Treason of the Senate," which disclosed in nauseating detail the corruption of the Senate by big business, particularly by the Standard Oil Company. It was the article that prompted President Theodore Roosevelt to give to Phillips and other writers the name by which we have known them ever since: "muckrakers."

The article was inspired by journalist Charles Edward Russell. While sitting in the press gallery of the U.S. Senate, he became aware of "well-fed and portly gentlemen," and that "almost nobody in that chamber had any other reason to be there than his skill in valeting for some powerful interest." In his book *Bare Hands and Stone Walls*, Russell explained that he conceived the idea that a series of articles "might well be written on the fact that strictly speaking we had no Senate; we had only a chamber of butlers for industrialists and financiers."[25]

Russell suggested the idea to his new boss, Hearst, who just purchased *Cosmopolitan*, and he liked it. However, Russell was busy on another assignment for *Everybody's* magazine, and Hearst's editors went looking for another writer. Phillips was tapped for the job. He was a prodigious and well-known novelist who had written a number of best sellers. After graduating from Princeton, he had worked as a political journalist for the *Cincinnati Star* and the *New York Sun* and *New York World*.

He stood out in any newsroom, not only because of his talents but because of his meticulous appearance. He was the only reporter who wore a white suit and large chrysanthemum in his lapel—an oddity at a time when many editors and reporters were disheveled sots.

Hearst hired Gustavus Myers, who had written *The History of the Great American Fortunes*, and Phillips' brother, Harrison, a Denver newspaperman, as research assistants to help his famous writer. With their help, he launched into writing the series with all the outraged fury and passion that marked his style.

In a personal message to his readers, Hearst described the sensational series that was to begin the next month, promising that its revelations would be so damaging that senators would have to resign. It said: "This convincing story of revelation, to be told in several chapters, and to run well through the magazine year, has been called 'The Treason of the Senate' for the reason that that is a fit and logical title for this terrible arraignment of those who, sitting in the seats of the mighty at Washington, have betrayed the public to that cruel and vicious Spirit of Mammon which has come to dominate the nation."[26]

The opening of the article charged:

> The Treason of the Senate! Treason is a strong word, but not too strong, rather too weak, to characterize the situation in which the Senate is an eager, resourceful, indefatigable agent of interest as hostile to the American people as any invading army could be, and vastly more dangerous: interests that manipulate the property produced by all, so that it heaps up riches for the few; interests whose growth and power can only man the degradation of the people, of the educated into sycophants of the masses toward serfdom.... The Senators are not elected by the people; they are elected by the "interest."[27]

The first article stripped bare the careers of New York senators Chauncey M. Depew and Thomas Collier Platt. He wrote that Depew had become a member of the boards of directors of seventy corporations, receiving more than $50,000 annually in fees for his services. He described Platt as having a "long ... unbroken record of treachery to the people."[28]

He also educated the public in how U.S. senators were selected. It was not by the vote of the people but by the vote of a closed tight little circle of bosses, the members of the senates in the individual states. What this meant, Phillips explained, was that "the interest," if it could pressure or bribe a majority of state senators, could name its own handpicked agents to sit in the powerful Senate of the United States, where they were appointed to important committees and where they worked their will on legislation, killing bills that might have hurt "the interest," and seeing that measures were passed that lined private pockets with literally millions of dollars extorted from the people.

What did this mean? Phillips asked. "The greatest single hold of 'the interests' is the fact that they are the 'campaign contributors'—the men who supply the money for 'keeping the party together,' and for 'getting out the vote,'" he wrote. "Did you ever think where the millions of watchers, spellbinders, halls, processions, posters, pamphlets, that are spent in national, state and local campaigns come from? Who pays the big election expenses of your congressman, of the men you send to the legislature to elect senators? Do you imagine those who foot those huge bills are fools? Don't you know they make sure of getting their money back, with interest, compound upon compound?"

"The Treason of the Senate" had a tremendous impact. Some exposed senators didn't even dare to seek office again; others were defeated. Six years after the article's publication, only four of the twenty-one senators Phillips wrote about still were in office. Even more important, Phillips scored the greatest success of any muckraker—a change to the U.S. Constitution. His article brought about the Seventeenth Amendment, calling for the popular election of senators.

The series also provoked President Roosevelt in an April 14, 1906, speech to warn the American people where such reporting was taking them.[29] He feared that articles such as Phillips' picture of important senators as corporate agents would threaten to carry the country beyond reform into radicalism.

Unfortunately, the talented and prolific writer did not realize the extent of his accomplishments. Phillips, forty-three years old, was shot six times by a deranged musician, Fitzhugh C. Goldsborough. The killer was obsessed with the mistaken idea that his sister had been the subject of one of Phillips' fictional female characters. Only one other muckraker, Upton Sinclair, would come close to equaling Phillips's accomplishments.

UPTON SINCLAIR

By 1906, muckraking articles were overflowing into books. Some writers, such as Upton Sinclair, whose revelations about the meatpacking industry in *The Jungle* shocked the country, chose that medium for their exposés.

In addition to exposing the horrid conditions of Chicago's meatpacking industry, Sinclair's aim was to illustrate the virtues of socialism. Fred D. Warren, editor of the socialist weekly *Appeal to Reason*, was impressed by Sinclair's manifesto published in his magazine. Sinclair began reading the magazine in 1904, at a time when he rebelled against the society he had come to know. It also was a time when a strike by 20,000 workers in the Chicago stockyards was crushed in the most shocking and brutal manner, moving Sinclair to become a passionate radical. An outraged Sinclair urged stockyard workers to fight on, telling them: "You have lost your strike, and now what are you going to do about it?"

Warren also was impressed with Sinclair's latest Civil War novel, *Manassas*, which centered around the struggle to abolish slavery. He suggested that Sinclair write a novel about a current topic, industrial slavery, and advanced him $500. Sinclair used his contacts from writing in *Appeal to Reason* to investigate the conditions under which the packinghouse workers labored.

He lived with the workers for seven weeks. He described the experience in his autobiography:

> I sat at night in the homes of workers, foreign-born and native, and they told me their stories, one after one, and I made notes of everything. In the daytime I would wander about the yards, and my friends would risk their jobs to show me what I wanted to see. I was not much better dressed than the workers, and found that by the simple device of carrying a dinner pail I could go anywhere. So long as I kept moving, no one would heed me. When I wanted to make careful observations, I would pass again and again through the same room.
>
> I went about the district, talking with lawyers, doctors, dentists, nurses, policemen, politicians, real estate agents—every sort of person. I got my meals at the University Settlement, where I could check my data with the men and women who were giving their lives to this neighborhood.[30]

He wrote *The Jungle* in three months and it is considered one of the most brutal American novels. It reads like a soap opera. The novel centers around Jurgis

Rudkus, a Lithuanian peasant, who wanted to attain the American dream. However, he was lured to the packinghouses by lies of high wages. But what followed was a nightmare. He must pay graft to keep his job and is cheated by a real estate man who sells him a home on an installment plan. If that isn't enough, he and his family contract horrible diseases from the packinghouses; his child dies; his wife has an affair with his boss; his wife dies in childbirth; he smashes the face of his boss; and he is sent to jail. But there is more. After being released from jail, he befriends his cousin, who has turned to prostitution. He wanders in despair until he hears a socialist, who can save him from this world.

The public was not swayed by his political philosophy but were stunned by the abuses and frightened by the meat they were eating. As Sinclair himself later said, "I aimed at the public's heart and by accident I hit it in the stomach."[31] For example, he wrote:

> There was never the least attention paid to what was cut up for sausages; there would come all the way back from Europe old sausage that had been rejected, and that was moldy and white—it would be dosed with borax and glycerine, and dumped into the hoppers, and made over again for home consumption. There would be meat that had tumbled out on the floor, in the dirt and sawdust, where the workers had tramped and spit uncounted billions of consumption germs. There would be meat stored in great piles in rooms; and the water from leaky roofs would drip over it, and thousands of rats would race about on it. It was too dark in these storage places to see well, but a man could run his hand over these piles of meat and sweep off handfuls of dried dung of rats. These rats were nuisances, and the packers would put poisoned bread out for them, and they would die, and then the rats, bread and meat would go into the hoppers together. This is no fairy story and no joke.[32]

The story appeared serially in *Appeal to Reason*. It was offered to five book publishers and rejected the first four times. Sinclair was going to publish the book himself when Doubleday Page and Company published it in 1906. It stayed on the best-seller list for one year. Sinclair became the most frequently translated author in the world as *The Jungle* was issued in seventeen other languages.

President Roosevelt, however, was not happy. The uproar in the nation was so great that the president appointed a commission to investigate the packers and their preparation of meats. Two New York social workers, Charles P. Neil and James B. Reynolds, were sent to Chicago to investigate the charges. Their report vindicated Sinclair.

In England Winston Churchill praised *The Jungle* as a masterwork. "This terrible book ... pierces the thickest skull and most leathery heart," he wrote.[33] In America, meat sales declined by half, and within six months after publication of *The Jungle*, in 1906 Congress passed the Meat Inspection Act, assuring the public it would no longer be poisoned by the meat it bought and ate.

MUCKRAKING'S IMPACT

Hundreds of articles were written during the era of the muckrakers by magazine writers who seemed to be Don Quixotes fighting windmills. Said the Weinbergs: "But from a historical perspective, their writings did have a part in changing the

AMERICAN MEDIA PROFILE | UPTON SINCLAIR 1878–1968

Murray Garrett/Getty Images

To Albert Einstein, Upton Sinclair was "one of the sharpest observers of our time." To Sir Arthur Doyle, Sinclair was "one of the greatest novelists in the world." To George Orwell, Sinclair was a "dull, empty windbag."

To most Americans, Sinclair has been reduced to the muckraker who described how capitalist meatpackers served tainted meat. However, he is one of the most translated authors in the world, and his books covered a broad range of subjects. He wrote about medicine in *Good Health and How We Won It* and *The Fasting Cure*; business in *The Flivver King, Money Writers*, and *Oil*; religion in *The Profits of Religion, What God Means to Me*, and *A Personal Jesus*; philosophy in *The Book of Life*; journalism in *The Brass Check*; psychology in *Mental Radio*; and education in *The Goose-Step*. And there are more than seventy-seven other books that could be listed.

The Jungle brought him his greatest fame. In his book *The American Outpost*, Sinclair explained the writing of that book: "I wrote with tears and anguish, pouring into the pages all that pain which life had meant to me. Externally the story had to do with a family of stockyard workers, but internally it was the story of my own family. Did I wish to know how the poor suffered in winter time in Chicago? I only had to recall the previous winter in the cabin, when we had only cotton blankets, and had rags on top of us. It was the same with hunger, with illness, with fear. Our little boy was down with pneumonia that winter, and nearly died, and the grief of that went into the book."

Sinclair was born in Baltimore, but his father, a wholesale whiskey salesman, was an alcoholic; he moved the family to New York City in 1888. "It took my good and gentle-souled father thirty or forty years to kill himself, and I watched the process week by week and sometimes hour by hour," Sinclair writes in his autobiography. That experience made him a prohibitionist. Though his immediate family was quite poor, Sinclair would spend time living with his wealthy grandparents. These extremes, he later argued, turned him into a socialist. He even used some of his *Jungle* royalties to establish Helicon Home Colony, a socialist community in Eaglewood, New Jersey. One of those who joined it was novelist Sinclair Lewis, who was influenced by Sinclair's views on politics and literature. The Socialist Party asked him to become its candidate for Congress. He lost, winning 750 out of 24,000 votes.

course of American political, economic, and social history and thought. They affected individual lives, as well as the community."[34]

The effect of muckraking on the soul of the nation was profound. Cook says: "It can hardly be considered an accident that the heyday of the muckrakers coincided with one of America's most yeasty and vigorous periods of ferment. The people of the country were aroused by the corruptions and wrongs of the age—and it was the muckrakers who informed and aroused them."[35] Muckraker Ray Stannard Baker said it best: "We 'muckraked' not because we hated our world but because we loved it. We were not hopeless, we were not cynical, we were not bitter."[36]

Some famous victories resulted from public pressure generated by muckraking. The Federal Reclamation Act of 1902 put a brake, although not a very substantial one, on the exploitation of natural resources. The Supreme Court dissolved the Northern Securities Company in 1904, and in the same year the man who had

He would run for political office again in 1934 as the Democratic candidate for governor of California. At the time the state's population was 7 million. One million were out of work, public relief funds were exhausted, and people were starving. Sinclair called his EPIC (End Poverty in California) gubernatorial campaign one of the great adventures of his life. His remedy to end poverty was obvious, he thought. "The factories were idle, and the workers had no money," he wrote in his autobiography. "Let them be put to work on the state's credit and produce goods for their own use, and set up a system of exchange by which the goods could be distributed." "Production for Use" was his slogan.

His EPIC campaign has been called one of the first modern political campaigns in U.S. history. His campaign issued an eight-page weekly paper called the *EPIC News*, and it held rallies up and down the state. He filled stadiums and auditoriums. However, the *Los Angeles Times* and advertising concerns did not want Sinclair to win. The *Times* would take a paragraph from one of Sinclair's books and place it on the front page with a black border outlining it. The paragraph would be taken out of context, making Sinclair look foolish. Even so, his campaign generated widespread support. He lost but won 879,537 votes to the winner's 1,138,620.

Following his defeat he wrote an eleven-volume novel series on American government. In 1942 he wrote *Dragon's Teeth*, a novel about the rise of Nazism, which was awarded a Pulitzer Prize.

When Sinclair was eighty-eight years old, a reader of his autobiography asked him the question: "Just what do you think you have accomplished in your long lifetime?" He responded that *The Jungle* helped clean and protect the meat that came to his table. *The Brass Check* helped to bring about improvements in journalism and encouraged newspapermen to form a union. *Mental Radio* helped to promote an interest in the investigation of psychic phenomena. *The Cup of Fury* informed the public about the ravages of alcoholism.

He also said his "mourning parade" before the offices of Standard Oil in New York ended slavery in the mining camps in the Rocky Mountains and changed the course of the Rockefeller family and other millionaire dynasties.

"Despite my fight and struggles of many others," he wrote, "communist dictatorships have taken over half the world. Meanwhile, for the first time, proud man, dressed with a little brief authority, has so perfected the instruments of destruction that he is in a position to put an end to the possibility of life on earth and condemn this planet to go its way through infinite space, lonely and forgotten."

prosecuted the "boodles" Steffens had exposed in St. Louis was elected governor of Missouri. In 1905, the leaders of the "beef trust" were indicted for conspiracy to restrain trade, and convicted and sentenced (only to see the conviction reversed). Insurance companies were regulated for the first time, and the fight for railroad regulation had some successes.

Tarbell's exposé of the Standard Oil Company was credited for the May 15, 1911, Supreme Court decision dissolving the oil company. Congress passed the Meat Inspection Act in 1906, following Sinclair's *The Jungle*, and the Pure Food and Drug Act in 1906, after Samuel Hopkins Adams's exposé of the patent medicine industry, "The Great American Fraud," was published in *Collier's*.

Still other legislative reforms followed from this literature of exposure. The Hepburn Act of 1905, which authorized the Interstate Commerce Commission to tighten railroad regulations, followed publication of Ray Stannard Baker's "Railroads on

Trial" for *McClure's*. Barton J. Hendrick's "Daughters of the Poor" for *McClure's* resulted in the Mann Act of 1909, which prohibited the transportation of females across state lines for immoral purposes. Edwin Markham's "The Hoe-Man in the Making" detailed the exploitation of children in sweatshops and factories. His work brought about the Child Labor Law of 1916, which excluded from interstate commerce products of factories that employed children. The U.S. Supreme Court later declared the law unconstitutional. However, child-labor regulations were finally adopted through the Fair Labor Standards Act of 1938 and its 1949 amendments. William Hard's "Making Steel and Killing Men" brought about the Workmen's Compensation Law.

Journalism in the Progressive Era failed, however, to increase political participation. If anything, the age of reform was an age of voter apathy. Overall, political participation declined in America as this reporting gained strength. The percentage of the electorate that voted was down sharply from the extraordinarily high turnouts in the decades when citizens could expect little in the way of inspired investigation of political ills on a national stage.[37]

"Progressives asked the public to overturn old assumptions and to view issues in new ways," according to Thomas C. Leonard. First, muckraking magazines attacked the notion that a citizen's vote should be an act of loyalty set by tradition and sprung by election spectacle. Political participation was redefined as a thoughtful search for true principle, which was obscured by the surface play of parties. Second, progressive journalism was a major, disruptive shift toward political education, confusing the voter's cues and teaching him to hesitate. Both parties, Leonard wrote, pursued citizens with open minds so well that they left some of their loyalists confused and distracted. Finally, party loyalty was itself a virtue of the old politics that progressive journalism helped turn into a vice. Gone was the notion of party voters with rings in their noses, pulled by the reins of party leaders. The muckrakers exposed the forced system of participation. Vote brokering and ballot box stuffing were over.[38]

By 1912 muckraking also would be over.

THE DEATH OF MUCKRAKING

According to Upton Sinclair, a number of factors contributed to the decline of muckraking. One reason, he said, was that muckrakers, particularly Phillips, in his "Treason of the Senate," went too far. People just got tired of reading about the ills of society.

With the advent of World War I, Americans turned their attention away from national issues to international issues. Meanwhile, President Woodrow Wilson solved many of the problems these reporter-reformers exposed. With President Wilson and the Democrats back in the White House in 1912, newspapers believed themselves in a better position in Washington, on the strength of the new president's assurance that he was in favor of "pitiless publicity" for public business. He backed this conviction by instituting the first formal, regular White House press conferences.

Sadly, at the end, muckrakers retreated in the face of organized counterattacks by business, which used advertising and public relations. Advertising was becoming too important economically to the magazines for them to continue their activist role. *Everybody's* magazine, for example, lost seven pages of advertising when a series on the beef trust was running. Advertisements for ham, preserved meats, soap, patent cleaners, fertilizers, and a railroad were pulled.

DIGESTS AND NEWSMAGAZINES

Although the magazines of the muckraking era succumbed to slow and sometimes painful deaths, the twentieth century saw new successes by publishers who were more in tune with the times. America was changing by the 1920s, and so were its magazines and the people who were buying them. For the first time, the nation was predominately urban and the period was filled with prosperity and optimism. Marked by bathtub gin, the Model T, the five-dollar workday, the first transatlantic flight, the movies, and radio, the "Roaring Twenties" exemplified the fast-paced life that followed World War I.

"Our lives, even in our so-called leisure hours," wrote a mechanical engineer in 1930, "are hectically speeded up." He asked:

> Do we settle down with a quiet smile to a thought-provoking or soul-enlarging book? No, we go to the movies, or to that gattling-gun variety of entertainment called a revue. We skim headlines on the way to the office and vote accordingly. On Sundays we rush about in cars at forty miles an hour (or more) cursing those ahead for blocking traffic. Or we play golf and yell "fore!" at every man we catch sight of.... We have roving minds. The novel is being replaced by the short story.... The two- and three-hour orations ... have to be compressed into twenty minutes or nobody will listen. Leisurely thinking, which means, or at least may mean, deep, continuous, sustained thinking, is rare.[39]

With more to do, Americans had less time to spend with their newspapers. They were looking to read something different, something they could read quickly and easily. Brevity was the key. Three trailblazers matched their needs. They were *Reader's Digest, Time,* and the *New Yorker.*

Reader's Digest was introduced by DeWitt Wallace in February 1922. The idea for a magazine designed for readers with little time available occurred to him while he was recovering from injuries sustained in World War I in the U.S. Army. While recuperating from shrapnel wounds, Wallace lay in bed going through one magazine after another. He found himself tightening stories, realizing that few people would have time to get through all the information. When he returned home to St. Paul, he submitted a sample magazine, which he called *The Readers Digest*, to publisher after publisher across the United States. They turned him down.

Wallace was disappointed but not deterred in his endeavor. He accepted a position in the publicity department of the Westinghouse Electric Company in Pittsburgh, but he was fired. More than ever, Wallace and his new bride, Lila Bell Acheson, were determined to get the magazine published. They borrowed $5,000 and moved to New York City, where they rented a storeroom in Greenwich Village, and promoted the magazine by mail. Some 5,000 copies of the publication were printed. That first edition included thirty-one articles, which the Wallaces copied by hand, because they were short of money, from publications in the

New York Public Library. Initially, some 1,500 people subscribed, paying twenty-five cents an issue.

From these humble beginnings grew one of the world's most widely read magazines. The Wallace formula was simple: "Is it quotable? Is it something the reader will remember, ponder and discuss? Is it applicable? Does it come within the framework of most people's interests and conversation? Does it touch the individual's own concerns? Is it of lasting interest? Will it still be of interest a year or two from now?"[40] Another part of the formula was keeping the operation a secret from those publications from which he was culling articles without paying for them.

That wasn't the only dishonest thing he did. He was on a mission to shape public opinion. Wallace would write articles on everything from sex to Communism, with a conservative bent to them. He placed these articles in major publications and then offered shorter versions of them in his magazine. This gave the *Digest* "power to propagandize its right-wing political views across a broad spectrum of the periodical press."[41] The publishers that received extra publicity from the reprints loved the idea. Others thought the practice dishonest.

The practice didn't appear to hamper the success of *Reader's Digest*. By 1935 circulation topped one million. Three years later the first international edition was published in Britain. During World War II, editions were published in South America, where it is the most widely read magazine, and Sweden. It was available in almost every European country by the end of the war. Today its forty-eight editions are issued in nineteen languages, with just fewer than 100 million readers every month.

The *Digest* has expanded its enterprise by launching its condensed books, venturing into the area of music and videos, and revolutionizing direct mail by introducing easy-to-enter sweepstakes.

TIME MAGAZINE

Henry Luce, who would publish a number of magazines to match the times, became the nation's single most powerful and innovative mass communicator. He was characterized by *Business Week* as the closest equivalent to "a Lord of the Press as America can now produce."[42] One out of every five Americans would come to look at a Luce periodical, such as *Time, Life*, or *Fortune*, during a given week. More correspondents in Washington read *Time* than any other magazine; there and elsewhere many admired and modeled their own work after *Time*'s peculiar newswriting style.[43]

Luce's newswriting formula involved little more than cleverly summarizing the week's news in print or pictures in ways that left readers with a concise, entertaining, and frequently inadequate version of an event or trend. The aim of this journalism of synthesis was to simplify complex stories, to give readers a succinct or "efficient" view of the world. Some subscribers wanted *Time* and other Luce publications to "mediate" information for them at a time when knowledge of government, technology, and business had expanded and complicated life. In time, Luce's formula of the directed synthesis could be found in radio, television, newspaper columns, and analyses. Simply, he transformed American journalism from information to synthesis.[44]

He would eventually bury competitors, such as the *Literary Digest*, which was founded in 1890 and reached an estimated 900,000 readers by 1922. In their prospectus for *Time*, Luce and his partner Britton Hadden argued that their publication, like the *Digest*, would give both sides of a question. However, *Time* would differ by clearly indicating which side it believed to have the stronger position.[45] *Time* also would spur imitators. Ten years after the founding of *Time*, a group of former *Time* writers began a rival newsmagazine called *Newsweek*. That same year David Lawrence, who had been a Washington correspondent, launched the *United States News*, which eventually would be combined with *World Report*, a magazine that dealt with international affairs. The new magazine, *U.S. News and World Report*, specialized in economic news and covered government with top businessmen in mind.

The "Lord of the Press" did not experience a typical American childhood, and this had an impact on his career and politics. The son of Presbyterian missionaries, Luce was born and spent all but one of his first fourteen years in China. At age ten he was sent to a British boarding school at Chefoo (now Yantai), on the Shantung (now Shandeng) north coast, where teachers offered strict, traditional instruction and flogged students who made mistakes on a translation or formula. To avoid that, Luce worked extra hard. Never again, he vowed, would school be such a challenge.

At Chefoo, he also got his first taste of journalism when he became the editor of the school newspaper.

His boyhood impressions of China never left him. Along with the other missionary children, Luce developed a special loyalty to America. He had a thesis: that U.S. foreign policy thrives when guided by traditional American principles and fails when it neglects them. Those principles were liberty under law; self-government by responsible and self-governing citizens; the reign of reason in argument and of constitutionally chosen majorities in power. He also believed that society needed an aristocracy—one of worth, not birth or money. His hope was that the American businessman might grow into an aristocratic role, since "those who have a sizable stake in the country ought, therefore, to yield to no other class in either the degree or the intelligence of their patriotism."[46] His political views changed with the trend of events. For example, mellowing in his later years, he stopped preaching his belief in aristocracy.

In 1912, at the age of fourteen, he traveled to England. He had won a scholarship at the Hotchkiss School, in Connecticut, but first he had to spend a year in a school at St. Albans, north of London. Luce was a stutterer, and this embarrassed him. The headmaster at St.Albans had great success in curing such problems.

At Hotchkiss he met Hadden, who came from a prosperous banking family in Brooklyn, had a passion for horseplay and baseball, and would ultimately join Luce in the strangest of partnerships. They measured each other in a singular relationship that always contained more of rivalry and respect than friendship, and continued on that basis for fifteen years.[47] Both won positions on the biweekly *Hotchkiss Record*, the school newspaper. Luce also assumed control of the *Hotchkiss Literary Monthly*.

Entering Yale in September 1916, Luce was drawn to journalism. He and Hadden won slots on the *Yale Daily News* despite keen competition. Hadden eventually

AMERICAN MEDIA PROFILE | MARGARET BOURKE-WHITE 1904–1971

Margaret Bourke-White/Time & Life Pictures/ Getty Images

Margaret Bourke-White—photographer extraordinaire—is a legend of firsts. Most significantly, she coined the term "photojournalism," combining the two crafts at the heart of the Fourth Estate.

Bourke-White started in the Bronx in New York. Her father, Joseph White, was an inventor, an engineer, and an amateur photographer. As a girl, Margaret relished tagging along with her father, using an empty cigar box as a pretend camera. Her mother, Minnie Bourke, worked in publishing, ran the household, and monitored with a firm hand the comings and goings of Margaret and her sister, Ruth.

For some reason, when it came time for college, Margaret had a tough time settling at any one school. Prior to getting her degree from Cornell University in New York, she attended Rutgers College, Columbia University, the University of Michigan, and, some accounts say, Purdue University, in Indiana.

During her meandering student career, she dabbled in herpetology (the study of reptiles and amphibians); studied under Clarence White, a portrait and landscape photographer who specialized in the creative subtleties of light; was photo editor for the yearbook at Michigan; and made a photographic architectural study of Cornell, which became her "selling portfolio."

It was her architectural pictures that launched her career as a photographer in Cleveland, Ohio, where she lived after graduation in 1927 to be near her family. Then, in 1929, a telegram came from Henry R. Luce. He wanted her to work for his new weekly magazine, *Time*. But she opted for his new business magazine, *Fortune*, becoming its first photographer. The lead story featured Swift & Company, a hog processing plant. Needless to say, she burned her camera equipment when the project was finished. But her documentation of the plant was the first step in the development of the photo essay—and the Bourke-White style.

It was 1930, and the Soviet Union was in the throes of an industrial and cultural revolution. Its doors were closed to Westerners, particularly photographers, so she was sent by *Fortune* to Germany instead. While there, she set out on her own to gain access to the Soviet Union—and did.

She came home with the first complete photo documentary of the emerging Soviet Russia, capturing the machinery and later, on a second trip, the people. The *New York Times Sunday Magazine* published six of her articles along with her photos, launching her career as a photojournalist. In 1931, she published *Eyes on Russia*.

defeated Luce for the position of chief editor of the *Daily News*. With Luce as his assistant, they reshaped the newspaper. The two shared the view that existing newspapers and magazines were disorganized and chaotic and gave inadequate coverage to world events. They introduced the formula that would be their trademark. That formula included packaging the news in an organized fashion and giving it in an orderly and coherent manner. It appealed to the college student who was busy with course work and athletics.

Luce obtained a position at the *Chicago Daily News*, considered at the time one of the nation's great newspapers. Hadden, on the other hand, worked at the prestigious *New York World*. Both were unhappy and saw that their innovations, tried at Yale and Hotchkiss, were not welcome.

Then in the mid-1930s, she connected with writer Erskine Caldwell and toured the South, documenting poor rural people and tenant farmers. This resulted in the book *You Have Seen Their Faces*. One of her most famous photographs comes from the South. It features black victims of a flood in Louisville, Kentucky, standing in a bread line beneath a billboard of a smiling white family in a car. The headline reads, "World's Highest Standard of Living—There's no way like the American Way."

Later, in 1936, Henry Luce started another magazine, *Life*, where "the pictures would tell the story." Margaret's photo of the Fort Peck Dam, located about twenty miles southeast of Glasgow, Montana, graced the cover of the first issue on November 23, 1936. She was one of the first four photographers for *Life* magazine.

She married Erskine Caldwell in 1939, and together they covered the war until their divorce in 1942. Margaret was the only foreign photographer in Moscow when the Germans attacked, and she became the first documented woman war correspondent, crossing the German border with Patton's troops. She also was the first photographer to document the German death camps. *Life* published her photos, breaking a tradition of abstinence from the horrors of war. *The Living Dead of Buchenwald* became a classic.

Following the war, *Life* sent her to India, where she followed Mahatma Gandhi with a camera for months and snapped her last shot of him just hours before he was assassinated. One of her most famous photos is "Gandhi at His Spinning Wheel."

From 1949 to 1953, the maverick photographer spent time in South Africa photographing life under apartheid, as well as the Korean War.

In the mid-1950s she was diagnosed with Parkinson's disease. Experimental surgery brought it under control, enough so she continued to work for *Life*, this time as a writer. Her friend, colleague, and mentor, Alfred Eisenstaedt, became her sidekick and photographer. Together they chronicled her story about the surgery and recovery. *Life* eventually published it, after much debate. It was a huge success.

However, the disease returned in 1961. And this time she settled for a less taxing assignment—her autobiography, *Portrait of Myself*. "Her postscript is both heartbreaking and uplifting, as she reveals plans to be the first photographer on the Moon, having snagged the assignment from *Life* magazine!" Her life more recently was captured in a movie for cable television, *Double Exposure*, starring Farrah Fawcett.

She died after a fall, an unfortunate aspect of her disease, on August 21, 1971.

Margaret Bourke-White prepared the palette for the new wave of photojournalists, ahead of her time in a man's world. She was spunky, tenacious, fearless, humane—an endless font of photographic sensitivity and talent. She had the "right stuff" to be the first woman photographer assigned to go to the moon.

In late 1921 they were reunited at the *Baltimore News*, where they began to plot their journalistic future. Their vision was to use their formula to produce a totally different weekly paper from anything being read by the American public.[48] With the help of their fellow Yale alumni, they raised $86,000, rented office space at 9 East 40th Street, and gathered a staff that included Stephen Vincent Benét and Archibald MacLeish. After a year of preparation, the first issue of *Time, the Weekly News-Magazine* was published on March 3, 1923. The purpose of *Time*, said the *New York Tribune* in a two-paragraph notice hidden on page 7, "is to summarize the week's news in the shortest possible space." Luce and Hadden promised fair news treatment without objectivity. Their publication also stressed personalities. Since the two lacked reporters for the first issue, which included twenty-two pages of editorial and six pages of advertising, most of the editorial copy was lifted entirely from the *New York Times*. That first issue sold 9,000 copies, rather than the expected 25,000 copies.

Time eventually appealed to many Americans. "Everyone reads it, everyone relies on it for part of his information about the modern scene," wrote *Harper's* editor Bernard De Voto in 1937.[49] By the end of the decade, *Time*'s circulation would near one million.

Luce and Hadden designed their publication for the small and large capitalist too busy to give his newspaper a close day-to-day reading. The bulk of *Time*'s readers were business executives and proprietors. A 1931 survey of readers in Appleton, Wisconsin, found that 60 percent of its subscribers had annual incomes of $5,000 or more. Nationwide, two years earlier, one percent of all families earned $10,000 or more; the average income was $2,335. *Time* advertising promoted products for the country club crowd—those who could afford expensive hotels, private schools, and air travel.[50]

Luce and Hadden both wanted to be editor of the new publication. By a toss of the coin, it went to Hadden, with the understanding that the two would alternate positions each year. Luce became the business manager. It was under Hadden that *Time* developed its peculiar style of writing, which came to be known as "*Time*-style." People in *Time* were gentle-spirited, beetle-browed, pot-bellied, tough-talking, or snaggletoothed. Also, people didn't talk. They barked, snapped, gushed, muttered, growled, grunted, cooed, or shrieked. People also didn't walk. They dashed, shuffled, ambled, sashayed, lumbered, or lurched.

The great problem of Luce's life was Hadden. So long as Hadden was there, Luce's missionary use of *Time* was limited to issues on which they agreed.[51] They had both shown an admiring interest in Mussolini since 1923. *Time* spoke of his "remarkable self-control, rare judgment and efficient application of his ideas." He was "daring," "brilliant," and "courageous." Stalin, on the other hand, was a coldblooded man of deeds, and uneducated in manner. Readers also noticed that *Time*'s use of terms conveyed its likes and dislikes in the political arena. Russia was "chill," "drab," "bleak." Italy was "warm," "gay," "genial."[52]

Hadden fell ill early in 1929. In late February he died of streptococcus infection of the bloodstream. Luce eventually bought enough of Hadden's stock to give him control of the magazine. He made Hadden's cousin, John S. Martin, who was fiercely devoted to his cousin's ideas, editor.

Hadden's death opened the way for a heavier print offensive against Soviet Russia. Luce began a propagandist effort to isolate Russia economically. He printed lists of American firms doing business with the Soviet Union, suggesting to the firms that they ought to know better. He specifically took a jab at publicist Ivy Lee, whom he called "the peripatetic representative extraordinary of U.S. Business," for his Moscow visits in search of contracts with American firms.[53]

Luce was most vocal, and biased, when it came to China. The Luce publicity promoted the Chinese as full-fledged members of the Grand Alliance, with Chiang Kai-shek on the same footing as Franklin D. Roosevelt, Churchill, and Stalin. Luce biographer W. A. Swanberg wrote that the publicity job Luce performed gratis for the Chiangs must rank as the greatest of its kind.[54] Luce also made sure that America was going to know Madame Chiang. Her picture appeared on the front page of

Time, and Luce arranged a major press tour for her in 1942. He arranged for her to meet the president and Eleanor Roosevelt, who became annoyed with her queenly habit of clapping her hands when she called for a household employee. The Roosevelts—and most prestigious U.S. newspaper publishers—did not share Luce's admiration of Madame Chiang.

By the time of Chiang's visit to the United States, Luce controlled an impressive media empire. *Time* had a weekly circulation of 1,160,000. *Fortune*, a magazine for business and industry, reached a weekly audience of 170,000. His *March of Time* radio program was heard by some 18 million. The *March of Time* newsreel, which presented a more dramatic summary of news than the radio broadcast, was seen by 20 million every month. He also owned *Architectural Forum*, which was read by 40,000. Finally, *Life* magazine had a weekly U.S. circulation of 4 million and a foreign circulation of 317,000.[55]

LIFE

For years, Luce believed that a "mind-guided camera can do a far better job of reporting current events than has been done." By the early 1930s, *Time* ran photographs that dailies refused to include. For example, a 1934 photo spread on the assassination of King Alexander of Yugoslavia gave readers the sensation of being there. *Fortune* also began to use illustrations, many by Margaret Bourke-White, who demonstrated the artistic possibilities of industrial photography, offering "unique angles upon the world of action—of blast furnaces erupting, of soup being cooked in kettles a thousand gallons at a time, of locomotives being hammered together red hot, of orchids growing under glass."[56]

Luce's marriage to Clare Boothe Brokaw also generated new interest in establishing a picture magazine. She had suggested to Luce before they were married that he should buy the humor magazine *Life* and turn it into a picture magazine. He eventually bought the magazine for $92,000. He did not want to compete with the *Saturday Evening Post* or *Collier's*, nor did he want to limit its readership to those "busy men" on Eastern commuter trains he and Hadden had targeted as potential readers for *Time*. Instead, he spoke of "half of mankind."[57]

Some $1.7 million in advertising contracts, based on a circulation of 250,000, were signed prior to *Life*'s publication—a very encouraging sign. Its first issue, scheduled for newsstands on November 19, 1936, included an impressive front cover shot of Fort Peck Dam by Bourke-White. That first issue sold out. After four weeks some 533,000 issues were purchased, making it the first magazine in American history to pass the half-million mark. It took *Time* ten years to reach that number. *Life* passed the one-million mark four months after the first issue.

However, the company was making only six cents for every issue sold. Time, Inc. was losing $3 million a year on *Life*. Luce rejected a suggestion to raise the price of the magazine. Instead he sought the largest possible circulation in order to raise advertising rates. Advertisers eventually fell in line as consumers clutching copies of *Life* literally rushed into showrooms to purchase automobiles and other products. By early 1939, *Life*'s circulation neared 2.4 million and it was beginning to make money.[58]

THE NEW YORKER

The *New Yorker*, which poked fun at Luce's writing style by publishing a profile of the media giant written in "Timese," was the third mass circulation magazine founded in the 1920s. It was a different magazine from the *Reader's Digest* and *Time*, which appealed to busy middle-class readers. The *New Yorker* appealed to upper-class readers, even boasting in its first issue, on February 21, 1925, that it was "not edited for the old lady in Dubuque." The *New Yorker* was looking for a highly literate, sophisticated, and educated audience.

The *New Yorker*, which initially concentrated on the social and cultural life of New York City, earned a reputation for publishing some of the best cartoons, biographical profiles, foreign reports, and arts reviews in the nation. It also would be one of the most important venues for modern fiction.

It was founded by Harold Ross, whom biographer Thomas Kunkel described as "a tramp newspaperman with a poor education, before he came to New York to build his career in publishing."[59] Kunkel also said that Ross made great professional (not personal) choices. And that he had a formidable intellect and curiosity, terrific taste, integrity, and an eye for talent.

Ross began writing for the *Salt Lake City Tribune* when he was thirteen years of age. He then worked for the *Marysville Appeal* in California before joining the U.S. Army during World War I. He went AWOL from duty in central France but reappeared in Paris as the army was establishing the *Stars and Stripes*, an eight-page newspaper based in Paris. Ross was able to talk his way into the position of editor in chief. While in Paris, he also edited and published *Yank Talk*, a book of jokes.

When he returned to the United States in May of 1919, he edited the *Home Sector* in New York, a weekly journal for former servicemen who had read *Stars and Stripes*. The journal went under, and Ross edited the humor magazine *Judge* for six weeks. He then set out to establish his own magazine. He obtained about $25,000 from investor Raoul Fleischmann, who also provided an office for the publication. Ross launched the *New Yorker* in 1925. In its early years, "serious fiction … simply was not a priority" for its founding editor. In his prospectus for the magazine, Ross wrote that he sought to publish prose and verse, short and long, humorous, satirical, and miscellaneous.

He also promised his readers "the whole truth without fear or favor," and he told his writers to push the bounds of convention. And humor was allowed to infect everything, as E. B. White wrote in his obituary of Ross in 1952.

In the meantime he frequented the Algonquin "round table," whose members were considered the "aristocracy of New York sophistication." They included Marc Connelly, Dorothy Parker, Alexander Woollcott, Edna Ferber, George S. Kaufman, and Heywood Broun. They became his board of editors.

Though it never attained the readership of the *Reader's Digest* or *Time*, the *New Yorker* was home to some of the nation's significant writers, including F. Scott Fitzgerald, Sinclair Lewis, John O'Hara, and John Cheever (who would have a half-century association with the magazine). Ernest Hemingway contributed only once, but declined further involvement because of the *New Yorker*'s chronic shortage of money. However, during the Depression, the magazine steadily attracted a generation of younger authors, including Irwin Shaw, Jean Stafford, and, by 1941, J. D. Salinger, E. B. White, and James Thurber.

THE BIRTH OF PUBLIC RELATIONS

More important to the muckrakers' demise was the hiring of America's first image-maker, Ivy Lee, by America's top industrial boss, John D. Rockefeller. Lee's job was to repaint the image of a man and his company for the public. This marked the beginning of the era of the press agent and the eventual emergence of public relations as a profession, under the leadership of Edward Bernays. Public relations professionals could fashion for business and industry a new image, to replace an image marred by muckraking journalists.

Modern public relations owes its being to the muckrakers, among other things, according to Bernays.[60] Certainly it didn't just begin in the 1900s. It is said that the great patriot Samuel Adams used every means of public relations available at the time to ignite the American Revolution. Adams, the "master of the puppets," developed techniques of persuading the public that foreshadowed the workings of the Committee on Public Information established by President Wilson at the start of World War I.[61] Among other things, Adams kept in touch with committees of correspondence, which he set up in eight towns; to each of them he sent copies of the *Boston Gazette*, the hotbed of revolutionary fever. To build support for the independence movement, he used the newspaper and his committees of correspondence to publicize the Boston Massacre of 1770 and the Boston Tea Party of December 16, 1773.

He was the "Father of the American Revolution" because he was a press agent who could outshine the feats of many successors. "[He] is to press relations experts what Benjamin Harris and Benjamin Franklin are to printers and newspapermen. Under tremendous handicaps he worked out methods similar to those in use today. He might be regarded as the 'father' of American press agentry."[62]

The rise of press agentry, the maturation of political campaigns, the rise of advertising, and the employment by business and industry of public relations writers in the nineteenth century spurred development of modern public relations in the twentieth century.

PRESS AGENTRY

Press agents emerged in the middle of the nineteenth century, when private interests wanted to influence the public press. Theatrical promoters like P. T. Barnum, the famous director of the Barnum & Bailey Circus, hired press agents to secure favorable comment in newspapers and magazines.[63]

Barnum's great discovery was not how easy it was to deceive the public but rather how much the public enjoyed being deceived. Barnum's success led to the hiring of publicists in politics, business, and industry.

POLITICAL CAMPAIGNS

Political groups had made use of the press long before 1900. For example, the nation's first contested election in which newspaper polemics, pamphlets, and

AMERICAN MEDIA PROFILE | P. T. BARNUM 1810–1891

Henry Guttman/Getty Images

Long before Ivy Lee and Edward Bernays were hailed as the founders of modern-day public relations, there was P. T. Barnum—press agent, museum proprietor, and publicist extraordinaire. During a career that spanned the better part of the nineteenth century, Phineas Taylor Barnum successfully promoted dozens of exhibitions and performers throughout the United States and Europe.

Today public relations practitioners and historians acknowledge Barnum's flamboyant style of press agentry as a form of early publicity practices, but many are reluctant to recognize him as one of the founders of the field. To Barnum's credit, however, much of this has to do with the times in which he lived. Barnum's career flourished during the era of the penny press, a time when newspaper editors thrived on the sensational and frequently did not question the promotional gimmicks and hyperbole behind the material submitted to them; if it were likely to sell papers they printed it.

Barnum used this to his advantage, taking on sensational show business acts and promoting them to the public through creative and often outlandish means. In 1835, for example, he purchased the rights to a slave named Joice Heth, who allegedly was one hundred sixty-one years old and claimed to have been George Washington's nurse in the early 1700s. He took her on tour throughout New York and New England, where she was a hit with the public.

Much of Barnum's questionable reputation can be traced to this first exhibition, given the improbability that Heth was actually one hundred sixty-one years old, not to mention being George Washington's nurse. Nonetheless, as several of Barnum's biographers have pointed out, whether Heth was authentic or a sham did not dissuade the American public from coming to see her and certainly did not discourage American newspapers from reporting on her appearances.

Throughout his career, Barnum continued this pattern of finding curiosities and then promoting and exhibiting them. In 1842, he opened The American Museum in New York City, a collection of curios and oddities, including, he claimed in his autobiography, "industrious fleas, educated dogs, jugglers, automatons, ventriloquists, living statuary," etc. It was Barnum's aim to make his museum a showplace, and he used every publicity trick he could muster to do so.

---

political rallies venerated and vilified the leading candidates occurred following President Washington's Farewell Address.[64] The Federalists and Jeffersonian Republicans, the Whigs and Jacksonian Democrats, all used party organs for their polemics. However, by the middle of the nineteenth century, newspapers obtained their revenues from advertising and expanded circulations, not from political parties. As newspapers changed their character, political parties began to hire newspaper people to serve as press agents, especially during election campaigns.[65]

ADVERTISING

The advertising field was still young and feeling growing pains. Between 1880 and 1890, the amount spent on newspaper advertising increased from $40 million to nearly $96 million annually. The period saw tremendous increases in advertising for patent medicines, soap, breakfast foods, and gas companies and for classified ads.

One of these tactics involved hiring a man to lay a trail of bricks leading into the museum. This both aroused the curiosity and inspired the ticket purchase of many an onlooker who followed the bricklayer to the museum's door. As biographer M. R. Werner noted, "Barnum's first object was publicity for the Museum and for the name of P. T. Barnum, and he went to any lengths to carry out those purposes. He soon succeeded in making his museum and his personality the talk of New York."

Barnum followed his museum triumph by becoming an international traveling showman. He took on a four-year-old midget, barely two feet tall and weighing only fifteen pounds, dressed him in a military uniform and promoted him as "General Tom Thumb." After crowds in the United States flocked to see the boy as a result of Barnum's promotion, Barnum took Tom Thumb to England to perform before Queen Victoria—a move that generated great interest from the British public at large, which was Barnum's ultimate goal.

Perhaps Barnum's most notable publicity endeavor involved opera singer Jenny Lind, a twenty-four-year-old Swedish soprano who had taken Europe by storm in 1844. Despite the fact that she was virtually unknown to the American public, Barnum set out to make Jenny Lind's name a household word. He did so by launching a publicity campaign more than six months before the opera singer's arrival in the United States. He painted such a romantic and innocent portrait of the young woman that the public was successfully enthralled: when the steamship carrying Lind pulled into New York harbor in September of 1850, thousands of people came to greet her.

Following his tour with Lind, Barnum retired from show business and settled down in Bridgeport, Connecticut, to write his autobiography and serve a brief stint in politics, first in the Connecticut State Assembly and subsequently as mayor of Bridgeport. Then in the 1881, he triumphantly returned to the world of show business by starting a traveling circus, ultimately joining up with James A. Bailey and launching the "Barnum & Bailey Greatest Show on Earth." It is perhaps for this final venture into entertainment promotion that Barnum is best remembered, despite the fact that he was already seventy-one years old.

Today Barnum is generally branded as the quintessential press agent rather than a forerunner of public relations as it is currently practiced. Nevertheless, his contribution to the arenas of publicity and promotion within the field of public relations cannot be ignored. As biographer A. H. Saxon observed, "Newspaper publishers of the nineteenth century were no less desperate for advertising and ready-made news than their counterparts of today, and throughout his career Barnum always took care to keep them supplied with a steady stream of both."

By Andi Stein

These businesses hired press agents or directly offered newspapers money or payment in kind to publish advertisements concealed as news or editorials.[66] In 1898 Standard Oil Company's advertising agency, the Jennings Advertising Agency, distributed articles to newspapers and paid for them on the condition that they appear as news or editorials. The Jennings Agency's contract with newspapers stated that the "publisher agrees to reprint on news or editorial pages of said newspaper, such notices set in the body type of said paper, and bearing no mark to indicate advertising, as are furnished from time to time by said Jennings Agency at the rate of ___ per line."[67]

BUSINESS AND INDUSTRY

The next step in the development of public relations was the employment of publicists by business and industry in the nineteenth century. As early as 1870 railroads began to stage publicity stunts. In that year the Pacific railroad invited 150 "ladies and gentlemen," Bernays wrote, to ride on the new line it had opened from New York to San Francisco.[68] Railroad executives hired publicists to write "puff" pieces to head off growing public criticism of their companies. Meanwhile, utility companies employed publicists to sway public opinion to hold that competition in public utilities was unfeasible. These attempts to minimize competition through public relations would achieve greater heights in the twentieth century with Ivy Lee.

IVY LEE

A former newspaperman, Lee undertook business publicity in a period when the muckrakers were at the height of their influence. As a matter of fact, the greatest era of trust-building in America occurred during Lee's years in college and as a young professional. For example, from 1895 to 1904 more than 3,000 companies were absorbed in mergers and disappeared.

A top economics student in the Princeton class of 1898, Lee understood what was going on. His yearbook said of Lee, "What he doesn't know about trusts is not worth knowing."[69] He was exposed to new thought at Princeton, where Darwinian ideas were applied to economic trends to show (supposedly) that movement toward larger economic units, and perhaps eventually one state economy, was a movement of inevitable economic progress.

In an article, "Coordinating Business Through Co-operation," Lee gives a hint of his economic philosophy. He opposed traditional competition and urged alliances of large corporations with each other and with the federal government.

Simply, Lee was jumping on the bandwagon for a new economic order—the notion that trusts backed by governments could produce many goods more efficiently than could a variety of small and mid-sized competitors. Supporters of the new economic order, such as J. P. Morgan and John D. Rockefeller, knew the public would consider this business philosophy un-American. Didn't capitalism demand liberty and competition?

A strategist who understood both economics and popular psychology was needed to convince skeptical businessmen and a skeptical public that government regulation could increase rather than stifle economic liberty. What they needed was a public relations professional. Who they needed was Ivy Lee.

Lee put into operation what he called the "psychology of the multitude." Give up attempts to explain economic laws through rational discourse, he advised businessmen, for people "will not analyze statistics…. Since crowds do not reason, they can only be organized and stimulated through symbols and phrases." Communications proceeded better when public relations spokesmen played on "the imagination or emotion of the public." Those favoring collaboration merely had to find "leaders who can fertilize the imagination and organize the will of the crowd … the crowd craves leadership."[70]

Lee made a career of telling leaders of the new economic order how to merge the new economics with the new psychology. For example, railroad managers were told that crowds are led by symbols and phrases. "Success in dealing with crowds ... rests upon the art of getting believed in. We know that Henry VIII by his obsequious deference to the forms of the law was able to get the people to believe him so completely that he was able to do almost anything with them," he said.[71]

If the appearance of truthfulness worked for Henry VIII, Lee thought, it would be useful to him. Listeners who believed him on small points, for good reason, were more likely to follow him to his collaborationist conclusions.[72] Lee championed a "Declaration of Principles." He explained what they were in an announcement sent to newspaper editors: all work would be done in the open; news—not advertising—would be distributed; factual accuracy would be the order of the day; necessary information would be supplied promptly; and editors would be assisted in all possible ways.

Lee's principles signaled the end of the "public-be-damned" attitude of business and the beginning of the "public-be-informed" era.[73] However, Lee didn't practice what he preached. He picked his words carefully. For instance, "I send out only matter every detail of which I am willing to assist any editor in verifying for himself."[74] Such a statement was factually correct in that all of Lee's details were generally verifiable, but Lee knew that effective propaganda contains in it only information that can be verified. Lee's goal was to slant the thinking of his readers and clients toward anticompetitive policies, but so subtly that he would leave with them a belief that they had made up their own minds.[75]

The master propagandist did that with his most important client, John D. Rockefeller, who employed Lee to repair damage caused to business-government collaboration by press coverage of the 1914 Ludlow Massacre. Violence erupted as the coal miners' strike in Colorado became heated. On April 20 strikers clashed with the Colorado state militia. By the end of day, fifty-three people, including two women and eleven children, were dead.

Following the violence, Rockefeller became one of the most hated and despised men in America. Something had to be done to protect the Rockefeller name and the capitalist class. Rockefeller Jr. hired Lee—and with that, modern public relations in industrial disputes was born.

He distributed documents listing a series of facts; some were dishonest. For example, he circulated a bulletin, "How Colorado Editors View the Strike," which contained statements made at a conference of Colorado editors. One would think from reading the bulletin that editors supported the coal company. However, the truth was that representatives of only 14 of the 331 newspapers in the state attended the conference and that eleven—all controlled by the coal companies—signed the report.[76]

The violence and such dishonest practices upset Upton Sinclair, who not only joined the protest against the Rockefellers but pinned Lee with the nickname "Poison Ivy." However, that didn't stop Lee's endeavors to turn around the image of Rockefeller, who came to be revered at the time of his death. Lee also was successful in fostering the notion that reducing competition was in the best interest of the public. Finally, he popularized the use of public relations in corporate America, paving the way for Edward L. Bernays.

EDWARD L. BERNAYS

Before his death in 1934, Lee told the young Edward L. Bernays, who would become the true father of public relations, that public relations was a temporary phenomenon that would die with the both of them. But to the contrary, the stock market crash and the Depression that followed accelerated public relations activities. Business realized that it not only had to sell products, but it had to resell itself to the public.

No longer could business afford to place its emphasis on getting attention for the organization, the product, or the service. Business had to explain its contribution to society. Corporations were open to the approach of Bernays.

The nephew of Sigmund Freud, Bernays taught shell-shocked business executives that "propaganda" would make them respected again. He wrote that intelligent individuals would defend public relations propaganda as "the modern instrument by which they can fight for productive ends and help to bring order out of chaos."[77] He contended that social manipulation by public relations counselors was justified by creating godhead figures who could assert subtle social control and prevent disaster.

Bernays' rationale for a public relations style that prized manipulation developed after he worked on very clever and important public relations campaigns. The turning point in his career was a stint with the Committee on Public Information, set up on April 13, 1917, one week after the United States entered World War I. It was the first time the government went into the business of opinionmaking.

"With the outbreak of World War I, nations in the conflict and out of it recognized how important public opinion was to the success of their effort," Bernays wrote. "Ideas and their dissemination became weapons and words became bullets. War publicity became an essential part of the war effort in each country."[78] President Woodrow Wilson and various government agencies mobilized every known device of persuasion and suggestion to sell the nation's war aims and ideals to the American people and to neutral countries, and to deflate the morale of enemy countries and get them to accept U.S. ideas.[79]

Bernays' public relations activities up to that point were fashioned by what he called "the engineering of consent based on Thomas Jefferson's principles that in a democracy everything depends on the consent of the people." According to Bernays, people like to go where they are led. In other words, clever public relations campaigns can direct "human herds" into appropriate corrals. "If you can influence the leaders, either with or without their conscious cooperation, you automatically influence the group which they sway."[80]

In his book *Propaganda*, Bernays argued for a new paradigm for public relations: to make a hero of "the special pleader who seeks to create public acceptance for a particular idea or commodity." This new paradigm for public relations also would consist of seizing the academics, applying the principles of social psychology to find out what the needs and wants of the people truly are.[81]

When he returned from the war, Bernays opened his own public relations business. His wife, Doris E. Fleischman, joined him as an equal partner in his venture. She was among the first women in public relations and became an early advocate of public relations as a profession for women. Other women public relations pioneers included Leone Baxter and Anne Williams Wheaton. Baxter and her husband, Clem Whitaker, formed the first public relations agency that specialized in political campaigns. Wheaton became President Dwight D. Eisenhower's associate press secretary in 1957.

"We called our activity 'public direction,'" Bernays wrote. "That was the best name we could think of at the time. We knew the term 'press agent,' of course, but it had bad connotations. 'Publicity' was too indefinite. At least 'direction' seemed to give greater dignity to our work and indicated that we were interested in the planning and directing phases of the field—the broad approach to problems."[82]

From 1919 to 1923 his work—and title—broadened. He now called himself a "counsel on public relations." His clients included presidents, business leaders, and entertainers. One of his assignments was to convince the nation that President Calvin Coolidge "was not the cold, silent iceberg many expected him to be. Instead he wanted people to see that the president was really human."[83] It was decided that the president should entertain at a breakfast at the White House. His guests for griddle cakes and bacon included Al Jolson, the Dolly Sisters, Charlotte Greenwood, and other stage and screen stars. Accounts of this hit the front pages of newspapers, including the *New York Times*. Its headline said: "President Almost Laughs."[84]

In 1928 Bernays was hired by the American Tobacco Company to bolster sales by helping women win the right to smoke in public; the current law prevented them from doing this. On Easter morning in New York City, Bernays organized a parade of women smoking their "torches of freedom," a gesture of protest for absolute equality with men. However, years later, after learning of the health dangers from smoking, he regretted being involved.

A high point of his career and of public relations was the 1929 Light's Golden Jubilee, designed to emphasize the significance of the electric light to America and world civilization. Committees were formed to promote the celebration, holidays were declared, speeches were made, and a commemorative postage stamp honoring Thomas A. Edison was issued by the United States. Henry Ford invited hundreds of prominent people to be his guests for several days. To dramatize the event, Edison, with the assistance of President Herbert Hoover and Ford, reconstructed the electric light at his old laboratory. When he lit the old lamp, people around the world did the same.

"While the Jubilee dramatized the importance of electric light, it had, in addition, a marked impact on the development of public relations," Bernays wrote. "The participation of President Herbert Hoover, Henry Ford, Thomas A. Edison, and many other personages in the Jubilee gave public relations a new meaning and new status."[85] It was the coming of age of public relations as muckraking moved into the shadows.

EXPANSION OF CORPORATE PUBLIC RELATIONS

Ivy Lee had told Edward Bernays that public relations would die with the both of them. He would be stunned to know that there were 243,000 "public relations specialists" in 2006, according to the U.S. Department of Labor. Lee, who described himself as "a physician to corporate bodies," also might be surprised at the growth in corporate public relations.

Since Lee's death in 1934, business, industry, and government have not only fought to sell the idea of free enterprise, but they have been plagued with trying to cope with government regulations and their corporate image in times of crises. Corporations began turning to corporate public relations firms such as Carl Byoir & Associates. Byoir, like Betrays, was educated in public relations during the time he spent with the Committee on Public Information during World War I. He turned to corporate counseling and industrial public relations from tourist travel promotion after an embarrassing incident involving the German Tourist Information Office.[86] The Freeport Sulphur Company, which owned large amounts of sulfur deposits in Louisiana and Texas, became Byoir & Associates' first major industrial account. Louisiana passed a bill that increased a tax on sulfur 200 percent. Legislators in Texas were going to do the same thing. Instead of stopping the bill in Texas, Byoir decided to work to overturn the Louisiana decision, which set a precedent for the region and public relations consulting. He gathered the most vocal public opinion groups in Louisiana and taught them how the tax was contrary to the economic interests of the company and the state. They descended upon the legislators, who rescinded and lowered the tax. Texas legislators then voted not to tax sulfur at a higher rate than Louisiana.

Some years later, Byoir & Associates was involved in what *Fortune* magazine called "the Railroad-Trucker's Brawl." The Pennsylvania Motor Truck Association lobbied the Pennsylvania state legislature to allow trucks to carry heavier loads on the state's highways. The Eastern Railroads Presidents Conference feared that the truckers would take business away from the railroads. Byoir planned an impressive public relations campaign by forming independent citizens' groups to support his client's position; he set forth the message that heavier loads were more dangerous and would ruin the state's roads. His firm also prepared negative ads and commissioned freelance writers to submit articles to magazines. The bill was vetoed.

However, the angry truckers charged the railroad presidents and Byoir with violating the Sherman Anti-Trust Act and the Clayton Act and questioning the use of the "third-party technique." The U.S. Supreme Court ruled in 1961 that attempts to influence the passage or enforcement of laws did not violate the Sherman Act.[87] It was a victory of sorts for public relations. The opinion gave First Amendment protection to public relations activities.

More corporate entities sought help from public relations consultants in the 1970s as they underwent corporate takeovers. That was followed in the 1980s by a surging interest in the stock market when corporations sought help to boost stock prices. This gave rise to a public relations specialty—investor relations.

Meanwhile, communications crises continue to keep public relations consultants busy trying to protect corporate images. For example, in 1982 McNeil Labs and Johnson & Johnson found their image and product under a cloud when six people in a Chicago suburb who took Tylenol capsules died of cyanide poisoning. Seven years later the tanker *Exxon Valdez* ran aground in Prince William Sound, causing the largest oil spill and public relations crisis in U.S. history. Pepsi's image was marred in 1993 when a syringe was found in a can of its soft drink.

CONCLUSION

America faced a rude awakening at the beginning of the twentieth century. It was a nation of many contrasts. At the top of the heap were the business tycoons who gorged themselves on the nation's wealth. They won favor with state legislators whom they bought and controlled. At the bottom of the heap were millions of immigrants and native-born Americans who lived in disease-infested tenements in the nation's largest cities. Among those providing cheap labor for the wealthy captains of industry were young boys and girls who worked long hours in factories, sweatshops, and mines for starvation wages.

By 1910 a number of Americans, including elected officials, had come to understand the dangers of unrestrained industrial capitalism. Helping them understand were muckraking journalists, "writers of exposure" whose aims were to expose the ills of society. Pointing to sore spots in business and politics, they named names while writing about businessmen colluding with corrupt politicians, criminal police, malefactions of capitalists, food adulteration, fraudulent claims for patents, and unscrupulous business practices. These muckraking journalists were aided by inexpensive and widely circulated magazines that also had huge resources.

The power of the muckrakers writing in these cheap magazines was tremendous. For example, muckraking journalism about the quality of food and drugs helped build a political constituency in favor of federal regulation. Food and drug bills had been proposed in Congress throughout the 1880s and 1890s. However, Congress did not enact federal food and drug bills (the Meat Inspection Act and Pure Food and Drug Act) until 1906. Before the muckrakers, competing producer, bureaucratic, and consumer interests with different opinions about the benefits of federal regulations prevented the formation of an effective coalition in favor of federal regulation.

Muckraking journalism also created a sense of crisis about child labor abuse, transportation of women across state lines for immoral purposes, industrial accidents, and prison reform. Muckraking journalism helped trigger reform legislation by highlighting these important social and economic problems to a broad audience. Their work also proved very profitable for the publishers of the magazines in which they worked. It has been estimated that by around 1905, each of the more popular muckraking magazines had expanded their circulation to approximately 500,000 to 1,000,000 readers. Some muckrakers became powerful political figures. Sinclair, for example, ran as the Democratic candidate for governor of California in 1934 on the platform "End Poverty in California" (EPIC). His EPIC campaign is considered one of the nation's first modern political campaigns. However, Sinclair, who romanced the Socialist Party at times, was defeated after major opposition from the *Los Angeles Times*. He did go on to win a Pulitzer Prize for fiction in 1942 for *Dragon's Teeth*, a book about the rise of Adolf Hitler.

The work of Sinclair and other muckrakers helped contribute to the growth of public relations. Companies, such as those owned by the Rockefellers, attacked by muckraking journalists sought help from public relations professionals such as Ivy Lee, whom Sinclair tagged "Poison Ivy" during the Ludlow Massacre, and Edward Bernays. Bernays learned his craft serving on the Committee on War Information during World War I. Lee, who thought public relations would die with Bernays, would be surprised at the growth of the profession today.

From 1865 to 1920, the press played a pivotal role in shaping the political and social fabric of the nation. It also influenced America's popular culture—in the comic strips, in pulp fiction, and in the movies. Many members of the newspaper and magazine press became popular folk heroes by this time, displacing the frontiersman, the whaler, the cowboy, the river pilot, and the railroad engineer. Even moviegoers became mesmerized by reporters and the workings of metropolitan newspapers and magazines. Some of the film's biggest stars sought roles as hard-boiled city reporters.[88]

1900–1950 MEDIA PROMISES IN A TECHNOLOGICAL SOCIETY

In this buoyant era of technology, America became the "can-do" nation. With the dream that riches would reward hard work, 8.8 million immigrants arrived in the United States in the first ten years of the twentieth century. With the era's wealth, much of it held by only 4,000 people, came leisure, a new experience.

Love of gimmickry matched by inventive genius produced a welter of labor savers and innovations, including the camera, motion-picture projector, radio, and television.

By 1900 some 1.25 million telephones buzzed with business and social talk; 20 million incandescent lamps glowed; buildings and elevators rose to giddy heights.

Movies exploded in popularity in the 1920s, a decade of radical change. Woodrow Wilson's prewar idealism and his "Crusade for Democracy" were replaced by the postwar alienation of Warren Harding's "Return to Normalcy." The nation turned conservative while fear of radical and foreign ideas, fueled by the Bolshevik Revolution in the future Soviet Union, resulted in a "Red scare."

There was a brief and bloody resurgence of the Ku Klux Klan. There was also a rise in religious fundamentalism, which blamed modern education for destroying traditional American beliefs. Americans raised their tariff barriers and passed restrictive immigration legislation and a prohibition on liquor—giving rise to a new national folk hero, the American gangster.

It was the Jazz Age. Sensationalism was fed by a mass journalism that focused on crimes of passion, freak accidents, bizarre divorce cases, and the private lives of movie personalities.

The ideal woman was now a flapper and not "the girl next door." She wore short skirts; danced the Charleston; and, thanks to Edward Bernays' successful public relations campaign, smoked cigarettes in public. She also won the right to vote in 1920. Hollywood in the 1920s was content to act as a barometer of American social and political well-being. The flapper, the new woman, the speakeasy, and liberal attitudes toward sex, marriage, and divorce became natural topics for the film industry.

But the fun was not to last. President Franklin D. Roosevelt stormed the country in 1933, calling for support of his controversial New Deal to pull the nation out of its economic doldrums. Almost immediately, he and all Americans were faced with a world crisis: the signing of the German-Soviet neutrality pact on August 23, 1939. The pact between the dictators Adolf Hitler and Joseph Stalin gave the Germans freedom to march against Poland and, later, their neighbors to the West without fear of Soviet intervention. The Soviet Union, in return, would annex eastern Poland. France and Britain would declare war against Germany on September 3. Roosevelt then called on the nation to become "the great arsenal of democracy." Using America's newest mass medium, the radio, most effectively, the president proclaimed an unlimited state of national emergency to prepare the nation for war. Until the morning of December 7, 1941, with the fateful Japanese attack on Pearl Harbor, the United States was technically a neutral nation.

The liberalism of the Roosevelt years, with its sweeping programs of social change, declined by 1947. The Soviet Union, America's ally in the fight against Fascism, emerged from the war as a strong, militant, and hostile power. The United States became locked into a fierce struggle with its former ally; it recognized the threat of international Communism and of Communist subversion in the media. Conservatives and frightened liberals now led the nation into a period of military belligerence and political repression that would reach a climax in the early 1950s, with the Korean War and with congressional committees investigating "un-American" activities in every area of the nation's life. No investigations were more persistent or more publicized than those concerning the motion picture industry.

AMERICAN FILM

CHAPTER **8**

The Birth of a Nation took America by storm in 1915. It was the first film to harness the power of "the magic wand of electricity" and use it to touch people's hearts and inflame their passions. President Woodrow Wilson, who had screened the film at the White House, is said to have quipped that it was "like writing history with lightning."[1] The passion and anger it aroused, the tensions it created lasted beyond the theater. They overflowed into the streets, and race riots and mob action followed in the wake of its presentation throughout the United States.

It was quite possibly the single most important film of all time. Certainly, this first American epic proved beyond any doubt that an entertainment medium could be a powerful social and political force.

Since *The Birth of a Nation*, the American film industry has evolved into a powerful communications entity that has shaped, and sometimes changed, the nation's perception and understanding of politics and society. This innovation laid the foundation for the communications revolution, and its power influenced American politics and society.

American film evolved in five stages: motion picture experimentation (1872–1914); storytelling motion pictures (1914–1919); economic expansion of the motion-picture industry (1919–1927); sound motion pictures (1927–1939); and challenges to the motion-picture industry (1940 to the present).

MOTION PICTURE EXPERIMENTATION

American film history began in a buoyant era when America became the "can-do" nation. Love of gimmickry matched by inventive genius produced a welter of labor savers and novelties. For example, in 1888 a Rochester, New York, bookkeeper introduced a toy and launched an industry: George Eastman's Kodak Brownie sold for $41.00 dollars, used roll film, and made everyone a photographer.

Confidently, Thomas Edison promised "inventions to order. "Among his 1,093 patents were those for the incandescent lamp and the phonograph. Still another was for the movie camera. The predilection of Edison and other inventors in the nineteenth century for machinery, movement, optical illusion, and public entertainment produced cinema, the dominant art form of the twentieth century. The development of this most modern of all arts was an evolutionary process: each new discovery or device inspired a fresh wave of emulation and experimentation, often in the cause of science alone but sometimes to create devices for entertainment. Most pioneers saw the moving picture primarily as a scientific aid. Even Louis Lumiére, who with his brother, Auguste, manufactured photographic equipment in France, claimed that his work had been directed toward scientific research.

Some have traced the motion picture's paternity to the ancient Greeks' discovery of electricity in amber and Leonardo da Vinci's example of a camera obscura. Its origin is the magic lantern, a device for reflecting the light of the sun from a mirror, through a lens, and onto a screen. But it had its actual beginning when Peter Mark Roget (of thesaurus fame) enunciated his theory, "The Persistence of Vision with Regard to Moving Objects," explaining the persistence of vision, that capacity of the retina to retain an image of an object seconds after its removal from the field of vision. Since then it has been shown that films seem to move because the brain, and not the eye, is accepting stimuli that it is incapable of perceiving as separate.[2] Though Roget's conclusions may have been inaccurate, scientists immediately invented a number of animating devices based on his idea that were critical to the development of the motion picture.

The English eccentric Eadweard Muybridge first recorded action spontaneously and simultaneously as it occurred. Though he never realized it, the itinerant photographer would produce America's first motion picture, *Occident Trotting*.

A $25,000 bet in 1872 prompted railroad king and California governor Leland Stanford to determine whether at some point a galloping horse, named Occident, had all four hooves off the ground at once. Muybridge's first attempt, in May 1872, was reasonably successful, though the rapid exposures could produce only shadowy silhouettes.[3]

Muybridge's work was interrupted when he was arraigned, but subsequently acquitted, for the murder of his young wife's seducer. In the summer of 1878, Muybridge resumed his photography at the Palo Alto racetrack, using a battery of twelve cameras alongside a specially prepared track. When the horse ran along the track, it broke a series of threads stretched across its path. Each thread in turn broke an electrical contact, and triggered the shutter of a camera. The series of still photographs attracted worldwide attention.

Edison, who had seen the motion photographs of Muybridge, had been interested in combining moving pictures with sound. By 1888 he perfected the phonograph, an instrument for recording and playing back sound, using wax cylinders. However, his earliest efforts were not directed toward movie projection. Instead, he succeeded with his first movie machine, the Kinetoscope, a coin-operated peep-show cabinet that contained a continuous loop of film about 50 feet long. It proved popular in the penny arcades, and Edison dismissed the potential of projection and concentrated on exploiting the peep-show cabinets, even though only one person at a time could watch the film.

Edison considered movies a passing arcade fad. So he ignored the sound aspects and concentrated on supplying one-minute subjects photographed in the "Black Maria," the world's first film studio, built in 1893 near his West Orange, New Jersey, laboratories. Although peep-show parlors were the rage throughout the United States and Europe, Edison had little confidence in long-term possibilities for his machine. He even neglected to pay the additional $150 for an international copyright when he first took out patents in 1891.[4]

That oversight would come to haunt Edison when inventors such as Robert W. Paul in England copied the Edison Kinetoscope and produced a hand-cranked portable camera. In France, the Lumiére brothers saw the Kinetoscope and invented their own Cinematographe, a machine that not only took pictures but also could print and project them as well. It weighed sixteen pounds, as compared with Edison's 500-pound apparatus, and it moved with ease and could follow events. And since the Lumiére camera was hand-cranked, films could be made and shown at speeds that varied from fourteen to twenty-four frames per second. Only with the coming of sound was film speed standardized at twenty-four frames per second.

They used their lightweight camera to record the happenings of everyday life and important events around France. Some of their most famous early films included *Arrival of a Train at a Station, Baby's Lunch*, and *Workers Leaving the Factory*.

No wonder the Lumiéres were the first to show a motion picture on a large screen. On December 28, 1895, a paying audience viewed films made with their Cinematographe in the Salon Indien, a basement room of the Grand Cafe in Paris, signaling the birth of the cinema.

Still other Europeans grasped the principles behind Edison's Kinetoscope and rapidly moved toward projecting their pictures on a large screen. Meanwhile, American inventors Eugene Lauste, Jean Le Roy, Thomas Armat, and F. Charles Jenkins were building machines to project the Edison Kinetoscope reels. Only Edison stood on the fringe. Borrowing from earlier discoveries, he finally joined forces with Armat, whose Vitascope incorporated the essentials to hold the filmstrip momentarily at rest in the aperture of the projector. On April 3, 1896, the Wizard of Menlo Park unveiled his invention at a press screening. Armat may have been in the audience, but it was Edison who stole the show, as the New York *Journal* reported the following day:

> For the first time since Edison has been working on his new invention, the vitascope, persons other than his trusted employees and assistants were allowed last night to see the workings of the wonderful machine. For two hours dancing girls and groups of figures, all of life size, seemed to exist as realities on the big white screen, which had been built at one end of the experimenting rooms.[5]

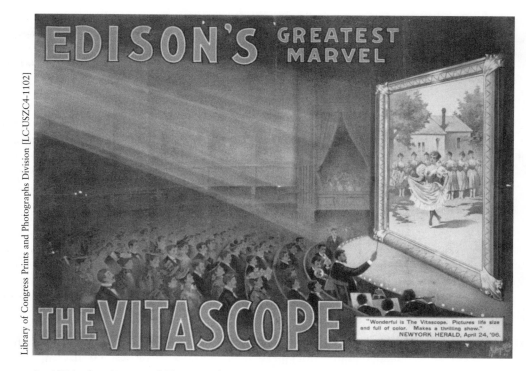

An 1896 advertisement of Thomas Edison's Vitascope in the *New York Herald* brought the public into theaters to see "thrilling shows" of life-size pictures in full color.

Even so, it was not until April 23, 1896, that Edison was prepared to present his projector. He unveiled his Kinetoscope during the vaudeville program at Koster & Bial's Music Hall at 34th and Broadway, in New York, on Herald Square. Audiences marveled at the large screen that displayed locomotives thundering down the tracks and rolling waves that looked so real that people ran for the exits. But the novelty wore thin as films continued to be brief, with shots from one camera position. The once-featured attractions were now relegated to function as "chasers"—shown while one audience was leaving and another was entering the theater—to vaudeville programs.

The Lumiéres' recording of actual events and Edison's entertainment films defined the principal forms of film as a mass medium, and the Lumiéres Cinematographe screenings and their initial popularity marked the end of the phase of invention of the movies.[6]

STORY-TELLING MOTION PICTURES

Few were willing to concede that film, with its roots in pulp fiction, comic strips, popular photography, and melodrama, was an art; they dismissed it as a fairground attraction or a magician's prop. The introduction of narrative, the second stage in the development of the motion picture, gave a new dimension to the movies.

The French illusionist George Méliés, considered by many "the father of the narrative film," became the screen's first true artist. Producer, writer, designer, director, cameraman, and actor, he was the first to use dissolves, superimpositions, time-lapse photography, art direction, artificial lighting effects, and optical effects; all these helped expand the parameters of the fictional film story. Charlie Chaplin called him "the alchemist of light."[7]

Méliés' films—witty, inventive, and filled with exuberant activity and fantastic imagination—were widely seen in this country through the first decade of the new century. The interest in his films proved to American producers that movies could and should be longer than the conventional fifty minutes on the screen.

Inspired by the work of Méliés, Edison projectionist, Edwin S. Porter, developed film's special visual potential. His *The Life of an American Fireman* (1903) and *The Great Train Robbery* (1903) rank among the most famous of pre-nickelodeon films. Porter concentrated on the effective use of innovative camera work; editing; and the use of actors, costumes, sets, and staged scenes.

In *The Great Train Robbery*, Porter established the basic principles of editing, the joining together of bits of film shot in different places and at different times to form a single, unified narrative. He began cross-cutting for rhythm and pace and overlapping shots to increase tension. "When I saw *The Great Train Robbery*, I discovered that you could tell a story in this medium and, in the telling, achieve both greater speed and greater detail than the stage allowed," Cecil B. DeMille stated.[8]

Innovative camera placement added to the success of *The Great Train Robbery*. Porter moved the camera from the studio stage to the outdoors, using "tilts" (a shot in which a tilting camera surveys vertical space while fixed to a stationary tripod) and "pans" (a shot in which a turning camera surveys horizontal space while fixed to a stationary tripod) to follow the action. His interior scenes were filmed as if they were scenes from a play, with the camera as the well-placed observer. Scenes taken on location were combined with shots staged against painted sets. Actors participating in these staged scenes were dressed in costumes.

The success of *The Great Train Robbery* established the single reel as the standard length (between eight and twelve minutes) for American films. And the public wanted to see more of these motion pictures as nickelodeons—about 10,000 of them by 1910—and store shows sprang up in almost every neighborhood. The demand for movies added a new dimension to the business. Distributors would buy or lease films from producers and then rent them to exhibitors, thus guaranteeing a market for the producer and availability for the exhibitor—a three-tier system still largely in operation.[9]

Overnight the movies became the poor man's theater. Porter left Edison in 1911 to found Rex, his own studio. Unable to keep up the pace, Porter, who probably never realized his important role in establishing American cinema, retired in 1915.

D. W. GRIFFITH AND THE ART OF FILMMAKING

While still an Edison employee, Porter was approached by David Wark Griffith with the script of his screen adaptation of Sardou's *Tosca*. Porter rejected it but offered Griffith the leading role in *Rescued from an Eagle's Nest* (1907). Griffith was a young stage actor and, like all actors in the legitimate theater, thought it degrading to perform in a movie. But, newly married, he badly needed money and accepted the role for five dollars a day.

That got his foot—and his scripts—into Porter's studio, where he became a fixture. His wife, Linda Arvidson, also joined the little company. Between 1908 and 1912, Griffith began directing films and established the basic film techniques and structures that moviemakers have used ever since. As late as 1959 director Frank Capra could state that there had been no major improvement in film direction since Griffith. "Griffith had no rivals," Cecil B. DeMille said. "He was the teacher of us all."[10]

The father of American film shaped the basic elements of filmmaking into the language and syntax that would serve cinema for more than a half century. He emerged as the master of film technique and the greatest American film storyteller. In the words of Erich von Stroheim, who graduated from extra to assistant director under Griffith, he "put beauty and power into a cheap and tawdry sort of entertainment."[11]

Griffith was more the refiner than the innovator. He took techniques of the camera, editing, and film that Porter had introduced, and developed film as an artistic medium. Working closely with cameraman G. W. "Billy" Bitzer, he refined Porter's tilts, pans, and tracks (a shot in which a camera moves toward, away from, or parallel to the action by means of a mobile support) into decipherable forms of expression, even cross-cutting between tracking shots in *The Lonedale Operator* (1911).[12] He broke the standard distance maintained between audience and actor by changing the camera's position in midscene.

Griffith's techniques of framing shots and alternating the tempo of shots added to the technique of film artistry. Unlike Porter, Griffith understood that a film's tempo could be affected through the editing of detached shots. Porter would shift from one scene to another without breaking up the run of the camera within scenes. What Griffith discovered, and what other filmmakers have learned and used since, is that rapid cutting, or a succession of short shots, can create excitement; slow cutting, or shots held longer on the screen, will support calm contemplation.

Griffith also became interested in composition and lighting. In *The Drunkard's Reformation* (1909), he used artificial lighting to suggest firelight. In *Pippa Passes* (1909), he employed what came to be called Rembrandt lighting—a technique achieved by placing the camera at an angle to the action, intensifying the mood and heightening the visual impact of scenes. Graphic techniques, such as the *dissolve* (a transition between scenes in which a second image is gradually superimposed over the first, which recedes at a similar pace), the *fade* (the gradual appearance or disappearance of an image from a darkened screen), the *iris* (a circular masking device that reveals or conceals an area of the screen to isolate key details, or to open or close a scene), and the *mask* (an opaque sheet placed before a camera or optical printer to block off part of a photographic image), were designated for narrative purposes, whereas split screens, triple split-screen shots, and soft focus were sparingly used for additional impact.

Griffith perfected Porter's editing techniques, eliminating some of the tedious business of having the actor open a door, step into a room, and close the door, and then walk to the center of the stage before the significant action begins. However, studio executives at Biograph, where he directed from 1907 to 1913, criticized his "jerky and distracting" editing techniques. Griffith shot back saying that Charles Dickens and other great novelists did the same thing, except that "these stories are in pictures, that's all."[13]

Griffith also led the movement for longer films. Again, the studio criticized him, this time for rebelling against the arbitrary single-reel restriction imposed by the American film industry. In 1913, lengthy Italian films, such as *The Last Days of Pompeii* and *QuoVadis?*, created a sensation in America. Working secretly that year in California, Griffith completed a four-reel version of the biblical story *Judith of Bethulia*. Biograph shelved the film and pulled Griffith from his directing duties. He left the studio, taking his best players and his best cameraman, Bitzer, with him.

Griffith joined the Mutual Company, where he supervised five-reel features and would produce the first American epic, *The Birth of a Nation* (1915), twelve reels (almost three hours) long. He became intrigued with Thomas Dixon's novel, *The Clansman*, a story of the Civil War, Reconstruction, and the rise of the Ku Klux Klan. He poured his finances and those of his friends into the production.

He devised unheard-of effects—battle scenes photographed in extreme long shot and reminiscent of Mathew Brady's Civil War photographs, action shots taken in extreme close-up, the climactic ride of Klansmen photographed with the camera mounted low on the back of a moving truck.

The Birth of a Nation broke many precedents in establishing feature-length motion pictures as a respectable and popular art form. It was three hours long, and it was the first American film to be accompanied by an original score, which was composed by Joseph Carl Briel and performed by a full symphony orchestra. Its cost, about $110,000, was five times greater than the next largest sum spent on an American film (*Judith of Bethulia*, which cost $23,000) until then. Overall production time went beyond the average of six weeks or less. For this American epic, Griffith spent six weeks in rehearsal, four months shooting, and three months editing. The film took in an unprecedented $50 million.[14]

The nation had never seen a film that pulsated with such emotion, creating tensions that moved tearful viewers to the edge of their seats. *The Birth of a Nation* also moved civil-rights groups, who attacked the film for its stereotypes of black people and its sympathetic account of the rise of the Klan; they called for boycotts and censorship of the film. This was the first time that Americans realized the social and political power of the entertainment machine.

MACK SENNETT DEFINES FILM COMEDY

One of Griffith's most fervent disciples, Mack Sennett, was defining American film comedy while Griffith demonstrated the power of motion picture drama. A gangling would-be opera singer, Sennett began working for Biograph in January 1909 with thoughts of playing a comic policeman. Griffith, however, cast him in straight roles.

But Sennett learned directing from Griffith. He said of his mentor, "He was my day school, my adult education program, my university."[15] He would eventually become a director, at sixty-five dollars a week. After three years at Biograph, he traveled to Los Angeles and began making pictures at his own studio, the

Keystone. There he developed his own comical Keystone Kops, arrayed in uniforms too big for them as they drove their collapsible tin lizzies.

Along the way, he generated his own cast of clowns, gargoyles, and grotesques, including "Fatty" Arbuckle, Charlie Murray, and, the most famous cop of them all, Charlie Chaplin. He also would discover actors Gloria Swanson, Carole Lombard, Marie Dressler, Harold Lloyd, W. C. Fields, Buster Keaton, Harry Langdon, and Bing Crosby. He would train directors Frank Capra, George Stevens, and George Marshall. He taught them timing and the need for physical movement on the screen, always stressing the importance of editing to tighten and sharpen a scene.

Though most noted for his slapstick comedy, Sennett was the film industry's first real producer. He was a versatile entrepreneur who recognized and encouraged talent and who created a systematic approach to production. This system yielded a bounty of films—some 1,000 silent and several dozen sound films—during his twenty-five-year career. In those films, he transformed slapstick comedy, a genre that had originated in French silent films, into a more complex art form, inventive and often even surrealistic.

Sennett also was responsible for developing the star system. Before 1910 actors and actresses were not given billing on their films. Studios, such as Biograph, were reluctant to identify them by name. They argued that a good picture was the result of "a good story, director, studio, and competent people as a class and not as individuals."[16] Still, audiences began to recognize their favorites and to write to studios and magazines asking for the players' names.

Placing the names of players on marquees would soon pay off as independent movie producers realized that they could develop their own stars. Chaplin, for example, joined Keystone in December of 1913 at $150 a week—a sizable sum for a former vaudeville circus performer who had been making $50 a week. By 1917, at the age of twenty-seven, Chaplin signed with First National for $1 million to deliver eight films in eighteen months—this time with a bonus of $15,000. Mary Pickford, a Canadian-born vaudeville performer, saw her salary increase from $100 a week in 1909 to $15,000 a week by 1917. That year, she, like Chaplin, earned more than $1 million because her films drew many to the box office.

The star system marked a milestone on January 15, 1919, when three of the biggest stars in the industry—Chaplin, Pickford, and Douglas Fairbanks—joined with director Griffith to create United Artists. They would extract the riches of their fame and drawing power at the box office by forming their own distribution company. For the first time in history, motion picture performers acquired complete autonomy over their work, controlling a corporate apparatus that set in motion approved production, advertising, and publicity.

HOLLYWOOD

Stars would become synonymous with Hollywood. Hollywood began to be the center of film production with the failure of the Motion Picture Patents Company (MPPC). With this organization, Edison and nine other leading producers of movies and manufacturers of cameras and projectors attempted in 1908 to form a cartel by pooling and controlling patents. Only cooperating companies licensed by the

MPPC could manufacture "legal" movies and movie equipment. Eastman Kodak agreed to supply film stock only to members. The MPPC received profits by charging for use of its patents. For example, to manufacture a projector, one had to pay five dollars a week, and to use projectors, exhibitors had to pay two dollars per week. MPPC's goal was to squeeze all profits possible from the production, distribution, and exhibition of motion pictures.

In addition, the MPPC set the single reel (ten minutes) as the length for all its films. It also blocked the identification of actors appearing in their films, fearing that they might demand more money if they became well known.

However, distributors such as William Swanson and Carl Laemmle went "independent" and began producing their own films. They were followed by William Fox, Adolph Zukor, and nine other companies. These producers formed the Motion Picture Distributing and Sales Company, and it sued the MPPC under government antitrust laws. MPPC's response to them was violent. Hired thugs destroyed their equipment and intimidated casts and crews.

Despite these tactics, the independents were successful. The courts finally outlawed the MPPC in 1917, though most of its members had already folded. With the MPPC's demise, the new companies cheerfully flouted all the rules of the MPPC and established principles underlying the economics of Hollywood. They increased the length of their pictures from two to three and, after 1914, to five reels, sometimes even to seven reels. They produced films with popular stories and developed stars to act in them; they discovered the value of publicity in promoting both films and stars. They marketed motion pictures in as many places as possible. It now was easy to translate and produce versions in French, Spanish, German, and other languages. Finally, they learned to take control of exhibition in the United States by developing chains of theaters in major urban areas. Thus, the independents succeeded where the MPPC failed—with the control of production, distribution, and exhibition.[17]

At this time, some independent filmmakers brought their operations to Hollywood. Filmmakers had been shooting in the sunbelts of Santa Fe, Jacksonville, San Francisco, and Cuba since 1907, in an effort to keep up production during East Coast winters. Southern California offered filmmakers more daylight hours, good weather, low taxes, diversity of scenery—from ocean to mountains to desert within easy traveling distances. It also had an abundance of cheap labor and cheap land, which companies bought for studios, standing sets, and back lots.

Hollywood, where 60 percent of films were made by 1915, became the cinema capital of the world for two reasons. First, the chaos of World War I halted European production, removing any serious competition. The war also created an economic boom in the United States, which caused costs and profits alike to soar. Second, Hollywood set the standard for proper filmmaking.

ECONOMIC EXPANSION OF THE MOTION PICTURE BUSINESS

The explosion in the popularity of movies in the 1920s took place in a decade of radical change. It was an era of big business, and movie moguls would write the blueprint for the motion-picture industry's financial and economic success, the

AMERICAN MEDIA PROFILE   THOMAS INCE 1882–1924

Melbourne Spurr/Getty Images

Americans appear more interested in Thomas Ince's death than his life, even though this film giant virtually invented the Hollywood studio system. Filmmaker Peter Bogdanovich, so intrigued with more than seventy-five years of rumors, tried to explain Ince's death in the movie *The Cat's Meow.*

Ince entered films as an actor with Biograph studios in New York, but his work as a director won him fame. His first directing job was with Carl Laemmle's Independent Motion Pictures Company. However, Ince was discouraged by the company's bad management and utter disorganization. He solved the problem by introducing Hollywood to an assembly-line system of film production. It was a simple idea for success. A film would be preplanned on paper and a shooting schedule would be developed so that related scenes could be shot sequentially. Eventually all studios adopted his formula.

To facilitate his theories of filmmaking, Ince bought 20,000 acres of land near the coast in Santa Monica. He called the tract Inceville.

In 1915 he teamed with D. W. Griffith and Mack Sennett to form the Triangle Company. His goal was to achieve the spectacular effects Griffith had accomplished in his films. He nearly achieved it with the spectacular antiwar film *Civilization.* Three years later he established another studio, designed in the form of an antebellum Southern mansion. It was taken over by David O. Selznick in the 1930s. It became the home of Desilu, the studio of Lucille Ball and Desi Arnaz, in the 1950s.

third stage in motion picture development. One moguls' blueprint would be followed for the next thirty years.

With an abundance of movie personalities and talent to make films, Hollywood needed an efficient and cost-effective apparatus to produce and distribute the films to theaters on a weekly basis. Actor-turned-director Thomas Ince devised the plan for successful studio management. Ince, Hollywood's first executive producer, introduced the concept of the creative producer—the man who knows so much about pictures that he can plan, organize, and supervise the work of others.[18]

Ince set up several shooting units, which worked on separate projects. He divided the studio's artistic and administrative functions and introduced detailed shooting scripts, tight schedules, and production notes, hiring accountants to keep a close eye on efficiency and ensure strict compliance with budgets. Hollywood would follow the Ince studio system for more than three decades.

Ince may have introduced the studio system to Hollywood, but Adolph Zukor taught the world how to fully exploit it. He would provide the plan for the industry's economic and financial success. By 1921, Zukor was in control of Paramount, the largest film company in the world. Paramount had the stars, the production outfit, the distribution channels, and the control of 2,000 theaters.[19] He developed his power by signing such popular stars as Pickford, Fairbanks, Swanson, Pauline Frederick, Blanche Sweet, and Norma Talmadge.

He would advance the concept of a vertical monopoly in the film business. He suggested that a company would have complete control of its product—from inception to final presentation—if it could produce, distribute, and exhibit that product.

AMERICAN MEDIA PROFILE   **CONTINUED**

Ince was at the height of his powers when he died mysteriously aboard the *Oneida*, William Randolph Hearst's yacht. Hearst had planned a forty-second birthday party for Ince. Hearst's mistress Marion Davies, columnist Louella Parsons, silent film star Charlie Chaplin, and Hearst's production manager Daniel Carson Goodman, a licensed but nonpracticing physician, were aboard the yacht on November 15, 1924. Ince fell ill and died forty-eight hours after boarding the yacht. His doctor listed the cause of death as heart failure. His body was cremated and his widow left for Europe. The headlines of the morning newspapers screamed: "Movie Producer Shot on Hearst Yacht!" One story goes that Hearst mistakenly shot Ince in the head, taking him for Chaplin, who was having an affair with Davies. Supposedly, Hearst found the couple in an embrace and went for his gun. Ince, hearing Davies scream, ran into the room and was shot in the scuffle.

Another story is that a struggle ensued belowdecks between unidentified passengers. A gun fired accidentally, shot through the boat's partition, and hit Ince, who was in a room on deck. Still another story has it that Ince raped Davies' secretary, Abigail Kinsolving, aboard the yacht that night. Kinsolving gave birth to a baby girl several months later. However, she died shortly after in a car accident near the Hearst ranch. Two Hearst bodyguards found her body with a suspicious suicide note. Her baby was sent to an orphanage that was supported by Davies.

Still another twist to the story is that Hearst awarded Louella Parsons with a lifetime contract after Ince's death. Was it to keep her silent?

Ince's death remains one of Hollywood's greatest mysteries—certainly a topic for a movie.

Along with that, he also advanced the economic blueprint—block booking and "blind booking"—for the film industry. Block booking forced theater owners to buy in "block" all of Paramount's films in order to be guaranteed play dates for "star" films. If a theater wanted a Paramount picture featuring a star such as Pickford, it also would have to take, sight unseen, pictures with less well-known stars. He pressured theater managers to sign with Paramount, which meant taking an entire year's supply, 104 of the studio's pictures, enough films to change the theater's bill twice a week. Blind booking allowed films to be presold on little more than a promise that they would be made in the future.[20]

Small, independent studios without theaters didn't have a chance. If they wanted to produce, screens weren't available to them. Meanwhile, some smaller studios were absorbed by larger companies; others closed their doors. One theater owner, Marcus Loew, purchased his own studio, Metro, in order to make sure there would be a flow of films to show in his vast array of movie houses. That studio would be the forerunner of the Metro-Goldwyn-Mayer company.

Zukor's concept of vertical monopoly and his all-or-nothing block booking system would eventually fail. However, he would thrive and maintain his importance in Hollywood. In 1917, he sought Wall Street backing and began buying theaters, transforming them into opulent movie palaces.[21]

This emphasis on motion picture exhibition made the twenties the great decade of motion picture theater construction. Approximately 80 million customers a week attended one of the more than 20,000 theaters in the country. Some 400 to 500 feature films a year were being produced for these movie palaces. Each of the large

companies released some fifty-two films a year to allow theaters to change programs weekly.[22]

FILM AS A SOCIAL AND POLITICAL POWER

As Hollywood came to rule the film industry, Americans slowly realized the power
that motion pictures could have on the nation's social and political fabric. They
were, after all, the first of the major mass media forms to attain the status of a
"massive" socializing national force, and society simply did not know how to
cope with them.

From early warnings that silent melodramas and comedies threatened the capitalist order, the purity of the Anglo-Saxon race, or the progress of womanhood, to
contemporary claims that *The Last Temptation of Christ* (1988) is anti-Christian
or that *Basic Instinct* (1992) is antihomosexual, would-be critics have always assumed that movies have the capacity to arouse passionate feelings and instill ideas
in audiences.

An uproar over social control was the first indication that this new entertainment machine had become a recognized social institution. No sooner were movies
exhibited publicly than attempts were made to censor them.

Ministers, social workers, civic reformers, police, politicians, women's clubs,
and civic organizations accused movies of inciting young boys to crime by glorify-
ing criminals and of corrupting young women by romanticizing "illicit" love affairs. A loose-knit confederation of reformers, who ranged from thoughtful and
perceptive critics like Jane Addams to religious reactionaries like Canon William
Chase, rector of the Christ Church in Brooklyn, claimed that movies were changing
traditional values, not reflecting them, and demanded that government use its licensing and regulatory powers to censor this new form of entertainment.[23] For
Chase, films were "the greatest enemy of civilization."[24]

These moral guardians began to agitate for legislation to control this new
"enemy" of civilization. Chicago, in November 1907, enacted the first movie censorship law in America. The ordinance required that a permit from the superinten-
dent of police had to be obtained before any film could be exhibited. Police censors
could ban films if they judged them immoral or obscene, or if they portrayed depravity, criminality, or lack of virtue of a class of citizens of any race, color, creed,
or religion and exposed them to contempt, derision, or obloquy, or tended to produce a breach of the peace or riots, or purported to represent any hangings, lynchings, or burning of a human being.[25] Film censorship gained national attention on
December 24, 1908, when New York mayor George B. McClellan ordered all
movie theaters in the city closed after a year of heavy lobbying by the city's fire
commissioner, who labeled movie theaters a fire threat, "a menace to life." The
police commissioner agreed and also recommended that the mayor close all of
them.[26]

These early attempts at censorship culminated with a U.S. Supreme Court decision on February 23, 1915, in *Mutual Film Corporation* v. *Industrial Commission
of Ohio*, which denied the motion picture the constitutional guarantees of freedom

of speech and press. The ruling relegated films to the same entertainment category as carnival sideshows. The Court's decision stated in part:

> It cannot be put out of view that exhibition of moving pictures is a business pure, simple, originated and conducted for profit, like other spectacles, not to be regarded, nor intended to be regarded by the Ohio constitution, we think, as part of the press of the country or as organs of public opinion. They are mere representations of events, of ideas and sentiments published and known, vivid, useful and entertaining no doubt, but, as we have said, capable of evil, having power for it, the greater because of the attractiveness and manner of exhibition.

The ruling legitimized prior restraint, allowing a governmental agency to evaluate a movie before it was seen by the public. Following the Supreme Court ruling, formal censorship bodies—whether the state or city boards, religious institutions, or even the industry's own self-regulatory agencies—were given some sense of legitimacy. Meanwhile, more than 100 anti-movie bills were introduced in state legislatures in 1921. The industry was determined to fight these bills, as well as any attempt at national censorship, and to set up a policy of self-censorship and regulation of its own films that would convince the public of the producers' good faith.

To combat censorship bills at the state and federal level, the industry created a trade association, the Motion Picture Producers and Distributors of America. The association hired Will H. Hays, the postmaster general in President Warren Harding's cabinet and chairman of the Republican National Committee, to oversee the upgrading of morals in the movies. His selection could not have come at a better time. It was a time when Hollywood films reflected the change in the nation's moral standards. Sophisticated sex had become big box office, while divorce, seduction, and the use of drugs were presented as marks of the fashionable life. DeMille took advantage of this trend and explored the sexuality of marriage in *Old Wives for New* (1918), *Don't Change Your Husband* (1919), *Male and Female* (1919), *Why Change Your Wife?* (1920), *Forbidden Fruit* (1921), and *The Affairs of Anatol* (1921).

In addition, the tangled lives of Hollywood stars would accelerate a demand for action against the movies. Within a few short months, Americans read about the rotund comedian Roscoe "Fatty" Arbuckle's rape case, director William Desmond Taylor's murder, matinee idol Wallace Reid's death from drug complications, Pickford's quickie divorce from actor Owen Moore and marriage to Fairbanks, and Ince's mysterious death aboard William Randolph Hearst's yacht.

Something had to be done with Hollywood—"Sin City." The urgency was underscored when word got out that sound would soon be combined with the visual image. Such a sensation, leaders in the Catholic Church believed, would be irresistible to the impressionable minds of children, the uneducated, the immature, and the unsophisticated—which, it said, comprised a large majority of the national film audience. It also believed this audience was incapable of distinguishing between fantasy and reality. Thus, self-regulation or greater control was necessary.[27]

The Catholic Church became a powerful force in film censorship. However, the industry received a greater jolt in October 1929 when the stock market crashed. Virtually everyone was affected as the nation's unemployment rate neared

25 percent. The hard facts of America's dying economy shook Hollywood's dream factory.

SOUND MOTION PICTURES

Sound movies, the fourth stage in the development of motion pictures, were introduced at the precise time that an economic depression was taking hold. This would prove to be a short-lived happy coincidence for the movie industry. Sound movies attracted approximately 100 million moviegoers per week by 1929.

American Telephone & Telegraph overcame the frustrating technological problems Edison could not resolve, and this allowed one of the nation's smallest studios, Warner Brothers, to become a leader in film production. AT&T perfected an electronic sound-on-disc recording-and-reproducing system to monitor and test its new long-distance telephone network. It also invented the first true loudspeaker and sound amplifier. Combining these inventions with movie technology produced a system that could record sound and project it in very large theaters.

A desperate minor Hollywood company, Warner Brothers, gambled on the technology in an effort to solve its financial difficulties. Sam Warner learned of AT&T's inventions and set out to convince the head of the family, Harry, to approve. "Who the hell wants to hear actors talk?" asked Harry. He finally agreed, and Warner premiered its Vitaphone system, which used disc recordings mechanically synchronized with the projector. On August 6, 1926, it added a sound track to a silent feature titled *Don Juan*, starring John Barrymore. The picture was a critical and commercial success. Harry Warner telephoned Hays and asked if he would speak on film on behalf of the industry before that night's showing of the film. It was the first speech ever recorded for talking pictures. He said:

> No story ever written for the screen is as dramatic as the story of the screen itself.
>
> Tonight marks another step in that story.
>
> Far indeed have we advanced from that few seconds of the shadow of a serpentine dancer thirty years ago when the motion picture was born—to this, the first public demonstration of the Vitaphone which synchronizes the production of sound with the reproduction of action.... It has been said that the art of the musician is ephemeral, that he creates but for the moment. Now, neither the artist nor his art will ever die.[28]

That was followed by *The Jazz Singer* (1927), in which audiences heard Al Jolson sing six songs and speak some 309 words of dialogue. Next was the first all-talking *The Lights of New York* (1928). Despite Warner's success with sound, other studios were not yet willing to buy into it. Some had a large investment in silent pictures and feared the financial investment required to change equipment and facilities for production and exhibition. Others dreaded the thought of paying royalties to Warner Brothers or Fox for use of its patented sound systems, and losing face to a competitor. Still others knew that some of their high-priced silent stars could not successfully make the transition to sound movies.

The industry would see synchronous sound film become universal. Only 16 such recording machines were in use in 1928. By the end of 1929, however, 116 were in use, and some 20,000 theaters in the country were equipped for sound reproduction. That year Warner Brothers' profits soared to $17 million; Loews, Inc. to nearly $12 million, and Fox and RKO to $1.5 million.

The movie industry would see those profits turn into debits from 1930 to 1933, as America's economy died. After its huge profits in 1929, Warner dropped to $7 million in 1930, and then to a loss of $7.9 million. It would stagger into 1933 with a $14 million deficit. About a third of all theaters closed as attendance fell. Almost half of the eight major studios neared collapse. Paramount went into bankruptcy, and RKO and Universal into receivership. Fox was reorganized and eventually taken over by Darryl Zanuck's Twentieth Century. United Artists and Columbia barely kept above water. Only MGM, with Louis B. Mayer and Irving Thalberg at the helm, showed a profit.

In a desperate move to lure back customers, the industry cut admission prices and offered double features, door prizes, games, and lotteries as well as live entertainment. The double bill, offering two movies for the price of one, not only stimulated attendance, from 70 million a week in 1934 to 88 million in 1936, it also energized production, since the second feature on the double bill was a low-budget "B" movie. B movies helped maintain full production during the Depression and served as training grounds for budding actors. Those who did well in B movies were moved up to those with bigger budgets.

PERIOD FILMS REFLECT POLITICS AND SOCIETY

If Americans wanted to escape the harshness of real life, what did the dream factory provide? Historian Arthur Schlesinger Jr., reflecting on the film industry of his youth, said that American film of the 1930s had "a vital connection with American emotion—more, I think, than it ever had before.... The movies were near the operative center of the nation's conscious."[29] The historian Andrew Bergman found that from 1930 to 1933 American films were preoccupied with depression, despair, and anomie. Moviemakers, he suggested, did not intuit the yearnings of a national subconscious, but rather felt the same tensions everyone else did and wanted to represent them in various ways. Gangsters, prostitutes, con men, sleazy back-room politicians, lawless lawyers: a dreary parade of characters peopled the movies, bred by a cynical, burnt-out culture.[30]

During the first unhappy years of the Great Depression, the public wanted recognizable images of their own problems on the screen. The popularity of Warner Brothers' *Little Caesar* (1930) sent the message that the public obviously wanted a hard-hitting, naturalistic form of drama that took its themes from the headlines of the day. They got it in *The Front Page* (1931), *The Public Enemy* (1931), and *The Secret Six* (1931). Some films even brought reforms. After the showing of *I Am a Fugitive from a Chain Gang* (1936), based on an actual case, public clamor forced changes in the chain-gang system.

Depression romances with heroines Constance Bennett, Tallulah Bankhead, Joan Crawford, Marlene Dietrich, Greta Garbo, and Barbara Stanwyck depicted ladies who took to the streets or became men's mistresses in order to obtain food for their babies, an education for their sisters, or medicine for their husbands. At the same time, Mae West emerged in Hollywood as the woman who best personified the sexual revolution of the 1920s. She was kept by no man, needed no nudity to suggest sexuality, and both delighted and infuriated moviegoers with the way she flouted tradition. If any single performer in the United States embodied what film reformers and the code did not want in the movies, it was Mae West.[31]

Something had to be done, according to the Catholic Church, to fix America's moral decay. By 1929 a small group of Catholics offered Hays and the movie industry a formula to control film's moral decay. For this task the church selected Father Daniel Lord, S.J., professor of dramatics at St. Louis University and editor of the widely read *The Queen's Work*, which preached morality and ethics to Catholic youth.

After studying the Hays Office's "Don'ts and Be Carefuls," state and municipal censorship codes, and the objections of Protestant reformers, Lord drafted a Catholic movie code. Thrown into its mix were conservative politics, pop psychology, and Catholic ideology. What came out were rules that would control the content of Hollywood films for three decades.[32] The Legion of Decency, the B'nai B'rith, the Elks, the Masons, the Odd Fellows, and the National Education Association joined in to pressure the film industry "to clean up its house."

The Hays Office embraced these new guidelines, but it did little to enforce them. Instead Hays formally established the Production Code Administration to evaluate all films. He gave it total control over film content and named a lay Catholic, Joseph I. Breen, as its director. Films could not project a positive image of "crime, wrong-doing, evil, or sin." Criminals, murders, and sexual activity had to be presented so as to discourage imitation. David O. Selznick even needed a special exception to have Clark Gable (as Rhett Butler) in *Gone with the Wind* (1939) say: "Frankly, my dear, I don't give a damn."

The true aim of this system of self-regulation policed by its own members was to create a public relations mechanism to squelch any attempts by the federal government to impose censorship laws. No federal laws were ever passed, and the Production Code lasted until the early 1950s.

CHALLENGES TO THE MOTION-PICTURE INDUSTRY

Until the fateful morning of December 7, 1941, with the Japanese attack on Pearl Harbor, the United States was a neutral nation in the great gathering war. Whatever sympathies Americans had, most studios walked a tight line between 1939 and 1942. Any overt partiality in their films could lead to economic reprisals on the part of the offended nation and actions against showing the films in those countries anxious to maintain neutrality.

As the threat of war grew nearer, Hollywood films began to depict the joys and glamour of military life. The War Department was happy to oblige. Bombers, battleships, and the Naval Academy at Annapolis itself were available to producers of any film that might serve as a recruiting poster or simply as publicity for the armed services.

At first, American war films dealt with training rather than actual combat, using the military as a romantic background for a love story or musical. By the end of the 1930s, with Europe in flames, American pictures took a different tone.

Foreign Correspondent, Alfred Hitchcock's 1940 spy thriller, told Americans to prepare for war. Films, like A *Yank in the R.A.F.* (1941), *This Above All* (1942), and *Mrs. Miniver* (1942), that paid homage to the beleaguered British followed. The danger of Fascism to the human spirit was the subject of *Confessions of a Nazi Spy* (1939) and Chaplin's *The Great Dictator* (1940). Russia came under attack in *Ninotchka* (1939) and *Comrade X* (1940).

Once America entered the war, German and Japanese people became stock villains in films, while Nazi and Niponese brutality was exposed and denounced in *Hitler's Children* (1943), *The Seventh Cross* (1944), *Behind the Rising Sun* (1944), and *Blood on the Sun* (1945). American troops in action were depicted in *The Story of G.I. Joe* (1945), *A Walk in the Sun* (1945), and *Pride of the Marines* (1945).

Problems associated with a postwar world, emotional adjustments of veterans, coping with the death and loss of loved ones in the war effort, war profiteering, the black market, and anti-Semitism were the subjects of such popular films as Samuel Goldwyn's *The Best Years of Our Lives* (1946) and Elia Kazan's *Boomerang* (1947).

Generally, the war years were good to the motion-picture industry. Although production dropped by 40 percent, it was a boom time for Hollywood. Full employment meant people had money to spend. More than 87 million people went to the movies every week, returning record annual receipts of $1.7 billion.

However, the motion picture business would soon be delivered three swift challenges. First, the federal courts would press the film industry to divest themselves of theater chains. The second challenge would be a series of investigations of the film industry by the House Un-American Activities Committee (HUAC). The third would be the unexpected rapid growth of television.

CHALLENGES BY THE COURTS

In 1944 the government renewed its interest in antitrust actions against the motion-picture industry. During Hollywood's Golden Age of the 1930s and 1940s, the major studios had controlled their own destinies, putting into operation the vertical monopoly concept devised by Zukor. These studios produced their own movies on their own lots and then distributed them to theaters that they owned.

As part of his effort to pull the nation out of the Great Depression, President Roosevelt took a renewed interest in antitrust laws. At the same time, independent exhibitors found support from women's groups and religious leaders who blamed Hollywood for many of the evils in society. Their logic was that if theaters were returned to hometown merchants, the producers would have to make good, clean family films.

On July 20, 1938, the Department of Justice filed a suit charging Paramount Pictures, Twentieth Century-Fox, RKO, Loew's MGM, Warner Brothers, Universal, Columbia, and United Artists with multiple violations of the antitrust laws.

However, before America's entry into World War II, the government and the major companies signed a consent decree that lasted three years. The government would refrain from pressing prosecution if the studios promised to eliminate certain abuses of power and settle disputes fairly between themselves and independent exhibitors.

AMERICAN MEDIA PROFILE | LOUIS B. MAYER 1885–1957

"Louie B. Mayer came out West with twenty-eight dollars, a box camera, and an old lion. He built a monument to himself—the Bank of America," quipped Bob Hope about the Hollywood movie mogul.

A former junkman, Mayer became one of the most influential and powerful men in Hollywood. He also became one of the richest. His $1.25 million annual salary made him the highest-paid person in America.

Born in Minsk, in Belarus, Mayer immigrated with his family to New York and then to St. John, New Brunswick, where the young Mayer helped out in his father's successful junk and scrap metal operation. His father soon realized that all his son wanted to do was to hang out at the new opera house every chance he got. There the youngster saw his first movie.

At nineteen, the restless Mayer traveled to Boston, where he set up his own successful junk business. With profits from the business, he purchased a rundown motion picture theater in Haverhill, Massachusetts. He continued to purchase movie houses until he became New England's largest theater-chain owner.

In 1914 he branched out into the new business of film distribution. Two years later he put up $50,000 and took in 90 percent of New England ticket sales for the D. W. Griffith blockbuster *The Birth of a Nation*. He earned $500,000. Mayer was now ready to produce his own pictures.

He traveled to Los Angeles and started a production studio, first called Alco and then Metro. There he produced a series of teary films. Entertainment tycoon Marcus Loew reached out to Mayer, buying

---

Studio executives did not hold up their end of the bargain during the war years, when Hollywood grew rich and prosperous. Hearing the cry of the independents, the government reopened the case in August 1944. It asked for the complete divorce from and divestment of studios owning theaters. After numerous decisions and appeals, in May of 1948 the U.S. Supreme Court in *United States* v. *Paramount* ruled that the practice of "vertical control" was in restraint of trade and tended toward a monopoly. It ordered studios to end block booking and to sell off their theaters. Studios could now produce and distribute their pictures, but they could not own theaters in which to show them.

By 1952, Hollywood would see a restructuring of the studio system. Production of motion pictures by the major studios declined because they could no longer bank on automatic bookings for all the pictures they could make. The first to go were low-budget movies without big stars, because they could not get enough bookings in open-market competition. The court's decision also forced the studios to reduce their roster of actors, ending the contract system that had trained and developed new stars for the industry. Reducing production also meant that studios were unable to make efficient use of their big back lots, vast resources, and large stock companies.

In the mid-forties about 400 features had been produced annually—300 by the major studies and 100 by the independents. Every week between 80 million and 100 million people paid admission to see them in 18,719 "hard-top" theaters and 300 drive-ins. By 1960 the average weekly attendance—in 13,200 indoor and 4,600

controlling interest in Mayer's picture company and the Goldwyn company. MGM was thus formed; its signature lion became one of the most recognized icons in the world. Mayer would rule MGM until his ouster in 1951.

During the 1930s and 1940s, Mayer set the standard that all others tried to follow. He cranked out major motion pictures weekly, employing thousands of artists and technicians. He raised the contract system to a new art, using it to rule over a stable of Hollywood's greatest stars. He operated MGM as one big family, rewarding obedience, punishing insubordination, and regarding opposition as personal betrayal.

He was respected for his insight, especially his understanding of what the public wanted. And he gave the public films such as *The Big Parade, Ben Hur, Grand Hotel, Dinner at Eight*, and the Andy Hardy series.

In 1927 he founded the Academy of Motion Picture Arts and Sciences, the organization that awards the Oscars. In this way he attempted to create a management-friendly Hollywood atmosphere and keep control at a time of threats by unions to control the movie industry.

Although his competitors were interested in making the best movies they could, Mayer attempted to use the power of film to exert what he believed was the proper moral influence on the American public. Thus, his films were quite family oriented. He was politically active, serving for many years as California state chair of the Republican Party.

"King Louie" was dethroned in 1951 by Dore Schary, one of his production chiefs. He then became adviser to the Cinerama corporation, while trying to regain some control over MGM. However, he would never again reign there.

outdoor theaters—had dropped to an estimated 46 million. Of the 136 features produced in that year, only 70 came from the major studios while 66 were from independents. The trend toward fewer pictures, more of which were by independents, smaller audiences, and a decrease in the total number of theaters would continue throughout the sixties and into the seventies.[33]

However, while Hollywood was battling in the courts, a more serious challenge to the motion-picture industry was taking place in the U.S. Congress.

CHALLENGE BY CONGRESS

By 1947, conservatives and frightened liberals led the nation into a period of military belligerence and political repression that would climax in the early 1950s in the Korean War; congressional committees would investigate "un-American" activities in every sphere of American life.

No investigations were more persistent or publicized than those of the motion-picture industry. The House Un-American Activities Committee (HUAC) chose the entertainment industry as its special target for three reasons, according to journalist Victor S. Navasky. First, HUAC was "the tail on the Communist Party's kite," following wherever it flew. It was no secret that two Communist Party activists, V. J. Jerome and Stanley Lawrence, traveled to the West Coast in 1936 to set up a movie-industry branch of the party. Hollywood represented prestige of its stars, a source of financial support, and a chance to influence or control "the weapon of mass culture."[34] However, party members were never a threat in the United States.

By 1950 party membership was at 31,608, and sank to 10,000 by 1957, including a healthy contingent of FBI undercover men.[35] Second, HUAC chose Hollywood for its glamour, giving the committee the publicity it couldn't get in Washington. In its more than thirty years of existence, the committee was responsible for only one piece of legislation. And Richard Nixon was one of only two men of any repute who ever sat on it. Despite its dismal track record, it received large appropriations from the House of Representatives, particularly after the war. Finally, HUAC provided an outlet for antiliberals to let off steam. Some believed the committee was in the thought-control business and out to break the left.[36]

At first, the motion-picture industry shrugged off any potential threat. Motion-picture executives united to oppose HUAC's inquiry as unnecessary, punitive, and un-American, infringing on civil liberties. "Hollywood is weary of being the national whipping boy for a congressional committee," complained the Association for Motion Picture Producers, as quoted in John Cogley's *Report on Blacklisting, Vol. 2, The Movies.* "We are tired of irresponsible charges made again and again and again and not sustained. If we have committed a crime we want to know it. If not, we should not be badgered by congressional committees."[37]

However, a chill went through the industry when HUAC, with the help of noted witnesses, cited pictures such as *Mission to Moscow* (1943) and *Song of Russia* (1943), which were made when the Soviet Union was an ally in the war against Fascism, as evidence that the big screen was used to win converts to Communism. For example, novelist Ayn Rand told HUAC that she found Communist propaganda in the smiling faces of Russian children in *Song of Russia.*

To protest HUAC's activities, directors William Wyler and John Huston and screenwriter Philip Dunne formed the Committee for the First Amendment. A delegation of its members, including Huston, Eric Johnston, president of the Motion Picture Association of America; Lauren Bacall; Humphrey Bogart; Gene Kelly; Danny Kaye; and Jane Wyatt appeared before HUAC in Washington to protest its activities. When HUAC chairman J. Parnell Thomas opened hearings in the fall of 1947, he found that the subpoenaed witnesses were either "friendly" ones who didn't really know any names of Communists in the motion-picture industry or "unfriendly" ones who wouldn't give them. From the "friendlies" who led off the testimony, HUAC got a list of names witnesses said were Communists, many of whom were not. For instance, Robert Taylor said: "I can name a few who seem to disrupt things once in a while. Whether or not they are Communists I don't know. One chap we have currently, I think, is Mr. Howard Da Silva. He always seems to have something to say at the wrong time." He added that if he had his way, the party would be outlawed, and "they would be sent back to Russia or some other unpleasant place." Still another "friendly" witness was studio mogul Jack Warner. He named Howard Koch, who participated in a 1945 strike against his studio.[38] Warner later admitted that he had been "carried away" by the hearings.

Following the "friendly" witnesses, the "unfriendly" witnesses were called to testify. The first was John Howard Lawson, screenwriter and leader in Hollywood guild and union organizing. He angrily denounced the committee and refused to answer questions. He stated: "For a week this committee has conducted an illegal and indecent trial of American citizens, whom the committee has selected to be publicly pilloried and smeared." He was followed by nine other "unfriendly" witnesses, who also refused to answer questions about their political beliefs and associations, invoking the First Amendment to the Constitution. In addition to Lawson, The Hollywood Ten, as they came to be known, included screenwriters Alvah Bessie, Lester Cole, Ring Lardner Jr., Albert Maltz, Samuel Ornitz, and Dalton Trumbo; directors Herbert Biberman and Edward Dmytryk; and producer Adrian Scott. All were cited for contempt of Congress. Then after court convictions, the ten served jail sentences ranging from six months to one year.

Their supporters, the Committee for the First Amendment, collapsed. But more damage to free expression in Hollywood occurred when studio heads and principal independent producers hastily met at the Waldorf-Astoria Hotel in New York City. They wrote the Waldorf Declaration, which deplored the actions of the Hollywood Ten, and pledged not to "knowingly employ a Communist or a member of any party or group which advocates the overthrow of the Government of the United States by force or by any illegal or unconstitutional methods."

Their actions ignited an era of blacklisting, which denied employment to people who were suspected of opinions and activities on the political left. HUAC named more than 200 motion-picture workers as suspected Communists or Communist supporters. The accused could be cleansed of their sins by being rehabilitated. Admitted Communists were required to publicly confess and recant, including naming associates. Non-Communists with suspicious liberal tendencies had to repudiate their past political attitudes, behaviors, and promises to sin no more in a letter to the studio executive employing them.

To further discredit the ideas of the Hollywood Ten and convince the public that Hollywood was purged of Communists, the industry launched a major public relations campaign in early 1948. The vehicle was the Motion Picture Industry Council. It was an amalgam of anti-Communist liberals such as Ronald Reagan, Walter Wanger, Dore Schary, and Allen Rivkin and conservative producers such as DeMille and Y. Frank Freeman. Its purpose was to fight the blacklist, to let the public know that Hollywood was innocent of the charges of subversion. And any "repentant" Communist had to get MPIC board member Roy M. Brewer's OK before going back to work. Brewer was one of Hollywood's most visible and most powerful anti-Communists.

The consequences of the HUAC investigation were many. It damaged careers and reputations. Some screenwriters were able to sell their work under assumed names and at greatly reduced rates; some directors worked under pseudonyms on low-budget productions abroad. Others left the country. In addition, the content of Hollywood films changed as Hollywood attempted to convince Americans that it was not a refuge for subversives.

HUAC developed an obsession with Communist infiltration in all phases of the professional and creative domestic arena. The blacklisting period provoked by that obsession particularly affected lives and careers in Hollywood. "As far as the industry's cooperation with HUAC is concerned, blacklisting was not about Communists or democracy," explains Hollywood screenwriter Garrick Dowhen, who has done extensive research on the period. "It was about economics. It was an overt attempt by Hollywood studio executives to squash, or at least cripple, the industry's trade unions."

The trade unions, Screen Actors Guild, Writers' Guild, and Directors' Guild were established to protect the rights of those working for the studios. "One must understand that studio heads ran their studios like dictators," Dowhen says. "Studio bosses such as Harry Cohn and Louis B. Mayer hated the unions. Additionally Walt Disney was one of the greatest anti-union icons in the industry. Studios did not want to pay higher wages or additional creative supplemental incomes, which included compensation for work hours and creative rights.

"Men as ruthless as railroad robber barons ran the studios. Those blacklisted, including the infamous Hollywood Ten, were or had been socialists in their ideological orientation at a time when the entertainment industry—like all other American industries—was undergoing a social convulsion of workers' rights," he says. "These liberals supported social and political causes, including the plight of the poor and working class and an end to racism and discrimination. The cinema represented a powerful platform or medium in which they could try and change society."[39]

A second HUAC inquiry in 1951 insisted that witnesses name names of party members. By the end of the third hearing in 1953, some 324 artists had been blacklisted. Meanwhile, some began to fight back with anti-HUAC films. Carl Foreman's *High Noon* (1952), starring Gary Cooper, for example, was one of the powerful allegories of its time. Cooper's character stood up to those who would run roughshod over the rights of the town's citizens. However, at the time the film was made, few understood what it was saying.

It wasn't until 1960 that the blacklisting era came to an end. Then Stanley Kubrick openly hired Dalton Trumbo, whose *The Brave One* had pseudonymously won the 1956 Academy Award for Best Original Screenplay, to write *Spartacus*. At the time, actor Kirk Douglas insisted that Trumbo be named in the credits. "It was Kirk Douglas who helped end the cowardly system that terrorized and tyrannized this industry for almost a generation," says Gerald Levin, former chairman and CEO of Time Warner.

The blacklisting period infected Hollywood with a cancer that destroyed some of its finest artists and creative personalities. Hollywood also lost some of its steam to fight motion pictures' biggest threat—television.

CHALLENGE BY TELEVISION

Only one million television sets were in operation ten years after the National Broadcasting Company began regular daily broadcasts in 1939. Within a decade 50 million sets would be in operation, delivering a mighty blow to movie attendance. A direct correlation existed between the increase in television viewing and the decease in moviegoing. In 1951 movie attendance held firm in cities without television stations, while it fell 20 to 40 percent where television broadcasting was available. By 1960 weekly movie attendance had dropped to 40 million.

Before 1948, the motion-picture industry ignored television. One studio even forbade the word *television* to be used in executive conversations. Once the industry realized television's potential, studios forbade their actors, writers, or directors to work for television. They also refused to offer television any feature films. If that wasn't enough, they would not advertise their films on television.

With complaints from stockholders about dwindling receipts at the box office, the motion-picture industry did an about-face. For example, Warner Brothers embraced the enemy (television) and became one of the industry's most prolific producers of television programming. It was the first company to produce action shows for television. Its successes included *77 Sunset Strip, Maverick, Surfside Six*, and *Cheyenne*.

Meanwhile, other motion picture companies suffering box office declines opened their vast vaults of feature films to television. By 1956, television was broadcasting such shows as *Twentieth Century–Fox Hour* and *MGM Parade*.

In addition, the motion-picture industry introduced several gimmicks to counter television's popularity. American audiences were treated to full-color spectacles. Cinerama, which utilized three synchronized cameras interlocked in an arc to record, introduced full-color, wide-screen, stereophonic pictures. Images were projected at six times the industry standard onto a curvilinear screen. Viewers could sit in their seats and feel as if they were on a roller coaster or airplane. However, the expense of conversion and unfamiliarity with the techniques required by the new system proved cumbersome to filmmakers.

A wide-screen system that didn't depart from existing standards was needed. Twentieth Century–Fox would introduce CinemaScope, with a screen smaller than Cinerama's, curved only enough to accommodate focus. The good thing was that it required no major change in production technology or even technique. It was simple and inexpensive to install in existing movie houses. Paramount would introduce VistaVision, which provided a sharper image than CinemaScope, which tended to distort close-ups and to have inconsistencies in clarity, coloring, and definition. Still other systems such as Todd–AO and Panavision–70 used wide-angle lenses. However, stereoscopic three dimensionality (3-D), which similarly attempted to reproduce depth of vision, bombed at the box office.

Besides technological advances to woo audiences, the motion-picture industry began to focus on a new audience and a new type of production. Convinced that families would rather stay home and watch television, the industry discovered the potential of the youth market. It replaced traditional family fare in 1969 with movies like *Easy Rider*, about young wanderers. It cost $400,000 to make and grossed more than $7 million.

With the success of disaster movies such as *The Towering Inferno* (1974), motion picture executives decided to reduce output and concentrate on the production of big-budget movies. Spectacles such as Steven Spielberg's *Jaws* (1975), which took in more than $100 million, and George Lucas's *Star Wars* (1976), which grossed $127 million, and their sequels—packed with big stars and lots of special effects—attracted new, younger audiences yearning for escapist entertainment.

Developing new merchandising campaigns, Hollywood focused on the teenage market and saw success with a number of genres, including comic-book adaptations, *Superman* (1978) and *Batman* (1989); science fiction, *Star Trek* (1979) and *Back to the Future* (1989); horror, *Gremlins* (1984) and *Ghostbusters* (1984); pop musicals, *Saturday Night Fever* (1977) and *Fame* (1980); and high-school comedy, *Fast Times at Ridgemont High* (1982) and *Ferris Bueller's Day Off* (1986).

To entice the more mature audience, motion pictures were filled with explicit sex and graphic violence, including horror, *The Texas Chainsaw Massacre* (1974 and 2003); gangsters, *The Godfather* trilogy (1972, 1974, 1990); body count crime, *Pulp Fiction* (1994); and the road movie, *Thelma and Louise* (1991).

A wave of profitable, innovative, but often irreverent movies by a new generation of moviemakers has revitalized the American independent cinema. Spike Lee, Steven Soderbergh, Kevin Smith, and Quentin Tarantino made movies such as *Do the Right Thing* (1989), *Sex Lies, and Videotape* (1989), *Clerks* (1994), and *Reservoir Dogs* (1992), respectively. To capitalize on this wave, major studios have developed subsidiaries, such as Fox Searchlight Pictures, to produce similar films. Add to that list U.S. Latino filmmaker Robert Rodriguez, whose films have been box-office successes. The young filmmaker began his phenomenal box-office run with *El Mariachi* (1995) and it has continued with four more U.S. Latino films— *Spy Kids* (2001), *Spy Kids 2* (2002), *Spy Kids 3-D* (2003), and *Once Upon Time in Mexico* (2003).

In addition, foreign-language films have become big box-office in America, such as *Crouching Tiger, Hidden Dragon* (2000) and *Hero* (2002); documentary films, such as *Super Size Me* (2004) and *March of the Penguins* (2005); and Michael Moore's *Bowling for Columbine* (2002) and *Fahrenheit 9/11* (2004) also have been big draws.

ECONOMIC CHALLENGES

To produce such films, their spiraling costs shook the motion-picture industry, whose primary purpose is to make money at the expense of creative autonomy.

For example, the Twentieth Century–Fox production of *Cleopatra* (1963), starring Elizabeth Taylor and Richard Burton, ripped a hole in the studio's budget and brought about the collapse of the studio system. Originally budgeted for $2 million, the spectacle's production costs soared to a record $30 million. To recoup its money, the studio sold off a chunk of its back lot, and it became Century City.

Such debacles brought about the absorption of studios by various multinational conglomerates. For example:

- MCA Inc. purchased Universal in 1962, was taken over by the Japanese Matsushita Company in 1990, and then changed ownership to the Seagram 6 company shortly there after.
- Gulf + Western Industries took over Paramount in 1966 until Viacom acquired it in 1994. In 2006, Viacom split into two companies. One retained the name Viacom, which continues to own and operate Paramount Pictures. The other operates as CBS Paramount Television.
- Kinney Services acquired Warner Brothers in 1969. In 1990, Time Inc. merged with Warner Brothers to form Time Warner, Inc. Since 2001, Internet Service Provider AOL has attained ownership.
- Twentieth Century-Fox changed ownership twice in 1981 and is now owned by Rupert Murdoch.
- The Coca-Cola Company purchased Columbia in 1982. Then merged with Tri-Star before the Sony Corporation of Japan purchased it in 1989, for $3.4 billion.
- United Artists merged with Transamerica group in 1967. Transamerica amalgamated with MGM in 1981, only to be passed to Turner Broadcasting

Systems in 1985. Then MGM was bought back by its 1981 owner, Italian financier billionaire Kirk Kerkorian, in 1996 for $1.4 billion. In 2005, Kerkorian sold MGM again to a grouping led by Sony Corporation.

- Walt Disney Company owns Touchstone pictures along with Pixar Animation Studios, and Miramax Films.
- During Chapter 11 bankruptcy proceedings, United Artists was purchased in 2007 by Merrill Lynch Capital Partners for $500 million.

In consequence, corporate decision making was placed in the hands of accountants, lawyers, and even hairdressers who knew little, if anything, about the movies. Sony, for example, learned the hard way after it placed Jon Peters, a semiliterate hairdresser, and his soul mate, attorney Peter Guber, in charge of Columbia Pictures. Sony lost $3 billion before firing them.[40]

Costs also kept filmmakers from gambling on untried formulas. This has resulted in a concentration on sequels, restorations, and remakes, one of the latest being *Titanic* (1997), which cost $200 million—the most ever spent to make a movie. It also was the first blockbuster to reap more than $1 billion at the box office. Such costs—and profits—would stun America's first movie master, D. W. Griffith, but the power of the motion picture would not.

CONCLUSION

After Edwin Porter's *The Great Train Robbery*, movies became the poor man's theater. However, what American moviemakers were producing was nothing compared to films made by the Italians and the French. Though the Italian films *The Last Days of Pompeii* and *Quo Vadis?* were creating a sensation in America, most U.S. filmmakers were content with shorter films. David W. Griffith led the movement for longer films and showed America how to make powerful dramatic movies.

Movies emerged in the 1920s as part of *a budding media-centered culture*. The nation's growing consumer-based economy saw the public reading tabloid newspapers, purchasing new gadgets, riding streetcars, and flocking to movie houses. Americans became enamored of the big screen and the celebrities on that screen.

However, as soon as the entertainment machine became a recognized institution in society, attempts were made to control it. The history of motion picture censorship in America presents an excellent illustration of the confusion caused by attempting to reconcile an unflagging allegiance to abstract liberty with traditional desire to censor personal morality.[41] Those who believe that film needs a watchdog point to the fact that it has tremendous impacts on the social and political fabric of the nation. Politicians complain that film violence increases violence in society. They also believe that certain films may give an untrue or harsh vision of America and its people.

The good news for the motion-picture industry is that after many disappointing years, the six major companies saw in 2007 money from home video, television, theatrical, and pay TV expand 8 percent to reach $42.6 billion. Of that number, the United States contributed $24.3 billion and international $18.3 billion.

Besides finding ways to increase its profits, the motion-picture industry today sees piracy of its creative works as one of its greatest challenges. The Motion Picture Association of America and its member companies have launched a multi-pronged approach to fighting piracy. It includes educating people about the consequences of piracy, taking action against Internet thieves, cooperating with law enforcement authorities throughout the world, and encouraging the development of new technologies that ensure movies can be made available legally over the Internet and other digital media.[42]

RADIO AND ITS PROMISES

Orson Welles never claimed that his Halloween eve radio broadcast of H. G. Wells' *War of the Worlds* was intended to panic a nation. It was, he said, "the Mercury Theater's own radio version of dressing up in a sheet and jumping out of a bush and saying 'Boo!'" However, millions of listeners on October 30, 1938, didn't take it as such. In adapting the play for radio, Welles made a number of changes to heighten the dramatic effect. Under his direction, the play was written and performed so it would sound like a news broadcast about the landing of an invasion force from Mars bent on destroying the United States.

Fake news bulletins reporting that a "huge flaming object" had dropped on a farm near Grovers Mill, New Jersey, interrupted dance music a number of times. At the start of the program, Welles informed the audience that it was listening to a fictional radio drama, but if the audience missed it, the next explanation didn't arrive until forty minutes later.

At one point in the broadcast, an actor in a studio, playing a newscaster in the field, described the emergence of one of the aliens from its spacecraft. "Good heavens, something's wriggling out of the shadow like a gray snake," he said, in an appropriately dramatic tone of voice.

Another interruption included a statement by a voice that sounded like President Franklin D. Roosevelt. "While we didn't say this is the president of the United States talking to you, the voice was sufficiently resemblant that the inference was obvious," actor John Houseman said later. "That was the only, I thought, naughty thing we did that night. Everything else was just good radio."[1]

Meanwhile, panic-stricken listeners ran for cover, packed the roads, hid in cellars, loaded guns, even wrapped their heads in wet towels as protection from Martian poison gas, in an attempt to defend themselves against aliens. They were caught in a kind of virtual world in which fiction was confused for fact.

News of the panic (which was conveyed via genuine news reports) quickly turned into a national scandal. Some called for government regulation of broadcasting, which never went anywhere, to ensure that a similar incident wouldn't happen again. Others threatened to bomb the CBS headquarters.

People believed what they heard on radio. Though Welles wanted to entertain a nation on Halloween night, he later said his purpose was "to destroy the belief that radio was a voice from heaven." "Let's do something impossible, make them believe it, show them it's only radio," Welles said.[2] Others saw it as a prelude to the power radio could have.

In a *New York Tribune* column, Dorothy Thompson said that Welles' broadcast may have been "one of the most fascinating and important demonstrations of all time." It revealed, she said, the way politicians could use the power of mass communications to create theatrical illusions to manipulate the public. "They have proved that a few effective voices, accompanied by sound effects, can convince masses of people of a totally unreasonable, completely fantastic proposition as to create a nationwide panic. They have demonstrated more potently than any argument . . . the appalling dangers and enormous effectiveness of popular and theatrical demagoguery."[3]

How did radio become such a voice from the beyond? No one ever sat down and plotted its development. Unlike other media, radio's history is a complex web of technological and scientific achievements that had to be tied together. Most of these achievements were not accomplished by scientists sitting with scientific plans in high-powered laboratories. Instead, individual inventors, or hobbyists, tinkering in their garages or basements, ignorant of what others were doing, helped bring about radio's development.

Radio's evolution can be understood by looking at its development in six phases: (1) scientific achievements and the rise of communications giants, (2) radio stations, (3) radio financing, (4) formation of networks, (5) radio programming, and (6) regulation of radio broadcasting.

SCIENTIFIC ACHIEVEMENTS AND THE RISE OF COMMUNICATIONS GIANTS

The development of radiotelephony, the transmission and reception of sound via radio waves, was the first step toward achieving broadcasting. It required a series of inventions, including telegraphy, uses of electricity, telephony, and wireless telegraphy.

TELEGRAPHY

Samuel F. B. Morse, a painter of some renown, was the first to succeed in developing an electromagnetic telegraph, in 1835. The Morse telegraph used electrical wire with electromagnetically equipped clicking keys. Combinations of dots and dashes, known today as Morse code, represented letters of the alphabet.

After more than six years of struggle and rejection, Morse received a $30,000 grant from Congress to build an experimental electrical telegraph line between Washington, D.C., and Baltimore. That line opened on May 24, 1844, with transmission of the familiar words borrowed from the Bible, Numbers 23:23, "What God hath wrought."[4]

Following the May 24 message, Morse astounded crowds in Washington when he reported James Polk's nomination for president. Even more astounding was the fact that Silas Wright, nominated for vice president, declined by telegraph. A delegation was immediately dispatched to Washington to confirm the news. The committee even tried to change Wright's mind by telegraph the next day, but the members failed.

However, the success in transmitting the convention results and Wright's decline of the vice presidency via telegraph was enough for Morse to raise even more funds to extend the line from Philadelphia to New York. Simply, what Morse had done was to revolutionize communication and open its modern era in America. Before his invention, no separation existed between transportation and communication, because the speed of transmitting information depended on the speed of the messenger who carried it.

ELECTRICITY

Thomas Edison, born in 1847, twelve years after Morse invented the telegraph, wanted to be a telegrapher and send messages over telegraph wires. While selling newspapers along the railroad, fifteen-year-old Edison saw a station official's child fall onto the tracks of an oncoming train. Edison saved the child, and, in return, the boy's father thanked Edison by teaching him how to use the telegraph.

The training paid off. Edison eventually moved to New York City, where he spent a lot of time studying the stock market ticker, a spin-off of the Morse telegraph that transmitted information about stock market prices. Once he fixed a broken stock ticker so well that the owners hired him to build a better one. Within a year he sold the patent for the stock ticker for $40,000.

With this windfall, Edison started building stock tickers and high-speed printing telegraphs. He also improved the typewriter. By 1876, he built a new science laboratory at Menlo Park, New Jersey, where he promised he would devise a small invention every ten days and a big invention every six months. He applied for as many as 400 patents a year.

His favorite invention was the phonograph, which he built by accident while attempting to record telegraph messages automatically. The first words he recorded were "Mary had a little lamb." His phonograph was sold to the public at prices ranging from $10 to $200.

His most important contribution would come two years later, when he promised he would invent a safe, mild, and inexpensive electric light. By 1876 he had become a business partner of some of New York's richest people, including J. P. Morgan and the Vanderbilts. Their company would be called the Edison Electric Light Company, though the electric lightbulb had not been invented. Edison's promised invention appeared in 1879 after the expenditure of $40,000 and 1,200 experiments. By 1882 he invented a system in which many lamps could get electricity at the same time. It led to the world's first electric power station in lower

Manhattan. Edison's work toward the electrification of America would provide the second ingredient for broadcasting.

The wizard of Menlo Park eventually sold his interest in electricity, but from this beginning emerged the General Electric Company. During World War I its efforts would direct wireless transmission research and development work for the United States and its allies.

TELEPHONY

Two years after Edison provided light for New York City, Alexander Graham Bell linked long-distance telephone connections between it and Boston. Bell's invention of the telephone would provide the third ingredient for broadcasting.

Bell's interest in the education of deaf people led him to invent the microphone and the telephone. His assistant, Thomas Watson, fashioned the device, a crude thing made of a wooden stand, a funnel, a cup of acid, and some copper wire. These simple parts transmitted the first telephone call, "Mr. Watson, come here, I want you!"

A successful teacher of the deaf, Bell filed for a patent on the telephone on February 14, 1876, just hours before his competitor, Elisha Gray, filed notice to patent a telephone himself. Bell was able to demonstrate its potential at the Philadelphia Centennial Exhibition, and by 1878, he set up the first telephone exchange, with twenty-one subscribers, in New Haven, Connecticut. That led Bell to form the Bell Telephone Company.

After an unsuccessful attempt to sell his invention to Western Union in 1877 for $100,000, Bell and his investors decided to improve the telephone by expanding its services while continuing to battle patent infringements. However, by the turn of the century the company had passed into other hands and, after purchasing the Western Electric Company, changed its name to the American Telephone & Telegraph Company.

WIRELESS TELEGRAPHY

While Bell worked on his invention, a group of scientific discoveries launched wireless telegraphy. James Clerk Maxwell, a Scottish physicist, theorized that energy passed through space as waves traveling at the speed of light. He called them electromagnetic radio waves; communication signals could be carried by them. They were similar to the signals that could be carried over telegraph wires.

His theory turned into reality in 1887 when German physicist Heinrich Hertz constructed a device that included two coils or hoops of wire, one of which was an oscillator that produced radio waves. He found that the oscillating coil excited electrical current in the other coil. As he moved the two coils farther apart, similar results were seen. The first transmission and reception of radio waves had taken place. So important was his contribution that his name has since been adopted as that of the measure of all radio frequencies. However, he never promoted the use of wireless communication.

A number of experiments followed; the most promising was the work of Nathan B. Stubblefield in 1892. From his Kentucky farm, using a wireless telephone, he talked to a friend some distance away. During the next ten years, Stubblefield conducted further experiments, including the first marine broadcast, when in 1902 he sent a wireless voice message from the steamship *Bartholdi*, off the Virginia bank of the Potomac River, to receivers on the shore. Eventually, he said, his invention "will be used for the general transmission of news of every description."[5]

A nonscientist, Guglielmo Marconi had read of Hertz's experiments, and was determined to apply this new discovery to communications. The young Italian put together several elements, including Hertz's oscillating coil, a Morse telegraph key, a coherer, a radio wave detection device, and grounded transmitting and self-designed receiving antennas. By 1896 he could transmit and receive two miles or more on his father's large estate near Bologna.

His family was impressed and took the lad to the Italian government, but it expressed no interest in the discovery. The family then sent him to England, where the head of the British Post Office, William Preece, who had dabbled in wireless experimentation, encouraged the twenty-two-year-old Marconi to improve his system. Using electricity without wires, Marconi was soon sending signals that traveled eight miles, and finally transmitted the letter S in Morse code across the Atlantic to Newfoundland.

By 1897 Marconi attracted investors who put together the first wireless firm, the Wireless Telegraph and Signal Company, which became the Marconi's Wireless Telegraph Company, or simply British Marconi. Two years later a U.S. subsidiary, American Marconi, was founded and became the dominant marine and transatlantic communication company until World War I.

While Marconi was sending wireless Morse code signals, Reginald A. Fessenden devised the theory of the "continuous wave," a means of superimposing sound onto a radio wave. This sound could then be transmitted to a receiver. After three years of experimentation, he succeeded in adding voice communication to a transmission. His voice was one of the first to be broadcast by radio waves and heard by another person. That was on December 23, 1900, on Cobb Island in the Potomac River, near Washington, D.C. He said, "One-two-three-four, is it snowing where you are, Mr. Thiessen? If it is, would you telegraph back to me?" Mr. Thiessen, one mile away, confirmed. Radio broadcasting was born.

The same year, Fessenden asked General Electric to build a high-speed generator of alternating current to use as a transmitter. It was in place on Christmas Eve 1906, when radio's first broadcast, from Boston, went on the air. Hundreds of miles out in the Atlantic, wireless operators in the harbor were astonished when they heard the inventor play his violin and his wife, Helen, and her friend sing Christmas carols.

However, lacking the showmanship of Marconi and the salesmanship of Edison, Fessenden had difficulty marketing himself or his inventions. Moreover, Fessenden's own backers were not interested in voice or music communication. Eventually the partnership began to sour. His patents were seized, and sponsors believed they did not need him anymore. Once hailed as "the greatest wireless inventor of the age—greater than Marconi," the pioneer in wireless radio died a forgotten man.

In 1899, however, ships in distress found Marconi's invention valuable. His reputation grew as more and more ships and their crews were saved from severe storms. One of the more serious incidents occurred in 1909 when a fog off the East Coast of the United States caused the liner *Republic* to collide with the *Florida*. A distress call by the radio operator saved almost all those aboard.

The most tragic peacetime maritime disaster, the sinking of the *Titanic* in 1912, underscored the importance of wireless radio. Radio operators assigned to the luxury ship did not heed the wireless warning that icebergs were in its path. They instead told other operators to clear the air so that they could complete sending personal messages from the ship's passengers to Europe and America. Once the crippled ship began to sink, SOS signals were sent, but most ship operators were off duty. Only the *Carpathia* responded.

A disputed legend tells us that on that night twenty-one-year-old David Sarnoff picked up the *Titanic*'s distress signal.[6] Sarnoff began his career selling Yiddish-language newspapers at age nine, shortly after arriving from Uzlian, in the Russian city of Minsk. He worked for the American Marconi Company in Nantucket, the Arctic, and Brooklyn. In 1912 he got a job as an operator at the John Wanamaker store in New York. Wanamaker, foreseeing the possibilities of wireless, had equipped both his Philadelphia and his Brooklyn stores with powerful commercial wireless equipment.

Sarnoff, who was studying engineering at Pratt Institute in Brooklyn, was sitting quietly at his Wanamaker instruments on a dull April afternoon when he heard signals in his earphones: "*Titanic* struck an iceberg. Sinking fast." Sarnoff immediately passed this news on to the world through the press, and concentrated on seeking further information from the air. Pounding away with his key, he alerted all ships at sea within range of his signals. One of these, the *Olympic*, gave him the information that the *Titanic* had sunk and that the *Carpathia* was bringing survivors to New York. Sarnoff then established communications with the *Carpathia*, to get the names of survivors. Sitting alone at his receiver for seventy-two hours, he gave the world the only story of this historic tragedy.[7] President William Howard Taft ordered every other wireless station in the country to shut down, to eliminate as much interference as possible. Even so, it took remarkable skill and endurance in those days of weak signals, primitive circuits, and deafening atmospheric interference to maintain contact.

Thousands of people milled in the streets outside the Wanamaker store, many of them friends and relatives of those on board the ship; these people were given names of survivors as soon as they could be identified and transmitted. After three days and nights on the key at Wanamaker's, Sarnoff identified the last of the 706 survivors before he rose from his instrument, pale and shaking.

The repercussions of the tragedy were far-reaching. In the investigative clamor that followed, it was pointed out that a ship equipped with wireless was much nearer to the *Titanic* than the *Carpathia*, the chief rescue vessel, but her only operator was in bed. Obviously better wireless was needed for ships, the public and newspapers cried. Congress, pressured to act, soon passed a law requiring wireless equipment and operators on all oceangoing vessels carrying more than fifty passengers. The act also required an around-the-clock watch, with two operators, and an independent auxiliary source of power for the equipment. Within a year, more than 500 American ships were so equipped.

"Wireless" was a word on everybody's tongue in the aftermath of the tragedy, but, oddly enough, its very usage doomed it as the common word for Marconi's invention. People began to saw off "radio" from its full name "radio wireless telegraphy" and use it as a kind of shorthand. Within a decade, "radio" was part of the language. The U.S. Navy preferred the term *radio-telegraphy* and adopted it, but in time "telegraphy" was stripped from its usage too.

The effect of the *Titanic*'s sinking on the fortunes of the Marconi Company and Sarnoff was nothing less than spectacular. Every newspaper story—and there were thousands of them—constituted free advertising for the company, which was virtually certain to be mentioned in all of them. Wireless was suddenly in the public mind all over the world, and the Marconi Company was the largest supplier in the United States. Years later, Sarnoff said that the *Titanic* disaster "brought radio to the front and incidentally me."[8] He was on his way to a career as the guiding genius of the Radio Corporation of America, the largest such company in the world.

Before World War I, the general public knew little or nothing about radio except what the *Titanic*'s sinking had revealed. Those who were informed about communications did not take seriously Lee De Forest's revolutionary invention that he called the Audion.

With only a few exceptions, people could not visualize the Audion, which became the heart of radio. In general, the experts still thought of wireless, or radio, as an interesting gadget, a comparatively unprofitable service that presented no real challenge to conventional telegraphy. Chief among the exceptions was Sarnoff. In 1916 he proposed the bold and imaginative use of the new medium in a home instrument for mass consumption. In a famous document, known in broadcasting history as the "Radio Music Box Memo," he wrote to the vice president and general manager of the Marconi Company: "I have in mind a plan of development which would make radio a 'household utility' in the same sense as the piano or phonograph. The idea is to bring music into the house by wireless."[9]

He predicted that his "Radio Music Box" would deliver perfectly audible lectures as well as accounts of events of national importance at home. In addition, he predicted that baseball scores could be transmitted in the air by use of one device installed at the Polo Grounds. The same would happen in other cities. He said that radio would be especially interesting to farmers and others living in outlying districts removed from cities. "By purchasing a 'Radio Music Box,' they could enjoy concerts, lectures, music, recitals, etc., which may be going on in the nearest city within their radius. While I have indicated the most probable fields of usefulness for such a device, yet, there are numerous other fields to which the principle can be extended."[10]

His company received the idea with polite silence. It was rejected as harebrained by Edward J. Nally, general manager of American Marconi.[11]

LEE DE FOREST

Lee De Forest would get most of the acclaim, including the title "father of radio." One week after Fessenden's historic broadcast, De Forest, who said he "never doubted his genius," transmitted and received code via radio waves from one side of his laboratory to other. This reception was based on his invention, the Audion, the first triode electron tube to successfully amplify radio waves. It became an essential component of not only commercial radio but the telephone, television, radar, and the computer.

He was a pilgrim striving for a goal.[12] That goal in 1906 was to use radio to bring voice and music into people's homes. Specifically, he wanted to bring opera into every home and along the way become rich and famous. By 1910 he broadcast a live performance by Enrico Caruso from the Metropolitan Opera.

De Forest turned Marconi's invention around. He did not think of it as point-to-point communication, as Marconi had, but as a technology that could transmit something from a particular location to many other points of reception. In other words, he, not Marconi, conceived mass broadcasting.

Some, however, considered De Forest a thief. Others blamed his many lawsuits on unscrupulous business associates who took the vulnerable inventor for a ride. He was accused on more than one occasion of dishonest business practices. As early as 1903 he was embroiled in a battle with Fessenden. He apparently visited the inventor's workshop and stole one of Fessenden's designs. After three court appearances, Fessenden obtained an injunction against De Forest for patent infringement. But that was only the beginning of court battles for De Forest.

At about the same time, De Forest was discredited by another business venture that went sour. In 1902 he and Wall Street promoter Abraham White formed the De Forest Wireless Telegraph Company. To dramatize the potential of wireless telegraphy, the company gave public demonstrations to businessmen, the press, and the military, and it sold radio equipment. The War Department and the navy eventually became its clients. As the company grew, White made a public offering of stock. White was a good talker, but his business practices were less than ethical. His promises of what the company could offer appeared too good to be true. The company became insolvent, and De Forest was squeezed out of its operation.

It wouldn't be the last time that De Forest was associated with stock fraud. Ten years after the first debacle, De Forest found himself in court with a pair of new business associates who were charged with fraud in giving absurd and misleading statements to potential investors. The business associates were found guilty. Meanwhile, the court appeared to go along with De Forest's prediction that someday human voice would be broadcast across the Atlantic. Why wouldn't they? They were hearing this prediction from one of the nation's leading physicists and inventors. He was acquitted. Broke, De Forest sold his patent rights to the Audion to AT&T for $50,000.

EDWIN H. ARMSTRONG

De Forest became embroiled in a decades-long court battle with Edwin H. Armstrong, who worked at eliminating static in radio reception. Those listening to radio in the summer of 1928, for example, listened on the AM band, which was subject to various types of atmospheric interference. Some newspapers even included a weather forecast on their radio listings page to help listeners predict how well stations would come in that day.

To solve this problem, Armstrong increased radio signals, making them loud enough to be heard across a room. This became the basis for transatlantic radio telegraphy. His sister, Ethel, remembered vividly: "Mother and Father were out playing cards with friends and I was fast asleep in bed. All of a sudden Howard burst into my room carrying a small box. He danced round and round the room shouting, 'I've done it! I've done it!' I really don't remember the sounds from the box. I was so groggy, just having been wakened. I just remember how excited he was."[13]

Not until the late 1930s would others support his technology, follow his lead, and make regular broadcasting on the FM band a reality. To bolster his efforts, in 1940 Armstrong's supporters began publishing *FM* magazine, displaying Armstrong's picture on the cover of its first issue.

Such public displays infuriated De Forest, who believed he, not Armstrong, should be given credit for this new invention. What emerged was the patent battle of the twentieth century. In 1912, De Forest had developed a feedback circuit that would increase the output of a radio transmitter and produce alternating current. Simply, it made weak signals strong. By the time he applied for a patent three years later, it had already been patented by Armstrong. De Forest sued, with legal action lasting from 1914 to 1934. The courts would finally decide for De Forest, although technicians sided with Armstrong. Distraught over the court loss to De Forest, Armstrong committed suicide in 1954. As a result of this court battle, De Forest was not taken seriously as an inventor or trusted as a colleague. Although solid-state transistors replaced the bulky Audion tubes originally used in these devices long ago, one cannot deny that De Forest's inventions and enthusiasm paved the way for the electronic age.

The communications revolution based on the development of wireless transmission would have to wait. Ahead was a period of confusion and patent turf wars that would block its development. Each of the communications firms that grew from the above inventions owned different patents that were collectively vital to radio's development. It appeared that none of these corporations was going to budge.

America's entry into World War I temporarily ended the patent wars. All commercial and amateur radio equipment was either sealed or appropriated by the U.S. Navy. Now war contractors, which included Westinghouse, General Electric, and AT&T's Western Electric, were able to manufacture tubes and circuits for military radios without worrying about infringing on the patents of others. The government's pooling of patents advanced wireless communications. But once the war ended, so did the military's control over the patents. Some congressmen introduced the Alexander Bill, which supported the notion that the government should be in control of the nation's wireless communication facilities. The cry of civilian wireless interests, however, drowned out any attempts to pass the bill. Its defeat in committee underscored the belief that electronic communication facilities should be privately owned. On July 11, 1919, President Woodrow Wilson ordered all seized stations returned to their owners.

THE RADIO CORPORATION OF AMERICA

Just four months after the end of World War I, it appeared that the Marconi Company would have a monopoly on radio communications. The thought of a foreign entity, such as Great Britain, controlling American communications repulsed many Americans, including President Wilson. With the help of two naval officers, Admiral William H. G. Bullard and Commander Stanley C. Hooper, known as "the father of naval radio," a plan was devised whereby GE would buy the controlling interest in American Marconi, and would allow British Marconi to use its generators only in Britain. In addition, GE, which wanted to manufacture radio receiving sets only, would be involved in creating a powerful American wireless communications organization.

By 1919, Owen D. Young, general counsel of GE, set up the new organization, the Radio Corporation of America (RCA). Young also devised a series of agreements that would enable GE, RCA, AT&T, Western Electric, and the United Fruit Company to pool their various wireless patents. GE, AT&T, and the United Fruit Company in return received RCA stock. Westinghouse also received RCA stock after it later acquired patents for radio. Under this new agreement, GE and Westinghouse had rights to use the pooled patents to manufacture receivers, which RCA would sell; AT&T would control all toll radiotelephonic communication and have the right to manufacture transmitters; AT&T and Western Electric would use the pooled patents for making telephone equipment; and GE and Westinghouse would make transmitters for themselves but not for others.

Once RCA bought the American operations of the Marconi Company, Sarnoff was appointed commercial manager. Two months later, he was taking up the "Radio Music Box" idea with Young, in a new memo that forecast not only home radio but radio programs and a broadcasting system. This time he was taken seriously.

RADIO STATIONS

In 1920, RCA placed its first production order with GE, and a few months later Dr. Frank Conrad, a Westinghouse engineer, began transmitting music on phonograph records from his garage in Pittsburgh, Pennsylvania. To determine if anyone was listening, he asked, "Will any of you who are listening in please phone or write me how the program is coming in. Thank you, Frank Conrad, station 8XK, signing off."

He received requests from listeners to play specific records. Once a week listeners were treated to a live band that included Conrad's son. His concerts became so popular that a local department store advertised that it had amateur wireless sets for $10 and up for those who wanted to listen to Conrad's programming. Harry P. Davis, a Westinghouse vice president, saw the ad and concluded that his company could provide a market for receivers if it had its own radio station. Davis called Conrad to explain his plan. A transmitter was installed in a shack atop the East Pittsburgh Westinghouse plant and assigned the call letters KDKA just in time to broadcast the results of the Cox-Harding presidential election on November 2, 1920. A Westinghouse information officer read the results; he got the vote counts from the *Pittsburgh Post*.

Conrad certainly wasn't the first to provide broadcasting. In San Jose, California, Charles "Doc" Herrold, headmaster of a wireless trade school, began broadcasting in 1909. From 1912 to 1917 he provided music, news, and talk on a regular basis on KQW, now KCBS in San Francisco. His wife, Sybil, may have been the first woman broadcaster. Her program, music for young people, received assistance from a nearby store, which set up a listening room and two receivers, plus two dozen telephone receivers. This allowed her to accept requests from listeners, a rather common programming idea today. Despite these innovations by the Herrolds, most historians consider Conrad the first to reach the general public with continuous programming.

Meanwhile, Sarnoff made the burgeoning radio business a national institution overnight when he proposed to broadcast the heavyweight championship fight between Jack Dempsey and Georges Charpentier from Boyle's Thirty Acres in Jersey City, New Jersey. Nearly 300,000 people heard Major J. Andrew White, the popular editor of *Wireless Age*, describe Dempsey's fourth-round knockout victory. Within a year, radio had become a national craze, and stations were springing up across the country.

In the first two years of radio, between 1920 and 1922, Americans spent an incredible $100,000 for sets, tubes, headphones, and batteries. In another two years, the number of home receivers reached an astonishing 3 million. Most radio owners in 1924 drew their chairs up close to the gooseneck speakers attached to the new super-heterodyne sets so that they might better hear the throaty, fading voice of William Jennings Bryan, in the sunset of his career, speaking from the Democratic National Convention in Madison Square Garden. Broadcasting, Bryan proclaimed, was a "gift of Providence," and so it seemed to those who heard him.

However, newspapers and the film industry didn't look upon radio as a "gift." If anything, they feared it. Take some of the call letters of stations at the time. The call letters KFWB, for instance, stood for "Keep Filming Warner Brothers," and KTAR's call letters stood for "Keep the Arizona Republic."

RADIO FINANCING

It cost money to run radio, and many feared the idea of radio stations broadcasting commercial messages. In the August 1922 issue of *Radio News*, J. C. McQuiston, a public relations officer at Westinghouse, wrote that "advertising by radio cannot be done; it would ruin the radio business, for nobody would stand for it." Even Commerce Secretary Herbert Hoover in a speech that year to the national Conference on Radio Telephony warned that "it is inconceivable that we should allow so great a possibility to be drowned in advertising chatter."

At first, station owners covered the cost of radio, but this became a financial drain on them and their businesses, which included newspapers, educational institutions, department stores, and radio manufacturers and dealers. The May 1924 issue of *Radio Broadcast* announced a $500 contest soliciting the best essay on the topic "Who Is to Pay for Broadcasting—and How?" Some suggested that radio be financed by a tax on radio receivers and tubes. Others suggested a city or state tax to finance radio or the development of a common fund that would receive contributions and distribute money to stations. Still others suggested that wealthy individuals support stations.

In February 1922, AT&T advanced an idea to establish a national radio network supported by advertising. At the time, AT&T believed that it was the only company in the United States allowed to operate broadcast stations, with the exception of a few that either purchased Western Electric transmitters or those that had cross-licensing agreements. It introduced "toll broadcasting," a suggestion first floated in Hoover's report on radio advertising.

AT&T would provide facilities but no programming. Anyone who wanted to distribute a message to the radio audience would pay a toll or fee to use the station. The first sponsored program over AT&T's WEAF station ran at 5 P.M. on

August 28, 1922. It was a fifteen-minute talk promoting a Queensboro Corporation apartment complex. The fee for this first commercial broadcast—though evidence exists that stations in New Jersey and Massachusetts may have been the first—was fifty dollars.

Eventually, AT&T dropped such talks, believing the public would not welcome the intrusion of direct advertising into their lives. Instead, it would be less intrusive if advertisers sponsored or bought a program. One was *The Eveready Hour*, sponsored by a battery company, which first aired on October 6, 1924. It became a quite successful program and paved the way for advertising to become the source of financing for network programming.

FORMATION OF THE NETWORKS

Sarnoff, who became general manager of RCA in 1921, would take radio, "this gift of Providence," and mold it to his liking. One year after his promotion, he suggested an RCA-controlled company to specialize in programming. Through a series of negotiations, representatives of the radio and telephone groups reached an agreement. First, AT&T would get out of broadcasting entirely and receive a monopoly of providing wire connections between stations. Second, licenses and patent pool agreements were redefined. AT&T and Western Electric would not market receivers. Western Electric and RCA would receive a monopoly in manufacturing and marketing transmitters. Third, AT&T would sell its broadcasting activities to RCA for $1 million. AT&T also agreed not to own any broadcasting stations for eight years, under penalty of having to refund part of the price.

NATIONAL BROADCASTING COMPANY

With the agreements in place, GE and Westinghouse founded the National Broadcasting Company on September 26, 1926. It went into service on November 15, 1926, with a four-and-a-half-hour special from the grand ballroom of the Waldorf-Astoria Hotel in New York. The 1,000 invited guests and the millions listening on twenty-five national stations heard popular singers and opera stars as well as leading orchestras. The venture was so successful that NBC soon had two networks with two New York stations as their flagships: the NBC-Red Network, with WEAF as the key station, and the NBC-Blue Network, with WJZ as the key station. The networks were named by the color of pencils executives used to draw the path of the planned networks on a map of the United States.

COLUMBIA BROADCASTING SYSTEM

While getting his network off the ground, Sarnoff received a visit in 1927 from George A. Coats and Arthur Judson. They hoped to supply programs and talent to NBC by organizing a bureau to represent concert artists who wished to perform on radio. Sarnoff, unwisely, showed them the door. He had already formed his own artists' bureau within NBC.

The two shunned businessmen were more determined than ever to start a rival network. In January 1927, they formed the United Independent Broadcasters network with $6,000 they had obtained from heiress Betty Fleischman Holmes. Eventually they would join together sixteen stations as affiliates.

As the cost of AT&T line charges soared, the two went looking for financial support. The Columbia Phonograph Company feared that a rival manufacturer, the Victor Company, was going to merge with RCA. Columbia forged a partnership with Coats and Judson for $163,000, which would cover their debts. In return, their network took the name of the Columbia Phonograph Broadcasting System, and it was launched on September 19, 1927. One year later, however, Columbia Phonograph withdrew from the venture as the new network went deeper into debt. Coats and Judson were allowed to keep the name, which was soon changed to the Columbia Broadcasting System. For capital, the two persuaded Philadelphia residents to invest in the network, but in time the investors grew weary and backed out.

Meanwhile, a successful cigar manufacturer, Sam Paley, realized the power of radio advertising. In the summer of 1927, Sam and his brother began to advertise cigars on WCAU, and sales soared. He signed on to sponsor another show, a serial called *Rolla and Dad*. His son William, vice president of advertising for the company, had been vacationing in Europe. Though fascinated with radio, he was infuriated when he learned what his father had done without consulting him. The irritated young man told his father, "I don't want anything to do with this pipsqueak radio network, this phony chain."[14] However, he finally agreed to supervise the half-hour program that Sam had bought on the Columbia network.

In time, William S. Paley, born September 28, 1901, in an apartment behind a cigar shop in a Chicago ghetto, would become the only media mogul to rival Sarnoff. His parents, Sam and Goldie, had arrived from Russia in the late 1880s. After trying his hand at several jobs, including selling newspapers and working in a piano factory, Sam Paley moved into the cigar-making business. By the time he was twenty-one years old, he had saved enough money to found Samuel Paley & Company. Two years later, he married sixteen-year-old Goldie Drell, who was born in Ukraine. Her father, it is said, came to America to escape the hand of government agents who discovered he was peddling illegal whiskey.

After a series of business setbacks, Sam Paley eventually took his family and his cigar business, now renamed the Congress Cigar Company, to Philadelphia. William Paley, who earned his degree from the University of Pennsylvania's Wharton School of Finance, became the production and advertising director of the family business. And the family's business thrived. From 1921 to 1926, net earnings increased from $75,000 to $1.7 million, and yearly production jumped from 55 million to 255 million cigars. Shares of the family business were eventually traded on the New York Stock Exchange. The family decided to sell 200,000 of its shares to the American Tobacco Company for $13,750,000. Bill Paley received $1 million and the title of vice president from the transaction.[15]

The young Paley used the money to invest in the Columbia Broadcasting System Company. Investors first suggested that Sam Paley buy the network for his son. Instead he told Bill that the network was for sale and eventually gave his blessing and some of his own money. The Paleys assumed control of the United Independent and its Columbia network on September 25, 1928. The next day Paley, then twenty-seven, was elected president of the company and bought Paramount

Pictures as a partner. The network lost more than $300,000 the year he took over. However, under his shrewd management, CBS would overtake NBC in profits.

MUTUAL BROADCASTING SYSTEM

Meanwhile, WGN (Chicago), owned by the *Chicago Tribune*; WPR (Newark, New Jersey), owned by the Bamberger Department Store; WLW (Cincinnati), owned by Powel Crosley Jr.; and WXYZ (Detroit), owned by George W. Trendle, banded together in 1934 as a cooperative network, the Quality Network, and offered a group rate to advertisers. On September 29, 1934, the group changed its name to the Mutual Broadcasting System (MBS).

Unlike NBC and CBS, which had a stranglehold on their affiliates, requiring them to sign five-year contracts, Mutual offered one-year terms. However, four years later Mutual, which would eventually attract more affiliates than any other network, would tighten its contracts to hold on to its affiliates.

Scandal rocked MBS in the 1950s, when ownership changed six times. One manager was convicted of stock manipulation while another was accused of guaranteeing Dominican Republic dictator Robert Trujillo favorable mention on its news programs. Some 130 affiliates left the MBS group after these costly debacles.

RADIO PROGRAMMING

Paley was extremely innovative when it came to radio programming. He devised the *network option*. With this, an affiliate contracted to carry the network's programs also could carry any or all network programs that were not sponsored. Such nonsponsored programs were called "sustaining," because the network, not a sponsor, sustained their costs. NBC charged its affiliates about $90 an hour for each sustaining program offered in the evening hours. But with Paley's plan, an affiliate gave CBS advance permission to use non-network time during its broadcast day. CBS affiliates were required to cancel local programming when a new sponsored program series started and to air the new series. This meant that Paley could sell a program to an advertiser and guarantee the time it would air. NBC could not make that guarantee.

Paley's plan proved a boon for CBS as it increased its affiliates from 16 in 1927 to 112 by 1940. In comparison, NBC-Red and NBC-Blue had 53 and 60, respectively. NBC adopted a plan similar to Paley's in 1935.

Like Joseph Pulitzer, who had a high-minded conception of what people wanted to read, Paley knew what people wanted to hear and see. He also was star driven and sought the most popular performers for his network. Simply, he knew how to entertain America. Like William Randolph Hearst, who hired the most talented of Pulitzer's staff, Paley raided his competitor, NBC, for its comedic talents.

He also enticed stars to his station by offering them a contract and bookkeeping arrangements they couldn't refuse. Personal income taxes were high. Those earning $70,000 or more a year were taxed at 77 percent. It was more advantageous for stars to form their own production companies and incorporate, with themselves as their chief assets, and then sell the companies' physical assets to CBS for millions plus a share of the profits from future shows. The amount paid by CBS for the assets would be considered a capital gain and taxed at a rate of only 25 percent. Moreover, stars would continue to receive salaries from CBS for their performances. Meanwhile, NBC's highly paid performers had to pay taxes at the higher personal income tax rate.

At the start of Radio's Golden Age, 1930 through 1953, Sarnoff became president of NBC and competed with Paley for stars of stage and movies to perform in radio plays—*dramas* for the theater of the mind. CBS was able to nab a young producer-director-actor named Orson Welles to host one of its dramas, the *Mercury Theatre of the Air*.

Meanwhile, NBC introduced Americans to *soap operas*, which attracted millions of listeners. By 1939, about thirty-eight soap operas were broadcast daily. De Forest called such programming "tripe." "They could be ordered off the air very easily without much of a cultural loss to the American people," he said.[16]

In August of 1929, Freeman Gosden and Charles Correll changed the appetite of listeners when they went on the air with their blackface characters; they started at WEBH in Chicago before moving to the NBC-Red Network. About 60 percent of the national radio listening audience was tuned to the program, which started out as *Sam and Henry*, then became *Amos 'n' Andy*. At one time some 40 million listeners were glued to their radio anticipating the next move by the duo.

It was said to be responsible for the sale of 4.4 million receivers in 1929. In addition, sales for radio sets and parts soared 23 percent from the previous year.

Amos 'n' Andy became the longest running show in radio history and introduced the craze for *comedies*. Programs featured Red Skelton, Edgar Bergen, and a number of husband-and-wife teams, including George Burns and Gracie Allen; Jim and Marion Jordan, whose stage names were "Fibber McGee and Mollie"; and Jack Benny and Mary Livingston.

Many stars were introduced to listeners by *comedy-variety shows*, which appeared at the same time as comedies, and, for a while, became radio's most popular type of entertainment programming. Such shows featured a master of ceremonies, who introduced various types of acts and guests. They included the *Rudy Vallee* show (also called the *Fleischmann Hour*).

By 1931, many, especially upper- and middle-class listeners, began to tire of *Amos 'n' Andy*. Ratings plunged from a high of 75 percent on an average evening in 1930 to 55 percent in 1933. To reinvigorate its programming, NBC introduced *dramatic series programming*, including such shows as *The Adventures of Sherlock Holmes* and *Rin-Tin-Tin Thrillers*.

Those in the studio or listening at home helped popularize *audience participation shows*. Major Bowes' *Original Amateur Hour*, which began in 1934, eventually soared to the top of the ratings chart. Of the more than 15,000 talents to perform for Bowes, only one major talent—Frank Sinatra, appearing in 1937 in a quartet called the Hoboken Four—was discovered. By 1938, audience participation programming led to the creation of another type of programming, *quiz shows*. The air was filled with sports quizzes, news quizzes, quizzes for children, and quizzes that pitted men against women. NBC-Red's *Pot O' Gold*, which began in 1939, became one of radio's top-rated shows. Movie houses complained that the show hurt their box office sales.

A variety of *talk shows*, especially religious talk shows, also filled the airwaves. Harry Emerson Fosdick launched a long-running Protestant program, which became *National Vespers* on NBC-Blue in 1929. One year later, the *Catholic Hour* appeared, and the flamboyant Catholic priest Charles E. Coughlin offered commentaries on CBS. Walter Winchell, who specialized in gossip, hit the airwaves in 1932; he would reign supreme for many years.

Radio also offered *educational programs*. NBC led the way in 1928 with the *Music Appreciation Hour*. CBS offered its first educational program, *American School of the Air*, two years later. Beginning in 1931, CBS also offered listeners the educational *March of Time*, a reenactment of the previous week's news. The program was created by *Time* magazine.

Specialty programs hosted by disc jockeys became the rage by 1950. During this time, AM stations soared along with the popularity of radios in automobiles. In 1946, for example, the number of AM stations went from 1,004 to 1,520, and by year's end some 35 million homes and 6 million automobiles had radios. Three years later, however, national radio network advertising sales took a tumble as billings dropped from 22.5 percent for 1944 to 0.8 percent for 1947. By 1950 network billings were down $100 million from their 1948 totals. To help lagging advertising sales, radio took a page from its past. Disc jockeys, who had been around since 1935, began to cater to young audiences by launching *top-40 programs*, which played the most popular single recordings and used promotional activities to attract listeners. Meanwhile, black radio stations found a niche by playing rhythm 'n' blues and gospel music.

Of course, *political broadcasting* and *news* had been a staple of radio ever since KDKA broadcast the results of the Cox-Harding election. H. V. Kaltenborn was the first to offer weekly radio commentaries, in 1923, at WEAF. In 1930, he switched to three times a week after Lowell Thomas introduced the first daily fifteen-minute newscast on NBC-Blue. Thomas retired in 1976 after forty-six years with the network.

POLITICAL BROADCASTING

President Franklin D. Roosevelt introduced the use of radio as a political instrument and probably best understood its potential and power, even though others had used it before him. For example, President Warren Harding delivered a radio Armistice Day address on November 11, 1921, and spoke on radio during his administration.

During the Great Depression, Roosevelt's *Fireside Chats* soothed a desperate nation. Approximately 50 million Americans tuned in to his first chat on March 12, 1933, when he attempted to stop a run on American banks. His conversational style not only invoked an intimacy his audience never before experienced, but it also showed the persuasive power radio could have. Newscaster Edwin C. Hill, in a June 1933 article in *Radio Stars* said: "It was as if a wise and kindly father had sat down to talk sympathetically and patiently and affectionately with his worried and anxious children, and had given them straightforward things that they had to do to help him along as the father of the family. That speech of the president's over the air humanized radio in a great governmental, national sense as it had never before been humanized."

The White House did not always indicate whether a particular radio address by Roosevelt was to be regarded as a Fireside Chat. Thus, the exact number of *Fireside Chats* is questionable. Information from the Franklin D. Roosevelt Library and Museum indicates that there were definitely twenty-eight such addresses. However, some seven were not given the fireside designation. Two other radio addresses could be considered Fireside Chats, although the evidence for this is not conclusive. He garnered huge audiences, and his ratings for each broadcast were near the top.

Roosevelt's opponents in the 1936 presidential campaign attempted innovative uses of radio. The Republican nominee, Kansas governor Alfred Landon, submitted to a lengthy radio interview prior to his nomination. Once the campaign got under way, the Republicans used frequent spot radio commercials to publicize their platform. They even employed what many believed a deceitful tactic by Senator Arthur Vandenberg. The GOP paid for time on CBS in which the senator mimicked a "debate," asking questions of an absent President Roosevelt. The audience heard answers from Roosevelt, but they were selections from Roosevelt's early speeches. Many CBS affiliates refused to air the program.[17]

Four years later, Roosevelt was running again. Results from surveys conducted during the 1940 presidential campaign suggested two things. First, most voters considered radio more important than newspapers as a source of political news. Second, they tended to listen to candidates they favored.

During Roosevelt's unprecedented election to a fourth term in 1944, political radio came of age as networks dropped their regular programs for the first time in favor of continuous election returns and analysis. This would become the standard format in future American elections.

Radio News Broadcasting

The public also turned to radio for *breaking news stories*. For example, in 1932 the networks interrupted scheduled programming for several days to report on the kidnapping of the Lindbergh baby. Five years later, on May 6, 1937, listeners were riveted to their radios as they heard Herbert Morrison of WLS, Chicago, describe the *Hindenburg* disaster, the German passenger dirigible that suddenly burst into flames before landing in New Jersey. Morrison's coverage turned out to be among the most dramatic in radio history. "This is one of the worst catastrophes in the world . . . oh, the humanity," Morrison sobbed.

Radio obtained its hard news from the Associated Press, United Press, and International News Service, news outlets controlled by the newspaper industry. Fearing radio's encroachment on advertising revenue, newspapers pressured wire services to stop selling their stories to radio networks. Newspapers also stopped printing free listings of radio programs.

As tensions mounted, a meeting was called in 1933 at New York's Biltmore Hotel between the newspaper industry and the radio networks. An agreement was reached that said that radio stations would issue only two five-minute newscasts per day; offer commentary and not hard news; cease all newsgathering and obtain news only from the newly created Press-Radio-Bureau, which would take wire copy and rewrite it in radio style; and broadcast only nonsponsored news.

However, the agreement didn't last a year. Independent stations set up their own newsgathering agencies, and the International News Service and United Press decided to sell news to stations without restrictions. As the press-radio war collapsed, a new war was brewing in Europe.

WORLD WAR II AND RADIO BROADCASTING

World War II took radio by surprise. No manual existed for wartime operations. Once war broke out in Europe, Americans depended on this new medium to make sense out of what was going on. They would come to rely on Edward R. Murrow,

---

AMERICAN MEDIA PROFILE

FRANKLIN AND ELEANOR ROOSEVELT
1882–1945 AND 1884–1962

AP Photo

Franklin and Eleanor Roosevelt were the first media couple to occupy the White House. The Washington press corps was captivated by the thirty-second president and first lady from the day of their first press conference. The tendency of the press to go along with whatever the president said earned him the titles of "the greatest managing editor of all time" and "the best newspaper man who has ever been president of the United States."

Theodore Roosevelt may have brought the press corps into the White House, but Franklin D. Roosevelt knew how to manipulate the press. And he did it better than any of his predecessors, including the first Roosevelt. This is not to say that Franklin Roosevelt was loved by the press. The truth is that a majority of newspapers opposed him, especially between 1935 and 1940, when he pushed domestic reforms such as Social Security.

However, the majority of the press corps liked the president, who didn't really understand the news process better than any other president. He did understand how to deal with the press. He gave journalists the information he wanted the public to know. He even fashioned the leads of stories and told reporters, "I would write the story this way. Now go along and write the story." He ended the long practice of having reporters submit written questions. Instead, he inaugurated the practice of providing long, off-the-record background discussions. And he supplied experts to explain complicated issues to reporters. They, in turn, appreciated the president's gesture, and that is why the traditional adversary relationship between the president and the press was not as hostile as in other presidencies.

The results of this relationship were stories that were largely uncritical of him and his policies. Some editors asked their reporters whether they were so hypnotized by the president that they were losing their objectivity.

At the time, in an article for *Collier's*, Walter Davenport perhaps put it best: "With Roosevelt, this is the only time that I had the feeling I was as important here as a member of the Cabinet or of Congress— even more important. I think you'll find that feeling general. . . . Here, at Hyde Park and on his special trains, we're not only welcome but we have the distinct feeling—for the first time—that we belong there, that he's *our* President. Ours. See?"

Roosevelt's view of the press remained consistent during his unprecedented three-plus terms. Even so, Australian researcher Graham White suggested that Roosevelt believed that the press, especially owners

who never anchored a nightly newscast, to explain it to them. He would become the most famous name in broadcasting history.

Paley ordered Murrow; Paul White, the CBS news chief; and Edward Klauber, the second in command at CBS in New York, to organize a news team to cover the widening conflict. And they put together the greatest news team in history. It included newspaper reporters Eric Sevareid, Charles Collingwood, Howard K. Smith, William L. Shirer, Ned Calmer, Richard C. Hottelet, Robert Trout, Bill Downs, John Daly, Cecil Brown, and Winston Burdett. They became known as "Murrow's boys." But Murrow couldn't find anyone to cover Hitler's entry into Vienna on March 3, 1938, so he went on the air himself. That broadcast included reports

---

AMERICAN MEDIA PROFILE   CONTINUED

of the media, opposed him and took out their hostilities against him with widespread editorial disapproval and distorted news reports.

Thus, Roosevelt used radio to go over the heads of the press to reach the people. He understood the power offered by access to a mass audience. And he effectively used that power. For Roosevelt, radio was not just a tool to deliver speeches. "He humanized radio in a great governmental, national sense as it had never before been humanized," wrote Edwin C. Hill, in the June 1933 *Radio Stars*. He said the president spoke as if "a wise and kindly father had sat down to talk sympathetically and patiently and affectionately with his worried and anxious children, and had given them straightforward things that they had to do to help him along as the father of the family." Some 50 million listened to the first "Fireside Chat," on March 12, 1933.

Like her husband, Eleanor Roosevelt used the media to inspire the nation with confidence and a feeling of unity. In 1933 she conducted the first press conference ever held by a U.S. president's wife. She tried to help women journalists who were operating in the male-dominated Washington sanctuary. She held her own press conferences for 500 women journalists. The first lady regularly met with the press—something no first lady had done before or since.

An accomplished writer, Mrs. Roosevelt was technically a working member of the press. Her column *My Day* was syndicated through hundreds of newspapers. She was involved in two radio programs: *The Eleanor and Anna Roosevelt Show*, on ABC radio from October 3, 1948, to December 15, 1949, and *The Eleanor Roosevelt Show*, on NBC radio, from October 11, 1950, to August 31, 1951. A lifelong liberal, she frequently spoke out on these programs about controversial issues, from civil rights for minorities to support for the poor. She contributed money earned from the radio programs to charitable organizations.

The nation's newspapers made fun of her tendency to stand up for the underdog. Some newspaper articles were unfair and cruel, attacking her personal appearance instead of the issues she championed. That did not stop her.

The first lady regularly attended meetings of the Washington chapter of the American Newspaper Guild. She would sit in the front row, knitting. She also saw to it that toilets for women were installed in the Capitol's press galleries.

After the president's death in 1945, she returned to a cottage at Franklin Roosevelt's Hyde Park estate. There she told reporters, "The story is over." However, within one year President Harry S. Truman appointed her to the U.S. Delegation to the United Nations. In the Kennedy administration she served as a member of the National Advisory Committee of the Peace Corps and chairman of the President's Commission on the Status of Women. She also made many guest appearances on radio and television programs.

Radio captured the imagination of America's young. Even President Franklin Roosevelt tailored a message to the youth of the world using the new medium.

from "Murrow's boys" stationed in other European cities and New York. It was the first news roundup in broadcasting history.

From 1939 to 1941, Murrow brought the war into living rooms with his nightly "This . . . is London . . ." broadcasts. Americans were again riveted to their radios on December 7, 1941, when the Japanese attacked the base at Pearl Harbor, Hawaii. The next day about 79 percent of U.S. homes—some 62 million people, the largest audience in radio history to date—were listening to Roosevelt's "day that will live in infamy" declaration of war.

In June 1942, President Roosevelt established the Office of War Information (OWI), which coordinated propaganda and information services. Some feared that the government would repeat its World War I practices, controlling broadcasting and closing all civilian wireless stations. The president put Elmer Davis, *New York Times* and CBS news commentator, in charge of the effort. Its task was to clear all government messages and establish priorities. It was intended to meet three needs of U.S. audiences. They included: (1) the need for news; (2) the need for information as to what the public should do and when and how to do it; and (3) the need for truthful explanations of war issues, including news about enemies and allies, war production at home, and sacrifices the war forced on everyone.[18]

The OWI took three approaches to disseminating this news. First, with the help of the War Advertising Council, organized by the advertising industry, special programs were aired with radio and film stars appealing for Americans to join the armed services, contribute scrap materials, and buy war bonds. Its most successful war bond appeal took place on February 1, 1944, when popular singer Kate Smith raised $112 million for the war effort.[19]

Second, it tailored war messages to specific publics and inserted them into popular programs. For example, the government put out a call for housewives to bring cooking fat, needed for processing into glycerin for gunpowder, to collection stations on certain days. Such messages were written into radio scripts for soap operas and variety shows.

The final approach was a thirteen-week series that focused upon the government's role in present and past wars. It was sponsored by government and network funds and aired simultaneously on all radio networks. Some music and variety programs, such as *The Army Hour*, *The War*, *In der Führer's Face*, *This Is the Army, Mr. Jones*, and *This Is Our Enemy*, were meant to inform and lift America's patriotic spirit.

Meanwhile, the Office of Censorship issued voluntary guidelines. At first, networks reported events after the fact, since live reports, distrusted by military censors, were banned. Even weather reports were censored, because enemy planes could use that information to their advantage. The National Association of Broadcasters also issued a voluntary set of rules concerning what information to broadcast dealing with war production, troop movements, scare headlines, commercials within broadcasts, and sound effects that might be confused with air-raid sirens.

Many, with Murrow as the most vocal, objected to these restrictions. Censors, however, finally realized that radio would not hamper the war effort and allowed Murrow and other reporters into war zones and neutral foreign capitals to file live reports.

No print journalist, and only one radio journalist, ever deliberately violated the World War II voluntary censorship code after being made aware of it and understanding its intent. Journalists who possessed military secrets kept them. Liberal crusading columnist Drew Pearson and *New York Times* reporter William L. Laurence, for example, revealed nothing about the atomic bomb, even though they knew about it many months before it was tested and dropped on Japan.[20]

A notable broadcast took place on D-day, on June 6, 1944, when the Allies invaded France and radio called upon resistance groups to hamper the German army. Another covered the death of Roosevelt on April 12, 1945. The networks and many local stations banned advertising for four days while they covered the president's death.

REGULATION OF RADIO BROADCASTING

Under Roosevelt, the Federal Communications Commission, radio's regulatory agency, was created. Roosevelt certainly wasn't the first to want to "supervise" radio, always distasteful to news gatherers. However, some type of regulation had existed since radio's inception.

Theoreticians of communications argue that the people have an inherent right to the air, that in effect they own it, and therefore the people's representatives have a right to regulate it. Broadcast law is based on that assumption, but it has little if any basis in reality.

AMERICAN MEDIA PROFILE | ERNIE PYLE 1900–1945

Alfred Eisenstaedt/Time & Life Pictures/ Getty Images

Ernie Pyle used his pen to offer a foxhole view of World War II: He reported on the life, and sometimes the death, of the average soldier, at the time when Edward R. Murrow used his microphone.

On April 18, 1945, Pyle, one of the war's most famous reporters, died as so many of the soldiers he wrote about did. A sniper's machine-gun bullets killed him when he stepped ashore with a group of infantrymen on Ie Shima, a small island just west of Okinawa.

For three years his columns had entered some 14 million homes. These columns read almost like personal letters from the war front. His daily reports were written in a folksy style and included the names and hometowns of countless soldiers. The *New York Times* obituary described him as "the chronicler of the average American soldier's daily round." Eleanor Roosevelt once wrote in her column, "I have read everything he has sent from overseas." She recommended that all Americans read his writings.

Pyle became a writer accidentally. He had no ambitions for anything, but he heard that journalism was "a breeze" of a major, so he enrolled in the program at Indiana University in Bloomington. However, he quit some months before graduating to work on the *La Porte* (Indiana) *Herald-Argus*. He then accepted a position as copyeditor on the Scripps-Howard *Washington* (D.C.) *Daily News* for an extra $2.50 a week.

For the last ten years of his life, he wrote feature columns six times a week, mostly for Scripps-Howard newspapers. As Pyle's fame grew, other dailies and weeklies published his work. His columns

The Constitution says nothing about this subject, nor is public ownership of the air among the Declaration's "unalienable rights." Indeed, if "life, liberty, and the pursuit of happiness" are to be taken seriously, government control of broadcasting would never be among these rights. In fact, the air is controlled by those who have some reason to control it. Governments, recognizing the power such control gives, regulate broadcasting in every country, including the United States, exercising varying degrees of repression and censorship.

In America amateur radio operators were among those who first sought some type of government regulation. Soon after Marconi equipped a small army of amateur radio operators, the air was filled with the crackling sounds of nonessential chatter, which began to annoy the United States armed forces, especially the Navy. The military considered itself the chief beneficiary of the new intervention. The Navy, no doubt, had a just grievance. Amateurs constantly jammed its wireless communications. If Marconi's "little black box" was going to have innovative military uses that the navy was certain it had, something had to be done about it. That something, obviously, was control of the airwaves. Nothing could have been simpler, or more in the pattern of American political life. The navy approached its friends in Congress, which passed a radio licensing law in 1912. It placed radio regulation under the secretary of commerce. President William Howard Taft (the friend of armed forces, as his predecessors had been) did not hesitate to sign the

could be read in approximately 400 dailies and 300 weekly newspapers worldwide. Before covering the war, he wrote about Alaska, where he traveled 1,000 miles down the Yukon and sailed the Arctic seas with the coast guard. He also wrote about the lepers at Molokai, one of the Hawaiian Islands, after spending five days with them. "I felt unrighteous at being whole and clean," he told his readers. It is said that he traveled across 150,000 miles in the Western Hemisphere, wearing out three cars and three typewriters.

In the fall of 1940 Pyle covered the Nazi bombings of London. He then traveled to Ireland and to Africa with American soldiers. The *New York Times* said, "His columns, done in foxholes, brought home all the hurt, horror, loneliness and homesickness that every soldier felt." They were the perfect supplement to the soldiers' own letters. He wrote of heartache and death, always naming names of the young soldiers on the front.

Nobel Prize-winning author John Steinbeck, Pyle's friend, told a *Time* magazine reporter: "There are really two wars and they haven't much to do with each other. There is the war of maps and logistics, of campaigns, of ballistics, armies, divisions and regiments—and that is General [George] Marshall's war. Then there is the war of the homesick, weary, funny, violent, common men who wash their socks in their helmets, complain about the food … and bring themselves as dirty a business as the world has ever seen and do it with humor and dignity and courage—and that's Pyle's war." Pyle won a Pulitzer Prize for distinguished war correspondence in 1944.

On the day Pyle was killed, General Mark W. Clark said: "A great soldier correspondent is dead, perhaps the greatest of this war. I refer to Ernie Pyle, who marched with my troops through Italy, took their part and championed their cause both here and at home… . He will be missed by all of us fighting with the Fifteenth Army Group. There could have been only one Ernie Pyle. May God bless his memory. He helped our soldiers to victory."

bill, the protests of amateurs notwithstanding. There was no support, either from the public or the press, for the amateurs. No one could foresee the ultimate effect of giving government the right to regulate broadcasting as a matter of national policy. This law governed broadcasting until the Radio Act of 1927.

RADIO ACT OF 1927

The turning point in government control of broadcasting came in 1926, when the 1912 radio law was tested in court by the Zenith Corporation. The U.S. Court for the Northern District of Illinois ruled that the secretary of commerce did not have the authority to regulate the airwaves, as he had been doing for fourteen years. The American system of government, said the court, did not permit "the play and action of purely personal and arbitrary power." Instead of appealing, the acting attorney general of the United States agreed with this verdict. Obviously, a new law would have to be passed, but by that time it was July and Congress had gone home.

During that summer, all government restraint had been removed, and chaos erupted. No force within the broadcasting industry itself was strong enough to regulate it. Stations increased their power, moved to better spots on the dial, and broadcast at the hours that suited them best. Moreover, many new stations went on the air. The result was a clamor for a new law, and the demand was led by the broadcasters themselves.

The Radio Act of 1927 proved a better law than the 1912 law. Its principal provisions were to maintain the control of the U.S. government over all channels, and to provide for the use of channels, "but not the ownership thereof," by licensees.

In granting a license or transfer of a station, the guiding standard would be the "public interest, convenience, or necessity," a legal phrase of such splendid ambiguity that it has been a subject of controversy ever since. Every applicant for a license had to sign a "waiver of any claim to the use of any particular frequency or wave length."

Recognizing the already thorny issue of censorship, the law read: "Nothing in this act shall be understood or construed to give the licensing authority the power of censorship over the radio communications or signals transmitted by any radio station, and no regulation or condition shall be promulgated or fixed by the licensing authority which shall interfere with the right of free speech by means of radio communications." Then the act abridged its own promise of free speech by forbidding "obscene, indecent, or profane language."

Anticipating another difficult issue, the act did not require broadcasters to give time to candidates for office, but obligated the stations to treat rival candidates equally and gave stations "no power of censorship over the material broadcast under the provisions of this paragraph."

Taking a stand against monopoly, the act forbade licensing "any person, firm, company, or corporation or any subsidiary thereof, which has been finally adjudged guilty by a Federal court of unlawfully monopolizing or attempting unlawfully to monopolize."

The most significant error in the bill was the assumption that stations would control their own programming, a concept already nullified by the creation of network broadcasting. The act made only a last-minute promise that the regulatory agency would be authorized to make "special regulations application to radio stations engaged in chain broadcasting." Nor did the act deal specifically with the vital matter of time sales, except to note that broadcast material must be "announced as paid for or furnished, as the case may be, by such person, firm, company, or corporation." The imminent impact of radio advertising was thus either unforeseen or evaded.

Who was to enforce these regulations? The act created a Federal Radio Commission, and even before it was fully organized, it was already subject to heavy congressional pressure. Secretary of Commerce Herbert Hoover gladly relinquished his authority over broadcasting, and drew up a list of five appointees to the commission that President Calvin Coolidge sent to Congress.

From the beginning, the commission was under the control of Congress and subject to constant pressure from it, as it is today. Louis Caldwell, the commission's first counsel, later noted the "political pressure constantly exercised ... in all manner of cases."

COMMUNICATIONS ACT OF 1934

As soon as Roosevelt entered the White House, there was talk of a new law to replace the one of 1927. Roosevelt wanted it as part of his broad-scale reform program, but it was not well understood at the time that he intended nothing more radical than to put the telephone and broadcasting in the same jurisdiction, taking the former away from the Interstate Commerce Commission. The impetus for real reform came mostly from educators, who were convinced that radio, which they saw as the best resource ever made available to them, had been sold out to business interests, with the support and connivance of the commission.

Commercial broadcasting was depicted as a cultural disaster. To remedy that, Congress approved the Wagner-Hatfield bill of 1934, which had wide support. It mandated, among other things, that financially hard-pressed educational stations, shoved into a corner by commercial interests, be permitted to sell enough of their time to make such stations self-supporting. But the supporters of the old Radio Act, who wanted to continue the status quo, had no intention of permitting the commercial broadcasters to suffer competition; they held up their hands in pious horror. They exclaimed that too much advertising existed on the air, and now the educators wanted more of it.

In settling the dispute by compromise, Congress as usual not only failed to satisfy either side but closed the door to any kind of really equitable settlement. The Communications Act of 1934 created a new seven-member Federal Communications Commission (reduced in 1982 to five) and included the telephone under its authority, as Roosevelt had desired. Meanwhile the Wagner-Hatfield bill was quietly buried. With only a few low-power stations operating for them, educators were shoved to the last row in broadcasting.

The former commission had operated on a level only slightly above that of the old-fashioned ward heelers. The new commission suffered from the same disease that still afflicts it; that is, it is a political body and it is, on the whole, conservative. Worse, it was administering a law that was obsolete in 1927 and wholly mythological in the 1934 revised version, since its basic premise—that broadcasting in America was locally responsible since it was comprised of individually licensed stations—was wrong. It was as though the networks did not exist, yet by this time they dominated broadcasting.

One omission in broadcasting legislation and the whole body of law that grew up around it was evident. In the increasingly vital matter of news broadcasting, the FCC—in short, the federal government—was given an implicit power of censorship. The idea that the protection of the First Amendment should be extended to broadcasting was not even considered.

The FCC's most publicized and controversial actions took place after it launched a radio-network "monopoly" probe, issuing its "Report on Chain Broadcasting" in 1938. That report, which the FCC said was meant to protect individual affiliate stations from undue pressure by the networks, had important and broad ramifications. First, it limited affiliate contracts to one-year renewable periods. Second, it permitted stations to use programs from other networks. Third, it prevented networks from interfering with station programming and scheduling prerogatives. Finally, it stopped networks from controlling affiliate stations' advertising rates for programs other than the networks'.

The most important problem, according to the FCC report, was NBC's ownership of two networks, NBC-Blue and NBC-Red. The report proposed "divorcement," and on October 12, 1943, NBC sold NBC-Blue, its weaker network, to Edward J. Noble, who made his fortune manufacturing LifeSavers candy. In 1945 it became the American Broadcasting Company.

RADIO'S BLUE BOOK

During the late 1930s and early 1940s the FCC received numerous complaints about programming. After Commissioner Clifford J. Durr investigated and found widespread programming abuses, the commission acted. It hired Charles A. Siepmann, a former British Broadcasting Corporation executive, to direct a study and suggest criteria the FCC might use to evaluate program service.[21] One year later on March 7, the FCC issued what may be its most important programming policy document, entitled *Public Responsibility of Broadcast Licensees*, familiarly known as the Blue Book, so called because of its deep blue cover.

The Blue Book had five parts, which reported on the state of programming and the need for stations to observe broad guidelines to ensure that they meet public service obligations. It criticized licensees for carrying excessive commercials and lacking local public interest and public affairs programming. Simply, radio licensees had not fulfilled the promises they made on their license renewal applications.

The Blue Book offered guidelines. These included devoting more time to sustaining programs or network-supported programs, in an effort to balance and limit advertiser-supported programming; to programs that serve minority tastes and interest as well as serve the needs of nonprofit organizations; to local live shows and discussion of public affairs issues; and to new types of experimental programs.

Finally, the FCC spelled out its policy for renewal of licenses. The FCC would favor those stations that met their public service responsibilities by adhering to the guidelines. It would no longer routinely renew licenses just because all technical requirements were met. It now would look at the station's past programming record.

In short, the Blue Book was a center of controversy. It did, indeed, document the melancholy character of local programming. It was hailed by the public—spirited everywhere as a step toward better radio fare. Supporters even cast Justin Miller, new president of the National Association of Broadcasters, as a villain when he said, at least by implication, that he believed broadcasters had been mistaken to allow the FCC any rights whatsoever over programming. FCC decisions made in that area were "censorship," he said bluntly, and violated the constitutional guarantees of freedom of speech, as well as the guarantees in the Communications Act itself. He also decried as "hooey and nonsense" the notion that the people owned the air. *Broadcasting* magazine, the voice of the industry, began to advance the idea that the government was emulating the totalitarian regimes so recently defeated by controlling what went on the air.

For the most part, the Blue Book won the praise of government officials and citizens' groups who championed putting interests of the public above those of the industry. It was the foundation for continuing FCC actions and policies. One of those policies was the Fairness Doctrine, which required all sides of controversial issues to be aired. However, President Ronald Reagan's deregulation policies dismantled public interest mandates, including the Fairness Doctrine.

RADIO BROADCASTING IN TRANSITION

From the time of the 1938 Blue Book to 1952, America and its broadcasting system changed drastically. The nation's military personnel returned home from the war to work, to live, and to enjoy life in a peaceful world—though that world would only be temporary. For radio, it was an even greater time of change as American broadcasting moved from a small radio system to larger AM-FM radio and television systems.

By mid-century, listening to radio was second only to sleeping as America's favorite leisure activity. As Siepmann put it:

> Here in America radio is our main pastime. More than 90 percent of American homes have at least one receiving set. Millions have several. The average man or woman spends more leisure hours in listening to the radio than in anything else—except sleeping. The poorer and less educated we are, the more we listen—and naturally so. For radio—cheap, accessible, and generous in its provision for popular tastes—has come to be the poor man's library, his legitimate theater, his vaudeville, his newspaper, his club. Never before has he met so many famous and interesting people, and never have these people been at once so friendly and so attentive to his wishes.[22]

Radio is still popular. Recent Arbitron ratings show that over the course of a week, radio reaches more than 224 million people, or 94 percent of all people aged twelve and older. And more than 181 million people, or 76 percent of all those twelve and older, are listening to radio on Saturday or Sunday.

Spanish-language radio continues to be one of the fastest-growing segments in the radio market. According to Arbitron, the number of Spanish-language radio stations increased by 100 in the past four years, to 664 stations in 2002. Hispanic people continue to listen to radio more than any other segment of the population. They spend more than nineteen hours per week listening, compared to sixteen and a half hours per week for non-Hispanic people. And Hispanics are not listening to the same thing. Some have their radios tuned to all-news, all-music, or all-talk stations.[23]

TALK, TALK, TALK

As music formats split into smaller and smaller divisions, talk radio, which came on the scene in 1960, has become one of the most popular radio programming formats in the country. Talk radio was largely local in the 1980s, then went national in the 1990s when one in ten radio programs on the air were call-in talk shows.[24] As talk radio programs increasingly went national, a few radio superstars emerged, including Rush Limbaugh, Larry King, Bill O'Reilly, Sean Hannity, and Howard Stern, one of the nation's first *shock jocks*, a modern term for the sensationalist monologuist. Limbaugh and Stern have become something of media phenomena— with books, fan clubs, and TV appearances—as they turned talk into show biz and entertainment.[25]

Stern's four-hour weekday morning "blabathon" pushes the boundaries of what is permissible on the airwaves. "His routines are spiced up with talk of masturbation, the size of sexual organs, and an array of other sexual topics. Stern disparaged virtually every ethnic group in the country."[26] FCC fines against Stern in the 1990s totaled some $1.7 million. However, in 1995 the FCC wiped the slate clean after accepting a $1.7 million "donation" from Infinity Broadcasting Company, a CBS-owned company that broadcasts the Stern show. The "donation" was in return for not citing violations when Infinity's license came up for renewal. Indecency fines don't count against stations at renewal time unless they have been paid.

A controversial "wardrobe malfunction" during the 2004 Super Bowl halftime with singer Justin Timberlake exposing Janet Jackson's breast to 90 million viewers became the rally point for Congress to take action. The result was the Broadcast Decency Enforcement Act of 2005 signed by President George W. Bush. The measure, which amends the Communications Act of 1934, sets fines for broadcasting obscene, indecent, or profane language not to exceed $325,000 for each violation or day of such violation, to a maximum of $3 million for any single act or failure to act.

While the bill was being debated, Stern claimed that Clear Channel was beholden to Republican leaders and that he was being punished for turning on President Bush, whom he vocally backed in the past. Stern ended his terrestrial radio stint and began broadcasting on subscription-based Sirius satellite radio on January 9, 2006. He received an $85-million bonus after increasing its subscriptions. Two years later the U.S. Justice Department approved the merger between Sirius and XM, despite outcries from politicians and traditional broadcast companies. Critics said the deal would be harmful to consumers. However, the Department of Justice said the merger was not anti-competitive, noting that other media companies such as Clear Channel, CBS, or even Apple with its iTunes software and iPod music player served as alternate options for music and media customers.

Talk radio programs such as Stern's offer a mediated interpersonal communications experience for their audience and provide listeners with a sense of personal contact, as well as a forum to discuss and to learn about societal issues.

Why the proliferation of talk radio? Some contribute the wave of recent talk shows to the September 11, 2001, terrorist attack on the World Trade Center in New York. September 11 may not be the day the music died on radio, but it came pretty close, according to Chris Baker in the *Washington Times*. Since the terrorist attacks, news and talk stations' ratings have soared while the audience for many music stations has shrunk. Baker writes that in Washington and other cities, low-key newsreaders talking about the attacks, the war in Afghanistan, and anthrax scares replaced "over-caffeinated disc jockeys" as the rulers of the airwaves. One in five adult listeners have reported listening to a call-in political radio program more than once a week; these listeners are politically active and regular consumers of the news media.[27]

SOCIAL AND POLITICAL IMPACT OF RADIO

What impact does radio, this "theater of the mind," have on the social and political fabric of the nation? The President's Research Committee on Social Trends, which observed social evolution in the United States from 1929 to 1932, concluded that early radio had 150 specific effects. For example, the committee's final report said that radio increased America's interest in sports. It noted that enrollments had increased at colleges whose athletic games were regularly broadcast. Attendance at baseball games also soared after radio began airing the sport that was as beloved as mom and apple pie.[28]

However, radio has done a lot more than increase attendance at sporting events. First, it became a *vehicle of news and entertainment*. Listeners, for example, could supplement news of World War II provided by Ernie Pyle and other print journalists with radio coverage by Edward R. Murrow and others. Radio also provided the public with a front-row seat to Charles Lindbergh's historic 1927 crossing of the Atlantic and the sensational 1935 trial of Bruno Richard Hauptmann for the kidnapping and murder of Charles and Anne Morrow Lindbergh's infant son. Radio also recorded the 1937 explosion and midair fire of the German dirigible *Hindenburg*. In modern times, the public turns to radio, especially those that are battery operated, in times of disasters, such as earthquakes, tornados, and hurricanes.

Second, radio became a *powerful and influential political tool* beginning with the first scheduled political program in America on November 2, 1920, the coverage of the election of Republican Warren Harding over Democrat James Cox. Since then presidents have used radio, and no one was more effective at it than Franklin D. Roosevelt. His *Fireside Chats* calmed a frightened and desperate nation during the Depression. Presidential candidates soon began to appreciate radio's nationwide reach and their ability to give one speech on radio to many thousands instead of going from city to city to give the same speech. One modern candidate, Bill Clinton, used radio for his successful bid for the White House. It allowed him to communicate to younger audiences previously ignored by politicians.

Third, radio continues to *influence political discourse* and may be creating a separate entity of power in a "talkocracy."[29] Radio talk shows, along with political Web sites and political newsmagazines on cable television, may have substantial implications for democratic discourse in the "marketplace of ideas."[30] Unlike newspapers, TV news, and major newsmagazines, talk radio shows, as well as political Web sites and cable television, do not attempt to uphold journalistic norms of objectivity and equal time in their coverage of political events.[31] Thus, talk radio listeners may become more misinformed, contentious, and polarized—resulting in legislative gridlock or restricted policy alternatives[32] as they listen to sources that appear kindred in spirit.

Results from a recent study on talk radio found that listeners were more likely than nonlisteners to accurately answer questions involving political information without any kind of ideological element—such as how large a congressional majority is needed to override a presidential veto. Those who listened to shows with conservative hosts, such as Limbaugh, also were much more likely to inaccurately perceive that the federal budget deficit had grown under the Clinton administration. At the same time, listeners to shows with moderate hosts tended to have the lowest levels of misinformation.[33]

Talk radio appears to enhance civic-mindedness and to spur listeners to believe they can make a difference in the political process. However, those who don't feel in sync with the talk show host may feel isolated and choose to silence themselves in the political arena.[34]

Finally, radio in its early years *helped unify the nation*. It cut across cultural, sectional, and regional boundaries. Network radio increased the similarity among Americans because it communicated the same messages throughout the nation. It developed a national constituency for its programs and commercials. In doing so it had to avoid offending sectional or regional preferences. Forced to find the common denominator among all groups within the United States, radio became the thread that tied together all people.[35]

CONCLUSION

Orson Welles showed the power of radio on Halloween night 1938. However, it took a long time to get to that point. Radio's development followed many scientific achievements and court battles, and it sustained a vision that many labeled harebrained. Along the way were awful battles for patents, recognition, profit, and, finally, regulation.

Once radio arrived, it changed America and mass communications. Guglielmo Marconi's protégé David Sarnoff helped make radio a *vehicle of big business*. As a youngster, Sarnoff envisioned a "radio music box" that would bring entertainment and information into the home. As an adult he shaped radio's future as an executive with the Radio Corporation of America and later as chairman of the powerful National Broadcasting Company. William S. Paley, as chairman of the equally powerful Columbia Broadcasting System, was his only equal. Both championed national advertising as a way to pay for their systems.

Sarnoff and Paley made radio a *vehicle for information and entertainment* as they introduced Bud Abbott and Lou Castello, Freeman Gosden and Charles Correll, Jackie Gleason, and Lucille Ball, as well as the musicians Bing Crosby and Kate Smith. They also offered religious programming with the flamboyant Catholic priest Charles E. Coughlin and gossip with Walter Winchell. And news personalities such as Edward R. Murrow explained events during war and peace.

Murrow also helped make radio a *vehicle for reform*. As CBS vice president and director of public affairs, he developed in-depth programs and documentaries that reported on national problems, such as race relations, public education, and health.

Radio also became a *vehicle for free expression*. From the start, radio frightened newspapers, which tried to prevent the new medium from encroaching on their news turf. For example, independent broadcasters were upset when Sarnoff and Paley joined the American Newspaper Publishers Association in creating the Press-Radio Bureau, which provided "limited" daily news bulletins to radio. To curb the crackling chaos of the airwaves, the government reigned in some of radio's freedom.

The Radio Act of 1912 gave the secretary of commerce the job of regulating the number of stations and assigning frequencies. The Radio Act of 1927 and the Communications Act of 1934 created commissions that would have broad powers over radio.

Radio offered many promises. Some thought it would advance peace, democracy, religion, and education. Early radio did deliver one thing. It made the nation homogenous for the first time. It became the thread that tied everyone and everything together.

Today's radio consumers can listen to a variety of stations that meet their needs, whether for talk or news or music. They can turn to stations that broadcast entirely in Spanish, Chinese, Japanese, Italian, or Armenian, to name a few. They can listen to all classical, jazz, disco, or Italian music radio stations. Thus, in modern America, radio may no longer be the thread that ties the nation together. It may be doing quite the opposite.

For some, such as William Jennings Bryan, radio was "the gift of Providence." For others, it was the "voice of Providence" that Orson Welles, on that fateful 1938 Halloween night, wanted to destroy. Instead, Welles, more than anyone, may have shown how powerful this "voice from heaven" could become.

However, by 1952 an even louder voice—whether it, too, was from Providence is debatable—was looming. It was the voice of television, and David Sarnoff could not have been happier.

TELEVISION: PROGRESS AND PROBLEMS

One day in January 1929 thirty-nine-year-old Vladimir Kosmo Zworykin, an engineer for the Westinghouse Electric and Manufacturing Company of East Pittsburgh, and thirty-seven-year-old David Sarnoff, vice president and general manager of RCA, held what is considered one of the most decisive meetings in industrial annals. It brought together television's leading inventor and the executive who would guide its development.

Sarnoff, sitting behind an immense desk and smoking an immense cigar, listened intently as Zworykin told his future boss about his dream of developing electronic television.

The RCA executive, who years earlier envisioned a "radio music box" that brought music, baseball games, and information into the house by wireless, heard Zworykin propose a television set cheap and small enough for an average family's living room. It would be maintenance free and could be operated as simply as a radio. Despite their excitement, the two dreamers had no way of foreseeing the long, long battle—which they would eventually win—to perfect television.

EARLY TV INVENTORS

By 1929 the dream of television was not new. For years inventors tried to perfect technology to bring about "visual telegraphy," "visual listening," "audiovision," "telectroscopy," "telephonoscope," or "hear-seeing." For example, in 1880 the French engineer Maurice LeBlanc published an article in *La Lumière Electrique* outlining a concept that would remain the basis of television. He described a scanning mechanism that capitalized on the retina's finite capacity to temporarily retain an image. He wrote that a single photocell could register part of the picture to be transmitted at a time. As with a typewriter, the transmission would start at the upper left corner of a picture, proceed across the page, and then return to repeat the process from a slightly lower point on the left-hand side.[1]

The picture would have to be scanned within a tenth of a second, and the receiving set would have to be perfectly synchronized in order to reproduce the picture. However, a method of scanning was needed. The solution came from German engineer Paul Nipkow, who at the age of twenty-three took out a German patent for a spinning disc in 1884 that would become the basis for the first working television system.

However, Nipkow faced insurmountable problems in refining his invention. He even abandoned the idea for a while. But the Nazi government, so proud that Nipkow planted the seed of television in the Fatherland, offered him a public rebirth of sorts. Hitler even signed an edict proclaiming him the only person he recognized as "the inventor of television."[2]

Nipkow's scanning disc ignited a series of experiments. Between 1890 and 1920 British, American, Russian, and German scientists made attempts to perfect the television set on the basis of Nipkow's invention. Scottish inventor John L. Baird proved the most successful. Baird was a character of sorts who attempted to market one idea after another. He failed at inventing a cure for hemorrhoids, failed at importing marmalade and soap, failed at developing a rustless glass razor, and failed at creating diamonds. His only success was the Baird Undersock. Baird suffered from cold feet, and after a number of trials, he found that an extra layer of cotton inside the sock provided warmth.

A visionary, Baird began dabbling with electricity. After a number of attempts, he began to build what would become the world's first working television set by purchasing an old hatbox and a pair of scissors, some darning needles, a few bicycle light lenses, a used tea chest, and a great deal of sealing wax and glue. Electric batteries were added, transformers and neon lamps appeared, and at last to his great joy he was able to show the shadow of a little cross transmitted over a few feet.[3]

His goal now was to attract investors who could see the commercial potential of his invention. However, no one came forward. So he bought an ad in the *London Times*:

> Seeing by wireless. Inventor of apparatus wishes to hear from someone who will assist, not financially, in making working model. Write Box S 686. The *Times*. E.C.4.[4]

He received two replies. Skeptics assailed Baird's invention, adding to his frustration as he attempted to perfect his system. Finally, on January 26, 1926, he conducted the first public demonstration of a live television picture in London. Faint and often blurred images were transmitted from one room to another. Two years later, however, he televised a woman's image from London to Hartsdale, New York. In that same year he transmitted to the liner *Berengaria*, which was a thousand miles at sea. Six years later, more than 4,000 people in a London movie house saw Baird's televised pictures of the English Derby on a large screen. Baird was on a roll—or so he thought.

However, a Russian immigrant and a Utah farm boy would challenge Baird's mechanical scanning system. Their electronic systems would eventually lead to

Baird's defeat at the hands of American corporate giants General Electric and Westinghouse—under the aegis of the Radio Corporation of America.

ZWORYKIN, SARNOFF, AND FARNSWORTH

Growing up in the provincial town of Mourom as a member of Russia's pre-Revolutionary upper bourgeoisie, Zworykin had a passion for science. As a university student, he was usually found assisting classmates in the physics laboratory. Seeing his enthusiasm for science, Professor Boris Rosing in 1910 invited Zworykin to help him get his television system to work. Rosing had applied for his first television patent, perhaps the most important television patent since Nipkow's 1884 spinning disc, in 1907. His system, a forerunner for an electronic television receiver, used a mechanical scanner at the pickup end and a cold cathode tube as a receiver. Though their rudimentary television receivers hadn't worked very well, Zworykin learned that the future of television's development lay in the potential of the cathode-ray tube.

After the tumult of the Russian Revolution and facing the prospect of a bleak existence, Zworykin traveled to New York, where he was determined to succeed as a scientist. He was hired by Westinghouse Research Laboratory in Pittsburgh, but when he and other employees were forced to take a 10 percent pay cut because of an economic downturn, he quit. He was eventually hired back with the promise that he could work part time on his television concept. Westinghouse's commitment paid off. In 1923, he began work on a camera tube that had been envisioned by Campbell Swinton in 1911.

Swinton proposed an electronic television, but Baird had convinced him that television's future lay in a mechanical, not electronic, system. Years later he realized that Baird was wrong. In July of 1928, he came close to calling Baird a fraud. He wrote in the *London Times*:

> At present, with the mechanically operated devices employed by all demonstrators, both in this country and in America, all that has been found possible is to transmit very simple pictures [which] can with a certain amount of imagination be recognized. Now, however, the public are being led to expect, in the near future, that, sitting at home in their armchairs, they will be able, with comparatively inexpensive apparatus, to witness moving images approximating in quality to those of the cinematograph.... Such achievements are obviously beyond the possible capacity of any mechanism with material moving parts ... and the only way it can ever be accomplished is by ... using the vastly superior agency of electrons.[5]

Drawing upon the works of Swinton, Zworykin developed the first electronic television camera tube—the iconoscope, which he patented in 1923. Three years later he invented the kinescope, a cathode-ray tube, the core of a receiving unit for an all-electronic system.

With Sarnoff's help, he joined the Westinghouse research unit in 1929. A year later, Westinghouse was embroiled in an antitrust lawsuit. The court finally ordered Westinghouse and General Electric to separate from RCA. Zworykin joined the large RCA research team in New Jersey, to the delight of Sarnoff. However, the duo would have to share the title of "father of television" with a brilliant farm boy.

While his classmates were reading *Superman*, Philo Farnsworth was reading *Science and Invention* as well as other popular technical magazines. He was fascinated by efforts to transmit pictures by radio and read of early television systems based on Nipkow's disc. He realized that a mechanical system would never be fast enough to produce a clear picture of live action.

Though he was only fifteen, he, like Swinton, was convinced that television's future lay in an electronic system. He spent his after-school hours explaining his system to his high school chemistry teacher, Justin Tolman. The baffled schoolteacher, who years later would serve as an important witness in patent suits between Farnsworth and RCA, encouraged the young inventor. The system Farnsworth outlined to his teacher almost mimicked that of Zworykin, whom he had never heard of.

Years later he received financial backing for his initial experiments from a professional fund-raiser, George Everson, who met Farnsworth while working on a community chest drive. He told Everson about his television idea. Everson asked how much and how long he thought it would take to develop it. "Six months and five thousand dollars," Farnsworth said. Everson took Farnsworth and Farnsworth's wife, Pem, who worked in his laboratory, back to California and set him up with equipment in an apartment—first in Los Angeles, later in San Francisco—while securing financial backers.[6]

However, it took more time and money than Farnsworth predicted. On September 7, 1927, he offered his first public demonstration, transmitting various graphic designs, including a dollar sign. He applied for a patent in the same year, to the shock of RCA, which contested the application. In August 1930, the twenty-four-year-old got his patent.

At the time, Zworykin had been taken off television work by Westinghouse, which, to his astonishment, saw a future in a mechanical, not electronic, system. He was advised by Sam Kintner, a Westinghouse vice president and one of Zworykin's few supporters, to discuss his system with Sarnoff. He took the advice and called Sarnoff 's secretary to make an appointment—the most important of his life—in 1929.

Sarnoff and the RCA patent attorneys were aware of Farnsworth's activities. A long series of patent litigation suits between the two groups had already begun. Sarnoff, meanwhile, asked Zworykin, who was now an RCA employee, to visit Farnsworth's laboratory. Zworykin realized that Farnsworth's cathode-ray picture tube could not produce as bright a picture as his own Kinescope. But Farnsworth's dissector camera tube, essential for picture transmission, was far superior to the first crude electronic camera tubes Zworykin was building. Zworykin also realized that Farnsworth was the only one to have perfected a working, fully electronic television system.

Sarnoff visited Farnsworth's laboratory himself, fearing that the young inventor's work might be a threat to RCA's future development of television. At first, Sarnoff agreed with Zworykin. He saw no use for Farnsworth's invention. However, the RCA executive offered Farnsworth $100,000 for his entire enterprise, including Farnsworth's services. Farnsworth wanted royalty payments instead. Sarnoff, who refused to pay anyone royalties, was dismayed.

Unlike the positive results Sarnoff negotiated during his first meeting with inventor Zworykin, the meeting with inventor Farnsworth would be the beginning of fierce competition leading to a series of court battles against the giant corporation.

After Sarnoff 's visit, Farnsworth struck up a deal with Philco Company, which allowed the inventor to perfect his television receiver and secure a patent to project a televised scene onto a screen two feet square. Farnsworth was now able to begin television broadcasts, and the Federal Radio Commission granted Philco a license with the call letters W3XE. A furious Sarnoff offered Philco an ultimatum. The company either had to drop Farnsworth or risk losing renewal of RCA licensing agreements.

Farnsworth realized that Philco only wanted to produce television sets. He also realized that Philco depended on RCA patents for their lucrative radio business. He left Philco and traveled to London, where he had been invited to demonstrate his system to Baird Television; they eventually persuaded him to sign a lucrative business agreement.

Returning to the United States, Farnsworth found that he was victorious in his first patent battle with Zworykin and RCA. On July 22, 1935, a forty-seven page decision was handed down by the court. Simply, it ruled that Farnsworth, not Zworykin, was the "father of electronic television." The court reasoned that Zworykin's system, unlike Farnsworth's, lacked a device to produce a scanned electrical image. With that decision, Sarnoff was denied total control of television.

Sarnoff soon realized that it would be impossible to succeed in the television market without Farnsworth's patents. After months of negotiations, RCA signed an agreement, its first ever, to pay continuing patent royalties to Farnsworth's company.

Months before the agreement was signed, Sarnoff was preparing to begin regular television broadcasting. On April 20, 1939, he invited about one hundred guests to Radio City to watch RCA's first broadcast. The highlight, as reported in the *New York Times*, was when Sarnoff appeared on the eight-by-nine-inch screen and said:

> Now we add radio sight to sound. It is with a feeling of humbleness that I come to this moment of announcing the birth of in this country of a new art so important in its implications that it is bound to affect all society. It is an art which shines like a torch in a troubled world. It is a creative force which we must learn to utilize for the benefit of all mankind.[7]

Ten days later television viewers saw the first official broadcast, President Franklin D. Roosevelt's talk opening the 1939 World's Fair in New York.

TELEVISION ARRIVES

The day following Roosevelt's TV appearance, sets were available in department stores. Screens ranged in size from three to twelve inches, and the sets cost from $125 to $600. Sarnoff predicted that 20,000 to 40,000 television receivers would be sold following the World's Fair introduction. However, three months later, only 800 sets had been sold.

The government had been slow in setting standards. The Communications Act of 1934 scrapped the seven-year-old Federal Radio Commission and created a seven-member Federal Communications Commission. Its duty was to ensure that radio and television broadcasters acted in the public interest. The new body had hoped that the television industry would standardize a television system. Farnsworth and RCA's system operated with 441 lines and 30 frames per second. Philco wanted 605 lines and 20 frames per second, while DuMont, a fourth television network that operated from 1946 to 1956, pushed for 625 lines and 15 frames per second. On April 20, 1941, the FCC finally approved 525 lines with 30 frames per second as the standard, and it authorized commercial broadcasting to begin on July 1, 1941.

The FCC approved eighteen stations for commercial operation. Among those were the New York stations of NBC and CBS. Eight more stations were approved nine months later. Altogether about 10,000 to 20,000 sets were in operation. Stations were allowed to present fifteen hours of programming per week.

However, within five months television's future was put on hold as America and its media giants—Sarnoff and William Paley—prepared for the nation's entrance into World War II. WCBW, the CBS station, distinguished itself on December 7, 1941, by giving viewers the latest bulletins on the Pearl Harbor attack and showing maps of the war zone.

POSTWAR TELEVISION

Following the war, more television sets were sold after customers saw for themselves store window displays pointing to the wonders and benefits of set ownership. By 1949, television set prices declined; some 1.7 million sets were sold that year.

By January 1949, there were forty-nine stations in twenty-eight markets. A year later, some ninety-eight operated in fifty-eight markets.

As the number of stations increased, interesting programs attracted viewers, and the viewers saw commercials. That encouraged advertisers to spend more on television programs; this led to even better programs.

THE COLOR WAR

As the new media toy found favor with American audiences, another battle loomed. There would be a vicious fight between Sarnoff and William Paley for dominance of the technology for color pictures on the home screen.

Scientists had been working on a color television system since 1889. Baird actually demonstrated a color television system in 1928. A year later, Bell Labs in New Jersey provided the first American demonstration of color television.

However, the 1930s saw very little work on color television; the industry concentrated on commercial black and white television. That changed in 1940 when thirty-four-year-old Peter Goldmark, a CBS engineer, became obsessed with the idea of color television after seeing his first color movie, the 1939 blockbuster, *Gone with the Wind*. He then cajoled Paley into supporting color television research. Goldmark's model for color television was in part an adaptation of the old mechanical spinning disc devised for black and white television in the 1920s.

He melded the wheel with electronic transmission and reception, unlike the old system. By 1946 Goldmark had perfected CBS's color television system, producing remarkably true colors, and he demonstrated it to the FCC. For Paley it was a direct challenge to RCA and a threat to Sarnoff's domination of the television industry.

As radio became popular, David Sarnoff, president of RCA and head of NBC, had his eye on television. He foresaw radio and television as mass media built around networks.

After serving as Eisenhower's top communications expert, Sarnoff returned to the United States in 1944 to fight another type of war—the color war. The media fed on the war between Paley and Sarnoff until an FCC commissioner called for a test of the two systems.

For years Sarnoff had been urging the FCC to develop a standard by which broadcast transmission technology is measured in the United States. The FCC agreed with Sarnoff. However, on October 10, 1950, the FCC approved CBS's color television and its corresponding broadcasting standards. The system could now be commercially marketed.

On June 25, 1951, CBS aired its first color broadcast, a one-hour show featuring Ed Sullivan and other CBS stars, but few were able to see it. Of the more than 10 million television sets in the nation, only twenty-five were equipped to watch CBS color. The rest of the industry, which wanted to unload their black and white sets, refused to cooperate with CBS.

To rectify the imbalance, CBS agreed to buy Hytron Radio and Electronics Corporation of Salem, Massachusetts, a manufacturer of television sets as well as tube components for radios and television. Instead of cash, CBS gave Hytron $18 million worth of CBS stock, or 26 percent of its total holdings.

CBS chairman William S. Paley (right) and CBS president Frank Stanton welcome comedian Jack Benny to CBS January 2, 1949, during Paley's notorious raid of NBC talent.

By the end of 1951, "radio's miracle man had not run of miracles," as reported in *Time* magazine. Sarnoff unveiled his own color television system to rave reviews. It was a blow to CBS.

Another problem faced CBS in the fall of 1951: the federal government told manufacturers to stop producing color television sets because they used materials needed for the Korean War. CBS's reason for purchasing Hytron was thwarted, but it probably saved the company in the long run. CBS would have had to produce 1 million color sets and absorb losses of at least $100 per set for an indefinite period. "It was the luckiest thing in the world," CBS president Frank Stanton would say years later. "It was a graceful way of getting out of color manufacturing."[8]

When the government lifted its ban on manufacturing color TV sets in March 1953, Stanton announced that CBS would end its plans to manufacture color TV sets.

During the suspension, Sarnoff perfected his color system. On December 17, 1953, the FCC officially reversed its 1951 decision and voted to accept the RCA system for commercial broadcasting. Sarnoff was victorious again. This same compatibility standard is still in effect as U.S. television stations and program suppliers move from analog to digital and HDTV production and distribution systems.

EARLY TV ENTERTAINMENT

For a while, Sarnoff had more to crow about. After years of financial losses, TV broadcasting began to show a profit in 1953. Some 39.4 million sets were in use in the United States; 70 percent of all U.S. homes had television; about 331 VHF and 106 UHF stations were operating in the United States.

Paley may have lost the technology war to Sarnoff, but by 1955 CBS made more money than NBC. CBS also became the most popular network in the ratings race, a position it would hold for twenty-one consecutive years.

Paley took chances on new TV formats. Sarnoff preferred live comedy-variety shows, and he turned to situation comedies. Both were safe as far as content was concerned. Both media giants were trying to avoid the wrath and accusations of Senator Joseph McCarthy, who was hunting for Communists in the film and television businesses.

Paley's greatest deal involved Lucille Ball, who was starring in the radio show *My Favorite Husband*. A CBS executive suggested that Lucy consider television. At the time Lucy and her bandleader husband, Desi Arnaz, had decided to set up a company to produce television programs on their own. They wanted the rights to television adaptations of Lucy's radio show. But she wanted Desi to play her husband. Paley objected. He didn't think Desi could act.

Lucy and Desi continued to develop a television situation comedy, *I Love Lucy*, on their own. The Philip Morris Company bought the show through Milton Biouw of the Biouw advertising agency, and it went looking for the best possible time period and station lineup. Stanton now wanted the show for his 9 to 9:30 P.M. time slot on Mondays, but CBS lacked television stations. Many cities had one station, and that was usually an NBC affiliate. Stanton, though, was able to pull it off by putting together a string of stations. By 1953, *I Love Lucy* became the nation's top-rated show, a position it held for four of its six full seasons, and Lucille Ball became the queen of CBS. When Lucy became pregnant, the nation waited for the big day. It came on January 19, 1953, when Desiderio Alberto Arnaz IV was born. It happened on the exact day of the Lucy-has-her-baby telecast. Some 68.8 percent of television sets were tuned to *I Love Lucy*. The birth was headline news and competed with the second presidential inauguration of Dwight Eisenhower the following morning.

NBC also had its share of comedies. Among its early offerings were *The Aldrich Family*; *The Life of Riley*, with Jackie Gleason and then William Bendix; *I Married Joan*, with Joan Davis and Jim Backus; *The Dennis Day Show*; and Wally Cox's *Mr. Peepers*.

And CBS also had its share of variety shows. It made an odd choice for host for what became one of its most popular shows. Stiff and serious Ed Sullivan couldn't tell jokes, sing, or play an instrument. He was a newspaper entertainment columnist. His program, *Toast of the Town* and later *The Ed Sullivan Show*, however, sustained its success for twenty-three years. Jackie Gleason in 1952 and Red Skelton in 1953 enjoyed similar successes in the comedy-variety format.

This was the golden age of television drama. Early entries were *The Kraft Television Theater*, *Robert Montgomery Presents*, *Studio One*, and *The Philco TV Playhouse*. These programs introduced America to such actor newcomers as Anne Francis, E. G. Marshall, Jack Lemmon, and Eva Marie Saint.

Except for *The Red Skelton Show*, by the late 1950s audiences and Paley looked to other TV formats for entertainment. Live quiz shows became the rage and eventually helped define the "decade of shame."

QUIZ SHOW SCANDALS

The $64,000 Question appeared on CBS in early June 1955. Not even Paley could have predicted America's fascination with game shows. *The $64,000 Question* supplanted *I Love Lucy* as the top-rated show, and reaped profits for its sponsor, Revlon. The three networks soon had a plethora of quiz shows: *The $64,000 Challenge*; *The Big Surprise*; *High Finance*; *Dotto*; *Treasure Hunt*; *Giant Step*; and *Twenty-One*, an NBC show launched in 1956 that raised the format's stakes by removing the limit on the amount of prizes.

Advertisers controlled TV programming, and advertisers hoped to attract large audiences with charismatic contestants on their quiz shows. These programs generated huge advertising revenues. Net revenues for CBS, for instance, went from $87 million in 1950 to $345 million in 1956. Such large profits were generated by an innovation in the way commercial time was sold. As television audiences grew, it became prohibitively expensive for smaller advertisers to sponsor half-hour or hour-long shows. To solve the problem, Sylvester L. "Pat" Weaver, who became president of NBC in 1953, invented the magazine concept. The network would produce and control the program and sell portions of time within it for commercial messages to advertisers. Each program would have a number of different advertisers. Using this concept, Weaver created the *Today* and *Tonight* shows. Instead of selling them as programs, he sold their commercial time by the minute. CBS soon did the same.

Weaver also had the idea of spectacular, one-time programs made with extra care and money and preceded by larger-than-normal publicity campaigns. They were designed to stand out from the usual programming, to create talk and excitement. Such programming events included Mary Martin in *Peter Pan*, and the 1952 Christmas Eve broadcast of *Amahl and the Night Visitors*, the first opera commissioned for television.

Television was riding high in the late 1950s. CBS and NBC had hit the equivalent of the Klondike gold strike. The quiz shows, however, would nearly do the networks in. *Twenty-One*, in particular, would take the ultimate step in quiz show fraudulence and corruption.

Twenty-One, first broadcast on September 12, 1956, was the brainchild of Dan Enright, the show's producer, and his longtime partner, Jack Barry, the show's master of ceremonies. It was modeled after the card game, pitting two contestants against each other; the winner was the one who stopped with the higher point total or with twenty-one points outright. Points were acquired by answering questions, which ranged in difficulty from one to eleven.

The first show was a dismal failure as contestants floundered in failure and scores were tied at zero to zero. "And next morning, the sponsor called my partner, Jack Barry, and me and told us in no uncertain terms that he never wanted to see a repeat of what happened the previous night," Enright said. "And from that moment on, we decided to rig *Twenty-One*."

Contestants became full partners in the deception. The partners' first target was army veteran Herbert Stempel, a City College student who had scored high on the qualifying exam. Enright rushed to Stempel's home and asked, "How would you like to win $25,000?" It was simple. Enright would provide the answers. However, after six weeks, the program's ratings began to drop. When Charles Van Doren, a Columbia University English teacher, turned up at Barry and Enright's offices to take the test for *Tic-Tac-Dough*, another daytime quiz show, Enright found a second potential partner in fraud. Van Doren would challenge Stempel on *Twenty-One*. After a dramatic series of tie games, Enright bluntly broke the news to Stempel. The show needed a new champion.

Van Doren would become one of the most popular and lauded figures on television. His students directed guests to "the smartest man in the world." He made the cover of *Time* magazine. And NBC awarded him a one-year $50,000 contract to appear each morning on the *Today* show.

Meanwhile, Stempel, as well as other contestants who participated in the quiz show fraud, began to knock on newspaper doors. It wasn't until May 20, 1958, that the quiz show empire would suffer its first blow. Contestants on a new daytime quiz show, *Dotto*, in which dots turned into pictures and pictures into dollars, realized that the show had been fixed. A standby, Eddie Hilgemeier, a part-time actor, waiter, comic, and butler who wangled his way into many quiz shows, was watching the game's champion peer into a notebook. A few minutes later, he watched how she trounced her latest challenger, an Osage Indian princess. Hilgemeier stormed back to the dressing room, opened the notebook, and found the answers to the questions the winner had just been asked. "This is a fixed show," he called out to the defeated princess. They walked out to hire a lawyer.

On August 25, 1958, New York County's district attorney, Frank Hogan, at the time a candidate for the U.S. Senate, announced that his office would be investigating *Dotto*. A time bomb began ticking, as Van Doren denied Stempel's charges of fraud on the *Today* show. He told United Press that at no time was he coached or tutored.

Congress became interested in quiz show fraud on July 20, when Senator Oren Harris, chairman of the oversight subcommittee, announced that he was going to uncover the facts about crooked quiz shows. On October 6, the quiz show hearings began on Capitol Hill. Following testimony from Stempel and another *Twenty-One* contestant, James Snodgrass, the *New York Times* front page read "TWO TESTIFY '21' QUIZ WAS FIXED."

On October 7, the subcommittee invited Van Doren to testify voluntarily the next day. NBC told him he faced suspension if he failed to appear. He fled to New England. He was ordered to testify on November 2. He returned to New York, held a news conference, and retired to his father's country place in Connecticut. On November 5, the district attorney said that of 150 witnesses who had testified under oath before the grand jury, about 100 of them, he estimated, had committed perjury (including Van Doren, who later pleaded guilty to the crime). No one involved in the scandal, however, suffered legal punishment. Van Doren lost his job at Columbia and lives a quiet life in New England as an editor of the *Encyclopedia Britannica*.

The quiz show scandal had wide-ranging consequences. Quiz show producers were forced out of television and unofficially blacklisted for years; many disgraced contestants hid from their past; networks took control of programs away from sponsors; big prize quiz programs were scrapped; and federal regulations were enacted against fraud.

Television had betrayed America. Famed newspaperman Walter Lippmann said it best in 1959: "Television has been caught perpetrating a fraud which is so gigantic that it calls into question the foundations of the industry.... The fraud was too big, too extensive, too well organized to be cured or atoned for by throwing a few conspicuous individuals to the wolves." Furthermore, he said that by constantly pandering to the largest possible audience in search of the most profitable advertising, television had become the opposite of free and that some saw it as the creature, the servant, and indeed the prostitute of merchandising. For example, the cosmetics firm Revlon was paying $80,000 for *The $64,000 Question*, which precipitated an industry-wide rush for quiz shows.

The scandal gave television a bad name. The shameful portrayal of stereotyping blacks and other people would give it a worse one.

SHAMEFUL STEREOTYPING OF BLACKS

Ebony magazine wrote that television, by its very nature, promised to be a medium "free of racial barriers."[9] The promise was broken right from the start, as it had been with other American media. When the popular twenty-year-old CBS radio program, *Amos 'n' Andy*, moved to television—with TV's first all-black cast—it divided the black community. On one side organized middle-class blacks winced at the thought of their collective image resting in the hands of two white men whose adult life had been devoted to creating weekly gags about blacks. On the other hand, blacks in show business saw this as another opportunity for black actors to work.[10]

When *Amos 'n' Andy* became available to the 12 percent of Americans with television sets in 1951, an organized black movement was ready to take on CBS and the rest of the industry. CBS, in particular, had often behaved as though black people did not exist. The network's arrogance in introducing *Amos 'n' Andy*, which depended for its humor on stereotypical racial traits, was another slap in the face to black people. It also provided an occasion for them to debate the issue.[11]

The debate was led by the National Association for the Advancement of Colored People (NAACP), whose membership had risen tenfold during the 1940s and whose power in post–World War II America was enhanced by the rise of the black middle class to postwar political awareness. A cautious optimism prevailed following World War II. President Harry S. Truman had desegregated the military, and returning black servicemen thought they should have a piece of the American pie they went to war to defend. In addition, some black people had been afforded greater economic opportunities at home during the war and were now poised to participate fully in the American dream.

The NAACP and organized black people were not so much shocked at the characters in *Amos 'n' Andy*, who were portrayed with "baggy pants, plug hats, foul cigars, pushy wives, misfired schemes, and mangled grammar," but by the timing of its release and its impact on the rise of black political consciousness.[12] The NAACP sued to block the first episode of the series. In the end, however, the NAACP failed to convince America that the show was an enemy of the entire black community. Instead it was looked upon as a slander against only the black middle class.

Even more stereotypical was *Beulah*, which reinforced the notion of a happy, grinning black woman working as a maid for a middle-class white family. Television was indifferent to Beulah's family, even to whether she had one. Viewers also saw the antics of the bumptious valet Rochester in *The Jack Benny Show*. TV then retreated from the race-relations conflict for most of the fifties as Hollywood presented America with *I Love Lucy*, *I Married Joan*, *Ozzie and Harriet*, *Father Knows Best*, *Leave It to Beaver*, *Dragnet*, and *Lassie*.

Famous black singer Nat King Cole had a show for one season. He couldn't get a sponsor for the next. Pressure from advertisers with Southern markets just wasn't going to allow television to be an equal opportunity employer, setting back the advancements, no matter how slight, television was making. One agency made it very plain: "No Negro performers allowed."[13]

TELEVISION NEWS

Before the quiz show scandal, Edward R. Murrow, who seldom watched any show preceding his, sat riveted and horrified when Hal March, the host of *The $64,000 Question* stood before an "isolation booth" and announced: "This is the *The $64,000 Question*." Murrow knew that the carny, midway atmosphere heralded by the big-money quizzes would soon be dominating the airwaves, Fred Friendly relates in *Circumstances Beyond Our Control*. That night Ed leaned over to Friendly in the control room and asked, "Any bets on how long we'll keep this time period?"[14]

Their respected documentary series *See It Now* was canceled by CBS in 1958 and replaced by another game show, *Do You Trust Your Wife?*, with ventriloquist Edgar Bergen and his three dummies. The quiz shows and CBS management had betrayed one of the greatest names in broadcast news history.

When television networks began broadcasting news in late 1948, it was televised radio. Edward P. Morgan's *Sunday News* program that year had no visuals. It was just "rip and read" from wire services and newspapers. He did provide some self-conscious choreography by pushing away from his desk and reading the news standing up.

By 1953 NBC offered fifteen minutes of the impeccably dressed John Cameron Swayze who hopscotched the world with his *Camel News Caravan*. In those pre-satellite days, hopscotching meant more news than pictures. However, the *Camel News Caravan* was the first to feature news film. The film had to be shipped, developed, and edited before it could be put on the air. Thus, immediacy, still a triumph of radio, was beyond television's grasp. When the film ran out, some primitive graphics were used. It was not uncommon to see hand-drawn pictures of car accidents or plane crashes on the screen. On one occasion a paper house was set on fire to illustrate a story.

When the anchor did not have actual footage of an event, he would improvise. For example, on CBS's fifteen-minute *Television News with Douglas Edwards*, viewers saw the anchor flipping through photos of England's very young Prince Charles.

Early sponsors did have some control over the news. R. J. Reynolds, for example, would not allow anyone pictured smoking a cigar. The company allowed one exception, Winston Churchill. Though the *Camel News Caravan* made Swayze the first star of television news, the real force was a man who never anchored a daily news program. Edward R. Murrow would become the "patron saint of broadcast journalism."

EDWARD R. MURROW

Murrow had to be dragged, kicking and screaming, into television. "We don't know anything about television," he told Friendly. "I wish it would go away." When Paley told him "the future belonged to television," he didn't want to hear it.[15] He was suspicious of television. It was not for Murrow or his boys. It was for novices breaking in. He did not want to be part of a medium that treated news superficially, with images instead of intellectual effort. He spelled out his feelings in February 1949, in an article intended for the *New York Times*:

> The interesting area of speculation is not whether TV news is here to stay, but rather what form it is likely to take after the shakedown cruise.... Is it to be a medium of entertainment or education? Do bathing girls on surfboards get preference over a first class but simple chart of the Middle East? ... So far ... there has been a tendency to tailor the news to fit the pictorial and animation possibilities rather than to give the news, as such, priority, and try to tailor up such pictorial support as may be possible.... If the editorial selection is based upon largely visual values, TV news will become an animated picture magazine or a newsreel.

The *New York Times* never published the piece.

Despite wanting no part of television, Murrow, along with 30 million other people, had his eyes glued to the box in March 1951. They were watching live coverage of Estes Kefauver's Senate investigation of organized crime and his star witness, mobster Frank Costello. His lawyers objected to Costello's being televised. Kefauver reached a compromise. The camera would focus upon Costello's hands. The most famous hands in America were seen clenching, fumbling with documents, shredding papers, reaching for a glass of water, and sweating as he described the underworld.

Following the Kefauver hearings, Murrow said, "The television performance has been fascinating." The magic of the new medium had happened, he said, when people realized "the midgets in the box have been real."[16] He realized that television had not substituted for thought and had not trivialized the subject of organized crime. However, he wanted no part of it. He was thinking of accepting a position as president of Washington State University.

In truth, he was not about to leave broadcasting. If anything, he was about to become more deeply involved. In June of 1951, he and Friendly decided to end their radio program *Hear It Now* and coproduce a new weekly half-hour television documentary series. *Hear It Now* would become *See It Now*. "TV in 1951 when we began *See It Now* was a no man's land, a vacuum. Alcoa came to us and wanted a program hosted by Murrow," Friendly related some years later.[17]

Joe Wershba, field producer for *See It Now*, called Murrow and Friendly "shatterers." "They shattered mountains. They moved into a new field. Neither of

CBS Photo Archive/Getty Images

Edward R. Murrow was sent by William S. Paley to hire on-air talent to cover World War II. He couldn't find anyone so he went on the air, becoming the most famous name in broadcast history.

them knew a thing about filmmaking." Meli Lerner Bonsignori, film editor of *See It Now*, said, "We learned from Fred Friendly and Ed Murrow. We learned to be journalists and in return we taught them film." Joining Wershba and Bonsignori was veteran filmmaker Palmer Williams, who had spent the war years making films for the army signal corps. They also contracted with the Hearst–MGM News of the Day for camera work and other technical services on a cost-plus basis and library footage as needed.[18]

On Sunday afternoon, November 18, 1951, viewers tuning into CBS television heard Murrow say, "Good evening. This is an old team trying to learn a new trade." On the first show he sat at a table, looking at live individual shots of the Statue of Liberty and San Francisco Bay, made possible after coaxial television cables and microwave relays knit the country together the month before. "We are impressed," he said, "by a medium through which a man sitting in his living room has been able for the first time to look at two oceans at once."

Murrow operated not from a set, but from the control room, with monitors, microphones, and control panel in full view. In the weekly half-hour program, which would be the forerunner of television documentaries, viewers would see three to a half-dozen stories on a variety of issues. Occasionally it would touch upon one subject. One such program was *See It Now*'s first full-hour show, the highly acclaimed "Christmas in Korea," in late 1952. The combat report openly showed that the war was stalemated.

Time magazine called *See It Now* "television's best and liveliest show." *Variety* awarded the program a special citation as "the most original, informative and entertaining type of journalism now riding the video waves." It also said of *See It Now*: "At a time when not only viewers but most industry toppers had started to believe that video had exhausted all possible facets of programming, Murrow and his co-producer, Fred W. Friendly, jolted them into discarding that cliché with this entirely new approach to news reporting, an approach which uncovered a power in TV's ability to report the news which most of them had never even suspected. Where it had been generally accepted that video could never equal radio's job of reporting, Murrow and Friendly exploited to the full ... the drama and excitement inherent in the news."

Don Hewitt, retired on-air director and creator of *60 Minutes* fame, said, "Television was never the same after the first *See It Now*. Ed Murrow made television respectable. All the big names in radio, Sevareid and Howard Smith and Collingwood, could stop looking down their noses at television. Ed was a hero of the intellectual establishment. So now it was respectable for them to own a television set—or admit they owned one."

THE CASE AGAINST MILO RADULOVICH

According to Friendly, Murrow was frustrated. Despite *See It Now*'s success, something was missing. Murrow realized that cameras need something more than emulsion and light values to create electronic journalism. The missing ingredients were conviction, controversy, and a point of view. The industry found them on the night of October 20, 1953, when Murrow looked up at the television camera and said: "We propose to examine ... the case of Lieutenant Radulovich." Television journalism was born.

"We had always been under pressure to do something about McCarthy. Ed kept saying to those who would come to see us about it. 'Look, we are not preachers. We cover the news. When there is a good news story about McCarthy that will give us a little picture, we'll do it. We are not going to make a speech against McCarthy,'" Friendly said. That "good" news story appeared in the *Detroit News*. The headline read, "Radulovich Fired from Job." "Ed handed it to me and said, 'Fritzel, this may be our McCarthy program.'"[19]

Radulovich, a twenty-six-year-old meteorologist in the Air Force Reserve and a senior at the University of Michigan, had been asked to resign his commission after eight years because he had been declared a security risk for having close associations with Communists or Communist sympathizers. The close associations were with his father and sister. His father was an old man who had come to America more than forty years before. He was a veteran of World War I and worked at the Hudson automobile factory. His only crime was that he read a Serbian-language newspaper said to support Marshall Tito of Yugoslavia. Meanwhile, Tito had broken with the Soviet bloc and was being wooed by the West. In addition, Tito was receiving loans from the same U.S. government that was persecuting Lieutenant Radulovich. The air force also said his sister was a Communist, but no proof was offered.

Radulovich refused to resign, and a three-officer board was convened to review the case. It recommended, without producing any evidence, that he be severed from the service. It was this story that Murrow found in the *Detroit News*.

Murrow and Friendly decided the Radulovich program was too important and too good not to be publicized. They paid $1,500 for a display ad in the *New York Times*. It was a simple layout in bold type that said: "The Case Against Milo Radulovich, A0589839," and listed the time and station. It did not include the CBS eye, just Murrow and Friendly's signatures.

New York Times journalist Jack Gould instantly understood what happened on the October 20 broadcast. He wrote: "The program marked perhaps the first time that a major network, the Columbia Broadcasting System, and one of the country's most important industrial sponsors, the Aluminum Company of America, consented to a program taking a vigorous editorial stand in a matter of national importance and controversy."[20]

According to author Joseph E. Persico, "What Murrow and Friendly had done for Milo Radulovich was to give the man what his government had denied him, the right to defend himself." What they had done for television was revealed in a telephone call Friendly received a month later.[21]

Murrow informed Friendly that a film crew was on its way to the Pentagon. That night on *See It Now*, Murrow introduced Secretary of the Air Force Harold E. Talbott. "I have decided," Talbott said, "that it is consistent with the interests of national security to retain Lieutenant Radulovich in the United States Air Force. He is not, in my opinion, a security risk."[22]

This important but obscure story showed for the first time the power of television. It also showed the extent of the fear, the cancer called McCarthyism, that was spreading from coast to coast. Perhaps *See It Now* film editor Bonsignori said it best: "All of us lived in fear of being accused of something that wasn't true or accused of something that was partially true. We were in a very sensitive business, and each one of us could have lost our jobs, could have lost our livelihoods because of this lunatic."[23]

JOSEPH MCCARTHY

Joseph McCarthy owed his political career to Wisconsin newsmen; he had been urged by his cronies in the newspaper business to run against twenty-year incumbent Senator Robert La Follette. Six years later, McCarthy went looking for a platform on which to run for reelection. He tossed around a lot of harebrained schemes. One idea was to give senior citizens one dollar a year. However, he heard about a professor, a Catholic priest, who told his class that Communists were serving in the U.S. government. He even attended the professor's lectures.

He would gain notoriety, much of it through televised hearings his committee conducted, by making largely unsubstantiated charges about Communist subversion in the U.S. government and other institutions, including the media.

The press aided McCarthy by its superficial coverage of his charges. Reporters believed they practiced objective journalism if they wrote down what he said and spelled his name correctly because he was a senator. But what they were writing down was meaningless as he made one charge after another. Journalists didn't bother putting all these charges into context in an attempt to provide perspective and meaning. McCarthy was a fascinating example to demonstrate the weaknesses of traditional journalistic objectivity, according to David Halberstam.[24]

Television had crossed the line with "The Case Against Milo Radulovich." It was the first time television's untested power had been brought to bear regarding an issue in which virtually the entire country had been cowed into submission. As Friendly put it, "Television journalism had achieved influence, like a great newspaper, like the *New York Times*. We found that night that we could make a difference."[25]

The show had another outcome. It put Murrow and McCarthy on a collision course. For it was this broadcast, the "Radwich junk," as McCarthy's agent, Don Surine, had called it, that led Surine to say that McCarthy had "proof" that "Murrow was on the Soviet payroll in 1934." At that point, Murrow decided to use the newfound power of television to expose the junior senator from Wisconsin.[26]

At that time, too, Murrow was being courted to present another television show that would give him even greater fame—but a show he was embarrassed to be part of.

PERSON TO PERSON

One of the early *See It Now* broadcasts was an interview with Senator Kefauver, who had catapulted himself into the Democratic presidential primaries by his investigation of organized crime. Murrow remained in New York and interviewed Kefauver, who was sitting in his home. That was followed by a live interview from the home of Senator Robert A. Taft in Ohio.

Following the successes of these two programs, Johnny Aarons and Jesse Zousmer, of Murrow's staff, convinced him to begin a weekly series of visits to the homes of celebrities. Friendly thought it beneath Murrow to whet America's appetite for voyeurism by playing the part of a Peeping Tom. However, to Friendly's dismay, Murrow agreed to the new series, *Person to Person*. He originally intended to interview a wide variety of noncelebrated Americans.

The half-hour program centered around two fifteen-minute visits to two homes each week. On the first program, which aired on Friday, October 2, 1953, Murrow visited baseball great Roy Campanella, who hit the winning home run that day in the Dodgers' World Series game with the Yankees. The second fifteen minutes was a visit with the conductor Leopold Stokowski and his wife, Gloria Vanderbilt. Later Murrow interviewed Marilyn Monroe, Elizabeth Taylor, Zsa Zsa Gabor, Sophie Tucker, Liberace, Lucille Ball, Arthur Godfrey, newly elected senator from Massachusetts John F. Kennedy, and Mary Martin, who said she received more mail after a single fifteen-minute appearance than she had during the entire run of *South Pacific*.[27]

Murrow did the show for obvious reasons. One was to broaden his base. Up to this time he was totally political and increasingly controversial. The new program gave Murrow a good-guy image. It made him a trusted figure, tolerated and liked in many more homes. He also did the show he hated in order to do the show he loved, he said.

Unlike *See It Now*, *Person to Person* was given a permanent time slot. *See It Now* continued to air at different times. Paley liked the new show and sent

Murrow a memo after its initial broadcast. It said, "You've got a sure winner in this show."[28]

The ratings proved that. Its audience and sponsors eager to support the show far outnumbered those of *See It Now*. On a week in 1956 when *See It Now*'s Nielsen rating was 11.3, *Person to Person*'s was 23.4. It was among America's top-ten most popular programs, attaining a 45 percent viewer share of all homes in 1957.

MURROW VS. MCCARTHY

America also would be riveted to *See It Now*'s most famous broadcast, "The McCarthy Broadcast." Murrow was not the first journalist to confront McCarthy. Columnists Drew Pearson, the Alsop brothers, and Walter Lippmann, as well as Murrow's boys, Sevareid, Smith, and Morgan, had already taken on the senator in the press and on radio. Until Murrow no one confronted the nation's demagogue on the powerful medium of television.

McCarthy's charge that Murrow had been on the Soviet payroll hastened the confrontation. He had indeed worked with Soviet officials twenty-two years earlier. In his job with the Institute of International Education, Murrow set up summer seminars at Moscow University for Americans interested in Russian studies.

Murrow decided a year earlier to expose McCarthy, using the man's own words. He asked his film crew to tape every McCarthy speech. He also had footage of McCarthy holding hearings and questioning witnesses.

Murrow and Friendly tried to persuade CBS to do some on-air promotion for its Tuesday, March 9, *See It Now*, but they found little support. Friendly had approached Bill Golden, the network's advertising chief, who agreed to buy an ad in the *New York Times*. Some time later, he contacted Friendly and reported that "management" said no. Murrow and Friendly said they would pay for the ad if Golden would place it for them. Again, Golden said no.

However, Paley did call Murrow on Tuesday morning before the broadcast. "I'll be with you tonight, Ed, and I'll be with you tomorrow as well."[29]

That night Friendly leaned to Murrow and whispered, "This is going to be a tough one." Murrow answered, "After this, they're all going to be tough."[30] The red light went on. "Good evening," Murrow said. "Tonight, *See It Now* devotes its entire half hour to a report on Senator Joseph R. McCarthy, told mainly in his own words and pictures."[31]

Friendly gave an account of what happened:

> For the next thirty minutes that control room was like a submarine during an emergency dive; fourteen technicians and a director were all responding to Murrow's cues and he to theirs. Murrow into a 1952 film of McCarthy ... Murrow to radio tape of the senator ... Murrow to Eisenhower ... Murrow live in the studio reading from a stack of American newspapers, most of them critical of the senator's attack on the Army ... Murrow introducing film of the senator laughing and scoffing at Eisenhower ... the Zwicker affair ... the senator attacking "Alger, I mean Adlai," which was how McCarthy referred to Stevenson.[32]

Finally, the show turned to McCarthy interrogating Reed Harris, a Voice of America official. McCarthy considered Harris part of the Communist apparatus because he had once canceled a Hebrew-language broadcast over the Voice of

America. McCarthy also hit Harris for being defended by the American Civil Liberties Union when he was suspended as a Columbia University student. McCarthy described the ACLU as "a front for doing the work of the Communist Party."

Murrow shot back: "Twice, McCarthy said the American Civil Liberties Union was listed as a subversive front. The Attorney General's list does not and has never listed the ACLU as subversive nor does the FBI or any other government agency. And the American Civil Liberties Union holds in its files letters of commendation from President Eisenhower, President Truman and General MacArthur."[33]

"That was the technique of the entire broadcast," Friendly related. "The viewer was seeing a series of typical attacks by the senator, which they had seen many times before, but for the first time on television there was a refutation—Murrow's correction of McCarthy's 'facts.' Each time the senator was his own worst witness; each time the facts countered his distortions."[34]

Murrow ended the broadcast with the following:

> Earlier the senator asked, "Upon what meat does this our Caesar feed." Had he looked three lines earlier in Shakespeare's *Caesar* he would have found this line, which is not altogether inappropriate: "The fault, dear Brutus, is not in our stars but in ourselves."
>
> No one familiar with the history of this country can deny that congressional committees are useful. It is necessary to investigate before legislating, but the line between investigation and persecuting is a very fine one, and the junior senator from Wisconsin has stepped over it repeatedly. His primary achievement has been in confusing the public mind as between [the] internal and ... external threat of Communism. We must not confuse dissent with disloyalty. We must remember always that accusation is not proof, and that conviction depends upon evidence and due process of law. We will not walk in fear, one of another. We will not be driven by fear into an age of unreason if we dig deep in our history and our doctrine, and remember that we are not descended from fearful men, not from men who feared to write, to speak, to associate with, and to defend causes which were for the moment unpopular.
>
> This is not time for men who oppose Senator McCarthy's methods to keep silent, or for those who approve. We can deny our heritage and our history, but we cannot escape responsibility for the result. There is no way for a citizen of a republic to abdicate his responsibilities. As a nation we have come into our full inheritance at a tender age. We proclaim ourselves—as indeed we are—the defenders of freedom, what's left of it, but we cannot defend freedom abroad by deserting it at home. The actions of the junior senator from Wisconsin have caused alarm and dismay amongst our allies abroad and given considerable comfort to our enemies and whose fault is it? Not really his. He didn't create this situation of fear; he merely exploited it, and rather successfully. Cassius was right: The fault, dear Brutus, is not in our stars but in ourselves.
>
> Good night, and good luck.[35]

The broadcast drew the greatest reaction to any single program in network history. By noon the next day, CBS received 12,348 comments. In the next few days, the total swelled to 75,000. They ran about ten to one in favor of Murrow.[36] He had become a national hero.

To Murrow's dismay, CBS allowed a thirty-minute response by McCarthy. The network even paid him $6,336.99 for production costs.[37] Following that broadcast, CBS logged 6,548 phone calls and telegrams favoring Murrow and 3,654 favoring McCarthy.[38]

However, no response came from CBS management until president Frank Stanton asked to see Friendly. He told Friendly that Murrow's "attack on McCarthy" might cost the company the network. Stanton then showed Friendly a public opinion survey that CBS had commissioned from Elmo Roper. The poll had been conducted on the Friday and Saturday after McCarthy's response, and he was most discouraged by the results. "The survey, neatly bound and annotated in Stanton's handwriting, indicated that 59 percent of the adult population had either watched or heard about the program, and thick orange-red brackets indicated that 33 percent of these believed either that McCarthy had proved Murrow was a pro-Communist or had raised doubts about Murrow."[39]

THE END OF MURROW AND McCARTHY

According to David Halberstam, the conversation provided "extraordinary insight into the way broadcasting management regarded journalism: "It was not whether it was the right show done in the right way, but according to the pressures that it had to bear. Not whether it was a good show but what the vote was."[40]

Friendly left the conversation wondering if Stanton was speaking for Stanton or Stanton for Paley. Stanton and Murrow were not friends, by any means. Stanton resented Murrow's close relationship, or what had been a close relationship, with Paley. He resented the fact that Murrow would walk past Stanton's office and go right into chairman Paley's office. If anyone was close to Paley at CBS, it was Murrow. But that was not to last.

Meanwhile, McCarthy was taking a pounding on the floor of the U.S. Senate. On the day of the broadcast, Senator Ralph Flanders, of Vermont, denounced McCarthy: "He dons war paint; he goes into his war dance; he emits his war whoops; he goes forth to battle and proudly returns with the scalp of a pink Army dentist."[41]

Just weeks after the broadcast, the Senate conducted what came to be called the Army-McCarthy hearings on television, an investigation of alleged pro-Communist activities within the U.S. Army itself. It would be the final blow for McCarthy. Senate colleagues repudiated him, as he sat there almost disintegrating before the nation. On December 9, 1954, nine months after the Murrow broadcast, the Senate declared that Joseph R. McCarthy "tended to bring the Senate into dishonor and disrepute, to obstruct the constitutional processes of the Senate and to impair its dignity, and such conduct is hereby condemned." He was censured by a vote of 67 to 22. Crushed, he left the spotlight, and died in 1957.[42]

Murrow's star also was fading. Sponsors began to drop *See It Now*. Alcoa had canceled sponsorship of the program. Pan American dropped out in November 1957. They were happy about the show but not about its Sunday afternoon time period, so the show was bumped from time period to time period.

According to Friendly:

Our budget was a source of constant irritation to the business-affairs managers, who claimed that we were reckless and irresponsible, and there were all kinds of cost studies to indicate how we were affecting corporate earnings. The fact that CBS's profits were at an all-time high of over $16,000,000 after taxes; that *See It Now*'s out-of-pocket expenses were comparatively favorable to those of an hour's entertainment program;

that the series was the single most prestigious project in all television, the winner of every conceivable award; that it was the standard against which all news and documentary broadcasts were measured—all these factors made little dent on those who believed that the burden exceeded the glory.[43]

Paley no longer appreciated the glory *See It Now* brought to CBS. Friendly recorded Murrow's conversation about the subject with Paley.

"Bill," Murrow pleaded at one point, "are you going to destroy all this? Don't you want an instrument like the *See It Now* organization, which you have poured so much into for so long to continue?"

"Yes," said Paley, "but I don't want this constant stomach ache every time you do a controversial subject."

"I'm afraid that's a price you have to be willing to pay," Murrow responded. "It goes with the job."[44]

After seven years and some 200 broadcasts, *See It Now* was dead. And with its demise, no broadcaster again would have the autonomy, the complete control of a program, that Murrow had.

Murrow also did not help himself with CBS management when he gave a historic speech to the Radio-Television News Directors Association in Chicago on October 15, 1958, just three months after the death of *See It Now*:

And if there are any historians … a hundred years from now and there should be preserved the kinescopes for one week of all three networks, they will find recorded, in black-and-white or color, evidence of decadence, escapism and insulation from the realities of the world in which we live.… . If we go on as we are, then history will take its revenge, and retribution will [catch] up with us.[45]

Murrow said that he was "frightened by the imbalance, the constant striving to reach the largest possible audience for everything"—which, of course, was the drive that created the quiz shows and, eventually, made them dishonest.[46]

One year later, Stanton accepted an award from the same group that Murrow had addressed a year earlier. He announced new program practices to do away with the "hanky-panky" of the quiz shows. He also promised that CBS would be master of its own house: "We [assure] the American people that what they see and hear on CBS programs is exactly what it purports to be."[47]

New York Times writer Gould telephoned Stanton, who told him that Murrow's *Person to Person* was an example of a show that endeavored to give the illusion that it was spontaneous, when in fact it was rehearsed. Stanton told Gould that guests should be denied advance questions, or that the audience should be told that the show was rehearsed.

Person to Person producers Zousmer and Aaron called Murrow to urge a strong statement to clear their names. Murrow's response shattered any further relationship he could have with Stanton. Said Murrow: "Dr. Stanton has finally revealed his ignorance both of news and of requirements of television production.… He suggests that *Person to Person*, a program with which I was associated for six years, was not what it purported to be. Surely Stanton must know that cameras, lights, and microphones do not just wander around a home. Producers must know who is going where and when and for how long.... The alternative ... would be chaos." He concluded by saying: "I am sorry Dr. Stanton feels that I have participated in perpetrating a fraud upon the public. My conscience is clear. His seems to be bothering him." The headline on the Sunday morning, October 25, *New York Times* front page read, "Murrow Says Stanton Criticism Shows Ignorance of TV Method."[48]

Murrow took a sabbatical leave from CBS. On his return in 1960 he was assigned a correspondent's role on the new *CBS Reports*, an hour-long informational program. Despite Friendly's plea that Murrow be designated the regular anchor and co-producer, Paley rejected the idea. Murrow could follow, but he could not lead. Murrow, however, did some stellar work, including "Harvest of Shame," which showed the plight of the migrant worker. "Not since McCarthy had we done a broadcast that created such impact, and never again would any of our programs create such clamor for change," Friendly said.[49]

Friendly, who threatened to resign if Murrow was not accepted as *CBS Report*'s anchor, was looking for some honorable solution. President Kennedy solved the problem. When Stanton declined the new president's offer of an appointment as head of the U.S. Information Agency, Kennedy asked Stanton to suggest other people for the post. He suggested "someone like Ed Murrow." Asked long afterward why he had not simply suggested Murrow, Kennedy replied, "I never believed Ed would accept the job."[50]

He did. As Arthur Schlesinger wrote in *A Thousand Days*: "[Murrow] revitalized the USIA, imbued it with his own bravery and honesty and directed its efforts especially to the developing nations.... . USIA became one of the most effective instruments of Kennedy's third-world policy; and Murrow himself was a new man, cheerful, amused, committed, and contented."[51]

Unfortunately, illness forced his retirement in December 1963. He died from cancer in April 1965, two days after his fifty-seventh birthday. At Murrow's death, Eric Sevareid, one of Murrow's boys, said: "He was a shooting star. We shall live in his afterglow a very long time ... we shall not see his likes again."[52]

60 MINUTES

One rising star at CBS was Murrow's associate Don Hewitt. After Murrow left CBS, Hewitt had assisted on a number of "snoozers" for television. One was called *Town Meeting of the World*, which linked up world statesmen via satellite to talk to each other. "The talking heads on *Town Meeting* weren't, for the most part, very scintillating—and I sure as hell didn't want to do documentaries for the rest of my life," Hewitt related. "So, I began to think there had to be a way to make information more palatable."[53] Richard S. Salant had become president of CBS News in 1966, and Hewitt proposed to him a program that would package sixty minutes of reality as attractively as Hollywood packages sixty minutes of make-believe. At the time he had no idea that *60 Minutes* would be the title.

With Mike Wallace and Harry Reasoner as correspondents and Hewitt as executive producer (who retired in 2004 after thirty-six years with the program), *60 Minutes* went on the air at 10 P.M. on alternate Tuesdays in 1968. It was no overnight success. That first program received lukewarm reviews and low ratings. CBS programming chief Oscar Katz recommended that the program be moved to 7 P.M. on Sundays as an alternative to *Wonderful World of Disney* on NBC and *Swiss Family Robinson* on ABC. It has remained in that spot ever since and continues to be among America's top-ten television programs—at times first in the ratings.

The success of *60 Minutes* had a number of far-reaching consequences. First, it saved the news division's budget in the nick of time. *60 Minutes'* top ratings and low costs made it a remarkable business phenomenon in network television. In the mid-1980s, the average cost of a single hour of an entertainment series approached $1 million. But programs produced by the network news divisions cost less than half that. As a result, *60 Minutes* was the most profitable program in network television history. Estimates of the program's annual profits are in the $60 to $70 million range—about a quarter to a third of the total network profits.[54]

The second consequence of the success of *60 Minutes* was its frustrating and costly ripple effect. It produced clones. NBC tried its first newsmagazine, *First Tuesday*, and it failed. NBC had more success some years later with *Dateline*.

AMERICAN MEDIA PROFILE | **WALTER CRONKITE 1916–**

CBS Photo Archive/Getty Images

When Walter Cronkite was in high school, his father brought home a fancy console radio with a record player that had a primitive recording device in it. On the attached large aluminum disk one could record a scratch soundtrack.

He used the device to interview most of his classmates until they fled if he moved anywhere near the device. When he was alone, he imitated announcers.

"It is strange, but I don't remember trying to do news broadcasts," Cronkite relates in his book *A Reporter's Life*. "However, despite the shortcomings of mid-thirties radio news, which I only later understood, I thought it to be glamorous. I was destined to bounce between it and print journalism for the next several years." At the time Cronkite's father didn't realize the impact that console radio would have in shaping his son's future. The son would define issues and events in America for almost two decades as anchor of the *CBS Evening News*.

In 1939 he became a reporter for United Press and covered World War II. While overseas, Cronkite flew bombing missions over Germany, covered the Nuremberg trials, and opened UP's first postwar Moscow bureau.

He joined CBS in 1950. There he served as host of *You Are There*, a re-creation of historical events, and the *CBS Morning Show*. Two years later, he impressed CBS brass when he anchored the presidential nominating conventions. In 1962 he was named anchor of the *CBS Evening News*. Within a year the fifteen-minute newscast was expanded, and Cronkite became the first broadcaster to anchor a daily thirty-minute news program. "And that's the way it is," became his exit trademark.

He told America about the death of President John Kennedy, which he considers one of the biggest stories of his career, and Apollo XI's space mission, staying on the air twenty-seven hours. And when the *Eagle* settled gently on the Moon's surface, all Cronkite could say was, "Oh, boy! Whew! Boy!"

Cronkite exercised a tremendous influence in his role as CBS anchor. He acknowledges that in his book. "The anchors do have tremendous power. Never in the history of journalism have single voices reached so many people on a daily basis. They can include or exclude an item, almost on a whim, in their broadcasts. By their presence at an event, they accentuate—perhaps even, on occasion, distort—its importance."

ABC presented its weekly newsmagazine, *20/20*. CBS also produced the clone *Who's Who*, which failed. However, by the late 1990s, a successful *60 Minutes II* was added to the CBS schedule.

The third and most profound consequence of the success of *60 Minutes* was that it spoiled management. By 1976, a new breed of senior managers expected a news division to be a profit center. They asked, "If *60 Minutes* could make all that money, why not everything else in the news division?" The program raised expectations and suggested a new criterion for news organizations—profitability— that had not existed before. The corporate rules and the demands of news were never the same.[55]

TV NEWS EXPANDS

Before the debut of *60 Minutes*, Salant was working on another news project—the first half-hour network evening news broadcast. On April 16, 1962, he had

---

AMERICAN MEDIA PROFILE   **CONTINUED**

He also noted that a problem with the anchor's exalted position is the tendency to slide from the role of observer to that of player. Cronkite was criticized for just that when he interviewed Egyptian President Anwar al-Sadat in 1977. He asked Sadat if he would go to Jerusalem to confer with the Israelis. The next day Sadat agreed to such a visit when he received an invitation from Israeli Prime Minister Menachem Begin. It paved the way for the Camp David accords and an Israeli-Egyptian peace treaty. One Egyptian source told Cronkite that Sadat was talking seriously with his inner circle of going to Jerusalem four months before CBS broke the story. "However, the important point is that television journalism, in this case at least, speeded up the process, brought it into the open, removed a lot of possibly obstructionist middlemen, and made it difficult for the principals to renege on their very public agreement," Cronkite said.

Cronkite was the first television anchor to make the Watergate issue intelligible to the American people, and he did it during a twenty-two minute overview. "It was a big kiss from Walter Cronkite," Bob Woodward of the *Washington Post* said later. Until then, no other newsperson had taken so much interest in the scandal, besides the *Post*. However, for the first time CBS management interfered with his broadcast, asking if he went a little too far in explaining the issue.

Cronkite contributed to President Lyndon B. Johnson's decision not to run for reelection in 1968.

The anchor had visited Vietnam after the Tet offensive and came away believing that America's intervention in that country had led to a stalemate. He urged the government to negotiate with the North Vietnamese.

His name is synonymous with reporting that separates reporting from advocacy. That may be his lasting legacy. In Sweden, for example, news anchors are called Kronkiters. In Holland they are called Cronkiters. His reporting style may have contributed to his being named "the most trusted figure" in America.

Cronkite retired from CBS in 1981 but continues to host a number of programs for PBS, Discovery, and the Learning Channel. He regularly hosts PBS's New Year's Eve broadcast of the Vienna Philharmonic Orchestra.

Cronkite returned to his journalism roots in 2003. He now writes a syndicated newspaper column. And that's the way it was—and is—for that young lad who was once mesmerized by a console radio.

AMERICAN MEDIA PROFILE | BARBARA WALTERS 1931–

AP Photo

Barbara Walters is one of the most recognizable television journalists on the air today. As host of *The Barbara Walters Specials*, in addition to her duties as executive producer and cohost of *The View*, Walters has become a television superstar. In large part this is because she has successfully covered hard news as well as in-depth celebrity features. She is so well known that her name and a brief biography are listed in the *American Heritage Dictionary*.

Walters was born on September 25, 1931, in Boston. Her father, Lou Walters, owned a famous New York City nightclub, the Latin Quarter. From an early age, Barbara was surrounded by celebrities who worked and socialized with her father, and because of that she wasn't intimidated by big-name stars.

After graduating from Sarah Lawrence College in Bronxville, New York, with a degree in English, Walters moved to New York City to pursue a career in television. In 1955, she got her first job in news as a gofer at the *CBS Morning Show*. Six years later, at the age of thirty, she landed a position as a writer for NBC's *The Today Show*. Within a year she was promoted to reporter, developing, writing, and editing her own stories and interviews. During this time, gender politics in the news business severely constrained her role as a reporter. According to Walters, she was not allowed to write for the male correspondents or to ask questions in male-dominated areas such as economics or politics, and she was forbidden to interview guests on-camera until all of the men on *The Today Show* had finished asking questions. The big stories at the network were given to men. Walters was at first given the feature segments of the show but slowly she proved herself; she helped pave the way for other women journalists. Her popularity among viewers rose primarily because of her unique ability to interview celebrities.

In 1972, Walters made history as the only woman journalist sent by NBC News to cover President Richard Nixon's historic visit to the People's Republic of China. In 1974, Walters was officially named the first female cohost of *The Today Show*. She remained there for another two years, until ABC lured her away with an offer to coanchor their prime-time news program for a record $1 million a year.

This was the first time a woman was allowed the privileged position of anchoring the network news. Walters's position as coanchor of the *ABC Evening News* with Harry Reasoner didn't last long. Public reaction to both her salary and her approach to the news, which critics claimed led to the creeping "info-tainment" mentality in newsrooms, caused many people in the business to speak out. Walter Cronkite said at the time, "There was a first wave of nausea, the sickening sensation that we were going under, that all of our efforts to hold network television news aloof from show business had failed." Public outcry alone wasn't enough to remove Walters from the evening anchor desk, but when ratings started to fall, her reign as coanchor of the *ABC Evening News* was over. Walters later said of that time in her life, "It

replaced Douglas Edwards as anchor of the fifteen-minute *CBS Evening News* with Walter Cronkite, who joined CBS in 1950. Salant thought that Edwards was fatigued after fourteen years of nightly television broadcasts. Edwards effectively and successfully continued to broadcast on radio and television for CBS.[56]

A year earlier, NBC had replaced John Cameron Swayze with Chet Huntley and David Brinkley on the evening news program. They were co-anchors of NBC's coverage of the 1956 political conventions. Huntley was deep-voiced and very serious. Brinkley was light and wry. They were just right for the national

AMERICAN MEDIA PROFILE   Continued

was the worst period in my professional life." But the lesson she learned, she said, "is that if you hang in and work your fanny off, it usually turns out all right."

The public relations disaster didn't keep Walters on the sidelines for long. She made a comeback at ABC with the highly rated *The Barbara Walters Special*s. Since 1976, her one-on-one interviews with Hollywood celebrities, sports figures, heads of state, and newsmakers consistently topped the ratings and made news in themselves. In 1977, Walters was the first person to conduct a joint interview with Egypt's President Anwar al-Sadat and Israel's Prime Minister Menachem Begin. Soon after, Walters landed another big first. She was the first journalist to interview Cuban president Fidel Castro on prime-time television.

Her empathetic style invited spontaneity and trust from the people she interviewed. For instance, Olympic diver Greg Louganis revealed to Walters that he was HIV–positive when he competed in the 1988 Olympics. Walters has interviewed every U.S. president since Richard Nixon, as well as interviewing such celebrities as John Wayne, Bette Davis, Halle Berry, John Travolta, Michael Douglas, and Catherine Zeta-Jones, just to name a few. One of her highest rated specials was a 1999 interview with White House intern Monica Lewinsky about her relationship with President Bill Clinton.

In 1984, at the age of fifty-three, Walters returned to the anchor desk as cohost with Hugh Downs of the newsmagazine show *20/20*. She retired from that program in 2004. In 1997, when she launched the successful panel show *The View*, Walters added daytime talk show host to her list of credits.

Walters's personal life has had its ups and downs as well. She was married three times. Her first marriage was annulled, and her second and third marriages ended in divorce. However, Walters calls her daughter, Jacqueline, her biggest accomplishment. She adopted Jackie as an infant in 1968. At that time, Walters was getting up at 3:30 A.M. to go to work on *The Today Show*. Walters said, "I told no one. I took one day off to get Jackie, took her right home from the hospital." Back then, women television journalists didn't talk about their kids on the air or in the office. Looking back, Walters says, "My daughter has given my life a meaning that none of my work could ever make up for." Barbara's daughter is equally proud of her mother, although Jackie admits that her mom is much better at work than at some of the domestic duties around the house. One day, as Walters was getting ready to go to an awards show where she was being honored, she overheard her daughter on the telephone: "My mommy can't drive. My mommy burns the meat loaf. The only thing my mommy can do is television."

In 2000, Walters renewed her contract with ABC News for an estimated $12 million a year. At the time it was a record for a news personality. However, she announced her retirement from *20/20* in 2004 to spend more time with her daily talk show *The View*, which she produces. Eventually Walters says she'd like to retire and have more time for her family and friends. But right now she's having too much fun to step out of the limelight. "I like my life. I am healthy and happy. I never imagined having a career like this. And I'm grateful almost every day."

By Beth Evans

political conventions and the evening news, and they dominated the evening news ratings until 1967.

On Monday, September 2, 1963, at 6:30 P.M., CBS launched the first network half-hour evening news broadcast. Cronkite interviewed President John F. Kennedy on the lawn of the Kennedy compound in Hyannis, Massachusetts. The interview focused on Vietnam, and Kennedy said it was a war for the South Vietnamese to win or lose. Eric Sevareid joined Cronkite four times a week to provide about three minutes of the news analysis, another Salant innovation.

NBC, with the Huntley-Brinkley team, also went to a half-hour format a week later. It, too, included an interview with Kennedy. Several years later, the struggling ABC went to a half-hour evening news format. ABC eventually pulled Peter Jennings as sole anchor of its *ABC World News Tonight* and replaced him with Harry Reasoner and Barbara Walters. The network then tried triple anchors with Frank Reynolds in Washington, Max Robinson in Chicago, and Peter Jennings in London. Finally, Peter Jennings was once again tapped to be the sole anchor, a position he held from 1983 until his death in 2005 of complications from lung cancer.

The half-hour news format arrived in the 1960s, at a time of tremendous change. There was too much news to squeeze into fifteen minutes: the civil rights struggle, the assassinations of John and Robert Kennedy and Martin Luther King Jr., urban riots, and the Vietnam War.

THE MEDIA AND CIVIL RIGHTS

Civil rights was an ongoing story; events moved fast after the U.S. Supreme Court on May 17, 1954, issued a landmark decision requiring school desegregation, in *Brown* v. *Board of Education of Topeka, Kansas*. The court ruled that segregation in public education was unconstitutional. In overturning an 1896 ruling in *Plessy* v. *Ferguson*, the court ruled unanimously that "in the field of public education the doctrine of 'separate but equal' has no place. Separate educational facilities are inherently unequal."

Despite the court's directive to integrate "with all deliberate speed," people in the Deep South and Virginia resisted. In September 1957, in Little Rock, Arkansas, Daisy Bates, the state president of the NAACP, personally escorted nine black students to the all-white Central High. Governor Orval E. Faubus called out the National Guard to prevent them from attending. A standoff continued for sixteen days, until federal district court judge Ronald Davies ordered the governor to remove the National Guard. The following Monday, several black journalists were mistaken for the students' parents and were beaten by a mob. While the uproar was going on outside the school, police slipped the students into the school by a side door. President Dwight Eisenhower had to send a thousand soldiers of the 101st Airborne Division to Little Rock to quell the mob, which numbered more than a thousand people.

Efforts to fight segregation in Congress were blocked by the Southern Democrats. Meanwhile, Southern states refused to repeal laws mandating racial segregation. In Greensboro, North Carolina, for example, Woolworth's refused, like any other chain store in the South, to serve black people at its lunch counter.

Two years before the Little Rock school integration fight, Rosa Parks, a forty-two-year-old black seamstress, refused to give up her seat on a Montgomery bus. She wasn't the first. A pregnant fifteen-year-old Claudette Colvin was pulled off a bus in handcuffs for refusing to give up her seat. E. D. Nixon, a former NAACP official, approached Parks with the idea of litigating to challenge bus segregation. She agreed. On December 5, 1955, black people were asked to boycott buses in Montgomery. The protest was supported by the city's black ministers, including the twenty-six-year-old Martin Luther King Jr.

A meeting was called at Holt Street Baptist Church the night of the boycott. Joe Azbell, a reporter for the *Advertiser*, remembered:

> I went up to the church, and they made way for me because I was the first white person there.... The audience was so on fire that the preacher would get up and say, "Do you want your freedom?" And they'd say, "Yeah, I want my freedom!" ... They were on fire for freedom. There was a spirit there that no one could capture again ... it was so powerful. And then King stood up, and most of them didn't even know who he was. And yet he was a master speaker.... I went back, and I wrote a special column. I wrote that this was the beginning of a flame that would go across America.[57]

King became the movement's voice and launched a new phase of mass protest. He was a disciple of the teachings of Gandhi and Thoreau, as well as of Jesus. He emphasized nonviolent civil disobedience. The civil rights struggle was not against whites, but against injustice; its most important weapons were not anger and hate but love and forgiveness, King declared.[58]

On November 13, 1956, the U.S. Supreme Court affirmed a lower court's opinion that bus segregation violated the Fourteenth Amendment. Eight days later, the city's blacks ended their 382-day boycott, riding buses and sitting at lunch counters. Seeing the success of the boycott, ministers from eleven Southern states met at King's father's Ebenezer Baptist Church in Atlanta and created the Southern Christian Leadership Conference to apply their successful principles elsewhere. Martin Luther King Jr. was elected its president. SCLC leadership then encouraged college students to form the Student Nonviolent Coordinating Committee. Both organizations staged sit-ins at restaurants, bus stations, and libraries, and encouraged blacks to register to vote. In addition the Freedom Riders, an interracial group, was formed to ride on interstate buses throughout the South. Their goal was to convince the new Kennedy administration to enforce the 1960 U.S. Supreme Court ruling in *Boynton* v. *Virginia* that segregation on interstate buses was illegal.

By 1960, President Kennedy sent U.S. marshals to protect James Meredith, a U.S. Air Force veteran, who attempted to become the first black student to enroll at the University of Mississippi. Two years later, the president federalized the Alabama National Guard to protect black students trying to enroll at the University of Alabama. Attorney General Robert F. Kennedy ordered Alabama Governor George Wallace to step aside and allow students to enter the university. That night President Kennedy addressed the nation about civil rights. That June he sent Congress a civil rights bill that outlawed segregation in all interstate public accommodations, empowered the attorney general to halt the funding of federal programs in which discrimination was practiced, and declared that any person with a sixth-grade education was presumed literate for the purpose of voting.

The SNCC declared that the Kennedy bill did not go far enough in ensuring civil rights. King and his supporters carried out an August 28, 1963, March on Washington. That day King approached the podium and delivered his "I have a dream" speech to a crowd of 250,000 at the Washington Monument.

Less than two weeks after the March on Washington, a bomb ripped through the Sixteenth Street Baptist Church, in Birmingham, Alabama, killing four black girls. Two months later, on November 22, 1963, President Kennedy was killed by an assassin's bullet in Dallas. Within months, President Lyndon Johnson proposed

AMERICAN MEDIA PROFILE | RUBEN SALAZAR 1928–1970

Bettman/CORBIS

Ruben Salazar, *la voz for la Raza*, the voice for his people, became the most articulate spokesperson for Chicano concerns to the Anglo community. He died a martyr but his work and words continue to guide those who fight ongoing repression.

His experiences on the campus newspaper, *El Burro*, at the University of Texas at El Paso, formerly Texas Western College, led to a career as one of the first Latino reporters to work for the mainstream press, the first Latino foreign correspondent, and the first Latino columnist.

His first job was at the *El Paso Herald-Post* where he covered the police and Juárez beats. There he earned a reputation as a hard-hitting, streetwise reporter. In his first investigative role, he posed as a drunk and spent twenty-five hours in El Paso's city jail. He then wrote an exposé—"25 Hours in Jail—I Lived in a Chamber of Horrors"—of filthy jail conditions and disclosed how drugs were smuggled to prisoners.

In 1959 Salazar joined *the Los Angeles Times*, where he covered the Mexican-American community, which had largely been ignored by the media. His stories about injustices against Mexican Americans and other minorities and working for better understanding among all racial groups proved to be the hallmark of his career.

By 1965 he was a *Times* correspondent in the Dominican Republic, where he covered the revolutionary outbreak, crawling over barricades to talk to members of both sides of the warring groups. From 1965 to 1968 he was with the paper's bureau in Saigon, where he narrowly missed being caught in the blast of a bomb at Da Nag. In 1968 he took charge of the *Times'* Mexico City bureau, covering Central America, the Caribbean, Cuba, and Mexico, where he was an eyewitness to the mass shooting of students by soldiers during the 1968 uprisings.

even tougher civil rights legislation than Kennedy had. The Civil Rights Act of 1964 outlawed racial discrimination in all public places, and ended discrimination in employment, union membership, and federally financed programs. Martin Luther King Jr. wanted to demonstrate what Southern blacks faced when they tried to register to vote, knowing that television would cover it. On February 1, 1965, King was arrested and jailed, joining 3,000 other demonstrators in jail. President Johnson then presented the Voting Rights Act of 1965 to Congress. This eliminated literacy tests and other obstacles to black registration. It also created a corps of federal examiners to make sure voter registrations would be fair and open.

Racial violence broke out across the country during the summers of 1964 and 1965. Violence erupted in the ghettos of Detroit and Newark, and elsewhere. Some 100 people died. Black people were frustrated by a lack of jobs and income. King then attempted to draw attention to these problems by a peaceful Poor People's March on Washington, D.C. On April 4, 1968, King, standing on the balcony of the Lorraine Motel in Memphis, was shot and killed by sniper James Earl Ray. That June Robert Kennedy was assassinated in a Los Angeles hotel while campaigning for the Democratic presidential nomination.

AMERICAN MEDIA PROFILE | **CONTINUED**

In 1969 the *Times* brought Salazar back to Los Angeles where he began writing news stories and a weekly column about Mexican Americans, whom he characterized as the "forgotten community." It was a time when East Los Angeles had become a hotbed of protest by activists who were calling themselves Chicanos instead of Mexican Americans. Thousands of students had staged walkouts at area high schools, demanding more Chicano teachers and improved facilities.

In April 1970 Salazar left the *Times* to become news director for the Spanish-language television station KMEX, where he again specialized in the Los Angeles Mexican-American community. He continued to write a column for the *Times*. Though no revolutionary, Salazar's writings became impassioned pleas for cross-cultural and cross-generational understanding. He called upon whites to listen to the needs of Chicano students. He also did some of his hardest-hitting reporting on law enforcement. He and his KMEX colleague, William Restrepo, began a major investigation into widespread allegations that police and sheriff's deputies had beaten residents and planted evidence when making arrests.

On August 29, 1970, Salazar, Restrepo, and a cameraman were covering a Chicano civil rights demonstration, which erupted into a riot. Deputies, responding to reports of lootings at a nearby liquor store, were hit by rocks and bottle. Salazar and Restrepo went into a café. What happened next is disputed to this day. A sheriff's deputy fired a 10-inch tear gas projectile inside, striking the 42-year-old Salazar in the head and killing him instantly.

His death made him a martyr of the Chicano/Latino civil right movement, and questions remain as to whether he was the victim of a tragic accident or whether he was assassinated.

In 2008 the U.S. Postal Service honored Salazar with a 42-cent stamp. It was supposed to come out one year earlier. For many, that stamp represented 42 years of a wonderful life which represented the best values of America and American journalism.

WOMEN IN TELEVISION NEWS

The Civil Rights Act of 1964 also opened doors for women journalists when President Lyndon B. Johnson asked Congress to include language preventing sexual discrimination. The Federal Communications Commission on December 21, 1971, went a step further. It made it possible to challenge television licenses if women were not given equal opportunity for employment or training for advancement.

Pauline Frederick in 1946 was the first and only woman in television news. At the time news writing was reserved for men because station managers and advertisers held that men's voices alone carried authority and believability.[59] Frederick understood that well. She was denied a permanent job because she was female, finally landing a position as a stringer for ABC, covering "women's stories." Her break came when her male boss had two important stories to assign. However, he had only one male reporter. He assigned her to cover a foreign ministers' conference. In just a few months, Frederick, who held a master's degree in international law, was assigned the United Nations as a regular beat. By 1948 she was assigned permanently to international affairs and politics. Five years later, however, NBC appointed her its United Nations correspondent.

AMERICAN MEDIA PROFILE   CHRISTIANE AMANPOUR 1958–

Michal Cizek/AFP/Getty Images

Christiane Amanpour is so identified over the world with war and disaster that people say jokingly that they shudder when they see her: "Oh my god. Amanpour is coming. Is something bad going to happen to us?"

U.S. soldiers joke that they track her movements in order to know where they will be deployed next. She says she has calculated that she has spent more time at the front than most normal military units. "I have spent the past ten years in just about every war zone there was. I have made my living bearing witness to some of the most horrific events of the end of our century, at the end of the 20th century," she explained at an Edward R. Murrow award ceremony.

Amanpour, the most celebrated war correspondent since Murrow, picked up a microphone during World War II and started broadcasting for CBS News. She arrived at CNN in 1983 with a suitcase, a bicycle, and $100. Today she is considered one of the world's most powerful women and among the highest-paid correspondents.

CNN's chief international correspondent fell into broadcasting almost by accident. Her younger sister had enrolled in a London-based journalism program then changed her mind about attending. The institution refused to allow a tuition reimbursement, so Amanpour was permitted to take her place. She would eventually add a bachelor's degree from the University of Rhode Island to her resume. The daughter of an Iranian airline executive and British mother, Amanpour worked for NBC affiliate WJAR in Providence, Rhode Island as an electronic graphics designer.

She arrived at CNN from one of the best local stations "who took me in right after college and sort of had pity on me and gave me a job." They then encouraged her to try CNN because they knew somebody who worked there. They basically said, "You know, this is a great opportunity for somebody like yourself who's foreign, who has a foreign accent. We hear foreign accents on CNN. It's crazy, it's wild, who knows, maybe they'll take you because you certainly don't fit in, in the American spectrum of news."

She was assigned to the foreign desk. "I kid you not, it's true. I was really just the tea boy to begin with, or the equivalent thereof, but I quickly announced, innocently but very ambitiously, that I wanted to be, I was going to be, a foreign correspondent."

CBS News tapped Nancy Dickerson as its first female network correspondent in 1960. At the time she recalled that *The Washington Daily News* offered her a job as women's editor but that she turned it down because "it seemed outlandish to try to change the world writing shopping and food columns." As network news was expanding on American television in the early sixties, she was the most visible woman on the air. She was described in a *Saturday Evening Post* article as "slim (five feet seven and 120 pounds) and social (she is a member of Washington's exclusive F Street Club), chic and charming, she looks and dresses like a fashion model, speaks like a professional actress, and goes about her job like a veteran newsman."[60]

However, once the FCC announced its anti-discrimination rule, the pressure to hire women was on. And CBS wasted no time. It feared legal repercussions if these criteria were not met in the workplace. That's when CBS hired 25-year-old Connie Chung, the first Asian-American network reporter, a move that would permanently launch her career.

AMERICAN MEDIA PROFILE	CONTINUED

Amanpour relates that her first experiences at CNN were not happy ones. "I am sorry to say that my first boss was a woman. You'd think this would have helped me, but it didn't, if I had thought I would get a sympathetic hearing from her, some female solidarity, I didn't, I was sorely mistaken. She hated me and my ambition. She made fun of me, she said, 'You'll never make it at CNN; you've got to go somewhere else and start.' In any event that was all character-building stuff."

Her assessment could not have been more off the mark. Today, Amanpour is one of the most respected television foreign correspondents. She has reported from the heart of war zones. Her coverage of the Persian Gulf War that followed Iraq's occupation of Kuwait in 1990 brought her fame and propelled her network to a new level of news coverage. Her coverage of conflicts in the Balkans, Africa, and the Middle East also has put her at the top of the class.

Her coverage hasn't come without criticisms. For example, viewers questioned her professional objectivity during her emotional delivery from Sarajevo during the Siege of Sarajevo. Some felt her reports were unjustified and favored the Bosnians. She told them: "There are some situations one simply cannot be neutral about, because when you are neutral you are an accomplice. Objectivity doesn't mean treating all sides equally. It means giving each side a hearing."

What gives her the courage to venture into war zones and disasters to get stories? "I believe many experiences shape a person" she said. "One of mine was riding horses competitively from age five. My teacher, a colonel in the Iranian army, was very tough—there was no mollycoddling. If I fell off or got kicked in the stomach, he put me right back on the horse. That teaches you fortitude. I also had several teachers—a biology teacher in secondary school, for example, and a Shakespeare professor in college—who infected me with their love of learning these difficult, complex subjects."

Her exclusive interviews with world figures also has landed her much praise. She conducted the first interview with Iranian president Mahmoud Ahmadinejad and has landed exclusives with former Pakistani president Pervez Musharraf and Syrian president Bashar el Assad on the U.N. investigation into Syria's involvement in the assassination of former Lebanese Prime Minister Rafiq Hariri.

An authoritative voice in the media on Islam, Amanpour was named by Queen Elizabeth II as a Commander of the Order of the British Empire, just one step shy of knighthood. She has won nine news and documentary Emmy awards and two George Polk awards. And the one she must be proudest of is the Edward R. Murrow Award for Distinguished Achievement in Broadcast Journalism.

Despite the progress concerning women's roles in the workforce—and specifically at the news desk—men still ruled the airwaves. They were paid more as evidenced by a 1977 out-of-court settlement where NBC awarded $2 million to its 2,600 women employees in back wages and increased salaries.[61]

A year earlier, ABC surprised the industry when it offered a $1-million contract to Barbara Walters to co-anchor the *ABC Evening News with Harry Reasoner and Barbara Walters*. It was obvious to viewers that it was not a good match. She injected the human element into her reporting, giving a more personal side to stories. Reasoner was hostile to this reporting style at a time when the credibility of ABC, television's youngest network, was questioned.[62] At first Nielsen reported strong ratings for the program, but when they began to slip, she realized her position would be short-lived.[63]

However, Walter was not the first female network anchor. ABC News appointed its correspondent, Marlene Sanders, a trailblazer for women in news, as its first female prime-time network news anchor in 1964 when she was asked to sub for an ailing anchor. Two years later she became the first TV newswoman to report from Vietnam, and in 1976, while a producer-correspondent for the network's documentary unit, became the first woman news vice president at the networks, when she was named vice president and director of documentaries.

These early pioneers paved the way for such notables as Diane Sawyer, who came to Washington to help President Richard Nixon write his memoirs. She decided to stay, landing the position as first woman correspondent for *60 Minutes*. In 1989 she moved to ABC to co-host *Prime Time Live* in 1989, eventually becoming the co-host of *Good Morning America* ten years later.

Lesley R. Stahl, who is nearing 20 seasons on *60 Minutes*, became a White House correspondent during the presidencies of Jimmy Carter, Ronald Reagan, and George H. W. Bush. On election night in 1974, she was finally included in the roundtable discussion on the night's events. She walked onto a set and found the male correspondents had their names in front of their chairs—"Cronkite," "Mudd," and "Wallace." Hers said, "female." They would soon come to know her name.

By the time Katie Couric was hired, CBS News asked Stahl to reduce her salary by $500,000 to accommodate Couric's salary. Before joining CBS, Couric was host of NBC's morning program *The Today Show* (reportedly signing a $65-million contract in 2001 to remain with the show until 2006). She not only gave a huge lift to the show's sagging ratings but became one of morning TV's most popular personalities. She took over anchor duties at *The CBS Evening News* on September 5, 2006, but she couldn't boost its ratings.

On the other hand, Christiane Amanpour helped put CNN on the map. And she also got the distinction of being named one of the world's most powerful women by *Forbes* magazine. She is also the world's highest-paid correspondent, and, according to *Time* magazine, the world's most influential correspondent since Murrow. President Bill Clinton called her the "voice of humanity." Clinton, no doubt, was referring to her acclaimed coverage of the war in the Balkans, a dangerous assignment as she attempted to bring the Bosnian tragedy into the international spotlight.

The Gulf War was her first major international story just two months after she was made a foreign correspondent. Since then she has covered CNN's biggest stories, including the conflict in the Middle East, natural disasters of Tsunami-hit Sri Lanka and the devastation wreaked by Hurricane Katrina in Louisiana. She also has been on the frontlines covering acts of terrorism, including the London tube bombings in July 2005, the Madrid railway bombings in 2004, riots in France, and the first democratic elections in Iraq. And she has traveled to Sudan to cover the crisis in Darfur. What drives her? "Because if the storytellers don't do this," she has said, "then the bad people will win."[64]

CONCLUSION

Though television broadcasting sputtered onto the scene in 1948, many minds had worked toward it for decades. Edward Bellamy's 1888 work *Looking Backward* predicted the transmission of "music and sermons" for the masses on "musical telephones." In 1936 Charlie Chaplin showed an uncanny vision of the future in *Modern Times*: he is discovered smoking in the washroom by his boss via TV monitor.

Guided by media giants such as David Sarnoff and William S. Paley, among others, television came into the homes of Americans, who were ready to be entertained and informed. Some of the early television entertainment programs, such as quiz shows and programs that stereotyped minorities, were shameful. Quiz shows cleaned up their acts and returned in the 1990s to even greater popularity. A Game Show Channel is now offered to most cable subscribers. And black performers, such as comedian Bill Cosby and actress Diahann Carroll, enjoyed great successes in television comedies.

Some say the new wave of television entertainment might be just as shameful. Reality television, from *An American Family* to *American Idol*, has become a ratings behemoth. The reality genre, however, has become a vehicle for presenting minorities and marginalized groups to a wide audience. It has brought issues of race relations and sexual identity to the mainstream and has helped foster a national discourse on these topics.

Television news programming has had an even greater impact on the social and political fabric of the nation. Edward R. Murrow used the power of television to expose Senator Joseph McCarthy. Martin Luther King Jr. also knew the value of television and used it to get his message out to Americans. For example, President John Kennedy and the nation were watching television on August 28, 1963, and witnessed the March on Washington, one of the largest rallies in the nation's history.

They heard and saw black leaders call for a revolution in jobs and freedom. In some ways television helped enlighten the public about the problems faced by black people, and it may have sped civil rights legislation.

Television, and the news media in general, would play an even greater role as the nation faced a series of national crises—the Vietnam War, Watergate, Iran-Contra, terrorism, and the fury of Hurricane Katrina. She walloped the Gulf Coast in one of the most catastrophic, costliest, and deadliest natural disasters in U.S. history, testing the very soul of news organizations on August 29, 2005. Flood waters, which reached some 20 feet, eventually engulfed 80 percent of New Orleans, shutting down as many as 50 to 100 radio and TV stations and the 169-year-old *New Orleans Times-Picayune*, the city's only daily.

News also would become profitable for the networks as advertising revenues reached new heights. Then the Internet and the information explosion would provide news organizations with their greatest challenge as mergers put fewer players on the field with a decreasing audience in the stands. It was a new media ballgame.

1950–PRESENT MEDIA CHALLENGES IN A CHANGING WORLD

PART | 5

For some, the late 1950s and early 1960s were the best of times. For others it was the worst of times. It was a period in which two generations clashed about what the proper goals for the nation should be. Older, more patient, and more conservative Americans found comfort in the steady and quiet leadership of Dwight D. Eisenhower. The younger, less patient, and more liberal were attracted to John F. Kennedy's vigor and call "to get this country moving again."

Television became a powerful and popular transmitter of entertainment and information, affecting the social and political fabric of America. "Never in the history of mankind has there been a medium with the impact of television. It . . . literally has brought the world home in a box," according to Walter Cronkite.

This has caught America at its best and its worse. For the first time, Americans were able to see—in the comfort of their living rooms—two presidential candidates debate. More than 85 million Americans tuned in to at least one of the Kennedy-Nixon debates. As president, Kennedy introduced live televising and broadcasting of presidential press conferences. But within 1,000 days of his inauguration, shocking bulletins told of his assassination. And within days, television audiences were shocked again when they witnessed the murder of the president's assassin. Television also made Americans uneasy as it captured violent and shocking pictures of race riots and combat engagements of the Vietnam War.

The nation stood with pride when television beamed Americans standing on the moon on July 20, 1969. In a matter of years, that pride turned to disgust as television captured a president in turmoil and his eventual resignation from office and the peccadilloes of another president and his eventual impeachment. And it wasn't television that broke the news. It was a nonjournalist writing on the Internet.

ADVERTISING AS A SOCIAL, ECONOMIC, AND POLITICAL FORCE

CHAPTER **11**

Although most people think of advertising as distracting pop-ups on the Internet or annoying interruptions of a favorite television show, in fact advertising is much more—a vital component of the nation's mass media, consumer economy, and political landscape. Beginning with the first ad in a colonial newspaper in 1704, advertising has steadily grown into such a powerful influence on our culture some theorize a connection between advertising and democracy.

Because advertising first became such a dominant force in the United States, those who see a parallel between advertising and democracy point out that Americans, born out of a hard-won political system requiring information-seeking from its citizens, became accustomed to looking for information on which to base their attitudes and opinions. It was this uniquely American characteristic of individuality and reliance on reason that shaped the role of advertising. Indeed, Americans who looked to the mass media for the political information needed for intelligent self-governance, also looked to the mass media for information to help make decisions on what products or services to buy.

ADVERTISING'S ECONOMIC ROLE

Out of this reliance on mass media for information comes one of the most important roles for advertising in democratic societies: providing the revenue for mass media to operate. The media that people look to for news, information, entertainment, and ideas would not exist in its present form without advertising.

Advertising's economic role in the United States, however, extends far beyond its support of the mass media. The mid-1800s saw the real beginning of advertising in America, as sweeping social and technological change were brought about by the Industrial Revolution. Technology drove mass production and an expanded transportation system distributed product and media on a national level. Advertisers began emphasizing brands in ads directed to a newly mobile American society, where people trusted and bought familiar brands even when they moved to a new location with unfamiliar shopkeepers. This brand-driven, national communication eventually led to America's consumer economy where advertising is essential to maintaining prosperity by driving demand, influencing buying decisions, and helping consumers make choices.

The advertising industry is a huge contributor to the U.S. economy. It is estimated that U.S. advertisers spend about 2 percent of the nation's gross domestic product to promote their products and services. Today's $284-billion ad industry is testimony that the relationship between advertising and a democratic and capitalistic society has always been and will continue to be one of mutual benefit.

Because it is social communication, advertising tells us a great deal about our past and present culture. When we view advertisements as cultural artifacts we see they reflect both social values and attitudes of the times. Advertising's influence on our culture is evidenced by the fact that the Archives Center of the Smithsonian Institute's National Museum of American History devotes a good portion of its collections to the category of advertising, along with music and technology.

Nowhere in American society does advertising play a more significant role than in the political process, where citizens often make voting decisions based on political ads. Although advertising truly became a political force with the advent of television in the 1950s, Americans saw political ad campaigns as early as 1840. Today's political candidates routinely use media consultants to develop advertising strategies to "sell" the candidate the same as a consumer product.

As advertising has become a more powerful force, some critics maintain that commercialism has gone too far in a society where people are exposed to more than 3,500 messages every day in a pop-culture landscape saturated with brands, slogans, and advertising characters.[1] Perhaps the critics have a point; during the 2007 season ABC television featured a new sitcom starring cavemen characters from an insurance commercial.

A SPECIAL RHETORIC

Simply, we accord advertising a place of special prominence in our lives. It has become a "privileged form of discourse," once reserved for church sermons, political oratory, and the words of family elders. Although these influences remain with us, their prominence, rhetorical force, and moral authority have diminished, replaced in part by talk and action about consumer goods, what they can do or should mean for us.

Advertisements, which now enjoy limited First Amendment protection though regulated to a degree by the federal government, are an ever more dominant part of life, not just in the mass media, but in every part of life, from the $3-million Super Bowl commercial to the local pizza sponsor on the Little Leaguer's uniform. Though sometimes subtle, ads are part of life on every level—the clothing we wear with a corporate logo, the T-shirts with a sales pitch, billboards which dot every road we drive or building we pass, sports events or venues which carry a corporate name, uniforms on sports teams flashing the famous "swish" logo before millions of fans watching them on TV—extending even to electronically generated logos flashed in strategic locations during televised sporting events.

Advertising's origin and impact is the subject of this chapter, which will trace early American advertising, the development of the advertising agency, the impact of branding, advertising self-regulation and advertising's role as a social, economic and political force in America.

COLONIAL ERA ADVERTISING

America's earliest newspaper publishers considered advertising a degrading and undesirable necessity. The colonies' first publication to resemble a newspaper, Boston's *Publick Occurrences, Both Forreign and Domestick*, carried no advertising in its first and only issue in 1690.

The earliest newspaper advertisements were published in the colonies' first continuously published newspaper, the *Boston News-Letter*, in 1704. Imported goods, runaway slaves, sales of slaves, and sailings from Boston were the concerns of these early ads; they resembled the modern classified or want ads. *Publick Occurrences'* editor, John Campbell, limited advertisements to a maximum space of twenty lines in his two-page newspaper. Another daily, the *Pennsylvania Packet and Daily Advertiser*, contained more advertisements than news.

Benjamin Franklin, whom some refer to as the father of American advertising, gave advertising its greatest boost when he purchased the *Pennsylvania Gazette* in 1729. He eventually increased his newspaper from two to four pages so he could print more advertisements and news stories. He carefully set off each ad with white space and a large type heading, later incorporating small illustrations. A talented writer, Franklin turned his genius to writing advertising copy, making him the first advertising copywriter worthy of the name in American history. He advertised glasses, wine, cheese, chocolate, mathematical instruments, codfish, tea, coffee, and stoves. Franklin found ads so valuable, he filled the entire front page of his papers with them, and also initiated the idea of printing ads throughout the paper, not in a special section.

Franklin also would have the distinction of being the first to print an advertisement in a magazine. On May 10, 1741, his *General Magazine* printed a notice about a ferry. It ran under the title "Advertisement." Prior to the start of the American Revolution, Franklin, like almost every other publisher, was affected when the British Parliament enacted the Stamp Act of 1765. Ads were now taxed. As shortages in paper increased, Franklin cut display advertising and filled advertising columns with small type and thumbnail-sized art.

By 1800 more than 300 newspapers were published in the United States. Despite the increase in advertising, very few newspapers depended on advertising revenue. Daily newspapers derived only about a third of their income from advertising; national magazines took in even less. Robert Bonner's *New York Ledger*, the first weekly publication to hit a national circulation of 400,000, carried no advertising at all.

Instead, private contributions, subscriptions, or political parties supported most newspapers. For example, the total amount of print advertising revenue in 1880 was $39,136,306. Revenues from subscriptions totaled $49,872,768.

ADVERTISING IN THE PENNY PRESS PERIOD

Prior to the penny press period, there was little need for elaborate advertising. The great majority of Americans lived in isolated areas and produced whatever they needed themselves. Whatever advertising existed was usually for local merchants selling their wares within the community.

Prior to the penny press period, editors sought specialized, differentiated audiences, catering primarily to members of a political party, business, or religion. That attitude toward advertising changed thanks to entrepreneurial editors and the enterprising advertising agents who appeared in the penny press period.

Benjamin Day's *New York Sun* began the changes in 1833. A single newspaper now appealed to everyone, including thousands of immigrants eager to learn about their new country and workers sharing in the exploding wealth created by industrialization and the labor movement. The result was a dramatic leap in the *Sun's* circulation to 20,000—more than twice that of any other newspaper in the United States—making the paper a favored medium for advertisers. Even with new printing technologies reducing costs, Day could not produce his paper for a penny per copy; therefore, he depended upon advertisers to show a profit.

Day acknowledged the importance of advertising when he wrote in his first issue, "The object of this paper is to lay before the public, at a price within the means of everyone, all the news of the day, and at the same time afford an advantageous medium for advertising." Day, who wrote most of the advertising copy, charged thirty dollars a year for advertising ten lines or less a day. He was more savvy than earlier editors. Having seen the importance of the want ad used by advertisers in London, he aggressively encouraged businesses and readers to purchase these small advertisements that he placed under the heading "Wants." Each two- or three-line ad cost fifty cents.

Day also instituted a cash-in-advance policy. Other penny press editors soon followed. Day was so successful in obtaining advertising that he had to increase the dimensions of his page, devoting thirteen of his daily columns to advertising. By 1836, the year he sold the *Sun*, the number of columns reserved for advertising grew to seventeen, in a twenty-four-column newspaper. No doubt, the paper's advertising revenue helped Day achieve a handsome profit when he sold the paper to Moses Yale Beach for $40,000.

James Gordon Bennett, the most successful of the penny press editors, was even more creative than Day in news and advertising content and style. He, too, instituted a cash-in-advance policy for adverting. He also required advertisers to change their copy daily.

An early ninteenth-century advertisement for Coca-Cola says the drink will relieve exhaustion "when the brain is running under full pressure." Note the cost—five cents.

Bennett's greatest achievement was instituting what came to be defined as display advertising. In 1836, his *Herald* published a two-column advertisement for the American Museum that contained a two-column illustration. Other New York newspapers followed the *Herald*'s lead. However, by the late 1840s, advertisers who placed small advertisements daily in Bennett's paper complained about the bigger display ads. In typical Bennett fashion, he banned all display advertising for a while, requiring all advertisements to be set in very small type.

THE ADVERTISING AGENT

The penny press period saw yet another innovation in advertising—the advertising agent and the brokering of newspaper ad space. Before the 1840s, those who wanted to advertise a product negotiated directly with owners of newspapers or magazines. Such a system worked when only one or two newspapers were available. However, as the number of publications increased, it became too time consuming for advertisers to correspond with every paper in which they wanted to advertise. Volney Palmer had an idea to solve that problem.

VOLNEY PALMER

Although some would give Volney Palmer the distinction of starting the first advertising agency, he was, in fact, primarily a space broker. Palmer, who worked in real estate, started advertising his ad brokering business along with his real estate business in 1842. Though he used the words "Advertising Agency" in one of his advertisements in 1849, Palmer was in fact America's first advertising "agent." He worked for the newspapers, not the advertisers. Functioning as a space salesman, he offered advertisers a list of publications in which he had exclusive space-selling rights. Palmer offered free estimates, and collected a 25 percent commission from the newspapers. He helped manufacturers and others realize how important and effective advertising was in the competitive arena.

SAMUEL PETTENGILL

The concept of brokering advertising space expanded rapidly and by the 1860s some thirty brokering agencies were operating in New York, the largest of which was owned by Samuel Pettengill, a former Palmer employee. By now brokering of ad space was beginning to take on the air of corruption, with agents selling space for publishers while giving expert and impartial advice to advertisers on how best to spend their advertising dollars.

In reality, agents wanted only to buy space from publishers as cheaply as possible and then sell it to advertisers as profitably as possible, without telling either what rates the other was paying. Pettingill's services differed from Palmer's in that he expanded the services of his firm, offering his clients copywriting services as well.

POST–CIVIL WAR: ADVERTISING AGENTS AND ADVERTISING AGENCIES

During the decades following the Civil War, specialized machinery expanded manufacturing production while advances in transportation—particularly the development of railroads—made distribution faster and easier. Both products and media became national and with that expansion came the development of advertising amid what most consider the beginning of the consumer economy. National advertising initially focused on patent medicines, which will be discussed later.

GEORGE P. ROWELL

In 1865 George P. Rowell took space brokerage to its logical conclusion by buying ad space in bulk on an annual contract and retailing it to advertisers at a profit. By buying in bulk, Rowell was in a position to bargain with publishers for lower rates. He guaranteed payment to publishers whether he collected his fees from advertisers or not. He also offered advertisers discounts for prompt payment. Some consider Rowell's company the first advertising agency.

Rowell offered small advertisers exciting new opportunities when he developed special contracts that allowed them to purchase advertising by the column-inch in 100 New England weeklies. Eventually he placed contracts on an annual basis and, with the use of thin stereotype plates that allowed advertisers to see their ad before it was printed, he became the largest advertising brokerage in New York by 1867.

A few years later, Rowell introduced yet another startling innovation to advertising—a directory of newspaper circulation figures. At this time no actual circulation figures were available and Rowell thought that if he could supply advertisers with accurate information about newspapers and their readers, they would have some indication of how much to pay for the space they purchased.

In 1869 his agency published the first issue of *Rowell's American Newspaper Directory*, which listed the circulations of more than 5,000 publications in the United States and some 300 in Canada. He didn't make a lot of friends. Many newspaper publishers lashed out at him for printing conservative circulation figures. However, his services were used, and eventually publishers followed his lead and adjusted their circulation figures to agree with the more accurate numbers published in Rowell's directory.

Another of Rowell's publications, *Printers' Ink*, eventually became the advertising industry's voice as the leading trade paper of the day. Initially containing suggestions for improving advertising copy, it grew into what has been called the greatest single influence for spreading information about improving advertising methods. As discussed later, *Printer's Ink* also influenced state legislation against misleading advertising.

J. WALTER THOMPSON

About this time a twenty-year-old with a name that would eventually become one of the most famous in the advertising business applied for a job as a clerk with Rowell's brokerage. Rowell didn't see much promise in J. Walter Thompson, and discouraged him from pursuing a career in advertising. Thompson went to work as a bookkeeper and assistant for a small, one-man brokerage and the rest is advertising history.

When Thompson was sent out to solicit new accounts, he was surprised to see that many magazines ran only a page or two of ads, and that these were accepted by reluctant editors. However, he saw that these magazines had a prominent place in people's homes, and they stayed there for some time.

Thompson was amazed that the publishing world had "failed to grasp the possibilities of such a medium in the advertising business."[2] To illustrate his point, he placed an ad for asbestos roofing in unlikely publications, two women's journals: *Godey's* and *Peterson's*. The company sold more roofing than at any promotion in its history. He then placed another ad in *Peterson's* and within twenty days merchants received more than three thousand dollars' worth of orders in sums no larger than thirty-five cents.[3]

Specialized magazines with their large circulations, Thompson reasoned, would become an effective medium to supplement the religious and other types of journals that he also serviced. By the end of the century, he had some thirty noted magazines taking their advertising from him. In 1878 he was able to buy out his former boss. He paid $500 for the business and $800 for the office furniture, and renamed the business the J. Walter Thompson Advertising Agency, considered by some to be the first advertising agency in America, though it did not initially offer full advertising services.

In 2005 the full-service J. Walter Thompson agency was re-branded as JWT and, as part of the past decade's move to consolidation, became part of the London-based WPP Group. According to *Advertising Age*, WPP ranks as the second-largest ad agency group in the world, with 90,182 employees and 2007 revenues of over $12 billion. JWT, which ranks eighth in the United States, had just over $1 billion in worldwide revenues in 2007.

FRANCIS WAYLAND AYER

Prior to J. Walter Thompson's acquisition of his employer's brokerage agency, another broker with another of the most famous names in advertising took the final step away from the role of space broker. Francis Wayland Ayer couldn't understand how Rowell and other space brokers could represent the advertiser while being paid by the publisher. Even at age twenty, Ayer also realized that most advertisers were too busy to write and produce their own ads. Ayer had a better idea—a full-service agency that would create, produce, and place ads while offering counsel and eventually a crude type of research.

He founded N. W. Ayer and Son in 1869 in Philadelphia, giving the agency his father's name to add credibility to an organization founded by such a young man. To address the conflict of interest he saw in the relationship between agents and advertisers, Ayer developed a media placement system still in use today. He called it the "Open Contract" plus commission. Ayer's agency would represent and be paid by the advertiser instead of the publisher; instead of acting as a space-seller, the company became a space-buyer, adding a commission of 8.5 to 15 percent to the cost of the ad space. Eventually the commission became a straight 15 percent of the rate. The contract would bind the agency and the advertiser for a period of time, usually a year, with the agency taking a standard percentage of the billing as its commission. Under this system, the agency no longer squeezed the advertiser to make a profit. It acted on the advertiser's behalf in finding the best publications for the advertiser's needs. The "Open Contract" would become the keystone of Ayer's success. It helped make Ayer the number-one agency of the 1890s.

The 1893 decision by the American Newspaper Publishers' Association to abide by Ayer's published rates and not to bargain with space brokers did much to make this billing system work. After the turn of the century, the policy of fixed commission was gradually accepted by other agents and endorsed by the agencies' professional association. The standard 15 percent commission remains the basic system for agency ad placement billing today.

The Ayer agency also was the first to base an advertising campaign on a market survey. It also issued the *American Newspaper Annual*, later to become the *N.W. Ayer & Son's Directory of Newspapers and Periodicals*, which listed every newspaper and magazine published in the United States and Canada. It is now published as the *Gale Directory of Publications and Broadcast Media*.

Sadly, the N. W. Ayer agency, once one of America's most successful ad agencies, began a downward spiral in the 1990s, and after several failed mergers was eventually bought by Chicago-based Bcom3. According to *Advertising Age*, when its parent company was acquired in 2002 by the gigantic Publicis Groupe, a French agency group now ranked number four in the world in revenue, Ayer ceased to exist when it was folded into New York–based Kaplan Thaler Group.

Ayer's influence over the years was validated when *Advertising Age* selected the twentieth century's top-ten advertising slogans. Ayer's slogan for DeBeers, "Diamonds are forever," was number one. Another Ayer slogan, "When it rains it pours," developed for Morton Salt, ranked number nine on the list.

ADVERTISING IN THE GILDED AGE

The last two decades of the eighteenth century were dubbed the "Gilded Age" by author Mark Twain, based on the enormous fortunes and luxurious lifestyles of the super-rich, whose unprecedented wealth came with the growth of industry and a huge wave of immigrants to work in the factories.

When the nineteenth century drew to a close, major agencies such as J. Walter Thompson, N. W. Ayer & Sons, and Batten and Company (forerunner of today's BBDO agency) were providing clients a variety of services and beginning to function in the same way as full-service agencies of the future. Their services included creative work, media placement, and basic research.

This period saw new developments in newspapers. In the 1880s and 1890s, Joseph Pulitzer and William Randolph Hearst introduced a new journalism and a new look for advertising. Marking the beginning of the modern commercial newspaper, Pulitzer introduced a new format for his papers, which included exciting headlines and page designs. These new techniques advanced Pulitzer's contribution to the development of advertising in three ways. First, these stylistic innovations opened up display advertising throughout the industry. Second, Pulitzer introduced a formula whereby a certain percentage of a newspaper's space would be devoted to advertising. Finally, he spurred the industry to determine advertising rates based on circulation, which was Pulitzer's measure of success. He proudly published his *New York World*'s high circulation figures on its front page, along with the fact that the paper printed more advertising than any other paper.

Pulitzer's circulation figures certainly justified his pride; in 1884, just one year after he bought the *World*, it boasted a circulation of 100,000, making it the most profitable newspaper ever published. Two years later the circulation stood at 250,000, eventually growing to 374,000 when he introduced the evening edition of his paper in 1887. Pulitzer's Sunday edition alone reached 250,000 in the late 1880s, with half of its thirty-six to forty pages carrying advertising.

MAGAZINES AND ADVERTISING

With more emphasis in this period on national advertising came more emphasis on a natural partner for advertisers—magazines, now with a national audience, giving them an advantage over newspapers' more geographically defined readership. Working off the successful business model developed by Benjamin Day and other penny press editors, many magazines began to address matters of concern to Americans and their families, such as health, fashion, and food. Major writers such as

Mark Twain and Sir Arthur Conan Doyle frequently contributed to magazines during this time, improving editorial quality.

Although magazine editors were still lukewarm to advertising, magazine publishers were not, as evidenced by these words from Cyrus H. K. Curtis, founder of *Ladies' Home Journal* who told an audience of manufacturers in 1883: "The editor of the Ladies' Home Journal thinks we publish it for the benefit of American women. This is an illusion, but a very proper one for him to have. The real reason, the publisher's reason, is to give you who manufacture things American women want, a chance to tell them about your product."[4]

By the end of the eighteenth century, magazines were supported primarily by advertisers rather than readers. These ads began to incorporate many of the aspects of advertising still in use today: seasonal placement, proximity placement next to editorial content of related interest, direct-response elements, professional design, and well-written text.

BRANDS AND THEIR INFLUENCE

One of advertising's most important developments also came into widespread use during this period—an emphasis on brands. A brand is a name and image associated with a particular product intended to be distributed on a national or broad regional scale. Manufacturers realized that in order to make a profit, these branded products had to be mass-produced for national consumption. This meant that new retail outlets for these brands had to be found, creating new relationships between retailers and consumers. Consumers now preferred national brands to the traditionally unbranded and often unpackaged items such as crackers, pickles, or candies sold in bulk and kept in barrels or jars.

As more products entered the national marketplace, advertisers quickly learned it was necessary to differentiate their products. For example, a company did not merely make soap, it made Kirkman's, Fairbank's Gold Dust, Breck, Pears', or Ivory soap.

One of the most successful and innovative brand management advertisers of all time, who ranked number one in advertising spending in 2007 with $4.9 billion, is Procter and Gamble (P&G). P&G introduced Ivory Soap nationally in 1879, when a bar cost ten cents. As one of America's longest-lived, branded consumer products, the advertising history for Ivory includes a number of "firsts": one of the first and most enduring slogans, "It floats," introduced in 1891; the first color magazine ad, appearing in *Cosmopolitan* in 1896; one of the first TV commercials, aired in 1939; one of the first sponsors of a TV soap opera, the *Guiding Light* in 1952. The "99 and 44/100% pure" campaign for Ivory, which was launched in 1882, was ranked in the top twenty of *Advertising Age*'s best advertising campaigns. The entire Ivory soap advertising archive was donated to the Smithsonian's National Museum of American History in 2001, where it can be viewed online through the Archive Center's *Ivory Project*.[5]

Today's advertisers consider branding the preeminent component of ongoing marketing success. Brands are actually assigned value in today's marketplace, with Coca-Cola ranked number one in value among global brands, with a brand value of $67 billion. Microsoft is second at $61 billion and IBM is third with a brand valued at $54 billion.

PATENT MEDICINE AND DEPARTMENT STORE ADVERTISING

Although soap manufacturers were heavy advertisers at the end of the 1800s, patent medicines and department stores dominated the advertising business, contributing half of ad agencies' revenues during this period.

As department stores and the products they carried became prominent in newspapers and magazines, they accounted for more than 20 percent of ad space by the early 1890s. These retailers brought consumers an entirely new shopping experience, where they browsed for brand names as opposed to shopping in small shops guided by the shopkeeper's recommendations. Much as retailing operates today, the department stores were able to spend more money on advertising because they purchased merchandise in larger volume, generally lowering their prices. In a pattern repeated today by Target and Wal-Mart, department store chains soon put small "mom and pop" shops out of business.

Patent medicines had already established themselves prior to this period. Before the Civil War they had a total annual sale of about $3.5 million. The most successful of these "wonders" included addictive doses of opium or morphine or a medicinal dollop of alcohol—sometimes as high as 44 percent. Civil War soldiers who used these medicines in the field often went home addicted.

By the 1880s, patent medicines became the first products advertised on a large national scale, accounting for one-sixth of all print ads. So successful was the advertising that by the turn of the century total patent medicine revenues climbed to $75 million. The most notorious products included one of the most advertised; St. Jacob's Oil, which was first promoted as Keller's Roman Liniment, with a picture of Caesar on the label and the assertion that his legions had used it to conquer the world.

Another was Lydia Pinkham's Vegetable Compound, which was prepared by Pinkham, a Quaker from a temperance family, in her kitchen as a remedy for "female complaints." It contained four plant ingredients and was 19 percent alcohol. The label at first intimated that Pinkham was a doctor. In 1879 her family changed to a new appeal, in which they stressed the natural ingredients of the product and the good name of the founder, pictured on the label in Quaker dress.

Still other products advertised included James' Fever Powder, Dr. Ryan's Incomparable Worm-Destroying Sugar-Plums, and mineral waters, such as Dr. Willard's Mineral Water and Godwin's Celebrated German Water. In addition, advertisements boasted of products that could cure consumption (tuberculosis) and numerous electrical devices that could restore the nervous system.

A number of contemporary products, most notably Coca-Cola, were initially marketed to consumers as having medicinal properties. In fact, Coca-Cola contained cocaine up until the turn of the century, when caffeine was substituted for the drug.

Patent medicines showed the power of advertising. Sales increased when advertising was applied and decreased when it was pulled. However, the exaggerated claims for these products were disreputable, contributing significantly to a growing bad reputation for advertising. Demand by product companies and department stores for advertising space was so heavy that the ratio of advertising to news changed drastically in most newspapers. In the mid-1880s the ratio was 75 percent editorial to 25 percent advertising. By the turn of the century this ratio was fifty-fifty.

The emphasis on advertising in newspapers continues today, with ads taking more than 60 percent of some daily newspapers' space. In summer 2008, illustrating the continuing pressures on newspapers to balance rising costs with declining revenues, the Tribune Company announced it was "right sizing" its newspaper network so its papers would contain no less than 50 percent advertising on any

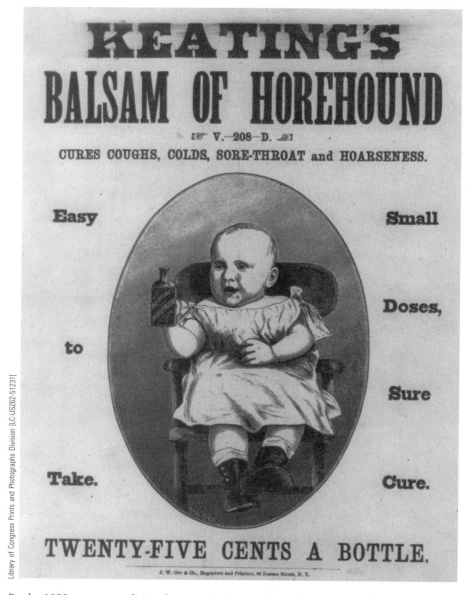

By the 1880s, patent medicines became the first products advertised on a large national scale, accounting for one-sixth of all print ads. Revenues soared to $75 million.

given day. For the company's largest paper, the *Los Angeles Times*, the new ratio meant a reduction of eighty-two pages per week, which management explained away by saying its newspapers were out of balance with production costs.[6]

INCREASED GROWTH IN AD AGENCIES

Growth at the N. W. Ayer and Son ad agency along with many other ad agencies coincided with the introduction of an enormous new range of branded household products. Manufacturers and retailers were forced to seek professional help in making their products stand out. By this time Ayer's agency was the largest in the nation, with more than 160 employees. In this new competitive environment, the number of agencies increased in order to keep up with demand.

The advertising agency evolved into its present form in the period leading up to the twentieth century. With the basic structure of the agency in place, product innovations of the late 1800s pushed advertisers to emphasize the ad itself—how it looked and what it meant. No longer was the emphasis on the selection of the medium or the size of the advertiser's budget.[7]

ADVERTISING AND THE PROGRESSIVE ERA

The turn of the century ushered in the Progressive Era in American society. This period brought essential change to the advertising industry, specifically a move to establish professional standards and self-regulation. This move to "clean up" fraudulent circulation figures and exaggerated, misleading claims coincided with the muckraking period when writers exposed social and economic corruption.

One of the first factors to influence this move toward professional standards in advertising was the outcry from the public and the medical profession against the outrageous lies in patent medicine ads. Fake medical data and ridiculous claims had been used for years to sell a product that was at best useless and at worst life-threatening. The ads became so bad that the *New York Herald Tribune* and *Ladies' Home Journal* restricted or completely banned medical advertising. Another factor was the scathing investigation and exposure of graft and corruption within many of the nation's institutions brought about by the muckrakers of the period. One such report, which acted as a catalyst to the public outcry, was a multi-part investigative exposure of the patent medicine industry called "The Great American Fraud" published by *Colliers* magazine in 1905. A third factor was legislation to protect consumers passed in 1906, and the establishment of a federal agency (Federal Trade Commission) in 1914 responsible for, among other duties, monitoring and regulating advertising.

ADVERTISING'S SELF-REGULATION

The advertising industry's self-regulation came about through individual and cooperative efforts of ad agencies, advertisers, and publishers directed against misleading advertising as well as exaggerated circulation claims by print media. Numerous organizations developed auditing systems and ethics codes to address the negative side of the business.

In 1914 the world's first not-for-profit auditing organization was formed; the Audit Bureau of Circulation (ABC) was a cooperative effort by advertisers, ad agencies and publishers to establish an industry watchdog to independently verify circulation figures. Calling itself "the gold standard in media audits," ABC has 4,000 members today and offers a wide range of services beyond verification of circulation claims.

Industry trade groups who develop and promote codes and standards were also begun at this time, all of whom are still in operation today. The precursor to the American Advertising Federation (AAF) was started in 1905. The AAF is the oldest national advertising trade association, representing 50,000 advertising professionals. AAF promotes a lengthy list of Advertising Ethics and Principles. With a national network of 200 ad clubs located in communities across the country as well as 215 college chapters, AAF's current slogan could date back to the time of its founding: "Advertising: the way great brands get to be great brands." The American Association of Advertising Agencies (AAAA) was founded in 1917 by 111 agencies (a dozen of which are still members today). It also has a Standards of Practice by which all members abide.

Though AAF was formed earlier, the Association of National Advertisers (ANA), which was founded in 1910, claims to be the advertising industry's oldest trades association. It was founded by forty-five companies to advance the interests of national advertisers. Today ANA's membership consists of 400 companies with 9,000 brands that together spend more than $100 billion in advertising and marketing communication.

Though it was established much later, in 1971, the National Advertising Review Council (NARC) was established by a joint partnership of the trade groups discussed above in conjunction with the Better Business Bureau (BBB). It is a self-regulatory group set up to deal with complaints against national advertisers.

THE GOVERNMENT RESPONDS AND REGULATES

Although there had been concerns over safety in the food supply for many years, it was not until after the Civil War that serious concerns brought increased pressure for national legislation to protect consumers. As the booming turn-of-the-century economy brought more and more mass-produced, nationally distributed consumer products to market, many food and drug products' lack of purity jeopardized consumers' health. This situation was worsened by the exaggerated claims of advertising.

Public opinion reached a high point by 1906, when Congress passed the Pure Food and Drug Act. Even though the legislation outlawed false claims for patent medicines, weak enforcement and minor penalties did little to address the problem. The first producer cited under the act marketed a headache remedy containing caffeine and alcohol. He was found guilty after a trial that took sixteen days and was fined $700. He had made about $2 million from the sale of his remedy.

It was only in 1939, when the Federal Food, Drug and Cosmetic Act came about that drug manufacturers had to provide scientific proof of new product's safety. Additionally, consumers no longer had to prove fraud in order to stop false advertising claims. Federal regulation came about in 1914 as Congress and the public were becoming more and more concerned over antitrust violations by big business, as exposed in such muckraking articles as Ida Tarbell's exposé of Standard Oil. The Federal Trade Commission (FTC), established by the 1914 legislation, was mandated to protect business owners from unscrupulous competition.

Eventually the FTC came to be the major federal agency to police and prevent fraudulent, misleading, or deceptive advertising; however, it has been criticized over the years for not being active enough. This changed in the 1960s, when the consumer movement pressured the agency to be more aggressive. The FTC has never ventured into attempts to regulate "good taste" or moral judgments.

Since the Reagan years and their impact on deregulation, critics again claim the FTC has not been aggressive enough. Consumer activists continue to bring pressure on the FTC, with much of the action in the area of advertising to children. State legislation against misleading advertising was heavily influenced by the 1911 model statute for state regulation prepared and sponsored by the industry's pioneer trade publication *Printer's Ink*. The *"Printer's Ink* Model Statute" is still operative, and has been modified or fully adopted by many states.

Today the FTC and the Food and Drug Administration (FDA) are only two of the federal agencies involved in regulating advertising. Others include the U.S. Postal Service (USPS), the Federal Communications Commission (FCC), and the Securities and Exchange Commission (SEC).

RADIO AND ADVERTISING

Radio was initially conceived as a service using airwaves in the public interest. As explained in Chapter 9, confusion and patent turf wars blocked the full development of radio in the United States until 1919. By 1922 there were 500 radio stations on the air but soon the overriding question became who was going to pay for radio broadcasting? Most entities felt advertising would be an unacceptable intrusion to listeners; however, in August 1922 the first commercial broadcast in America came about when a New York real estate company bought fifteen minutes of broadcast time for $50 to talk about its apartment complex.

This was the beginning of sponsored programs, which most felt would be less intrusive than direct advertising. Until the advent of the networks, radio's early developers paid little attention to the role it could play in promoting consumer goods. The sponsored programming concept paved the way for advertising to become the source of financing for network programming when the two National Broadcasting Company's (NBC) networks started in 1926 soon followed by the Columbia Broadcasting System (CBS) network in 1928.

Though radio started out as a local medium, advertisers soon realized its value as a vehicle to reach millions of listeners across the country. Radio was in the right place at the right time. A national audience was needed by manufacturers to advertise new consumer products, such as refrigerators and washing machines, introduced to meet pent-up consumer demand after the end of World War I in 1918.

Even as the booming 1920s gave way to the devastation of the great depression of the 30s, radio was one of the few businesses that thrived. As radio receivers became more affordable, the free news and entertainment source was so popular set ownership increased from 12 million households in 1929 to more than 28 million by 1939.

Although other advertising media suffered during the depression, radio advertising revenues grew along with its audience, starting at a healthy $18.7 million in 1929 and skyrocketing to more than $80 million in 1939. By the end of World War II in 1945, radio penetration was nearly total, with 95 percent of households owning at least one radio.

WORLD WAR II AND PUBLIC SERVICE ADVERTISING

Just as it had during World War I, wartime demanded sacrifices from Americans. Beginning with the U.S. entry into World War II in 1941, nearly all consumer goods were rationed or in short supply, as manufacturers turned to meeting wartime production demands. In spite of limited availability, national advertisers continued to promote their brands, taking the long-range view that peacetime would bring back consumer demand. Within these marketing messages most advertisers encouraged patriotism and cooperation even while promoting their brands.

The government's need to have people adhere to the rationing system, practice conservation, and avoid buying goods through the black market brought a series of advertising messages sponsored by the government and private industry. This unique advertising was the beginning of an enduring specialty type of advertising—public service advertising. In 1942, with the support and cooperation of the government, advertisers formed the War Advertising Council to create, produce, and disseminate advertising to support the U.S. war effort on a volunteer basis at no cost to the government. The J. Walter Thompson agency created the first and perhaps best known of these campaigns with a series of ads to encourage women to enter the badly depleted workforce. Built around a now-famous "Rosie the Riverter" character, the campaign was very successful.

The long-running Smokey Bear fire prevention campaign began during the war based on the fear that Japanese submarines might start a forest fire by shelling the West Coast of the country. The work of the War Advertising Council produced the greatest volume of advertising and publicity ever developed on a voluntary basis.

After the successful wartime campaigns, President Franklin Roosevelt urged advertisers to continue the Council's activities. The Advertising Council was the result and the shift was to a focus on campaigns aimed to "enhance public opinion of and co-opt liberal opposition to advertising by using it to promote liberal and patriotic causes."[8] Now-familiar slogans such as "a mind is a terrible thing to waste" for the United Negro College Fund and "friends don't let friends drive drunk" are just a few of the many campaigns produced for charity and government agencies pro bono by ad agencies and placed for free by the media, who donate more than $1 billion in time and space for messages created by the Ad Council.

TELEVISION AND ADVERTISING

As with radio after World War I, the pent-up demand for consumer goods at the end of World War II in 1945 produced unprecedented growth in manufacturing and advertising. The volume of advertising media in 1950 was nearly three times the amount from ten years earlier. By the mid-1950s commercial television was back in business after being interrupted by the war. Mirroring the earlier explosive growth of radio, television reached 90 percent of households by 1960, and its advertising revenues grew right along with its viewers. In 1951, advertisers spent $128 million on television advertising; by 1955 that amount grew to more than $1 billion.

Most of the early television programs came straight from radio, and structure of the television industry, like radio, centered on networks, chains of stations carrying the same programming nationwide. As with radio, early television shows were sponsored; however, as television viewership grew and production costs grew, sole-sponsor advertising was becoming too costly, even for the largest national advertisers.

The man who created a system to make television advertising affordable was a former advertising vice president who became one of the television industry's most innovative executives—Sylvester "Pat" Weaver, better known to younger Americans as the father of actress Sigourney Weaver. Weaver's greatest impact came while he was head of programming at NBC television in the late 1940s and early 1950s (he became chairman of the network in 1956), when he not only developed programming but advertising placement strategies that are still in use today.[9]

Weaver's experience at the Young and Rubicam ad agency gave him a unique insight into advertising's relationship with programming. He realized that sponsors, not network executives, actually controlled the programs and their content, sometimes even dictating when a show would appear on the network's broadcast schedule.

In a move to shift that power back to the networks, Weaver pressured NBC to produce programs and then offer multiple sponsors blocks of time within the show. He called the practice the "magazine concept" because it was so similar to the way in which print advertisers bought space in magazines without exercising any editorial control. Other networks soon followed and by the 1960s the 30-second commercials for multiple sponsors became the norm.

Although Weaver's "magazine concept" initially took programming control away from advertisers, many critics contend that today's huge ad budgets have given control of programming back to advertisers. They contend advertising-dependent mass media have become mere audience delivery systems, with a life-or-death dependence upon ratings and circulation. It is a fact of life that in the 21st century network television schedules are sliced and diced weekly, as ratings numbers rise or fall, with lower-rated shows canceled after a few weeks. Network television advertising revenues continue to fall yearly, as its audiences grow smaller and smaller, fragmented by new technologies and so many other media choices such as cable, pay-TV, DVDs, and the Internet.

So, as we saw in Chapter 10, television not only changed advertising, it changed American society, quickly challenging all other mass media for audience and becoming a particularly powerful force in politics.

ADVERTISING AS A SOCIAL FORCE

Some of the attention to the body paid off and actually made people healthier. It also implied a "liberation from Victorian denials of the body." The ads fitted the spirit of the 1920s, a decade of short skirts, the demise of the corset, open discussions of sexuality and birth control, Hollywood sheiks and vamps, and the general flouting of prohibition. Gargling Listerine did no body much good, or much harm.

Advertising's discovery of the body also projected a vision of tasteless, colorless, odorless, and sweatless world. Ethnic minorities cooked with vivid spice—even garlic!—and might neglect toothpaste, mouthwash, deodorants, and regular bathing. Advertisements would show them how to cleanse themselves.[10] We are Sinclair Lewis said, "the first great nation in which all individuality, all sweetness of life, all saline and racy earthiness has with success been subordinated to a machine-ruled industrialism."[11]

With the work of Resor and others, advertising became a social force in America by the 1920s. The Roaring Twenties witnessed the emergence of America's first youth culture, newfound freedoms for women, and unprecedented technological advances. For example, electrification brought about a new consumer culture. Convenience and efficiency—in products from appliances to food—were the order of the day. Consumers, especially women, now had some control over their lives. Advertisements promoted the concept of a society of leisure. Advertisements by the American Laundry Machinery Company, for example, stressed the time saved by sending family washing to a commercial laundry and described the activities women might choose to engage in instead.

Besides promoting a society of leisure, advertising became a unifying force that brought new communities together. Expenditure patterns among consumers

AMERICAN MEDIA PROFILE | MARY WELLS LAWRENCE 1928–

AP Photo

Plop plop / fizz fizz / Oh what a / relief it is! Say those words and most Americans can immediately sing them and identify the product they advertise. What many may not realize is they were conceived as part of a very successful advertising campaign by one of the advertising industry's most famous executives: Mary Wells Lawrence.

Originator of such famous advertising slogans as "Quality is job one," "Flick your Bic," and "I love New York," Lawrence has been called the first great woman in advertising. During the 1960s, she became the world's highest-paid female executive, advertising's most glamorous superstar, and the first woman CEO of a company listed on the New York Stock Exchange.

A native of Ohio, Lawrence originally aspired to be an actress. After attending Carnegie Institute of Technology, she returned to Ohio and became an advertising writer for a department store. Soon she was in New York, writing copy for Macy's, and from there she moved to a series of jobs with top New York ad agencies.

During the 1950s, Lawrence worked at McCann-Erickson and at Doyle Dane Bernbach (DDB), where, as a young copywriter, she worked with the innovative advertising genius Bill Bernbach. She was part of the hottest agency in New York when Bernbach was making advertising history with two campaigns that are considered classics: one for Avis, an obscure rental car company, saying that it was Number Two, therefore it tried harder; the other, the celebrated "Think Small" campaign that started America's love affair with the lowly Volkswagen beetle, an unlikely automobile for a post–World War II American society obsessed with huge cars adorned with shiny chrome and tail fins.

After seven years at DDB, Lawrence moved to Jack Tinker and Partners. There the brightest creative advertising minds would set about making advertising history during the 1960s; many people feel that

became a principal force for social cohesion in the new century. "Consumption communities," according to Boorstin, replaced the ethnic bonds that people had brought with them to the industrial city.

A famous 1929 sociological study, Middletown, traced the transition from older to newer forms of community. In depicting the cultural changes that had occurred in the preceding thirty years, Helen and Robert Lynd chronicled what they saw as the systematic replacement of personal interactions with "services" for which cash payment was made.

They also detected a shift in attitudes toward work. What had once been a considerable source of intrinsic personal satisfaction was becoming chiefly a means of earning income. The authors also noted that in the 1920s consumption had begun to serve as "compensatory fulfillment" for the older, largely interpersonal, forms of life satisfaction that were disappearing. The transition from industrial culture to consumer culture had taken place.

ADVERTISING AS A POLITICAL FORCE

With the arrival of television in the 1950s, advertising became a political force, particularly in presidential campaigns. Political advertising had been around since the election of 1840, when William Henry Harrison's campaign produced a series

---

AMERICAN MEDIA PROFILE | **CONTINUED**

was the golden age of advertising creativity. She had been lured away from DDB with a salary offer of $60,000 per year, at a time when most salaries averaged around $10,000. At Tinker, Lawrence formed relationships that shaped her ascent to the top of the advertising industry.

Lawrence worked with two other top creative people who would ultimately become her partners in the agency she would head. She created the *Plop plop / fizz fizz* campaign for Alka Seltzer and a campaign for Braniff Airlines that would turn the staid airline industry upside down. Calling for the end of the "plain plane," Lawrence had Braniff paint its airplanes vivid colors and outfit its flight attendants in equally bright outfits designed by Italian couturier Emilio Pucci.

With two major successes, in 1966 Lawrence was offered a raise to $80,000 and a long-term contract, both of which she refused. She resigned from Tinker, as did her copywriter and art-director partners, Dick Rich and Stew Greene. In April 1967 the three formed Wells, Rich, Greene (WRG), and the rest is advertising history.

The new agency was quickly assured success when Braniff Airlines became its first client. The $7 million Braniff account was quickly joined by others, and after six months WRG was billing $30 million.

The first major agency headed by a woman had shaken up male-dominated Madison Avenue.

As CEO, chairman, and president of WRG, Lawrence was one of the most powerful people in advertising, male or female. By 1969 she was making $225,000 a year, and advertising industry trade journal *Ad Age* called her "advertising's most widely publicized symbol of glamour, success, wealth, brains and beauty." Later Lawrence took WRG public, and by 1971, the agency was billing $100 million yearly. It had clients like Alka Seltzer, Proctor and Gamble, TWA, and Benson and Hedges. Lawrence, who married former Braniff Airlines president Harding Lawrence, retired in 1980. Sadly, in the early 1990s WRG became a victim of the "merger mania" that swept the advertising industry. It closed in 1998.

By Gail Love

of firsts in political advertising history. He was the first to use what is called image advertising on a systematic and widespread basis in politics. "Its modern-day equivalent would be the 30-second television spot commercial, which ignores issues, ignores party label, and concentrates on some aspect of the candidate's personality, usually one that links him closely with the ordinary voter," Wilcomb Washburn argued in the October 1972 *American Heritage.*

In his 1840 race against Martin Van Buren, Harrison used the symbol of a log cabin and cider to transform himself from the wealthy son of a governor into a farmer and backwoodsman, while revealing little of his past and less of his future. Log cabins were carried in parades, pictured on kerchiefs, bandannas, and banners. Log cabin pins, songs, and badges served as the outward signs of inward political convictions. Even hard cider was distributed along the campaign trail. Supporters were successful in painting a picture of Harrison as a hardy, healthy, heroic candidate. However, the image soon proved to be wrong. He won the election but died within a month.

By 1860, image advertising became a staple of political campaigns. Abraham Lincoln became the rail candidate, taken presumably by a story that Lincoln split a rail in his youth. Other examples of image advertising included teddy bears for Theodore Roosevelt's campaigns, and a "hole in the shoe" in Adlai Stevenson's 1952 campaign.

It was unfortunate for Harrison that radio was so far in the future. By 1928 a presidential candidate could preserve his health by communicating with millions in front of a microphone instead of making exhausting campaign appearances around the country. Over the course of 100 days in the campaign of 1896, William Jennings Bryan, by his own account, had made 600 speeches in twenty-seven states and had traveled more than 18,000 miles to reach 5 million people. Franklin Delano Roosevelt reached twelve times that number by radio. Once elected, he broadcasted famous *Fireside Chats,* which reached more than 60 million listeners.

Radio also transformed the content of political messages. As the *New York Times* observed in 1928, "Radio 'hook-up' has destroyed the old-time politician's game of promising the Western farmer higher prices for wheat without arousing the Eastern factory population against higher bread prices."[12]

Candidates were expected to pay for air time. They were given free air time up until their acceptance speeches during the presidential conventions. After that, they were charged the same commercial rates as department stores or manufacturers.

It was only a matter of time before the techniques used to sell a product would be taken up by advertising gurus to sell a presidential candidate. Television was an island waiting to be invaded, according to Rosser Reeves, a student of advertising's "hard-sell" approach. He was the first to apply the same technique that had been successful in selling M&Ms candy and the headache remedy Anacin to presidential candidates.

Reeves crafted the first political advertisements for Dwight D. Eisenhower, in 1952. He went to NBC's New York studio with a film crew and picked various citizens to ask Eisenhower a question or two. Later he filmed Eisenhower's answers and edited the questions and answers together to produce a series of "Eisenhower Answers America" political commercials. His success developed the profession of media consulting. With the publication of Joe McGinniss' *The Selling of the*

President, which documented the packaging of presidential candidate Richard M. Nixon, emphasis on consultants and their services increased. Until the late 1960s, a political advertisement would make news only if it was controversial. President Lyndon Johnson's 1964 "Daisy" ad, which was pulled from television after one airing, was considered too offensive to viewers.

The ad showed a girl picking petals from a daisy. As she picked the last petal, a nuclear explosion occurred and Johnson was heard saying, "Either we learn to live with one another, or we die." By the late sixties, firms specializing in political media consulting emerged. The hiring and firing of these consultants by presidential contenders became news. Eventually the consultants stepped out of the shadow of their candidates and held their own press conferences. By the 1970s they were being interviewed by the likes of CBS's Mike Wallace. By the 1990s, political television ads were the subject of daily critiques by newspaper and broadcast journalists.

Among the most critiqued were three credited with George H. W. Bush's victory over Michael Dukakis in 1988. One attacked Dukakis' environmental record, another his criminal justice policy when he was governor of Massachusetts. The "Boston Harbor" commercial depicted images of garbage in the water. The "Willie Horton" commercial focused on a revolving prison door and Dukakis' purported soft policy toward criminals. A third commercial also contributed to Dukakis' defeat. The Bush camp produced a video of Dukakis' helmeted head jutting out from a military tank. It looked as if Dukakis was aboard a popular Disneyland ride wearing a Mickey Mouse hat.

In the 1996 primaries, little-known millionaires, such as Steve Forbes and Ross Perot, used their personal funds to finance advertising commercials to place their names before the public. In his presidential race two years earlier, Perot bought large blocks of television time for infomercials, in which he used data and charts to teach Americans about various issues. Unfortunately, in their efforts to appeal to the average voter, political commercials have become simple, trivial, and emotional, like Ronald Reagan's 1980 "Morning in America" commercials. These were beautifully choreographed, with happy citizens surrounded by waving American flags. Though they made viewers feel good about the country and themselves, they contained little substance. Information that may be crucial for voting decisions is often too complex and technical to appeal to much of the audience.

THE DIGITAL WORLD AND ADVERTISING

The current explosion of digital media and marketing made only one thing clear: The pace of technological change makes it difficult for media and marketers to stay on top. The advent of new mobile applications, and the advertising potential they present, are exciting; however, more than half of consumers have made it clear they are not willing to watch ads on their phones in return for free mobile phone applications.

The newest mass medium, the Internet, has quickly taken its place as the fastest-growing vehicle for advertising, particularly that directed to a younger demographic. *Advertising Age* reports U.S. advertisers spent nearly $10 billion on

Internet advertising in 2006, 6.5 percent of the total $150 billion advertising expenditure. Although that figure is still far below the amount spent on traditional media (20 percent on newspapers, 20 percent on magazines, 18 percent on network television, just over 11 percent each on cable and spot television and 7 percent on radio), Internet spending was up 17.3 percent from the previous year, the largest increase of any media. *Advertising Age* also reports advertisers project spending between 5 and 8 percent of their online advertising budgets on social networking sites in 2008.

Still in its infancy, Internet advertising has already gone through changes and many new formats are promised. The earliest type of Internet advertising, the banner ad, lost favor by 2001, as click-through rates fell below one percent. Newer and larger ads, embedded within the Web page text, soon became the way to increase click-through rates. These new formats, which came to resemble layouts in print media, were not the only new type of ad introduced; there was the pop-up, the pop-under, and interstitials, the ads that pop up when a user accesses a new Web page. Although provocative, these new formats also became more annoying, driving users to buy software to block pop-ups.

Currently, the dominant type of Internet advertising is the paid search format, with 27 percent of 2006 online media budgets allocated to it. Online video was second, accounting for about 15 percent. Paid search advertising meant search engine sites such as Google and Yahoo! have quietly become advertising media companies, selling advertising links associated with search terms as well as separate advertising messages and links within the search results themselves. Google moved ahead in the fiercely competitive search advertising arena, emerging in 2006 as the top U.S. search engine, with 56.5 percent of the U.S. search share. Google had generated nearly all of its revenue from selling keyword searches on its own site and its partner sites; however, in late 2006 Google acquired YouTube, which opened a whole new source of revenue: video.

Now that Google is able to push search into video, it is giving its partner sites a real bonus: the ability to display ad-supported video content. With its recent growth, Google ranked nineteenth on Ad Age's list of the 100 largest U.S. media companies, generating $4.1 billion in U.S. ad revenue in 2006 (up 70 percent).

ADVERTISING'S FUTURE

Early in the decade of the 90s, a major trend emerged among marketers—a concept called "integrated marketing communications (IMC)," which is the process of mixing various promotional tools so that all marketing communication messages are unified and send a consistent, persuasive message. As the marketplace became more crowded and consumers received more and more messages, it became imperative that marketers remind themselves that all promotional tools deliver messages, not just advertising, and all must work together to create a coherent brand message. Although advertising is one of the most important marketing communication tools, it is not the only tool. Others include sales promotions, special events, direct mail, product placement, and public relations.

Big national advertisers such as McDonald's spend over a billion dollars yearly on media advertising, but they also spend millions more on giveaway premiums tied to blockbuster movies, contests, philanthropy, and sponsorships of special events such as national rock concerts.

Although some would say IMC is the "new advertising," veteran advertisers continue to spend billions every year on media advertising. Why? Because media advertising can do what no other marketing tool can do as effectively—create an image for a brand. Though results from media advertising are not as easy to track as direct mail or coupons, it retains a secure place in the future of marketing communication in America.

CONCLUSION

"If I were starting life over again," Franklin D. Roosevelt once said, "I am inclined to think that I would go into the advertising business in preference to almost any other. . . . It is essentially a form of education; and the progress of civilization depends on education." Advertising, which makes up most of today's media, has a place of special prominence in the United States. However, it wasn't always like that. Most New World settlers could not imagine advertising as a vehicle for education. Colonial and revolutionary printers, for example, considered advertising a degrading element to include in their newspapers. It wasn't until the penny press era that advertising came into its own.

The development of the advertising agency made advertising a *privileged form of discourse*, a rubric once reserved for church sermons, political oratory, and the words of family elders. Today, a significant portion of our daily talk and action is about consumer goods and what they can do or should mean for us.

By the 1920s advertising became a social force in America, moving the nation from an industrial to consumer culture. It became a *unifying force* by creating consumption communities that replaced ethnic bonds. National advertising campaigns successfully integrated the melting pot of working-class people and immigrants into the American way of life by appealing to consumers in ways that bridged their cultural differences. Those once isolated now became part of the national culture.

National advertising campaigns began touting brand names, and they asked consumers to try the products at their local stores. This created demand for the products. Advertising created a nation of homogenized taste. National brand advertising also shifted consumers' allegiances and trust. They no longer had a personal relationship with the local shopkeeper as they moved toward national labels.

Advertising became an important political force when Rosser Reeves showed candidates how to apply the principles of selling products like M&Ms to selling candidates. Today, candidates for national and state offices spend most of their campaign budgets on media advertisements. And some voters know about presidential candidates only from a thirty-second media advertisement.

Advertising, the privileged discourse, will continue to shape the social and political outlook of the nation. Today, about $108.2 billion is spent on advertising to influence consumers—or as FDR might say, "educate consumers to further the progress of civilization."

THE MEDIA AND NATIONAL CRISES

For some, the 1970s marked an irresistible rise of news-media power. The mass media, especially television, not only held up a mirror to society but also became a significant force that shaped the nation's cultural and political fabric.

For others, it was not the mass media that shaped public opinion but rather the holders of power who shaped public opinion by using the media as their agents. They were aided by the rise of masterful image makers, such as CNN commentator David Gergen, who did his spinning for presidents from Richard Nixon to Bill Clinton. Under Nixon, Gergen modeled what he called "a systematic program of propaganda," a formula for marketing the president and his policies.[1]

Whichever view one takes, it is hard to dispute the fact that during the last years of the twentieth century, the power of journalists, especially broadcast journalists, clashed with the power of the presidency in what could be called "an era of deception." The upshot was a crisis in credibility, with part of the public doubting the press and the other part doubting the presidency.

Following on the heels of deception about the Vietnam War in the late sixties, the crises in credibility were heightened by the lies of Watergate, Iran-Contra, and those that arose from a White House sexual tryst. Each had an impact on the public, press, and government. The impact was so deep, according to James Fallows, former Washington editor of the *Atlantic Monthly*, that its reverberations may eventually bring about the decline of American democracy.[2]

The latter part of the twentieth century did see a dramatic transition of the role of the press from "lap dog" to "watchdog" to "pit bull," particularly in covering politics. This created the phenomenon of "gotcha" journalism, according to Ellen Hume, an Annenberg Senior Fellow and former executive director of Harvard's Joan Shorenstein Barone Center on the Press, Politics, and Public Policy. "The watchdog that barks at everything loses its bite. The apparently endless flow of scandals and feeding frenzies has damaged, rather than enhanced, journalism's credibility."[3]

JOURNALISTS' CHANGING VALUES

Evidence of Hume's analysis could be seen in the latter part of the twentieth century with the growth of the news media's power, its "pit-bull" approach to reporting, precipitated by an increasingly adversarial view of politicians, who, in turn, employed image makers to manipulate their adversaries. The end result was the loss of the essence of real journalism—the search for information of use to the public, according to Fallows.[4] What evolved was celebrity oriented, sensational journalism, a throwback to the Gilded Age, and a lack of public trust in both journalists and politicians.

The great power of the news media is often looked at in the context of the political arena. During the 1970s, coverage of that arena introduced the term *pack journalism*. "Journalists, as we have seen, are sometimes likened to roving packs of beasts with a bloodthirsty urge to destroy their prey," according to critic J. Herbert Altschull. "When a 'big story' emerges, reporters descend on it in droves, with such intense concentration that the story rapidly becomes the nation's chief topic of conversation, and other 'news' disappears from the television screen and the front pages." He refers to it as the "jackal syndrome," the case in which journalists wait about for a lion among them, often the *New York Times*, to interpret events, and then move quickly to adopt the lion's interpretation as their own.[5] The most celebrated case, the O. J. Simpson murder trial, was an example; so was the struggle in the Senate over Clarence Thomas' nomination to the Supreme Court; and so were the many sexual peccadilloes of Bill Clinton. His alleged trysts with Paula Jones, Gennifer Flowers, and the biggest headline grabber of all, Monica Lewinsky, produced much fodder for the press.

When one adds to these the lies of Vietnam, Watergate, and the Iran-Contra scandal, no wonder journalists became locked in the negative assumption that the government and its political leaders are lying most of the time. This produced journalists who became adversaries of those in power as they moved away from traditional "objective" reporting to more analytical journalism. Such reporting calls for packaging the news in ways that interpret what political figures, presidents in particular, really mean in those sound bites that appear on the air.

By the end of the century, journalists received help—whether they liked it or not—in the "packaging of information." A growing image industry employed by political leaders and candidates emerged in the 1980s. This group of image makers came to be known as "spin doctors." Simply, it was the politician or candidate's staff interpreting information—whether it is polls or election results or stands on pending legislation. Their job was to put a "spin" favorable to their candidate on the information. Journalists decried the practice but at the same time reported what the image industry provided.

What arose was a "fear of flacking," according to media specialist Michael Robinson.[6] Manipulative efforts by this new industry became obvious to journalists, and some were determined to fight back. According to critic Daniel C. Hallin, there arose what politicians often speak of as negative reporting.[7] For example, the bad news generated by Watergate, fully reported by television, was more than large segments of the public wanted to take. The mirror had been held up once more, and millions did not like what they saw. Characteristically, some minimized the scandal or even denied its existence, whereas others blamed the media for bearing the bad news. From that point it was easy to blame the media for the whole monstrous affair. Take Nixon and those close to him in late August 1973, at a San Clemente press conference in which he answered press questions about Watergate for the first time. The president not only blamed the press for his difficulties but also did it with scarcely concealed hostility, masked only by the usual rhetoric, which reporters present had heard—especially during Vietnam and Watergate—many times before.

VIETNAM

Barbara Tuchman called Vietnam America's "march of folly."[8] David Halberstam called it "the making of a quagmire."[9] In Vietnam, as in the Civil War a century earlier, America found itself deeply and violently divided about its national purpose. It was a war in which journalists made their reputations and generals lost theirs. It was the first of two national crises—Watergate being the second—in which the essential combatants were not the president and the opposition party or the president and the Congress but the president and the press.

AMERICA'S ROAD TO VIETNAM

How did America get involved in Vietnam? Japan replaced the French in 1940 as the dominant power in Vietnam, proclaiming Asia for the Asian people. After Japan surrendered in 1945, the Vietnamese, led by Ho Chi Minh, declared their independence. Ho had hoped the Allies would support him, but the British, who came to take Japan's surrender, rearmed the French and drove Ho's Viet Minh out of Saigon. The United States, though, perceived Ho Chi Minh as part of an international movement to spread Communism. In April 1954, President Dwight Eisenhower made his famous prediction that if Indochina fell, the rest of Southeast Asia would "go over very quickly like a row of dominoes." He also added "the possible consequences of the loss are just incalculable to the free world."[10]

That perception was wrong, former Secretary of Defense Robert McNamara said many years later. "We looked upon Ho Chi Minh as a servant, a vassal, if you will, of Khrushchev and Mao Tse-tung. He wasn't that. He was a patriot. He was an Asian Tito. And he was leading a civil war, the force of nationalism, and it was far stronger than we understood. We were wrong. We didn't have our history. We didn't have our culture correct."[11]

President Harry S. Truman responded to Ho Chi Minh and what he saw as a Communist threat by sending the French eight transport planes. In 1950 he also gave the French $15 million, and this ballooned to $40 million under President Dwight D. Eisenhower. The number of American military personnel in Vietnam rose rapidly during the Kennedy administration to more than 12,000. That began a decades-long commitment, which eventually cost 58,000 American lives.

With the United States carrying 80 percent of the cost, the French placed ex-emperor Bao Dai as chief of state in Saigon. However, the French defeat at Dien Bien Phu, a siege that lasted fifty-five days, ended France's presence in Indochina. It was the end of the French empire. The Geneva Peace Agreement was signed in 1954, ending hostilities and partitioning Vietnam at the seventeenth parallel. It also called for reunification through national elections in 1956. However, South Vietnam's new premier, Ngo Dinh Diem, decided to ignore the peace agreement and refused to hold elections. He then launched a campaign to wipe out some 8,000 to 10,000 Viet Minh cadres left in the south. The CIA and Diem's army rooted them out and shot them on sight. There were no trials. The Viet Minh decided that the only way to survive was to fight back. They fought back, and ignited a civil war.

As the enemy became more energetic, the U.S.-backed government of President Diem became more corrupt. He refused to conciliate the large Buddhist population, making his Roman Catholic government unpopular. Hatred spread as Buddhists partook in self-immolations on Saigon streets when Americans caught this on the evening news. Efforts to rid Vietnam of Diem spawned on December 20, 1960, a new united front, called the National Liberation Front (NLF). Membership was open to anyone who opposed Diem and sought a unified Vietnam. Washington denounced the party, calling it the "Viet Cong," a derogatory slang term meaning Vietnamese Communist. The NLF began to score a number of successes in the Vietnamese countryside, while the South Vietnamese government was on the verge of political collapse. In 1963 some of Diem's generals approached the American Embassy in Saigon with a plan to overthrow him. With Washington's approval, the plan was carried out on November 1, 1963. Diem and his brother, Ngo Dinh Nhu, were captured and later killed. Three weeks later, President Kennedy was assassinated on the streets of Dallas.

At the time of Diem's death, approximately 16,000 American military advisers were in Vietnam. However, continuing political problems in Saigon convinced President Lyndon B. Johnson that a more aggressive plan was needed. After an enemy raid on two U.S. ships in the Gulf of Tonkin, the new president asked for and received expansive war powers. In July 1965 Johnson chose to Americanize the war, increasing U.S. combat strength in Vietnam from 75,000 to 125,000. That number rose to 500,000 by January 1968. So did the U.S. press and TV contingent in Saigon: 131 in December 1965, 175 in December 1966, and 207 at the end of 1967. By January 1968, the collective strength—all nationalities—of accredited media representatives in Saigon was sizable, involving a combined multimillion-dollar annual outlay (mostly by TV networks for logistics) and a payroll for support staff covering perhaps 100 messengers, secretaries, and translators.[12]

As America and its journalists became more involved in Vietnam, three major conflicts developed. They were conflicts between the media and the military, between the media and the public, and between the media and the government.

THE MEDIA IN VIETNAM

The clashes didn't come about because of any type of formal censorship. While official ignorance and evasion were present in Vietnam, no formal censorship existed; rarely did the Vietnamese president expel an offending U.S. newsman.[13] Vietnam became the first war in which journalists were routinely accredited to accompany military forces but not subject to formal censorship. For the most part, relates Hallin, "journalists in Vietnam were free to go where they pleased and report what they wished. Vietnam was in this sense genuinely an uncensored war."[14]

The military did consider the feasibility of formal censorship, but decided that it would not be practical for at least three reasons. First, they felt that censorship in the field would be of limited use in an undeclared war. Thus, reporters could get around the rules by filing stories from Hong Kong or Tokyo. Second, since the United States was fighting as guests of a foreign government, effective censorship would have required U.S. court-martial jurisdiction to be extended not only to American civilians in South Vietnam, but also to third-country nationals—reporters from Asia and Western Europe. Finally, American officials felt that the voluntary guidelines distributed provided adequate military security. These guidelines included fifteen categories of information reporters were not allowed to write about without authorization. They included writing about troop movements or casualty figures until they were officially announced in Saigon.[15]

Despite the lack of censorship, some journalists felt the military interfered with their reporting in at least two ways: military embargoes placed on information and restrictions to the front lines. Information, such as U.S. casualty figures, was withheld. Such information was not released until 1967. The military also placed restrictions on access to the front lines, accessible only by military transportation. The military said the restrictions were meant to protect military security. Journalists said they were politically motivated.[16]

Any attempt at censorship may also have been hampered by the introduction of television news, which came of age on the eve of the Vietnam War. It was America's first real televised war, since television news had not been a staple during the Korean War. Technological changes, including lightweight sound cameras, satellites, and jet air transportation, allowed images to be transmitted as fast as words. However, by the time the coverage got onto the small screen, it was about twenty-four hours old. Most television news reports filmed in Vietnam consisted of a few sentences rewritten from AP and UPI dispatches and read aloud on camera by anchor people in "visual" variations on the nightly radio news of previous decades.[17] Nine network employees—correspondents, camera operators, and sound technicians—were killed in Indochina and many more were wounded.[18]

Some Vietnam revisionists say that television's coverage of this conflict, the most divisive and unsuccessful in American history, turned the public against the war.[19] President Johnson's favorite ploy was to blame the messenger. He said in an interview on September 20, 1967, "NBC and the *New York Times* are committed to an editorial policy of making us surrender."[20]

THE PRESS VS. THE MILITARY

The handful of reporters assigned to Vietnam during the early stages of the conflict eventually became split about America's efforts in Indochina. One group traveling in and out of Saigon included Joseph Alsop, a columnist; Keyes Beech, of the *Chicago Daily News*; and Marguerite Higgins, of the *New York Herald*. All were veterans of World War II and the Korean press corps. They were joined by Jim Lucas, of Scripps Howard. Though ready to fight any attempt at censorship, they were more on the team and saw the war as a necessary evil.

Another group of reporters included Neil Sheehan, of United Press International; Malcolm Browne, of the Associated Press; David Halberstam, who replaced Homer Bigart, a Pulitzer Prize–winning writer for the *New York Times*; and Harrison Salisbury, of the *New York Times*. They took a more activist role in probing the humaneness of military action. They also were more critical of the Diem dictatorship as protestors, especially Buddhists, became more vocal.

Aware of the growing criticism of the Diem regime, Carl T. Rowan, of the State Department, issued a warning in 1962 that "newsmen should be advised that trifling or thoughtless criticism of the Diem government would make it difficult to maintain proper cooperation between the United States and Diem." If that wasn't enough, a year later *Time* magazine gave those critical of the Diem regime a tongue-lashing. It attacked the Saigon press corps as propagandists plotting to overthrow the Diem government and, through distorted reporting, "helping to compound the very confusion that it should be untangling for its readers at home."[21] *Time* correspondents Charles Mohr and Mert Perry resigned in protest.

A sorry estrangement developed between the top military and civilian levels in Vietnam and the media as reporters found that the military sometimes deliberately falsified information and often withheld information detrimental to the continued belief in the eventual success of U.S. efforts in Vietnam. At daily Saigon press briefings, dubbed "The Five O'Clock Follies" because it was folly to attend, reporters were given elaborate statistical accounts to justify the policies of the White House and the Pentagon. It would not do any good to probe further because officers knew only what was in their communiqués.

These briefings included "body-count statistics," the number of enemy killed the previous day. Defense Secretary McNamara instituted the daily statistical ritual in an effort to show that the enemy was being exhausted. Correspondents also heard daily accounts of "precision bombing" raids of enemy convoys, roads, factories, and troop concentrations at an unprecedented saturation level. But correspondents were becoming increasingly uncomfortable with the rosy predictions being given out at the top. They worked their way down the command level to junior combat officers who had a bleaker view. In effect, many correspondents became rogue reporters working on a different side of the story from the official one.

THE PRESS VS. THE PUBLIC

The conflict between the media and the public is best illustrated by CBS newsman Morley Safer's reporting from Vietnam. In August 1965, Safer was having coffee with some young marine officers who eventually asked him if he would like to join them in an operation the next day. Safer found himself on an amphibious carrier to a place called Cam Ne. He was told that the marines were going to level it, because they had been taking a lot of fire from the village and the province chief wanted it leveled.

"The Burning of Cam Ne" was shown on the CBS *Evening News with Walter Cronkite*. "This is what the war in Vietnam is all about," Safer narrated as he stood in front of the burning huts. The Viet Cong were long gone... the action wounded three women, killed one baby, wounded one marine and netted four old men prisoners."[22]

Years later *Washington Star* reporter Richard Critchfield, who wrote a book on villages in Vietnam, told Safer that the reason Cam Ne was leveled had nothing to do with the Viet Cong but simply with the province chief. The potentate was furious with the locals, who refused to pay their taxes, and he wanted their village punished.[23]

Before Safer's report, the media in general portrayed the U.S. government as unified, decisive, optimistic, and sure of its course in Vietnam. Television, in particular, had trivialized the debate and confirmed the legitimacy of the president. Those who opposed the administration appeared to be outcasts. "The Burning of Cam Ne" changed those perceptions. Critics said the film was too realistic, one-sided, and negative, and portrayed American soldiers in a bad light. However, it helped legitimize pessimistic reporting by all other television correspondents. For some Americans, Safer's report paved the way for a different perception of the war and for a recognition that something was wrong in Vietnam.[24]

A year after Safer's report, the military's "precision-bombing" statistics came under attack by Salisbury. After visiting Hanoi, the *New York Times* senior editor began filing stories and photographs that contradicted accounts of the successes of the U.S. bombing program. He wrote that fliers who needed to lose their payloads dropped bombs indiscriminately. He also reported that such bombing missions did not stop the enemy. After the stories, the *Times* and Salisbury received verbal lashings from the public.

THE PRESS VS. THE GOVERNMENT

Salisbury was vindicated during the Tet offensive of 1968.The offensive began January 30–31, 1968, the beginning of the lunar year, with the aim of toppling *the U.S.-backed* South Vietnamese government headed by President Nguyen Van Thieu and its American allies. The North Vietnamese and their southern allies, the NLF, sent some 84,000 men against most of South Vietnam's major cities and towns.[25] For the first time, American television audiences saw the enemy fighting in cities, including Saigon, during daylight hours.

Cronkite, America's most trusted newsman at the time, decided to go to Saigon. His hurried tour of Vietnam (Hue and Saigon) shocked the commentator.[26] His half-hour news special, which he wrote himself, stunned a president and a nation. Cronkite reported that the war didn't work, that an increase in troop strength would not turn it around, and that the United States should think of a way to get out. He told a national audience:

> We have been too often disappointed by the optimism of the American leaders, both in Vietnam and Washington, to have faith any longer in the silver linings they find in the darkest clouds.... For it seems now more certain than ever that the bloody experience

© Express Newspapers/Getty Images

War photographers Terry Fincher, of the *Express*, and Harry Burrows, of *Life* magazine, follow the United States advances against the Viet Cong from an encampment at "Hill Timothy" on April 11, 1968.

of Vietnam is to end in a stalemate. To say that we are mired in stalemate seems the only realistic, yet unsatisfactory, conclusion.[27]

It was the first time in the nation's history that a television anchor declared a war to be over. President Johnson told his press secretary, George Christian, that Cronkite's report was the turning point. If he had lost Cronkite, he had lost the average citizen. It helped him make up his mind not to seek reelection.

Richard M. Nixon defeated Vice President Hubert Humphrey in the 1968 presidential election, campaigning on the slogan "peace with honor." However, President Nixon began a massive invasion of Cambodia on April 30, 1970. He believed that the Viet Cong were planning to take over Cambodia and turn it into an arsenal and a refuge. By May U.S.–financed mercenaries were flown into Phnom Penh to augment the 50,000 troops that were in Cambodia. By June, troops were being withdrawn into South Vietnam, as American military strategy changed. The president instituted a "Vietnamization of the War" plan in which ground troops, other than advisers, would be withdrawn and U.S. presence maintained by way of massive air support, including the use of B-52 strategic bombers as well as tactical aircraft.

At home Nixon was facing campus riots, disgruntled church and labor groups, peace organizations, and the emergence of a radical and underground press. Nixon told the American people in a November 3, 1969, speech that he was being pounded by TV network news organizations with their biased and distorted "instant analysis" and coverage. "Unless the practices were challenged, it would make it impossible for a President to appeal directly to the people, something I considered to be the essence of democracy."[28]

Nixon speechwriter Pat Buchanan urged the president to attack the network commentators directly. Nixon tapped Vice President Spiro Agnew, the former governor of Maryland, to do the job. All three networks decided to carry his thirty-minute speech live. On November 13, 1969, in Des Moines, Agnew referred to the president's earlier speech, saying his words had been unfairly subjected to "instant analysis and querulous criticism." He had harsh words to say about the "unaccountable power in the hands of the 'unelected elite' of network newsmen." He said: "A small group of men, numbering perhaps no more than a dozen anchormen, commentators, and executive producers, settle upon the film and commentary that is to reach the public. They decide what 40 to 50 million Americans will learn of the day's events in the nation and in the world."[29]

It was the first time a high-ranking federal official made direct attacks on those reporting and commenting on the news. His attacks were twofold: Networks and newspapers exercised too powerful an influence over public opinion, and network management used commentators with a preponderant "Eastern Establishment bias" and failed to provide a "wall of separation" between news and comment.

Faced with a growing animosity toward the war, Nixon began maneuvering to find a way to get out of Vietnam, and jump-started the Paris peace talks. Between January 8 and 13, 1973, Secretary of State Henry Kissinger and Vietnamese official Le Duc Tho met secretly in Paris. Finally, in January a cease-fire agreement was reached. However, Nixon, the nation, and the media faced another battle of deception.

WATERGATE

Though millions of Americans may not have liked what the mirror showed in the 1970s, Watergate was no aberration. Granted, it wasn't the first political scandal to rock the nation, but the deception and thwarting of the constitutional process of government was unprecedented.

To understand Watergate, one must understand the events leading to one of the greatest political scandals in the nation's history. Nixon won a close victory against Vice President Humphrey in 1968 with the promise "to bring the boys home" from Vietnam. Instead of keeping his promise, Nixon began a secret bombing campaign against neutral Cambodia. Americans turned from an unthinking patriotism to dismay at the mounting casualty lists. As the media began to expose another administration's lies about the course of the war, protests against the continuation of the war erupted in cities, including Washington, and on college campuses. In one protest at Kent State University, four students were killed by National Guard troops.

Nixon feared the November 15, 1969, peace rally, which drew 250,000 to the Capitol. He ordered 9,000 troops into Washington, backing up thousands of police, and other armed forces. So fearful was the president that forces patrolled White House corridors. He also feared threats by militant groups, including "the

Weathermen and Black Panthers." The fear was justified, according to Nixon. In August 1970 a policeman was killed and six others were wounded in a series of gun battles with the Black Panthers and another black militant group in Philadelphia. On October 8, 1970, the Weathermen reportedly were responsible for several bomb explosions at the University of Wisconsin. And on March 1, 1971, the Weather Underground bombed the U.S. Capitol.[30]

Nixon also feared news leaks at the White House. To tighten White House security, he advanced a secret plan by staffer Thomas Huston to use illegal methods to get intelligence on left-wingers who organized demonstrations and leaked information. Nixon described these methods as "resumption of covert mail-opening, increased electronic surveillance, and an increase in campus informants."[31] Within a month, the CIA, the Defense Intelligence Agency, the National Security Council, and the president supported the plan. Only FBI chief J. Edgar Hoover thought the plan "unnecessary," though he did not object to its obvious illegality. Nixon eventually withdrew his support, and Huston was heard no more.

Its demise did not stop the president, who, with Secretary of State Kissinger's approval, ordered FBI wiretaps on four newsmen and thirteen government officials between May 1969 and February 1971. But a gusher in June 1971 turned into a tidal wave with the publication of parts of the "Pentagon Papers" in the *New York Times*.

THE "PENTAGON PAPERS"

Four years earlier, then–Secretary of Defense McNamara ordered an in-depth history of American involvement in Indochina, including Korea and Vietnam, from its start in 1945. Its forty-seven volumes, entitled *History of the U.S. Decision-Making Process on Vietnam Policy*, revealed that four administrations had lied to Congress and the public about U.S. military and political actions in these countries. The report was kept under wraps until the Rand Corporation, a Santa Monica, California–based think tank received a copy. Rand employee Daniel Ellsberg, who vehemently opposed the Vietnam War, took parts of the history, copied them, and sent them to several newspapers.

The *New York Times* began publishing long sections of the document on Sunday, June 13, 1971. Horrified that his own secret maneuvering might be placed in the open, Nixon authorized the establishment of a White House surveillance team known as the "plumbers." Their job was to detect and plug leaks of classified information.

Meanwhile, Attorney General John Mitchell asked the *New York Times* to discontinue publication of the document. It refused. On June 15, 1971, at Nixon's insistence, the Justice Department was ordered to issue a restraining order against further publication. Federal District Judge Murray Gurfein ordered the *Times* to suspend publication of the documents after the third installment by issuing a temporary restraining order. The *Washington Post* then began printing excerpts from the "Pentagon Papers," and the administration went to court to force it to cease publication of the stories. Shortly afterward, Deputy Attorney General Richard Kleindienst threatened the *Post* with criminal prosecution, according to *Washington Post* publisher Katherine Graham. Kleindienst suggested that if the criminal charges were successfully prosecuted, the Washington Post Company could lose the licenses of its three television stations.[32]

On June 19, 1971, the judge refused to grant a permanent restraining order, noting that the government did not prove its case. When the *Washington Post* began publishing sections of the "Pentagon Papers," Judge Gerhard A. Gesell ruled that the government could not "impose a prior restraint on essentially historical data."

The U.S. Court of Appeals for the District of Columbia upheld Gesell's ruling, and on June 25 the two cases reached the U.S. Supreme Court, which voted 5–4 to hear testimony and continue the temporary order of prior restraint. It was then that the attorneys argued that the government could not prove that national security was involved. The Supreme Court finally decided in favor of the newspapers.[33]

THE BREAK-IN

Having lost the fight over the publication of the papers, the Nixon administration wanted to punish Ellsberg. It launched an investigation, and he was indicted in a California court. The plumbers also broke into his psychiatrist's office in the Watergate complex in Washington, D.C., on September 3, 1971, in order to find personal information that might discredit him.

That same week White House aide Charles Colson gave White House counsel John Dean a priority list of twenty political enemies, which included politicians, journalists, and movie stars, among others. In addition, the White House hired operatives, including Newport Beach, California, attorney Donald Segretti, to disrupt the campaigns of Democratic candidates.

After the midterm election setback of November 1970, Nixon and his cadre became increasingly focused on the 1972 presidential reelection campaign. Polls at the time showed that the popular U.S. senator from Maine, Edmund Muskie, would win the election in a match with Nixon. The White House did not want to run against Muskie; they wanted to run against U.S. Senator George McGovern, a liberal Democrat.

The goal was to destroy the Muskie campaign by taking the "low-road" approach to winning the election. With White House chief of staff H. R. "Bob" Haldeman's knowledge, a destructive campaign filled with "dirty tricks" prevailed. Techniques included tapping the phones of newspaper and TV people and writing phony letters and making phony phone calls.[34] The most destructive was a letter suggesting that Muskie had used the term "Canuck" (for French Canadian) derogatorily and the dissemination of pictures of Muskie crying tears of rage in front of a New Hampshire newspaper office.[35]

The most notorious act was the break-in by White House "plumbers" of the Democratic National Committee, located in the Watergate apartment complex, on June 17, 1972. The plumbers were going to plant listening devices in the office of Lawrence F. O'Brien, chairperson for the Democratic Party. It was their second attempt, having bungled the job the first time. With professional locksmith tools and wearing rubber gloves, the five entered the office again. But Frank Willis, the security guard for the building, heard them and called the Washington police, who caught them red-handed. The break-in, however, was only a small part of a grand spy scheme on Democratic leaders that was financed by contributions to the Committee to Re-Elect the President, referred to at the time as CREEP.

The next day the *Washington Post* ran an 83-inch story linking one of the burglars, James McCord, to the CIA. "Not your average burglar," *Post* reporter Bob Woodward thought at the time.[36] Woodward also traced the name of burglar E. Howard Hunt to a White House office.

THE COVER-UP

Woodward and his *Post* colleague Carl Bernstein reported in an October 10, 1972, article that the Watergate break-in was only the tip of the iceberg. Aided by an anonymous source by the name of "Deep Throat," derived from a popular porno film at the time, Woodward and Bernstein learned that a "massive campaign of political spying and espionage" by CREEP and the White House was under way.[37] (Deep Throat was finally revealed on May 31, 2005, by *Vanity Fair* magazine. "I'm the guy they used to call Deep Throat," confirmed Deputy Director of the FBI William Felt, Sr.)

Despite this breakthrough, Watergate got little attention from the media. It wasn't until Cronkite took fifteen minutes of his *CBS Evening News* broadcast the Friday before Nixon's reelection to explain the players and their activities that anyone paid attention. "It was a giant kiss from Walter Cronkite," Woodward said later.[38] However, CBS News President Dick Salant told Cronkite that too much air time was spent on the Watergate story that evening. "I went through life saying this was the purest form of journalism I ever worked, including magazines and newspapers," Cronkite said. "I had to back off of that when I learned the truth about the Watergate episode because clearly management had interfered with the Watergate broadcast."[39]

By March 20, 1973, however, Watergate would become a big story. On that day McCord, leader of the hit men, delivered to Judge John Sirica a letter stating that political pressure had been applied to the defendants to keep silent. He also wrote the judge that perjury had occurred during the trial, and that others involved in Watergate had not been identified. Meanwhile, the Senate Select Committee on Presidential Campaign Activities, with Chairman Senator Sam J. Ervin Jr., of North Carolina, began hearing testimony. Chief Senate Watergate counsel Sam Dash began to question McCord, who implicated White House counsel John Dean, and Jeb Magruder, CREEP deputy director.

A Pandora's box opened on July 13, 1973, when Alexander Butterfield, a former White House Communications aide, admitted out of the Senate chamber that Nixon had taped himself and all those he talked to since 1970. Senator Ervin announced this in open session. In the midst of the tape battle, Vice President Agnew resigned on October 10, 1973, after pleading no contest to tax evasion.

While governor of Maryland, Agnew accepted more than $20,000 in payments — "bribes"—from agents of consulting and engineering firms. House Minority Leader Gerald Ford was sworn in as the new vice president.

"Nixon Quits Tonight" was the front-page headline in the *New York Post* on August 8, 1974.

Meanwhile, a series of events centering on the tapes rocked the nation, tagged the "Saturday night massacre" by the media. On October 12, 1973, the Court of Appeals ruled that the tapes requested by Special Prosecutor Archibald Cox must be delivered. On October 20, 1973, Nixon ordered Attorney General Elliott Richard to fire Cox. He refused and resigned. Then Nixon asked his deputy attorney William Ruckelshaus to do the job. He refused and resigned. Then Robert Bork, third in line at the Justice Department, accepted the post and fired Cox. Finally, on July 24, 1973, the Supreme Court voted 8 to 0 that Nixon had to turn over his tape recordings to Judge Sirica.

Among the nine tapes that Nixon finally agreed to yield to Cox's replacement, Texas lawyer Leon Jaworski, was a crucial one of June 20, 1972. The tape between Nixon and Haldeman contained an eighteen-and-a-half-minute gap caused by manual erasure. The damn burst as many assumed Nixon himself blotted out incriminating parts of the tape, bolstering the public's perception of a deceitful president who was obstructing justice, a criminal offense.

Next, the House voted 410 to 4 to begin impeachment hearings, culminating in a vote by the bipartisan House Judiciary Committee for three articles of impeachment: obstruction of justice, abuse of power, and contempt of Congress for refusing to turn over the tapes.

On August 5, 1974, Nixon released a transcript of the tape of June 23, 1972, nine days after Watergate. It was "the smoking gun," a damning tape showing that the man in the Oval Office was intimately involved all the way, and all his protestations were shown to be outright lies.

On August 8, 1974, more than two years after the notorious Watergate break-in, the president announced his resignation. The impeachment resolution, the unanimous Supreme Court decision, and the defections of his long-term supporters in the Congress and the media left him without friends.

NIXON AND THE PRESS

Nixon's method of dealing with the press and television had been on display long before he came to the White House. These incidents had certainly conditioned his attitude toward the media and had shown him the way they could be used to seize power and influence votes. He discovered the power of the press to set events in motion when his part in the unlikely discovery of the incriminating "pumpkin papers" led to the trial of Alger Hiss. Hiss was a former high-level State Department official who was publicly accused of being a Communist by Whittaker Chambers, a *Time* magazine editor, a reformed Communist himself. Chambers claimed that typed copies of State Department documents were given to him for transmission to the Soviet Union. Chambers said he held on to the pages in case he was threatened by Communist agents after he left the party. Chambers thought Hiss forces were plotting to steal the evidence. To protect himself, he took the film and placed it in a hollowed-out pumpkin behind his home. Then he alerted investigators for the House Un-American Activities Committee to what he had done. Here was a real discovery. A young and relatively obscure congressman, who just two years earlier was elected on a tough-line-toward-Communism platform, would become a national figure overnight simply by having his name associated with a major event.[40]

As a vice presidential candidate on the Eisenhower ticket, and more accomplished by this time, Nixon had employed basic emotional appeals in the famous Checkers speech, named after the Nixon family's dog. It was designed to vindicate Nixon, who was beset by charges concerning his handling of campaign financing, after the *New York Post* published a story under the headline "Secret Nixon Fund" on September 18, 1952. It was the first political speech ever to be made famous by television as some 9 million sets were tuned in—half of the nation's television households.

People also remembered the often-quoted remark he made in the course of his rambling, hysterical press conference of 1962, after he lost the California governorship. He told a shocked and embarrassed assemblage of reporters, "You won't have Nixon to kick around any more."[41] Yet the facts are that most of the state's newspapers backed him in that campaign; and since then, in both of his presidential campaigns, he was supported by nearly 80 percent of the country's newspapers.

Once elected president, Nixon and his associates entered the White House with a scheme in mind to manipulate, intimidate, control, and evade the press. His premise was that the national press was not essential and, later, that Watergate was a public relations problem. The press was to be serviced with innocuous material to write about, but the grand strategy was to "end run" the press, go above and around the press, as he abused his welcome into the nation's living rooms with a continuous series of television appearances during prime-time hours.

The plan worked until March 1973 when Judge Sirica read in open court the infamous McCord letter that he and his six codefendants had been subjected to political pressure and that perjury had been committed during the trial. Only then did the press realize it had been bamboozled for months by White House denials, disseminations, and lies.[42]

As the Watergate scandal unfolded, Nixon became more irritated with the press. He fumed on October 20, 1973, when the press reported the firing of Cox and the resignations of Richardson and Ruckelshaus. He said news correspondents that night were "almost hysterical" and "talked in apocalyptic terms." "Some called it the 'Night of the Long Knives' in a tasteless and inflammatory comparison with Adolf Hitler's murderous purge of his opposition in 1934. Within twenty-four hours the television and press had labeled the events with the prejudicial shorthand of 'Saturday Night Massacre,'" Nixon said.[43] He found John Chancellor's NBC broadcast most infuriating. Chancellor reported: "The country tonight is in the midst of what may be the most serious constitutional crisis in its history.... That is a stunning development and nothing even remotely like it has happened in all of our history.... In my career as a correspondent, I never thought I would be announcing these things."[44]

Nixon raged against journalists; he confounded them, damned them, called down curses upon their heads.[45] He referred to them as "clowns who write for the media"[46] or, simply, "sons of bitches."[47] America and its media were tiring of Nixon's deceptions and name-calling. President Ford would be a refreshing replacement—or so they thought.

THE POST-WATERGATE PARDON

It has been said that there is a temptation to dismiss the presidencies of Gerald Ford and Jimmy Carter as a protracted yawn between those of Nixon and Reagan: afterthought presidents. Yet, even in this desert of mediocrity there is something to be learned about the president–press relationship.

First of all, a certain sympathy exists for these presidents, both of whom inherited a nation suffering from the worst traumas since the Depression and confronted with new and terrifying prospects in the nuclear arms race and explosions in the Middle East. As another accidental president, who had not even been elected vice president, Ford had little opportunity to be anything more than a caretaker, nor did he seem to want to be anything more.

Ford's relations with the press began on a troubled note, but there was no subsequent rancor or alienation. Reporters found it impossible to dislike him, and although they might respect the office more than his actions, and even make him the subject of running jokes, they could not help having affection for him. He was, as has been frequently said, a nice guy who was trying to do his best in a job for which he was eminently unqualified, and the press appreciated his position.

Twenty days after he took office, Ford held his first press conference, on national television, an occasion for which he had spent ten hours of careful preparation. He even had dress rehearsals with staff members, who spared him even less than the reporters were expected to. His advisers thought of a splendid public relations touch.

AMERICAN MEDIA PROFILE   HELEN THOMAS 1920–

© Getty Images

Helen Thomas was a fixture of the White House press corps for more than forty years. As White House bureau chief for UPI, Thomas covered eight presidential administrations, beginning with that of John F. Kennedy. She became famous for her trademark line that signaled the end to the presidential press conference: "Thank you, Mr. President."

During her long career in journalism, Thomas helped women reporters break though barriers. She became the first woman White House bureau chief of a wire service in 1974. She was the first woman president of the White House Correspondents Association and the first woman member, later president, of the Gridiron Club, an exclusive press organization. Thomas was also the only woman print journalist to travel with President Richard Nixon to China on his breakthrough trip in January 1972. Thomas was known for helping generations of younger reporters, especially women, learn the ropes of the White House beat.

Thomas became famous for the hard-hitting, yet insightful questions she asked at White House news conferences. Her tough questioning earned her the respect of her colleagues, including CBS anchor Dan Rather. He said: "Helen Thomas is not only one of the smartest and savviest Washington reporters ever, she's also one of the most admired."

The eighth of ten children born to Lebanese immigrants, Thomas found her life's work after publishing an article for her high school newspaper. "Seeing my byline for the first time was an ego-swelling event. Printer's ink was in my veins," she said. Thomas admired the work of many of the journalists of her time, but says her parents were her most important role models. They came to the United States as young adults with hopes for a better life for their children. To make ends meet, they ran a grocery store in Detroit; they kept the accounts in their heads because they could not read or write.

After graduating from Wayne State University, the young reporter landed a job as a copy girl for the Washington *Daily News* for $17.50 a week. Besides cutting copy from the Teletype machine, she

Instead of appearing before Nixon's presidential blue drapes, such unpleasant reminders of the most imperial of presidencies could be avoided by having Ford speak before an open door in the East Room. Some of the press swallowed this bait. *Time* magazine's headline read: "Plain Words before an Open Door."

As Jerald F. terHorst, his press secretary, and the Ford staff had anticipated, the conference got around to the pardon with the first question, asked by Helen Thomas, of UPI, who as senior wire service correspondent had the privilege of the initial thrust. "Mr. President," she said, "do you agree with Governor Rockefeller that former President Nixon should have immunity from prosecution? And specifically, would you use your pardon authority if necessary?" The president gave her the evasive answer that might have been expected, providing no indication that only eleven days later he would grant "a full, free, and absolute pardon unto Richard Nixon for all offenses against the United States which [he]... has... or may have committed."[48]

It was the major mistake of Ford's brief presidency, and whether it was done out of unabashed party and personal loyalty, from inner conviction, or as the result of a prior deal with the former president has never been unequivocally established,

AMERICAN MEDIA PROFILE   C**ONTINUED**

fetched coffee for the editors. In 1943, Thomas began her work with the United Press International wire service. She was hired to write stories of interest to women, but it was politics that Thomas longed to cover. She got her chance in 1961, when she marched herself into the White House press room on President Kennedy's inauguration day and never left. It was during this first White House assignment that Thomas delivered her famous line, "Thank you, Mr. President." "President Kennedy had been given a very difficult question and he kept talking, hoping to hit on the answer. I got up and, finally extracting him from dilemma, I said, 'Thank you, Mr. President,' and he shot back, 'Thank you, Helen.'"

Thomas helped define the way modern reporters covered the White House. She was there from the glowing years of President Kennedy's administration, through the dark years of Watergate, all the way to the age of the Internet and the new millennium. Unlike many of her colleagues, Thomas never bothered with modern technology such as a cell phone or a laptop computer. Instead, from her perch in the front row at White House press conferences, she relentlessly asked tough questions and wouldn't take "no comment" without a fight. She insisted on access, information, and truth.

Her personal life was inseparable from her professional one. One of the stories that Thomas didn't break was that of her engagement. In 1971, President Nixon held a farewell reception for Thomas's chief competitor, Douglas B. Cornell, of the Associated Press. Nixon surprised the guests by announcing that Thomas and Cornell were going to be married now that they were no longer news rivals. Thomas cried but continued to take notes as the president spoke.

In 2000, Thomas retired from UPI after fifty-seven years, but she hung on to her White House press credential. She continued to cover the White House as a syndicated columnist for the Hearst newspaper chain. Even into her eighties Thomas worked harder than just about any other reporter, arriving earlier than most and staying later. At her retirement party from UPI, Thomas told colleagues, "I was so lucky to pick a profession where it's a joy to go to work every day."

By Beth Evans

although a strong case for the latter has been made. In any event the immediate effect was to reverse what *Time* had called the "mood of good feeling and even exhilaration in Washington that the city had not experienced for many years." The effect on the public and press opinion was even more dramatic. Overnight the Gallup poll showed that the president's public approval rating had dropped from 70 percent to 50 percent, whereas press approval, which had been nearly unanimous, plummeted to near zero. The move also cost Ford the services of terHorst, who resigned his post.[49]

Ford did make an honest effort to raise the level of president–press relations from the abysmal depths of the Nixon days. He held thirty-nine regular press conferences during his two and one-half years in office: five in the balance of 1974, nineteen in 1975, and fifteen more in 1976. His press conferences—often in the East Room, which he preferred—were conducted in a different spirit by far from Nixon's. He spoke bluntly and plainly.

Ford's run for the presidency in 1976 was a foredoomed affair. The public image of the president was marred by television. The public saw Ford on the nightly news playing golf in Palm Springs while Da Nang, in Vietnam, fell in blood and terror. Then Agriculture Secretary Earl Butz's tasteless jokes about black people cost him his job. Ford's acknowledgement that as a congressman he had accepted free golf holidays from corporate friends also didn't help his image. Ex-Nixon aide John Dean chimed in with the accusation that the Nixon White House had recruited Ford to suppress an early congressional investigation of Watergate.

In August Ford was thirteen points behind in his bid for his own term. He almost caught up with his opponent, but it was too late. By November, Governor Jimmy Carter came on strong and held a slight advantage in the polls.

In the public mind, the nice guy was still nice but tainted, and they turned to the honest farmer from Georgia who wanted to be called "Jimmy" and promised to exorcise the devil from the White House and from government in general.

MIDDLE EAST CRISIS

Carter had convinced the electorate of his superior morality, so the shock to some of the people was all the greater when a notorious interview with him appeared in *Playboy* magazine. There he confessed he had lusted in his heart after women and employed such otherwise common words as "screw" and "shack up." Fellow moralists were horrified, others were highly amused, and some hardly knew whether to laugh or cry at the prospect of such a man in the White House. In the end, opinion remained divided whether religion had plagued him all the way to Washington and afterward or whether it was religion that had been responsible for his being there at all. Certainly it was Richard Reeves' article, "Carter's Secret," that propelled religion into the campaign and led Carter to assert his "intimate relationship" with Jesus.[50]

As president, he successfully negotiated the gradual return of the Panama Canal to Panama, earning the respect of the people of Latin America. Even more important, he brought warring President Anwar al-Sadat of Egypt and Prime Minister Menachem Begin of Israel to finally agree on peace terms during talks at Camp David in 1979.

His brother Billy also caused Carter heartaches. His brother, whose jovial, wisecracking, beer-drinking, life-loving personality was the antithesis of the sober, God-fearing, intensely serious image the president presented. The media found Billy a welcome relief from the austerity of the Carter regime, and Billy found the media a welcome vehicle for his own good-natured aggrandizement of his family's position.

Soon after his brother's election, Billy himself ran for office as mayor of Plains, campaigning from the typical small-town Georgia gas station he owned, often filled with his drinking buddies, a place redolent of beer and grease. "Roll Out the Barrel" was his campaign song. The magic did not rub off, however, and Billy was defeated a month after his brother's victory.

In any case Carter had a great deal more to worry about than Billy. Of his many problems at home in 1979, the worst was the energy crisis created by the sharp reduction of oil from the Middle East. The country expected him to do something about it, and indeed he had a highly controversial energy bill he hoped to get through Congress, but the public had heard little from him, and it was becoming irritable and impatient. The oil shortage had produced rising inflation, with long lines at the gasoline pumps as well as higher supermarket bills.

Late in June, Carter gave up a Hawaii vacation and retreated to Camp David, where he had already made history by bringing the Israeli and Egyptian leaders together in the Camp David agreements, optimistically intended to achieve lasting peace in the Middle East. Now Carter meant to come up with a speech on energy that would get vital public support behind his program. Yet his first national address on energy fell on deaf ears. He looked at several drafts, heard conflicting views from his advisers, and then, only twenty-four hours before his scheduled appearance on television to address the nation, he abruptly canceled his speech.

Rumors spread rapidly. It was said that Carter was ailing from a variety of supposed diseases. The dollar plunged so rapidly that in order to stop it Carter had to announce that he would give the wire services a general statement promising that he would act decisively on the energy problem. Political advisers were rushed to Camp David by helicopter, and it was decided to call in leaders in politics, the media, businesses, unions, ethnic groups, and religious and civil rights organizations for a ten-day national summit conference on the crisis. These guests represented a cross-section of people who had been close to Carter's or earlier Democratic administrations, and among the 134 people invited were 20 governors, 10 professors, a sprinkling of congressmen, and others representing special-interest groups.

The president ate with his visitors three times a day, presenting to them an unruffled façade that seemed quite out of keeping with the emergency nature of the meeting. He had consulted only his wife, Rosalynn. In addition, he had decided that it was useless to make any more speeches on energy, he said, because he had already spoken on the same subject to decreasing television audiences. No one was listening, he believed, and he was becoming convinced that the electorate was not ready to make necessary sacrifices. He talked about spiritual exhaustion and his need to exert moral leadership in the country. In that case, some of his listeners suggested, he should fire his aide, Hamilton Jordan; his energy secretary, James Schlesinger; and his press secretary, Jody Powell.

Like Moses, Carter came down from the mountain eventually, but without exactly having talked to God. He delivered a speech written for him that presumably embodied what he had learned from the conference. He had rehearsed it several times beforehand, even practiced clenching a visible fist as a symbol of determined leadership. In thirty-two minutes he made a bold and typical attempt to separate himself from responsibility for the crisis, laying it at the door of "government" caught in "paralysis... stagnation, and drift." He had resolved to go back to the people, he said, and be their moral leader, after which he laid out a specific new energy policy for them to support.[51]

Somehow, in the press, what emerged most memorably was the president's remark about these same people whose support he sought, whose man he had claimed to be from the beginning. He confessed that they had been disappointing him. A malaise had appeared in the land, bringing with it too much self-interest, even despair—no doubt deepest among those at the end of the gas lines.

THE IRAN CRISIS

If there was despair, it would be directed at Carter, after militant Iranian students, fanatic followers of the Ayatollah Khomeini, seized the American Embassy in Teheran on November 4, 1979, and held ninety people, sixty-three of them

Americans, hostage. The action was taken because Carter had admitted the ailing shah of Iran to the United States for cancer surgery. The hostages would be detained for 442 days, while America wallowed in anger, pity, and frustration.

The media added to that frustration by reminding audiences of the number of days the hostages were being held. And no one was more effective than Cronkite. He would end a broadcast to this effect: "And that's the way it is, Wednesday, October 29, 1980, the three-hundred and sixty-first day of captivity of American hostages in Iran." Viewers also saw humiliating pictures of the embassy surrounded by chanting mobs burning the American flag and denouncing America as the "Great Satan." At Christmas they also saw grim captives receiving gifts and visitors. The crisis gave birth to ABC's *Nightline*, with Ted Koppel.

The results for Carter were disastrous as his reelection campaign approached. He was expected to do something, to restore national honor and bring the captives home. He attempted the slow process of negotiating through a mediator, Algeria. However, Americans were becoming impatient; they pointed to an Israeli rescue of hostages from the Entebbe airport in Uganda. A desperate Carter decided to rescue the hostages in what proved to be a harebrained military plan by using a small force, equipped with helicopters, launched from a battleship. He soon found out that Teheran was not Entebbe. The helicopters malfunctioned, and eight Americans were killed. Carter's presidency was finished, well before the votes were counted in 1980. His negotiations finally succeeded, but the Iranians clouded his victory by keeping the released hostages on the ground at the Teheran airport until the moment Ronald Reagan was sworn in as president.[52]

During his last four months in office, Carter held no press conferences. By this time he blamed the media for his approaching downfall. However, he never held the press in high esteem. Carter "thinks he's ninety-nine percent smarter than anybody who's around him," said *New York Times* reporter James Wooten, who covered the Carter campaign and the first year of his administration. "He has no respect for scribes; he hates the press."[53]

Yet, he did get good press coverage at the start of his administration and again with his successes. *National Journal* correspondent Dom Bonafede concluded after Carter's first two months in office that "few modern presidents have enjoyed more favorable treatment at the hands of the news media."[54] Carter also received extensive coverage and high marks for his successes—the Camp David summit meeting between Begin and Sadat, the Panama Canal treaties, and the human rights campaign, among others. As important as these events were, they were not enough to overcome the reality awaiting him with the candidacy of Ronald Reagan.

Although Carter rarely attacked the press as president, once he was out of office the rage emerged, and in an interview with *Parade*, the Sunday magazine supplement, he rehearsed the familiar litany of presidents before him. He said: "The press is superficial and inaccurate. The papers publish stories they know are lies and treat rumors as facts without checking. They do not want to check because they do not want to see a good story killed. They never apologize for an inaccurate story."[55]

In all fairness, however, it must be said that Carter made headlines in 1994 when he brokered a peace agreement between the war-torn factions of Bosnia and again when he did the same in North Korea and in Haiti. In 2002, he became the first former president to visit Cuba and address the Cuban people on television. In that same year, he was awarded the Nobel Peace Prize, adding support to the claim that he is one of the most respected ex-presidents in U.S. history.

AMERICA'S NEW DAWN—OR SO THE ADS SAID

Voters wanting to forget about Johnson, Nixon, Ford, and Carter saw something refreshing in Reagan. His TV commercials, among the most effective in campaign history, promised a new dawn for America. "The Time Is Now," "The Time Is Now for Leadership," and "The Time Is Now for Reagan" were comparable to Eisenhower's "It's Time for a Change." The slogans also whispered that the electorate had waited four years too long for Carter's promises to be kept.[56] Reagan also said to voters: "Ask yourself, are you better off now than you were four years ago?" The answer was overwhelming. Once elected, Reagan asked Americans to "dream heroic dreams"[57] and discard what he considered the corrosive pessimism of the Carter years.

Reagan's path to the White House was unlike that of any other president. Although his political philosophy was deeply rooted in the McKinley era, at the same time he was peculiarly a man of his own period—paradoxically an antiquarian relic of the past and at the same moment a product of the American era that began with the Depression.[58]

He was, observed Lou Cannon, White House correspondent for the *Washington Post*, "on one level the 'citizen-politician' he claimed to be, almost completely ignorant of even civics-book information about how bills were passed or how an administration functioned. But on another level, he seemed the most consummate and effective politician I had ever met."[59]

Before he became governor of California in 1967, Reagan was "Hollywood's child, citizen, spokesman, and defender." He was a "B-grade" star in generally mediocre movies, the most famous being *Bedtime for Bonzo*, in which he costarred with an ape, and *Knute Rockne—All American*, in which he portrayed George Gipp, the Notre Dame football player who died from pneumonia.

A Democrat in the 1950s, Reagan became a conservative Republican at the time he accepted a new job as TV host of *General Electric Theater*, in which he introduced dramas and sometimes acted in them. He also traveled throughout the country for ten weeks every year to promote GE products and meet company personnel at the (then) large salary of $125,000 a year, which was soon raised to $150,000.

As governor, he freely lied to reporters for what he considered good reasons. He was, as he himself jokingly admitted, playing the role of a governor, just as he had played movie roles, and as he would play his greatest starring role as president.[60] By 1968 Reagan was already being promoted for president. An oil millionaire named Tom Reed spent a good deal of time and money on the promotion, but Reagan did not believe the time was right. He refused a run for the U.S. Senate when he left the governorship after two terms. Instead he lectured on his favorite theme, New Federalism, attacking food stamps, welfare costs, and government spending. No doubts existed that he would run for president, and he made an unsuccessful try in 1975. He tried again in 1980.

He was tagged "the Teflon man" after surviving a series of blunders in that 1980 campaign. For example, he announced his intention to establish official relations with Taiwan while George Bush was on his way to mainland China; told a fundamentalist Christian rally in Dallas (avoided by the born-again Carter) that he thought creationism should be taught in the schools; and he implied unintentionally in a Michigan speech that Carter was linked to the Ku Klux Klan. Since all these mistakes occurred in the first seventeen days of the campaign, the press was beginning to hover over him in anticipation of the next startling pronouncement.[61] As the first actor ever to occupy the White House, Reagan appeared at ease in front of the cameras with his relaxed "aw-shucks," "there-you-go-again" style. However, the press could not deal with Reagan in the usual way. For one thing, press conferences became more formal as reporters were told to stay in their assigned seats and raise their hands if they wanted to ask a question. It allowed him to call upon whom he wanted.

AMERICAN MEDIA PROFILE | **I. F. STONE 1907–1989**

© Grey Villet/Getty Images

I. F. Stone continued the great American tradition of muckraking, independent journalism that stretches back to Tom Paine and in part shared the all-too-common fate of being marginalized in life and lionized in death.

Stone himself put it this way: "If you live long enough, the venerability factor creeps in; first you get accused of things you never did, and later, credited for virtues you never had."

Stone's major stories over the years included his early opposition to Adolf Hitler, his whistle-blowing on Pentagon spending debacles when such stories were rare, and his discovery of falsification of testing data by the Atomic Energy Commission. Additionally, he was one of very few major journalists, if not the sole one, to challenge President Johnson's account of the Gulf of Tonkin incident in 1964.

Isador Feinstein Stone was born in Philadelphia on December 24, 1907. His parents were Russian immigrants who owned a store in New Jersey. He studied philosophy at the University of Pennsylvania. (Toward the end of his life he devoted more than ten years of study to the Platonic world of ancient Greece, and published *The Trial of Socrates*, which became a best seller.)

After the university, where as a student he wrote for the *Philadelphia Inquirer*, Stone worked for a stint at the *Camden Courier-Post* before moving to the *New York Post* in 1933.

The Court Disposes was his first book, published four years later; it was his justification for President Franklin Roosevelt's attempts to expand, and "packing" of the Supreme Court, a controversial move which failed.

Stone left the *New York Post* in 1939 and became associate editor of *The Nation*, a left-oriented weekly. He published his second book, *Business as Usual*, in 1941. It was a critique of U.S. foot-dragging in preparations for what was to become World War II. After the war, he wrote a book about the migration of Eastern European Jews, *Underground to Palestine*. He joined the *New York Star* in 1948. He published *The Hidden History of the Korean War* in 1952, a statement of his criticism of the Cold War.

THE STRUGGLE FOR ACCESS

After eight months in office, Reagan had become the most inaccessible of modern presidents, with the exception of Nixon during the Watergate period. At that point, he had held only three news conferences, whereas Carter had held fourteen and Ford twelve. Reagan was to average three per year.

The press conferences were only a relatively small part of the media machine that had grown so explosively since Nixon's days. Ford had a press office staff of only forty-five people, about seven times more than in 1960; most of the increase had taken place under Nixon, and it constituted about 10 percent of the entire White House staff of 500 people. Reagan's staff numbered about 600 people, possibly more. Of these, 150, at a minimum, and nearly 500 at a more reasonable maximum, were devoting most of their time and talents to public relations efforts. In 1978 the Office of Media Liaison had been averaging 35,551 press release items each month, sending them to 6,500 news organizations, interest groups, and individuals. The figure under Reagan swelled to even larger proportions.

AMERICAN MEDIA PROFILE | **CONTINUED**

Stone started his own publication, *I. F. Stone's Weekly*, in 1953. With this paper, Stone attacked the blacklist, racial segregation, nuclear proliferation, military spending, the war economy, and both the Korean and Vietnam wars.

His secret was simple—consistent, unceasing research. He pored over Defense Department reports, Pentagon documents, congressional testimony. Ralph Nader said in an obituary tribute, "Notwithstanding poor eyesight and bad ears, he managed to see more and hear more than other journalists because he was curious and fresh, with the capacity for both discovery and outrage every new day." As Victor Navasky, now *The Nation*'s publisher, put it, "His method [was] to scour and devour public documents, bury himself in the *Congressional Record*, study obscure congressional committee hearings, debates, and reports, all the time prospecting for news nuggets, contradictions in the official line, examples of bureaucratic and political mendacity, [and] documentation on incursions on civil rights and liberties."

At one student journalism conference he was introduced as an investigative reporter. "That's redundant," he said. "All reporters should be investigative."

Stone believed that you could not report well as an insider, and that you could not be friends or drinking buddies with the subjects you covered. And as an outsider, he broke scoop after scoop, stories often ignored by the mainstream press for years afterward. As he told Navasky years ago: if you didn't attend background briefings, you weren't bound by the rules; you could debrief correspondents who did, check out what they had been told, and as often as not reveal the lies for what they were.

Ill health forced him to stop the *Weekly* in the early 1970s, but he kept up a stream of writing, speaking, and research until his death from a heart attack, July 17, 1989. As he said:

The only kinds of fights worth fighting are those you're going to lose, because somebody has to fight them and lose and lose and lose until someday, somebody who believes as you do wins. In order for somebody to win an important, major fight 100 years hence, a lot of other people have got to be willing—for the sheer fun and joy of it—to go right ahead and fight, knowing you're going to lose. You mustn't feel like a martyr. You've got to enjoy it.

By Fred Glienna

Early coverage of the Reagan presidency was surprisingly fair, as he acknowledged. But then leaks began, as they always do, and Reagan was as irate as his predecessors had been. At first it appeared to be his policy to punish, if he could (or at least chastise), those who had printed information he wanted suppressed, rather than those who were the leakers. But then, in 1982, he issued an order forbidding speaking to reporters on a background basis by everyone in the White House, with a half-dozen exceptions, including his closest advisers and Gergen.

One unexpected leak turned into a gusher when the November 1982 *Atlantic* appeared on the newsstands with an article titled "The Education of David Stockman," in which the thirty-five-year-old director of the budget admitted that he had deployed his figures so that they would not appear as "voodoo economics," a term Vice President Bush had used to describe the Reagan plan during the Republican primary. Most damaging of all, Stockman admitted that the grand theory of supply-siders was really a cover for the older, largely discredited idea of "trickle-down"—the view that tax cuts for corporations and the wealthy produce beneficial effects for those on the lower rungs of the economic ladder.[62]

The article could not have come at a worse moment. Only a few weeks earlier the national debt had soared beyond a trillion dollars, meaning $100 billion annually would be spent on interest payments; simultaneously, unemployment had reached its highest point since 1975. How to pay for the deficit and his grandiose plans for military spending without raising taxes was at that juncture a dilemma that the president had no idea how to solve, except by means that would be politically difficult and dangerous.

Complaining about the media's coverage of such issues, Reagan asked: "Is it news that some fellow out in South Succotash has just been laid off?"[63] The *Los Angeles Times* replied: "The answer is, it is news. It is news in Los Angeles, Detroit, New York and yes, South Succotash. Unemployment is news." The editorial was headlined, "Let Them Eat Succotash." In the same issue, a Paul Conrad cartoon captioned "Reagan Country" showing a sign reading, "Welcome to South Succotash, Population: 9,000,000 Unemployed."

Conrad's cartoon was almost prophetic. On October 19, 1987, the stock market crashed as the Dow plunged 500 points. Investors' losses were nearly double those of the historic Black Monday in 1929. Reagan apparently didn't understand that his policy of massive tax cuts would lead to a sharp rise in the volume of savings. However, the savings rate as a percentage of disposable income after taxes had dropped from 7.1 percent in 1980 to less than 3 percent in 1987. Private and public debt had doubled.

Meanwhile, Reagan made a systematic effort to suppress and control the flow of information from such government agencies as the Justice Department, the Pentagon, and the Central Intelligence Agency. In 1981, he quietly attempted to gut the Freedom of Information Act (FOIA), while exempting the CIA and FBI from it entirely. He declared a moratorium on the publication of government documents, deprived citizens of due process by excluding the public from oversight of federal rule-making proceedings, invoked the president's personal executive privilege to justify withholding Interior Departments document from Congress, and authorized the CIA to monitor the private conversations of American citizens.[64]

Reagan again went after the FOIA in 1982, reversing Carter-era provisions that forbade classification of a document after a request had been made for it. The administration also sought to control public dissemination of private scientific research, and ordered the reclassification of millions of previously declassified government documents.

Reagan also tried to tinker with the constitutional doctrine of separation of powers by pushing to have the federal budget office decide which acts of Congress it could afford to enforce. He then defied congressional subpoenas for Environmental Protection Agency documents on toxic waste. A year later the FBI was awarded the right to infiltrate political organizations in the name of "domestic security." An interagency task force also recommended that the administration request legislation that would make it a federal crime for government employees to disclose classified information. Punishment for breaking the law would be as much as three years in prison and a fine of $10,000. The task force also recommended that unauthorized recipients of classified information, including journalists, be subjected to civil penalties.[65]

The "secret" government needed a fine-tuned media to get its message out. By early 1983 the president and his advisers had raised the manipulation of television news, begun in the Kennedy administration, to a fine art. These new efforts included ten-minute daytime mini–news conferences; making of public appearances with high-technology executives and auto workers; an intense multiplication of "photo opportunities" (really high-level press agentry); and the briefing (that is, propagandizing) of local television news anchors and news directors, as well as the few news conferences he held.

GRENADA AND PRESS CONTROL

Government secrecy and media manipulation allowed Reagan to quietly invade the tiny island of Grenada. Questions of media access to combat operations had changed dramatically by the time of the invasion. No access existed. It was the first military strike in American history that was produced, filmed, and reported by the Pentagon. At the time, the administration believed the media would only get in the way.

On October 25, 1983, President Reagan ordered some 1,200 troops to invade the island. Why? The president and his administration were concerned that the Marxist government of Prime Minister Maurice Bishop was allowing Cuba to gain undue influence in Grenada, specifically by constructing a military-grade airport with Cuban military engineers.

The administration line was that 1,000 American medical students were in danger and had to be rescued after the Grenadian army seized power in a bloody coup twelve days earlier. As U.S. troops soared to 7,000 within days, the island fell to U.S. combat forces, and a pro-American government took power. Some nineteen Americans, forty-eight Grenadians, and twenty-nine Cubans died in the invasion.

More importantly, it was the first war conducted by the government in which the press was denied access. An even greater challenge exposed by the press was on the horizon for this administration.

IRAN-CONTRA SCANDAL

The White House's greatest challenge followed the publication of an October 31, 1986, story in *Al Shira'a*, the Beirut magazine, about how the Reagan administration had been secretly selling arms to Iran in exchange for the captive American hostages, an act in violation of U.S. foreign policy. U.S. reporters in the Middle East picked up the story a few days later, and all hell broke loose, with the public, politicians, and news organizations demanding a full-scale investigation. Evidence indicated that what occurred was an impeachable offense no less virulent than those carried out during the Watergate crisis. Legislation had barred Reagan from providing military assistance to Nicaraguan rebels known as the Contras, who were waging a civil insurrection to unseat the revolutionary (later elected) Sandinista government of President Daniel Ortega. Reagan, at the time, pledged not to make a deal with the Iranians that would benefit them for freeing American hostages held by Arab insurgents backed by Iran.

Ignoring the law, an unknown lieutenant colonel named Oliver L. North, backed by the president's national security adviser, engineered a deal that sent arms to Iran in exchange for money that was in turn supplied to the Contras for their civil war effort, which the president publicly endorsed. North would admit later that he, along with security chief Admiral John M. Poindexter, had, indeed, swung the deal, which they had hoped would bring about the release of the hostages.

Ironically, the very day the Lebanese story was published, November 3, 1986, an article by John Wallach, foreign editor of the Hearst Newspapers, appeared reporting that secret negotiations with Iran had been going on for a year.

Opposition to Reagan's sinister plot could be heard in the halls of Congress. North and Poindexter were summoned to Capitol Hill to testify in closed-door hearings. Three weeks after the article appeared, Attorney General Edward Meese called a news conference, in which he said for the first time that weapons for the Contras had been purchased with proceeds from the sale of arms to Iran. The news forced the resignations of Poindexter and North.

North appeared before the Senate and House Select Investigative Committee that began meeting on May 25, 1987. He told the committee that an Iranian munitions dealer had suggested the idea of diverting arms sales profits to the Contras. Furthermore, he revealed that he had shredded documents—evidence.

The American public no longer believed the president, who feared that he could be impeached. Some 53 percent of Americans said Reagan was lying about his knowledge of the Contra arms diversion. Even more damaging was the rumor that was to plague the first Bush administration: it was said that a deal had been finalized in Paris whereby the American hostages would not be released prior to the November presidential election. Thus, Carter would be prevented from obtaining their release and winning reelection. If true, the participants would have been guilty of treason. The story appeared in several alternative publications and in the European press. The U.S. press did not take it seriously.

According to investigative journalist Mark Haertsgaard, the Iran-Contra affair was widely regarded as a vindication of the American press, "but this interpretation owed more to the remarkable passivity of the press during Reagan's first six years in office than to any valiant behavior on its part during the scandal that shook his presidency." He said the press all but missed the Iran-Contra story in three ways—by coming to it too late, leaving it too soon, and failing to convey its full significance along the way.[66]

Bill Moyers exposed the misdeed in his November 1990 PBS show *High Crimes and Misdemeanors*. Moyers believed that Reagan and Bush had lied about their involvement in the scandal.

"THE NEW WORLD ORDER"

Questions about Vice President Bush's involvement in the Iran-Contra scandal did not hamper his 1988 presidential bid. However, it did produce one of the most controversial moments in television news history. Bush confronted anchor Dan Rather on his *CBS Evening News*. The vice president was annoyed that Rather was using his appearance to cross-examine his role in the Iran-Contra scandal. Bush shot out: "It's not fair to judge my whole career by a rehash on Iran. How would you [Rather] like if I judged your career by those seven minutes when you walked off the set in New York?" Bush was alluding to an incident five months earlier when Rather refused to appear on air as a protest over a tennis match that ran over into the news slot. For seven minutes, the network telecast went dead. Rather responded that Bush's race for the presidency was more important than Rather's action.[67]

Bush became the first sitting vice president since Van Buren to win the presidency, in what many consider the nastiest television advertising campaign in American history. Bush defeated Massachusetts Governor Michael S. Dukakis after airing a number of negative advertisements that portrayed his opponent as soft on crime, antimilitary, and an ineffective state executive unable to clean up a polluted Boston harbor.

Once in office, Bush's presidency witnessed a "new world order." The news media captured these fast-paced events with some of the most dramatic pictures in American history. Within the first year of his inauguration, Bush and the media would deal with the end of the Cold War, the disintegration of the Soviet Union and the Eastern European bloc countries from Poland to Romania, and the dramatic fall of the Berlin Wall.

On April 2, 1989, the *New York Times* declared "The Cold War Is Over" as Soviet leader Mikhail Gorbachev's policy of glasnost swept across borders that had been closed since World War II. Gorbachev, furthermore, attempted to hasten the collapse of Communism with his perestroika, the restructuring of the Soviet economy. At the time, Gorbachev and President Boris Yeltsin appeared on ABC television as the Soviet Union and its Communist system disintegrated. A Russian TV newscast began with: "Today, September 5, 1991, we all began living in a new country: the Soviet Union is no more."

However, a faltering economy continued to threaten the Soviet's new political freedoms and media openness. Despite fears that pro-Communist forces would undermine Gorbachev's mission, the government allowed contested elections for the first time in its history. Employing American campaign consultants, Yeltsin became Russia's first democratically elected president, as a wave of democracy spread throughout the Eastern European bloc countries.

Nothing was more dramatic than the pictures capturing the fall of the Berlin Wall on November 9, 1989, as thousands of East Berliners streamed into the West. Others danced on the wall in front of the Brandenburg Gate. Still others began hacking away at the massive unnatural barrier with any tool available. By June 22, 1990, the famed allied control booth at Checkpoint Charlie, the main crossing point between East and West Berlin, was lifted by crane in the presence of foreign ministers and other politicians.

However, this new wave of freedom had come to an abrupt halt on June 3, 1989, when Chinese soldiers massacred thousands of students who demanded their version of democracy in Beijing's Tiananmen Square. A stunned world witnessed the emotional event on television; the broadcasts were a weapon the demonstrators believed would help their fight for democracy.

Still another event would stun Americans in this era of a changing world order. At the end of his first year in office, Bush hoped to install a democratic government in Panama. He ordered U.S. troops into the Central American country with a mission to capture Manuel Noriega, the Panamanian leader, who had been involved in international drug smuggling and espionage. The mission also was undertaken, according to the president, to protect U.S. interests in the Panama Canal as well as the lives of U.S. residents. Noriega surrendered at the Vatican Embassy and was taken to Florida and jailed on drug trafficking charges. As head of the CIA, Bush for years had a relationship with Noriega; then his activities could be excused in exchange for information about Cuba and Nicaragua. However, his drug activities made him a liability. However, Bush came under heavy criticism for the invasion, which resulted in hundreds of civilian deaths. The media that were denied access to the action also criticized him.

THE GULF WAR AND PRESS ACCESS

Bush earned high marks from the press as he established his own personality. He was more accessible to the press than Reagan had been. As commander in chief, Bush won equally high marks from the public during his conduct of the Gulf War. Promising during his campaign for the presidency to provide a "kinder and gentler America," Bush sent U.S. troops to Saudi Arabia on August 7, 1990. Iraq's President Saddam Hussein had seized neighboring Kuwait. The action was puzzling to some Americans, who believed Iraq was a U.S. ally, having borne the brunt of the eight-year war against America's number-one enemy, Iran. Hussein charged that Kuwait had been stealing oil from a field on a disputed boundary.

For the first time in American history, the public watched live coverage of an air war, as bombs were being dropped from U.S. Stealth fighter-bombers and Patriot missiles were hitting incoming Iraqi Scuds. A series of polls in early 1991 showed that the public approved of the news media's war performance, giving television and newspapers 90 percent and 89 percent favorable ratings, respectively. Some 89 percent of those polled said they used television as the main source of war news. Some 67 percent said follow-ups in newspapers gave them the same basic coverage.

From the administration's point of view, the Gulf War showed how top officials became sophisticated in their approach to controlling the news media. Public relations expert and former Reagan adviser Michael Deaver said, in the *New York Times*: "The coverage on television has been a combination of Lawrence of Arabia and Star Wars, and since television is where eighty percent of the people get their news, it couldn't be better."[68]

What the public got was something right out of a Madison Avenue public relations firm; the media were reduced to being a conduit for official information offered by commanders who could scarcely disguise their disgust with the delivery system they were forced to use. The media got all the pictures and quotes they needed. However, they were supplied by the military. They also got access to the front lines. However, they were personally escorted after being assigned to press pools to locations determined by the military. Officers closely monitored field interviews with the troops. Pictures showing soldiers in distress were suppressed, and television coverage of flag-draped coffins arriving in the United States was banned.

John R. MacArthur, *Harper's* magazine publisher, said that the obstacles to producing good journalism during the Gulf War were considerable. At the top of the list, he said, was military censorship—the 1,200 U.S. journalists covering the mostly American side in Saudi Arabia simply weren't permitted to file much that was worth reading or watching. Another obstacle may have been the brevity of the fighting, and that it was conducted mostly from the air. Still another was fear, since most reporters want to survive to tell the story.[69]

Others criticized the media for being caught flat-footed in the gulf because military beats had been poorly covered. It is one thing to cover the antics and waste at the Pentagon, such as purchasing five-hundred-dollar hammers. It is another to cover the people who were going to be responsible for any future military action. As an example of how poorly the media had been covering the military beat, for the last twenty years the public lacked information on General "Stormin'" Norman Schwarzkopf. The media began to focus on him as American troops started to move toward the desert. His victory over the press was total and devastating.

"We covered the politics of the military but not its mission," says Bill Kovach, curator of the Neiman Foundation for Journalism at Harvard University. "A huge industry has grown up to shape public opinion by controlling what goes into the media in the last twenty years and in all that time, the press doesn't seem to have thought about the problem at all. We tend to be a responsive apparatus that reacts to whatever comes along."

Despite the military's and Bush's rout of the media, as well as his high approval rating handling international tensions, the president could not be awarded high marks for handling domestic matters. He broke his "read-my-lips" promise not to raise taxes; he refused to halt a burgeoning federal deficit that went out of control during the Reagan administration; he was criticized for his controversial nomination of Judge Clarence Thomas to the U.S. Supreme Court; and he was embarrassed by a son's involvement in a savings and loan scandal. Such issues were too much to overcome. Bush was defeated handily in the 1992 election, 43 to 38 percent, by Arkansas governor Bill Clinton.

TABLOIDIZATION OF THE MEDIA

Clinton's rough-and-tumble presidency was marked by investigations into land dealings in his native Arkansas, which cleared him and his wife in the final months of his presidency, and sexual misconduct that led to his impeachment (he was the second president in America history to have that distinction). Despite it all, Clinton continued to receive relatively high public approval ratings for his job. During the 2000 presidential race, polls showed that he would beat both major candidates if he could have sought a third term.

The first baby boomer to become president, Clinton was compared to John Kennedy, his childhood idol whom he met at the White House as a teenager. Like Kennedy and Reagan, Clinton had charisma, and lots of it, and he conquered television. He used television in his unconventional presidential campaign, appearing on radio and TV talk shows, playing his saxophone on the Arsenio Hall program, and becoming the first presidential candidate to appear on MTV.

Once in the White House, Clinton received the shortest honeymoon from the press accorded a modern president. Though he was able to field tough questions at news conferences, he held them very seldom—only three in his first twenty months in office. When he did meet the press, it was usually contentious. On the nomination of Supreme Court Justice Ruth Bader Ginsburg, for instance, ABC's Brit Hume asked a question that the president found insulting. He rebuked Hume and then stalked off. Instead, the president favored televised meetings with average citizens, appearing on talk shows, or discussing policy on his weekly radio broadcast.

Perhaps Jack Nelson, Washington bureau chief of the *Los Angeles Times*, in a talk to the Los Angeles World Affairs Council on February 2, 1994, described Clinton best:

> He has turned out to be one of the most activist, ambitious, controversial, undisciplined, procrastinating presidents.... He's into everything. He's late for almost everything, even for making the State of the Union address.... One of his aides said he's inventing a new form of chaos that works for him.... But despite his eccentricities and many ups and downs... I think his harshest critics would agree that he's delivered on one or two of his major promises. Whether you like him or whether you don't like him, he has delivered on diversity and he has delivered on change.

He delivered on diversity by appointing more people of color to government posts than his Republican predecessors had. Ronald Brown became the first black secretary of commerce and Joycelyn Elders became the first black surgeon general. Her tenure was short. She was fired for making a controversial suggestion that masturbation was a proper subject for sex education. However, the president was not willing to fight for a strong liberal to follow in the footsteps of Thurgood Marshall, when he left the Supreme Court.

Keep in mind that Clinton did not ride into the White House on a liberal agenda or a formula for social change. It was a formula for electoral victory—moving the Democratic Party to the center, doing enough for minorities and working people to keep their support while trying to win over white conservative voters with a program of toughness on crime and a strong military. "The era of big government is over," Clinton proclaimed as he ran for president, seeking votes on the belief that Americans supported the Republican position that government was spending too much for social programs.

In search of support for the centrist vote for his reelection, in the summer of 1996 Clinton took up the Republican agenda and signed a welfare reform law ending the federal government's guarantee of financial help to poor families with dependent children, a program begun during the New Deal. To the dismay of labor unions, he signed the North American Free Trade Agreement (NAFTA), which was enthusiastically supported by corporate interests. NAFTA cut tariffs and allowed businesses to move freely across the Mexican and Canadian borders. However, it offered no protection for exploited Mexican workers living in squalor just south of the U.S. border.

Despite hugging a Republican agenda, Clinton was delivered a devastating blow in the 1994 midterm elections. Republicans captured both the House and Senate for the first time since 1954. Speaker of the House Newt Gingrich and his Republican colleagues fashioned a "Contract with America," specific campaign pledges signed with much media fanfare on the steps of the Capitol.

The Republican onslaught did not prevent Clinton's election for a second term. He soundly defeated Senate Majority Leader Robert Dole by eight percentage points. However, he faced a Republican Congress and an aggressive media.

The Clinton era brought with it a new or lower standard for covering public affairs. Extreme "tabloidization" was heightened by excessive coverage of the O. J. Simpson trial. Tabloids were given greater credibility when major newspapers and the networks quoted them while covering the story. Meanwhile, the mainstream press became obsessed with financial dealings dating back to Clinton's term as governor. The so-called Whitewater affair involved financial dealings of his wife, Hillary, and close friends. Some of these friends went to jail, but investigations, which lasted the entire Clinton presidency, cleared both of them.

Investigations of Whitewater expanded to allegations of sexual misconduct. The remainder of Clinton's term would be absorbed with disclosures of his affair with a White House intern. It wasn't the mainstream media that broke the news of the president's latest sexual tryst. Matt Drudge reported on his Internet site that *Newsweek* had delayed publication of a report that Clinton had a sexual relationship with White House intern Monica Lewinsky from 1995 to 1997. Within hours the major media pursued the story, relying on anonymous sources and rumor to get a new angle.

Lewinsky was a witness in an earlier sexual harassment lawsuit against Clinton by Paula Jones, a former Arkansas state clerk. Jones' attorneys were seeking evidence of a pattern of sexual misbehavior by the president. Lewinsky's onetime friend Linda Rattrap, who worked in the Bush White House, taped her talking about conspiring with Clinton to lie in the case and turned the recordings over to independent counsel Kenneth W. Starr.

Meanwhile, Clinton told the nation that he did not have sex with Lewinsky. After being called to testify before a federal grand jury, he admitted in a televised speech that he lied but was adamant that he broke no laws.

Starr thought differently. Eleven months after the investigation began, Starr delivered to Congress a 445-page report alleging eleven impeachable acts, charging that Clinton "has betrayed his trust as president and has acted in a manner subversive of the rule of law and justice" in trying to impede Jones' suit and Starr's resulting criminal investigation. The document contained explicit descriptions of sexual acts committed in the White House. In addition, Starr released a videotape of Clinton's grand jury testimony.

On December 19, 1998, the House of Representatives voted 228 to 206, largely along party lines, to approve two articles of impeachment, accusing the Democratic president of perjury before a grand jury and alleging tampering with witnesses and helping to hide evidence. Two articles of perjury and abuse of power were rejected.

The vote came hours after the newly anointed House speaker, Bob Livingston of Louisiana, admitted to having extramarital affairs. He called on Clinton to resign and then, abruptly and unexpectedly, took his own advice. He stepped down, saying, "I must set the example that I hope President Clinton will follow."

In early 1999 the U.S. Senate acquitted Clinton of the two articles of impeachment that the House had passed against him. Brushing aside calls for his resignation, Clinton vowed to serve "until the last hour of the last day of my term." Despite excessive coverage by the nation's media, the Clinton sexual affairs did not hurt the president's standing in the polls. Results indicated that Americans did not consider the story important.

Instead, Americans took the press to task for its obsession with Clinton's sexual affairs. Cronkite criticized journalists for using excessive unidentified sources and investigative leaks. Steve Brill, publisher of *Brill's Content*, went further than Cronkite, pointing fingers at NBC correspondent David Bloom and ABC's Jackie Judd for being virtual extensions of Starr's investigation.

Still others found parallels with the age of yellow journalism. Some serious journalists and news consumers found it hard to digest that major news organizations, both print and broadcast, freely quoted the *National Enquirer* and the *Star* and thought they now had to compete with *Hard Copy* and *Inside Edition*.

By the 2000 presidential race, Texas governor George W. Bush and Vice President Al Gore had to answer "probing" questions related to drug and alcohol use as well as to extramarital affairs. Americans wanted to know, or so some members of the "press" thought. On election night television anchors received another black eye in the tight presidential race. Anchors, their reports based on exit polls, declared Florida for Gore. Minutes later they gave the state to Bush. As Gore was making his way to congratulate the Texas governor, television called it a toss-up. Gore never made his concession speech that night.[70]

It would take weeks until the nation knew who its next president would be. Florida electors finally were declared in Bush's column, after numerous court battles, including a decisive one at the Supreme Court. Once inaugurated, Bush was bumped from the nation's front pages for weeks by the Clintons: Hillary Clinton won the U.S. Senate race in New York and became the first wife of a president to win political office, and the Clintons bought a new home. The press also was busy covering Clinton's controversial last-minute pardons, which included one for a jailed drug dealer, and his taking furniture and other items from the White House.

Within nine months of his inauguration, however, President Bush would have to deal with the bloodiest day on American soil since the Civil War, "a modern Antietam played out in real time, on fast-forward, and not with soldiers but with secretaries, security guards, lawyers, bankers, janitors," as Nancy Gibbs, writing in *Time* magazine, put it.[71] It was September 11, 2001, the day the American empire was threatened and the president and the nation faced a new enemy.

A NEW KIND OF ENEMY

"Terror works like a musical composition," Gibbs wrote, following the September 11 attack, "so many instruments, all in tune, playing perfectly together to create their desired effect."[72] That effect was to maim what America's enemies saw as the nation's defining sanctuaries—money and power. At 8:45 A.M. American Airlines Flight 11, a Boeing 767 carrying eighty-one passengers that left Boston on its way to Los Angeles, slammed into the north tower of New York City's World Trade Center. Twenty-six minutes later, a United Airlines flight from Boston to Los Angeles careened into the center's south tower. Meanwhile, American Flight 77, a Boeing 757 that departed Dulles, hit the Pentagon's west side. The terrorists' carefully crafted composition crumbled when a commandeered United Airlines flight from Newark, New Jersey, bound for San Francisco, with thirty-eight passengers and seven crew members, crashed in a Pennsylvania field.

In a speech before Congress, President Bush told the nation that evidence gathered by investigators "all points to" the al Qaeda organization, led by Saudi terrorist Osama bin Laden, as the perpetrator of the suicide hijackings that killed an estimated 3,047. He ordered Afghanistan's Islamic government to hand over every terrorist within its borders—or face destruction. American troops, as well as fighting forces from Europe, were called to Afghanistan. The media were not. Journalists were frustrated by their limited access to the conflict. Meanwhile, the public once again blamed the media for the uncertainty and confusion generated by the attack.

By November 2001, John Barry, *Newsweek*'s Pentagon reporter, said that access was restricted precisely because the Bush administration and the Defense Department "don't really know how well the war is going" and are reluctant to permit coverage that "might not be consistent with their basic message that they're making inexorable progress toward inevitable victory."[73]

David Shribman, Washington bureau chief for the *Boston Globe*, told the late *Los Angeles Times* media critic David Shaw that reporters are "so separate from the action that we don't even know what questions we should be asking." Mark Thompson, Pentagon correspondent for *Time* magazine, said, "They'd like to fight the whole war at night and we like to shine a light."[74]

The savvy secretary of defense, Donald H. Rumsfeld, told reporters that he recognized the need to provide the press—and, through them, the American people—with information to the fullest extent possible. "Defending our freedom and way of life is what this conflict is all about, and that certainly includes freedom of the press," he said.[75] However, the gulf of distrust between the military and reporters appeared to have widened during the new war as military commanders on the ground feared security leaks.

The military's skepticism increased because MSNBC and Fox News now programmed a twenty-four-hour news cycle, and they were rushing to be first. In the

Gulf War, the military had to contend only with CNN. "It used to be that a reporter worked as hard as he could to get something right. Now you just put it out there as soon as you know it and figure that if it's wrong, you can fix it fifteen minutes later. That's a really big deal with a commander in the field. The fact that you can fix your mistake in fifteen minutes is not a real big comfort to a commander," according to Major Patrick Gibbons, a longtime public information specialist with the marines. He also said the media sometimes invoke "the public's right to know" to justify their pursuit of scoops and sensationalism, especially stories that show military failure.[76]

The major may have a point. The news media reduced time and space for foreign coverage by 70 to 80 percent during the past fifteen to twenty years. In that time, international news bureaus were closed. Some media critics blame these cutbacks for the uncertainty and confusion among many Americans as to why terrorists committed such horrible acts on September 11. "I think most Americans are clueless when it comes to the politics and ideology and religion in [the Muslim] world and, in that sense, I think we do bear some responsibility," said Martin Baron, editor of the *Boston Globe*.[77]

EMBEDDED REPORTERS IN IRAQ

The Bush administration attempted to bridge the gulf of distrust between the military and the press as it prepared for its next phase in the war on terrorism—in Iraq. After Afghanistan, the Pentagon promised to increase press access by opening up slots for several hundred journalists to be "embedded" with military units. Reporters were assigned to one squad, in one platoon, in one company, placing some journalists closer than others to military battles. To prepare journalists to be embedded, the navy, army, and marines treated some fifty-eight journalists from thirty news organizations to an eight-day media boot camp. "The virtue of embedding is that it allows reporters to eat, breathe, sleep and experience war firsthand with soldiers," said Tom Rosenstiel, director of the Washington, D.C.–based Project for Excellence in Journalism. "But the danger is that you're liable to start reporting from the point of view of the troops who are protecting you. In a way, you owe your life to them, and the Pentagon knows that."[78]

The Pentagon's about-face on access was intended to reduce the tensions that have marked media-military relations since Vietnam, the last major U.S. war in which reporters had close access to the troops and their commanders. The press was shut out in Panama, Grenada, and the 1991 Gulf War. "In Desert Storm, what with restrictive pools and a choke chain continuously yanked by military public affairs officers, only 10 percent of reporters in theater actually made it into battle," *Weekly Standard* reporter Matt Labash said.[79]

Some 500 journalists joined U.S. forces poised for the assault on Iraq, which began March 20, 2003. President Bush told Americans that he had ordered a strike on Iraq in an effort to disarm the Iraqi regime and drive its leader, Dictator Saddam Hussein, from power. The thundering bomb and missile attack on Baghdad was launched after the president had given Hussein forty-eight hours to relinquish power and flee. It was aimed at a "target of opportunity," Bush said, after he received word that evening that "senior elements of Iraqi leadership" were meeting in a "residential facility" near Baghdad. The administration was convinced that Hussein housed weapons of mass destruction, but questions continue to loom whether such weapons existed.

Meanwhile, television launched a small-scale invasion in Iraq with the largest operations that network news divisions have ever mounted. The three networks, as well as CNN, Fox, MSNBC, and the Associated Press, were each given twenty-six embedded slots. CNN alone had some 250 in the region, expecting to spend approximately $25 million for war coverage. The networks expected to spend about $1 million a day. CNN even purchased a couple of used Humvees in Kuwait City to aid its reporters.[80]

The military's embedded policy, which provided more access, coupled with advances in technology, promised a new kind of war coverage. According to *Los Angeles Times* correspondent Josh Getlin, the arrangement provided the public a "grittier, grunt's-eye view of modern war than the remote, video-game clash that was beamed into living rooms twelve years ago."[81] Technology in the Vietnam War was clumsy. Filmed reports flown to the United States were two days old before they got on the air. Though quantum leaps in technology took place at the time of Panama, Grenada, and the 1991 Gulf War, the press had little access. Veteran ABC reporter and *Nightline* host Ted Koppel could have covered the Iraqi war from a comfortable anchor-chair perch in either Washington or Kuwait. "But I wanted to do it [Kuwait]," Koppel said, "because this is the first time there has been a complete convergence of the satellite technology that allows us to report on the war immediately and the promise of total access."[82]

Before President Bush declared victory on May 2, 2003, aboard the USS *Abraham Lincoln*, the world saw incredible coverage, including the fall of Baghdad, Hussein's bombed palaces, and prisons where the regime tortured Olympic athletes and others. But did the convergence of access and technology bring about better reporting? Veteran Vietnam War reporters meeting at California State University, Fullerton, gave the press, especially broadcast journalists, a failing grade for its reporting in Iraq. The consensus was that despite the improvements in technology, reporters were caught up with their status as celebrities. Take Erin Moriarity, of CBS's *48 Hours*. She reported from the field with a gas mask attached to her face. The veterans also criticized the shallow reporting coming out of Iraq and the reporters who failed to humanize the soldiers they were accompanying and interviewing.

Iraq also provided a wake-up call for the networks. They learned that about 53 percent of Americans got their news about terrorism and the war from cable TV, as compared to 34 percent from newspapers, 19 percent from radio, 18 percent from local TV news, 17 percent from network TV, and 13 percent from the Internet. CNN Chairman Walter Isaacson said that the attacks helped his network rediscover its "true mission and the vital importance of what we do... to be reasoned and calm and to cover international news in a serious way."

More negative opinions of press coverage of America's most recent war were to come. Results of the most recent poll by the Pew Research Center for the People and the Press showed that wall-to-wall media reports did not result in significant improvement of the public's view of the media's coverage of this war, compared with the first Persian Gulf conflict. The survey showed that more Americans have a great deal of confidence in the accuracy of military reports on the war than they do in media coverage (40 percent to 30 percent).The number expressing a high degree of confidence in military reports also rose since the Persian Gulf War (40 percent now, 29 percent then).[83]

Even more disturbing were poll results showing that almost half of the people in America think that the news media are generally inaccurate and politically biased. More than half also said that the media try to cover up their mistakes and get in the way of society solving its problems. Perhaps that is why 80 percent of the 1,500 polled said that censorship of the news from Afghanistan is a "good idea." When asked which is more important—the government's ability to censor any news it believes is "a threat to national security" or the media's ability to report news they believe is "in the national interest"—respondents favored the government 53 to 39 percent. Some 50 percent also said that the military should have more control over the media.[84]

However, five years later the Bush administration's popularity plummeted as well as that of the U.S. Congress, which fell even lower—to single-digit numbers. Some 54 percent said the United States made the wrong decision in using military force in Iraq, while 38 percent said it was the right decision.[85]

In addition to 9/11 and the deceptions dealing with the Iraq invasion, the Bush administration was hit with a trifecta of disasters. First, on July 14, 2003, Robert Novak in his syndicated *Washington Post* column, identified Valerie Elise Plame as a CIA operations agency officer who just happened to be the wife of former Ambassador Joseph C. Wilson, IV. Her covert identity was classified. Wilson had written a piece for *The New York Times* in which he stated that the Bush administration exaggerated unreliable claims that Iraq intended to purchase uranium yellowcake from Niger to support the administration's arguments that Iraq was proliferating weapons of mass destruction so as to justify its preemptive war in Iraq.[86]

Novak's revelations led to a CIA leak grand jury investigation which resulted in the indictment, conviction and commuted sentence by President Bush of I. Lewis "Scooter" Libby, assistant to the president, in *United States v. Libby* on charges of perjury, obstruction of justice, and making false statements to federal investigators.

The second was the fury of Hurricane Katrina, which not only walloped the Gulf Coast on August 29, 2005, in one of the most catastrophic, costliest, and deadliest natural disaster in U.S. history, but caught the administration unprepared and tested the very soul of news organizations. It shut down as many as 100 radio and TV stations and the 169-year old *New Orleans Times-Picayune*, the city's only daily. Katharine Q. Seelye reporting in *The New York Times* online edition said that papers such as the *Times-Picayune* connected with readers the way newspapers did before the arrival of television. She reported that the paper regained about two-thirds of its readers, with a circulation of 176,000 daily and 196,000 on Sunday. However, only 10 percent of the city's businesses had reopened, adding a mighty blow to the newspaper's revenue.

The president and his administration did not fare as well. TV showed vivid pictures of citizens in their life-and-death struggle caused by Katrina. They sent shockwaves through the nation. TV images showed shaken residents who remained in New Orleans without water, food, or shelter, and deaths of citizens from thirst, exhaustion and violence days after the storm had passed. TV also showed local and federal agencies that weren't prepared and frustrated political leaders. CNN's Soledad O'Brien asked Michael Brown, then Federal Emergency Management Agency director, on national television: "How is it possible that we're getting better info than you are getting... We were showing live pictures [and] reporting that officials had been telling people to go to the Convention Center... I don't understand how FEMA cannot have this information." Brown admitted that he learned about the hungry crowds at the Convention Center from media reports.[87] However, the administration was very prepared when Hurricane Ike's destructive force ravaged the United States three years later.

A third catastrophe on the Bush administration's watch was the September 2008 collapse of Wall Street and fears of another Great Depression. Simply, households and financial institutions accumulated debts beyond what was sustainable. Such actions drove families and banks into bankruptcy, as more assets got dumped on the market, producing a downward spiral that financial experts called deleveraging.[88] Congress responded with a $700-billion Wall Street rescue package. Explaining why it happened challenged the nation's most outstanding financial reporters. And the news media did their best trying to explain its causes—including financial policies pushed by current and past Republican and Democratic administrations. Many Americans skipped the traditional media and turned to the Internet to monitor the state of their economic portfolio or to get up-to-date information on the worst financial collapse since 1929.

CONCLUSION

"Television is moments," writes retired Pulitzer Prize–winning *Los Angeles Times* columnist Howard Rosenberg. "It was such moments—converging sights and sounds that instantly convey lasting impressions of dramatic change—that helped make television so memorable in earlier times."[89] By 1970 television took its place as a powerful news and entertainment medium and captured the moments of an era of change and deception.

It captured the bloody combat in Vietnam, America's first "living-room war." And what people saw in their living rooms they did not like. Before the broadcast of Morley Safer's "The Burning of Cam Ne," on the *CBS Evening News with Walter Cronkite*, television trivialized the debate on Vietnam and confirmed the legitimacy of the president. "Cam Ne" presented for the first time a different side of the war, an ugly side showing that something was not right. The television event helped legitimize pessimistic reporting by all other television correspondents and, with it, America's hatred of the media.

Cronkite's report from Vietnam following the 1968 Tet offensive, when television viewers saw the enemy battling in the south for the first time, was another defining moment. Cronkite, the "most trusted man in America," told the television audience that the war didn't work, that an increase in troop strength would not turn it around, and that the United States should think of a way to get out. It was the first time in the nation's history that a television anchor declared a war over and motivated a president's decision not to run for reelection.

Television captured the Watergate caper and showed its symbolic moments—a president declaring, "I am not a crook," the "Saturday Night Massacre," an impeachment hearing, and, finally, the revelations of dirty deeds and cover-ups in an attempt to circumvent the Constitution and the democratic electoral process.

Television also contributed to the end of the Carter presidency by showing the grim pictures of sixty-three American hostages and giving a constant reminder of their captivity. Television also captured the changing world order with its coverage of the symbolic and dramatic fall of the Berlin Wall and of the thousands of East Berliners streaming into the West, the disintegration of the Soviet Union and the Eastern European bloc countries from Poland to Romania. It showed a lone dissident defying the Chinese military by using his body to block Chinese tanks in Beijing's Tiananmen Square. Before the "living-room audience" could take a breather, it witnessed live coverage of the Persian Gulf War. Viewers saw scud missiles dropped from U.S. Stealth fighter-bombers as Patriot missiles hit incoming Iraqi scuds.

In the 1990s television held up a mirror to society and showed symbols of sleaze—allegations of sexual misconduct by a charismatic president, who was eventually impeached; a House Speaker who resigned because of an extramarital affair; and a popular football player turned movie star who was accused of killing his wife.

Perhaps the greatest moment in television history was its reporting of September 11, 2001, when the symbols of power and wealth were crippled by hatred. Stunned viewers saw two jetliners careen into the World Trade Center, leaving a legacy of death and destruction. The small screen also displayed an angry nation that wanted revenge.

Television is moments. It also is a powerful medium that has changed the social and political fabric of America. And it will continue to capture the symbolic moments in the tides of history. In capturing these moments, the media, television in particular, have made the world a much smaller place. The Internet has made it even smaller and advanced an information explosion beyond one's imagination, challenging the economic health and future of traditional media.

THE INTERNET REVOLUTION AND THE INFORMATION EXPLOSION

Without German printer Johannes Gutenberg, "the person of the millennium," it is unlikely the world would ever have known the genius of computer industry pioneer Bill Gates, number 41 on the same millennium list. Gates ushered in the fourth technological revolution and, perhaps, the most revolutionary after the invention of writing and the invention of the alphabet and the invention of the printing press.

The best-known entrepreneur of the personal computer revolution and the software that goes with it, Gates' inventions may not have been the first or the best. However, he succeeded with strategy and tactics in the battlefield of advanced technology, eyeing what the world wanted and giving it to them.

Gates must have been as happy as a proud parent when *Time* magazine bumped its annual tradition of naming a Man of the Year in 1982, and chose to name the computer its Machine of the Year. "Several human candidates might have represented 1982, but none symbolized the past year more richly, or will be viewed by history as more significant, than a machine: the computer," *Time* publisher John A. Meyers said.[1]

The successes of the Machine of the Year may be at the expense of other mediums. Consider, for example, that it took 38 years for radio to reach a market audience of 50 million and television 13 years. However, it took the computer only four years. And its advancements are knocking on the door. For example, a third generation of fiber optics has recently been tested that pushes 10 trillion bits per second down one strand of fiber. That is 1,900 CDs or 150 million simultaneous phone calls, every second. Only in a matter of time, a supercomputer will be built that exceeds the computation capability of the human brain. By 2049, it is predicted that a $1,000 computer will exceed the computational capabilities of the human race.

Those are amazing predictions when one considers that the first computers were nothing more than calculating machines and tabulators. As evolution of the computer advanced, the concept of it doing logical steps and thinking through problems was included to improve the quality of the output. From the first calculators to the massive computers built at the end of the World War II, to the invention of the personal computer, computers were always thought of as calculators of one scale or another. That all changed between the 1960s and the 1980s when "computing technology underwent a dramatic transformation: the computer, originally conceived as an isolated calculating device, was reborn as a means of communication."[2]

This chapter looks at this modern marvel, the PC, and what Gates wrought—the Internet; the World Wide Web; and social networks, including YouTube, MySpace, Facebook, and Second Life, a virtual kaleidoscope of mediated messages. This chapter also spends time with another revolutionary figure, Steve Jobs, who at 21 unveiled the Apple II personal computer and then thirty years later introduced the iPhone, a technology and design triumph. Finally, this chapter discusses the growth of the alternative and ethnic press and an important, perhaps tragic outcome of the information revolution—the fact that only a few media giants are in this playground.

FROM ABACUS TO COMPUTER

Throughout history humans have been absorbed with counting and counting machines.

"If you cannot calculate," Plato writes in *Philebus* ("On Pleasure"), "you cannot speculate on future pleasure and your life will not be that of a human, but that of an oyster or jellyfish." Throughout the ages, humankind has found the calculation of numbers slow, difficult, and tedious. That is why scientists have always sought to simplify their various calculations.

The abacus, in the fourth century, was the first device to help simplify those calculations. Many consider it the prelude to modern computers. For example, during the European Renaissance, developments in mathematics, science, and technology were progressing so fast that astronomers and mathematicians needed more efficient ways to solve more complicated and difficult problems. Also driving this need was a revolution of sorts in the sixteenth century when the old numerals and counter-boards dating back to Roman times were supplanted by the Indian number system and the Indian methods of arithmetic. It sent European scholars scurrying for more rapid and reliable methods of calculating.

Many from every corner of the world and from every period of history sought ways to make more challenging calculations easier. The Industrial Revolution in the nineteenth century spurred the greatest progress with the spread of machines and automation, culminating in the technological revolution of the twentieth century. English economist and inventor Charles Babbage, considered the true father of the modern computer, in the first half of the nineteenth century reasoned that a machine could do more than calculate mathematical problems. He even thought it could be used to play computer games[3] or be asked to solve chess problems or play draughts (similar to checkers) against a human opponent.[4]

Babbage's "analytical engine," which he developed in 1823, had all the elements of a modern computer. It had a set of input devices, an arithmetic processor to do the calculating, a control unit which allowed the task ordered to be completed, enough memory storage, and an output mechanism.[5] However, his machine, the first programmable computer, could not be manufactured because the technology to produce it was not available.[6]

The computer became a reality owing to the emergence and expansion of industrialized societies which were stimulated by, among other things, need and competition. Its inventors were under pressures from many directions—social, economic, commercial, scientific, and, most crucially, the political and military urgency during World War II to oppose Nazism.[7]

The first attempt to harness electronic technology was at Iowa State University where professors John Vincent Atanasoff, the "forgotten father of the computer," and Clifford Berry built the first electronic digital computer. From 1939 until 1941 they worked at developing and improving the ABC, Atanasoff-Berry Computer, as it was later named. However, at the start of World War II on December 7, 1941, the work on the computer came to a halt.

Once the war broke out, scientific and military needs pushed computer development. First, a simple, reliable, fast and effective method of cracking enemy communications was needed. Second, the military was looking for a way to achieve more accurate gun aiming. Third was the ever growing requirement to solve simulation problems. Finally, a need existed to resolve complex problems such as those associated with the use of radar to intercept enemy aircraft.[8]

What was needed was a general-purpose instrument that allowed a broad range of operations to be performed. The first major breakthrough in the field came at Bletchley Park, home to the British Code and Cipher School. There engineer Tommy Flowers and mathematician Max Newman and their team constructed the Colossus, the first of the electronic digital machines with programmability. Its aim was to help the English decipher German military codes in an effort to halt the advantage of Nazi troops. The huge computer remained highly secret for many years after the war, depriving its founders a prominent place in the history of computing hardware.

Harvard mathematician Howard Aiken would have more luck and fame. While a grad student in Harvard's Department of Physics, he planned to build a large computer to solve complex mathematical problems that were too time consuming to be done by human hand alone. Harvard funded some of the research but a far greater investment was needed. He contacted IBM president Thomas Watson, Jr. who enthusiastically agreed to foot the bill for the project. The new machine would be called the The Harvard Mark I. And in the waning days of World War II, it was used by the U.S. Navy for gunnery and ballistics calculations.

The Harvard Mark I was essentially a huge machine with its moving parts driven and synchronized by gears connected to a drive mechanism system that ran for practically the entire length of the machine. This computer weighed about five tons, had about 750,000 different components, including 1,000 ball bearings and a little more than 850 kilometers of electrical wiring with 175,000 connections and three million solder joints.[9]

Meanwhile, two University of Pennsylvania physicists, Presper Eckert and John W. Mauchly, inspired by the achievements of Atanasoff and Berry, developed the first electronic computer, which they called the Electronic Numerical Integrator and Computer, better known by its acronym ENIAC. Like Aiken's computer, it was used by the military for gunnery and ballistic calculations. And the machine was as huge as Aiken's. It took less than a second to solve addition problems, six seconds for multiplication, and twice as long for division.[10]

Eckert and Mauchly also developed the UNIVAC, the Universal Automatic Computer. It became the first commercial computer—and the fastest up to that time. One was delivered to the U.S. Census Bureau on March 31, 1951, becoming the first computer to be used for non-military purposes. Another was used by CBS to predict the result of the 1952 presidential election. With a sample of just 1 percent of the voting population, it correctly predicted that Gen. Dwight Eisenhower would defeat Illinois Gov. Adlai Stevenson.

Hulton Archive/Getty Images

The earliest computers were massive pieces of equipment.

FROM DINOSAUR TO DESKTOP

MIT researcher Vannevar Bush saw these huge computers as "an enlarged supplement to his memory." He appropriately labeled them "memex" or memory machines "in which an individual stores all his books, records, and communications, and which is mechanized so that it may be consulted with exceeding speed and flexibility."[11] He pictured this device as an ordinary desk with slanting translucent screens on which material can be projected for convenient reading. It also would have a keyboard and buttons and levers, with content (such as books, pictures, periodicals, and newspapers) being purchased on microfilm ready for insertion. All one had to do was tap a code on the keyboard, and the title page of a book would promptly appear. He saw this device benefiting lawyers needing to call up opinions and decisions, physicians wanting to look up similar cases in an effort to diagnose a patient's reaction to drugs, chemists struggling with the synthesis of an organic compound, and historians seeking a vast chronological account of civilization.

Douglas C. Englebart, a young sailor stationed in the Philippines during World War II, was intrigued by Bush's vision and pictured a user-friendly tool that average persons, not just trained scientists, could use. Users would sit in front of computer screens, flying around in what today we call the World Wide Web, obtaining information that would augment the human intellect. Englebart saw computers as the engines that could give the human intellect the same kind of boost received when people first learned to turn grunts into words. Some referred to it at the time as Artificial Intelligence. However, he shunned that concept and didn't think computers would ever think for humans. If that happened he thought man and computers would just exchange places, and that is what he wanted to avoid. Instead, he wanted computers to be used to help people make the best of their abilities and work in teams, pooling their resources for maximum benefit. His goal was to find the most productive working environment, and the computer was an essential part of this environment.[12]

As director of the Stanford Research Institute, he worked to make that vision a reality, inventing or contributing to several interactive, user-friendly devices, including the computer mouse, word processing, windows, computer video teleconferencing, hypermedia, groupware, e-mail, and the Internet.

To realize his vision, a number of inventions were necessary, and they came quickly during the 1950s and 1960s. The *transistor*, invented in 1948 by John Bardeen, Walter Battain, and William Shockly at AT&T labs in New Jersey, did away with the unreliable and expensive vacuum tubes. Jack Kilby and Robert Noyce's invention of the *integrated circuit* or *microchip*, a single chip with all the circuitry that formerly occupied large cabinets, led to Englebart's dream—the proliferation of personal computers. Noyce, by the way, took his invention and started a tiny company called INTEL. It became the largest producers of microchips in the world.

Early personal computers, or microcomputers, were sold often in kit form and in limited volumes. For example, the world's first personal computer, the Altair 8800, was sold as a kit in 1975 at the astonishingly low price of $379. However, a video display terminal, storage disks, a printer set, plus programming languages BASIC (an acronym for Beginner's All-purpose Symbolic Instruction Code, a family of high-level programming languages), FORTRAN (a blend word derived from the IBM Mathematical Formula Translating System), COBOL (an acronym for Common Business-Oriented Language, one of the oldest programming languages still in active use), and PL/I (Program Language One), as well as word processing and file management put the true price at $5,000. One great disadvantage of the computer was the long and tedious process to enter data. Switches, instead of a keyboard, on the front panel were used to enter instruction codes and data. The Altair 8800, developed by a small company called Micro Instrumentation Telemetry System (MITS), was an instant hit with amateur computer enthusiasts. They placed thousands of orders during the first few months of advertisement.[13]

A *Popular Electronics* article written by H. Edward Roberts and William Yates of MITS entitled "Altair 8800—The Most Powerful Minicomputer Project Ever Presented—Can Be Built for under $400," caught the eye of Paul Allen. He and his high school friend Bill Gates saw that this computer used the new Intel 8080 microprocessor for which he and Gates had wanted to develop a BASIC interpreter. They realized now they had a potential market for the software. Within months, Gates and Allen signed a contract with MITS to provide BASIC interpreter programs. MITS would pay a royalty on each sale and Gates and Allen would retain ownership of the software. MITS also agreed to promote and commercialize the program to other companies.[14]

A month after the first personal computer hit the market, Gates and Allen founded a partnership called Micro-Soft in Albuquerque, New Mexico. They eventually deleted the hyphen and capitalized the "S" to form MicroSoft, with Gates owning 60 percent interest and Allen the remaining 40 percent. (Gates felt he made a larger contribution.). On November 26, 1976, they dropped the hyphen and registered the name "Microsoft." Thus, the history of the personal computer began.

THE IBM & MACINTOSH ERA

Within two years, Americans were eager to buy computer machines such as the Apple II, the Commodore PET, and the Tandy/Radio Shack TRS-80. IBM joined the market in 1981 with its own PC, which quickly became an industry standard. The basic system unit, with sixteen kilobytes of RAM and a keyboard, sold for $1,565. A system unit with forty-eight kilobytes of RAM, a keyboard, a single floppy disk drive and a disk-drive adapter card was $2,235. A monochrome video display was $345.[15]

Several dealings with IBM, beginning in 1980, led Microsoft to become a leader in the computer industry. IBM needed a BASIC interpreter for the personal computer it was creating—the IBM PC—and approached Microsoft to provide it. The company also needed an operating system, and Gates was able to find one and put together a deal to became full owner of 86-DOS. Altering the operating system for the PC, Microsoft sold it to IBM as PC-DOS for a one-time fee of $80,000. But Gates was adamant about keeping the copyright on the operating system. He also devised an agreement with IBM allowing the corporation to bundle

Microsoft's PC-DOS software with IBM personal computers. In return, Microsoft received a fee for every computer sold, making Gates a very rich man.

The IBM-PC was an outstanding success. Some 30,000 were ordered from its own U.S. employees on announcement day. The only thing holding up sales was the production capacity. IBM took a group of twelve people in 1980 to a work force of 9,500 in 1984. Around 750,000 IBM personal computers were sold by the end of 1983.[16]

Meanwhile, Steve Jobs with Apple cofounder Steve Wozniak helped popularize the personal computer in the late 1970s. At twenty-one Jobs unveiled the Apple II personal computer which quickly became one of the most successful home computers, the standard computer in American education, and popular with business users because of its ease of use and features. It put Jobs and the Apple company on the map. By the end of its production in 1993, somewhere between 5 and 6 million Apple II series computers, including approximately 1.23 million Apple II$_{GS}$ models had been produced. Apple II and its associated community of third-party developers and retailers became a billion-dollar-a-year industry.

The Apple II was eclipsed by the company's new Macintosh in 1993. It was announced with great fanfare, including a $1.5-million television commercial, "1984," directed by Ridley Scott and aired during the third quarter of Super Bowl XVII on January 22, 1984. It was the first affordable computer which advanced the concept of a new user-friendly graphical user interface and a mouse. Its Motorola 6800 chip was significantly faster than the previous processors, running at eight megahertz. The smart-looking Mac came in a small beige case with a black-and-white monitor built in, and sold for $2,495. However, Apple devised a unique sales strategy. The company formed an Apple University Consortium that offered the Macintosh to students and faculty for a flat $1,000. The program was a huge success, enabling the Macintosh to penetrate the educational market.[17]

Gates was not about to take the growing interest in graphical user interfaces sitting down. He wanted his Windows program to be more like the Macintosh and to simplify the adaptation of Microsoft's application software to either the IBM Personal Computer or the Macintosh. A number of Macintosh features were added, including a calendar, clock, control panel, games, and an elementary word processor. Gates also wanted keyboard equivalents for all mouse operations.[18]

On May 22, 1990, he got what he wanted. Windows 3.0 was introduced in New York City with a $10-million promotional campaign. It allowed DOS systems to be as user-friendly as the Macintosh but with the speed of the DOS microcomputer. Simply, it popularized computers, making them easy to use. In addition, people soon realized that if they purchased a PC with Windows and a dial-up modem, they could drive the Internet and send e-mails through their phone lines with the help of an Internet Service Provider. Before Windows, these activities were predominately used by government and computer scientists. Microsoft Windows came to dominate the world's personal computer market with approximately 90 percent of the client operating system market.

In the 2000s, Apple began to focus on video, music, and photo production solutions, with a view to promoting their product as a "digital hub." In October 2001, it unveiled the iPod, the company's first venture into the digital music market.

AMERICAN MEDIA PROFILE | Bill Gates 1955–

Ed Wray/AP Photos

Listed by Forbes.com as the world's third richest man, William Henry Gates III, chairman of Microsoft—the software company he co-founded—is one of America's foremost business magnates and philanthropists.

His career at Microsoft has included stints as CEO and chief software architect, and he is still the major individual shareholder with more than 9 percent of the common stock. Although Gates is one of the best-known entrepreneurs of the personal computer revolution and is admired by many, some industry insiders criticize his business tactics as anti-competitive. At times, the courts have upheld that sentiment.

Born on Oct. 28, 1955, in Seattle, Wash., to wealthy parents, Gates was praised as an excellent student from his earliest school years. His parents had hoped he would pursue a career in law. As an eighth-grade student at Lakeside School, an exclusive preparatory academy in Seattle, Gates took full advantage of free computer time that had been purchased for the students by the Mothers Club with rummage sale profits. Working on a General Electric computer, he was intrigued by the machine and was excused from math class to pursue his interest in programming it in BASIC. Gates' first computer program was written on this machine—it was a version of tic-tac-toe that pitted students against the computer.

"There was just something neat about the machine," Gates wrote in his 1996 book, "The Road Ahead," as he recalled his initial fascination with this grade school computer.

Later, Gates was one of several students who devised a way to obtain additional free computer time despite expiration of the Mothers Club donation to the corporation that had made the machine available. He and three others students were banned for the summer from using the machine after it was discovered that they had been taking advantage of bugs in the operating system to gain free time.

In exchange for free computer time at the end of the ban, the four students made a deal to debug the corporation's software. Gates was later employed with the same students to write a payroll program in COBOL. For his work he earned computer time and royalties.

At his school, administrators learned of his programming abilities and selected Gates to write the school's computer program to schedule students in classes. The young programmer altered the code to place himself in classes with the highest female enrollment.

Along with Paul Allen (one of those school friends), Gates, 17, formed a partnership called Traf-O-Data, making traffic counters based on the Intel 8008 processor. He wrote in his 1996 book that the first year he earned $20,000. However, after clients learned how young he was, he said business slowed.

Gates was attending Harvard College when he read in the January 1975 issue of *Popular Electronics* about the Altair 8800, a new microcomputer created by Micro Instrumentation and Telemetry Systems

It became the most popular digital music player in the world. Three years later it raised the bar for portability in a hard disk music player when it introduced the iPod mini, which was the height and width of a business card and built around a one-inch, four-gigabyte hard drive. Small enough to wear comfortably on an armband, it was large enough to hold nearly 1,000 songs. It sold for $249, and demand outstripped supply.

If that wasn't enough, Jobs, thirty years after introducing the Apple II personal computer, unveiled the iPhone in January 2007. It was named that year *Time*'s

AMERICAN MEDIA PROFILE | **CONTINUED**

(MITS). Inspired by the development, he and Allen decided that now was the time to make their move as they believed with the impending drop in the price of computers, it would soon be profitable to sell software. In a bold move, Gates contacted MITS boasting that he and a partner were creating a BASIC interpreter for the platform.

Flying by the seat of their pants, Gates and Allen offered something they had not yet created. They did not possess an Altair nor had they written any code for it. However, the duo snagged a meeting with MITS. Hitting the ground running, they created an Altair emulator and then the BASIC interpreter. After a stunning demonstration, Allen was hired in November 1975 to work in MITS's Albuquerque, N.M., offices and Gates took a leave from Harvard to work with him. "Micro-soft" was the name they chose for their new venture and they established an office in Albuquerque.

In late 1976, Microsoft became independent of MITS and continued to create programming language software for various systems. With a need for more room for expansion, the company relocated to its new home in Bellevue, Wash., on Jan. 1, 1979. Despite turning his attention to business details, Gates still continued to write codes. He personally reviewed every line of code the company shipped in the first five years of operation, often rewriting it.

Another milestone for Gates and Microsoft came with restructuring on June 25, 1981, when the company was re-incorporated in Washington. Overseeing the reorganization, Gates became president and chairman of the board. On Nov. 20, 1985, the company launched its first retail version of Microsoft Windows. In another effort with IBM, Gates and the company struck a deal to develop a separate operating system. However, mounting creative differences undermined that partnership. On May 16, 1991, Gates told employees that the IBM partnership was over and Windows NT kernel development became the company's major effort.

As for his personal life, Gates married Melinda French from Dallas, Texas, on Jan. 1, 1994, and they have three children. His home life befits a man once recognized as the world's richest (No. 1 until 2007 on the *Forbes'* magazine list) as he lives in a 21st century earth-sheltered home in the side of a hill overlooking Lake Washington in Medina, Wash. The land and his home were valued in 2006 at $125 million.

In his more recent years, Gates has made news in connection with huge donations to various charitable organizations and scientific research programs. In 2000, he created the Bill & Melinda Gates Foundation to steer his philanthropic endeavors. As he prepares to give up day-to-day involvement in Microsoft that he co-founded 33 years ago, he said he plans to devote himself to a full-time career in philanthropy working on his global health and education projects at the foundation. His agency aids causes working to equip the poor with financial tools, working toward development of vaccines (AIDS, malaria, tuberculosis), and working to improve faltering U.S. high schools.

By Suzanne Schenkel

Invention of the Year and provided the path for Apple's entry into the cellular phone marketplace. It blended three products into one: an iPod, a phone, and a device to access the Internet. It was a technology and design triumph for Jobs, bringing the company into a market with an extraordinary potential for growth, and pushing the industry to a new level of competition in ways to connect us to each other and to the Web.[19]

Paul Sakuma/AP Photos

Steve Jobs unveiled the iPhone in January 2007. It blended three products into one: an iPod, a phone, and a device to access the Internet.

THE INTERNET

The computer, originally conceived as a tool to solve mathematical problems, was reborn between the 1960s and the 1980s as a means of communication. The worldwide system, called the Internet, placed computers at the center of a new communications medium.

The Internet is like a network of electronic roads crisscrossing the planet—the much-hyped information superhighway. The World Wide Web is just one of many services using that network, just as many different kinds of vehicles use the roads. The arrival of the Web in 1990 was to the Internet like the arrival of the internal combustion engine to the car. Internet transport would never be the same again. Before the Internet, electronic communication was only possible via the telephone.[20] Between the 1960s and the 1990s, the Internet grew from a single experimental network serving a dozen sites in the United States to a globe-spanning system linking millions of computers, allowing Americans to experience the possibilities of cyberspace for the first time.[21]

The story of the Internet begins with the Soviet Union's launch of Sputnik 1 on October 4, 1957. Sputnik 1 changed the course of American research thinking. President Eisenhower declared that never again would the United States be caught off guard by the USSR, and he tuned his defense research and development strategy to making sure that America stayed one step ahead. A single agency, the Advanced Research Projects Agency (ARPA), under the secretary of defense, was proposed. Its task was to mobilize research resources, particularly from the university world, toward building technological military superiority over the Soviet Union.[22] In the 1960s and 1970s ARPA scientists drove forward technological advances in microelectronics, computing, and network communications. Its scientists and engineers also advocated and subsequently implemented a fundamental change in how computers would be used and for what purposes.[23]

That change began with the arrival of MIT Professor Joseph Licklider, the appointed director of the Information Processing Techniques Office of ARPA. He would oversee the building of the ARPANET, a computer network that would become the origin of the Internet.

Licklider's task at the ARPA was to harness the analytical power of the computer to assist commanders on the field to make the right decisions in battle. He saw that constraints on time, combined with the highly dynamic battlefield environment, did not allow for the delays and discontinuity inherent in the present system (called batch processing). This process required handing off data to a remote computer operator, who then had to feed the data into the computer, run the program and wait for the response, and communicate results back to the command center or battlefield. Using this process, two problems had to be solved. One was how to provide multiple users with direct and immediate access to a computer. The other was how to provide remote access directly from a battlefield or another distant location.[24]

To build this interactive computer network, Licklider's office would rely on a revolutionary telecommunications transmission technology called "packet switching," which was developed by Paul Baran at the Rand Corporation and Donald Davies at the British National Physical Laboratory. Packet switching allows a computer to know when a packet of data has been sent, allowing for the efficient sharing of network resources and guaranteeing the delivery of data. The next step was to make ARPANET's connection with other computer networks possible. Two computer scientists, Robert Kahn of ARPA and Vint Cert, who as a graduate student at UCLA, were involved in the early design of the ARPANET. Their TCP/IP protocol (software codes that enable one computer to communicate with another—a prerequisite for the Internet) allowed ARPA to connect various independent networks together to form one large network of networks—the Internet. It made Cert, some say, the true "father of the Internet."

Strange as it may seem, the Internet was not developed as a message system. It was engineered to connect computers, not people. Its goal was to allow scientists, mathematicians, and the military to share resources—access expensive computer equipment with the intention of facilitating the sharing of computational power and resources. E-mail introduced a human element onto the network. It became a communications network that connected people.[25] The rise in electronic mail would be the catalyst for the Internet's growth and development. E-mail was to the ARPANET what the Louisiana Purchase was to the young United States. Things only got better as the network grew and technology converged with the torrential human tendency to talk.[26]

The Internet then went from a technological achievement, an information-age tool for the pursuit of scientific, mathematical, and military objectives, to a force for societal change. E-mail turned the Internet into something personal and something anyone could use, which in small, tangible ways as well as subtle, far-reaching ones, changed the way we live, communicate, and interact with others.[27]

THE WORLD WIDE WEB

The arrival of the World Wide Web made personal computers popular and made the Internet into something accessible, usable, and empowering. It also introduced commercial ventures on the Internet.[28] The latter was certainly not what its founder, Tim Berners-Lee, had in mind when he invented the World Wide Web in 1989 and made it public in 1993. He set out to design a global space that would allow all information stored in computers everywhere on the planet to be accessible to everyone, particularly researchers.

His innovations included hyperlinks (electronic cross-references), which, with a click of the mouse, allow users to move from one site to another with ease. It didn't take long for the public to realize how simple it now was to drive the Web highway once Marc Andreeseen, a student at the University of Illinois at Urbana-Champaign, unveiled the first Web browser, Mosaic, in 1993.[29] With the help of Mosaic, traffic on the World Wide Web proliferated at an astonishing rate. Some 40,000 copies were downloaded in the first month; by the spring of 1994 a million or more copies were estimated to be in use.[30] Web servers also proliferated. In April of 1993, some sixty-two Web servers existed; by May of 1994 it climbed to 1,248.[31]

That year Andreeseen and his team, four other former students, began work on a commercial version of Mosaic called Netscape, which eventually was bought by America Online (AOL). Thus, Netscape started the commercial browser wars. Other companies, such as Microsoft with its Internet Explorer, joined the commercial browser competition and new businesses sprang up offering service that made it easier to locate information on the Web. One was Amazon.com, which relies entirely on its Internet storefront, presented through the Web, to bring products to consumers. Yahoo!, though an information service provider, is another that generates revenue through pay services and advertising as well as providing a rich and diverse selection of information sources, such as news, weather, and stock information, and information management tools, such as a calendar, online bill paying, and e-mail access.[32]

In 1995 the Internet moved from military hands to the public sector upon the realization that with so many online, it could not be useful for national security purposes. Today, the World Wide Web Consortium (W3C) is the main international standards organization for governing the World Wide Web. Its current 434 members come from businesses, nonprofit organizations, universities, and governmental entities. Individual memberships are not allowed. Membership cost is determined on a sliding scale, depending on the character of the organization applying and the country in which it is located. Countries are categorized by the World Bank's grouping by gross national income per capita.

The Consortium's main purpose is to lead the World Wide Web to its full potential by developing protocols and guidelines that ensure long-term growth for the Web. It also engages in education and outreach, develops software, and serves as an open forum for discussion about the Web. Its director is, of course, none other than its founder, Berners-Lee.

SOCIAL NETWORKING IN CYBERSPACE

Berners-Lee's invention also opened the floodgates to a vast array of social networking sites. Here members create profile pages, share information, and connect to other members. Members may interact by chatting, messages, video, blogging, games, contests, or group discussions. During the past ten years, online social networks have evolved from general friendship sites—SixDegrees, Frienster, Classmates, MySpace, and Facebook—to more specific hobby-related and career-focused sites.

The first social networking sites began appearing in the late 1990s with Classmates.com and SixDegrees.com. Classmates.com helped people find former classmates, whereas SixDegrees.com focused on networking friends (and friends of friends) together. However, these sites failed to keep their members actively engaged within the communities and lost audiences in 2002 to Frienster.com—considered the first official social networking site. It was different from Classmates.com and SixDegrees.com because it allowed members to manage their own personal Web pages. There they could list their friends and interests. Technological problems hampered its development, and it became encumbered by a board of directors which began censoring profiles. Its demise opened the doors to MySpace in 2003, where anyone can create profiles and look up members' profiles.

MySpace, with approximately 65,744,241 visits per month, is currently among the top twenty social networking sites. With their headquarters in Beverly Hills, California, the website offers an interactive, user-submitted network of friends, personal profiles, blogs, groups, photos, music, and videos internationally. It currently occupies 73.45 percent of the market share across all social networking sites and receives about 230,000 new registrations per day on average.

MySpace has been described as nothing short of a cultural phenomenon. It's been likened to the equivalent of one's high school lunchroom, the college quad, or a favorite bar, except that it doesn't sell much of anything. It's just a place to hang out and express oneself.[33] MySpace operates solely on revenues generated by advertising, attracting the eye of the search engine Google, which paid on August 6, 2006, some $900 million to provide a Google search facility and advertising on MySpace. In 2005 Rupert Murdoch's News Corporation paid $580 million for MySpace and its parent company eUniverse (renamed Intermix Media). The value of MySpace in this deal was said to be approximately $327 million.

Facebook, launched February 4, 2004, is currently the second dominant player in social networking. It has captured about 14.56 percent of the market share. Facebook.com was originally only open to students at Harvard, where its founder Mark Zuckerberg attended. It then opened its doors to students at other college campuses as long as they had a school-based e-mail address (.edu). A year later, it expanded to include university students, then high school students, and, finally, to anyone older than thirteen years old. Some 70 million people have been known to visit Facebook in a given month.

Facebook differs from MySpace in that its content is easy to read and organized in a systematic way. The information section, for example, lists the member's favorite television shows, movies, musicians, and other items the person wants to share. Each of these items is a link which can connect the person with other people in his or her network with similar interests.

Some sites have become big business and new sites are cropping up daily. Craigslist features free classified advertisements—another blow to newspapers. Its sole revenue source is paid job ads in select cities ($75 per ad for the San Francisco Bay Area and $25 per ad for Los Angeles; San Diego; Seattle; Portland; Chicago; Washington, D.C.; New York; and Boston). Meanwhile, Jeff Taylor's Monster.com is trying to do for obituary sections what Craigslist did for classified sections of traditional newspapers. He is trying to cash in on death by taking one of the newspapers' last mainstays—obituaries—online. With financial backing from the *Wall Street Journal*, Taylor is attempting to partner with funeral homes to cut newspapers directly out of the loop.

Another site, Twitter.com, is essentially a hybridization of traditional social networking sites, blogs, and text messaging. A user creates an account and adds "friends" and sets alert types. A person then "twitters" on the go by sending text messages, which are disseminated to everyone on the user's "friends" list. It lists around 30 million new classified advertisements each month. Also gaining popularity is Treasuremytext.com, where users can archive their text messages. A user signs up for an account and then forwards text messages to a specific phone number listed on the website. The user can then access, archive, and organize text messages into folders for later viewing.

And then there is Digg.com, a website that wields a lot of power on the World Wide Web. It is essentially an online news aggregator that is developed, promoted, and maintained by its online community members (referred to as "Diggers"). Members vote stories up and down (referred to as "digging" and "burying"). Lots of stories are submitted daily, but only the most "digged" appear on the front page. It has received more than 20 million unique visitors from the United States, surpassing nytimes.com and foxnews.com. Its popularity also has generated other social networking sites that employ story submissions and voting systems.

SECOND LIFE IN THE METAVERSE

Once dismissed as "a playground for the ultra-nerdy," Second Life is a 3-D, Internet-based virtual world that was launched in 2003. This is not like computer games, which tend to be static environments where users can explore but cannot modify the environment. The Second Life Viewer enables users, called "residents," to interact with each other through avatars (an object representing the embodiment of the user).

Philip Rosedale, its founder, has been called "the Bill Gates of the virtual realm." He first began programming computers in the fifth grade. This led to a start-up company that created database systems for car dealerships and architecture firms. At this time, Rosedale was seventeen. Rosedale used his proceeds to fund a B.S. degree in physics from the University of California, San Diego.

His interest in creating a life in cyberspace was inspired by the cyberpunk literary movement driven by Neal Stephenson's novel *Snow Crash*. The novel takes place across two worlds: the real world and the highly realistic online space called the "metaverse." Here people interact, play, do business, and communicate. His creative energies led to the founding of Linden Lab on Linden Alley in San Francisco. At the time, Rosedale would readily tell you that he was not out to build a game, he was out to build a new country.

Second Life was originally released with a barren landscape and a set of tools that users could manipulate to create objects and structures. It began generating revenues primarily from the sale of virtual land. Customers rent space on the 1,750 servers that store the digital representation of tens of thousands of acres of new land that are being developed every month. Uses have created more than a billion unique digital objects—including houses, blimps, ski mountains, beach umbrellas, and body parts.

Like eBay, Second Life is slowly becoming an avenue where businesses can develop. Companies are exploring whether this 3-D world can support corporate commerce and markets. IBM, Dell Computers, Cisco Systems, Intel, Nissan, Toyota, American Appeal, the American Cancer Society, Starwoods Hotels, and Reuters hold virtual events, media conferences, and training seminars within the metaverse.

Toyota has provided avatars the ability to test-drive its Scions or purchase American Apparel products at its virtual online stores. Even Reuters has set up a virtual Second Life news bureau, offering the latest crop of politicians another campaign avenue.

Second Life also provides grants of virtual land to educators, attracting some 400 universities to date. One is Harvard Law School, which is offering a course on how legal codes are applied to a virtual world by Harvard Law School. Another is California State University, Fullerton, which offers courses in visual communications in the metaverse. And USC's Center on Public Diplomacy created a Virtual World Project to explore possibility of the virtual world hosting international program initiatives.

Despite its potential, Second Life has had to deal with legal problems. It even lost a noted court case focusing on whether virtual property is real property. Another problem involves taxes. Should a federal tax be applied to assets, especially real estate, owned in the virtual world? Still other legal questions center around copyright issues and the role of the Digital Millennium Copyright Act.

VIDEOS IN CYBERSPACE: YOUTUBE

YouTube, a video-sharing website phenomena where one can upload, view, and share clips, is also under heavy criticism for failing to ensure that its online content adheres to principles in the Digital Millennium Copyright Act. Despite its warnings to users, YouTube participants continue to upload unauthorized television clips, films, and music videos. Viacom has demanded $1 billion in damages in a lawsuit filed against YouTube, which, it says, has done little or nothing to stop infringement. Furthermore, it said that former Vice President Al Gore's documentary, *An Inconvenient Truth*, has been illegally uploaded to YouTube, and received an "astonishing" 1.5 billion views by site users.

Such lawsuits are now the headache of Google Inc., which acquired YouTube for $1.65 billion in Google stock on November 13, 2006, making its founders, former PenPal employees Chad Hurley, Steve Chen, and Jawed Karim, very rich.

Their venture started when they were looking to make an easier way to share videos online and earn an extra buck to pay college tuition. After four months of tinkering with their invention in a Palo Alto, California, garage, the trio previewed their site in May 2005. The following year it was named *Time*'s Invention of the Year and sold to Google.

What they did was to make it possible for anyone, anywhere to post a video that millions of people could watch within a few minutes. Estimates place the total daily YouTube uploads to be approximately 150,000 to 200,000.[34] It receives some 350 million U.S. visits each month.[35] To underscore its popularity, Google.com receives about 125 million monthly U.S. visits, myspace.com about 45 million U.S. visits, and CNN.com about 23 million U.S. visits.

Delivering these free video clips costs Google plenty, and YouTube has not been a moneymaker for the giant search engine. YouTube sends about 1,000 gigabytes of data every second, or nearly 300 billion gigabytes each month. Industry insiders estimate that YouTube spends approximately $1 million a day to pay for the bandwidth to host the videos. That is about 3 percent of Google's operating costs. The site receives much of its revenue from selling display ads that run on the right side of the site's homepage.[36]

YouTube came of age when it hosted the CNN/YouTube Presidential Debates in 2008. Questions were submitted to YouTube via thirty-second videos where voters asked questions to the respective candidates. Around 200 videos were posted daily with questions geared toward various social issues. Google, its corporate mother, must have been proud of its youngster.

THE FIRST INTERNET ELECTION

The YouTube Presidential Debates helped label the 2008 presidential campaign the first Internet election. Candidates Hillary Clinton, Barack Obama and John McCain made more extensive use of the Web than at any time in American history. They used it for organizing, fund-raising, networking, and announcing news.[37] Obama even skipped the traditional media and announced his vice presidential nominee, Senator Joseph Biden, via text message on Twitter.

It certainly wasn't the first time the Internet had been used in presidential political campaigns. Howard Dean, the obscure former governor of Vermont, started his campaign in early 2003 with virtually no campaign funds and only around four hundred known supporters. With help from Meetup.com (a Web tool for forming social groups) and hundreds of bloggers, he was widely regarded as the front-runner within a year. He had raised more than $40 million, some eight times more than Massachusetts Senator John Kerry, the eventual primary winner for the Democratic Party, and had more than half a million supporters across the country. These volunteers went door-to-door and helped write personal letters to likely voters, host meetings, and distribute flyers.[38] Despite his failed campaign, it is not too far fetched to say that his candidacy forever changed the American political landscape. Simply, he found that if money is the mother's milk of politics, the computer is the milking machine.

Besides bringing in money, the Internet has become the major source for news about the presidential campaign. In 2008, a record-breaking 46 percent of Americans used the internet, email or cell phone text messaging to get news about the presidential campaign, share their views and mobilize others. Three online activities became especially prominent. First, 35 percent of Americans said they watched on-line political videos—a figure that nearly tripled 2004 figures. Second, 10 percent said they used social networking sites such as Facebook or MySpace to gather information or become involved. Third, 6 percent of Americans said they made political contributions online, compared with 2 percent who did that during the entire 2004 campaign.[39]

And more and more bloggers had an influence on the political scene as they circulated all kinds of information, some of which found its way into mainstream media coverage. In 2006 some 12 million people were active bloggers in the United States, and 57 million were readers of these blogs. Many of these bloggers have been successful in keeping a factual check on media stories. For example, bloggers questioned the veracity of some documents used in a CBS News story about President George Bush's National Guard service. The documents suggested that the president disobeyed an order to appear for a physical exam and that friends of the Bush family tried to "sugar coast" his Guard service. The story relied on four documents allegedly written by one of Bush's Texas Air National Guard commanders in the early 1970s, Lt. Col. Jerry Killian, who is now dead. Critics said the documents were most probably forgeries prepared on a modern word processor. When the bloggers turned out to be correct in their claim that the documents were false, four CBS News employees, including three executives, were fired for their role in preparing and reporting the story. CBS News anchor Dan Rather, who eventually retired under pressure some months later, was left with egg on his face. The story tarnished his twenty-four year record with the network.

Bloggers also have uncovered news stories either intentionally or unreported or unnoticed by the mainstream media. For example, photographs of a mysterious bulge under President Bush's suit coat during one of the 2004 presidential debates and Howard Dean's scream (which contributed to his failed campaign) on the night of the Iowa caucuses gave these two campaign episodes more attention than they might otherwise have warranted.

The use of YouTube videos on blogs, especially the *Saturday Night Live* skit of the vice presidential nominee, Alaska Governor Sarah Palin, by actress Tina Fey also played a role in the 2008 campaign. And for the first time in a presidential race, readers got to comment online about individual news stories by major publications. This may have contributed to one of the bitterest presidential campaigns between senators Barack Obama and Hillary Clinton for the Democratic presidential nomination.

AMERICAN MEDIA PROFILE | STEVE JOBS 1955–

Markus Schreiber/AP Photos

Steve Jobs doesn't mince words. When he lured John Sculley away from Pepsi-Cola to serve as Apple's CEO, he simply said, "Do you want to spend the rest of your life selling sugared water, or do you want a chance to change the world?"

In 1984 Jobs did change the world. That year he introduced the Macintosh, the first commercially successful computer with a graphical user interface. And he did it in a grand fashion with a Super Bowl television commercial titled "1984." Two days later, on January 24, 1984, he introduced the Macintosh at Apple's annual shareholders meeting.

Perhaps his success is due to his persistence. The first evidence of this trait was when he was assigned a project at the high school he was attending in Cupertino. He needed a part for the project and did not hesitate to call William Hewlett, the president of Hewlett-Packard. Not only did Hewlett send him the part but offered him a summer job. That summer he met and worked with Stephen Wozniak, a University of California, Berkeley dropout, who had a passion to invent electronics. He would again met up with Wozniak at the Homebrew Computer Club meetings.

He took a job as a technician at Atari, a popular video game manufacturer. While there he reunited with Wozniak and the rest is history. They designed their first computer, the Apple I, in Jobs' bedroom, and pieced the prototype together in his garage. The Apple I was the first single-board computer with a built-in video interface. In 1976, Jobs marketed the machine to a local electronics retailer for the price of $666. The retailer was so impressed with the product he ordered twenty-five of them. In the first year of sales the Apple I generated $774,000.

The following year, Jobs and Wozniak created the general purpose Apple II equipped with the ability to interface with a color monitor. Jobs also encouraged local programmers to create applications for the Apple II, resulting in more than 16,000 software programs. Setting the standard for personal computers, the Apple II had earnings of $139 million within the first three years, and a growth of 700 percent. Apple went public in 1980 with a price of $22 a share, and went up the same day to $29 per share. With a 150-percent growth rate per year and essentially no competition in sight, things at Apple were continually getting better.

In 1981, Apple introduced the Apple III and had to recall 14,000 units due to design flaws. Shortly after the Apple III fiasco, Jobs announced the release of the first mouse controlled, user-friendly Lisa with an un-friendly price of $10,000. By 1983, IBM had dominated the industry with the PC and created an operating system that wasn't compatible with any of Apple's products. With the design recalls and

The viciousness spilled over into the general election between the Obama-Biden and McCain-Palin camps.

What is next? Text messaging to register and mobilize voter and greater use of the blogsphere will undoubtedly play an even greater role in political campaigns. Also expect spin-doctors using google-bombing to frame debates. (Google bombing is a technique where many links are created so that certain search terms become associated with certain individuals and organizations.) Or, expect video emails from candidates that inoculate them against embarrassing YouTube moments. Further

AMERICAN MEDIA PROFILE   CONTINUED

outrageous pricing, Jobs had come up with a way to revitalize his company, or fall victim to his new competitors at IBM. He introduced the Macintosh.

After skirmishes with Sculley, he sold $20 million in Apple stock in 1985 and left for Italy to find a new purpose in life. A year later he found that purpose. He purchased The Graphics Group from Lucasfilms computer graphics division for $10 million. Feeling betrayed by the company he had co-founded, Jobs decided he'd rather run his own computer company than focus his efforts in the computer graphics business. Jobs kept The Graphics Group and renamed it Pixar, but focused all his efforts toward his new venture instead. In 1989, the NeXT computer company was born.

Jobs' intent was to revolutionize the personal computer and put Apple to shame for their wrong doings. The NeXT workstation was technologically advanced, but it wasn't really able to take off because of its high cost of $3,000. As NeXT struggled, Jobs had success with Pixar and signed a deal to produce three movies for Disney.

Jobs continued to market NeXT computers to scientific and academic fields in hopes the new technologies they possessed would justify the cost. Sales weren't what they were projected, and Jobs continued to push his line of NeXT products. After only selling 50,000 machines in seven years, NeXT computers transformed into a software company. After several years of development the NeXTSTEP operating system was released and again couldn't get off the ground. Even though NeXTSTEP never really took off, it did pave the way for some major developments in the technology field. For example, Berners-Lee created the original World Wide Web at CERN (European Organization for Nuclear Research) on a NeXT workstation running NeXTSTEP as an operating system. NeXTSTEP also was used in the development of the game Doom and later the series Quake. Apple saw the potential of all this and purchased NeXT computers for $429 million.

In 1996 the deal with Apple and NeXT was finalized and Jobs returned to the company he co-founded. To get Apple back on track, Jobs cancelled several projects and went back to NeXTSTEP for more development, which later evolved into the Mac OS X. A few months later the iMac was introduced and significantly boosted Apple's sales as well as their creditability. Not ready to stop there, Jobs began to develop Apple's version of the portable music player called the iPod. More than 110 million iPods have been sold, and more than three billion songs have been downloaded from the iTunes online store. Add to that the success of the new mobile phone venture with the iPhone.

By 2006, Jobs had built his company back up, revolutionized the technology industry, and made the *Guinness Book of World* records as the lowest paid CEO in world, with a salary of $1 per year. He sold Pixar to the Walt Disney Company and now serves on its board of directors. His roller-coaster ride on the technology superhighway has been nothing short of "extraordinary."

By Darren Williams

technological advances will push the Internet's role in politics to even greater heights. And someday the iconic Internet president may emerge, dominating the media like FDR dominated radio and JFK and Ronald Reagan did with television.[40]

THE ETHNIC AND ALTERNATIVE MEDIA IN THE INFORMATION AGE

The challenges posed by the Internet and the cable TV era may offer new opportunities to America's ethnic and alternative media. "The new media are tailor-made for the niche market in which black-oriented media always have operated," according to nationally syndicated columnist Clarence Page. "Today almost anyone with Web access has the ability to be a publisher, with all the joys and headaches that come with that lofty position." However, fear exists that the major media conglomerates will eventually gobble the ethnic and alternative media.

THE BLACK MEDIA

When the Reverand Samuel Cornish and John B. Russwurm launched America's first black newspaper, *Freedom's Journal*, in 1827, they proclaimed, "Too long have others spoken for us... We wish to plead our own cause." It is still the mantra for the National Negro Publishers Association, formed in 1941 by John Sengstacke of the *Chicago Defender* and representatives from twenty-two publications. In 1956 it was renamed the National Publishers Association (NNPA).[41]

Today, more than 200 black newspapers in the United States and the Virgin Islands are part of the NNPA. Its newspapers have a combined readership of 15 million and have joined the digital age with the creation of an electronic news service and the BlackPressUSA.com website, enabling it to provide immediate news coverage to its national constituency. Meanwhile, from 2002 to 2006, some eighty-five magazines targeting African-Americans were launched. However, the black press has been hampered in virtually all areas of publishing—advertising, circulation, production, financing, editorial, and promotion. Each of these has caused extraordinary concern in the black press world.[42]

There were 30 African-American-owned broadcast facilities in the United States in 1976. In 1998 blacks owned 168 of 10,315 commercial AM and FM radio stations with most concentrated in the southern region of the country. In 2005 blacks owned 240 radio stations. Today, local black radio news is near extinction after black owners were enticed to join the game of consolidation that began in the 1980s and reached fever pitch after passage of the Telecommunications Act of 1996. Those black "stand-alone" stations operated by business leaders who had roots in the community were forced out or cashed out. Media giants such as Clear Channel gobbled up station after station. No better example is Clear Channel's purchase of US Radio, the black-owned chain of 17 stations.[43]

During 2007 and 2008 black TV station ownership dropped by 60 percent with the total number falling from nineteen to eight and making black ownership almost nonexistent. "Minority television ownership is in such a precarious state that the loss of a single minority-owned company results in a disastrous decline," said S. Derek Turner, research director of *Free Press* and lead author of *Out of the Picture 2007*, an updated analysis of the impact of consolidation on minority and female television station ownership.[44]

THE SPANISH-LANGUAGE MEDIA

Unlike the English-speaking media, the Spanish-language media are thriving. Spanish-language newspapers are experiencing a rise in circulation. In Los Angeles alone, two out of the three top morning drive-time spots belong to Spanish radio stations. And distributors of U.S. Latino films have a growing target audience with skyrocketing purchasing strength over the first two decades of the twenty-first century.

The future continues to look bright for the Spanish-language market. For example, Hispanic buying power grew from $630 million in 2002 to $798 million in 2006 and is expected to exceed black buying power.[45] By the end of this decade, Latino purchasing power is expected to reach $1 trillion[46] and by 2020 about $2.5 trillion.[47]

That is good news for the media market because U.S. Latinos generally tend to be heavy consumers of mass media. They read newspapers, listen to radio, and see more films than the mainstream. For example, Hispanic newspapers alone have increased 55 percent in the past decade from 355 to 550 newspapers, while Hispanic magazines grew from 177 to 352.

Television is the medium of choice for Hispanics, regardless of the language learned. Spanish-language programming is the choice for some 49 percent of U.S. Hispanics who watch television during prime-time hours, with Univision being the leading network. They also spend about twenty-six to thirty hours per week listening to radio, around 13 percent above the general population; some listen all day.

Latinos also go to nearly ten films per year, making up the second-largest segment of U.S. moviegoers. They are expected to account for 20 percent of the U.S. box office by 2012. And the film studios are not losing any time in their efforts to attract more U.S. Latino moviegoers. Studios are developing deals with well-known Latino-owned production companies. Universal and Focus Features made a $100-million, five-picture deal with Cha Cha Cha, a production company run by a trio of Oscar-nominated directors including Alfonso Cuaron, Alejandro Gonzalez Inarritu, and Guillermo del Toro. Meanwhile, Metro-Goldwyn-Mayer developed a partnership with actress Salma Hayek's production company, Ventanazul, which will deliver motion pictures with Latino talent or have a Latino flavor to them.

THE GAY AND LESBIAN MEDIA

Information aimed at a gay or lesbian audience can be found just about anywhere today in the Western world. Slick mass-market, ad-based magazines such as *Out*, *The Advocate*, or *Genre* are just a few of the dozens of national and regional magazines in the United States alone that earmark the gay audience. In 2005 a free cable network, LOGO, was launched to compete with pay cable here! for the gays and lesbians wanting 24/7 news coverage and entertainment. Satellite radio SIRIUS has a gay-oriented news and entertainment channel, while Internet sites such as gay.com and planetout.com provide social networking and immediate access to information on everything from travel and fashion to the latest national news of interest to the gay community.

The first stirrings of the modern gay press took place in 1967 when two Los Angeles men started *The Los Angeles Advocate* to provide coverage of the local gay community, which was being ignored by the mainstream *Los Angeles Times*. By 1970, the *Advocate* was turning a profit. This same period was the beginning of gay newspapers outside California. *The Gay Blade*, later renamed *The Washington Blade*, *Gay Community News* in Boston, *NewsWest* in Los Angeles, *Gay News* in Pittsburgh, and *Gay Life* in Chicago all covered local and national politics and stressed change, rather than cooperation.[48]

In 2006 the combined circulation of all publications constituting the gay and lesbian press was 3,777,488.[49] Although local gay newspapers continue today, and are particularly strong in cities such as San Francisco (*Bay Area Reporter*) and Washington, D.C. (*The Washington Blade*), the focus in gay publishing during the past thirty years has been more on the development of the mass-market glossy bimonthly or monthly magazine with a strong advertising base. Over the years gay publications have turned from news to lifestyle and entertainment. *The Advocate*, under new owner David B. Goodstein, was reinvented in the mid-1970s from being the nation's largest gay newspaper into a gay newsmagazine, with a focus on coverage of gay culture and lifestyles. Today the *Advocate*, along with its website advocate.com, provide both news and lifestyle coverage for gay and lesbian Americans.

Though not as strong as the Hispanic market, the gay and lesbian market is significant because it is both affluent and influential. In 2006, the buying power of this market was estimated at $641 billion, a vital contributor to the U.S. economy.[50]

Corporate mergers of the gay and lesbian press also threaten to reduce minority voices, some analysts fear. The growth of the Internet has spurred sales of gay publications, with copies of books, DVDs, and same-sex oriented magazines easier to purchase from the anonymity of one's computer at home instead of walking into a bookstore. Further consolidation appears likely in the future, as witnessed by the sale in April 2008 of LPI's magazines, which include *The Advocate* and *Out*, to Regent Publishing, which owns *here!*, a premium cable television network for the gay and lesbian audience.

MEGAMERGERS AND THE FUTURE OF MEDIA AND DEMOCRACY

In less than twenty-five years, the number of companies that own the major American media, including ventures on the Information Highway, has gone from fifty to five. A mere five U.S. corporations now control the flow of news and information: what is heard or not heard, what is seen or not seen. Those five corporations are Time Warner, Walt Disney, Rupert Murdoch's News Corp, NBC Universal/GE, and the CBS Corporation. The Big Five have similar boards of directors; they currently have a total of 141 joint ventures, which makes them business partners with each other. And they even go through motions that, in effect, lend each other money and swap properties when it is mutually advantageous.[51]

Of course, media conglomerates are not the only industry whose owners have become monopolistic in the American economy. However, media products are unique in one vital respect: They do not manufacture nuts and bolts, they manufacture a social and political world.[52] Simply, they decide what most citizens will—or will not—learn.[53]

Two questions arise: What has brought about this rush to merge and concentrate? and What impact have these megamergers had on the political and social fabric of America?

American media scholar Robert McChesney states that Washington, D.C., has been very kind to media corporations. Why? He says the most important commercial broadcasters are now part of the giant media conglomerates which have their own lobbying machines, and these firms are generous supporters of politicians through powerful lobbyists.[54] The *Wall Street Journal* calls the commercial broadcasters "the most powerful lobby in Washington," and most other analysts place broadcasters in the top tier of influence.[55]

According to Bagdikian, these powerful lobbyists have pushed legislation that once again favors vertical integration, in which corporations have control of a total process, from raw material to fabrication to sales. Today, government has become sympathetic to dominant vertical corporations that have merged into ever-larger total systems. These corporations, including those in the media, have remained largely unrestrained.[56]

CNN founder Ted Turner agrees. He says that in 1990 the major broadcast networks—ABC, CBS, NBC, and Fox—fully or partially owned just 12.5 percent of the new series they aired. By 2000, it was 56.3 percent, and by 2002, it had surged to 77.5 percent. In this environment, he says, most independent media firms either get gobbled up by one of the big companies or get driven out of business altogether. He argues that instead of balancing the rules to give independent broadcasters a fair chance in the market, Washington continues to tilt the playing field in favor of the biggest players.[57]

McChesney argues that the major beneficiaries of the so-called Information Age are wealthy investors; advertisers; and a handful of enormous media, computer, and telecommunications corporations. Simply, he states, "The history of American media is one continual victory of powerful corporate interests over everyone else."[58]

The powerful Big Five have become major players in altering the politics of the country, according to Bagdikian. "They have been able to promote new laws that increase their corporate domination and that permit them to abolish regulations that inhibit their control," he writes. He says their major accomplishment was the Telecommunications Act of 1996. It was the first major overhaul of U.S. telecommunications law since the Communications Act of 1934 and opened the floodgates to media consolidation.[59]

When such a handful of powerful corporations control the flow of information, McChesney and Bagdikian say, the place of individual citizens diminishes. The interests of the corporate entity win out over the interests of the citizenry. "In the history of the United States and in its Constitution, citizens are presumed to have the sole right to determine the shape of their democracy," Bagdikian writes. "But concentrated media power in news and commentary, together with corporate political contributions in general, have diminished the influence of voters over which issues and candidates will be offered on Election Day."[60]

He says the inappropriate fit between the country's major media and the country's political system has starved voters of relevant information. "It has eroded the central requirement of a democracy that those who are governed give not only their consent but their informed consent."[61]

CONCLUSION

Coffeehouses played a pivotal role in forming communities and disseminating information in Colonial America. In fact, they were the primary subscribers to newspapers. At times, stories were read aloud and certainly commented upon by the men who frequented these meeting places. Sometimes newsrunners would take the conversations and opinions they overheard in the coffeehouses and print them in the newspapers that would be returned to the coffeehouses. At other times, it was not above those men who had political or financial interests to plant stories in the coffeehouses for newsrunners to hear. Coffeehouses, too, were usually locations of mail delivery since they were public and easy to locate. In a sense, they were reincarnations of what John Milton envisioned in his "marketplaces of ideas." They served as laboratories for experimentation in some of the various freedoms articulated in the American Bill of Rights later in the eighteenth century: freedom of the press, freedom of association and assembly, freedom of speech. The coffeehouse then provided access to information and opinion beyond the official disseminators of news.[62]

Coffeehouses fostered a sense of community, especially when those commenting on the news and offering opinions were of like mind. Communications, then, fostered political discourse. That political discourse hurried the American Revolution and the type of government the new nation would pursue.

Like the eighteenth-century coffeehouse, the Internet has provided users with unlimited access to information and opinion beyond the official disseminators of news. Users of the Internet, like the denizens of coffeehouses, have access to information unlike anytime in history. And they have a greater advantage: Not only can they access information at the modern coffeehouse, Starbucks, for example, but in the privacy of their home. Instead of newsrunners, we have spin doctors who twist facts to foster their point of view. They were evident during the 2008 presidential contest when supporters of the three major contenders tried to fashion news and opinion on newspaper blogs. Also, all can readily get their mail at the new coffeehouse.

In earlier times, many ideas could be heard at the coffeehouse. Those with incompatible ideas argued. Those whose ideas clicked with one another formed political partnerships. It is not too naïve to say that these political partnerships helped form the experiment in government we call America. And many of those women, but mostly men, some bombastic, rude, and crude, and others brilliant, excited a people by what they said and, more importantly, what they penned. They, along with the thousands who died on the battlefields at home and in foreign lands, have shaped this country, protected its democracy, and fostered the greatest media system in the world.

In a short time that media system may look nothing like today. We hear daily that newspapers will go the way of the dinosaur and the press as we know it will vanish. However, mankind will always want stories and need stories to be informed and entertained. The goal of the new storytellers, whether on the Internet or some other electronic medium, is to continue the journalistic adage—comfort the afflicted and afflict the comfortable.

May those frequenting the new coffeehouse have a sense of where we've been, the ability to discern truth and falsity, and the vision to carry forward the best values of American democracy and protect the freedoms guaranteed in the First Amendment.

ENDNOTES

Introduction: Before the American Experience

1. J. Herbert Altschull, *Agents of Power: The Media and Public Policy* (White Plains, NY: Longman, 1995), p. xviii.
2. J. Herbert Altschull, *Agents of Power: The Media and Public Policy,* p. xviii.
3. John Man, *Gutenberg: How One Man Remade the World with Words* (New York: John Wiley and Sons, 2002), p. 2.
4. John Man, *Gutenberg: How One Man Remade the World with Words,* pp. 252–253.
5. Elizabeth L. Eisenstein, *The Printing Revolution as an Agent of Change* (Cambridge: Cambridge University Press, 1977), p. 66.
6. John Man, *Gutenberg: How One Man Remade the World with Words,* pp. 256–257.
7. John Man, *Gutenberg: How One Man Remade the World with Words,* pp. 259–260.
8. Myron P. Gilmore, *The World of Humanism 1453–1517* (New York: Harper and Row Publishers, 1952) p. 190.
9. Walter M. Brasch and Dana R. Ulloth, *The Press and the State: Sociohistorical and Contemporary Interpretations* (New York: University Press of America, 1986), p. 24.
10. Van Vechten Veeder, "History of Law of Defamation," in Committee of the Association of American Law Schools, ed., *Select Essays in Anglo-American Legal History* (Boston, 1909, 3 vols.), Vol. III, pp. 453–454.
11. Leonard W. Levy, *Emergence of a Free Press* (New York: Oxford University Press, 1985), p. 6.
12. Philip II was considered the most barbaric European ruler, having put to death Jews, Moors, and other "heretics."
13. Walter M. Brasch and Dana R. Ulloth, *The Press and the State: Sociohistorical and Contemporary Interpretations,* p. 37.
14. Mitchell Stephens, *A History of News* (New York: Penguin Books, 1988), pp. 161–162; Ian K. Steele, *The English Atlantic, 1675–1740: An Exploration of Communication and Community* (New York: Oxford University Press, 1986), pp. 133–134.
15. B. Williams, *A History of English Journalism to the Foundation of the Gazette* (London: Longmans, Green, 1908) p. 186. See also *Rex v. Twyn,* in T. J. Howell, *A Complete Collection of State Trials to 1820* (London, 1816–1828), Vol. 6, pp. 513, 536.

16. The *areopagetica* (from the Greek *Ares*, the god of war; *pagos*, hill) was taken from a hill in Athens called the Areopagus, where the Athenians placed their highest court, the tribunal. A speech before the court was called an areopagetica. Milton took his title concerning free expression from the tribunal as well as from the Areopagetica discourse of Isocrates (436 BC–338 BC). Here lawyer Isocrates made a famous speech in which he appealed for a system of government in which all people possessed equal political power.

17. George H. Sabine, *A History of Political Theory*, 3rd ed. (New York: Holt, Rinehart and Winston, 1965), p. 509.

18. J. Herbert Altschull, *From Milton to McLuhan* (New York: Longman, 1990), p. 40. See also Harold L. Nelson, ed., *Freedom of the Press from Hamilton to the Warren Court* (Indianapolis: The Bobbs-Merrill Company, 1967), pp. 28–34.

19. John Milton, *Areopagetica* (New York: Payson and Clarke, 1927), p. 36.

20. John Milton, *Areopagetica*, p. 13.

21. J. Herbert Altschull, *From Milton to McLuhan*, p. 40.

22. Walter M. Brasch and Dana R. Ulloth, *The Press and the State: Sociohistorical and Contemporary Interpretations*, p. 44.

23. Michael Oakeshott, ed., *Leviathan: Or the Matter, Forme and Power of a Commonwealth Ecclesiastical and Civil* (Oxford: Basil Blackwell, 1946), pp. 113–120.

24. John Locke, *Second Treatise of Civil Government*, ed. Thomas I. Cook (New York: Hafner, 1947), p. 132.

25. J. Herbert Altschull, *From Milton to McLuhan*, p. 51.

26. *A Letter Concerning Television*, in *The Works of John Locke* (London: 1812), Vol. XI, p. 4.

27. *A Letter Concerning Television*, in *The Works of John Locke*, Vol. XI, p. 46.

28. *A Letter Concerning Television*, in *The Works of John Locke*, Vol. XI, p. 51.

29. Walter M. Brasch and Dana R. Ulloth, *The Press and the State: Sociohistorical and Contemporary Interpretations*, p. 64.

30. Leonard W. Levy, *Emergence of a Free Press*, p. 117.

31. Elizabeth Christine Cook, *Literary Influences in Colonial Newspapers* (New York: Columbia University Press, 1912), p. 81.

32. *New-England Courant*, July 9, and September 21, 1721.

33. *Boston Gazette*, September 27, 1773.

34. John Adams, *Works; with a Life of the Author, John Adams*, ed. Charles Francis Adams, (Boston: Little Brown, 1850–56), Vol. 10, p. 202.

35. Paul Leicester Ford, ed., *The Writing of John Dickinson* (Philadelphia, 1895); *Memoirs of the Historical Society of Pennsylvania*, Vol. 14, p. 343; *Letters of a Farmer*, No. 7; E. Millicent Sowerby, *Catalogue of the Library of Thomas Jefferson* (Washington, 1952), Vol. 3, p. 133.

36. Leonard W. Levy, *Emergence of a Free Press*, p. 114.

37. Walter M. Brasch and Dana R. Ulloth, *The Press and the State: Sociohistorical and Contemporary Interpretations*, p. 68.

Chapter 1: The Colonial Years

1. Samuel Green Jr., a newsletter writer, published a one-sheet broadside, *The Present State of the New-English Affairs*, with the approval of Massachusetts authorities in the fall of 1689. Although it looked like a contemporary English newspaper, it was published only once, leaving some question whether it was intended to be a newspaper. He died less than one year after publishing the broadsheet.

2. *Publick Occurrences*, September 25, 1690.

3. John Tebbel, *The Compact History of the American Newspaper* (New York: Hawthorn Books, 1963), p. 16.

4. In Leonard W. Labaree et al., eds., *The Autobiography of Benjamin Franklin* (New Haven and London: Yale University Press, 2003), p. 67.

5. About one-third of Boston's population was struck by smallpox from 1751 to 1752. However, no newspaper in the town alerted the population that it was a major epidemic.

6. Robert E. McGrew, in *The Encyclopedia of Media History* (New York: McGraw-Hill, 1985), pp. 155–156.
7. *New-England Courant*, August 7, 1721; John Blake, "The Inoculation Controversy in Boston: 1721–1722," *New England Quarterly* (1952), pp. 489–506.
8. This view is not shared by all media history scholars. David Sloan labeled James Franklin a mean-spirited religious bigot whose crusade against the smallpox inoculation showed his indifference to the plight of those afflicted or to the health of the colony.
9. John Tebbel, *The Compact History of the American Newspaper*, p. 19.
10. Benjamin Franklin wrote fourteen letters of Silence Dogood, printed in the *Courant* between April 12 and October 8, 1722. These are Franklin's earliest surviving writings. He was sixteen years old at the time. See *The Autobiography of Benjamin Franklin, Papers 1*, pp. 8–45.
11. Walter Isaacson, *Benjamin Franklin: An American Life* (New York: Simon and Schuster, 2003), p. 29.
12. Leonard Levy, *Emergence of a Free Press* (New York: Oxford University Press, 1985), p. 30.
13. *New-England Courant*, January 14–21, 1723.
14. Carl Van Doren, *Benjamin Franklin* (New York: Viking Press, 1939), p. 32.
15. In Leonard W. Labaree et al., eds., *The Autobiography of Benjamin Franklin*, p. 70.
16. Walter Isaacson, *Benjamin Franklin: An American Life*, p. 39.
17. Carl Van Doren, *Benjamin Franklin*, p. 41.
18. See an account of this story in Sidney Kobre's *Development of American Journalism* (Dubuque, IA: William C. Brown Company, 1969), pp. 31–32; and Walter Isaacson, *Benjamin Franklin*, p. 53.
19. *Pennsylvania Gazette*, June 10, 1731.
20. Water Isaacson, *Benjamin Franklin: An American Life*, p. 67.
21. Carl Van Doren, *Benjamin Franklin*, p. 100.
22. In Leonard W. Labaree et al., eds., *The Autobiography of Benjamin Franklin*, p. 121.
23. Sidney Kobre, *Development of American Journalism*, p. 33.
24. Walter Isaacson, *Benjamin Franklin: An American Life*, p. 68.
25. *Pennsylvania Gazette*, October 24, 1734.
26. Carl Van Doren, *Benjamin Franklin*, p. 99.
27. Sidney Kobre, *Development of American Journalism*, p. 33.
28. Leonard Levy, *Freedom of Speech and Press in Early American History: Legacy of Suppression* (New York: Harper and Row, 1963), p. 18.
29. Isaiah Thomas, *The History of Printing in America*, Marcus A. McCorison, ed., from Thomas's second edition (New York: Weathervane Books, 1970), p. 344. An account can also be found in Norman Rosenberg, *Protecting the Best Men: An Interpretive History of the Law of Libel* (Chapel Hill: University of North Carolina Press, 1986), p. 35.
30. Isaiah Thomas, *The History of Printing in America*, p. 350.
31. Isaiah Thomas, *The History of Printing in America*, pp. 354–355.
32. *New-York Weekly Journal*, January 7, 1733.
33. *New York Gazette*, January 28–February 4, 1734, as cited in Stanley Katz, *Introduction to James Alexander, A Brief Narrative of the Case and Trial of John Peter Zenger*, 2nd ed. (Cambridge: Harvard University Press, 1971), p. 13.
34. Catherine L. Covert, "Journalism History and Women's Experience: A Problem in Conceptual Change," *Journalism History* 9:1 (Spring 1981), p. 4. She writes that John Peter Zenger was used by rich and powerful people in an effort to assist their own "flagging social and economic power."
35. *Cato's Letters*, essays by John Trenchard and Thomas Gordon, were originally published from 1720 to 1723 in the London *Journal* and the British *Journal*. They were issued in a four-volume collected edition in 1724. The essays were reprinted throughout the American colonies and were influential in spreading the concept of political liberty in the New World. Examples of Trenchard and Gordon's work can be found in James Franklin's *New-England Courant*, Andrew Bradford's *Mercury*, and John Peter Zenger's *Weekly Journal*.
36. Isaiah Thomas, *The History of Printing in America*, p. 488.
37. *New-York Weekly Journal*, November 25, 1734.

38. Anna Janney DeArmond, *Andrew Bradford: Colonial Journalist* (Newark: University of Delaware Press, 1949), pp. 84–113.

39. Quotations from Andrew Hamilton's defense are cited in Stanley Katz, *A Brief Narrative of the Case and Trial of John Peter Zenger,* (Cambridge, MA: Harvard University Press, 1963), pp. 62–101. See also Leonard Levy, *Emergence of a Free Press*, pp. 37–45.

40. Catherine L. Covert, "Journalism History and Women's Experience: A Problem in Conceptual Change," p. 4.

41. *New York Weekly Journal*, November 18 and 25, 1734.

42. Marion Marzolf, *Up From the Footnote: A History of Women Journalists* (New York: Hastings House, 1977), p. 3.

43. Maurine H. Beasley and Sheila J. Gibbons, *Taking Their Place: A Documentary History of Women and Journalism* (State College, PA: Strata Publishing Company, 2003), p. 8.

44. Maurine H. Beasley and Sheila J. Gibbons, *Taking Their Place: A Documentary History of Women and Journalism*, p. 5.

45. Susan Henry, "Ann Franklin: Rhode Island's Woman Printer," in *Newsletters to Newspapers: Eighteenth Century Journalism*, Donovan H. Bond and W. Reynolds McLeod, eds. (Morgantown, WV, 1977), pp. 129–143.

46. Isaiah Thomas, *The History of Printing in America*, pp. 325–326.

47. *South-Carolina Gazette*, January 4, 1739.

48. Madelon Golden Schilp and Sharon M. Murphy, *Great Women of the Press* (Carbondale: Southern Illinois University Press, 1983), p. 5.

49. Marion Marzolf, *Up From the Footnote: A History of Women Journalists*, p. 5.

50. Leona Hudak, *Early American Women Printers and Publishers, 1639–1820* (Metuchen, NJ: Scarecrow Press, 1978), p. 231.

51. Madelon Golden Schilp and Sharon M. Murphy, *Great Women of the Press*, p. 15.

52. Maurine H. Beasley and Sheila J. Gibbons, *Taking Their Place: A Documentary History of Women and Journalism*, p. 11.

53. Madelon Golden Schilp and Sharon M. Murphy, *Great Women of the Press*, p. 18.

54. Marion Marzolf, *Up From the Footnote: A History of Women Journalists*, p. 6.

55. Marion Marzolf, *Up From the Footnote: A History of Women Journalists*, p. 6.

56. Leonard Levy, *Emergence of a Free Press*, p. 15.

57. Isaiah Thomas, *The History of Printing in America*, p. 97.

Chapter 2: The Press and the Revolution

1. Arthur M. Schlesinger, *Prelude to Independence: The Newspaper War on Great Britain, 1764–1776* (New York: Alfred A. Knopf, 1958), p. 20.

2. John Tebbel, *The Media in America* (New York: Thomas Y. Crowell Company, 1974), p. 35.

3. Richard Frothingham, *The Rise of the Republic of the United States* (Boston: 1872), p. 153.

4. In Leonard W. Labaree et al., eds., *Benjamin Franklin* (New Haven and London: Yale University Press, 1964), pp. 91–92.

5. In Leonard W. Labaree et al., eds., *Benjamin Franklin*, pp. 147–148.

6. In Leonard W. Labaree et al., eds., *Benjamin Franklin*, p. 211.

7. Arthur M. Schlesinger, *Prelude to Independence: The Newspaper War on Great Britain, 1764–1776* (New York: Alfred A. Knopf, 1958), p. 262.

8. Allen Weinstein and David Rubel, *The Story of America: Freedom and Crisis from Settlement to Superpower* (New York: DK Publishing, Inc., 2002), p. 80.

9. Bernard Bailyn and John B. Hench, eds., *The Press & the American Revolution* (Worcester, MA: American Antiquarian Society, 1980), p. 23.

10. *Boston Gazette*, July 22, 1765.

11. *New-York Gazette and Post Boy*, December 12, 1765.

12. *Pennsylvania Journal*, October 31, 1765.
13. Carl Van Doren, *Benjamin Franklin* (New York: Viking Press, 1938), p. 334.
14. Carl Van Doren, *Benjamin Franklin*, pp. 334–335.
15. Carl Van Doren, *Benjamin Franklin*, p. 352.
16. Carl Van Doren, *Benjamin Franklin*, p. 353.
17. Carl Van Doren, *Benjamin Franklin*, p. 528.
18. *Rivington's New-York Gazetteer*, October 13, 1774.
19. *Massachusetts Gazette* and *Boston News-Letter*, April 1, 1773.
20. Arthur M. Schlesinger, *Prelude to Independence: The Newspaper War on Great Britain, 1764–1776*, p. 166.
21. John Tebbel, *The Media in America*, p. 44.
22. *Rivington's New-York Gazetteer*, July 14, August 11, December 8, 1774.
23. *Rivington's New-York Gazetteer*, April 20, 1775.
24. John Tebbel, *The Media in America*, p. 45.
25. Theodore Sedgwick, *A Memoir of the Life of William Livingston* (New York: J. and J. Harper, 1833), p. 247.
26. John L. Lawson, "The Remarkable Mystery of James Rivington, 'Spy,'" *Journalism Quarterly*, Vol. 35 (Summer 1958), p. 395.
27. *New-York Mercury*, December 16, 1776.
28. Jeffrey L. Pasley, *"The Tyranny of Printers": Newspaper Politics in the Early American Republic* (Charlottesville: University Press of Virginia, 2001), p. 35.
29. Allen Weinstein and David Rubel, *The Story of America: Freedom and Crisis from Settlement to Superpower*, p. 82.
30. Arthur M. Schlesinger, *Prelude to Independence: The Newspaper War on Great Britain, 1764–1776*, p. 89.
31. Arthur M. Schlesinger, *Prelude to Independence: The Newspaper War on Great Britain, 1764–1776*, p. 88.
32. Arthur M. Schlesinger, *Prelude to Independence: The Newspaper War on Great Britain, 1764–1776*, p. 91.
33. Arthur M. Schlesinger, *Prelude to Independence: The Newspaper War on Great Britain, 1764–1776*, p. 90.
34. Paul Lewis, *The Grand Incendiary: A Biography of Samuel Adams* (New York: Dial Press, 1973), p. 7.
35. A. J. Langguth, *Patriots: The Men Who Started the American Revolution* (New York: Simon and Schuster, 1988), p. 30.
36. A. J. Langguth, *Patriots: The Men Who Started the American Revolution*, p. 31.
37. A. J. Langguth, *Patriots: The Men Who Started the American Revolution*, p. 32.
38. William V. Wells, *The Life and Public Services of Samuel Adams*, Vol. 1 (Boston: Little, Brown, 1865), p. 48.
39. Frank Luther Mott, *American Journalism: A History: 1690–1960* (New York: The Macmillan Company, 1962), p. 75.
40. Frank Luther Mott, *American Journalism: A History: 1690–1960*, p. 75.
41. Allen Weinstein and David Rubel, *The Story of America: Freedom and Crisis from Settlement to Superpower*, pp. 100–101.
42. Allen Weinstein and David Rubel, *The Story of America: Freedom and Crisis from Settlement to Superpower*, p. 90.
43. Allen Weinstein and David Rubel, *The Story of America: Freedom and Crisis from Settlement to Superpower*, p. 81.
44. Allen Weinstein and David Rubel, *The Story of America: Freedom and Crisis from Settlement to Superpower*, p. 90.
45. *Pennsylvania Evening Post*, July 2, 1776.
46. Arthur M. Schlesinger, *Prelude to Independence: The Newspaper War on Great Britain, 1764–1776*, p. 282.
47. Arthur M. Schlesinger, *Prelude to Independence: The Newspaper War on Great Britain, 1764–1776*, p. 282.
48. Arthur M. Schlesinger, *Prelude to Independence: The Newspaper War on Great Britain, 1764–1776*, p. 281.

49. Frank Luther Mott, *American Journalism: A History: 1690–1960*, pp. 104–105.
50. Arthur M. Schlesinger, *Prelude to Independence: The Newspaper War on Great Britain, 1764–1776*, p. 296.
51. Frank Luther Mott, *American Journalism: A History: 1690–1960*, pp. 105–106.
52. Arthur M. Schlesinger, *Prelude to Independence: The Newspaper War on Great Britain, 1764–1776*, p. 297.
53. Frank Luther Mott, *American Journalism: A History: 1690–1960*, p. 102.
54. Frank Luther Mott, *American Journalism: A History: 1690–1960*, pp. 101–102.
55. John Adams, "Dissertation in the Canon and Feudal Law," in *The Works of John Adams*, Charles Francis Adams, ed. (Boston, 1851), p. 3; Alden Bradford, ed., *Speeches of the Governors of Massachusetts from 1765 to 1775* (Boston, 1818), p. 121.
56. Bernard Bailyn and John B. Hench, eds., *The Press & the American Revolution* (Worcester, MA: American Antiquarian Society, 1980), p. 59.
57. "To the Inhabitants of the Province of Quebec," October 24, 1774, in Worthington Chauncey Ford, et al., eds., *Journals of the Continental Congress, 1774–1789* (Washington, D.C., 1904–1937), p. I:108.
58. Leonard W. Levy, *Freedom of Speech and Press in Early American History: Legacy of Suppression* (New York: Harper and Row, Publishers, 1963), p. 177.
59. Leonard W. Levy, *Freedom of Speech and Press in Early American History: Legacy of Suppression*, p. 176.
60. Arthur M. Schlesinger, *Prelude to Independence: The Newspaper War on Great Britain, 1764–1776*, p. 189.
61. Leonard W. Levy, *Freedom of Speech and Press in Early American History: Legacy of Suppression*, p. 180.
62. Arthur M. Schlesinger, *Prelude to Independence: The Newspaper War on Great Britain, 1764–1776*, p. 298.
63. Arthur M. Schlesinger, *Prelude to Independence: The Newspaper War on Great Britain, 1764–1776*, p. 299.
64. Arthur M. Schlesinger, *Prelude to Independence: The Newspaper War on Great Britain, 1764–1776*, pp. 299–300.

Chapter 3: The Press and the Founding of a Nation

1. *Columbian Centinel*, January 1, 1799.
2. David McCullough, *John Adams* (New York: Simon and Schuster, 2001), p. 397.
3. David McCullough, *John Adams*, p. 397.
4. Thomas Jefferson to George Washington, 1793, in Paul Leicester Ford, ed., *The Writings of Thomas Jefferson* (New York: G. P. Putnam's Sons, 1894), Vol. VI, p. 106.
5. David McCullough, *John Adams*, p. 379.
6. Thomas Jefferson to Edward Carrington, 1787, in Andrew A. Lipscomb and Albert Ellery Bergh, eds., *The Writings of Thomas Jefferson*, Vol. VI, p. 387.
7. James Madison to Thomas Jefferson, 1788, in *The Papers of Thomas Jefferson*, Vol. XXIV, pp. 19–20, cited in Jeffrey A. Smith, "Public Opinion and the Press Clause," *Journalism History* 14:1 (Spring 1987), p. 15.
8. John C. Miller, *Alexander Hamilton: Portrait in Paradox* (New York: Harper and Row, 1959), p. 317.
9. Curtis P. Nettels, "The Money Supply of the American Colonies before 1720," *University of Wisconsin Studies*, no. 20 (1934), pp. 279–283.
10. Claude G. Bowers, *Jefferson and Hamilton* (Boston: Houghton Mifflin, 1925), p. 31.
11. *Gazette of the United States*, April 27, 1791.
12. *Gazette of the United States*, September 18, 1790.
13. *Porcupine's Gazette*, March 5, 1797.
14. *Porcupine's Gazette*, November 14, 1797.
15. *Columbian Centinel*, October 5, 1798.
16. Thomas Jefferson to Edward Carrington, 1787, in Paul Leicester Ford, ed., *The Writings of Thomas Jefferson*, Vol. IV, p. 360.

17. David McCullough, *John Adams*, p. 436.
18. It should be noted that the Republican Party of Thomas Jefferson's day has no relationship to the Republican Party of today.
19. *Aurora*, December 23, 1796.
20. Thomas C. Leonard, *The Power of the Press: The Birth of Political Reporting* (New York: Oxford University Press, 1986), p. 79.
21. Thomas C. Leonard, *The Power of the Press: The Birth of Political Reporting*, pp. 76–77. It should be noted that the *Congressional Record* has sometimes been considered inaccurate compared with what is actually said or reported on the Senate floor, for example.
22. May 5, 1777, in John C. Fitzpatrick, ed., *The Writings of George Washington* (Washington, D.C.: United States Government Printing Office, 1939), vol. VIII, p. 17.
23. John Tebbel and Sarah Miles Watts, *The Press and the Presidency: From George Washington to Ronald Reagan* (New York: Oxford University Press, 1985), p. 18.
24. John Tebbel, *The Media in America* (New York: Thomas Y. Crowell Company, 1974), p. 82.
25. Samuel Miller, *A Brief Retrospective of the Eighteenth Century* (New York: B. Franklin, 1970), p. 255.

Chapter 4: A Press for the Masses

1. James L. Crouthamel, *Bennett's New York Herald and the Rise of the Popular Press* (Syracuse, NY: Syracuse University Press, 1989), p. 20.
2. James L. Crouthamel, *Bennett's New York Herald and the Rise of the Popular Press*, p. 20.
3. Frank Luther Mott, *American Journalism: A History: 1690–1960* (New York: The Macmillan Company, 1962), p. 222.
4. Dan Schiller, *Objectivity and the News: The Public and the Rise of Commercial Journalism* (Philadelphia: University of Pennsylvania Press, 1981), pp. 76–80.
5. Frank O'Brien, *The Story of the Sun, New York: 1833–1928* (New York: D. Appleton and Company, 1928), pp. 62–63.
6. *New York Herald*, May 6, 1835.
7. Douglas Fermer, *James Gordon Bennett and the New York Herald: A Study of Editorial Opinion in the Civil War Era, 1854–1867* (Woodbridge, United Kingdom: The Boydell Press, 1986), p. 18.
8. *New York Herald*, October 8, 1835.
9. *New York Herald*, August 31, 1835.
10. James L. Crouthamel, *Bennett's New York Herald and the Rise of the Popular Press*, pp. 19–20.
11. *New York Evening Post*, December 30, 1899.
12. *New York Herald*, July 27, 1836.
13. *New York Herald*, August 19, 1836.
14. *New York Herald*, July 20, 1836.
15. Paul Peebles, "James Gordon Bennett's Scintillations," *Galaxy* 14 (August 1872), pp. 258ff.
16. Madelon Golden Schlipp and Sharon M. Murphy, *Great Women of the Press* (Carbondale: Southern Illinois University Press, 1983), pp. 85–87.
17. James L. Crouthamel, *Bennett's New York Herald and the Rise of the Popular Press*, p. 34.
18. Oliver Carlson, *The Man Who Made News: James Gordon Bennett* (New York: Duell, Sloan and Pearce, 1942), p. 199.
19. Victor Rosewater, *History of Cooperative Newsgathering in the United States* (New York: Appleton, 1930), pp. 41–42; Frederic Hudson, *Journalism in the United States from 1690 to 1872* (New York: Harper & Brother, 1873), p. 480.
20. Oliver Carlson, *The Man Who Made News: James Gordon Bennett*, pp. 198–199.
21. *New York Herald*, March 4, 1854.
22. James L. Crouthamel, *Bennett's New York Herald and the Rise of the Popular Press*, pp. 26–27.
23. Frank Luther Mott, *American Journalism: A History: 1690–1960*, p. 235.
24. Frank Luther Mott, *American Journalism: A History: 1690–1960*, p. 20.

25. Isaac Pray, *Memoirs of James Gordon Bennett and His Time* (New York: Stringer and Townsend, 1855), p. 263.
26. Isaac Pray, *Memoirs of James Gordon Bennett and His Time*, p. 263.
27. Oliver Carlson, *The Man Who Made News: James Gordon Bennett*, p. 185.
28. Oliver Carlson, *The Man Who Made News: James Gordon Bennett*, p. 185.
29. Oliver Carlson, *The Man Who Made News: James Gordon Bennett*, p. 185.
30. Oliver Carlson, *The Man Who Made News: James Gordon Bennett*, pp. 170–171.
31. A discussion of Bennett's struggles with Catholic and Protestant churches can be found in his "Memoirs of James Gordon Bennett and His Times," pp. 276–279, and in Oliver Carlson, *The Man Who Made News: James Gordon Bennett*, pp. 213–217.
32. Richard O'Connor, *The Scandalous Mr. Bennett* (Garden City, NY: Doubleday and Company, 1962), p. 27.
33. Oliver Carlson, *The Man Who Made News: James Gordon Bennett*, p. 214.
34. Isaac Pray, *Memoirs of James Gordon Bennett*, p. 266.
35. Oliver Carlson, *The Man Who Made News: James Gordon Bennett*, pp. 209–210
36. Don C. Seitz, *The James Gordon Bennetts: Father and Son, Proprietors of the New York Herald* (Indianapolis: The Bobbs-Merrill Company, 1928), p. 84.
37. Richard Kluger, *The Paper: The Life and Death of the New York Herald Tribune* (New York: Alfred A. Knopf, 1986), pp. 13–14.
38. John Tebbell, *The Media in America* (New York: Thomas Y. Crowell Company, 1974), p. 172.
39. Don C. Seitz, *Horace Greeley: Founder of the New York Tribune* (New York: AMS Press, 1970), pp. 3–4.
40. Advertisement in *Log Cabin*, April 3, 1841.
41. James Ford Rhodes, *Historical Essays* (Port Washington, NY: Kennikat Press, 1909), p 90.
42. Don C. Seitz, *Horace Greeley: Founder of the New York Tribune*, pp. 116–117.
43. Horace Greeley, *Autobiography of . . . , or Recollections of a Busy Life* (New York: E. B. Treat, 1872), p. 508.
44. A full account of Brook Farm can be found in the January 1842 issue of *Dial*, which was edited by Margaret Fuller.
45. Don C. Seitz, *Horace Greeley: Founder of the New York Tribune*, p. 119.
46. Jules Archer, *Fighting Journalist: Horace Greeley* (New York: Julian Messner, 1966), p. 42.
47. Glyndon G. Van Deusen, *Horace Greeley: Nineteenth-Century Crusader* (New York: Hill and Wang, 1953), p. 69.
48. Neil W. Chamberlain, *Collective Bargaining* (New York: McGraw-Hill Book Company, 1951), pp. 23–31.
49. Though attributed to and popularized by Greeley, this slogan was not originated by him. He gave credit for it to John B. L. Soule, of the *Terre Haute* (Indiana) *Express*.
50. *New York Herald*, May 12, 1846.
51. *New York Tribune*, May 12, 1846.
52. *New York Tribune*, May 19, 25, 29, 1846; Robert A. Rutland, *The Newsmongers: Journalism in the Life of the Nation, 1690–1972* (New York: Doubleday, 1973), p. 156.
53. Richard Kluger, *The Paper: The Life and Death of the New York Herald Tribune*, pp. 63–64.
54. *Baltimore Sun*, April 12, 1847.
55. Richard A. Schwarzlose, "Harbor News Association: The Formal Origin of the A.P.," *Journalism Quarterly*, 45 (1968), pp. 253–60; "Early Telegraphic News Dispatches: Forerunner of the A.P.," *Journalism Quarterly* 51 (1974), pp. 595–601.
56. Tom Reilly, "The War Press of New Orleans: 1846–1848," *Journalism History* 13 (1986), pp. 86–95.
57. Richard Kluger, *The Paper: The Life and Death of the New York Herald Tribune*, pp. 63–64.
58. *New York Herald*, February 22, 25; March 11, 13, 15, 16, 1848.
59. James L. Crouthamel, *Bennett's New York Herald and the Rise of the Popular Press*, pp. 49–50.
60. *New York Tribune*, May 13, 1846.
61. Richard Kluger, *The Paper: The Life and Death of the New York Herald Tribune*, p. 64.
62. *New York Tribune*, July 3, 1848.
63. Francis Brown, *Raymond of the Times* (New York: W.W. Norton and Company, Inc., 1951), pp. 97–98.
64. *The New York-Daily Times*, September 17, 1851.

65. Francis Brown, *Raymond of the Times*, p. 98.

66. Frederic Hudson, *Journalism in the United States* (New York: Harper's, 1872), pp. 540–542.

67. Walter Lippmann, "Two Revolutions in the American Press," *Yale Review* 20 (March 1931), pp. 433–441.

68. Augustus Maverick, *Henry J. Raymond and the New York Press for Thirty Years, Progress of American Journalism from 1849 to 1870* (New York: Ayer Company Publishers, 1970), p. 53.

69. William David Sloan and James D. Startt, *The Media in America: A History* (Northport, AL: Vision Press, 1996), p. 155.

70. Michael Schudson, *Discovering the News: A Social History of American Newspapers* (New York: Basic Books, 1967), pp. 31–43.

71. Michael Schudson, *Discovering the News: A Social History of American Newspapers*, pp. 43–50.

72. Isaac Pray, *Memoirs of James Gordon Bennett*, p. 84. See Michael Schudson, *Discovering the News: A Social History of American Newspapers*, p. 46.

73. Mitchell Stephens, *A History of News* (New York: Penguin Books, 1988), p. 202.

74. Michael Schudson, *Discovering the News: A Social History of American Newspapers*, p. 22.

75. George H. Douglas, *The Golden Age of the Newspaper* (Westport, CT: Greenwood Press, 1999), pp. 2–3.

76. George H. Douglas, *The Golden Age of the Newspaper*, p. 9.

Chapter 5: A Divided Nation, a Divided Media

1. Robert Penn Warren, *The Legacy of the Civil War* (New York: Random House, 1961), p. 3.

2. Delivered June 16, 1858, at Springfield, Illinois.

3. William Hesseltine and David Smiley, *The South in American History* (Englewood Cliffs, NJ: Prentice-Hall, 1960) p. 147.

4. Merton L. Dillon, *Benjamin Lundy and the Struggle for Negro Freedom* (Urbana: University of Illinois Press, 1966), p. 18.

5. *The Liberator*, January 1, 1831.

6. *The Liberator*, May 31, 1844.

7. John Tebbel, *The Media in America* (New York: Thomas Y. Crowell Company, 1974), p. 185.

8. Saint Louis *Observer*, April 16, 1835.

9. *The Liberator*, December 8, 1837.

10. Frederick Douglass, *The Narrative and Selected Writings* (New York: The Modern Library, 1984), p. 154.

11. Frederick Douglass, *The Narrative and Selected Writings*, pp. xxii–xxiii.

12. *The North Star*, December 3, 1847.

13. J. Cutler Andrews, *The North Reports the Civil War* (Pittsburgh: University of Pittsburgh Press, 1955), p. 638.

14. Rollo Ogden, *Life and Letters of Edwin Lawrence Godkin* (New York: Classic Books, 1907), I, pp. 204–205.

15. Emmet Crozier, *Yankee Reporters, 1861–65* (New York: Oxford University Press, 1956), p. 4.

16. J. Cutler Andrews, *The North Reports the Civil War*, p. 6.

17. Brayton Harris, *Blue & Gray in Black & White: Newspapers in the Civil War* (Washington, D.C.: Batsford Brassey, 1999), pp. 6–7.

18. J. Cutler Andrews, *The North Reports the Civil War*, p. 60.

19. J. Cutler Andrews, *The North Reports the Civil War*, p. 63

20. *Cincinnati Daily Commercial*, December 29, 1862.

21. Brayton Harris, *Blue & Gray in Black & White*, p. 16.

22. Maurine Beasley and Sheila Silver, *Women in Media: A Documentary Source Book* (Washington, D.C.: Women's Institute for Freedom of the Press, 1977), p. 8.

23. Madelon Golden Schlipp and Sharon M. Murphy, *Great Women of the Press* (Carbondale: Southern Illinois University Press, 1983), p. 80.

24. Marion Marzolf, *Up From the Footnote: A History of Women Journalists* (New York: Hastings House, 1977), pp. 16–17.

25. Maurine H. Beasley and Sheila J. Gibbons, *Taking Their Place: A Documentary History of Women and Journalism* (State College, PA: Strata Publishing, 2003), p. 50.
26. Ishbel Ross, *Ladies of the Press: The Story of Women in Journalism by an Insider* (New York: Harper and Brothers, 1936), p. 332.
27. Frank Luther Mott, *American Journalism: A History: 1690–1960* (New York: The Macmillan Company, 1962), p. 363.
28. J. Cutler Andrews, *The South Reports the Civil War* (Princeton, NJ: Princeton University Press, 1970), p. 523.
29. James E. Pollard, *The Presidents and the Press* (New York: Macmillan, 1947), pp. 348, 352, 364–365.
30. Louis M. Starr, *Bohemian Brigade: Civil War Newsmen in Action* (New York: Alfred A. Knopf, 1954), p. 154.
31. Louis M. Starr, *Bohemian Brigade: Civil War Newsmen in Action* p. 158.
32. John Tebbel, *The Media in America*, pp. 194–195.
33. John Tebbel, *The Media in America*, p. 195.
34. John Tebbel, *The Media in America*, p. 197.
35. John Tebbel, *The Media in America*, pp. 197–198.
36. Murat Halstead, "Recollections and Letters of General Sherman," *Independent* 51 (June 15, 1899), pp. 1611–1612.
37. John F. Marszalek, *Sherman's Other War* (Kent, OH: Kent State University Press, 1981), pp. 63–100.
38. John Tebbell, *The Media in America*, pp. 199–200.
39. John Tebbell, *The Media in America*, p. 201.
40. John Tebbell, *The Media in America*, p. 205.
41. Frank Luther Mott, *American Journalism: A History: 1690–1960*, p. 401.
42. J. Cutler Andrews, *The North Reports the Civil War*, p. 34.
43. *Chicago Daily Tribune*, June 10, 1897.
44. *New York Times,* September 25, 1901.
45. B. Stutler, "An Eyewitness Describes the Hanging of John Brown," *American Heritage* (February 1955), pp. 4–9.
46. *Frank Leslie's Illustrated Newspaper*, November 24, 1864.
47. Michael Schudson, *Discovering the News: A Social History of American Newspapers* (New York: Basic Books, 1978), pp. 66–67.
48. David Mindich, "Edwin M. Stanton, the Inverted Pyramid, and Information Control," in David B. Sachsman, S. Kittrell Rushing, and Debra Reddin van Tuyll, eds., *The Civil War and the Press* (New Brunswick, NJ: Transaction Publishers, 2000), pp. 203–204.

Chapter 6: The Yellow Press and the *Times*

1. Geoffrey C. Ward, *The Civil War, An Illustrated History* (New York: Alfred A. Knopf, 1990), p. 273.
2. Ted Curtis Smythe, *The Gilded Age Press, 1865–1900* (Westport, CT: Praeger, 2003), p. 1.
3. Sidney Kobre, *Development of American Journalism* (Dubuque, IA: William C. Brown, 1969), p. 351.
4. Sidney Kobre, *Development of American Journalism*, p. 355.
5. James Parton, in *Harper's Monthly*, July 1874 (XLIX), p. 274.
6. John Tebbel, *The Media in America* (New York: Thomas Y. Crowell Company, 1974), p. 259.
7. John Tebbel, *The Media in America*, pp. 259–260.
8. Denis Tilden Lynch, *"Boss" Tweed: The Story of a Grim Generation* (New York: Boni and Liveright, 1927), p. 363.
9. As quoted in John Tebbel, *The Media in America*, p. 260.
10. James Wyman Barrett, *Joseph Pulitzer and His World* (New York: Vanguard Press, 1941), p. 3.
11. James Wyman Barrett, *Joseph Pulitzer and His World*, p. 3.
12. Julian S. Rammelkamp, *Pulitzer's Post-Dispatch* (Princeton, NJ: Princeton University Press, 1967), p. 19.
13. Walt McDougall, *This Is the Life* (New York: Charles Scribner's Sons, 1926), p. 138.
14. *St. Louis Post-Dispatch*, December 12, 1878.

15. *New York World*, May 11, 1883.
16. Frank Luther Mott, *American Journalism: A History: 1690–1960* (New York: The Macmillan Company, 1962), pp. 434–435.
17. Denis Brian, *Pulitzer: A Life* (New York: John Wiley and Sons, 2001), p. 66.
18. Julian S. Rammelkamp, *Pulitzer's Post-Dispatch*, p. 299.
19. *Journalist*, March 16, 1887.
20. Frank Luther Mott, *American Journalism: A History: 1690–1960*, p. 436.
21. Z. L. White, "A Decade of American Journalism," *Westminister Review*, CXXVIII (October 1887), p. 858.
22. *World,* October 3, 1883.
23. Quoted in Denis Brian, *Pulitzer: A Life*, p. 2.
24. John A. Cockerill, "Some Phrases of Contemporary Journalism," *Cosmopolitan* 13, 1892.
25. *Journalist,* August 22, 1885.
26. Denis Brian, *Pulitzer: A Life*, p. 144.
27. *New York World*, March 16, 1885.
28. Frank Luther Mott, *American Journalism: A History: 1690–1960*, pp. 437–438.
29. Michael Schudson, *Discovering the News: A Social History of American Newspapers* (New York: Basic Books, Inc., Publishers, 1978), p. 93.
30. Michael Schudson, *Discovering the News: A Social History of American Newspapers,* p. 93.
31. Frank Presbrey, *The History and Development of Advertising* (Garden City, NY: Doubleday, Doran, 1929), p. 356.
32. James Wyman Barrett, *Joseph Pulitzer and His World*, p. 154.
33. W. A. Swanberg, *Pulitzer,* p. 206.
34. Sidney Kobre, *Development of American Journalism*, pp. 384–385.
35. Sidney Kobre, *Development of American Journalism*, p. 385.
36. Joseph Campbell, *Yellow Journalism: Puncturing the Myths, Defining the Legacies* (Westport, CT: Praeger, 2003), p. 25.
37. Frank Luther Mott, *American Journalism: A History: 1690–1960*, p. 539.
38. Frank Luther Mott, *American Journalism: A History: 1690–1960*, p. 539.
39. Will Irwin, "The American Newspaper: The Spread and Decline of Yellow Journalism," reprinted in Will Irwin, *The American Newspaper* (Ames, IA: Iowa State University Press, 1969), pp. 18–20. See also Joseph Campbell, *Yellow Journalism: Puncturing the Myths, Defining the Legacies*, p. 51.
40. Frank Luther Mott, *American Journalism: A History: 1690–1960*, p. 598.
41. Joseph Campbell, *Yellow Journalism: Puncturing the Myths, Defining the Legacies*, p. 52.
42. Lydia Kingsmill Commander, "The Significance of Yellow Journalism," *Arena* 34 (August 1906), pp. 154–155.
43. *Raleigh News and Observer*, March 27, 1898. See also Joseph Campbell, *Yellow Journalism: Puncturing the Myths, Defining the Legacies*, p. 52.
44. W. A. Swanberg, *Citizen Hearst: A Biography of William Randolph Hearst* (New York: Galahad Books, 1961), p. 59.
45. *New York Evening Post*, March 17, 1898.
46. James Creelman, *On the Great Highway: The Wanderings and Adventures of a Special Correspondent* (Boston: Lothrop, 1901), pp. 177–178. However, Joseph Campbell, in *Yellow Journalism: Puncturing the Myths, Defining the Legacies,* suggests that no evidence exists that such a message was ever sent.
47. Ferdinand Lundberg, in *Imperial Hearst* (New York: Modern Library, 1937), suggests that Hearst may have had some connection with the explosion.
48. David Nasaw, *The Chief: The Life of William Randolph Hearst* (Boston: Houghton Mifflin Company, 2000), p. 125.
49. *New York Sunday Journal*, February 23, 1896.
50. David Nasaw, *The Chief: The Life of William Randolph Hearst*, p. 126.
51. David Nasaw, *The Chief: The Life of William Randolph Hearst*, p. 128.
52. *New York Journal*, October 12, 1897. See David Nasaw, *The Chief: The Life of William Randolph Hearst*, p. 129; Cora Older, *William Randolph Hearst, American* (New York: Appleton-Century, 1936), pp. 164–180;

Wilbur Cross, "The Perils of Evangelina,"*American Heritage* 19 (1968), pp. 36–39, 104–107; James Creelman, *On the Great Highway: The Wanderings and Adventures of a Special Correspondent,* pp. 258–259.

53. David Nasaw, *The Chief: The Life of William Randolph Hearst,* p. 139.
54. William Randolph Hearst's "In the News" column, July 1, 1940. See also Edmond D. Coblentz, *William Randolph Hearst, a Portrait in His Own Words,* p. 59.
55. John Stevens, *Sensationalism and the New York Press* (New York: Columbia University Press, 1993), p. 97.
56. James Creelman, *On the Great Highway: The Wanderings and Adventures of a Special Correspondent,* pp. 211–212.
57. David Nasaw, *The Chief: The Life of William Randolph Hearst,* p. 139.
58. *Pearson's Magazine,* September 1906.
59. *Collier's,* September 22, 1906.
60. *New York Journal,* April 19, 1901.
61. *New York Journal,* April 10, 1901.
62. Frank Luther Mott, *American Journalism: A History: 1690–1960,* p. 541.
63. W. A. Swanberg, *Citizen Hearst: A Biography of William Randolph Hearst,* p.159.
64. Frank Luther Mott, *American Journalism: A History: 1690–1960,* p. 540.
65. David Nasaw, *The Chief: The Life of William Randolph Hearst,* p. 428.
66. David Nasaw, *The Chief: The Life of William Randolph Hearst,* p. 428.
67. Richard Harwood, "The Fourth Estate," in *The Washington Post Guide to Washington,* Laura Longley Babb, ed. (New York: McGraw-Hill Book Company, 1976), p. 85.
68. Frank Presbrey, *The History and Development of Advertising* (Garden City, NY: Doubleday, Doran, 1929), p. 354.
69. Alva Johnson, "Twilight of the Ink-Stained Gods," *Vanity Fair,* February, 1932, pp. 36, 70.
70. Harrison E. Salisbury, *Without Fear or Favor* (New York: Times Books, 1980), p. 24.
71. Elmer Davis, *History of the New York Times: 1851–1921* (New York: The New York Times, 1921), p. 218.
72. Meyer Berger, *The Story of the New York Times 1851–1951* (New York: Simon and Schuster, 1951), p. 109. See also Michael Schudson, *Discovering the News: A Social History of American Newspapers.*
73. Elmer Davis, *History of the New York Times: 1851–1951,* pp. 223–224.
74. George Herbert Mead, "The Nature of Aesthetic Experience," *International Journal of Ethics,* XXXVI (July 1926), p. 390; see also Michael Schudson, *Discovering the News: A Social History of American Newspapers,* p. 89.
75. Walter M. Brasch and Dana R. Ulloth, *The Press and the State: Sociohistorical and Contemporary Studies* (New York: University Press of America, 1986), p. 160.
76. Richard L. Kaplan, *Politics and the American Press: The Rise of Objectivity, 1865–1920* (New York: Cambridge University Press, 2002), p. 184.
77. George H. Douglas, *The Golden Age of the Newspaper* (Westport, CT: Greenwood Press, 1999), p. 234.

Chapter 7: Magazines, Muckraking, and Public Relations

1. Louis Filler, *Crusaders for American Liberalism* (New York: Harcourt Brace Jovanovich, 1939), p. 12.
2. Louis Filler, *Crusaders for American Liberalism,* p. 13.
3. Fred J. Cook, *American Political Bosses and Machines* (New York: Franklin Watts, Inc., 1973), p. 9.
4. Fred J. Cook, *American Political Bosses and Machines,* pp. 11–12, 27.
5. Louis Filler, *Crusaders for American Liberalism,* p. 13.
6. Richard Hofstadter, *The Age of Reform: From Bryan to F.D.R.* (New York: Alfred A. Knopf, 1955), p.185.
7. Richard Hofstadter, *The Age of Reform: From Bryan to F.D.R.,* p. 186.
8. Alfred McLung Lee, *The Daily Newspaper in America* (New York: Macmillan Company, 1947), pp. 716–717.
9. John Tebbel, *The Media in America* (New York: Thomas Y. Crowell Company, 1974), p. 280.
10. Hofstadter, *The Age of Reform: From Bryan to F.D.R.,* pp. 187–188.

11. S. S. McClure, *My Autobiography* (New York: Frederick A. Stokes Co., 1913), p. 245.
12. Ellery Sedgwick, *The Happy Profession* (Boston: Little, Brown and Company, 1946), p. 142.
13. *McClure's*, January 1903.
14. Ida M. Tarbell, *The History of the Standard Oil Company* (Gloucester, MA: Peter Smith, 1904), p. 292.
15. Lincoln Steffens, *The Autobiography of Lincoln Steffens* (New York: Harcourt, Brace and Company, 1931) p. 364.
16. *McClure's*, October 1902.
17. *McClure's*, October 1902.
18. *McClure's*, October 1902.
19. Minneapolis *Tribune*, June 1, 1902.
20. Fred J. Cook, *The Muckrakers*.
21. *McClure' s*, October 1902.
22. Arthur M. Schlesinger, *Political and Social History of the United States, 1829–1925* (New York: Macmillan Company, 1925), p. 442.
23. Lincoln Steffens, *The Shame of the Cities* (New York: Peter Smith, 1948), pp. 3–4.
24. Lincoln Steffens, *The Autobiography of Lincoln Steffens* (New York: Harcourt, Brace and Company, 1931), pp. 448–449.
25. Charles Edward Russell, *Bare Hands and Stone Walls* (New York: Charles Scribner's Sons, 1933), pp. 142–143.
26. *Cosmopolitan*, February 1906.
27. *Cosmopolitan*, March 1906.
28. *Cosmopolitan*, March 1906.
29. *New York Tribune*, April 15, 1906.
30. *Appeal to Reason*, April 29, 1905.
31. *Cosmopolitan*, October 1906.
32. Upton Sinclair, *The Jungle* (New York: The Modern Library, 2002), pp. 148–149.
33. Mark Sullivan, *Our Times: The United States, 1900–1925* (New York: Charles Scribner's Sons, 1927), II, p. 479.
34. Arthur and Lila Weinberg, *The Muckrakers* (New York: Simon and Schuster, 1961), p. xxiii.
35. Fred J. Cook, *The Muckrakers* (Garden City, NY: Doubleday and Company, Inc., 1972), p. 179.
36. Ray Stannard Baker, *American Chronicle* (New York: Charles Scribner's Sons, 1945), p. 226.
37. Thomas C. Leonard, "Did the Muckrakers Muck Up Progress?" in Robert Miraldi, ed., *The Muckrakers: Evangelical Crusaders* (Westport, CT: Praeger, 2000), p. 132.
38. Thomas C. Leonard, *The Power of the Press: The Birth of American Political Reporting* (New York: Oxford University Press, 1986), p. 198.
39. Harvey N. Davis, "Spirit and Culture under the Machine," in Charles A. Beard, ed., *Toward Civilization* (Longmans, Green and Company, 1930), p. 289.
40. John Heidenry, *Theirs Was the Kingdom: Lila and DeWitt Wallace and the Story of the Reader's Digest* (New York: Norton, 1993) pp. 80–81.
41. John Tebbel and Mary Ellen Zuckerman, *The Magazine in America* (New York: Oxford University Press, 1991), p. 185.
42. *Business Week*, March 6, 1948, p. 6.
43. James L. Baughman, *Henry R. Luce and the Rise of the American News Media* (Boston, Twayne Publishers, 1987), p. 2.
44. James L. Baughman, *Henry R. Luce and the Rise of the American News Media*, p. 6.
45. James L. Baughman, *Henry R. Luce and the Rise of the American News Media*, pp. 30–33.
46. John K. Jessup, *The Ideas of Henry Luce* (New York: Atheneum, 1969), p. 13.
47. W. A. Swanberg, *Luce and His Empire* (New York: Charles Scribner's Sons, 1972), p. 32.
48. James L. Baughman, *Henry R. Luce and the Rise of the American News Media*, p. 24.
49. Bernard De Voto, "Distempers of the Press," *Harper's*, March 1937, p. 447.
50. James L. Baughman, *Henry R. Luce and the Rise of the American News Media*, p. 51.

51. W. A. Swanberg, *Luce and His Empire*, p. 75.
52. W. A. Swanberg, *Luce and His Empire*, pp. 75–78.
53. W. A. Swanberg, *Luce and His Empire*, pp. 89–90.
54. W. A. Swanberg, *Luce and His Empire*, p. 200.
55. W. A. Swanberg, *Luce and His Empire*, p. 214; James L. Baughman, *Henry R. Luce and the Rise of the American News Media*, p. 81.
56. James L. Baughman, *Henry R. Luce and the Rise of the American News Media*, pp. 83–84.
57. James L. Baughman, *Henry R. Luce and the Rise of the American News Media*, p. 91.
58. Robert T. Elson, *The World of Time Inc.* (New York: Atheneum, 1968), Vol. 1, pp. 342–343.
59. Thomas Kunkel, *Genius in Disguise* (New York: Avalon Publishing Group, 1966), p. 306.
60. Edward L. Bernays, *Public Relations* (Norman, OK: University of Oklahoma Press, 1952), p. 64.
61. Edward Bernays, *Public Relations*, p. 32.
62. Alfred McLung Lee, *The Daily Newspaper in America*, p. 427.
63. Alan R. Raucher, *Public Relations and Business 1900–1929* (Baltimore: The Johns Hopkins Press, 1968), p. 1.
64. Page Smith, *John Adams II: 1784–1829* (Westport, CT: Greenwood Press, 1963), p. 898.
65. Alan R. Raucher, *Public Relations and Business 1900–1929*, p. 2.
66. Ellis Paxon Oberholtzer, *A History of the United States since the Civil War* (New York: Macmillian Co., 1928), p. 2.
67. Edward L. Bernays, *Public Relations*, p. 60.
68. Edward L. Bernays, *Public Relations*, p. 59.
69. Ray Hiebert, *Courtier to the Crowd* (Ames: Iowa State University Press, 1966), p. 29.
70. Ray Hiebert, *Courtier to the Crowd*, p. 72.
71. Peter Collier and David Horowitz, *The Rockefellers* (New York: Holt, Rinehart and Winston, 1976), p. 152.
72. Marvin N. Olasky, *Corporate Public Relations: A New Historical Perspective* (Hillsdale, NJ: Lawrence Erlbaum Associates, Publishers, 1987), p. 50.
73. Edward Bernays writes in *Public Relations*, p. 51–52, that the phrase "the public be damned" characterized the period. One version says the phrase arose when a reporter, interviewing William Vanderbilt, head of the New York Central, asked him why he was eliminating the fast extra-fare mail train between New York and Chicago. The magnate replied that the train wasn't paying. But the public found it useful and convenient, the reporter said; shouldn't Mr. Vanderbilt accommodate the public? "The public be damned!" Mr. Vanderbilt is said to have exclaimed. "I am working for my stockholders; if the public wants the train, why don't they pay for it?" Another version, Bernays writes, was related in Roger Butterfield's *The American Past* (New York: Simon and Schuster, 1947). He relates that two reporters asked Vanderbilt about the new fast train he had just put on to cut the New York–Chicago running time. Did it pay? "No, not a bit of it," snapped the railroad king. "We only run the limited because we're forced to by the action of the Pennsylvania Railroad." "But don't you run it for the public benefit?" one reporter insisted. "The public be damned!" Vanderbilt exploded.
74. Scott Cutlip and Allen Center, *Effective Public Relations*, 5th rev. ed., (Englewood Cliffs, NJ: Prentice-Hall, 1982), p. 79.
75. Olasky, *Corporate Public Relations: A New Historical Perspective*, p. 51.
76. Olasky, *Corporate Public Relations: A New Historical Perspective*, p. 51.
77. Edward L. Bernays, *Propaganda* (New York: Liveright, 1928), p. 159.
78. Edward Bernays, *Public Relations*, p. 71.
79. Edward Bernays, *Public Relations*, p. 71.
80. Edward Bernays, *Propaganda*, p. 37.
81. Edward Bernays, *Propaganda*, p. 47.
82. Edward Bernays, *Public Relations*, pp. 78–79.
83. Edward Bernays, *Public Relations*, p. 84.
84. See Bill Moyers, "The Image Makers," *A Walk through the 20th Century*, 1984, for an account of Edward Bernays' clients, including President Calvin Coolidge, the American Tobacco Company, and Light's Golden Jubilee.

85. Edward Bernays, *Public Relations*, p. 86.
86. Carl Byoir & Associates accepted a contract in 1933 to distribute press releases to improve Germany's image in the United States, in response to publicity about German antisemitism. The account caused adverse publicity for the firm when Texas congressman Wright Patman accused the firm of Nazi propaganda.
87. *Eastern Railroad Presidents Conference* vs. *Noerr Motor Freight, Inc.*, 365 U.S. 127 (1961).
88. George H. Douglas, *The Golden Age of the Newspaper* (Westport, CT: Greenwood Press, 1999), p. 234.

Chapter 8: American Film

1. Lewis Jacobs, *The Rise of the American Film* (New York: Harcourt, Brace & Co., 1939), p. 175. After controversy arose over *The Birth of a Nation*, the White House disavowed any approval on the part of the president.
2. David Parkinson, *History of Film* (New York: Thames and Hudson, 1995), p. 7.
3. Gordon Hendricks, *Eadweard Muybridge: The Father of the Motion Picture* (New York: Grossman, 1975), p. 46.
4. Arthur Knight, *The Liveliest Art* (New York: New American Library, 1957), p. 17.
5. New York *Journal*, April 4, 1986.
6. Douglas Gomery, *Movie History: A Survey* (Belmont, CA: Wadsworth Publishing Company, 1991), p. 10.
7. David Parkinson, *History of Film*, p. 18.
8. Donald Hayne, *The Autobiography of Cecil B. De Mille* (New York: Garland Publishing Company, 1989), p. 69.
9. Noel Burch, "Porter, or Ambivalence," *Screen*, Winter 1978/79; Charles Musser, "The Early Cinema of Edwin Porter," *Cinema Journal*, Vol. 19, No. 1 (Fall 1979).
10. Edward Wagenknecht, *The Movies in the Age of Innocence* (Norman: University of Oklahoma Press, 1962), p. 89.
11. Erich von Stroheim's impassioned tribute to D. W. Griffith can be found in Peter Noble, *Hollywood Scapegoat* (London: The Fortune Press, 1950), pp. 23–28.
12. David Parkinson, *History of Film*, p. 24.
13. Richard Schickel, *D. W. Griffith: An American Life* (New York: Simon and Schuster, 1984), p. 112.
14. Jack C. Ellis, *A History of Film* (Englewood Cliffs, NJ: Prentice-Hall, 1990), p. 28.
15. Mack Sennett, *King of Comedy* (New York: Doubleday, 1954), p. 51.
16. Mack Sennett, *King of Comedy*, p. 51.
17. See Benjamin B. Hampton, *A History of the Movies* (New York: Covici Friede Publishers, 1931), pp. 64–82.
18. Arthur Knight, *The Liveliest Art* (New York: New American Library, 1957), p. 38.
19. Jack C. Ellis, *A History of Film*, pp. 101–102.
20. Richard Koszarski. *An Evening's Entertainment: The Age of the Silent Feature Picture, 1915–1928* (New York: Charles Scribner's Sons, 1990), p. 72.
21. David Parkinson, *History of Film*, p. 40.
22. Jack C. Ellis, *A History of Film*, pp. 101–103.
23. Gregory D. Black, *Hollywood Censored* (New York: Cambridge University Press, 1996), p. 9.
24. Kevin Brownlow, *Behind the Mask of Innocence* (New York: Alfred A. Knopf, 1990), p. i.
25. Garth Jowett, "A Capacity for Evil: The 1915 Supreme Court Mutual Decision," *Historical Journal of Film, Radio and Television* 9 (1989), pp. 59–78.
26. Charles M. Feldman, *The National Board of Censorship of Motion Pictures, 1909–22* (New York: Arno Press, 1975), p. 4.
27. Gregory D. Black, *Hollywood Censored* (New York: Cambridge University Press, 1996), p. 40.
28. Will H. Hays, *See and Hear* (New York: Motion Picture Producers and Distributors of America, 1929), p. 48.

29. Arthur Schlesinger Jr., "When the Movies Really Counted," *Show*, April, 1963, p. 77.
30. Andrew Bergman, *We're in the Money: Depression America and Its Films* (New York: Harper and Row, Publishers, 1971).
31. Gregory D. Black, *Hollywood Censored*, p. 72.
32. Gregory D. Black, *Hollywood Censored*, p. 39.
33. Jack C. Ellis, *A History of Film*, p. 252.
34. Victor S. Navasky, *Naming Names* (New York: Penguin Books, 1991), p. 78.
35. Victor S. Navasky, *Naming Names*, p. 26.
36. Victor S. Navasky, *Naming Names*, p. 78.
37. John Cogley, *Report on Blacklisting, Vol. 1, The Movies* (The Fund for the Republic, Inc., 1956), p. 3.
38. Victor S. Navasky, *Naming Names*, p. 79.
39. Garrick Dowhen, interview with the author, 1998, Westwood, CA.
40. See Nancy Griffin and Kim Masters, *Hit and Run* (New York: Simon and Schuster, 1996).
41. Walter M. Brasch and Dana R. Ulloth, *The Press and the State: Sociohistorical and Contemporary Studies* (New York: University Press of America, 1986), p. 215.
42. *USA Today*, January 8, 2004, pp. 1–2.

Chapter 9: Radio and its Promises

1. See Richard France, *The Theatre of Orson Welles* (Canbury, NJ: Associated University Press, Inc., 1977), pp. 171–179.
2. John Russell Taylor, *Orson Welles* (Boston: Little, Brown and Company, 1986), p. 38.
3. *New York Tribune*, November 2, 1938, pp. 6–8.
4. Christopher H. Sterling and John M. Kittross, *Stay Tuned: A Concise History of American Broadcasting* (Belmont, CA: Wadsworth Publishing Company, 1990), p. 9.
5. *Washington Post*, August 10, 1904. See Thomas W. Hoffer, "Nathan B. Stubblefield and His Wireless Telephone," *Journal of Broadcasting*, XV (Summer 1971), pp. 317–329.
6. Erik Barnouw, *Tube of Plenty: The Evolution of American Television* (New York: Oxford University Press, 1982), p. 17.
7. Carl Dreher, *Sarnoff: An American Success* (New York: Quadrangle/The New York Times Book Co., 1977), pp. 28–29, gives a different account of Sarnoff's activities on April 14, 1912, explaining that he was not on watch and could not possibly have heard the signal from the *Titanic*.
8. Eugene Lyons, *David Sarnoff* (New York: Harper and Row Publishers, 1966), p. 60.
9. David Sarnoff, *Looking Ahead: The Papers of David Sarnoff* (New York: McGraw-Hill Book Company, 1968), p. 31.
10. David Sarnoff, *Looking Ahead: The Papers of David Sarnoff*, p. 32.
11. Erik Barnouw, *Tube of Plenty: The Evolution of American Television*, p. 36.
12. Erik Barnouw, *Tube of Plenty: The Evolution of American Television*, p. 15.
13. Interview on *Empire of the Air*.
14. Sally Bedell Smith, *In All His Glory: The Life of William S. Paley* (New York: Simon and Schuster, 1990), p. 59.
15. Sally Bedell Smith, *In All His Glory: The Life of William S. Paley*, p. 46.
16. *Variety*, August 31, 1948, p. 1.
17. Christopher H. Sterling and John M. Kittross, *Stay Tuned: A Concise History of American Broadcasting*, pp. 179–180.
18. Christopher H. Sterling and John M. Kittross, *Stay Tuned: A Concise History of American Broadcasting*, p. 214.
19. Christopher H. Sterling and John M. Kittross, *Stay Tuned: A Concise History of American Broadcasting*, p. 213.
20. Michael S. Sweeney, *Secrets of Victory: The Office of Censorship and the American Press and Radio in World War II* (Chapel Hill: University of North Carolina Press, 2001), pp. 3–4.

21. F. Leslie Smith, *Perspectives on Radio and Television: Telecommunication in the United States* (New York: Harper and Row Publishers, 1990), p. 350.
22. Charles A. Siepmann, *Radio's Second Chance* (Boston: Little, Brown, 1946), pp. 82–83.
23. Arbitron, December 2003.
24. Howard Fineman, "The Power of Talk," *Newsweek*, February 8, 1993, pp. 24–28.
25. Gini Graham Scott, *Can We Talk? The Power and Influence of Talk Shows* (New York: Insight Books, 1996), p. 60.
26. Edmund L. Andrews, "F.C.C. Delays Radio Deal by Howard Stern Employer," *New York Times*, December 31, 1993, p. D2.
27. Chris Baker, *The Washington Times*, November 23, 2001.
28. J. Fred MacDonald, *Don't Touch That Dial! Radio Programming in American Life, 1920–1960* (Chicago: Nelson-Hall, 1979), p. 37.
29. Peter Laufer, *Inside Talk Radio: America's Voice or Just Hot Air?* (New York: Birch Lane Press, 1995) p. 14.
30. David C. Barker, *Rushed to Judgment: Talk Radio, Persuasion, and American Political Behavior* (New York: Columbia University Press, 2002), p. 1.
31. Many critics disagree that the traditional mass media are objective. Some argue that journalists are predominantly Democratic in their party affiliation and have a liberal bias (See Bernard Goldberg, *Bias,* New York: Dimensions, 2003). Others argue that the media are owned by large corporations and depend on advertisers to pay the bills; thus they reflect a rightward-leaning pro-business slate (See Ben Bagdikian, *The Media Monopoly,* Boston: Beacon Press, 1997).
32. David C. Barker, *Rushed to Judgment: Talk Radio, Persuasion, and American Political Behavior*, p. 1.
33. David C. Barker, *Rushed to Judgment: Talk Radio, Persuasion, and American Political Behavior*, p. 125.
34. David C. Barker, *Rushed to Judgment: Talk Radio, Persuasion, and American Political Behavior*, p. 125.
35. J. Fred MacDonald, *Don't Touch That Dial! Radio Programming in American Life, 1920–1960*, p. 41.

Chapter 10: Television: Progress and Problems

1. David E. Fisher and Marshall Jon Fisher, *The Tube: The Invention of Television* (San Diego, CA: Harcourt Brace & Company, 1996), pp. 15–16.
2. David E. Fisher and Marshall Jon Fisher, *The Tube: The Invention of Television*, p. 19.
3. David E. Fisher and Marshall Jon Fisher, *The Tube: The Invention of Television*, p. 31.
4. *London Times*, July 27, 1923.
5. *London Times*, July 19, 1928.
6. David E. Fisher and Marshall Jon Fisher, *The Tube: The Invention of Television,* pp. 131–134.
7. Printed in a booklet, "The Birth of an Industry," address by David Sarnoff, April 20, 1939.
8. Sally Bedell Smith, *In All His Glory: The Life of William S. Paley*, p. 286.
9. *Ebony*, June 1950, p. 22.
10. John E. O'Connor, ed., *American History/American Television: Interpreting the Video Past* (New York: Frederick Ungar Publishing Co., 1958), p. 39.
11. John E. O'Connor, ed., *American History/American Television: Interpreting the Video Past*, p. 33.
12. John E. O'Connor, ed., *American History/American Television: Interpreting the Video Past*, p. 39.
13. *Variety*, June 20, 1956, p. 17.
14. Fred W. Friendly, *Circumstances Beyond Our Control . . .* (New York: Random House, 1967), p. 77.
15. Joseph E. Persico, *Edward R. Murrow: An American Original* (New York: McGraw-Hill Book Company, 1988), p. 209.
16. Joseph E. Persico, *Edward R. Murrow: An American Original*, p. 300.
17. Discussed in Fred W. Friendly's, *Circumstances Beyond Our Control. . . ,* p. xix.
18. See PBS, "Edward R. Murrow: This Reporter," *American Masters*, 1990.
19. Fred W. Friendly, *Circumstances Beyond Our Control . . . ,* p. 5.
20. Joseph E. Persico, *Edward R. Murrow: An American Original*, p. 372.

21. Joseph E. Persico, *Edward R. Murrow: An American Original*, p. 372.
22. Fred W. Friendly, *Circumstances Beyond Our Control . . .* , pp. 19–20.
23. See PBS, "Edward R. Murrow: This Reporter," *American Masters*, 1990.
24. David Halberstam, *The Powers That Be* (New York: Alfred A. Knopf, 1979), p. 141.
25. Joseph E. Persico, *Edward R. Murrow: An American Original*, pp. 372–373.
26. A. M. Sperber, *Murrow: His Life and Times* (New York: Freundlich Books, 1986), p. 416.
27. Joseph E. Persico, *Edward R. Murrow: An American Original*, p. 345.
28. Joseph E. Persico, *Edward R. Murrow: An American Original*, p. 345.
29. Fred W. Friendly, *Circumstances Beyond Our Control . . .* , p. 35.
30. Fred W. Friendly, *Circumstances Beyond Our Control . . .* , p. 36.
31. *See It Now*, March 9, 1954.
32. Fred W. Friendly, *Circumstances Beyond Our Control . . .* , p. 37.
33. Fred W. Friendly, *Circumstances Beyond Our Control . . .* , p. 40.
34. Fred W. Friendly, *Circumstances Beyond Our Control . . .* , p. 40.
35. Fred W. Friendly, *Circumstances Beyond Our Control . . .* , pp. 40–41.
36. Alexander Kendrick, *Prime Time, The Life of Edward R. Murrow* (Boston: Little, Brown and Company, 1969), p. 54.
37. Fred W. Friendly, *Circumstances Beyond Our Control . . .* , p. 53.
38. Edward R. Murrow statement rebutting Senator Joseph McCarthy, April 6, 1961.
39. Fred W. Friendly, *Circumstances Beyond Our Control . . .* , p. 60.
40. David Halberstam, *The Powers That Be,* p. 145.
41. Joseph E. Persico, *Edward R. Murrow: An American Original*, p. 393.
42. Joseph E. Persico, *Edward R. Murrow: An American Original*, p. 393.
43. Fred W. Friendly, *Circumstances Beyond Our Control . . .* , pp. 87–88.
44. Fred W. Friendly, *Circumstances Beyond Our Control . . .* , p. 92.
45. Fred W. Friendly, *Circumstances Beyond Our Control . . .* , p. 99.
46. Fred W. Friendly, *Circumstances Beyond Our Control . . .* , p. 99.
47. Joseph E. Persico, *Edward R. Murrow: An American Original*, p. 447.
48. *New York Times,* October 25, 1959.
49. Fred W. Friendly, *Circumstances Beyond Our Control . . .* , p. 121.
50. Joseph E. Persico, *Edward R. Murrow: An American Original*, pp. 464–465.
51. Arthur M. Schlesinger Jr., *A Thousand Days* (Boston: Houghton Mifflin, 1965) p. 612.
52. Stanley Cloud and Lynne Olson, *The Murrow Boys: Pioneers on the Front Lines of Broadcast Journalism* (Boston: Houghton Mifflin Company, 1996), pp. 356–357.
53. Don Hewitt, *Minute by Minute* (New York: Random House, 1985), p. 26.
54. Richard S. Salant, *Salant, CBS, and the Battle for the Soul of Broadcast Journalism* (Boulder, CO: Westview Press, 1999), p. 66.
55. Richard S. Salant, *Salant, CBS, and the Battle for the Soul of Broadcast Journalism*, p. 67.
56. Richard S. Salant, *Salant, CBS, and the Battle for the Soul of Broadcast Journalism*, p. 38.
57. Allen Weinstein and David Rubel, *The Story of America: Freedom and Crisis from Settlement to Superpower* (New York: DK Publishing, Inc., 2002), pp. 290–291.
58. Allen Weinstein and David Rubel, *The Story of America: Freedom and Crisis from Settlement to Superpower*, p. 591.
59. Maurine H. Beasley & Sheila J. Gibbons, *Taking Their Place: A Documentary History of Women and Journalism* (Washington: The American University Press, 1933), p. 165.
60. David H. Hosley & Gayle K. Yamada, *Hard News: Women in Broadcast Journalism* (Westport: Greenwood Press, 1987), p. 157.
61. Patricia Bradley, *Women and the Press: The Struggle for Equality* (Evanston: Northwestern University Press, 2005), p. 115.
62. Judith Marlane, *Women in Television News Revisited* (University of Texas Press, 1999), p. 76.
63. David H. Hosley & Gayle K. Yamada, *Hard News: Women in Broadcast Journalism*, p. 131.

64. Marurine H. Beasley & Sheila J. Gibbons, *Taking Their Place: A Documentary History of Women and Journalism*, p. 227.

Chapter 11: Advertising as a Social, Economic, and Political Force

1. *USA Today,* June 20, 2005, p. B5.
2. *Appleton's,* May 1908.
3. Stephen Fox, *The Mirror Makers: A History of American Advertising and Its Creators* (New York: William Morrow and Company, 1984), p. 30.
4. C. H. Sandage et al., *Advertising Theory and Practice*, 1989, p. 32.
5. http://www.americanhistory.si.edu/archives
6. *Advertising Age,* June 6, 2008, p. 1.
7. Stephen Fox, *The Mirror Makers: A History of American Advertising and Its Creators,* p. 40.
8. TBD
9. http://adage.com.
10. Stephen Fox, *The Mirror Makers: A History of American Advertising and Its Creators,* p. 101.
11. *Nation*, March 6, 1929.
12. http://www.museum.tv/archives/etv/W/htmlW/weaversylve/weaversylve.htm

Chapter 12: The Media and National Crises

1. Michael Kelly, "David Gergen, Master of the Game: How Image Became the Sacred Faith of Washington, and How This Insider Became Its High Priest," *New York Times Sunday Magazine*, October 31, 1993, pp. 57, 97.
2. James Fallows, *Breaking the News: How the Media Undermine American Democracy* (New York: Pantheon Books, 1996), p. 267.
3. Ellen Hume, "Tabloids, Talk Radio, and the Future of News: Technology's Impact on Journalism" (Washington, D.C.: The Annenberg Washington Program in Communications Policy Studies of Northwestern University, 1995).
4. James Fallows, *Breaking the News: How the Media Undermine American Democracy,* p. 7.
5. J. Herbert Altschull, *Agents of Power: The Media and Public Policy* (New York: Longman Publishers, 1995), p. 158.
6. Daniel C. Hallin, "Whose Campaign Is It Anyway?" *Columbia Journalism Review* (January/February 1991), p. 44.
7. J. Herbert Altschull, *Agents of Power: The Media and Public Policy,* p. 158.
8. Barbara W. Tuchman, *The March of Folly: From Troy to Vietnam* (New York: Alfred A. Knopf, 1984), pp. 244–245.
9. David Halberstam, *The Making of a Quagmire* (New York: Random House, 1965).
10. *Public Papers, Dwight D. Eisenhower, 1954* (Washington, D.C.: U.S. Government Printing Office, 1960), pp. 382–384.
11. Robert S. McNamara and Brian VanDeMark, *In Retrospect: The Tragedy and Lessons of Vietnam* (New York: Times Books, 1995), pp. 321–323. McNamara also had a frank discussion about his changing beliefs about the Vietnam War on Charlie Rose's PBS broadcast in 1995.
12. Peter Braestrup, *Big Story: How the American Press and Television Reported and Interpreted the Crisis of Tet 1968 in Vietnam and Washington* (New Haven, CT: Yale University Press, 1977), p. 9.
13. Peter Braestrup, *Big Story: How the American Press and Television Reported and Interpreted the Crisis of Tet 1968 in Vietnam and Washington,* p. 20.
14. Daniel C. Hallin, *The Uncensored War: The Media and Vietnam* (New York: Oxford University Press, 1986), pp. 128–129.
15. Daniel C. Hallin, *The Uncensored War: The Media and Vietnam,* pp. 127–128.
16. Daniel C. Hallin, *The Uncensored War: The Media and Vietnam,* p. 128.

17. Peter Braestrup, *Big Story: How the American Press and Television Reported and Interpreted the Crisis of Tet 1968 in Vietnam and Washington*, p. 38.

18. Peter Braestrup, *Big Story: How the American Press and Television Reported and Interpreted the Crisis of Tet 1968 in Vietnam and Washington*, dedication.

19. See Guenter Lewy, *America in Vietnam* (New York: Oxford University Press, 1978), pp. 433–434.

20. Larry Berman, *Lyndon Johnson's War* (New York: W.W. Norton and Company, 1989), p. 183.

21. *Time*, September 20, 1963.

22. *CBS Evening News with Walter Cronkite*, August 5, 1965.

23. David Halberstam, *The Powers That Be* (New York: Alfred A. Knopf, 1979), p. 488.

24. David Halberstam, *The Powers That Be*, p. 491.

25. Peter Braestrup, *Big Story: How the American Press and Television Reported and Interpreted the Crisis of Tet 1968 in Vietnam and Washington*, p. ix.

26. Don Oberdorfer, *Tet!* (New York: Doubleday and Co., 1971), pp. 246–249.

27. Larry Berman, *Lyndon Johnson's War*, p. 175.

28. Richard Nixon, *The Memoirs of Richard Nixon* (New York: Grosset and Dunlap, 1978), p. 411.

29. Richard Nixon, *The Memoirs of Richard Nixon*, p. 411.

30. Richard Nixon, *The Memoirs of Richard Nixon*, p. 475.

31. Richard Nixon, *The Memoirs of Richard* Nixon, p. 424.

32. "The Post's Peril of '71," *Quill* 62:9 (September 1973), p. 9.

33. See Wayne Overbeck, *Principles of Communications Law* (Belmont, CA: Wadsworth Publishing Company, 2003) for a comprehensive account of the legal maneuverings associated with this case.

34. Carl Bernstein and Bob Woodward, *All the President's Men* (New York: Simon and Schuster, 1974), p. 196.

35. Carl Bernstein and Bob Woodward, *All the President's Men*, p. 127. The "Canuck letter" ended the Muskie presidential campaign.

36. Carl Bernstein and Bob Woodward, *All the President's Men*, p. 18.

37. Carl Bernstein and Bob Woodward, *All the President's Men*, p. 71.

38. CBS News, "Watergate: The Secret Story with Mike Wallace," 1992.

39. CBS News, "Watergate: The Secret Story with Mike Wallace," 1992.

40. Morton Levitt and Michael Levitt, *A Tissue of Lies: Nixon vs. Hiss* (New York: McGraw-Hill Book Company, 1979), p. xi. Hiss was convicted after two trials and sent to prison for perjury, since the statute of limitations precluded a charge of espionage.

41. Richard Nixon, *The Memoirs of Richard Nixon*, p. 249.

42. Joseph S. Spear, *Presidents and the Press: The Nixon Legacy* (Cambridge, MA: The MIT Press, 1984), p. 43.

43. Richard Nixon, *The Memoirs of Richard Nixon*, pp. 934–935.

44. Richard Nixon, *The Memoirs of Richard Nixon*, pp. 934–935.

45. Joseph S. Spear, *Presidents and the Press: The Nixon Legacy*, p. 42.

46. David Frost, *"I Gave Them a Sword": Behind the Scenes of the Nixon Interviews* (New York: Morrow, 1978), p. 134.

47. Arthur Woodstone, *Nixon's Head* (New York: St. Martin's Press, 1972), p. 40.

48. John Tebbel and Sarah Miles Watts, *The Press and the Presidency: From George Washington to Ronald Reagan* (New York: Oxford University Press, 1985), p. 516.

49. John Tebbell and Sarah Miles Watts, *The Press and The Presidency: From George Washington to Ronald Reagan*, p. 517.

50. *New York*, March 1976.

51. John Tebbel and Sarah Miles Watts, *The Press and the Presidency: From George Washington to Ronald Reagan*, p. 529.

52. John Tebbel and Sarah Miles Watts, *The Press and the Presidency: From George Washington to Ronald Reagan*, pp. 529–530.

53. Peter Meyer, *James Earl Carter: The Man and the Myth* (Kansas City, Kansas: Sheed, Andrews and McMeel, 1978), p. 144.

54. Don Bonafede, "Beat the Press," *National Journal*, December 9, 1978.
55. John Tebbel and Sarah Miles Watts, *The Press and the Presidency: From George Washington to Ronald Reagan*, p. 531.
56. Kathleen Hall Jamieson, *Packaging the Presidency: A History and Criticism of Presidential Campaign Advertising* (New York: Oxford University Press, 1984), p. 445.
57. Inaugural Address, January 20, 1981.
58. John Tebbel and Sarah Miles Watts, *The Press and the Presidency: From George Washington to Ronald Reagan*, p. 531.
59. Lou Cannon, *President Reagan: The Role of a Lifetime* (New York: Simon and Schuster, 1991), p. 12.
60. John Tebbel and Sarah Miles Watts, *The Press and the Presidency: From George Washington to Ronald Reagan*, p. 535.
61. John Tebbel and Sarah Miles Watts, *The Press and the Presidency: From George Washington to Ronald Reagan*, p. 535.
62. Lou Cannon, *President Reagan: The Role of a Lifetime*, p. 261.
63. *Washington Post,* March 18, 1982.
64. Mark Hertsgaard, *On Bended Knee: The Press and the Reagan Presidency* (New York: Farrar, Straus and Giroux, 1988) pp. 221–222.
65. Mark Hertsgaard, *On Bended Knee: The Press and the Reagan Presidency*, pp. 221–222.
66. Mark Hertsgaard, *On Bended Knee: The Press and the Reagan Presidency*, p. 341.
67. *CBS Evening News with Dan Rather*, January 25, 1988.
68. *New York Times*, February 15, 1991.
69. John MacArthur, *Second Front: Censorship and Propaganda in the Gulf War* (Berkeley: University of California Press, 1992), pp. 146–147.
70. The *Los Angeles Times* reported on November 20, 2001, that a comprehensive study of Florida's uncounted ballots showed that Bush would have won the state by several hundred votes.
71. *Time*, September 11, 2001.
72. *Time*, September 11, 2001.
73. *Los Angeles Times*, November 1, 2001.
74. *Los Angeles Times*, November 1, 2001.
75. *Los Angeles Times*, November 1, 2001.
76. *Los Angeles Times*, November 1, 2001.
77. *Los Angeles Times*, November 1, 2001.
78. *Los Angeles Times*, November 11, 2002.
79. *Weekly Standard*, March 3, 2003.
80. *Washington Post*, March 11, 2003.
81. *Los Angeles Times*, March 11, 2003.
82. *Los Angeles Times*, April 7, 2003.
83. Pew Research Center for the People and the Press, March 28, 2003.
84. Pew Research Center for the People and the Press, March 28, 2003.
85. Pew Research Center for the People and the Press, March 19. 2008.
86. Joseph C. Wilson, IV, "What I Didn't Find in Africa," *The New York Times,* July 6, 2003.
87. See Anthony R. Fellow's "The Information Function: Mediating Reality," in *Mass Communication in the Global Age,* David Copeland and Anthony Hatcher, eds. (Northport, AL: Vision Press, 2007), pp. 53–55.
88. *Time*, October 13, 2008.
89. *Los Angeles Times*, April 10, 2003.

Chapter 13: The Internet Revolution and the Information Explosion

1. *Time Magazine*, January 3, 1983, Vol. 121, No. 1.
2. Janet Abbate, *Inventing the Internet* (Cambridge, MA: The MIT Press, 2000), p. 1.

3. James Gillies & Robert Cailliau, *How the Web was Born: The Story of the World Wide Web* (New York: Oxford University Press, 2000), p. 126.
4. James Gillies & Robert Cailliau, *How the Web was Born: The Story of the World Wide Web*, p. 150.
5. Christopher Evans, *The Micro Millennium* (New York: Viking Press, 1979), p. 25.
6. Martin Campbell-Kelly & William Aspray, *A History of the Information Machine*, 2nd ed. (New York: Westview Press Books, 2004), pp. 4–9.
7. George Ifrah, *The Universal History of Computing* (New York: John Wiley & Son, Inc., 2001), p. 109.
8. George Ifrah, *The Universal History of Computing*, pp. 210–211.
9. George Ifrah, *The University History of Computing*, p. 212.
10. Roy A. Allen, *A History of the Personal Computer: The People and the Technology* (London, Ontario, Canada: Allan Publishing, 2001), pp. 1/5.
11. Roy A. Allen, *A History of the Personal Computer: The People and the Technology*, pp. 1/14–1/15.
12. James Gillies & Robert Cailliau, *How the Web was Born: The Story of the World Wide Web*, pp. 96–97.
13. Janet Abbate, *Inventing the Internet*, p. 137.
14. Roy A. Allen, *A History of the Personal Computer: The People and the Technology*, p. 6/5.
15. Roy A. Allen, *A History of the Personal Computer: The People and the Technology*, p. 9/8.
16. Roy A. Allen, *A History of the Personal Computer: The People and the Technology*, p. 9/8.
17. Roy A. Allen, *A History of the Personal Computer: The People and the Technology*, p. 10/23.
18. Roy A. Allen, *A History of the Personal Computer: The People and the Technology*, p. 12/19.
19. Johnathan Zittrain, *The Future of the Internet and How to Stop It* (New Haven: Yale University Press, 2008), p. 1.
20. James Gillies & Robert Cailliau, *How the Web was Born: The Story of the World Wide Web*, p. 1.
21. Janet Abbate, *Inventing the Internet*, pp. 1–2.
22. Manuel Castells, *The Internet Galaxy: Reflections on the Internet, Business, and Society* (New York: Oxford University Press, 2001), p. 10.
23. J. R. Okin, *The Internet Revolution: The Not-For-Dummies Guide to the History, Technology and Use of the Internet*, p. 55.
24. J. R. Okin, *The Internet Revolution: The Not-For-Dummies Guide to the History, Technology and Use of the Internet*, p. 56.
25. J. R. Okin, *The Internet Revolution: The Not-For-Dummies Guide to the History, Technology and Use of the Internet*, p. 207.
26. Katie Hafner & Matthew Lyon, *Where Wisards Stay Up Late: The Origins of the Internet* (New York: Simon & Schuster Paperbacks, 1996), p. 189.
27. J. R. Okin, *The Internet Revolution: The Not-For-Dummies Guide to the History, Technology and Use of the Internet*, p. 208.
28. J. R. Okin, *The Internet Revolution: The Not-For-Dummies Guide to the History, Technology and Use of the Internet*, p. 109.
29. J. R. Okin, *The Internet Revolution: The Not-For-Dummies Guide to the History, Technology and Use of the Internet*, p. 110.
30. Bruce R. Schatz & Joseph B. Hardin, "NCSA Mosaic and the World Wide Web: Global Hypermedia Protocols for the Internet, *Science 265* (1994), pp. 897, 900.
31. Tim Berners-Lee, Robert Cailliau, Ari Luotonen, Henrik Frystyk Nielsen, & Arthur Secret, "The World-Wide Web." *Communications of the ACM 37* (1994), p. 80.
32. J. R. Okin, *The Internet Revolution: The Not-For-Dummies Guide to the History, Technology and Use of the Internet*, p. 111.
33. Patricia Sellers, "MySpace Cowboys", *Money,* CNN.com, April 9, 2006.
34. Michael Wesch, "YouTube Statistics," *Digital Ethnography*, Kansas State University, 2008.
35. This number comes from Quantcast.com, a media measurement service that lets advertisers view audience reports on millions of websites and services.
36. Yi-Win Yen, "YouTube Looks for the Money Clip," *CNN.com,* March 25, 2008.
37. Pew Research Center for the People and the Press, September 15, 2008.

38. Andrew Chadwick. *Internet Politics: States, Citizens, and New Communication Technologies* (New York: Oxford University Press, 2006), p. 162.
39. Pew Research Center for the People and the Press, July 19, 2006.
40. Michael Cornfield and Lee Rainie, "The Impact of the Internet on Politics," *Washington Post*, November 5, 2006.
41. Roland E. Wolseley, *The Black Press, U.S.A.* (Ames, IA: Iowa State University, Press, 1990), p. 306.
42. Patrick S. Washburn, *The African American Newspaper: Voice of Freedom* (Evanston, Illinois: Northwestern University Press, 2006), pp. xii–xiii.
43. Annette Walker, "Black-Owned Radio Stations Struggle to Survive," *The Black World Today*, July 27, 2005, on http://www.tbwt.org/index.php?option=content&task=view&id=525&Itemid=2.
44. "Black-Owned TV Stations Nearly Extinct," *New American Media*, January 2, 2008, on http://news.ncmonline.com/news/view_article.html?article_id=e62b69d9845c083523c04dd0d9cda407.
45. "Where the Action Is," *Brandweek* 44 (2003), pp. 48, 50, 52–54, 56; Ray Richmond, "Now You See Them, Now You Don't," *Hollywood Reporter* 377 (2003), pp. 70–72; Jeffrey M. Humphreys, *The Multicultural Economy* (Athens, GA: The University of Georgia. 2006), p. 15.
46. Denis Seguin, "In Search of America's El Dorado," *Screen International* (2006), pp. 10, 12.
47. Scott McClellan, "Telemundo Trumpets Hispanic Power," *Broadcasting & Cable* 133 (2003), p. 19.
48. Edward Alwood, *Straight News: Gays, Lesbian, and the News Media* (New York: Columbia University Press, 1996), p. 79.
49. *The 2006 Gay Press Report*, sponsored by Prime Access Inc., a New York advertising agency, and Rivendell Media Company Inc., a media placement firm based in Westfield, NJ, p. 5.
50. *The 2006 Gay Press Report*, p.3.
51. Ben H. Bagdikian, *The New Media Monopoly* (Boston: Beacon Press, 2004), pp. 3–6.
52. Ben H. Bagdikian, *The New Media Monopoly*, p. 9.
53. Ben H. Bagdikian, *The New Media Monopoly*, p. 16.
54. Robert W, McChesney, *Rich Media Poor Democracy: Communication Politics in Dubious Times* (Urbana, II: University of Illinois Press, 1999), p. 64.
55. Alan Murray, "Broadcasters Get a Pass on Campaign Reform," *Wall Street Journal*, September 29, 1997, p. A1; Leslie Wayne, "Broadcast Lobby's Formula: Airtime + Money=Influence," *New York Times*, May 5, 1997, pp.C1, C9; Jeffrey H. Birnbaum, "Washington's Power 25," *Fortune*, December 8, 1997, pp. 144–58.
56. Ben H. Bagdikian, *The New Media Monopoly*, 6th ed. (Boston: Beacon Press, 2000), p. xvii.
57. Ted Turner, "My Beef with Big Media," *Washington Monthly*, July/August 2004.
58. Robert W. McChesney, *Communication Revolution: Critical Junctures and the Future of Media* (New York: The New Press, 2007), p. xiii.
59. Ben H. Bagdikian, *The New Media Monopoly*, p. 10.
60. Ben H. Bagdikian, *The New Media Monopoly*, p.10.
61. Ben H. Bagdikian, *The New Media Monopoly*, p. 192.
62. David Porter, *Internet Culture* (New York: Routledge, 1996), p. 166.

ANNOTATED BIBLIOGRAPHY

Introduction: Before the American Experience

Altschull, J. Herbert. *From Milton to McLuhan*. White Plains, NY: Longman, 1990. The author's chief purpose is to demonstrate that American journalists, in their pursuit of facts, do indeed have a professional philosophy, which has been arrived at through the assimilation of intellectual concepts that form the basis of Western civilization.

Brasch, Walter M., and Dana R. Ulloth. *The Press and the State: Sociohistorical and Contemporary Interpretation*. New York: University Press of America, 1986. Among the finest books to explain the concepts that define the limits of expression within the state.

Eisenstein, Elizabeth L. *The Printing Press as an Agent of Change*. Cambridge: Cambridge University Press, 1997. A classic on the shift from script to print in Western Europe and the relationship between the communications shift and other developments conventionally associated with the transition from medieval to early modern times.

Man, John. *Gutenberg: How One Man Remade the World with Words*. New York: John Wiley & Sons, 2002. The author attempts to present as much information as is known about the creator of the "third revolution." It is the most current biography of Johannes Gutenberg and the impact of his invention.

Stephens, Mitchell. *A History of News*. New York: Penguin Books, 1988. An investigation into man's enduring need to gather and spread news. It sketches the long history of news and explores its implications for the understanding of news, of journalism, and of history.

Chapter 1: The Colonial Years

Beasley, Maurine H., and Sheila J. Gibbons. *Taking Their Place: A Documentary History of Women and Journalism*. State College, PA: Strata Publishing Company, 2003. A history of the vital roles women have played in U.S. journalism.

Boorstin, Daniel J. *The Americans: The Colonial Experience*. New York: Random House, 1958. Stresses the notion that America grew in search of community. This is the first of three volumes.

Brigham, Clarence S. *A History and Bibliography of American Newspapers, 1690–1820*. 2 vols. Worcester, MA: American Antiquarian Society, 1947. Provides brief descriptions, names, dates, and locations of existing copies of colonial newspapers to 1820.

Franklin, Benjamin. *The Autobiography of Benjamin Franklin*. 2nd ed. New Haven, CT: Yale University Press, 1964. Prepared and annotated by the editors of *The Papers of Benjamin Franklin*. Contains a Foreword by Edmund S. Morgan.

Isaacson, Walter. *Benjamin Franklin*. New York: Simon and Schuster, 2003. A contemporary analytical perspective of one of the nation's most fascinating and inventive citizens.

Kobre, Sidney. *The Development of the Colonial Newspaper*. Pittsburgh: The Colonial Press, 1944. A classic study that focuses on political, economic, and social forces that influenced the development of American journalism.

Marzolf, Marion. *Up from the Footnote: A History of Women Journalists*. New York: Hastings House Publishers, 1977. The author reassesses the contributions of women journalists, moving them from footnotes to roles as major players.

Morgan, Edmund S. *Benjamin Franklin*. New Haven, CT: Yale University Press, 2002. The author dissects Benjamin Franklin's personality and mind as well as his social self and political beliefs in this short biography.

Mott, Frank Luther. *American Journalism: A History: 1690–1960*. New York: Macmillan, 1941; rev. eds., 1950, 1962. A detailed account of the history of American journalism by one of the nation's outstanding scholars.

Schlipp, Madelon Golden, and Sharon M. Murphy. *Great Women of the Press*. Carbondale: Southern Illinois Press, 1983. In-depth biographies of important women and their contributions to American journalism.

Thomas, Isaiah. *History of Printing in America*. 2 vols. Worcester, MA: Isaiah Thomas Jr., 1810; Albany, NY: Joel Munsell, 1874. An encyclopedic account of the printers and newspapers in each of the colonies.

Van Doren, Carl. *Benjamin Franklin*. New York: Viking, 1938. Biography of America's most famous printer-journalist.

Chapter 2: The Press and the Revolution

Bailyn, Bernard. *The Ideological Origins of the American Revolution*. Cambridge, MA: Harvard University Press, 1967. Utilizing the Harvard Library pamphlet collection, shows the American Revolution was primarily an ideological struggle for greater political freedom and equality.

Davidson, Philip. *Propaganda in the American Revolution, 1763–1783*. Chapel Hill, NC: University of North Carolina Press, 1941. Propagandists using pamphlets, books, and broadsides fomented and helped the country win independence.

Langguth, A. J. *Patriots: The Men Who Started the American Revolution*. New York: Simon and Schuster, 1988. Detailed account of battles and patriots, including James Otis, Samuel Adams, Patrick Henry, and John Hancock.

Miller John C. *Sam Adams: Pioneer in Propaganda*. Boston: Little, Brown, 1936. Adams, a consummate politician, prodded others to accept that his way was the right way toward independence.

Schlesinger, Arthur M. *Prelude to Independence: The Newspaper War on Great Britain, 1764–1776*. New York: Knopf, 1958. Documents role of newspapers in promoting the spread of revolution.

Teeter, Dwight L. "King Sears, the Mob, and Freedom of the Press in New York, 1765–76," *Journalism Quarterly*, XLI (Autumn 1964), 539. Patriots didn't extend freedoms they were fighting for to James Rivington, whose business was destroyed.

Woodward, W. E. *Tom Paine: America's Godfather*. New York: E.P. Dutton and Company, 1945. The author attempts to refute the accumulation of lies, false impressions, twisted remarks, and untrue and slanderous episodes surrounding America's godfather.

Chapter 3: The Press and the Founding of a Nation

Boorstin, Daniel. *The Americans: The National Experience*. New York: Random House, 1965. With a focus on consensus history, Boorstin traces social history to the Civil War.

Fay, Bernard. *The Two Franklins: Fathers of American Democracy*. Boston: Little, Brown, 1933. Contrast between Benjamin Franklin and his grandson Benjamin Franklin Bache.

Leary, Lewis. *That Rascal Freneau*. New Brunswick, NJ: Rutgers University Press, 1941. The challenges and failures of the Anti-Federalist editor.

Leonard, Thomas C. *The Power of the Press: The Birth of American Political Reporting*. New York: Oxford University Press, 1986. Traces the rise of political reporting; has an excellent chapter on the "unfeeling accuracy" of the party press era.

Levy, Leonard W. *Emergence of a Free Press*. New York: Oxford University Press, 1985. A detailed account of the fight for press freedom, with the author's interpretation of what the framers meant by it.

McCullough, David. *John Adams*. New York: Simon and Schuster, 2001. Perhaps the best written account of the life, mission, and impact of one of the nation's founders.

Schudder, Horace E. *Noah Webster*. Boston: Houghton Mifflin, 1882. A concise biography of this man of letters who fought on the side of the Federalists.

Stewart, Donald H. *The Opposition Press of the Federalist Period*. Albany: State University of New York Press, 1969. A study on the content of Federalist and Republican newspapers.

Woodward, W. E. *Tom Paine: America's Godfather*. New York: E.P. Dutton and Company, 1945. The author works to present a true picture of the much maligned Tom Paine and his place in American history.

Chapter 4: A Press for the Masses

Archer, Jules. *Fighting Journalist: Horace Greeley*. New York: Julian Messner, 1966. A short biography of Greeley as journalist.

Brown, Francis. *Raymond of the Times*. New York: Norton, 1951. Biography.

Carson, Oliver. *The Man Who Made News*. New York: Duell, Sloan and Pearce, 1942. Biography of James Gordon Bennett Sr.

Crouthamel, James L. *Bennett's New York Herald and the Rise of the Popular Press*. Syracuse, NY: Syracuse University Press, 1989. Details of Bennett's contributions to journalistic practices.

Fermer, Douglas. *James Gordon Bennett and the New York Herald: A Study of Editorial Opinion in the Civil War Era 1854–1867*. Woodbridge, United Kingdom: The Boydell Press, 1986. Explores Bennett's editorship from 1854 until after the Civil War, when he transferred the active duties of management to his son.

Kluger, Richard. *The Paper: The Life and Decline of the New York Herald Tribune*. New York: Alfred A. Knopf, 1986. Detailed account of the publication of the *Herald Tribune* and its founder, Horace Greeley.

O'Connor, Richard. *The Scandalous Mr. Bennett*. Garden City, NY: Doubleday and Company, 1962. Focuses on the younger Bennett, who, as Elmer Davis wrote, with his father "invented almost everything, good and bad, in modern journalism."

Parton, James. *Life of Horace Greeley.* New York: Mason Brothers, 1855. Biography.

Pray, Isaac. *Memoirs of James Gordon Bennett and His Times.* New York: Stringer and Townsend, 1855. An unauthorized memoir and very positive compliment "to the man whose mind and industry have left such marked traces of his progress through the thorny ways of journalism, as to furnish ample materials for a history."

Schudson, Michael. *Discovering the News: A Social History of American Newspapers.* New York: Basic Books, 1978. Five essays examine the development of the penny press, reporting, and objectivity.

Seitz, Don. C. *Horace Greeley: Founder of The New York Tribune.* New York: AMS Press, 1970. An account of Greeley and what he did, how he did it, and what manner of man he was.

Seitz, Don C. *The James Gordon Bennetts: Father and Son, Proprietors of the New York Herald.* Indianapolis: The Bobbs-Merrill Company, 1928. Makes the point that had the son been less a sybarite he would have excelled the father.

Shiller, Dan. *Objectivity and the News: The Public and the Rise of Commercial Journalism.* Philadelphia: University of Pennsylvania Press, 1981. The penny press spurred objectivity in reporting.

Van Deusen, Glyndon G. *Horace Greeley: Nineteenth-Century Crusader.* New York: Hill and Wang, 1953. An account of Horace Greeley and his America.

Chapter 5: A Divided Nation, a Divided Media

Andrews, J. Cutler. *The North Reports the Civil War.* Pittsburgh: University of Pittsburgh Press, 1955. A story of the men in the North who collected, wrote, and transmitted the news.

Andrews, J. Cutler. *The South Reports the Civil War.* Princeton, NJ: Princeton University Press, 1970. A story of the men in the South who collected, wrote, and transmitted the news.

Beasley, Maurine H. and Sheila J. Gibbons. *Taking Their Place: A Documentary History of Women in Journalism.* State College, PA: Strata Publishing, 2003. An overall view of the issues faced by women working in journalism.

Beasley, Maurine H. and Sheila Silver. *Women in Media: Documentary Source Book.* Washington, D.C.: Women's Institute for Freedom of the Press, 1977. An account of Jane Grey Swisshelm and Sara Clarke Lippincott.

Belford, Barbara. *Brilliant Bylines: A Biographical Anthology of Notable Newspaperwomen in America.* New York: Columbia University Press, 1986. Biographies of famous women journalists, including Civil War crusader and feminist Jane Grey Swisshelm.

Crozier, Emmet. *Yankee Reporters, 1861–65.* New York: Oxford University Press, 1956. Details the work of Civil War "specials," conveying the color and tension of the period.

Douglass, Frederick. *The Narrative and Selected Writings.* New York: The Modern Library, 1984. The early works of Frederick Douglass, focusing upon his struggle for freedom and autonomy.

Filler, Louis. *Crusade Against Slavery: Friends, Foes and Reforms, 1820–1860.* Algonac, MI: Reference Publications, Inc., 1986. The author provides an account of the changing winds in public awareness of the abolitionist saga.

Genovese, Eugene D. *The Political Economy of Slavery.* Middletown, CT: Wesleyan University Press, 1989. His central point is that slaveholders were honorable and admirable people who could be neither bought nor frightened and who therefore had to be crushed as a class.

Harris, Brayton. *Blue & Gray in Black & White: Newspapers in the Civil War.* Washington, D.C.: Batsford Brassey, Inc., 1999. A guided tour of highlights as covered by, and at times influenced by, the press.

Marszalek, John F. *Sherman's Other War: The General and the Civil War Press.* Kent, OH: Kent State University Press, 1999. An account of the Civil War general's battle with the press.

Marzolf, Marion. *Up from the Footnote: A History of Women Journalists.* New York: Hastings House, 1977. Discusses the women journalists' contributions to the abolitionist press.

Morison, Samuel E., and Henry S. Commager. *The Growth of the American Republic.* vol. 1. New York: Oxford University Press, 1962. In-depth history of the United States.

Mott, Frank Luther. *American Journalism: A History: 1690–1960.* New York: Macmillan Company, 1962. One of the major media history texts; provides an account of journalism's development during the decade of the 1850s.

Perry, James M. *A Bohemian Brigade: The Civil War Correspondents— Mostly Rough, Sometimes Ready.* New York: John Wiley and Sons, 2000. A newspaperman's perspective on the reporters, rogues, and heroes of the Civil War.

Reynolds, Donald E. *Editors Make War: Southern Newspapers in the Secession Crisis.* Nashville, TN: Vanderbilt University Press, 1970. Analyzes the evolution of newspaper opinion in the eleven Confederate states from a unionist position in early 1860 to a predominantly secessionist viewpoint a year later.

Sachsman, David B., S. Kittrell Rushing, and Debra Reddin van Tuyll. *The Civil War and the Press.* New Brunswick, NJ: Transaction Publishers, 1999. Compilation of papers presented at a conference on the Civil War.

Schlipp, Madelon Golden, and Sharon M. Murphy. *Great Women of the Press.* Carbondale: Southern Illinois University Press, 1983. An account of famous women journalists from Elizabeth Timothy, the first woman publisher, to Marguerite Higgins, the war correspondent.

Starr, Louis M. *Bohemian Brigade: Civil War Newsmen in Action.* New York: Alfred A. Knopf, 1954. Documents news coverage of Civil War battles and the effects of newspaper reporting on the war.

Warren, Robert Penn. *The Legacy of the Civil War.* New York: Random House, 1961. Meditations on the centennial of the Civil War.

Chapter 6: The Yellow Press and the *Times*

Barrett, James Wyman. *Joseph Pulitzer and his World*. New York: The Vanguard Press, 1941.An in-depth look at Joseph Pulitzer in a good and a bad light. The author writes that America's debt to Pulitzer resides in the fact that he not only gave to journalism its most distinctive impulse and its most sensational success, but also provided its most moving tragedy.

Brian, Denis. *Pulitzer: A Life*. New York: John Wiley and Sons, Inc., 2001. The most current biography of Pulitzer, who is praised by the author as the Shakespeare, Einstein, and Churchill of journalists.

Brown, Francis. *Raymond of the Times*. New York: W.W. Norton and Company, 1951. An exhaustive study of Henry Raymond, his journalism, and his politics.

Campbell, W. Joseph. *Yellow Journalism: Puncturing the Myths, Defining the Legacies*. Westport, CT: Praeger, 2003. A study of yellow journalism, its origin and its myths.

Hearst, William Randolph Jr. *The Hearsts: Father and Son*. Niwot, CO: Roberts Rinehart Publishers, 1991. A revealing book about one of the most influential families in American history.

Milton, Joyce. *The Yellow Kids: Foreign Correspondents in the Heyday of American Journalism*. New York: Harper and Row, 1989. Discusses noted correspondents from 1895 to 1898.

Nasaw, David. *The Chief: The Life of William Randolph Hearst*. Boston: Houghton Mifflin Co., 2000. A definitive and one of the best written biographies of the man of prodigious appetites—for politics, for women, and for personal possessions—based on private and business papers and interviews that were unavailable to previous biographers.

Salisbury, Harrison E. *Without Fear or Favor*. New York: New York Times Books, 1980. Known as a controversial inside look at the *New York Times* break with the Establishment and its coming of age as the world's greatest newspaper.

Schudson, Michael. *Discovering the News: A Social History of American Newspapers*. New York: Basic Books, 1978. Explains the development of two forms of journalism that emerged in the 1890s.

Seitz, Don C. *Joseph Pulitzer: His Life and Letters*. New York: Simon and Schuster, 1924. The first study of Pulitzer, written by his business manager.

Smythe, Ted Curtis. "The Reporter, 1880–1900: Working Conditions and Their Influence on the News," *Journalism History*, VII (Spring 1980), 1.

Swanberg, W. A. *Pulitzer*. New York: Scribner's, 1967. An interesting account of the complex newspaper publisher.

Swanberg, W. A. *Citizen Hearst*. New York: Scribner's, 1961. A well-written biography of one of the most colorful publishers in the nation's history.

Chapter 7: Magazines, Muckraking, and Public Relations

Baughman, James L. *Henry R. Luce and the Rise of the American News Media*. Boston: Twayne Publishers, 1987. The character and accomplishments of the builder of the greatest publishing empire in twentieth-century America, revealed in a readable and fascinating story.

Bernays, Edward L. *Crystallizing Public Opinion*. 2nd ed. New York: Liveright Publishing, 1961. The father of public relations describes the scope and function of his profession.

Bernays, Edward L. *Propaganda*. New York: Liveright, 1928.

Bernays, Edward L. *Public Relations*. Norman: University of Oklahoma Press, 1952. Bernays' interpretation of the history of public relations.

Cook, Fred J. *The Muckrakers: Crusading Journalists Who Changed America*. Garden City, NY: Doubleday and Company, 1972. An account of the evolution of muckraking and its major players.

Filler, Louis. *Crusaders for American Liberalism*. New York: Harcourt Brace Jovanovich, 1939. A study of the 1902 to 1914 muckrakers.

Heidenry, John. *Theirs Was the Kingdom: Lila and DeWitt Wallace and the Story of the Reader's Digest*. New York: W.W. Norton and Company, 1993. An account of how *Reader's Digest* became one of the world's most influential periodicals.

Jessup, John K., ed. *The Ideas of Henry Luce*. New York: Atheneum, 1969. The purpose of this volume, according to the editor, is to reveal the mind of Henry Robinson Luce in his own words.

Kobler, John. *Luce: His Time, Life and Fortune*. London: MacDonald, 1968. One of the first biographies written about Luce with interviews by his wife, Clare Boothe Luce.

Leonard, Thomas C. *The Power of the Press: The Birth of American Political Reporting*. New York: Oxford University Press, 1986. Excellent chapter on the impact of muckraking on voting.

Olasky, Marvin N. *Corporate Public Relations: A New Historical Perspective*. Hillsdale, NJ: Lawrence Erlbaum Associates, 1987. A story of convoluted philosophy and tawdry practice. Tells how major corporate public relations leaders have worked diligently to kill free enterprise by promoting government–big business collaboration.

Phillips, David Graham. *The Treason of the Senate,* George E. Mowry and Judson A. Grenier, eds. Chicago; Quadrangle Books, 1964. Discussion and text of Phillips's famous work.

Raucher, Alan R. *Public Relations and Business, 1900–1929*. Baltimore: The Johns Hopkins University Press, 1968. An examination of the interrelationship of ideas and actions in the study of public relations.

Serrin, Judith and William. *Muckraking! The Journalism That Changed America*. A compilation of work by "writers of exposure."

Sinclair, Upton. *The Jungle*. New York: Doubleday, Page and Co., 1906. Famous novel about the meatpacking industry.

Steffens, Lincoln. *The Autobiography of Lincoln Steffens*. New York: Harcourt, Brace and Company, 1931.

Steffens, Lincoln. *The Shame of the Cities*. New York: McClure, Phillips, 1904. Brings under one cover the author's six magazine articles exposing the corruption of American municipal government.

Swanberg, W. A. *Luce and His Empire*. New York: Charles Scribner's Sons, 1972. The definitive biography of a complex and intriguing media giant.

Tarbell, Ida M. *All in the Day's Work*. New York: Macmillan, 1939. The first woman muckraker looks at her work.

Tarbell, Ida M. *The History of the Standard Oil Company*. Gloucester, MA: Peter Smith, 1904. Considered one of the most controversial works in the muckraking period.

Tedlow, Richard S. *Keeping the Corporate Image: Public Relations and Business, 1900–1950*. Greenwich, CT: JAI Press, 1979. A study that focuses on those who not only act as press liaisons but also have exerted, or at least tried to exert, influence on policy.

Weinberg, Arthur, and Lila Weinberg, eds. *The Muckrakers*. New York: Simon and Schuster, 1961. Includes the most significant magazine articles of 1902–1912.

Chapter 8: American Film

Balio, Tino. *The American Film Industry*. Madison: University of Wisconsin Press, 1976. A systematic survey of the history of the industry, focusing on the economics, legal restraints, technological advances, studio organization, and procedures that have influenced the form and content of the movies.

Bergman, Andrew. *We're in the Money*. New York: Harper and Row Publishers, 1971. Studies the role moving pictures played in the lives of Americans during the abysmal days of the early thirties.

Black, Gregory D. *Hollywood Censored*. New York: Cambridge University Press, 1996. Examines how hundreds of films were censored to promote a conservative political agenda during the golden era of studio production in the 1930s.

Couvares, Francis G., ed. *Movie Censorship and American Culture*. Washington, D.C.: Smithsonian Institution Press, 1996. The book's eleven essays explore nearly a century of struggle over cinematic representations of sex, crime, violence, religion, race, and ethnicity, revealing that the effort to regulate the screen has reflected deep social and cultural cleavages.

Ellis, Jack C. *A History of Film*. Englewood Cliffs, NJ: Prentice-Hall, 1990. A study of the world history of narrative fiction film.

Giannetti, Louis. *Masters of the American Cinema*. Englewood Cliffs, NJ: Prentice-Hall, 1981. Eighteen representative fiction filmmakers—beginning with D. W. Griffith and concluding with Robert Altman—are the focus of this comprehensive survey of American cinema.

Gomery, Douglas. *Movie History*. Belmont, CA: Wadsworth Publishing Company, 1991. A methodological basis for studying film is advanced in this survey of major films, filmmakers, and cinema institutions. Four perspectives on American film history are presented: as artistic expression; as economic proposition; as production of and catalyst for social influence; and as representation of technological advance.

Griffin, Nancy, and Kim Masters. *Hit and Run*. New York: Simon and Schuster, 1996. An improbable and often hilarious story—good enough for a motion picture—of how two film packagers, Jon Peters and Peter Guber, took the Sony Corporation for a ride in Hollywood after they were put in charge of Columbia Pictures.

Hampton, Benjamin B. *A History of the Movies*. New York: Covici, Friede Publishers, 1931. The story of motion-picture development from peep shows to the early 1930s.

Higham, Charles. *Louis B. Mayer, M.G.M. and the Secret Hollywood*. New York: Donald I. Fine, 1993. The character and genius of this complex "merchant of dreams" is revealed in a tell-all book of little-known Hollywood tales. A gripping account of the public successes and private agonies of the man who personified the Hollywood mogul.

Knight, Arthur. *The Liveliest Art*. New York: New American Library, 1957. A complete and very readable history of motion pictures from their birth to the late 1950s.

Navasky, Victor S. *Naming Names*. New York: Penguin Books, 1991. The definitive book on the House Committee on Un-American Activities and its 1950s investigation of Hollywood.

Parkinson, David. *History of Film*. New York: Thames and Hudson, 1996. Film from its prehistory to developments in world cinema since 1970 is explored.

Toll, Robert C. *The Entertainment Machine*. New York: Oxford University Press, 1982. The chapter on motion picture as medium provides a very readable history of the development of movies in America.

Wagenknecht, Edward. *The Movies in the Age of Innocence*. Norman: University of Oklahoma Press, 1962. An attempt to record what the first motion pictures looked like to the generation for which they were created.

Chapter 9: Radio and Its Promises

Czitrom, Daniel J. *Media and the American Mind: From Morse to McLuhan*. Chapel Hill: University of North Carolina Press, 1984. An intellectual history of modern communications, which looks at media development not merely as a formal history of ideas but as the history of symbolic action and meaning, and its relation to human behavior.

Dreher, Carl. *Sarnoff: An American Success*. New York: Quadrangle/ The New York Times Book Co., 1977. A biography of David Sarnoff.

Hilliard, Robert L., and Michael C. Keith. *The Broadcasting Century and Beyond: A Biography of American Broadcasting*. Boston: Focal Press, 2001. Depicts the events, people, programs, and companies that made television and radio dominant forms of communication.

Lyons, Eugene. *David Sarnoff*. New York: Harper and Row Publishers, 1966. A biography of an untypical success story.

MacDonald, J. Fred. *Don't Touch That Dial*. Chicago: Nelson-Hall, 1979. An account of radio programming in American life from 1920 to 1960.

McChesney, Robert W. *Telecommunications: Mass Media and Democracy: The Battle for the Control of U.S. Broadcasting*,

1928–1935. New York: Oxford University Press, 1994. Focuses on the success of commercial interests in radio's early development.

Siepmann, Charles A. *Radio's Second Chance.* Boston: Little, Brown, 1946. Looks at the impact of radio on America.

Smith, F. Leslie. *Perspectives on Radio and Television: Telecommunications in the United States.* New York: Harper and Row, 1990. A comprehensive history of broadcasting.

Smith, Sally Bedell. *In All His Glory.* New York: Simon and Schuster, 1990. An outstanding biography of William S. Paley, television's greatest tycoon.

Smulyan, Susan. *Selling Radio: The Commercialization of American Broadcasting 1920–1934.* Washington, D.C.: Smithsonian Institution Press, 1994. Argues that the emergence of commercialized broadcasting was not an inevitable development but rather the result of a bitter struggle over the form and content of the new technology.

Sterling, Christopher H., and John M. Kittross. *Stay Tuned: A History of American Broadcasting.* Third Edition. Mahwah, NJ.: Lawrence Erlbaum, 2001. Traces the history of broadcasting from radio to cable to the internet.

Sweeney, Michael S. *Secrets of Victory: The Office of Censorship and the American Press and Radio in World War II.* Chapel Hill: University of North Carolina Press, 2001. Examines the World War II censorship program and analyzes the reasons for its success.

Chapter 10: Television: Progress and Problems

Barnouw, Erik. *Tube of Plenty.* New York: Oxford University Press, 1982. An anecdotal history of the evolution of American television.

Fisher, David E., and Marshall Jon Fisher. *The Tube: The Invention of Television.* San Diego: Harcourt Brace & Company, 1996. The definitive story of the inventors of television, including details of the systems they built.

Friendly, Fred W. *Due to Circumstances Beyond Our Control...* New York:

Random House, 1967. An interesting first-person account of his years with Edward R. Murrow.

Goldenson, Leonard H. *Beating the Odds.* New York: Charles Scribner's Sons, 1991. A personal saga of Goldenson, who helped guide Paramount from bankruptcy to film industry leadership and built ABC into the number-one network.

Karp, Walter. "The Quiz-Show Scandal." *American Heritage* 40 (May/June 1989): 77–88. A detailed account of the dark days of television entertainment.

MacDonald, Fred. *One Nation Under Television.* Chicago: Nelson-Hall Publishers, 1994. Traces the rise and decline of network television.

Paper, Lewis J. *Empire: William S. Paley and the Making of CBS.* New York: St. Martin's Press, 1987. Traces Paley's drive for success and the empire he built, which influenced entertainment and politics.

Persico, Joseph E. *Edward R. Murrow: An American Original.* New York: McGraw-Hill Book Company, 1988. An interesting, well-written, and documented account of one of America's greatest broadcasters.

Chapter 11: Advertising as a Social, Economic, and Political Force

Brozen, Yale, ed. *Advertising and Society.* New York: New York University Press, 1974. Worth reading, if only for Daniel J. Boorstin's chapter about advertising and American culture.

Fox, Stephen. *The Mirror Makers: A History of American Advertising and Its Creators.* New York: William Morrow and Company, 1984. For Fox, it is not the ads themselves but the colorful personalities of the men and women creators of them who have had the greatest influence on the industry.

Hower, Ralph M. *The History of an Advertising Agency: N.W. Ayer & Son at Work, 1869–1949.* Cambridge, MA: Harvard University Press, 1949. The history of an advertising agency, whose founder, Francis Wayland Ayer, started with no money but good judgment, to build one of the nation's most successful ad agencies.

Jamieson, Kathleen Hall. *Packaging the Presidency: A History and Criticism*

of Presidential Campaign Advertising. New York: Oxford University Press, 1984. The definitive book on presidential campaign advertising.

Marchand, Roland. *Advertising and the American Dream: Making Way for Modernity 1920–1940.* Berkeley: University of California Press, 1985. A look at two decades when advertising discovered striking new ways to play on anxieties and to promise solace for the masses.

Sandage, Charles H., Vernon Fryburger & Kim Rotzell, *Advertising Theory and Practice.* London: Longman Group United Kingdom, 1989. Theoretical foundations of advertising and how it is practiced.

Chapter 12: The Media and National Crises

Bernstein, Carl, and Bob Woodward. *All the President's Men.* New York: Simon and Schuster, 1974. A fascinating account of the toppling of a president as reported by the two Washington Post reporters. See also Bob Woodward and Carl Bernstein, *The Final Days* (New York: Simon & Schuster, 1976).

Braestrup, Peter. *Big Story: How the American Press and Television Reported and Interpreted the Crisis of Tet 1968 in Vietnam and Washington.* 2 vols. Boulder, CO: Western Press, 1977. The *Washington Post*'s Saigon bureau chief analyzes the war.

Cannon, Lou. *President Reagan: The Role of a Lifetime.* New York, Simon & Schuster, 1991. A look at the "Great Communicator" by a reporter who covered the phenomenon for more than a quarter century.

Ford, Gerald R. *A Time to Heal: The Autobiography of Gerald R. Ford.* New York: Harper and Row Publishers, 1979. An account of Ford's controversial decision to pardon Nixon.

Gitlin, Todd. *The Whole World Is Watching.* Berkeley: University of California Press, 1980. Focuses upon the antiwar movement of the 1960s.

Halberstam, David. *The Powers That Be.* New York: Knopf, 1979. A very readable account of the *Washington Post, Los Angeles Times, Time* Inc., and CBS. Detailed accounts of press and broadcast performance and influence in covering the Vietnam War.

Hallin, Daniel C. *The "Uncensored War": The Media and Vietnam.* New York: Oxford University Press, 1986. The networks did not lose the war, according to Hallin.

Hertsgaard, Mark. *On Bended Knee: The Press and the Reagan Presidency.* New York: Farrar, Straus and Giroux, 1988. A history and indictment of the relations between the major news media and the Reagan administration.

Karnow, Stanley. *Vietnam: A History.* New York: Viking, 1983. A companion to the PBS series.

Kearns-Goodwin, Doris. *Lyndon Johnson and the American Dream.* New York: Harper & Row, 1976. Portrays LBJ's strengths and weaknesses; as seen by one of the nation's popular historians and former Johnson aide.

Lashner, Marilyn A. *The Chilling Effects in TV News: Intimidation by the Nixon White House.* New York: Praeger, 1984. White House attempts to intimidate television journalism.

MacArthur, John R. *Second Front: Censorship and Propaganda in the Gulf War.* Berkeley: University of California Press. An examination of the government's assault on constitutional freedoms during Operation Desert Storm.

Macdougall, Malcolm D. *We Almost Made It.* New York: Crown Publishers, 1977. An irreverent account of how Ford almost won the presidency.

Nixon, Richard. *In the Arena.* New York: Simon and Schuster, 1990. Nixon shares his views on Vietnam and Watergate, and on political leaders he has known firsthand.

Salisbury, Harrison. *Behind the Lines.* New York: Harper and Row, 1967. The author's reporting from behind enemy lines enlightened the nation to what was really going on in Vietnam.

Sheehan, Neil. *A Bright, Shining Lie: John Paul Van and America in Vietnam.* New York: Random House, 1988. Sheehan analyzes the war in this Pulitzer Prize–winning book.

Shoup, Laurence H. *The Carter Presidency and Beyond: Power and Politics in the 1980s.* Palo Alto, CA: Ramparts Press, 1980. A guide to understanding the 1980 candidates and the political role of the media.

Spear, Joseph C. *Presidents and the Press: The Nixon Legacy.* Cambridge, MA: The MIT Press, 1986. An investigative journalist tells how the Nixon, Ford, Carter, and Reagan administrations have controlled and manipulated the press.

Tebbel, John, and Sarah Miles Watts. *The Press and the Presidency: From George Washington to Ronald Reagan.* New York: Oxford University Press, 1985. An account of the relationship and interaction between the White House and the news media from George Washington to Ronald Reagan.

Chapter 13: The Internet Revolution and the Information Explosion

Abbate, Janet. *Inventing the Internet.* Cambridge, MA: The MIT Press, 2000. Traces the key players and technologies that allowed the Internet to develop, but focuses upon the social and cultural factors that influenced its design and use.

Allan, Roy A. *A History of the Personal Computer: The People and the Technology.* London, Ontario, Canada: Allan Publishing, 2001. Comprehensive coverage of the history of the personal computer revolution with descriptions of the hardware and software as well as the companies and people who made it happen.

Bagdikian, Ben H. *The New Media Monopoly.* Boston: Beacon Press, 2004. The definitive book dealing with media mergers and the impact of consolidation on American democracy.

Gillies, James & Robet Cailliau. *How the Web was Born.* New York: Oxford University Press, 2000. This first book-length account of the Web's origins and development covers the history of computer networking from the 1950s.

Hafner, Katie & Matthew Lyon. *Where Wizards Stay Up Late: The Origins of the Internet.* New York: Simon & Schuster Paperbacks, 1996. The story of the pioneers who created the Internet.

Ifrah, Georges. *The Universal History of Computing: From the Abacus to the Quantum Computer.* New York: John Wiley & Sons, Inc., 2001. Traces the development of computing from the invention of the abacus to the first modern computer.

McChesney, Robert W. *Rich Media Poor Democracy: Communication Politics in Dubious Times.* Urbana, Ill.: University of Illinois Press, 1999. He argues that the media has gone astray from providing a bedrock for freedom and democracy, to a significant antidemocratic force in the United States, and, to varying degrees, worldwide.

Okin, J. R. *The Internet Revolution: The Not-For-Dummies Guide to the History, Technology, and Use of the Internet.* Winter Harbor, ME: Ironbound Press, 2005. The author reviews the history of the Internet and discusses how it is changing society and the interconnectedness of the world.

Washburn, Patrick S. *The African American Newspaper: Voice of Freedom.* Evanston, IL: Northwestern University Press, 2006.

Wolseley, Roland E. *The Black Press, U.S.A.* Ames, IA: Iowa State University Press, 1990. One of the seminal works about the history of the black press in America.

Index